INROADS: PATHS IN A
MODERN WESTERN PHILOSOPHY

This unique introduction to philosophy is designed as a companion volume to a number of classic philosophical texts widely used in first- and upper-year philosophy courses. While remaining clear and readable at all times, it provides detailed, sometimes fairly technical analyses of fundamental issues in metaphysics and morals. These include the existence of God, the meaning of death, and the nature of the good life for man.

Combining a historical with a systematic approach, Murray Miles's work straddles the customary divisions between ancient and modern, but also between Anglo-American and continental European philosophy. In each of five main parts devoted to Socrates, Plato, Descartes, Hume, and Sartre, respectively, *Inroads* discusses, from a philosophical rather than a religious or scientific perspective, those questions that make up the common inheritance of academic philosophy and ethico-religious thought of other kinds. Other features include a detailed glossary of philosophical terms, suggestions for further reading, and questions for reflection and review. *Inroads* is a useful text for first- or upper-year undergraduate courses or, equally, a sound resource for the general reader looking for a good grounding in philosophy and its history.

(Toronto Studies in Philosophy)

MURRAY MILES is a professor of philosophy at Brock University.

MURRAY MILES

Inroads: Paths in Ancient and Modern Western Philosophy

UNIVERSITY OF TORONTO PRESS
Toronto Buffalo London

© University of Toronto Press Incorporated 2003
Toronto Buffalo London
Printed in Canada

ISBN 0-8020-3744-5 (cloth)
ISBN 0-8020-8531-8 (paper)

Printed on acid-free paper

Toronto Studies in Philosophy
Editors: James R. Brown and Amy Mullin

National Library of Canada Cataloguing in Publication

Miles, Murray
  Inroads : paths in ancient and modern western
philosophy / Murray Miles

  (Toronto studies in philosophy)
  ISBN 0-8020-3744-5 (bound)   ISBN 0-8020-8531-8 (pbk.)

  1. Philosophy – Introductions. I. Title. II. Series.

  BD21.M44 2003   100   C2003-902473-3

University of Toronto Press acknowledges the financial assistance to its publishing program of the Canada Council for the Arts and the Ontario Arts Council.

University of Toronto Press acknowledges the financial support for its publishing activities of the Government of Canada through the Book Publishing Industry Development Program (BPIDP).

FOR SIMON

εἰ δ' ἄγ' ἐγὼν ἐρέω αἵπερ ὁδοὶ διζήσιός εἰσι νοῆσαι·

Contents

ACKNOWLEDGMENTS XI
PREFACE XV
NOTE ON TEXTS AND QUOTATIONS XXIII

INTRODUCTION: WHAT PHILOSOPHY IS 1

1 Problems, Periods, Genres 3
2 Philosophy and Higher Education 24
3 The Order of Knowing 37
4 The Order of Being 47
5 Philosophy and Mythico-Religious Thought 66
6 Philosophy and Science 92
7 Philosophy and Logic 110

Recommended readings and references 145
Questions for reflection, discussion, and review 146

PART ONE: SOCRATES AND THE ROAD TO WISDOM 147

8 Sources and Outline 149
9 Life and Character 158
10 Defence of the Philosophic Life 187
11 Socratic Piety 204
12 Virtue and Happiness 225
13 Concluding Appraisal 248

Recommended readings and references 255
Questions for reflection, discussion, and review 256

PART TWO: PLATO AND THE ROAD TO REALITY 257

14 Doctrines and Influences 259
15 New Defence of the Philosophic Life 267
16 Soul, Death, Immortality 275
17 Cyclical Argument 287
18 Recollection Argument 295
19 Affinity Argument 309
20 The Metaphysics of Form 318
21 Concluding Appraisal 350

Recommended readings and references 359
Questions for reflection, discussion, and review 360

PART THREE: DESCARTES AND THE ROAD TO CERTAINTY 361

22 Subjectivism and Dualism 363
23 Doubt and Certainty 369
24 Mind and Matter 383
25 Truth and Circularity 406
26 The Existence of God 424
27 Man and World 456

Recommended readings and references 482
Questions for reflection, discussion, and review 484

PART FOUR: HUME AND THE ROAD BACK TO COMMON LIFE 485

28 Philosophical Works and Outlook 487
29 An Empiricist Critique of Reason 497
30 The Unmaking of Miracles 517
31 The Undoing of Divine Justice 536

Recommended readings and references 553
Questions for reflection, discussion, and review 554

PART FIVE: SARTRE AND THE ROAD TO FREEDOM 557

32 Life, Work, and Basic Philosophical Outlook 559
33 Atheistic Humanism 568

34 Criticisms of Existentialism   576
35 Slogan and Basic Doctrines   581
36 Human Reality   592
37 Will and Emotion   601
38 Decisionism   610

Recommended readings and references   629
Questions for reflection, discussion, and review   630

CONCLUSION   631
GLOSSARY OF PHILOSOPHICAL TERMS   637
INDEX OF NAMES   663

Acknowledgments

Neither these Acknowledgments nor the Preface that follows is intended for beginning students of philosophy or lay readers, who should proceed straight to the subsequent Note and Introduction. Advanced readers, however, especially philosophy instructors considering this volume as a text or teaching resource, may find these preliminaries helpful in assessing its suitability for their purposes.

The first acknowledgment is a general one concerning those works listed at the end of each of the five main parts of this book under the heading "Recommended readings and references." Often enough, key ideas of the part in question were originally suggested to me by the writings listed there. If I have nevertheless omitted detailed acknowledgment of my sources, even when conscious of some quite specific debt, the intent is only to avoid the clutter of footnotes, which are not customary in a work of this kind and can easily prove more distracting than helpful. There are doubtless other publications that could have been included among the references, but the reader astute enough to spot some unacknowledged source will probably know from experience just how hard it is in practice to recall each and every influence on a book that has been many years in the writing.

Apart from a couple of unusual features mentioned in the Preface, this work makes no claim to great originality of interpretation. No one familiar with Gregory Vlastos's writings can fail to recognize his illuminating insights in the part on Socrates; the same is true of David Gallop's and T.M. Robinson's influence on the interpretation of the *Phaedo*. The whole discussion of Plato's theory of Forms owes much to R.E. Allen's book on the *Euthyphro*. Descartes is a speciality of mine; here I have presented, in condensed form, the results of my own published research. My reading of Hume has been shaped by Antony Flew, among others, from whose writings I have learned most of what I know about analytic philosophy. My approach to Sartre focuses largely on his extensive borrowings from Heidegger's early work, *Being and Time*, with which I have a specialist's acquaintance from my doctoral studies at the University of Freiburg. As for the ethical theory in the first and last parts of the book,

I have drawn heavily on the well-known presentation of the subject by William Frankena. Finally, my conception of philosophy owes as much to Father Joseph Owens CSsR as to Heidegger—two names not usually mentioned in the same breath, though their synoptic views of the history of thought have more in common than one might think. At most, then, there is a significant shift in overall perspective, with few daring departures from the well-trodden paths of scholarship, except in the case of Descartes; that too seems fitting in a work of this nature, the aim of which is to promote the spread of philosophical culture, and only incidentally to advance the system of ideas in any particular domain of scholarly research. I am conscious of having a fairly novel idea of philosophy, of organizing familiar material in new ways, and of introducing a couple of useful ideas and distinctions that have been generally overlooked in the scholarly literature; but if there are indeed any appreciable additions to professional scholarship in this volume, I must admit that they are largely inadvertent. My aims are more educational than scholarly, though a scholarly introduction to philosophy is, I confess, an idea that intrigued me in these times of educational decline.

In addition to the foregoing, I must acknowledge one very special debt. I am well aware that much that I have to say, especially about Greek philosophy, is the fruit of discussions over the years with my friend and colleague Martha Husain, though I am no longer able to say exactly where her brainchildren leave off and mine begin. In addition to her many indirect contributions to this book, she gave generously of her time at the end, reading the entire manuscript and tactfully recommending ways to improve it. Her reactions, as she read and returned portions of the manuscript with her comments, occasioned a discovery on my part not unlike that made by the eminent British art historian and educator, Kenneth Clark, while preparing the book version of his BBC television series *Civilisation*. "Just as the Bourgeois Gentilhomme was delighted to find that he spoke prose," writes Lord Clark in the Foreword, "so I was astonished to discover that I had a point of view." I too was surprised to learn that I had, if not a philosophy, at least a point of view. On the whole, I prefer analysis and argument to what Lord Clark, in one of those programmes, calls "vivid assertion." I am drawn to philosophies of the type designated 'realist,' and wary of idealism in all its forms. I favour what I call 'philosophies of immanence,' down-to-earth philosophies like those of Aristotle, Hume, and Heidegger, over philosophies of transcendence, like those of Plato and Descartes. Concrete phenomenological description and analysis comes closer to my idea of successful philosophical understanding than the formal methods employed in the mathematical sciences. I am averse to reductivist techniques that ignore or explain away things that form part of ordinary pre-philosophical experience; and though firmly convinced that experience is the great teacher of mankind, I take strong exception to philosophies that diminish the role of reason, or understand it too narrowly, as the perquisite of the mathematical sciences, or of the 'hard' physical sciences, or of the empirically proceeding natural and social sciences in general. It would be very surprising if there were any domain of what Lord Clark calls 'civilization' without its own pattern of rationality, not excepting the fine arts. Indeed, I think that what distinguishes different modes of discourse—moral and prudential from aesthetic value judgments, and philosophical from religious and scientific theories of various kinds—is precisely the distinctive pattern of rational argument and justification belonging to each. If I were able to say exactly how they differ, I would presumably have more than a point of view, a philosophy in fact; if that is what is required for a genuine "dialogue between thinkers" (Heidegger), a point of view seems enough for intelligent critical engagement with the great philosophies of the past.

Of course, it is not just the discovery, but the point of view itself, that comes of having had the good fortune to land, almost twenty years ago, in a philosophy department in which at least one colleague already thought much as I do now. It hardly mattered that she was influenced by Aristotle and I by recent German phenomenology. I probably owe more to her and to my students over the years than I realize. The latter provided me with the opportunity for extensive classroom testing of the book, which has led to many improvements. An attentive reading of earlier drafts of the manuscript by Scott Stapleford and Stefan Rodde, at different times my teaching and research assistants respectively, resulted in the correction of many minor errors. Errors no doubt remain, major as well as minor; for these I am alone responsible. Any brought to my attention will be remedied to the best of my ability before any subsequent printing. Finally, I offer sincere thanks to the Toronto-based painter John Anderson, who kindly furnished a slide of his magnificent landscape "Track to the Wheat Field" for the cover. Thanks, too, to Mr Roberto Navarro of the Navarro Gallery (Toronto), which represents Mr Anderson.

This book is dedicated to my son, Simon, who has always displayed a healthy mixture of curiosity and scepticism about whatever it is that keeps his father closeted in his study so much of the day. The answer is here, as accessible as I know how to make it, should he ever care to find out for himself. The Greek of the dedication is a slightly bowdlerized version of the opening lines of fragment 2 of Parmenides's great poem, in which a goddess exhorts the philosopher in these words: "Come, I shall tell you … what paths of inquiry … there are for thinking" (Gallop translation).

Murray Miles
St Catharines, Ontario

Preface

The present introduction to philosophy was originally designed for use in first-year undergraduate courses such as are offered at nearly every institution of higher learning in the English-speaking world today. In the course of successive elaborations it has grown to accommodate some more advanced material, though the ground plan and purpose remain substantially unaltered. In its present form, the book may also be of use to upper-year philosophy students, as well as to those general readers who want to acquire the proverbial intelligent layman's knowledge of philosophy and its history, but crave more technical detail than is found in most popular outlines and sketches of the subject. Philosophy instructors who prefer to use only primary sources, but would like to cover some or all of the works dealt with here, may find this volume useful as a teaching resource. It has even been put to me that a work of this kind could be of value to doctoral students preparing for the historical part of their comprehensive examinations—but about that I reserve judgment.

So much for the audiences I had in mind in writing this book. Its distinctive features are (1) its format as a companion volume to a number of widely used introductory texts; (2) a unified conception of philosophy so old as to seem almost novel today; and (3) its design as both an introduction and a *vademecum*. Each of these points will be expanded in what follows. Another conspicuous feature worth mentioning here is (4) the effort to pay both ancient Greek and contemporary continental philosophy fuller and more sympathetic attention than they receive in most available introductions to philosophy in English. Just in terms of bulk, the portions of the work devoted Socrates, Plato, and Sartre amount to well over half; and while I have sharply critical things to say about both Plato's arguments and Sartre's unargued assumptions, I have gone out of my way to read them sympathetically as well as critically. In discussing Socrates the situation was reversed: here it cost me a similar effort to temper my admiration with criticism.

The two approaches favoured by university teachers of introductory courses in philosophy are commonly labelled (a) 'problems' or 'topics' and (b) 'historical' or 'philosophical classics.' The first typically employs articles by contemporary writers on one or two issues of metaphysics, epistemology, ethics, political theory, and other sub-disciplines of philosophy. These are often collected in anthologies of readings that include a few short excerpts from classical works. By contrast, the historical approach is generally based on the study of a few, usually brief, classical texts by great dead authors—Plato, Aristotle, Aquinas, Descartes, Hume, Kant and so on. These are studied either in separate, complete editions or, more frequently, as reprinted in abbreviated form in anthologies. Another, though somewhat less popular, historical approach is the single-authored introduction incorporating classical texts as (sometimes very long) quoted passages. A good example is Antony Flew's *Introduction to Western Philosophy*, which canvasses the issues by analyzing an apparently timeless tissue of philosophical arguments drawn freely from every period of thought. A steady stream of complimentary copies of each type of text comes across the desks of first-year instructors every year.

The present work is a blend of the two historical approaches. It is designed as an interpretive commentary to be read and discussed in conjunction with a number of fairly short but important historical works available in separate editions. A concerted effort has been made to place each work in its historical context. Some instructors may find it more suitable as a resource for their own lectures than as assigned reading for first-year students; certainly, the historical works themselves should be the main focus of any introductory course. I have not attempted to interpret them exhaustively so much as to exploit them for opportunities to get across some fairly technical philosophical points, vocabulary, and distinctions, or to stimulate reflection on some particular issue of importance. Instructors who share my view of philosophy as a technical discipline may want to have the students grapple with the interpretations given here while reading the primary texts; those who find this approach somewhat too dry may want to make their own selection of the terms and distinctions for in-class presentation, devoting the bulk of the lecture time to interpretative discussion of the primary texts and leaving students a freer hand to come to terms with the historical works on their own.

In view of the former of these two possibilities, I have attempted to write in a manner that presupposes no prior knowledge of philosophy, carefully explaining all technical terms and distinctions as I introduce them and placing them, for ease of reference, in a glossary at the end of the volume. I am confident that the present work *can* be understood by first-year undergraduates willing to read it attentively, though it is up to the individual instructor to decide whether that is the best use to make of it. The alternative 'teaching resource' approach has much to recommend it; that, indeed, is how this work began life, as a set of detailed notes on which my own lectures were rather loosely based. Even students whose introductory courses are of the other kinds described above may find this a useful addition to their libraries, either as supplementary reading or as a reference work.

The book as published here grew not only out of my introductory philosophy lectures since 1991, but also out of my scholarly research on Descartes and a series of team-taught comparative seminars on ancient Greek and early modern philosophy offered over the same period in collaboration with the Greek philosophy specialist in my department, Martha Husain. It was in pondering the similarities and differences between ancient and modern metaphysics that I arrived at the conception of the subject outlined in the Introduction and illustrated throughout the text. It is not the standard view of 'primary philosophy'—at least not any more, and especially not among those writing in English. The test of its worth is its ability to shed fresh light on the individual works and the sweeping historical developments examined. But along with the metaphysical outlook goes a constant emphasis on gaining a command of the tools of philosophical analysis, so that the goal of fostering in students a more critical cast of mind can be pursued quite independently of my own, no doubt one-sided views about philosophy and its history. For those students who think of philosophy in terms of 'personal growth' and 'spiritual development,' I am afraid there is not much here, something I have tried to make clear in the Introduction.

Apart from (1) its format and (2) the unifying idea of philosophy behind it, the present work may recommend itself as filling a gap in the existing literature by providing (3) a *vademecum* of philosophy. By this I mean a digest or manual of philosophical concepts, distinctions, and interpretations designed to accompany the student on his journey through the undergraduate years of a philosophy programme. Although it is aimed primarily at the potential philosophy major rather than the masses of students reluctantly fulfilling some university requirement, even the latter may be best served by an introduction that makes few of the usual concessions to waning literacy and conceptual skills among first-year students. The material tends at times to go beyond what one could reasonably expect even a talented beginner to *master* in an introductory course; my hope is that in later, specialized courses on Plato, Descartes, Hume, and Sartre the student will revisit his first-year text, coming to understand some of the finer nuances and broader historical perspectives that may have eluded him on first reading. Partly for this reason I have tended to cover only part of the works discussed: segments of the *Meno* and *Euthyphro*, about half of the *Phaedo*, five of Descartes's six *Meditations*, two sections of Hume's *Enquiry* (in detail), and a minor essay in the case of Sartre.

As for the classical philosophers and works selected, my choice pretty much reflects the collective wisdom of the profession, with which I am in substantial agreement. Where, for reasons of space, I have had to omit philosophers and themes I should have liked to include, I have generally sought a pretext to incorporate at least some important material into one of the five main parts of this book. Thus, I have taken the opportunity to sketch Kant's moral theory (along with that of Hobbes) as a foil to the moral philosophy of Socrates in Part One. The Kantian notion of the synthetic a priori comes up both within an early chapter on logic, in the context of the distinction between conceptual and factual truths, and again later, where Descartes's a priori and a posteriori proofs of God's existence are introduced. In the same contexts I have briefly outlined the main bone of contention between rationalist and empiricist philosophies as well. The empiricist position appears in fleshed-out form in the part on Hume, whose views on the origin of ideas are discussed at length. Similarly, I have used the discussion of Descartes's two proofs of God's existence as a jumping-off point for a brief look at Aquinas's Five Ways and at Anselm's famous argument—two standard themes of introductory works of this kind. I have also woven an important strand of Aristotelianism into the fabric of the discussion of metaphysics in the parts devoted to Plato and Descartes; I refer to what Heidegger has aptly called "the onto-theological constitution of metaphysics." In the same context I provide a brief sketch of the Aristotelian doctrine of the four causes—a standard piece of introductory philosophy. Finally, I seized the opportunity, in discussing the relation of metaphysics to physics, of describing the astronomical picture of the universe that remained the dominant world-view from later Greek times until the end of the Middle Ages. I did so as much from a conviction that this is something students ought to be exposed to as because of its strict relevance to metaphysics.

Another doctrine out of the same Aristotelian stable as those mentioned above is the famous faculty psychology of medieval scholasticism. It is contrasted with the new, distinctively modern concept of the soul as self-consciousness in Descartes's Second Meditation. As for the other central 'isms' of philosophy (rationalism and empiricism have been mentioned already), ontological idealism is opposed to realism in one context (Descartes's causal proof of the existence of matter) and to materialism in another (the discussion of mind–body union in Descartes). All three 'isms' are first broached in the Introduction, along with nominalism, conceptualism, and the particular form of realism (essentialism) that is usually contrasted with them both. Causal and representative realism, the components of so-called naive realism, are discussed in the part on Descartes. Epistemological direct realism and its counterpart, representationalism, come up at the end of the part on Hume. All these are matters that should at least be touched on in any introductory textbook; for the most part, I have done more than touch upon them.

I have also exploited the opportunity afforded by the Introduction to clarify the concepts that form the stock-in-trade of the intellectual historian (Renaissance, Reformation, Enlightenment, and so forth), with which students taking their first university course in a humanities discipline ought to have at least some acquaintance. It would have been desirable to include entire parts on Aristotle, Aquinas, and Kant, but, in my experience, the five parts of this volume represent pretty well all one can reasonably expect to cover in an introduction to philosophy of this sort, devoting roughly six or seven weeks each to Socrates, Plato, and Descartes, and about three or four each to Hume and Sartre. Besides, the thinkers singled out for close study here are particularly well suited to the first-year level in a way that Aristotle, Aquinas, Kant and Hegel, for example, are not. Even as it is, some portions of the work may have to be left out or assigned as independent reading, particularly the philosophy of science and logic portions of the Introduction (chaps. 6 and 7), which would be too tedious for lectures. (I myself simply leave them to the students to study on their own, testing them on the material afterwards.) The same is true of the historical sketch of Presocratic philosophy (chap. 5); I included it partly as a means of introducing the 'philosophy and religion' theme, partly to satisfy the beginner's curiosity about the beginnings of philosophy itself. Yet I have never actually lectured on the subject.

Thematically, the emphasis of the book lies squarely on metaphysics, in the first instance, particularly on those questions, like the existence of God and the immortality of the soul, that are central to religious thought as well. With the secondary emphasis on moral philosophy, it is probably fair to say that the focus of each of the five main parts is on the domain of the ethico-religious. These are the traditional philosophical issues that reflective young people are likeliest to have thought about, questions about science having, in most cases, hardly crossed their minds up to this point in their lives. The approach taken to the issues discussed is, however, strictly philosophical rather than religious or scientific.

The contrast may seem odd since, on at least one still widely held (and, in my opinion, respectable) view of the relationship between philosophy and religion, the goal of philosophical reflection is to deepen one's understanding of truths already accepted on grounds of faith. This need not signify that philosophical enquiry is strictly subordinate to faith in the manner conveyed by the famous dictum of St Anselm, *credo ut intelligam* ("I believe so that I may understand"), a view which harks back to St Augustine and is echoed by St Bonaventure and the whole Augustinian tradition. It may just mean that some religious truths are taken for granted, the job of philosophy being to deepen our understanding of them in ways that would be perfectly intelligible and cogent even for an unbeliever. While allowing philosophy some measure of autonomy, this still casts her in the role of a handmaiden to theology or religion. This, or something like it, is Aquinas's view of the relationship between philosophy and religion.

The most widespread view nowadays, however, is that of the scientifically-minded philosopher for whom the goal of philosophical reflection is to clarify or deepen our understanding of "the scientific image" of the world, as Wilfrid Sellars has called it. Together with this goes a reflection on the assumptions, methods, logical structure, and rationality of the scientific enterprise itself. In the normal case, philosophy, so understood, sets up to be sole arbiter of conclusions about ethico-religious matters as well. Their acceptance or rejection depends upon the outcome of critical philosophical scrutiny of the relevant evidence and arguments in accordance with the canons of scientific rationality. This is essentially Hume's attitude, at least in one of his moods; only his understanding of scientific method is now outdated, not his philosophical outlook, which is more in vogue than ever. While again perfectly respectable, this makes philosophy ancillary to science rather than religion, leaving one to wonder just what an autonomous philosophical approach might be.

As philosophers, we may wish to understand things, neither as modern science nor as traditional faith and scripture tell us they are, but as we experience them in our day-to-day living. Like science and religion, everyday lived experience is an authority whose lessons require careful scrutiny if they are to be kept free of distortion by alien schemes of representation. Not that we do not already understand ourselves and the world even before engaging in philosophical reflection; on the contrary, the job of an autonomous philosophy, as I understand it, is to develop conceptual tools that are continuous with that pre-theoretical understanding that we already have, and must have, in order to get on successfully with the business of living. In doing so, philosophy enables us to deepen our understanding of what we in fact already know (perhaps without fully knowing that we know it); it makes explicit what we have hitherto understood only implicitly; it does not supplant our pre-theoretical way of looking at things with theories that are incompatible with it, but makes the content of ordinary experience more transparent by fixing it in a framework of clarified concepts. By contrast, both modern science and traditional religion impose interpretive schemes that may be felt to be at odds with that pre-theoretical way of understanding ourselves and the world already implicit in ordinary experience. It would be hard to deny this of scientific efforts to supplant the world of ordinary experience with what Cornford, speaking of ancient atomism, has called "the dance of material particles"; and traditional religion, too, introduces alien divisions into the self (body, soul, spirit, etc.), bringing other-worldly perspectives to bear (this life and the next, above and below, and so on) that seem to trample underfoot the plain facts of immediate lived experience.

If this idea of philosophy is defensible, an autonomous philosophical approach is one that borrows nothing from either science or religion or any other authority except reflection upon experience itself as it is pre-theoretically understood and interpreted. The prescription has proved very hard to live up to. It seems to have been Aristotle's ideal (despite lapses), and it is Heidegger's understanding of philosophy as well. Hume wrote (in another of his moods) that "philosophical decisions are nothing but the reflections of common life, methodized and corrected"; yet if this was his goal, Hume, as we shall see, fell astoundingly short of it.

In its search for truth, autonomous philosophy may not even go beyond the "manifest image" of the world to that of science, let alone to the next world or to

God; but it could do so, in principle, if rational reflection on experience provided the warrant—and 'experience,' even 'ordinary experience,' it is argued at several places in this book, is an elusive concept. In any case, this is the idea of autonomous philosophical enquiry that underlies the critical remarks that conclude the parts on Descartes and Hume, and it may be better understood from the way it is put to work there than from this brief sketch.

So much for the general thematic focus on the ethico-religious domain. One specific theme running through the parts of the work devoted to Socrates, Descartes, and Sartre is the famous Euthyphro dilemma. The theological voluntarism briefly mooted in a moral context in the *Euthyphro*, yet hardly deemed worthy of serious consideration there, becomes, in the *un*orthodox Christian perspective of Descartes, the central tenet of metaphysics. I refer to the doctrine of God's creation of truth and value. It is then transformed by Sartre into a non-theological voluntarist doctrine that straddles metaphysics and moral philosophy: *man's* creation of truth and value. The broad outlines of this historical development may pique the interest of students for whom it is a matter of course that truth is subjective and morals relative. For the Greeks, value, including moral value, was part of the very fabric of the cosmos; far from making the moral law, the gods are subject to it in just the way mankind is. Descartes's unorthodox idea that God makes the good good, *and* the true true is dispelled indeed by Sartre's atheism, but only to be replaced by the even more startling claim that man creates the good and (at least as far as his own nature is concerned) the true. In this case (as so often), the journey from Socrates via Descartes to Sartre is as interesting as the destination is (in my view) disappointing. The Conclusion contains some reflections designed to shake the uncritical confidence which undergraduates embrace relativism without any very clear idea of the historical developments that led up to and underlie it. That seemed the right place for a retrospective look at some of the main trends and perennial postures noticed along the way.

A second recurring theme is the conception of the mind or soul in Plato, Aristotle, and Descartes. (A related issue, life after death, occurs in the part on Hume as well.) The Cartesian concept of the mind as self-consciousness, though still canonical for Hume and even nineteenth-century psychology, has come increasingly under attack from various quarters in contemporary philosophy. It has, of course, been famously derided as a 'ghost in a machine' by behaviourist philosophy and psychology since Ryle. This attack is only briefly mentioned here. Nor has much attention been paid to contemporary materialism or neuro-philosophy. In the final part, however, the bodiless, worldless, solipsistic *ego cogitans* of Descartes is juxtaposed with the radical conception of the self as a Being-in-the-World, taken over by Sartre from Heidegger. This may be more important than any of the various Anglo-American critiques of Cartesian dualism, though that is debatable; in any case, it forms the main attempt at criticism here.

A third theme that is carried right through the work is the persecution and defence of philosophy. First encountered in the *Apology*, it resurfaces in the *Phaedo* and again in Epicurus's harangue (as Hume calls it) in "Of a Particular Providence and a Future State." The relation of philosophy to religion (theology) and irreligion is another topic that crops up in some guise or other within each part. Philosophical agnosticism and atheism are explored in some depth in the parts on Hume and Sartre.

Since the life and martyrdom of Socrates may be more effective than the consideration of his moral philosophy in awakening the beginner's interest in philosophy ('getting the hooks in,' as I call it), the portrait of Socrates has been drawn in more detail than is customary in works of this kind. As I have said, I expect a sustained focus on ethico-religious questions and the 'lived' aspect of philosophy to reflect the interests of first-year students to a far greater extent than scientific questions, though I have no doubt that some instructors will feel that I should have given much more attention to philosophical issues related to science.

Be that as it may, the fact remains that, both extensively and intensively, this book either treats, or at least alludes to, a large and important segment of what one would normally expect an undergraduate to have mastered by the time of graduation. If this is too much for the beginning, it may at least set students on the right path.

Note on Texts and Quotations

This work is a companion volume to a number of short philosophical texts, all widely used as introductory readings for students embarking on a first study of philosophy. All but the last are undisputed classics of the philosophical literature, and even the last is by an author with strong claims to have produced at least one of the masterpieces of twentieth-century philosophy. This volume is accordingly no more than a secondary source, an interpretation or critical exposition, not a free-standing introduction to be read on its own, except by those already well versed in the primary sources.

References to the dialogues of Plato and the other works interpreted are to the following readily available separate editions or translations (dates are those of first printing):

Plato. 1981. *Five Dialogues*. Translated by G.M.A. Grube. Indianapolis: Hackett Publishing Co.
Descartes, René. 1986. *Meditations on First Philosophy. With Selections from the Objections and Replies*. Translated by John Cottingham with an introduction by Bernard Williams. Cambridge: Cambridge University Press.
Hume, David. 1988. *An Enquiry Concerning Human Understanding*. Introduction, notes, and editorial arrangement by Antony Flew. LaSalle, Illinois: Open Court.
Sartre, J.-P. 1948. *Existentialism and Humanism*. Translation and introduction by Philip Mairet. London: Methuen.

Quotations from Plato's dialogues are referenced in the usual way, by Stephanus pages. (Stephanus was a Renaissance editor of the works of Plato whose Greek and Latin edition of the dialogues was divided horizontally into five sections on the printed page. Thus, '18e' refers to segment e of page 18. The Stephanus pagination is reprinted in the margins of almost all modern editions.) In the case of Descartes, references are to the pagination printed in the margins of the above edition, that is, to the page numbers of the standard Franco-Latin edition of Descartes's works by Adam and Tannery. This makes it easy to find the cited passages in the standard three-volume English translation prepared by Cottingham, Stoothof, Murdoch and Kenny, which includes the Adam and Tannery references in the margins. (See the Recommended readings and references to Part Three for the exact bibliographical details concerning these editions.) Otherwise, references are to the page numbers of the above editions. In the case of Sartre, however, I have included the page numbers (separated by an oblique) of Walter Kaufmann's *Existentialism from Dostoevsky to Sartre* (New American Library, 1975) which contains the same Mairet translation and may be easier to come by than the Methuen edition.

All page references are inserted parenthetically into the running text. Where parts of quotations have been italicized by the author, the letters 'e.a.' (emphasis added) appear after the page reference. 'Ibid.' (short for the Latin *ibidem*, 'in that very place') is used whenever the reference is to the same page of the work cited in the previous quotation. So too when the same section or sub-section of this work is cross-referenced twice in a row. Changes to the text as printed, or explanatory interpolations of the author, including numbering of sections in longer passages, are placed within square brackets. Foreign words (mainly Greek or Latin, occasionally French) are italicized, following standard scholarly practice, except where their use in English is so well established that their foreignness seems doubtful. The terms 'genus,' 'a priori,' and 'motif,' for instance, are not recognizably foreign any longer; nor, for that matter, is 'ibid.' *Proprium*, on the other hand, and *definiens* are still sufficiently foreign-sounding to require italicization throughout.

With the exception of Plato, passages from other works of the main authors (for example, Descartes's *Principles* or the Replies to the Objections to the *Meditations*) have not been referenced in the text. Nor have the writings of other classical or modern authors, be it Aristotle or A.H. Armstrong, St Anselm or R.E.Allen, Aquinas or Quine, Hobbes or Cornford. I realize that this may be frustrating for instructors and more advanced students, who may wish to know the sources from which these quotations are drawn, but having decided against footnotes I also rejected the idea making an already bulky volume bulkier by adding a separate section at the end giving bibliographic references to other works cited.

Technical and semi-technical terms are generally explained in detail when first introduced and included in the Glossary at the end of the book. On encountering them again, a quick glance should suffice to recall to mind the main connotations of the term in question. The Glossary also serves as a complete subject index, since every entry ends with a list of those sections in which the term is used, every important term having been included in the Glossary. A separate index of names follows the Glossary at the end of the volume.

INTRODUCTION

WHAT PHILOSOPHY IS

There are many strange and exotic specimens in the gardens of philosophy: Epistemology, Ontology, Cosmology, to name but a few. And clearly there is much good sense—not only rhyme but reason—to these labels.

The American philosopher Wilfrid Sellars on the flora of philosophy.

1

Problems, Periods, Genres

1.1 Introductory

For purposes of introduction, it may be useful to conduct a rapid survey of the traditional, current, and perennial issues discussed by philosophers today. From these we can then select those problems that will occupy us in the five main parts of this book (see 1.2). Proceeding in this way will make it clear from the start which issues are *not* to be pursued; the reader whose interests tend that way should consult one of the many other excellent introductory texts available. Something needs to be said at the outset, too, about the standard periodization of the history of philosophy; for we shall have to confine our attention to a few key epochs, and it is useful to have the bigger picture before us at least once before narrowing our focus (see 1.3). In this connection we can consider the relation between actually doing philosophy and studying its history. Although the two are widely held to be not just different but separately pursuable, the view to be taken here is that philosophy and the history of philosophy go hand in hand (see 1.4). The first chapter concludes with a quick overview of the literary forms philosophical writing has taken down through the history of the discipline (see 1.5).

The second chapter addresses the question of the approach to be taken to the problems selected in the first. There is reason to believe that the philosophical approach to problems of all sorts reflects the goals and nature of university education to an extent unequalled by any other academic discipline. In academic as opposed to popular philosophy, moreover, the sort of understanding sought is universal rather than confined to a particular time, place, or individual. This is why philosophy is bound to initiate a dialogue with its own history. Since all this may appear far too ambitious for a start, the chapter concludes with a description of the more modest goal of acquiring the rudiments of philosophical culture.

Chapters 3 and 4 revert from the how to the what of philosophy, sketching two basic yet complex issues that run through the history of the discipline: the order of being and the order of knowing. These chapters explain what philosophy is by describing what it is about. (The other chapters of the Introduction complete the picture of what philosophy is mainly by saying what it is *not* about.) Here the universality of philosophy comes to the fore in a new guise: *primary* philosophy or metaphysics is about absolutely everything, the whole order of knowing and of being of which we ourselves, together with all other things, are a part. The discussion of the order of being focuses on two main problems, labelled the mind–body problem and the problem of universals, respectively.

Chapter 5 attempts a sketch of the origins of philosophy, its emergence as a separate kind of enquiry from mythico-religious thought, outlining its history up to the time of Socrates. As we shall see, early Greek philosophy lays most of the groundwork for the metaphysical tasks described in chapters 3 and 4. On the discussion of philosophy and myth in chapter 5 follows a consideration of philosophy and science in chapter 6 and of philosophy and logic in chapter 7. The former considers the main patterns of rationality recognizable in the sciences, while the latter introduces those elements of logical theory to be employed in the analysis of the texts dealt with in the five succeeding parts of the book.

This, incidentally, is the pattern to be followed in each of the five main parts of this book: the initial chapter states the subject matter, setting out the stages of the itinerary to be followed in the first and subsequent chapters. For purposes of orientation, then, an attentive reading of the initial chapter is essential.

1.2 Philosophical issues

Over the millennia, those calling themselves philosophers have discussed and debated a vast array of different, though often related, problems and puzzles. To avoid the charge of starting with a highly selective tradition dictated by personal tastes and interests, it may be best to include as much as possible in this initial survey of philosophical problems. However, there is no point in trying to deny that a value judgment is implicit in the four headings of the table on the next page: (a) traditional issues that are no longer current; (b) current issues that are not traditional; (c) current and traditional issues that are not perennial; and (d) the perennial issues of philosophy. The point of the designations is admittedly to suggest that the perennial issues of philosophy are particularly deserving of our attention. With this emphasis not everyone will agree, and it has to be conceded that the other problems, those *not* to be pursued here, are perfectly legitimate philosophical issues and may, for various reasons, have an urgency about them that the perennial issues, having been around for a very long time, appear to lack.

Chapter 1: Problems, Periods, Genres 5

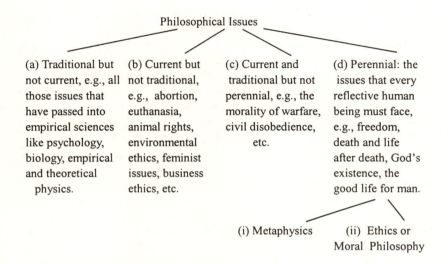

1.2.1 Traditional issues that are no longer current

Under (a), traditional but not current, belong all those subjects of philosophical speculation that, over the past few centuries, have become amenable to empirical scientific investigation, thus passing from the domain of philosophy into that of some special science. For example, not very long ago, in the late seventeenth and throughout the eighteenth century, the empirical psychological and physiological study of the human mind or brain was regarded as a branch of philosophy. It was carried on within the philosophical faculty, or the faculty of letters, of the great European universities, by professors whose official university titles usually included the word 'philosophy.'

In the eighteenth century it was especially the brilliant associationist psychology of David Hume (1711–1776), which we shall get to know in the fourth part of this work, that revealed the great promise of empirical psychology as a sub-discipline destined to revolutionize philosophy from the ground up. Well before Hume, the empirical investigation of the human mind had already been recognized as a fledgling discipline under the umbrella of philosophy. At the end of the eighteenth century the great German philosopher Immanuel Kant (1724–1804) proposed that empirical psychology continue to be accorded a place within philosophy, but only as a temporary measure and a matter of courtesy, until that science was sufficiently well established to command a place of its own in the university curriculum, alongside another empirical science that had once been a sub-domain of philosophy, namely physics. Although it grew steadily both in extent and importance after Kant's time, psychology continued to be studied as a branch of philosophy right through the nineteenth century; no separate department of psychology existed in the universities, and no sharp division was made between (1) general theoretical or conceptual matters bearing on the classification of mental phenomena or on the mind–body relation; and (2) empirical enquiry (both descriptive and explanatory) into special psychical and psycho-physical phenomena under controlled experimental or laboratory conditions. Once this distinction was drawn, however, a whole raft of questions about the mind ceased to be regarded as part of the subject matter of philosophy, becoming the special province of psychology and neuro-physiology as empirical sciences of the mind. And so too in biology and physics. As theories about the origins of the universe, of the earth, and of the human species became amenable to scientific testing through empirical observation and experimentation, they passed from philosophy into the jurisdictions of such special sciences as physics, astronomy, geology, biology, and so forth. Of course, certain questions, namely those purely conceptual or theoretical issues *not* amenable to empirical scientific investigation, remained for philosophers or philosophically minded scientists to deal with. Thus, the so-called philosophy of mind (or philosophical psychology), philosophy of biology, and philosophical cosmology remain sub-disciplines of philosophy to this day. But it is a much-chastened philosophy that stakes out its claim to these as sub-disciplines; the bulk of what was once philosophy is no longer within her province.

1.2.2 Current issues that are not traditional

So much for those issues about the mind, the universe, the earth, and the life-forms on it that were traditionally, but are now no longer, considered philosophical. As for those that are (b) current but not traditional, we note that advances in science and technology have led to the emergence of many issues in present-day moral philosophy that simply could not have arisen, or taken the same form, in traditional ethics. The classical Greek philosophers, like the ancient Hebrews, certainly discussed both suicide and letting die, debating whether or not either was morally permissible; but they did not even have a word for what we call (adopting a late-Greek coinage) 'euthanasia' or, in plain English, 'mercy-killing.' By this we mean, roughly, bringing about another's death (with or without consent) in order to provide release from a painful or debilitating disease, where the condition is known to be incurable or irreversible. Hastening death may involve taking active measures to end a life, or simply ceasing to prolong it—by shutting down a life support system, for example. This distinction, together with the idea of consent, gives rise to the notions of voluntary and non-voluntary (with and without consent) and active and passive euthanasia (killing and letting die).

These questions obviously did not arise in their present-day form for ancient peoples; nor did they have the same urgency, since, given the state of medical knowledge at the time, it would in most cases have been uncertain just when a disease was degenerative or incurable or when death was imminent. No doubt religious taboos on killing, reinforced by the threat of blood pollution, played an important role in suppressing discussion of questions of the kind; but Greek philosophical thought was remarkably free of the constraints that were imposed on Greek popular morality. As for killing by the state rather than by individuals, both Plato (429?–347BC) and Aristotle (384–322BC) have certain—decidedly unpleasant—things to say on the subject of ending the lives of the sick and the congenitally deformed, although these are not cases of mercy-killing as we understand it; Plato and Aristotle both hold that if a life is such that it can never be worthwhile for one to live it, it should be ended. More will be said of the criteria by which a life might be adjudged not worth living in the survey of Greek moral philosophy in Part One.

The reason these questions, so urgent today, occupy a relatively minor place in earlier philosophical debate has as much to do with the predominantly secular character of contemporary philosophy as with the state of modern science and technology. It is true, of course, that there are nowadays special sub-disciplines of philosophy like Jewish and Christian or even Catholic bioethics. These draw on authoritative religious texts that are centuries old or ancient, as well as on institutional traditions. But the very fact that the word 'bioethics' is a recent coinage highlights the fact that most of these issues are current rather than traditional. Similarly, ethical questions regarding the environment (so-called environmental ethics), abortion, and the equality of women might have been, or were actually, raised by individual thinkers from time to time in the recent and remoter past; but they did not become widely discussed social issues until major technological and social developments rendered them pressing matters for large numbers of people the world over. Thus, what were at best relatively minor issues in the remoter past often loom large in the philosophical debates of the present. Some current issues, like human cloning for example, could not even be conceived of before the advances in scientific knowledge and technology of the past few years. This is accordingly a particularly good example of an issue that is current but not traditional.

1.2.3 Issues that are traditional, current, and perennial

Finally, we may consider our last two categories together: (c) traditional and current issues that are not, and (d) those that are, perennial. Of course, the word 'perennial' comes from the Latin *per* ('through') and *anni* ('years'), so it might be objected that any issue that is very old but still debated is perennial by definition. And so it is, given the nominal (that is, the literal, etymological) meaning of the word. Yet it is possible to maintain a distinction between (c) and (d) by giving 'perennial' an enriched sense. That sense can only be hinted at here; it will be explained fully in the discussion of primary philosophy in chapters 3 and 4.

To begin with, a very brief word on (c). While the issues described in the previous sub-section are current but not traditional, some social and political issues—the examples given above were civil disobedience and the morality of warfare—are both traditional and current, since they are a constant in human society, and therefore in the life of most individuals, once social life develops beyond the stage of primitive tribalism. (Up to that point one cannot legitimately speak of people's consciousness of themselves as individuals apart from the tribe.) Plato treated the former of these issues, civil disobedience, in one of the dialogues we shall be studying (see chap. 12). Problems concerning the individual and state authority and conflicts among sovereign nations are still very much a topic of philosophical debate, as they were in Plato's day; and they will pose themselves afresh as the domestic social order and the international political landscape continue to undergo change.

Turning now to (d), the moral questions about right and wrong and the good life for man (What is moral? and Why be moral?) are relatively self-explanatory; what is meant by 'metaphysics,' on the other hand, requires a good deal of careful elaboration. Nevertheless, the nominal meaning of the word seems clear: problems concerning those things, if any, that lie outside or beyond (Greek: *meta*) the physical or sensible world—*super*sensible things, in other words. The questions of God's existence and the soul's survival of death obviously belong to this domain; in chapters 3 and 4, however, they will be shown to form part of two larger issues concerning the whole order of being and of knowing. Metaphysics, accordingly, concerns itself with the sensible no less than the supersensible. That should be clear from the talk of *man's* place within the totality of all things; for unlike the soul, a human being is clearly a physical entity. As with 'perennial,' then, the nominal meaning ('beyond the physical') gives only a rough idea of the tendency of metaphysical thinking. For metaphysics, as we shall see, includes much more—everything, in fact, of which we can say, in any sense, that it 'is.' Throughout this work we shall subsume the metaphysical issues of perennial philosophy under the heading 'primary philosophy,' excluding from this domain the perennial moral issues concerning right, wrong, and the good life.

The moral and metaphysical issues under (d) were described as those that arise from the universal human condition and must be faced as soon as we begin to reflect upon our nature as human beings and on our place in the order of things. Historically, therefore, the perennial issues confront human reflection earlier than, and provide the basis and outer framework for, the enduring social and political issues mentioned under (c). They underlie many of the issues addressed in other sub-disciplines of philosophy as well. In the next chapter it will be argued that the perennial issues underlie *all* those studies carried on in the arts and science faculties of universities today. The purpose of university education as described there is to examine the moral and intellectual basis of human life without which genuine human flourishing is just not possible. This examination is not focused upon the perennial issues alone, but it has not so far either gone back *behind* them to anything more fundamental or *beyond* them to any perspective more encompassing; whether or not their founding and framing role is acknowledged, they are presupposed by all the other philosophical and non-philosophical pursuits in which the examination of the moral and intellectual basis of human life is carried on.

While philosophy is only one discipline within the arts and science faculty of the modern university, it is nevertheless central to the university enterprise precisely because its primary focus is on the perennial issues. These, however, are not the sole prerogative of philosophy, being in fact much older than philosophy itself. The perennial issues were first addressed in a *pre*-philosophical manner in mythico-religious thought, well before the birth of philosophy (see chap. 5 below); and they continue to be addressed, whether constructively or dismissively, directly or obliquely, in *extra*-philosophical religious, scientific, and social scientific thought, both within and outside the university, right down to the present day. While the dominant perspective in which the questions regarding human mortality, the divine, the good life, and man's place in the encompassing order of things may shift from religion to philosophy to science and back again to philosophy or religion, the issues themselves remain substantially the same, furnishing a basis and outer framework for all the other beliefs that go to make up the constantly shifting moral and intellectual basis of our lives.

The mention of religion and even science should make it clear that the designation 'perennial' is not intended to preclude sweeping historical changes in the dominant *way* in which these questions have been asked. This is true even of philosophical thought itself. For the rise of Christianity, on the one hand, and the advent of the modern science, on the other, had a decisive shaping influence on the metaphysical and moral reflections of philosophers. Given the way in which the Christian and scientific world-views have revolutionized philosophy itself, the very distinctness of the latter from religion and science is open to question. The short answer to the question, How is philosophy essentially different? seems to be that religious thought employs scriptural authority as well as tradition, including interpretive and institutional traditions, as final tests of the fruits of rational reflection; philosophy, by contrast, relies on unaided human reason and our common human experience alone. The same may be said of science, of course, except that modern science understands rationality exclusively in terms of its own highly successful investigative techniques. Philosophy, as will be seen more clearly in chapter 6, is open to other methodologies, other patterns of rational enquiry, than those found in either the exact mathematical or the empirical natural and social sciences.

1.2.4 The issues to be pursued

In this work, we shall be concerned only with the perennial issues of philosophy. Body and soul, life and death, will be the main topics in the discussion of Plato, where we shall focus on the doctrine of immortality in particular. Truth (or certainty) and knowledge will occupy us primarily in the parts on Descartes and Hume. Such questions are termed 'epistemological' today, from the Greek word for knowledge, *epistēmē*. While now generally treated as a separate sub-discipline of philosophy, distinct from metaphysics, theory of knowledge was originally part and parcel of metaphysics itself. The reasons for this will be explained in chapter 3. Faith and the existence of God will be central to our study of Descartes, Hume, and Sartre, while morality and the good life will be the focus of our study of Socrates, in the first part, and of Sartre, in the last.

This approach to philosophy, by way of the perennial issues, is admittedly partial and selective; yet it seems on the whole the best way to convey a sense of what philosophy is and has been since its inception, and of what it still can be—provided there are individuals willing to pursue it in the same spirit, if not exactly in the same manner, as the Greek thinkers of the first great classical age of philosophical exploration. If there were need of an authority to endorse this approach, we might turn again to Kant. At the conclusion of his monumental work, the *Critique of Pure Reason*, Kant wrote that all the problems of philosophy "combine in the three following questions: 1. What can I know? 2. What ought I to do? 3. What may I hope?" The first of these questions concerns metaphysics, or rather that portion of metaphysical enquiry that Kant was apt to take for the whole of it: the problem of the order of knowing to be discussed in chapter 3. This comprises questions about the starting point, the kinds, and the scope or extent of human knowledge—in short, what are now called 'epistemological' issues. Kant's assignment of them to metaphysics accords well enough with the idea of metaphysics to be elaborated in chapters 3 and 4, except that problems concerning the order of knowing must share centre stage with the other chief object of metaphysical enquiry, problems regarding the order of being. The latter were clearly the principal focus of metaphysics long before Kant (see 3.2–3); and they survive in Kant's thought, too, even if he himself was apt to stress the epistemological unduly.

The second of Kant's questions has to do with duty. This is the basic question of Kant's moral philosophy. As in the case of metaphysics, so too in that of morals, Kant's understanding of the basic issues is narrower than that of the Greeks. In the mainstream of Greek ethics, doing one's moral duty was not diametrically opposed to the quest for the good life (happiness) but a key part of it. This exclusive

Chapter 1: Problems, Periods, Genres   11

disjunction—duty or inclination—is a peculiarly Kantian innovation, about which we shall have more to say in the part on Socrates. It probably owes a lot to Kant's own austerely Protestant upbringing and faith, with its emphasis on doing what one ought in order to be worthy of the next world while staunchly resisting the many enticements of pleasure in this one.

Finally, the question "What may I hope?" is none other than the problem of personal immortality. For the issue is: if I do as I ought, that is, in Kant's words, if I "so behave as not to be unworthy of happiness, may I hope to obtain happiness?" Since "a system in which happiness is bound up with and proportioned to morality" is not to be found in this world—in which the wicked often prosper and the good are trampled underfoot—the question is whether I may hope to be part of such a system in the next world, in the afterlife. That presupposes the existence of a supremely just God who metes out reward and punishment in the afterlife in accordance with men's deserts.

These then—the order of being and of knowing, morality and the good life, death and immortality, the existence and nature of God—are among the perennial questions that stand in the forefront of philosophical enquiry, despite important variations in emphasis and interpretation in the pagan Greek, medieval Christian, and modern scientific periods. For that reason they have a special claim upon our attention as we take our first steps in the field of philosophy. How they fit into the framework of the questions of the order of knowing and of being will be discussed more fully in chapters 3 and 4.

1.3 Periods in the history of philosophy

So much for the perennial problems of philosophy to be dealt with here (with occasional side-glances at other issues). The next task is to provide a rough overview of the main epochs making up the western philosophical tradition according to a periodization that would probably be acceptable to most historians of the subject nowadays. The starting and end points of each period are admittedly somewhat arbitrary, disguising the real overlap among them; but something like the following divisions seem to be agreed upon by intellectual historians today.

1.3.1 Overview of the periodization of the history of philosophy

To begin with, we may distinguish five broad periods of intellectual history.

(1) Ancient or Greek and Roman (from the early sixth century BC to the end of the fourth century AD, that is, between 599 BC and 399 AD). There are three or four main sub-divisions here, roughly describable as the (1) pre-classical, (2) classical,

and (3) post-classical periods, with the last divisible into (a) the Hellenistic period (from the Macedonian conquest in the late fourth century BC down to the completion of the Roman conquests around 30 BC); and (b) the return to classicism marked chiefly by the emergence of what is usually called 'Neoplatonism' (literally, 'new Platonism') in the mid-third century AD. The pre-classical era began in Asia Minor (modern-day Turkey) and southern Italy some time after the turn from the seventh to the sixth century BC, while ancient Greek philosophy reached its apogee at Athens in the fourth century. Although the conquests of Alexander of Macedon brought the era of the independent city-states of classical Greece to a close, they and the subsequent Roman conquests fostered a tremendous spread of Greek learning throughout the known world. From this process (called 'hellenization,' from the Greeks' own words for their country, *Hellas*, and people, *Hellenes*), the first post-classical or Hellenistic period derives its name. Athens remained an important centre of learning throughout this period, though it was gradually supplanted by Rome, with important outposts of Greek culture situated in North Africa (Alexandria in Egypt and Antioch in Syria) and in the eastern part of the Roman empire (Constantinople, that is, ancient Byzantium or modern-day Istanbul). The final date assigned is rather arbitrary, Neoplatonism having continued to be a force for centuries thereafter.

(2) Medieval (from the fourth to the fourteenth century). This includes what is known as 'Byzantine philosophy' that is, the philosophy of the Greeks (many of them by now Christians) of the Middle Ages, centred first in Constantinople, later in Alexandria. The Christian philosophy of the Middle Ages is usually divided into two main sub-periods: the time of the Church fathers, or the Patristic period, and the so-called high Middle Ages, that is, the twelfth and thirteenth centuries, when the until then lost writings of Aristotle gradually filtered back into Europe from the Arabic countries of North Africa, along with the works of the great Arab commentators (see 2.2), bringing about a revolution in philosophy and theology throughout Christian Europe. The outstanding centres of learning in the high Middle Ages were the great universities of Oxford, Paris, and Cologne. The teachers at these great schools during the High Middle Ages are called 'the schoolmen' or 'the scholastics.'

(3) Renaissance and Reformation (from the middle of the fourteenth to the end of the sixteenth century). The Renaissance emanated to all the great centres of European culture from Italy (especially Florence), to which certain influential Greek scholars and philosophers had emigrated before the fall of Constantinople (see below); the Reformation, which only began in the sixteenth century, arose first in Germany and Switzerland, gradually spreading throughout northern Europe. Though the strictly philosophical achievements of Renaissance and Reformation were not of the first rank, the artistic legacy of such giants of the Italian Renaissance as Michelangelo and

Leonardo da Vinci remains unequalled, while the theology of the Reformation was to have the greatest influence on the history of western Europe for centuries to come.

(4) Modern (from the seventeenth to the nineteenth century). This encompasses the traditions known as 'British empiricism' and 'continental rationalism,' as well as Kant, who sparked the nineteenth-century movement known as 'German Idealism.' The first two centuries together are sometimes referred to as 'the Age of Reason.' The eighteenth century in particular is usually called 'the Age of Enlightenment' or simply 'the Enlightenment.' Nineteenth-century German Idealism has been aptly described as a Romantic reaction to the rationalism of the Enlightenment, though one that still shared many of the Enlightenment's ideals. The entire century is often called 'the Romantic era,' not just, or even primarily, in philosophy, of course, but especially in music, literature, and the fine arts.

(5) Contemporary (twentieth-century philosophy). The contemporary continuators of the British tradition are the proponents of so-called analytic philosophy (roughly coextensive with the term 'Anglo-American philosophy'), while the German tradition has been carried on by certain original French and German thinkers, usually lumped together under some such heading as 'contemporary continental philosophy.' This includes the movements known as 'existentialism,' 'phenomenology,' 'hermeneutics,' and more recently 'post-modernism.' The first and last of these have deep roots in nineteenth-century continental thought—in Romanticism or (as some would describe the Romantic revolt against the Enlightenment) in irrationalism. It is probably fair to say that contemporary philosophy, along with much else in the twentieth century, remains torn between the Enlightenment and the Romantic traditions. This unresolved tension is evident on many levels, right down to that of the ongoing debates about public policy issues in our own time.

1.3.2 Renaissance, Reformation, and Enlightenment

The summary above will have to do by way of overview, though a word or two may still be in order concerning the Renaissance, Reformation, and Enlightenment. Like 'ancient,' 'medieval,' 'modern,' and 'contemporary,' these terms are used in many departments of cultural history apart from philosophy—in art history, literary history, political history, Church history, and theology, to name just a few. Yet their content is even harder to pin down. 'Ancient,' as we have seen, refers not just to the classical Greek period, but to everything thereafter right down to the fall of Rome; while 'medieval' covers not just a few centuries (say, the eleventh to the thirteenth) but an entire millennium. Even 'contemporary' and 'modern' are at least slightly misleading. If we consider what is usually meant by contemporary painting, for example (roughly, the current decade or two, as opposed to everything since the end of the nineteenth century, which is called 'modern'), we realize that both terms are used very differently in philosophy and art history. 'Contemporary music,' too, covers a shorter span than 'contemporary philosophy,' though perhaps not so short as 'contemporary painting.' Still, the danger of misunderstanding is relatively small in all these cases by comparison with those of 'Renaissance,' 'Reformation,' and 'Enlightenment.'

In terms of the history of thought, the so-called Renaissance (the word is of nineteenth-century French coinage meaning 'rebirth,' but has been adopted in its French spelling by several other European languages) should be dated roughly from the fall of Constantinople in the mid-fifteenth century, when certain Greek scholars, fleeing the Turks, arrived in Italy, bringing with them Greek manuscripts that were to form the basis of new schools of philosophy devoted to the study of Greek ideas, principally in Florence. (If our primary focus were literature and the fine arts rather than philosophy, we should have to date the start of the Renaissance a century earlier, in the time of the poet Petrarch and the painter Giotto). The Renaissance may be said to have ended in the first half of the seventeenth century, when the innovations of Galileo (1564–1642) in natural science shifted the focus of intellectual pursuits decisively from man, the arts, and literature, to the study of nature. As already mentioned, the geographical epicentre of the Renaissance was Italy, from which it spread to France, England, and Germany, all of which became major centres. In this general rebirth of the literary, philosophical, and artistic heritage of ancient Greece and Rome, all the main schools or sects of Greek philosophy described under (1) experienced some sort of rebirth of their own. Moreover, the classical legacy was made available to a far wider audience than ever before owing to the invention of the printing press and the consequent spread of education to a much broader segment of the population. It was to the Roman lawyer-statesman and philosopher Cicero (106–43 BC) that the Renaissance 'humanists,' as they were called, looked for the ideal of a civilized way of life based on the study of Greek cultural monuments. The first so-called humanists were university teachers of grammar, rhetoric, and poetry, who harboured a deep animosity to the traditional medieval or scholastic (Aristotelian) learning of the universities based on handbooks and commentaries rather than the study of original texts (particularly Plato); but the term 'humanist' came to be applied ever more widely to university and private scholars engaged in the study of the ancient languages and the whole cultural legacy of antiquity. Today, it can mean anyone engaged in the pursuit of the liberal arts ('the humanities,' as we say) as opposed to narrowly technical or professional training.

By 'Reformation,' on the other hand, is meant, first and foremost, the sixteenth-century religious protest or reform movement that resulted in the permanent division of the Christian church into Roman Catholicism and a plethora of different Protestant denominations. Symbolically, it dates from a day in 1517 when Martin Luther (1483–1546), rebelling against the authority of the papacy, nailed his famous ninety-five theses to the door of the Castle Church in Wittenberg. Some humanists, notably Erasmus of Rotterdam (1466–1536), figured among, or were close to, the reformers, so the separation of Renaissance and Reformation is not always sharp. The Reformation proper was over once the split in the Church had become irreversible, around the middle of the sixteenth century, though other reform movements began within the Catholic Church, and the different Protestant confessions continued to contend among themselves, leading to new schisms and sects. Philosophically, the great significance of the Reformation lay in the severing of the bond forged between Christian theology and Aristotelian science by the philosophy of the high Middle Ages, particularly in the work of St Thomas Aquinas (1225–1274). The weakening of centralized ecclesiastical authority and the new emphasis placed on the individual's own immediate access to spiritual truth prepared the way for the new individualism and independence of thought that inaugurated the modern era. The philosophy of Descartes (1596–1650), the so-called Father of Modern Philosophy, has been characterized as "Protestant individualism secularized" (see 23.3.2), and we shall see that there are in fact excellent grounds for thinking of it in these terms. What this perspective overlooks, however, is the extent to which Descartes was above all a Christian philosopher with strong roots in the Catholicism of the Middle Ages. Nevertheless, if it is true that Galileo and his predecessors shifted attention away from man to the surrounding physical cosmos, Descartes restored man to his place at the centre.

The Renaissance having brought about a spread of learning to a much wider segment of the European populace, the eighteenth-century Enlightenment went much further in the same direction. In this particular phase of modern European thought, the mathematical natural science of Galileo and especially Sir Isaac Newton (1642–1727)—'natural philosophy,' as physics and astronomy were still called at the time—bulked much larger than ever before, without, however, completely eclipsing the man-centred outlook inaugurated by Descartes. Thus, political and social ideas, particularly the ideals of equality, the rights of man, and progress, played an important role in enkindling the revolutionary spirit of the Age of Reason, notably in France and the American colonies. The educated public absorbed the new belief in the ennobling and emancipating power of universal human reason—an important part of the Cartesian legacy—as much through the works of gifted writers and compilers of encyclopedias of knowledge as through study of the great philosophical and scientific works on which those encyclopedias were based. Accordingly, the spread of Enlightenment went on mainly outside the universities, in salons or clubs and in the correspondence of the greatest minds of the day. The work of the great creative geniuses of the age was more apt to be supported by the new national

Academies of the Sciences than by the universities, which became bastions of conservatism. What is most characteristic of the Enlightenment, however, is the violence of its reaction against the social, intellectual, and political inheritance and institutions of the past—the Old Regime, as it was called—as well as its faith in human reason as the agent of liberation and of practical, political progress. Even those who, like Hume, made a very sober estimate of the capacities of human reason, still shared this outlook to a very great extent (see chap. 28).

Perhaps the only periodization that is universally subscribed to by historians of philosophy is the basic tripartition, ancient, medieval, and modern. On this undisputed basis, further divisions are introduced, usually according to the research interests of the individual historian. This is naturally susceptible of change as intellectual history is rewritten in each generation, though the above periodization reflects the current consensus of thought on the subject.

1.3.3 Periods to be studied

In this work, we shall study two figures from the ancient Greek period (Socrates and Plato), two from different centuries of the modern era (Descartes and Hume), and one contemporary thinker (Sartre). But frequent reference will be made to certain central features of medieval philosophy, too, especially to St Augustine (354–430 AD) and Aquinas, even if no works from the early or the high Middle Ages are to be studied. The omission of such nineteenth-century figures as Friedrich Nietzsche (1844–1900) and Gottfried Wilhelm Hegel (1770–1831) is regrettable, but, in the eyes of most historians of ideas, the nineteenth century has not quite the same claim to be regarded as one of the great classical ages of philosophy as the sixth through fourth centuries BC or the seventeenth and eighteenth centuries AD. Only Sartre, the sole representative of contemporary philosophy, falls outside these two great classical epochs. Though he may not have the same claim as the others to be a great philosopher in his own right, Sartre is nonetheless an interesting and influential exponent of contemporary thought on the European continent. As we shall see, he stands squarely on the shoulders of two undisputed giants of twentieth-century thought, Edmund Husserl (1859–1938) and Martin Heidegger (1889–1976), many of whose most important ideas he takes over and presents in much more accessible form.

1.4 Philosophy and its history

Does the decision to begin with the works of great thinkers representing key epochs of the past mean that we are embarking on a study of the *history* rather than the *problems* of western philosophy? By no means. To see why not, let us consider three different senses of 'self-knowledge' roughly identifiable as (1) the Greek sense, (2) the contemporary, popular sense (the one that comes most readily to mind today), and (3) the special sense in which self-knowledge is the aim of *academic* philosophy, of which the study of the history of ideas is an integral part.

There was a very old tradition among the Greeks according to which the pinnacle of human wisdom lay in understanding what it is to be human and not divine, that is, in *self*-knowledge. For the Greeks, this did not mean plumbing the depths of one's individual psyche—the sort of thing we find endlessly fascinating today, turning to popular psychology and social science or to literature and 'pop' philosophy in search of insights into the perplexing selves that we are. In this Greek tradition, the inscription 'know thyself' on the temple of the Oracle at Delphi—the closest thing to a Vatican known to the Greeks—was taken to mean: understand what it is to be mortal; think only 'human thoughts,' as befits the weakness of your race; enjoy such meagre and transitory pleasures as human life affords, yet 'nothing in excess'—the other famous inscription on the temple—lest you get above yourself and the gods cast you down again. This impersonal self-understanding aims at knowing something universal about human nature and the condition of all mankind. Among the Greeks, the perennial philosophical questions about the divine, about human mortality, and about the good life for man formed part of the outer framework of a quest for self-knowledge in this strictly impersonal sense.

Now since each of us, aside from being a unique individual personality, is also a member of the human species, we too may aspire, in our reflective moments, to self-knowledge in this impersonal Greek sense. That is, we may decide to confront the perennial issues regarding mortality and morality, the human condition, and man's place in the greater scheme of things. But as individuals who happen to have been educated in a contemporary western language, we are also members of a very old (though by no means the oldest) civilization, one that grew up in Athens, Rome, Constantinople, Florence, evolving in various centres in western Europe for centuries until it finally achieved world-wide dominance in the last century. In spreading to non-western countries, western or European culture has sometimes all but supplanted local or indigenous cultures, sometimes changed them radically, sometimes had only a very limited influence. So when we ask the perennial questions concerning God, the soul, death, and the good life for man, we are asking questions that are rooted *both* in the universal human condition *and* in the long history of the particular civilization of which we are part—in virtue of our language and geographic location, which may or may not be that of our parents and remoter ancestors. We *can* ask these questions without considering the ways in which they have been answered for millennia in western philosophy; we can even ask them exclusively in the light of the way they have been asked and answered in other, non-western civilizations (if we have the knowledge and linguistic equipment to do so). But the most immediate way for us to approach them is in the terms in which they have been posed in the western tradition. Only thus do we start from where we *are* rather than selecting a point of departure that must first be reached, perhaps through long preparation.

To ask these questions in dialogue with the western traditions of philosophy is not to pursue the history of western philosophy; it is, rather, a way of pursuing philosophy itself. For to 'do' philosophy is to become a participant in a philosophical conversation of the present with the past. The dialogue is carried on primarily as a debate among those living in the present, but it is also a conversation with the past. It has been aptly said of the Greek philosophers that they "have been not just the fathers but the companions of western philosophy" (Bernard Williams); and much the same holds of every truly great philosophical figure of the past. In the mathematical and the experimental sciences, where debate turns very largely on measurement, calculation, and the repeatable experiment, on the interpretation of data and the canons of logic and proof, this historical dimension is hardly significant; but in philosophy, where the system of ideas is advanced by the illuminating insight, the trenchant criticism, the compelling argument, and the original approach, we may expect to find that peculiar "involvement in its own history" (Williams again) that is a constant in all the arts or humanities and in philosophy in particular.

Nor is it indicative of a parochial 'Eurocentrism' that we select as our starting point certain influential philosophies of the west. We have to start somewhere, and our western traditions, without being in any way intrinsically superior to others, are the intuitively obvious place to begin—given the hemisphere we inhabit and the language we speak. True, its historical "involvement" makes our way of proceeding very different from anything in the Greek wisdom tradition—but then, the Greeks did not have the Greeks and two millennia of Judeo-Christian culture behind them! It is accordingly a third path of reflection or self-understanding, as different from the Greek pursuit of wisdom as it is from the contemporary preoccupation with the self; it is the path of academic philosophy, and it is on this path that we are about to set foot.

In fairness to other points of view it should be acknowledged that some of the greatest thinkers of the past have themselves treated the prior history of their discipline as largely irrelevant to their aims. Historical studies may be useful in alerting philosophers to pitfalls, or in providing them with a foil to set off the truth of their own insights, they hold; but otherwise the philosophical thought of the past is largely irrelevant to the enterprise of the present, or no more relevant than is alchemy (the pseudo-science of turning base metals into gold) to the rigorous science of chemistry, or astrology to scientific astronomy. Kant may have been the first to characterize the relationship of his own to all previous metaphysical systems of thought in terms such as these. In a work as short as its title is long, *Prolegomena to Any Future Metaphysics That Will Be Able to Come Forward as Science*, he writes that his own metaphysics "stands in the same relation to the common metaphysics of the Schools [that is, the universities] as does chemistry to alchemy, or astronomy to the astrology of the fortune teller." In this way Kant (the proto-typical learned German university professor!) introduced an analogy which was to be used by the antagonists of intellectual history in the present century to dismiss the entire preceding philosophical tradition—including poor Kant himself! In their more provocative moods, some of these modern critics of historical studies are apt to say that genuine philosophy only began around 1900, with the birth of so-called analytic philosophy in the early work of the British thinkers Bertrand Russell (1872–1970) and G.E. Moore (1873–1958). Analytic philosophy, in which logic and the analysis of language bulk very large, is still the dominant trend in the Anglo-American universities today, although its stranglehold on the minds of those who write in English appears to be relaxing. Still, the brash overstatement that all philosophy before 1900 was about as worthless as the alchemy and astrology of earlier, less enlightened times still has considerable shock effect—and is therefore heard on occasion in the ranks of the despisers of intellectual history even today.

1.5 Literary form in philosophy

So much for philosophy and its history. To round out this initial chapter, a word is in order on literary form in philosophical writing.

Thales (c.[from the Latin *circa*, 'around'] 624–546 BC), by general agreement the first philosopher, seems to have written nothing, while the prose works written by his immediate pupils and successors, Anaximander (c. 610–546 BC) and Anaximenes (c. 585–528 BC), are lost. The thought of all three is known to us only through the indirect testimony of later writers. So too the ideas of Pythagoras (c. 571–497 BC), another pre-classical thinker who will figure centrally in our study of Plato. Pythagoras, incidentally, may have been the first thinker to call himself a philosopher. When asked what this meant—the literal meaning is obviously 'lover (*philos*) of wisdom (*sophia*)'—he is reported to have replied that life "is like a festival; just as some come to the festival to compete [for honours and distinction, at the Olympic games, for example], some to ply their trade [and accumulate wealth], but the best people come as spectators, so in life the slavish men go hunting for fame or gain, the philosophers for the truth." These 'Three Lives' were much discussed in antiquity; despite its open disdain for wealth and honours, the so-called Parable of the Festival is still a nice way of expressing the perennial choice that faces each one of us in life.

Like this anecdote about the man, most of what we know about Pythagoras's philosophical teachings stems from much later sources, especially the Pythagoreanism of the classical and Hellenistic periods. A considerable body of fragments of the early Greek philosopher Heracleitus of Ephesus (*fluorit* [*fl.*]that is, 'bloomed,' was at his peak or acme, around 504–501 BC) has come down to us in literal form. They consist of what is now sometimes referred to as 'oracular prose': short, pithy, sometimes highly enigmatic, utterances resembling the pronouncements of divinely inspired oracles or soothsayers. Such sayings are marked by the complete absence of justification or formal argumentation as we know (and expect) it nowadays. With Heracleitus's contemporary, Parmenides of Elea (born around 515–510 BC), the formal argumentative or dialectical style (from the Greek word *dialegesthai*, meaning 'to converse,' 'to exchange words' or even arguments) makes its first appearance, although Parmenides recorded his meticulously reasoned findings in the apparently incongruous literary form of a long poem, only part of which has been preserved. His pupils Zeno of Elea (*fl.* c. 465–455 BC) and Melissus of Samos (born around 480 BC) developed the argumentative style of their master further, virtually pioneering the now common practice of examining commonly accepted beliefs based on ordinary experience in order to bring out unsuspected incongruities; to escape these puzzles they recommended acceptance of the decidedly *un*common and counter-intuitive conclusions of Parmenides himself (see 5.6 and 20.10.2). A later anti-Eleatic, Empedocles of Acragas (*fl.* c. 444 BC), followed Parmenides's example, writing philosophy in verse form, even beginning his philosophical poem, as had Parmenides, with a mythological introduction reminiscent of the Greek epic tradition; but whereas Parmenides puts his philosophical doctrine into the mouth of a goddess, Empedocles at least speaks in his own person, even if he too claims the authority of divine revelation for all he has to say. The other main schools of anti-Eleatic thought before Socrates were the atomists, Leucippus (*fl.* c. 440–435 BC) and Democritus (born c. 460 BC), and Anaxagoras, a rough contemporary of Empedocles. In the *Apology* Socrates mentions a book written by Anaxagoras as purchasable at the price of only one drachma—probably, therefore, not a very long work. It seems also to have been his only work. Democritus was a much more prolific prose writer on a wide variety of subjects, apparently one of the most prolific, in fact, though all that survives are fragments taken from his ethical works.

As for Socrates (470–399 BC), he wrote nothing at all. His teachings were transmitted to his contemporaries orally, in conversation, and were neither recorded verbatim nor reliably transcribed by anyone who heard them. (A contemporary writer on Socrates, the soldier-historian Xenophon, claims to be recalling Socrates's actual conversations, but his testimony is not generally regarded as credible.) Following the example of others in the circle of Socrates, Plato (427–347 BC), without doubt Socrates's most gifted student and follower, wrote dramatic dialogues or literary conversations in which Socrates was almost always the main character. These dialogues, particularly the earliest of them, are the main source of our knowledge of the moral philosophy of Socrates. However, the fact that it was Plato who wrote them gives rise to a vexing problem. How are we to make out anything about the philosophy of Socrates when our chief sources are the writings of another, who was no mere disciple but a creative philosophical genius in his own right? More will be said about this problem later (see chap. 8). Aristotle (384–322 BC), like most philosophers after him, wrote mainly systematic prose treatises, although the treatises of Aristotle, as they have come down to us, are part of a traditional literary genre known as 'school discourses.' These are neither just lecture notes nor systematic works intended for publication, but highly condensed treatments of different philosophical topics probably intended to serve as the basis of discussions in specialized circles of students in Aristotle's philosophy school. Aristotle's earlier works, written in dialogue form, are unfortunately lost.

Ever since Aristotle it has become customary to write philosophy in expository and argumentative prose, be it shorter essays or longer, systematic treatises. This was in fact just a return to the practice of the earliest natural investigators who pioneered this literary form. Two notable exceptions in the post-Aristotelian tradition are (1) the commentaries on the works of Aristotle that became the standard form of philosophical expression starting around the first century AD, persisting throughout the Middle Ages and until the end of the sixteenth century; and (2) the formal disputations of the medieval schoolmen, or 'scholastics,' as they are more frequently called. The works of St Thomas Aquinas provide examples of the best of both genres. The medieval commentaries on Aristotle (and other Greek authorities) are, in all interesting cases, by no means merely elucidations of Aristotelian texts but, above all, bold speculative transformations of the doctrines of Aristotle and other pagan authorities in the new Christian perspective of medieval philosophy. ('Pagan,' incidentally, is used here in contradistinction to 'Christian' and 'Judeo-Christian'; it is a historical term having none of the negative connotations of 'paganism' and 'heathenism' as employed by Church Fathers concerned to develop a truly Christian philosophy.) Instead of reproducing Greek ideas, the medieval thinkers attempted to move the philosophical problems forward in decisive ways. In this they differ significantly from the explanatory commentaries on classical philosophical texts that began to be written in late Greek times. The philosophical genre of commentary writing remained in vogue right down to the sixteenth century, when a Spanish Jesuit named Francisco Suarez (1548–1617), whose *Metaphysical Disputations* appeared in 1597, brought about a radical innovation in the literary form in which metaphysics was treated. This work had, directly and indirectly, a profound influence on Protestant scholasticism in Germany in the seventeenth and eighteenth centuries, which in turn shaped the literary form that Kant gave to his major work, the *Critique of Pure Reason*. And as in metaphysics, so in many other areas of philosophy, the history of the literary forms employed is essentially the history of successive modifications of the original Aristotelian model. What is true of the form holds for the content as well: successive epochs of philosophy can be distinguished by the way the original Aristotelian matrix of philosophy, or of some sub-discipline like moral or natural philosophy, is modified, often by introducing Platonic or Neoplatonic elements, though sometimes in more radical ways—as in Kant, for example.

Many philosophers after Aristotle and the medieval Schoolmen tried their hand at the dialogue form pioneered by Plato and certain of his contemporaries. Thus, while Hume wrote mainly essays or treatises, he also wrote several short dialogues, one of which ("Of a Particular Providence and a Future State") we shall be examining in Part Four. In this he followed the lead of his immediate predecessor, George Berkeley (1685-1753), Bishop of Cloyne, who recast his philosophy, first published in treatise form, in the shape of three masterful dialogues. Even Descartes left behind in his private papers an unfinished dialogue entitled *The Search for Truth*. One of his best-known followers, Nicholas Malebranche (1638-1715), wrote a couple of works in dialogue form. Another seventeenth-century giant, Gottfried Wilhelm Friedrich Leibniz (1646-1716) wrote an extended dialogue, the length of a very substantial treatise, entitled *New Essays on Human Understanding*. Some philosophical writing has even taken the form of intellectual or spiritual autobiography. Examples are St Augustine's *Confessions* and the first part of Descartes's *Discourse on Method*. Even the famous work by Descartes that we shall be studying, the *Meditations on First Philosophy*, incorporates elements of autobiography into what is essentially a connected treatise developing a single, very complex line of argument. And one must not forget epistolary philosophy, the writing and exchange of philosophical letters that was one of the main forms of philosophical expression in the seventeenth century. No one interested in the thought of Descartes or Leibniz can afford to ignore their philosophical correspondence.

Some later philosophers have even attempted to write philosophy in verse form again, as did certain of the Presocratics. One thinks here primarily of the great poem of the Roman philosopher-poet, Lucretius (c. 99–55 BC), who renewed the atomistic philosophy of Epicurus (see 2.1 and 4.6 below); but as recently as the middle of the last century a leading German thinker, Martin Heidegger, published a small volume of what he designated 'thought-lyrics.' Apart from this unique work, many of Heidegger's later writings exemplify a style that has a certain affinity with the oracular mode of speech characteristic of Heracleitus. This absence of formal argumentation has earned him both dismissive criticism and a devoted following of true believers, in different quarters. In the preceding century, Nietzsche had written important works in an aphoristic style reminiscent of certain Greek models (particular in the tradition of ancient medicine). In this use of aphorism he was preceded by an older contemporary he very much admired, Arthur Schopenhauer (1788-1860), though both thinkers wrote important works in the more conventional treatise form as well. Even earlier, the *Thoughts* of Blaise Pascal (1623-1662) were, as the title suggests, cast in a similar aphoristic form. Perhaps the oddest of literary forms is the rare attempt, found in the major work of Benedict de Spinoza (1632–1677), as well as some minor works of Descartes, to write philosophy *more geometrico*, that is, in the geometrical manner of Euclid's famed mathematical treatise, starting with definitions, axioms, and postulates, and proceeding to theorems. More will be said of this strange phenomenon in the discussion of scientific method in chapter 6.

Summing up, then, the history of philosophy provides notable examples of a wide variety of literary genres, from philosophical poems and 'thought-lyrics' to dialogues of varying length and collections of aphorisms, not to mention letters, school discourses, and formal disputations. The more conventional forms, however, are sentence-by-sentence commentaries on or interpretations of earlier writers regarded as classical or authorities, as well as essays, and, of course, lengthy treatises—the *magnum opus* ('major work') that has come to be expected of every major philosopher. In this work we shall be examining some dialogues and a few short connected treatises. To what extent the form is suited to the content of each will become apparent as we interpret the works in question.

2

Philosophy and Higher Education

2.1 Introductory

In this chapter it will be suggested that the philosophical approach to problems epitomizes university studies, embodying all that sets so-called higher education apart from the primary and secondary levels. The very first universities were essentially philosophy schools in which the perennial issues identified in the last chapter were central to the course of studies. It was in these schools, too, that the first halting attempts at scientific research and scholarly enquiry began. The very first of them, the school founded by Plato some time in the 380s BC, was called 'the Academy,' the name Plato's house took from the nearby grove on the outskirts of Athens named for the Greek hero Academus. From it comes our modern term 'academic' and the expression 'the grove of academe' as a highbrow—or mock-highbrow—designation for the university.

The form of instruction practised at the first university is a matter of conjecture, but there were, we know, teachers other than Plato himself, and the curriculum, if not the length of the course of studies, probably bore some resemblance to that described in Book VII of Plato's long dialogue on political and social matters, the *Republic*. It was at this school that a young Macedonian named Aristotle, Plato's most gifted pupil, received his philosophical and scientific training. Many years later, somewhere in the late 330s, Aristotle founded a similar school just outside Athens. It was known as 'the Lyceum' for the grove sacred to the god Apollo Lyceius near which it stood. The words *lycée* and *liceo* are still used in French and Italian for institutions of secondary education. The buildings on the site included a covered walkway (*peripatos* in Greek) of some sort, whence the followers of Aristotle were known as 'the Peripatetics.' Aristotelian philosophy has been known as 'Peripateticism' or 'the Peripatetic tradition' ever since. However, as mentioned earlier (see 1.3.1), medieval

Aristotelianism is often referred to as 'scholasticism' and the medieval followers of Aristotle as 'the schoolmen' or the 'the scholastics.' 'Scholastic-Aristotelian' is a phrase that will be used frequently in this work to designate a philosophical outlook widely shared in the Middle Ages, its origins clearly traceable to the late-Greek science codified in the works of Aristotle. It still has many adherents in Roman Catholic colleges and universities today.

Two other schools of a similar type had been founded by the end of the fourth century BC. Their emphasis, however, was more on training in a particular system of thought than on independent enquiry or research. Around 306 BC Epicurus (341–270), who was born of Athenian parents on the island of Samos (off the coast of Asia Minor) founded an influential school at Athens known as 'the Garden,' while Zeno of Citium (336–264 BC), a town on Cyprus, came to Athens around 313 BC and founded a school near the so-called Painted Porch (*Poikilē Stoa* in Greek). His followers were called 'Stoics.' The Stoic tradition was to play a major role in not just the intellectual but the social, political, and even the military life of ancient Rome.

2.2 The medieval and the modern university

The university as we know it today is an indirect descendant of these philosophy schools and the direct descendant of certain medieval institutions fostered, from the twelfth century on, by the Catholic Church and the European aristocracy. These institutions were in turn an outgrowth of the still earlier cathedral and palace schools. The so-called *universitas societas magistrorum discipulorumque* of the Middle Ages (whence our word, 'university') was essentially a guild of the teachers and students of a town, not unlike the guilds formed by various classes of artisans to defend or promote their collective interests. It was devoted largely to training the so-called learned professions—doctors, lawyers, and priests. In addition to the three main faculties, medicine, jurisprudence, and theology, the medieval university included a philosophical faculty, the so-called faculty of arts. Here were taught those disciplines that made up the old trivium (logic, rhetoric, and grammar) and quadrivium (arithmetic, geometry, harmonics, and astronomy) of Roman and Hellenistic education—the 'seven liberal arts,' as they were called. From about the start of the thirteenth century, the old curriculum of the arts faculty began to be supplemented by the addition of natural philosophy or physics, moral philosophy or ethics, and metaphysics, all owing to the fact that around this time the works of Aristotle and his Arabic commentators began to be available on the European continent in Latin translations (see 1.3.1). The closest thing in the contemporary North American university to the philosophical faculty, which still exists and is still so designated in many European countries today, is the faculty of arts and sciences.

What was taught by the teachers or masters (*magistri*) of the arts faculties of medieval universities was the core university curriculum. It was distinct from, and the basis for, the professional training received by teachers, doctors, lawyers, and priests, the chief products of the universities right down to the nineteenth century. Of course, things began to change rapidly after the industrial revolution, until, in the contemporary university, professional training has come to be seen, by government, university administrators, and the general populace alike, as the university's main contribution, as a public institution, to contemporary society at large. This distorting view is no doubt owing in part to what Aristotle called a 'lack of culture,' that is, the so-called mechanic's preoccupation with practical benefit; but it is due in large part also to the fact that there are so many more professions to train in today's complex industrial or post-industrial society, including all manner of practitioners of applied sciences and the hordes of skilled technicians required to man key positions in a diverse technology-based economy. ('Knowledge-based economy,' an expression much used nowadays, is a misnomer on any understanding of 'knowledge' worth taking seriously.) Things have long since reached the point where these developments threaten the very existence of the traditional academy. As the professional schools become increasingly dominant, the original purpose of the university may be lost sight of altogether. That purpose, simply put, is the cultivation of the arts and sciences as the chief means of providing a moral and intellectual basis for human life.

Here we revert to a theme first touched on in the last chapter. It seems obvious, even on slight reflection, that human beings require an intellectual and moral as well as a material basis for living if they are to thrive and flourish. For humankind it is apparently not enough to possess the bare means of biological subsistence, nor even such material prosperity as is enjoyed in the so-called advanced nations of the world today; if we are truly to flourish as individuals and as a species, we require a comprehensive framework of ideas for understanding ourselves and our social and natural environment as a whole. If the word 'practical' is taken narrowly in the sense of whatever contributes *materially* to human life, the chief practical use of the universities may indeed be as described above; but if promoting genuine human fulfilment—happiness in a Greek sense to be discussed more fully later—is a practical, even *the* practical end to which all others are subordinate, then university education may be more practical in this sense the less practical it is in the other.

From this perspective the customary distinction between practical and intellectual or theoretical pursuits begins to appear questionable. While a great variety of things, including science, and especially medicine, make human *life* possible, providing the material basis for everything from simple biological survival to leisure and luxury, the cultivation of the arts and sciences makes a fully *human* life possible, securing the intellectual and moral basis without which genuine human flourishing is impossible. This is the purpose to which the university is dedicated. In this pursuit philosophy has always occupied a central place, having been at the outset, as noted already, not so much the centre as virtually the whole of the university enterprise.

2.3 Religion, philosophy, science, and the arts

It was noted in the last chapter that the western tradition has thus far produced three principal frameworks for understanding ourselves and our human and non-human environment, namely, (1) myth or religion, (2) philosophy, and (3) modern science. The divisions among them are not clear-cut, for no sooner did the second separate from the first and the third from the second than they began to interpenetrate. Nevertheless, these three, or one or two of them, have always furnished the moral and intellectual basis of human life, depending on the stage of civilization reached.

The moral and intellectual basis of life comprises several distinct patterns or textures of rationality (see chaps. 5 and 6). Even particular 'families' of sciences, like mathematics, for example, display distinctive types of rationality of their own. So too both mythico-religious thought and philosophy. If any *one* thing singles the human species out from others, it is perhaps the need for some such *rational* basis for living. This, at all events, is one way of understanding the hoary Scholastic-Aristotelian definition of 'man' as 'a rational animal' (see 7.14). It raises interesting questions about reason and the emotions that may shed further light on the modern university.

On the face of it, there would seem to be much more to leading a fully human life than just religious, philosophical, and scientific *understanding*. The fine arts, too, have always been prized for their humanizing effect and accorded a place within university studies. It has become customary to regard the experience of art as contributing neither morally nor intellectually but emotionally and aesthetically to a fully human way of life. This is one way of explaining why the fine arts are studied and practised within the contemporary arts and science faculty of the university. Yet this manner of isolating the aesthetic and emotional from the moral and intellectual is just as open to question as the customary distinction, considered in the last section, between intellectual and practical pursuits.

It is tempting, no doubt, to describe university studies in the arts and sciences as devoted to the examination of the whole *cultural* basis of human flourishing, distinguishing the rational (moral and intellectual) from the non-rational (emotional and aesthetic) dimension. Yet it is not at all clear that either the emotions or the fine arts have to do primarily with feeling rather than understanding. In the last part of this work, we shall see that Sartre, following Heidegger, regards certain key emotions as conveying a more immediate and profound understanding of the human condition than rational reflection alone can provide; and Heidegger himself has furnished a brilliant analysis of artworks designed to show that they convey, first and foremost, an understanding of the world—although, admittedly, not in the ordinary sense of that term. If it is true that the arts furnish not just pleasurable emotional experiences, but above all insight and understanding, and if 'understanding' is taken to refer to a process that must be rational to some degree, then we ought to be wary of the customary juxtaposition of reason or intellect with feeling or emotion. In what follows, we shall use the expression 'moral and intellectual basis of life' to cover the whole domain of culture, the whole basis of civilized life, including art, literature, and all varieties of emotional experience. Of course, to pin down the peculiar texture of rationality belonging to emotional experience or even artworks is much more difficult than the corresponding tasks in the three principal domains of religion, philosophy, and science. Only when we come to Sartre shall we pause to consider the question briefly.

2.4 Philosophy and university studies

The previous section may help to explain the rather fluid boundaries between the liberal arts studied in the arts and science faculties and the so-called fine arts. Moreover, the historical fact that the sciences themselves (arithmetic, geometry, harmonics, and astronomy) once figured among the seven liberal arts of traditional humanistic education suggests that, on that side, too, the boundaries were once much more fluid than they are today, especially where the so-called humanities disciplines are housed in a separate part of the university from the sciences.

Philosophy, we have said, is one of three dominant approaches to the perennial issues concerning life, death, and man's place within the totality of things, though hardly the leading one any longer. Science and religion have vied for that honour for centuries now. Globally speaking, the outcome is hard to assess. The spread of education, including higher education, to ever larger segments of the population in so-called developed countries, and from these to more and more of the undeveloped countries of the world, might be expected to seal the fate of traditional religion in the long run. Yet it would be a mistake to underestimate the hold of mythico-religious thought on most minds, even in the leading scientific nations of the world, let alone elsewhere. This much seems clear, however: within the contemporary secular university modern science reigns supreme. Despite pockets of Romantic resistance to the Enlightenment ideal of scientific progress, the place of philosophy is nothing like the proud position it once occupied in the academies of Greece, while theology has its principal seat in other, specifically religious institutions.

Though only two amidst a vast proliferation of subjects studied within the arts and science faculties of our post-secondary institutions today—and marginal ones at that—philosophy and religion share a common focus upon those perennial issues that science treats only peripherally, often with scepticism, even dismissively at times. Accordingly, both are marginal in this sense as well: their subject matter provides the outer framework and foundation for the examination of the whole cultural basis of human life, which is the chief purpose of higher education. Moreover, philosophical enquiry in particular epitomizes university studies in the arts and sciences in a way having to do with the *how* of philosophical exploration rather than its subject matter. Not that the approach taken in philosophy is altogether different from that of other disciplines; it is rather a question of the relative importance of each of three dimensions of what we shall call 'the educational experience.'

To understand why philosophy epitomizes university studies, we shall have to consider briefly the nature of the educational experience. The present chapter as a whole can be regarded as a thumbnail sketch of a sub-discipline of philosophy known as 'philosophy of education.' We have noticed several such sub-disciplines already: philosophy of mind (or philosophical psychology), philosophy of biology, philosophical cosmology, and so on (see 1.2.1). Epistemology is often regarded as an autonomous sub-discipline of philosophy nowadays, though, as has been pointed out (see 1.2.4), it was originally part of metaphysics. As we proceed, we shall have occasion to note further sub-disciplines of the same order.

2.5 The elements of the educational experience

The three principal dimensions or elements of the educational experience are (1) the *indoctrinational*, (2) the *informational*, and (3) the *interpretive*. The last can be called the *conversational* or the *reflective* dimension as well. All three can be briefly summarized as follows:

1 *indoctrinational*: instilling attitudes and belief in certain doctrines, theories, ideas, methodologies, or life-styles through example, repetition, habituation, positive and negative reinforcement.
2 *informational*: information and skills transfer, including information about cultural traditions, practical know-how, and factual data.
3 *interpretive*: promoting critical and independent thinking, debating issues, confronting conflicting ideas, theories, interpretations (of data or texts), methodologies, etc.

Every type of teaching and learning involves at least one of these elements, and some—university education, for example—may involve all three. This can be shown by expanding on the above descriptions and comparing the focus of tertiary education with that of the primary and secondary levels.

2.5.1 Indoctrination

At what must be considered the lowest level of education, there is learning by rote or through repetition of a set of practices, precepts, or dogmas (for example, learning a catechism). The aim is to shape the individual's belief system and/or behaviour, to make something 'stick' through repetition, habituation, reward and punishment. Examples are, say, making school children 'safety conscious,' 'health conscious,' 'environmentally aware' or 'biology conscious' (that is, sensitive to differences of race and gender). This is done by shaping the desired pro and con attitudes, mostly through approval and disapproval, but sometimes through more palpable rewards and punishments. Or, to take another example, the aim might be to change the attitudes of high school students toward smoking, drugs, or unsafe sex by means of slogans and images that suggest that certain choices are not really so 'cool' after all. The aim of indoctrination is direct benefit to the learner and indirect benefit to the community as a consequence of the learner's heeding certain warnings; the point is *not* to get the learner to *think* about what is being taught, but to *modify* his beliefs, behaviour, habits, or attitudes. All forms of promoting a doctrine, an outlook, or a 'life-style' belong to this category—that is, all forms of what is best called 'advocacy.'

Obviously, a lot of indoctrination goes on in schools, both at the primary and secondary levels, and—for the most part—rightly so. Nevertheless it is quite possible to have reservations about some aspects of what goes under the name of promoting what was just termed 'biology consciousness.' Such misgivings may be warranted because, as some would say, attempts to indoctrinate in these areas often take as established many conclusions with which reasonable people can and do disagree. No reasonable person would object to promoting safety- or health-consciousness; some social attitudes, however, are another matter.

2.5.2 Information

At a somewhat higher level, the aim of education is to transfer information and skills from teacher to learner. The skills are usually valuable, ones the learner wants to acquire, like literacy, numeracy, and computer skills; similarly, the information imparted is usually uncontroversial in the sense that it is almost universally accepted by those competent in the field, be it some set of mathematical formulae or some body of historical fact about a certain period of the past. The formulae 'work,' whether or not one understands why; the facts are accurate, or at least sufficiently so for the purposes at hand. There is not much discussion or questioning, not because they are frowned upon (as they usually are in advocacy and indoctrination), but simply because there is little to discuss or question.

Obviously, a lot of this goes on at all levels of education: primary, secondary, and tertiary. And again: rightly so. Enhancing literacy and numeracy skills (including scientific, cultural, and computer literacy), learning foreign languages, mastering historical facts, grasping the rudiments of scholarly research (everything from using or compiling bibliographies to—at the post-graduate level—advanced paleography) all belong in this category, and this is a big part of education, including so-called higher education.

2.5.3 Interpretation

In higher education, however, the main goal is neither indoctrination nor information and skills transfer, but reflection and interpretation or evaluation of competing points of view. The emphasis lies squarely upon independent critical thinking as the only means of participating in an ongoing conversation or debate. This is so much the case that attempts at indoctrination are regarded, not just as out of place, but even as offensive, by many in the field of higher education. For while information and skills transfer are important, the real focus of higher education must be upon the clash of ideas, methods, theories, analyses, interpretations, and assumptions; upon thinking critically, assessing evidence and arguments impartially (including counter-evidence and counter-arguments), upon reaching one's own conclusions—perhaps under the guidance of a teacher, but ultimately by working things out for oneself. The aim here is neither conformity to some norm imposed from without nor blind discipleship (as in some forms of indoctrination) nor information and skills acquisition, but rather achieving intellectual independence and maturity through the honing of analytical powers, development of reasoning skills, of critical judgment, of those capacities necessary for spotting fallacies and falsehoods and for weighing the strength of evidence or argument—or, for that matter, the aesthetic merits of a work of art, literature, or music. For in the realm of higher education, cultural literacy—for example, acquaintance with the graphic arts and music—is at least as important as 'print' literacy or scientific and computer literacy, perhaps much more important—though that is a quite legitimate matter of dispute. Developing these capacities amounts to acquiring the qualities necessary to become a participant in a conversation that has been going on for millennia, in Athens, Rome, Alexandria, Constantinople, Paris, Oxford, Cologne, Florence—to name only some the greatest centres of ancient, medieval, and modern culture (see 1.3.1). It is carried on all around us still today, though mostly in our universities, a conversation among ourselves, in the first place, but also with the great books, great works, and great minds of the past, a conversation that also goes on within each one of us, as we attempt to come to grips with our own social, political, religious, artistic, philosophical, and scientific heritage.

2.6 The Socratic strain in higher education

These things—interpretation, reflection, conversation—figure centrally in the ideal of education pioneered thousands of years ago by Socrates. He was critical of the education of his day as carried out by a class of itinerant teachers called 'sophists,' men who, for a fee, promised to inculcate in the youth, merely by associating with them, the habits and attitudes that led to public and private success. The Socratic ideal of education received a new impetus in the eighteenth century, when it was absorbed into the ideal of rational enlightenment. About this more will be said later on (see 9.4.2 and 12.8.5). The Socratic element is still the vital thing in university education today, though it has been betrayed again and again throughout the ages, beginning with Socrates's own student, Plato, who at times displayed dogmatic and authoritarian tendencies of thought at which his teacher would have shuddered. It was Plato who, in the dialogue *Republic,* mentioned earlier, developed the first comprehensive scheme of indoctrination as the core of his educational theory.

Now, obviously, thinking critically, whether in private reflection or public conversation, is itself a skill; and habituating people to exercise this skill appropriately by positive and negative reinforcement (good and bad grades, for example) is indoctrination of sorts; so the boundaries between indoctrination, information, and interpretation are perhaps not so sharply drawn as they may have seemed at first. Moreover, if one were to enquire about any truly cultivated person—someone who, say, speaks several foreign languages, plays a musical instrument, possesses a high degree of visual literacy in the graphic arts, and so on—one would discover that the whole basis of that individual's culture is in fact fairly mindless practice, drill, and repetition over many years, often starting in childhood. But the point that must be insisted upon here is that this is *only* the basis; higher or university education has to do primarily with taking consciously critical approaches to all sorts of things; indoctrination and drill in anything but the habit of thinking for oneself is suspect, while information and skills acquisition are really only the necessary prerequisites to confronting issues and challenges calling for the exercise of independent critical thought and judgment.

This last is the real business of universities. And it is conducted in all faculties and departments to a greater or lesser extent. The notable thing about philosophy is that here the interpretive dimension preponderates to a degree scarcely imaginable in most other disciplines. There is comparatively little in the way of straightforward skills to be acquired, relatively much less uncontroversial information to be conveyed, while indoctrination is usually regarded as inimical to the very spirit of philosophy. The clash of ideas, whether privately, in reflection, or publicly, in conversation—dialogue and debate in all their forms—makes up almost the whole of the study of philosophy. And that is what makes philosophy unique and uniquely typical of university studies as such.

2.7 Philosophical culture

The foregoing may provide some idea of the approach to be taken to the issues selected in chapter 1. From this it appears that philosophy, as an academic pursuit, has little, if anything, to do with personal self-understanding, with clarifying one's most fundamental beliefs or values, with spiritual growth, finding oneself, or the like. It is rather a matter of examining critically the *common* intellectual and moral basis of life formed by a set of living traditions in the arts, sciences, philosophy, and religion, extending right back to the Greeks. This resembles that Greek sense of wisdom or self-knowledge discussed earlier (see 1.4), the main difference being that, for us, the historical dimension of self-understanding is incomparably richer and more complex than it could have been for the Greeks thousands of years ago.

Taking 'self-understanding' very broadly to include not just our social and natural environment but mankind's place in the totality of things, it appears that the very breadth of scope and historical depth of academic philosophy make *doing* philosophy in the sense just described too much even to contemplate at the outset. For the beginning it will be enough to plant some seeds of philosophical culture so that, after an initial exposure to the discipline, one may find oneself in a position to read philosophical works with a degree of comprehension, knowing what to be on the lookout for and how to cope with a modicum of technical vocabulary. Among the rudiments of philosophical culture are also sensitivity to the subtleties of argument, appreciation of the historical antecedents, perhaps also of the influence, of the ideas under consideration, maybe even a measure of critical detachment and independence of judgment, so as not to be over-awed by the towering figures and great works of the past.

A technical term, incidentally, is literally a 'term of art,' that is, a word invented or given a special meaning within a particular field or sub-field for some discipline-specific purpose. 'Technical' is therefore much closer in meaning to 'artificial' (as when we distinguish human artefacts, like tables and chairs, from things that arise naturally and reproduce themselves, like plants and animals) than to 'technical' in the contemporary sense—the sense in which electronic gizmos, gadgets, and gimmicks are called 'technical,' and those qualified to operate, maintain, or repair them 'technicians.' Of course, the term 'technical' is loosely applied to any out-of-the-way expression not in everyday use. It is because academic philosophy is a 'technical' discipline in the literal rather than this loose sense that much of its content, the point of which is to develop conceptual tools and learn how to apply them, seems dry or lacking in intellectual excitement. The unfortunate truth is that there is no way to deal with the really provocative ideas of the past in a competent manner except via preparatory exercises—much as one cannot interpret the keyboard works of a Bach or a Beethoven without sitting daily at the piano and laboriously honing one's skills through hours of unexciting finger exercises.

These technical skills are the rudiments of philosophical culture. There is arguably no better way to acquire them than through the encounter with the great minds of the past. To see the critical, at times downright sceptical, spirit at work in the questioning of a Socrates, Descartes, or Hume is, for many, to become imbued with it. To follow a carefully crafted argument like Descartes's first proof of the existence of God is to grasp that technical vocabulary is something different from jargon; that an arsenal of sharply honed philosophical distinctions can be something other than hair-splitting or logic-chopping; that in the absence of either of these, rigour and precision of thought are just not attainable; and that the usual effect on us of a truly disciplined mind is—to discipline our minds!

Part of this discipline is the ability to identify and evaluate arguments, to pick out their formal structure by distinguishing premises and conclusion, to assess their logical validity, and to evaluate the evidence adduced for the premises. Of course, most philosophical works are an extended tissue of such arguments, set off, in most cases, against counter-arguments or objections. The ability to break down such writings into their constituent stages or phases, to synopsize accurately each successive stage as well as the argument as a whole, to recognize point and counter-point almost immediately—this is another of the elements of philosophical culture. So is the ability to express oneself clearly and precisely and to argue in a logically coherent manner. Whether or not these are important 'life-skills'—'practical' in the narrow sense identified above (see 2.2)—will depend on what one does in life. For a profession like the law, they are undoubtedly crucial. For most people something will hinge some day on the ability to make a case clearly, succinctly, and cogently—though perhaps at no greater length than a memorandum to the boss. Of course, some things are useless because they are *above* use. The possession of philosophical culture may be among these things.

Useful or useless, philosophical like other skills can, once acquired, become second nature to us—which is perhaps what all genuine culture really is at bottom. A trained mind, one that possesses "some tincture of philosophy," as Hume once said, does not have to apply rules or techniques. It spots the arguments, their historical antecedents, their strengths and weaknesses, almost 'without thinking,' as the expression goes; and it constructs arguments and undertakes analyses in much the same way: with very little attention, if any, to rules. It is disciplined, or rule-governed, without mechanical rule-following—as in all domains of what we call 'culture.'

Anyone who has ever become proficient at speaking a foreign language is familiar with the effect of repetition and drill. Much the same applies to philosophy. At first it may be as though a philosophical text were written in a foreign language. Only after a time do the strange sounds of a conversation in another language become recognizable words forming meaningful sentence-patterns, some of which challenge us by *what* they say. The conversation of philosophy is at bottom no different. At the outset we may expect to understand little or nothing of what the great philosophers have to tell us, at least until we become attuned to their discourse. And that requires time and practice, as does the attunement of the ear to foreign languages. If it was correct to say, as was said a short time ago, that the study of the great works of philosophy is the best form of practice, then no adequate introduction to the subject can afford to neglect the history and classics of philosophy. But whether this or another form of practice is best, the fact remains that practice, drill, and repetition are an integral part of acquiring technical competence in philosophy, as in every other realm of culture.

Given its nature, it is not difficult to understand why an enterprise like philosophy has always been confined to relatively few of the outstanding minds of each epoch. Nevertheless, every age has its own philosophical, just as each has its own literary and artistic, culture; that is, every period has an informed and educated public capable of appreciating the work of the philosopher, just as it has a public, however limited, capable of a critical appreciation of the work of the poet, the musician, the dancer, the actor, the painter, or sculptor. As the aim of, say, English or Art History departments within universities is not to produce poets or painters, but to transmit the rudiments of literary and artistic culture, so the business of the Philosophy department is to transmit the elements of philosophical culture, enabling the student to become an informed observer of, though perhaps not yet an active participant in, the contemporary 'trade' in ideas.

That the study of the philosophical classics is indeed the best way to achieve this end is disputed by those who favour a 'topics' or 'problems' approach. This is a strictly *philosophical* disagreement, about which something has been said already (see 1.4). Of course, if it were only a matter of skills-sharpening and technical mastery of the means of philosophical enquiry, the antagonists would be fairly evenly matched; for as there are different skills involved, so there are different ways in which they are best developed. On the other hand, if philosophy has, as will be argued more fully in the next two chapters, a perennial content that both antedates the proliferation of sub-disciplines and will probably outlast the various special problems that continue to emerge, then the arguments for the historical or 'philosophical classics' approach become much stronger. For in the classic works of past ages the perennial questions loom large.

How this particular dispute should be settled is unclear. As was just suggested, much depends on whether being alive to a special set of enduring issues anchored in our universal human condition is an aspect of the possession of philosophical culture that outweighs technical proficiency in importance. The present work as a whole is an attempt to demonstrate that this is so.

2.8 Conclusion

From all that has been said in this and the preceding chapter, it should be clear by now that philosophy is above all a matter of acquiring and learning to apply the tools of critical analysis and reflection; of interpreting and weighing evidence, arguments, and counter-arguments; and of assessing critically and impartially the fruitfulness of various approaches to a special set of problems arising out of the universal condition of mankind. To these problems some solution must be given if human life is to have that moral and intellectual basis without which, it seems, genuine human flourishing is just not possible. By the same token, it must be clear that philosophy has little, if anything, to do with the exchange of strictly personal viewpoints, the clarification of one's own private system of values, or the purely individual search for value, meaning, or something to believe in.

Nor is the business of philosophy confined to, though it may include, the clarification and critical examination of the doctrines of some religious creed or of the findings of science. True, philosophy *can* be engaged in for the purpose of deepening one's understanding of beliefs held for extra-philosophical reasons, convictions that form part of one's early religious or later scientific training, for example; but autonomous philosophy takes nothing for granted that is borrowed from extra-philosophical sources. Its only authorities are universal human reason and that lived experience of self and world that is the shared estate of all mankind. Since philosophy was once an autonomous alternative to religion and science, both among the Greek thinkers and again among the German intelligentsia of the nineteenth century, it can presumably still be pursued in the same spirit of autonomy and universality today. Perhaps autonomous philosophy can even set up to be the judge of the limits and legitimacy of the claims of its hereditary competitors, science and religion. That would be a very high calling. Nevertheless, it remains perennially tempting, particularly for beginners, to confuse philosophy with something like spiritual development and personal growth, with elaborating one's own individual world-view by pondering 'the big questions.' There are two main reasons for this.

One is the fact that philosophy does not fit any of the familiar paradigms of rationality generally believed to confer objectivity on the sciences. This will be discussed in chapter 6. The fact that many of its most important arguments conform to no known pattern of reasoning or proof suggests that philosophy may not be a kind of rational discourse at all; that it is more akin to our most fundamental personal, religious, or political commitments, that is, to the whole realm that Northrop Frye has termed 'the ideological.'

The second reason for the confusion is the unparalleled scope of the issues addressed by academic philosophy, many of which are, owing to their sheer breadth, *unsettleable* in principle. The scope of metaphysics or primary philosophy is to be the subject of the next two chapters.

3

The Order of Knowing

3.1 Introductory

In chapter 2 it was suggested that the way philosophy typifies university studies has to do with the *how*, the approach taken, rather than its specific content. We turn now to the distinctive *what* or subject matter of philosophy. Obviously, we can only begin to understand what philosophy is when we have some idea of what it is about. The aim of this and the next chapter, accordingly, is to explain what philosophy is. This is a question every beginner rightly asks, and it may as well be faced sooner rather than later.

What, then, is philosophy? We have already illustrated its subject matter by means of examples—a wide array of sample questions of the sort that philosophers ask (see 1.2). Of these, those issues belonging to metaphysics have generally been regarded, not just as perennial, but as central to philosophy—as *first or primary philosophy*, to use Aristotle's phrase, that is, *philosophy in the chief and fullest sense*. The existence of God and the nature and destiny of the human soul were described as perennial metaphysical questions of this sort, but they belong to a much larger complex of problems to be described in this and the next chapter.

Consideration of that larger problem complex will make clear why epistemology or theory of knowledge was included within metaphysics earlier (see 1.2.4). It will also shed fresh light on the peculiar breadth of scope that fosters confusion between philosophy and the business of developing a personal world-view (see 2.8). As for moral philosophy, the other domain of perennial philosophical problems, its subject matter will be discussed first in the part devoted to Socrates (see 10.2) and then in that on Sartre (see 38.2–3). Here it can only be suggested that moral philosophy, too, has its roots in metaphysics, and that, from a certain vantage point, it is debatable whether the two are really as distinct as their separate treatment here will suggest.

3.2 The subject matter of metaphysics

The short answer to the question concerning the subject matter of metaphysics can be put in many ways, the most concise being: 'everything.' Metaphysics is about absolutely everything that is or exists in any sense at all. It has from the start been regarded as (1) the *highest* science, the science that deals with the highest beings, the supersensible divine; 'highest' is in fact the original sense of 'first' alluded to a moment ago. But metaphysics has always been regarded as (2) the *universal* science as well, the attempt to bring within the compass of thought the unrestricted totality of what is, both sensible and supersensible. That is why it was remarked earlier (see 1.2.3) that the nominal word meaning ('beyond the physical things') is misleading. Furthermore, if we attend carefully to the way in which the earliest Greek thinkers understood the totality of things (see chap. 5), what will be found to include what *was* as well, the whole spatio-temporal order of causes from the very beginning; and since the encompassing order of things was regarded by them as one that is necessary in a moral sense as well, the totality of what is may be taken to include what *will* and *must* (ought to) be, too. From this we see already that the sharp separation of metaphysical from moral enquiry reflects a modern outlook that has not always been the dominant view; indeed, it is still not accepted by all schools of metaphysical thought today.

In the light of the foregoing, we can say, by way of preliminary definition, that metaphysics is mankind's attempt to orientate itself within the totality of what is, to discover the ultimate *order* governing all things, including man's place within that order. The reflective talk of 'orientating *oneself*' underscores the fact that understanding everything includes *self*-understanding; the same point is at least implicit in the talk of 'order' since, assuming there is one to be discovered, we ourselves most certainly belong somewhere in that universal scheme of things, along with the rest of our social and natural environment. It may be worth trying to make this point clearer now by disengaging two pertinent senses of 'order' that are frequently run together.

In a metaphysical context, 'order' means, for one thing, the order or sequence in which things are known. This sequence is not temporal (a time sequence: this *earlier* than that) but *epistemological*. Alternatively, philosophers speak of the order of knowing as a *conceptual* or a *logical* order among the objects of knowledge. There are nuances of difference among these designations, but that need not concern us now; it is important only that we distinguish carefully between the order of knowing, to be discussed in this chapter, and the order of being, the subject of the next.

The questions concerning the order of knowing and the order of being circumscribe the whole sphere of metaphysical enquiry. Are they of equal importance? To say so would be to flout a long tradition according to which *metaphysics is the science of being*. Whatever the order in which the totality of things may stand in relation to our minds (the order of knowing), the final aim of first or primary philosophy is to make out the order in which they stand among themselves (the order of being). Consideration of the order of knowing is only a means, though apparently an indispensable means, to this end.

This already suggests that philosophy may, after all, have a special role to play in university education by virtue of its subject matter. The cultivation of the arts and sciences, it was said in the last chapter, examines the intellectual and moral basis without which a rich, fulfilling human existence—and coexistence—just is not possible. Now the goal of metaphysics as the science of being is to achieve an understanding of the totality of what is. Without metaphysics, then, the intellectual and moral basis of life would lack a foundation or, to vary the metaphor, an encompassing outer framework. Admittedly, religion and science are capable of providing a framework of founding principles too. But, as we have seen, philosophy is distinctive in having at its disposal fewer resources than the former and more than the latter; its principles are drawn from a single source—rational reflection on our common human experience—whereas religion has recourse to faith, scripture, and institutional traditions, while science tends to understand reason and experience narrowly, in terms of its own methodology. From the perspective of autonomous philosophical enquiry, then, the framework of religion includes too much, that of science too little; or if that is not obviously the case, the question, at least, seems to be one that must be asked from a philosophical rather than a religious or scientific perspective.

3.3 Five questions

The problem of the correct order of knowing can be circumscribed in five distinct though inter-related questions. The first three are: (1) What things are known best, that is, most immediately and reliably? In other words, what truths are basic or primitive? Next, (2) What things are known only indirectly, on the basis of (by logical inference from) those things known best and most reliably? Or, in other words, which truths are derivative, and how remote are they from the so-called first truths or *principles* (as first truths are customarily called) of knowledge? And furthermore, (3) What things, if any, cannot be known at all? At issue, then, are (1) the starting point, (2) the extent or scope, and (3) the limits of human knowledge: what it commences with, what it encompasses (and in what order), and what it terminates or culminates in.

The first two questions have always been asked by metaphysicians, at least implicitly, while the third has a distinctively modern ring to it. When Kant asks "What can I know?" (see 1.2.4), it is the question of the limits of human knowledge that is uppermost in his mind. There are, however, those who deny that reliable knowledge is attainable at all. These are the so-called philosophical sceptics. On their account we must add another question to the original three: (4) Is there is any genuine knowledge at all? A fifth question will be added once we have considered (4) briefly, followed by a sixth in the next section (3.4).

3.3.1 Scepticism, relativism, and critical rationalism

The philosophical sceptics should not to be confused with *sceptical relativists*. The relativist, we might say, denies that there is such a thing as objective truth, a way things are, just in themselves. If there *is* no absolute or non-relative truth to be known, then, of course, there can be no knowledge of such truth. The sceptic *may*, but need not, be a relativist in the sense just described. That is, he can perfectly well concede the existence of absolutely objective states of affairs, and yet emphatically deny that we can discover them reliably. In the last two parts of this work we shall encounter a philosophic sceptic in the person of David Hume, and an out-and-out relativist, or sceptical relativist, in Jean-Paul Sartre.

Scepticism was already well represented in the Greek period by figures who could trace their lineage back, with more or less plausibility, to the very earliest philosophers, men like Xenophanes (*fl.* around 540 BC), Parmenides, Zeno of Elea (see 5.6), as well as to the so-called sophists (see 9.1.2.2), chief among them Gorgias of Leontini (*fl.* c. 444) and Protagoras of Abdera (483–414 BC). Even Socrates was at times claimed as the patron saint of the sceptics, though that seems to have been wishful thinking on their part. We shall examine the varieties of Greek scepticism in more detail later (see 9.1.4).

As for relativism, it too is nothing new. According to a very old saying ascribed to Protagoras, "Man is the measure of all things, of what is, that it is, and of what is not, that it is not." In one of his dialogues, Plato explains what he took to be the point of this dictum by posing a question:

[I]s the essence of things private to each of us, as Protagoras used to say, declaring 'Man is the measure of all things'—that such as things appear to me, such they are for me; while such as they appear to you, such they are for you? Or do you believe that they have some stability of essence of their own? (*Cratylus* 385e–386a)

Whether this is exactly what Protagoras had in mind is debatable. The probability is against it. But it shows nevertheless that relativism was pretty clearly staked out as a philosophical position by the time of Plato's *Cratylus*. From the relativist's viewpoint, which has persisted, if not prevailed, in one form or another throughout the entire history of philosophy, what is real, what is true, and what is good are determined by mankind, even if not always by the individual human subject, as suggested in the above passage from the *Cratylus* and reasserted over two millennia later by Sartre. There is, accordingly, no truth, no reality, no goodness to *discover*, but only the truth, reality, and goodness that human beings, individually or collectively, invent or *create*, what they agree upon (or are compelled by those wielding power to accept) as true, real, good, and so forth. Since Greek times this has been referred to as goodness 'by convention,' as opposed to that which is good independent of our thoughts and wishes, the good 'by nature,' as it is called. To this corresponds the idea of that which is true only by convention rather than by nature.

From scepticism and relativism we must distinguish, further, what is sometimes called *critical rationalism*. Like some sceptics, but unlike relativists, the critical rationalist holds (i) that there is objective truth, valid for everyone and always. He even concedes (ii) that we can lay hold of it, 'hit on' the truth. In addition to this, the critical rationalist *may* concede (iii) that we have in fact laid hold of it, at least in part; that is, that we do have at least some knowledge (beliefs that we shall never have to revise or abandon). What he flatly denies, however, is (iv) that, having got it, we can or could ever know that we have got it. So what the critical rationalist denies is neither the existence of objective truth, like the relativist, nor that we can get at it, like the sceptic, but that we can ever be certain that we have got at it *even when we have*, declaring the question definitively settled and closing the book on it.

The early Greek thinker Xenophanes (see 5.5.4) may have been the first to express an outlook of this sort. For he wrote: "if [any man] succeeds to the full in saying what is completely true, he himself is nevertheless unaware of it." Even if critical rationalism as just described is not exactly what Xenophanes had in mind, it was at least read into this saying by later Greek thinkers like Plato; so something like critical rationalism has clearly been around since Greek times too. The Anglo-Austrian philosopher of science Sir Karl Popper (1902–1994) is the most recent thinker to defend this theory in a sophisticated version that has found wide acceptance.

Dogmatic relativism and extreme scepticism are obviously radical responses to the question, (4) Is there is any genuine knowledge at all? Critical rationalism is more moderate, though, as anyone hankering after infallible certainty must feel, still a disappointingly pessimistic view of human knowledge.

3.3.2 Reason and experience

At issue in discussions of the order of knowing are not just (1) the starting point, (2) extent, and (3) limits of human knowledge, together with the question of (4) whether there can be any genuine knowledge at all; there is also the question of (5) the nature of experience. After all, it seems likely that what we know directly and most reliably is that of which we have *immediate experience*. Yet there have been, and continue to be, conflicting views of what is to count as immediate experience.

Is it (a) the sensible things around us, the objects of ordinary sense perception (sight, hearing, touch, taste, smell), that we experience immediately? Or do we perhaps not experience such things immediately at all, but only indirectly, via the intermediary of (b) images or concepts of them in the mind, these latter being the *sole* immediate objects of experience? If (b) is the correct alternative, then 'experience' refers to *inner* experience; it must be understood primarily as *intro*spective (literally, 'inward looking') awareness of one's own mental contents, in a word, introspection. This is certainly not what we normally take 'experience' to mean. Yet we shall see in Part Three that Descartes takes 'experience' in just this novel sense—with revolutionary effect on the subsequent course of modern philosophy.

Or do we have, in addition to (a) and (b), immediate experience of another kind, (c) *non*-sensory experience or intuition of non-sensible and/or supersensible entities? Such experiences could be either (i) insights into the hidden or non-sensible structure or order of the material world itself; or they could be glimpses of the existence and/or nature of (ii) immaterial realities like the immortal soul and the supersensible divine. The philosophical tradition has not been lacking in those who speak of 'grasping' the reality (i) behind or (ii) beyond the world of sensory experience by means of the intellect alone—yet in a way that must be at least somewhat analogous to ordinary sensory apprehension, if the customary metaphor of vision is at all apt. Those who speak of 'religious experience,' on the other hand, seem to have (ii) in mind. Many would deny that such experience, which, in addition to being inner, is often intensely personal and private, can have any bearing on the philosophical problem of *human* knowledge at all.

However that may be, (c), like (b), certainly stretches the familiar meaning of 'experience' captured by (a). That is why philosophers who posit both lower and higher faculties or powers of the mind generally do not treat the higher as a form of experience at all, but call it 'intellect' or 'the understanding' or 'reason' instead. Ordinary experience they sometimes regard as a dependent, inferior mode of knowledge, valuable perhaps in applying our fundamental insights to particular cases or else in sparking those insights themselves, but nevertheless lacking the authority to contradict that special *non-sensory* vision that the intellect or reason provides. Some even go so far as to regard ordinary experience (seeing, hearing, etc.) as inherently deceptive, as the source, not of truth, but of our most persistent illusions and errors. So, for example, not just Plato, but Descartes, and Platonists, and Cartesians generally. ('Cartesian,' incidentally, is the adjective derived from the name 'Descartes.')

For Plato, as we shall see in Part Two, reason furnishes an intuitive vision of a supersensible world of imperceptible objects altogether different and distinct from the things that populate this world; that alone is knowledge, opinion being all that is possible concerning the world 'down here.' For Descartes, by contrast, reason furnishes knowledge both of non-sensible or supersensible immaterial objects and of the material world; for truths about the nature of material things are implanted in the mind by God, along with truths about God himself and the human soul. We have only to turn our mental gaze inward to discover them there. Such inner experience coincides with reason for Descartes. But while reason and inner experience coincide in the case of truths implanted in the mind, when what we experience inwardly are ideas acquired through the senses, reason and experience are opposed.

About the nature of experience, then, philosophical opinion has always been sharply divided. Those, like Plato and Descartes, who emphasize reason at the expense of ordinary sense experience are called 'rationalists' (from the Latin *ratio* 'reason'), while those who stress experience in opposition to reason go by the name of 'empiricists' (from the Greek *empeiria*, experience). Empiricism and rationalism will be discussed more fully in 7.5.1–2, 21.3.1–2, and 26.2.

3.4 Epistemological realism and idealism

To summarize the previous section let us list briefly once again the five questions at issue in determining the correct order of knowing: (1) the starting point, (2) extent, (3) limits, and (4) the very possibility of human knowledge, along with (5) the nature of experience. To these we must add a further question in the present section: (6) the nature of truth.

The two main types of answers given to the questions regarding (1) the starting point of knowledge, the (5) meaning of 'experience,' and (6) the nature of truth are commonly labelled 'epistemological realism' and 'epistemological idealism.' These are at best rough-and-ready labels for numerous different shades and gradations of opinion. For one thing, both go together with forms of what were just termed empiricism or rationalism, giving us empiricist and rationalist varieties of epistemological realism and idealism that differ widely. Still, the designations are instructive in making it clear that the one sort of approach gives primacy to ordinary sensible things ('thing' in Latin is *res*, whence 'realism'), whereas the other considers the contents of the mind as first in the order of knowing, the *ideas* accessible in inner experience (whence 'idealism').

According to epistemological realism, (1) we perceive or experience ordinary material things immediately, and do so, for the most part, reliably. Moreover, (6) we judge truly about such things when we take them for what they really are in themselves; the rules for distinguishing true from false judgments may be fairly elaborate, but truth consists in the agreement of thought with an extra-mental object. ('Extra-mental object' is just a semi-technical expression for the things that exist outside, and independently of, our minds.) Depending on (5) whether the particular mode of consciousness by which such agreement is optimally achieved is ordinary sensory experience, or whether it is designated 'reason' and set over against ordinary experience, this or that particular form of epistemological realism is either empiricist or rationalist in outlook. What they all have in common, though, is this: whether or not our beliefs constitute knowledge depends on the way the world is in itself, independently of us.

According to the epistemological idealist, on the other hand, (1) all that we experience directly are ideas of things in our own minds, not the extra-mental material things themselves. All our judgments about external things are therefore just inferences from other, incomparably more secure judgments about images or concepts of them in our minds. Direct apprehension of the things themselves being assumed to be impossible, (6) the criteria for distinguishing true from false judgments have to be internal, having to do with the order of perceptions or ideas within the totality of experience, not their agreement with extra-mental things. According as (3) our access to the 'true' in this sense is ordinary experience or non-experiential (rational or inborn) ideas, empiricist and rationalist varieties of epistemological idealism can again be distinguished. What they all have in common is this: whether or not our beliefs constitute knowledge cannot depend on any alleged state of affairs existing independently of the mind, since we have no access to things as they are in themselves such that we could check our inferences about them directly.

Sometimes the titles 'epistemological realist' and 'epistemological idealist' are given to thinkers who subscribe to only one of the three tenets just described under (1), (5), and (6). While there is no universally acknowledged definition of either, and while there are many different shades of both, some more, others less 'pure,' the above seem nonetheless helpful descriptions of the epistemological realist and idealist 'in the full-bodied sense,' as we might put it. If space permitted, we could discuss different varieties of epistemological idealism and realism, as was done with degrees of scepticism earlier. That would allow us to consider how the questions itemized as (2), (3), and (4) figure in the order of knowing.

3.5 Subjectivism and objectivism

In the course of our study of Plato, Descartes, Hume, and Sartre we shall encounter an unmistakable shift in the main current of thought away from epistemological realism (primacy of ordinary sensible things, the objective) toward idealism (primacy of ideas in the mind, the subjective). In the next chapter (see 4.5), we shall see that there is a trend in the order of being similar to that in the order of knowing. This remarkable switch can also be described as a move from 'objectivism' to 'subjectivism.' For, beginning with Descartes, the ordinary sensible things believed by the Greeks and medievals alike to be immediately experienced and knowable with at least a reasonable degree of certainty cease to be the starting point of philosophy at all. Henceforth the *only* thing knowable with the degree of certainty requisite for a secure starting point is the human *subject* and the contents of the human mind. 'Subjectivism' and 'objectivism' are just two more designations for the transition from epistemological realism to epistemological idealism, though fairly non-technical ones; after all, we frequently speak of this or that as being 'merely subjective' rather than 'objective.'

A radically new concept of experience lies behind this changed conception of the order of knowing within the philosophical tradition. For the Greeks, and in the mainstream of medieval thought, the meaning of 'experience' is just ordinary outer experience by means of the five bodily senses, the 'doors of perception' in Aldous Huxley's memorable phrase. Yet this standard philosophical and everyday use of 'experience' was supplanted in the thought of Descartes and his successors by the concept of *inner* experience described above. Descartes's new concept of experience was instrumental in effecting the shift from objectivism to subjectivism; this, in turn, fostered both the scepticism of Hume and the relativism of Sartre, developments that Descartes could not have foreseen and at which he would—quite frankly—have been appalled.

The reorientation of philosophy toward the human subject and inner experience in the seventeenth and eighteenth centuries was, however, in some respects just a return to the perspective of one of the early Christian Church Fathers of the fifth century AD, St Augustine. It took over a millennium for Augustine's pioneering insights, epitomized in the famous maxim "Go back into yourself; in the inner man dwells truth," to take root, grow, and blossom into a philosophical outlook that completely revolutionized western metaphysics. Between the fifth and the seventeenth centuries the Augustinian maxim received a great deal of attention but without producing the extraordinary effects it was to have once seized upon by Descartes. Given its hoary past, it is not surprising that Descartes could not foresee the future direction of subjectivism.

When we speak of trends toward subjectivism, scepticism, and relativism, the point is not, of course, that these attitudes first emerged in modern times, but only that they achieved unprecedented importance. In a certain sense the whole course of classical Greek, medieval, and even modern philosophy can be seen as a rearguard action against this unholy alliance of three. And yet the course of western philosophy to be charted in the five main parts of this book ends up, willy-nilly, right back at the position regarding being, knowing, and goodness so chillingly formulated by old Protagoras. For Sartre, too, *man is the measure*, both of truth—not of *all* truth, admittedly, but at least of the truth about *human* nature—and of good and evil, right and wrong. And so too for a host of contemporary (again largely French, so-called post-modern) thinkers, who incline to the view that the true, the right, and the good are, as it is fashionable to say nowadays, 'linguistically' and 'socially constructed,' not indeed, as Sartre believed, by the individual, but by the collectivity. So Protagoras and his ilk win after all, it seems—at least if Sartre has the last word, as he will in the sequence of thinkers to be studied here.

Ultimately, of course, the last word belongs to the reflective reader, for criticisms of subjectivism, relativism, and scepticism aplenty will be included in these pages.

It is up to us to decide whether the historical development sketched here represents real progress; whether scepticism and relativism are indeed the outcome of a gradual process of intellectual emancipation from a naive and groundless traditional objectivism; or whether they are at bottom a counsel of despair, a refuge to which one should only repair when all hope of obtaining secure knowledge of the real, the true, and the good has been abandoned. As an eminent historian of Greek philosophy (A.H. Armstrong) once wrote: "philosophy must be either a search after attainable truth or a solemn game played with words to the advantage of those who are paid in our Universities for playing it, but of nobody else." No doubt, philosophy *could* be such a game; and maybe *some* philosophy is. But we had better have pretty compelling reasons before concluding that *all* philosophy is just a solemn game of this kind. Unless and until such reasons are produced, the principle of charity dictates that we take philosophy, provisionally at least, for what its name ('love of wisdom') conveys: the search for wisdom and truth.

For the time being, then, let us just say that the ancient, medieval, early modern, and contemporary outlooks, both sceptical and anti-sceptical, absolutist and relativistic, subjectivist and objectivist, represent basic philosophical postures or starting points concerning the order of knowing, each with its peculiar strengths and weaknesses. Among them we must decide for ourselves, perhaps modifying any traditional posture we are inclined to adopt in accordance with our own ideas. It would be a mistake, however, to interpret the remark that all have their strengths and weaknesses to mean that there is not really much to choose among them. There may in fact be very cogent arguments for embracing one and rejecting another, even if not everyone will agree; about this we must keep an open mind, or else cede the field to the doubters and scoffers without offering so much as token resistance.

4

The Order of Being

4.1 Introductory

The previous chapter was devoted to the order of knowing as a key dimension of mankind's attempt to orientate itself within the totality of what is. 'Order' refers, secondly, to the order of being. Whatever the order in which we come to know things, whatever the order in which those things stand *in relation to our minds*, to the human cognitive capacity, it is still possible to ask a very different question, namely: Which things are first and primary *in themselves*? When we refer to this as the 'ontological' order of things, distinguishing it from the 'epistemic,' 'epistemological,' or 'cognitional' order, we are just applying the standard term derived from the Greek word for an entity or being, *on* (or, with the definite article 'the' added, *to on*). Both 'ontological' and 'epistemological' are relatively late coinages, from the seventeenth and nineteenth centuries, respectively, notwithstanding the fact that their etymologies are Greek.

Now obviously the things we experience and know first or immediately, the epistemologically first things, are not necessarily the first things *in themselves*, those on which all others depend *for their existence and nature*, that is, ontologically. Theoretically, the things first in the order of being could even be *last* in the cognitional or conceptual order. And indeed, that is precisely the way many prominent philosophers have seen it. Throughout the Peripatetic tradition, for instance, God or the divine is understood as first in the ontological but last in the epistemological order, last to be known in the order of inference from the already known to the as yet unknown. So there is a further order of things to be considered in primary philosophy or metaphysics, one quite distinct from, and possibly even opposed to, that considered in the last chapter.

4.2 Four questions

What is at issue in determining the correct order of being is the dependence, independence, interdependence, or inter-independence between entities of different sorts, namely, (1) between full-fledged *things* like material bodies, living or non-living, and their essential and other *properties*; (2) between material things generally, including living plant, animal, and human organisms, and immaterial things (assuming there are such) like animal and human minds or souls, perhaps also higher spiritual beings like angels; and (3) between finite things of all these kinds—properties and substances, both material or immaterial, living or non-living—and the infinite immaterial being, God—should such a being exist.

As just described, the order of being has to do with beings within the world, chiefly mental and physical things, with their properties, qualities, or attributes (sometimes called 'forms'), and with something outside the world, God. And the question whose answer decides the *order* of being is: What depends on what for its existence and nature? Such relations of dependence, independence, and so on, have been the central focus of metaphysics throughout most of its history. Dependence, moreover, has always been understood as causal dependence, though here an important difference crops up. Throughout the modern period, there has been a reluctance to recognize any type of causality or dependence other than efficient or productive causality, the cause of existence, which is the only thing meant by 'cause' in modern science. The order of being is accordingly understood as the order of existence. In the older tradition, however, another type of causality called 'formal' figured prominently. It was in terms of this latter type of causality that (1) above, the dependence of properties (under the name of 'forms') on things, and of one type of form on another, was understood, particularly in scholastic philosophy. This relationship of dependence in the order of formal causality was reinterpreted in terms of efficient or productive causality in the modern tradition. For purposes of simplification, we shall confine ourselves to the order of efficient causality, taking the order of being as the order of existence and ignoring the order of being in the sense of form, essence, or nature. But in doing so we leave out an interesting chapter in the story of metaphysics.

In the order of being or existence the relation of the mental to the material has clear implications for the understanding of man as a psycho-physical entity, an embodied soul. So (4) the question of human nature—sometimes called 'philosophical anthropology' and treated as a separate sub-discipline of philosophy—is likewise rooted in the metaphysical study of the order of being. Accordingly, the nature of man, what it is to be human, may be regarded as a metaphysical question of the perennial sort, though not one specifically mentioned in 1.2.3 above. Nevertheless, its inclusion was implicit in the talk of mankind's attempt to orientate *itself* within the totality of what is (see 3.2), that is, in the notion of *self*-understanding that has been part of our description of metaphysics all along.

In this connection it may be worth taking another look at Kant, who was quoted in chapter 1 as marking out adjoining domains of philosophy with the aid of three questions: "1. What can I know? 2. What ought I to do? and 3. What may I hope?" In certain writings Kant expanded this list to include a fourth question, "4. What is man?" Of this last question Kant remarked enigmatically (leaving his readers to puzzle out his meaning) that the first three questions are "related" to it. He probably meant that the first three were just part of the fourth question. This is an intriguing idea. In terms of our own list of questions, it is not hard to see that the first three have a bearing on the fourth. For the way in which we answer the question of the nature of man obviously depends on how we understand thing and property, mind and matter, finite and infinite being and the relations of dependence among them. On the face of it, then, the fourth question is not special. If Kant thought otherwise, this presumably has a lot to do with his role in that movement described in the last chapter as the trend toward subjectivism and idealism. Outside the setting provided by Kantian epistemological and ontological idealism, however, the question of the nature of man seems subordinate to the others. The talk of self-understanding should not mislead us into thinking otherwise.

If the question of human nature is included within metaphysics as one of the perennial questions, though a derivative rather than basic one, what are we to say of the relations between man and man? The social and ethical would seem to be at least as important a dimension of the order of being as the puzzling God–world and mind–matter (or mind–body) relations that have figured so prominently among the perennial problems of metaphysics in the past. If so, then perhaps the traditional and current issues addressed in such sub-disciplines of philosophy as ethics and politics are at least rooted in the perennial problems of metaphysics, even though not themselves perennial questions in our enriched sense. From this perspective, metaphysics is not so much a sub-discipline of philosophy as the master-discipline *under* which the others are subsumed, the foundation or, as we said earlier, the outer framework, not just of the others but of the non-philosophical arts and sciences as well.

The 'master-discipline' or 'overlord' idea of metaphysics, while very old, is nonetheless controversial. One thing that makes it difficult to accept is the fact that philosophy is beset by the same trend toward specialization as is found in most other disciplines, so that the metaphysical roots of politics, ethics, and other branches of knowledge dealing with man and society are largely ignored in favour of all sorts of derivative questions in these fields. It was just suggested that this was not always so, although it is substantially true already of the very first moral philosopher, Socrates, who, as we shall see in Part One of this work, shunned metaphysical speculation entirely, even about human nature, confining his enquiries to a fairly circumscribed sphere of strictly moral issues regarding the good life.

The whole question of metaphysics as overlord or handmaiden of religion or the sciences is not easily settled. To conclude the present section with a rapid summary, we may say that the task of determining the order of being comprises four questions regarding the relations of dependence, independence, interdependence and interindependence between (1) full-fledged things and their properties; (2) material and immaterial beings; (3) finite things of both kinds and the infinite being, God; and (4) the human mind and body (the nature of man).

4.3 Ontological realism and idealism

To understand better what is at issue in determining the order of being, let us get down to cases by returning for a moment to our earlier question about death and immortality: Does the mind or soul of man depend upon the body for its continued existence? Or is it—as certain philosophers have rather brazenly maintained—the other way round? Do material things actually depend for their existence on minds perceiving them?

There is more at issue here than just (4) the mind–body relation; for that problem is just an instance of (2), the more general problem regarding material and immaterial beings. As we shall see presently, (1), the substance–property relation is involved in the mind–body problem as well. To begin with, then, let us consider briefly three metaphysical postures involving (1), (2), and (4), namely ontological idealism and a couple of varieties of ontological realism known as reductive and non-reductive materialism, respectively. This parallels the procedure followed in the previous chapter, where epistemological idealism and realism were distinguished.

The trivial and misleading form in which something like question (2) has filtered down into the popular mind runs something like this: 'When a tree falls in the forest, with no one around to hear it, does it actually make a sound?' Most people find it very difficult to take this question seriously, and rightly so. But consider: Do sounds exist unheard? Not if sounds, colours, tastes, and other sensory qualities are just like pains. For pains quite clearly do not exist when not felt by anyone. A pain that no one feels, a pain said to exist but not to be felt by any sentient being, is a manifest absurdity. Are, then, sounds, colours, tastes, odours, and so forth just like pains? Consider again: as the fire in the fireplace produces a sensation of pain in me when I come too near it, so it produces in me, along with sensations of light and colour, a pleasing feeling of warmth as I enter the room and approach it. Where, then, is the difference between pain and warmth or colour? Granted that pains cannot exist unfelt, can then colours exist unsensed?

Now suppose that by such words as 'tree,' 'mountain,' 'river,' 'house,' and 'fire' all we really mean, or all we can legitimately mean if we are not just talking nonsense, is the actual or possible occurrence together of certain sensory qualities like those just mentioned. What is being suggested now is that (a) an apple, for instance, is just a collection of sensations like a certain redness of hue, roundness of shape, tartness of taste, and a distinctive odour, together with solidity, heaviness, and so forth; and that (b) all these sensations are just like the sensation of pain: they cannot, without absurdity, be said to exist unperceived.

That (a) is the case is just what the seventeenth-century British philosopher John Locke (1632–1704) maintained, using the philosopher's term 'substance' for what we have called a 'thing,' and 'simple idea' for sensations of colour, odour, taste, and so forth, through which the properties of such substances are known: "all the ideas we have of particular distinct sorts of substances," writes Locke, "are nothing but several combinations of simple ideas." Or again: "The mind ... takes notice that a certain number of these simple ideas go constantly together; which being presumed to belong to one thing ... are called by one name," for example 'apple.' From this Locke was quite prepared to conclude that the term 'substance' or 'thing' does not really designate anything over and above the sum total of sensible qualities or properties sensed, and to do away with the time-hallowed philosophical idea, going back to Aristotle, that properties depend on things or substances for their existence. So our question (1) plays into the problem about the dependence of matter on mind, at least as formulated by Locke.

Now consider (b) again. If Locke is right about what an apple really is, could things like apples exist unperceived? Apparently not. Although Locke did not draw this conclusion, it was drawn for him by his philosophical successor, one George Berkeley, Bishop of Cloyne. For Berkeley, a tree could no more be said to exist deep in the primeval forest unperceived and 'un-thought of' by any mind whatever than the sound of its fall could exist unheard or a pain exist unfelt by any sentient being. All three cases are on exactly the same footing for Berkeley, who can therefore be called an 'ontological idealist.' For him, ordinary material things like trees are really just collections of ideas that depend for their existence on their being perceived, on the existence of ideas (of leafy green things called 'trees') in minds—just the opposite of our commonsense assumption that the idea or perception of a tree depends for its existence on a real tree that causes it and on the existence of sense organs and a body by means of which we perceive it. After all, we say we see the tree because it exists, not that it exists because we see it. For Berkeley it is just the other way round.

Maybe Berkeley and other defenders of ontological idealism got this aspect of the order of being all wrong. Maybe it really is the other way round, as ontological realists and common sense tell us. After all, mind or consciousness appears to depend for its existence on the living human body. Both common experience and a great deal of empirical scientific evidence attest to this fact. When someone is sleepy or under the influence of drugs or alcohol, or when head trauma causes brain lesions, consciousness is affected too; the mind just works differently. That is a well-known fact. Now if the mind's capacities can be thus affected by the body's and brain's state, then, surely, when the body dies and all electrochemical activity in the brain shuts down completely, the mind or soul ceases to act and to exist as well. So say all those ontological realists who place material things, *res*, ahead of minds, ideas, in the order of being, yet without attempting to argue that minds just *are* brains, that what we call 'consciousness' and 'the mental' is *only* a matter of physical processes going on in the brain *and nothing more*. For this reason they are frequently called 'non-reductive materialists': they insist on the primacy of the material, but make no attempt to elide the difference between the mental and the physical as Berkeley did by absorbing the physical into the mental or as so-called reductive materialists do by absorbing the mental into the physical. Non-reductive materialism, or something like it, is widely endorsed in modern psychology and contemporary neuro-science, though some of its defenders might balk at the idea of holding a metaphysical theory concerning the order of being. It goes back at least to Aristotle and his followers in ancient Greek and medieval times. And it seems fair to say, as indicated above, that non-reductive materialism is the viewpoint of plain common sense as well. (Even common sense is not without a metaphysical dimension!)

So far we have contrasted one form of ontological idealism, the reductive ontological idealism of Berkeley, with one form of ontological realism, usually dubbed 'non-reductive materialism.' But we really ought to consider a third possibility intermediate between these two, namely, that mind and body are separate and independent entities (hence: 'inter-independent'), *each* capable of existing in its own right. This form of ontological realism, famously championed by Descartes, is universally known as Cartesian dualism. Both the non-reductive materialist and the Cartesian dualist take material things to exist in their own right, independently of minds. Both, in other words, are ontological realists. The key difference is that dualism (rather improbably) regards the mind as capable of existing in its own right as well, whereas non-reductive materialism denies this. The mind–body problem, then, with which the question of immortality is closely tied up, is a prime example of a metaphysical question regarding the order of being. As we have just seen, at least three of the four questions distinguished in the last section—(1), (2) and (4)—are implicated in it in various ways.

To illustrate the problem of the ontological order further, consider our other example of a metaphysical question: the existence of God. Does everything else depend for its existence and nature on some creator God or other First Cause that itself depends on nothing else? This too is a metaphysical question concerning the order of being—*all* being, in fact, the totality of what is. It coincides with item (3) in the earlier list of questions, that about finite and infinite being. Ever since Aristotle first drew the inference from the changing sensible world to supersensible beings or movers (causes of change) and thence to a First Mover (see 20.5.1), philosophy has never wanted for alleged proofs of the existence of God. Between the thirteenth and eighteenth centuries the controversy was at its most intense.

4.4 The analysis of mind and matter

The metaphysical postures sketched so far have to do with the order of dependence discernible *within* the totality of what is, namely with relations between properties and substances, between minds and bodies, and between finite things like minds and bodies, on the one hand, and the infinite divine being, God, on the other. The questions to which (a) ontological idealism, (b) non-reductive materialism, and (c) Cartesian dualism are answers are central to metaphysical enquiry now, and have been so for centuries, if not millennia. Of course, determining the place of mind and body within the cosmos, in the order of sensible (physical) and non-sensible (mental, psychical) phenomena—or even in the order of *all* being whatsoever, sensible, non-sensible, *and* supersensible—presupposes some understanding of the *nature* of mind and the nature of matter. For this reason, what may be called the *analysis of mind* and the *analysis of matter* have always occupied a central place within metaphysics. After all, before we can determine reliably what they depend on, if anything, we must know what mind and matter are, their respective natures. Do animals have minds or souls too, and if so, what is the difference between a human mind and an animal soul? How are the different sorts of psychical or mental phenomena in humans to be classified? These are just some of the philosophical questions that can and must be pursued in the analysis of mind or philosophical psychology. As for body, how does the human or any living animal body differ from inert or lifeless matter? What does 'life' mean? (This should not be confused with the popular and much-satirized question of the meaning of life.) What are the most basic features that set the material off from the mental, and what are those that separate living from lifeless matter? What role does the body or brain play in purely mental operations?

From this last question it should be obvious that the analyses of mind and matter play a vital role in establishing the order of knowing as well as the order of being. For problems regarding the nature of mind, its faculties, and operations, like the question of the nature of matter or body, are not so much separate issues in their own right, as they are part and parcel of attempts to encompass in thought the totality of what is by fixing the exact epistemological and ontological order of all things. And that, to repeat, is what metaphysics is all about.

4.5 Varieties of realism and idealism

We have seen that and why the analysis of mind and matter figure prominently in discussions of the order of being in modern metaphysics since Descartes. As for the range of basic metaphysical postures, we have so far touched only on (1) Berkeleian idealism, (2) Scholastic-Aristotelian non-reductive materialism (which is also the attitude of common sense), and (3) Cartesian dualism. In addition to the latter two, both of which are forms of ontological realism, it may be useful to take at least a brief look at (4) reductive materialism, a further realist posture. On the other side of the realist–idealist divide, in company with Berkeley, stand such towering metaphysical geniuses as Leibniz, Kant, and Hegel. While detailed consideration of the varieties of idealism is beyond the scope of this Introduction, it may be worth setting out in graphic form the full range of basic metaphysical postures before going on to say a word about reductive materialism in the next section:

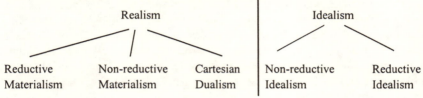

Regarding the temporal sequence of these metaphysical postures, it is interesting to note that they appeared on the historical scene roughly in the order in which they are presented here, starting from the left. Descartes developed his dualistic metaphysics, not as a mean between existing extremes, but in response to the dominant forms of reductive and non-reductive materialism elaborated in the pre-modern period. His dualism is accordingly still fundamentally realist, like that of his materialist opponents, although, as noted earlier (see 3.5), Descartes took the first step in the direction of *epistemological* idealism, a new order of *knowing*, which led eventually to new forms of scepticism and relativism or subjectivism. The only qualification that must be added, and it is an important one, is that a position not unlike Descartes's was already pioneered by Plato, so that Descartes was really going back to a quasi-Platonic view of the soul and its relation to the body when he championed dualism, rejecting both reductive and non-reductive materialism.

Ontological idealism, as a fully developed metaphysical posture, emerged only after Descartes, as a critical reaction to the realism of Cartesian dualism and the puzzles to which it gave rise (see chap. 27). That too has been mentioned already. Leibniz prepared the ground for this development on the European continent, introducing a moderate form of metaphysical idealism that reduced the mathematically describable spatio-temporal objects posited in modern natural science (what has been called 'the scientific image' of the world) to ideal entities dependent for their existence upon the human mind. Still, unlike Bishop Berkeley on the other side of the English channel, Leibniz left completely unreduced another domain of mind-independent (though themselves mind-like) entities, called 'monads.' So his is a moderate idealism. Kant and Hegel moved forward on the basis of Leibniz's research to more radical forms of idealism, with Hegel expanding the notion of the ideal, mental, or mind-*dependent* (the 'phenomenal,' as they called it, following Leibniz) to include the totality of what is. That is the reason for the term 'reductive idealism' in the above chart, which applies to Berkeley as well as Hegel, though in different senses. Kant followed Leibniz in reducing one sort of entity and leaving another mind-independent or unreduced; the details are unimportant for our purposes. These varieties of idealism are distinguished by their differing interpretations of (i) the *sense* of 'ideal' or 'mind-dependent' no less than of (ii) the precise *extent* of the entities so designated, whether all or only some. But these differences among idealisms lie, as already noted, beyond the scope of this Introduction. Still, a quick scan of the above chart from left to right gives at least some sense of the trend of the history of metaphysics described in the last chapter as a shift toward subjectivism. Here the emphasis is on the ontological dimension of the shift; there it was on the epistemological.

4.6 Reductive materialism

While idealism is opposed to realism on the chart in the last section, it is frequently also contrasted with materialism, and it is to *reductive* materialism that we turn last, having said a good deal about non-reductive materialism already.

A good example of the way in which idealism can be contrasted with reductive materialism is provided by Berkeley, who appeals to the authority of the Neoplatonist philosopher Proclus (c. 410 to c. 485 AD): "Proclus, in his *Commentary on the Theology of Plato*," writes Berkeley,

> observes that there are two sorts of philosophers. The one placed Body first in the order of beings, and made the faculty of thinking dependent thereupon, supposing that the principles of all things are corporeal; that Body most really or principally exists, and all other things in a secondary sense, and by virtue of that [i.e., as dependent upon body]. Others, making corporeal things to be dependent on Soul or Mind, think this to exist in the first place and primary sense, and the being of bodies to be altogether derived from and presuppose that of the Mind.

Here Berkeley juxtaposes idealism with materialism in very much the way it was opposed to realism above. But while all forms of materialism are forms of ontological realism, not all ontological realisms are materialistic. Cartesian dualism, for instance, is not. Far from it. Nor do all forms of materialism set out to *eliminate* the immaterial altogether. That is why we distinguished non-reductive materialism of the sort espoused in the Scholastic-Aristotelian tradition, from the reductive materialism here described by Berkeley. The latter has been championed not just by the ancient Greek and Roman atomists, but also by such contemporaries of Descartes as Thomas Hobbes (1588–1679) and Pierre Gassendi (1592–1655), not to mention the Stoics among the later ancients and certain prominent figures in twentieth-century neuro-philosophy (as contemporary reductive materialism is called).

The key point of difference between non-reductive and reductive materialists is the flat denial by the latter that the distinction between the mental and the material, between mental operations and physical (electrochemical) activity in the brain, has any basis in reality. Mental states and processes just *are* brain states or processes *by another name* for the reductive materialist—they are nothing really different from the latter in reality, however differently we may be accustomed to conceiving (or rather misconceiving) and designating them. The mental is thus eliminated as a separate realm of being really distinct from body or matter (distinct *in fact*, not just *in thought*); and so, according to some forms of reductive materialism, is the supersensible divine. Hence the frequency with which the phrase 'atheistic materialism' occurs in modern philosophy. The alternative is brought out nicely by that prominent historian of ancient philosophy cited earlier, A.H. Armstrong, who sums up the materialism of the Stoics in this curious inference: "For them only bodies could act and be causes. Only bodies had a real substantial existence. God and the soul were therefore bodies." This casts the main contention very neatly in the form of an argument. It also permits a nice contrast with Berkeleian idealism, since, for Berkeley, "only minds had a real substantial existence." Armstrong's Stoic, however, does not argue that there is no God or that there are no minds, but rather that both exist—as bodily substances!

4.7 Immanent and transcendent realism

The foregoing account of the order of being is all very well so long as our main aim is to understand *modern* metaphysics since Descartes. For of the modern era it is fair to say that the main metaphysical bone of contention is the order of dependence (independence, interdependence, etc.) among (1) finite particular things called 'bodies,' (2) finite particular entities called 'minds,' and (3) the infinite mind of the creator God. By distinguishing these three types of entities it is possible to contrast the main realist and idealist postures in a manner reasonably adequate for purposes of understanding modern metaphysics, perhaps also for certain pre-modern forms of realism like Aristotle's non-reductive or Stoic and atomistic reductive materialism. But the schema will be found wanting as soon as the term 'metaphysics' is taken to include *all* the major varieties, including ancient and medieval versions, of realism and idealism. For in the ancient tradition another aspect of the order of being predominates, namely the order of dependence (independence, interdependence, etc.) between universals and particulars. In this context, the terms 'realism' and 'idealism' have a different sense, as must be shown now.

The Greek expressions to which the medieval and modern terms 'universals' (*universalia*) and 'particulars' (*particularia*) correspond were first coined by Aristotle (*ta kath'holou* and *ta kath'hekasta*, respectively) based on expressions (*kata holou, kata meros, hekaston, polla hekasta*) already used in a similar way by

Plato. Even before this time the ancient tradition distinguished what is common (*koinon*) from what is individual. For convenience, we shall designate this second main problem concerning the order of being as 'the problem of universals.' Similarly, all problems discussed earlier regarding property, thing, mind, body, God, man, and so on can be subsumed under the simple heading 'mind–body problem,' taking 'mind' to include both the infinite mind of God and finite minds like our own. Thus, the problem complex designated 'the order of being' includes the mind–body problem and the problem of universals. As we explicated the former in terms of various special lower-level problems, so now we must try to survey all issues covered by the latter. What follows now is slightly more difficult than the foregoing, though what may remain puzzling here should be fully cleared up in the part on Plato.

4.7.1 The problem of universals

In pre-modern philosophy there were some highly influential and important problems concerning the nature of universals that have not even been touched upon in the account of the order of being so far. The problems in question are often put in terms such as these: Do universals—for example that which is designated by the abstract noun 'humanity' and by the common noun 'man' as opposed to the proper names 'Socrates' or 'Plato'—do such universals exist (i) only in the mind? Or do they not even exist in the mind (everything in the mind being a concrete individual item or idea and hence particular), but only (ii) in language as abstract nouns? Or, finally, do universals exist, (iii) not just in the mind as abstract concepts *and* in language as abstract nouns, but *also* outside the mind, in sensible things, as their essences, perhaps even (iv) apart from those sensible things, just on their own?

These competing views are known as (i) conceptualism ('only in the mind'), (ii) nominalism ('only in language'), (iii) immanent realism ('in the mind, in language, *and* in things'), and (iv) transcendent realism ('in the mind, in language, in things, *and* apart from those things'), respectively. They will become clearer in the course of the fuller consideration of the order of being to be undertaken now. It should be noted, however, with respect to (iii), immanent realism, that the claim is not that something universal actually resides in particular things; that seems scarcely intelligible since it only stands to reason that whatever is in a particular thing, whether as a part or a property or in some other sense, must itself be particular. The point is rather that the concrete particular nature or essence that really exists in each thing of a certain species or kind is something common or the same in all particular things of that species. It is undoubtedly the mind's apprehension of this particular essence or nature or form (as it is also called) common to all members of a certain class of thing that makes possible the formation of abstract universal concepts like 'humanity' in the mind itself; and for this the mind has to perform all those mental operations necessary to universalize that which it apprehends in the concrete particular entity. What those operations are for the immanent realist is controversial and need not concern us. The point just now is that the form or essence really exists in the things and not *just* in the mind or in language. This, as we shall see, is more than conceptualists and nominalists are prepared to admit, though less than the transcendent realist maintains.

4.7.2 Four questions

The problem of universals is at the very heart of the first full-blown metaphysical theory or system, the Platonic theory of Forms (see Part Two, especially chap. 20). It was prefigured in the enquiries of Plato's great teacher, Socrates, whose goal was to arrive at precise definitions of certain words widely used in moral discourse, words like 'just' and 'unjust,' 'piety,' 'virtue,' and so on. To define such terms, Socrates believed, is indispensable if we are to recognize the corresponding characteristics reliably when and where we actually encounter them, and to pass informed moral judgment on human actions, including our own. Now the first and most important requirement for any definition that will enable us to do this, Socrates held, is that it be strictly universal. That is, to use language more like his own, it must apply to *all and only* those things that are just or pious or virtuous, as the case may be. And as the definition or defining formula must be universal, so that which is defined, too, may be regarded (with a certain distortion, as already noted) as *a* universal, as an 'essence' that is one and the same, though met with *in* all the many particulars that share a common name or designation.

Now for Socrates himself the real existence of such essences *in things* seems to have been a tacit assumption rather than an epistemological or metaphysical doctrine. Socrates was, after all, a moral philosopher who disclaimed all interest in intellectual controversies outside the ethical sphere (see 4.2). But for Plato, who was influenced by certain earlier Greek philosophers engaged in epistemological and ontological pursuits, questions like the following arose.

(1) (a) *Are* there such universal essences; that is, do they really *exist*? And if so, (b) do universals exist for *every* class of particular things to which a single generic class name applies (as 'just' applies to all just actions, just men, just wars, just laws, and so forth)? If only particular things exist, then, of course, the second question, concerning the range of entities for which there are universals, does not even arise. After some wavering on (b), Plato apparently came to the conclusion that there were indeed really existing universals corresponding to *all* particular things of a given class, even artefacts like tables and beds, and such unseemly items as dirt and hair, though his exact views remained largely unsettled through his long philosophical career. Universals for negations like 'not-beautiful' and relations like 'greater than' proved a particularly intractable problem.

Moreover, (2) do these universals really exist *in* particular things, in the individual members of every class of things, or do they have being only in the mind, as universal concepts? Plato remained firmly convinced that they exist outside the mind as well as in it. Whether and how they exist in particular things was a more difficult question for him to answer.

Furthermore, assuming that such universals somehow exist *in* all particulars, (3) do they depend upon those particulars for their being? Or is it the other way around: do the particulars depend upon them for their being? Plato never wavered in his adherence to the latter alternative.

Finally, (4) do these universals, regardless of whether they exist in things, also exist apart and separate from particular things, in their own right, so that even if all individuals of a certain kind were to perish, those universals (or Forms, as Plato called them) would continue to exist? Or would, in that case, the universals cease to exist too? Here Plato decided without hesitation for the former alternative.

4.7.3 Platonic realism

No small amount of confusion arises if, as often happens, the metaphysical theory just sketched is styled 'Platonic idealism,' using the very term employed earlier to characterize the varieties of modern metaphysical idealism from Berkeley and Leibniz to Kant and Hegel. For one thing, the theory in question concerns universals and their relationship to particulars, not—as in modern metaphysics—different kinds of particulars, material and immaterial, finite and infinite. True, the problem of universals persists in modern metaphysics, but more as a side issue; the central issue is the relationship among particulars of a material and immaterial, finite and infinite kind—the 'mind–body problem,' as we call it for convenience. Conversely, it is true that Scholastic-Aristotelian non-reductive materialism addresses the core mind–body problem that preoccupied modern metaphysics, while Plato and his followers championed the ontological independence of the soul from the body, very much in the later manner of Descartes. Still, for the two giants of Greek metaphysics, Plato and Aristotle, this central debate of modern philosophy can be regarded as important though secondary; the central question separating them has to do with universals or essences, and in this context the use of the term 'idealism' must inevitably spawn confusion.

The most decisive consideration against the designation 'Platonic idealism' is the fact that Plato's universal Forms are, in the decisive respect, real rather than ideal; that is, they are *independent of the human mind*, existent in their own right, not mind-dependent, which is the principal meaning of 'ideal.' Even for Socrates, essences exist *in fact, in reality*, and not just *ideally, in the mind*, in the way in which universal concepts are present in thought. As for Platonic Forms, they exist not just *in*, but also apart from and independently of, all particulars. Here too real existence, being in reality, real being, is opposed to existing in thought, in consciousness, ideal being—although for Plato the real Forms exist beyond this world in another realm outside space and time, in a transcendent realm as well as in particulars *and* in the mind. Accordingly, 'Platonic realism' is usually contrasted with the *immanent* realism of both Socrates and Aristotle. It is best labelled 'transcendent realism,' as above. Instead of 'immanent realism,' philosophers nowadays speak of 'essentialism' (roughly, belief in the extra-mental reality or being of essences). It is under this name that we shall discuss the viability of immanent realism later (see chap. 21).

4.7.4 Three senses of 'ideal'

Since the Forms of Plato are both immanently and transcendently real rather than ideal entities (1) *existing in, and dependent upon, the human mind*, Plato's metaphysics can be aptly labelled 'realism' without danger of confusion with the three varieties of metaphysical realism (non-reductive materialism, reductive materialism, Cartesian dualism) discussed earlier (see 4.5–6). For, to repeat, Platonic realism concerns the order of being as regards universals and particulars, not two kinds of particulars, minds and bodies. Nevertheless, the same Forms are undeniably ideal in at least two other, secondary senses of the term. For one thing, the Forms are (2) *non-sensible* (inaccessible to sense perception) *and immaterial*, and thus altogether unlike the real particular *material* things and events that populate the physical world around us. Moreover, as the universal essences of material things, the same for many different individuals, the Forms are in some sense (3) *abstract, not concrete* like the individuals or particulars that populate this world. In this third sense, too, it is customary to speak of Platonic Forms as 'ideal.' Add to this Plato's staunch opposition to materialism concerning the human soul, not to mention his teaching concerning the World Soul, the divine Spirit of the cosmos (see 16.2 and 20.5.1), and there seem to be many reasons to speak of Platonic idealism in characterizing the very theory described above as 'Platonic realism' above.

Still, the expression 'Platonic realism' is preferable, mainly because 'Platonic idealism' almost inevitably invites confusion of 'ideal' in senses (2) and (3) with 'ideal' in the primary sense, that is, (1) mind-dependent. If intellectual historians give way to the powerful temptation to speak of a 'metaphysics of spirit' running through the entire western tradition, starting with Plato and revived by Descartes, they should at least take care to distinguish the Platonic and Cartesian as two distinct phases of the metaphysics of spirit, corresponding to two distinct problems, the problem of universals and the mind–body problem. But, on the whole, it is better not to give in to the temptation at all.

4.8 Conceptualism and nominalism

It was suggested in the preceding section that ancient thought on universals was predominantly realist, at least among the towering figures of the classical period. Socrates presupposed (perhaps unconsciously) a kind of immanent realism in his quest for the universal definitions in the moral sphere; Plato generalized and transformed this Socratic enquiry, positing transcendently real Forms for all things designated by a single name, not just moral attributes; Aristotle emphatically rejected Plato's theory, providing immanent realism with the clear theoretical underpinnings that Socrates (as a moral philosopher) never undertook to give it. Only in the medieval and modern periods were these attitudes challenged by those approaches to the problem of universals referred to earlier as 'conceptualism' and 'nominalism.'

According to conceptualists, we said, universals are ideal, not real; they exist only in the mind, as general concepts (including concepts of genera like 'animal' and species like 'man' as well as abstractions like 'animality' and 'humanity'); they do not exist in things, let alone apart from them. Individual things have similarities on the basis of which *we* group them into classes or collections according to our purposes and interests; but only ideas or class concepts *in the mind* are universal, while everything real or mind-independent is particular. Of course, not all the contents of the mind are universal; universal concepts (from the Latin *concipio* 'seize or take together') must be distinguished from those contents of the mind, notably sense perceptions, that have concrete individuals as their objects. Yet both depend upon the mind for their existence. That is the key thing as regards the order of being.

The ancient Stoics and Epicureans (see 2.1) were conceptualists in the sense just described. So were Locke and Kant in the modern period. Like the Stoics and Epicureans, moreover, Locke and Kant recognized that *some* class concepts are not of our own devising but 'natural': all human beings have an innate or inborn disposition to form, and think in terms of, just these concepts. To that extent there are some universals that do not depend on the human will; they do not exist in things, of course, much less outside them, but only in the mind, and yet not as the arbitrary products of the will. Most universals existing in the mind are, however, precisely that: arbitrary or conventional. Notwithstanding this difference with respect to the will, Locke, following the Stoics, took both types of universals to have their sole origin in experience; Kant disagreed, calling those that depend on the mind's own nature but not on the will 'pure' or 'a priori' (roughly: 'non-empirical,' 'not dependent on experience') concepts. His predecessors in the seventeenth century, notably Descartes, had called them 'innate' or 'inborn.' What concerns us now is not this difference between Locke and Kant but their shared conceptualism on the question of universals. The difference between them over innateness or a priori (non-empirical) concepts will be considered in other contexts.

Opposing this conceptualist theory, those called 'nominalists' dispute the very existence of abstract general ideas in the mind, maintaining that mental contents are invariably particular. This position was defended with wit and eloquence by Berkeley. Universals, Berkeley urged, are a feature of our language, of words (Latin, *nomen*, whence 'nominalism'), all nouns being either proper names for particulars or else common names for classes or groups of things or, finally, abstract nouns. These last are universal. And as language as a whole is a human artefact, different in different times and places, so the universal terms we devise differ from time to time and place to place. There is no universal predisposition to think in any one set of concepts rather than another; rather, thought follows language, which is indefinitely malleable or plastic. For the nominalist, then, there are neither inborn, universal concepts nor natural dispositions to form them, since all the contents of the mind are just particular ideas; nor, of course, are there universal natures really existing in things outside the mind, let alone apart from them in a higher realm.

It is not hard to see how nominalism, if true, might be thought to have a great liberating effect on philosophy. For it proudly proclaims the freedom to think and speak in terms quite different from those of the dominant philosophical sects and systems of the past—to consult experience directly and attempt to shape or reshape our thought and language freely in accordance with the dictates of immediate experience. It is not surprising, therefore, that nominalism has generally gone hand in hand with radical empiricism, even with materialism (as in the cases of Hobbes and Gassendi). In the Middle Ages, William of Ockham (c. 1285–1349) was a prominent proponent of nominalism, as were the empiricists Hobbes and Berkeley in the modern era. In contemporary philosophy this particular anti-realist (or anti-essentialist) attitude has dominated the Anglo-American tradition of philosophy with its emphasis on language over both thought and things as the starting point of philosophical reflection (see chap. 21).

Just as Plato's theory of universal Forms can be called 'idealism' in the two senses specified above (Forms are *immaterial* and *abstract* essences), though not in the first and primary sense (Forms are definitely not *mind-dependent*), so nominalism and conceptualism can be labelled 'idealisms' in the first or primary sense: both assert the mind-dependence of the universal. Still, in the interests of clarity it is best to stick with the customary labels, reserving the term 'idealism' for that conception of the order of knowing and of being that makes mind and the mental ontologically and/or epistemologically prior *to the material world*. So understood, metaphysical idealism is a distinctively modern phenomenon that began with Berkeley, Leibniz, and Kant, while epistemological idealism began earlier, with Descartes. Idealism is a key factor in the development away from objectivism toward subjectivism and relativism described in 3.5. As for the Platonic Forms, their being nonsensible and immaterial as well as abstract takes nothing away from their perfect objectivity or being in themselves, apart from all relation to the human mind or subject. It is understandable, therefore, that some scholars prefer to speak of Plato's metaphysics as a form of 'immaterialism' or 'spiritualism,' shunning 'idealism' altogether. Indeed, 'Platonic immaterialism' and 'Platonic realism' both seem apt, particularly when conjoined, to capture the objectivism of this first great metaphysical theory.

4.9 The regions and guiding idea of being

The relevance of this preliminary discussion of immanent and transcendent realism, nominalism, and conceptualism to the central theme of Part Two of this work will become apparent later. The point we have been leading up to for some time is this: If we wish to understand the chief philosophical accounts of the order of being, starting with the Greeks, the simple binary division of the totality of what is into (1) matter and (2) mind will not get us very far. Nor will a tripartition consisting of (i) finite material things, (ii) finite minds, and (iii) the infinite divine mind. For the problem of universals is not even mooted in this schema, though it is central to the metaphysical contest between Plato and Aristotle, overshadowing even the problem of the relation of material particulars (bodies) to immaterial particulars (souls).

Interestingly, the very notion of the infinite was unknown in Greek thought prior to the fifth century, when it first attracted the attention of mathematicians rather than philosophers. It acquired importance as a physical and metaphysical concept first among the Pythagoreans, in the work of Melissus of Samos and Zeno of Elea, and in the atomists' theories of the infinite void containing an infinitude of material particles or atoms. Aristotle, however, rejected the notion of a real or actual (as opposed to a mathematical) infinite, and his view was to remain decisive for all pre-modern science. Accordingly, the real physical world of Greek and medieval science is a closed or bounded cosmos (see 20.4.1). The notion of an actual infinite first gained wide acceptance in the Christian *theology* of the Middle Ages, where infinity became the chief attribute of God. Only subsequently, in early modern natural science, was it applied to the cosmos, the closed world of the ancients giving way to an infinite universe, unbounded in space and time—with all the insoluble puzzles that Zeno had shown to attend that strange idea. So what is needed for purposes of understanding *all* metaphysical conceptions of the order of being is a more extensive map of the *regions of being* than has been developed thus far, one that includes both the real and the ideal, universals and particulars, the finite and the infinite, the sensible and the non-sensible, as well as different types of ideal entities.

This is not the place to attempt a fuller description of the principal domains of being—much less of the different possible orders of dependence, independence, interdependence, and inter-independence among them. For purposes of contrasting the figures and periods to be studied in this work, the preceding sketch of the order of being will suffice. Nevertheless, it may be worth noting the important place in metaphysical enquiry occupied by certain key concept pairs. These include not just prior (that on which something else depends for its being or being known) and posterior (the ontologically or epistemologically dependent), but one and many, universal and particular, being and non-being, sensible and non-sensible (or supersensible), mental (immaterial) and physical (material), ideal and real, abstract and concrete, finite and infinite, immanent and transcendent. To these may be added part and whole, simple and composite, form and matter, existence and essence, possible and actual, changing and unchanging, temporal and eternal. Metaphysicians in the western tradition have constantly relied on these concept pairs (or some subset of them) as their basic theoretical framework. Questions in which they figure are invariably metaphysical questions.

What, then, determines the order of being posited in a given philosophical system? On what basis does one philosopher—say, an Aristotle or a Leibniz—relegate infinite space or time to the realm of the merely ideal, the abstract, the universal that exists only in the mind, while another—Newton, for instance—regards both space and time as fully real, concrete things, infinite container-like entities existing in their own right? How does it come about that one thinker regards the transitory and changing as merely ideal, mind-dependent, even illusory, acknowledging only the permanent and unchanging as truly real, while another takes the real to be coextensive with the concrete individual changing things that we observe all round us, treating the permanent and changeless as a mere idealization existing only in the human intellect or imagination? Why, finally, does one thinker or school of thought set the divine completely apart from the world, in the manner of Aristotle, while another treats the very cosmos itself as divine (see 5.5.3–4)? Why does one period or tradition stress the will, when another consistently subordinates the will to the intellect? How is it that one dominant sense of being, say essence or finite form in Greek philosophy, comes to be supplanted by another—for example, infinite existence in the Christian philosophy of the Middle Ages (see 20.5.2)?

The short answer to these questions is that every great metaphysical system of thought grows up under some *guiding idea of being*. If we wish to understand the sequence and variety of metaphysical postures *in depth*, we must try to grasp the underlying concept of being in each. Though something of the sort would appear to be the ultimate goal in studying the metaphysics of the past, it is obviously a very tall order for the start. The most we can hope to achieve at the outset is a better understanding of the regions and order of being posited in some few of the major metaphysical systems of the past.

Still, if examples of guiding ideas of being are wanted, it is not hard to provide them. One of the most influential seems to derive from mathematics. Thus, for Plato, as for Parmenides before him, the (1) idea of being as permanence and perfect intelligibility served to set true beings apart from the less-than-perfectly real or the altogether unreal. Traces of this guiding idea of being reappear in one form or another in most subsequent metaphysics. Others seem to derive from religion and philosophical theology, for example the (2) idea of being as infinite existence that shaped medieval Christian metaphysics, persisting right down to the end of the seventeenth century. For Aquinas, the "Angelic Doctor" of medieval thought, the ultimate source of all finite existence does not merely *have* existence; the infinite being, God, *is* existence itself. Other guiding ideas of being have a lowlier origin in what we see all around us everyday. An example is that (3) idea of being circumscribed in the concepts 'life,' 'growth,' and 'organism,' which put its stamp on early Greek philosophy and to the great synthesis of Greek science carried out by Aristotle at the end of the classical period. Here it is above all the philosophical concept of finite form, an outgrowth of earlier ideas like 'balance,' 'measure,' 'harmony,' and 'proportion' (see 5.5.1), that emerged as the guiding idea of being in Greek art and intellectual contemplation. Different again is that (4) idea of being implicit in the conception of all things as objects of scientific knowledge (*ens cognitum*, a cognized thing). It came into its own with Berkeley and Kant in the eighteenth century, the proud age of scientific Enlightenment. Despite the apparent differences in provenance, all these guiding ideas of being may have a common root—say, in the idea of time, as Heidegger maintained. To show anything of the kind would be a monumental task. (Heidegger himself barely got started before abandoning it.) These few examples of guiding ideas of being will have to suffice as we focus our attention on certain influential conceptions of the order of being in ancient, modern, and contemporary philosophy in four of the five main parts of this book.

5

Philosophy and Mythico-Religious Thought

5.1 Introductory

The present chapter deals with the relationship of Greek philosophy to the non-philosophical literature of the ancient Greek world, including poetry, drama, and history. Myth and legend were the stuff of Greek literature during most of antiquity. The birth of philosophy around the turn of the sixth century BC meant a sharp break with the older mythological ways of thinking that continued to hold sway in most spheres of Greek life long after philosophy appeared on the scene. Some intellectual factors behind the rupture will be touched on in this sketch of the history of Greek philosophy before Socrates; social and other historical developments working in the same direction lie outside its scope.

Though sharply discontinuous at one level, mythological and philosophical understanding display a striking continuity as well. In fact, late developments in mythology, on the one hand, and Presocratic philosophy, on the other, can be regarded as successive phases in mankind's quest for a more rational intellectual and moral basis for life. That is how they are to be presented here. 'Myth' is accordingly shorthand for mytho-poetic or mythico-religious *thought* as distinct from legend and folktale. A third stage in this development begins in the latter half of the fifth century with Socrates himself, who shifted the intellectual focus from natural philosophy and rational theology to moral matters or ethics (see chap. 9). Accordingly, to understand Socrates's ethical teachings a knowledge of earlier developments is not strictly necessary. Still, anyone who feels, as beginners often do, that the study of philosophy should begin at the beginning, will want to consider the new texture of rationality that emerged with philosophy itself a century and a half before Socrates. Those impatient to get on to the first classical text may, however, omit the present chapter without serious detriment to their understanding of Part One. In fact, since this

Introduction is getting long, the next two chapters can be skipped as well, provided the back references to the chapter on logic (chap. 7) are followed up as they occur in the five main parts of the book.

As for the Greek literature of the two succeeding centuries, the purpose of the whirlwind tour of the classical period at the end of this chapter (see 5.9) is to provide a few salient points of cultural reference for the appreciation of the philosophical achievements of the same epoch.

5.2 Philosophy, literature, art, and religion

The similarities and differences between philosophical and mythological thinking are just one aspect of the very involved historical relationship between philosophy and the great works and major developments of world literature and the fine arts. Detailed reflection on this topic is obviously beyond the scope of the present Introduction. Nevertheless, the theory or philosophy of literature ('criticism,' as it is sometimes called) should perhaps be added to the growing list of philosophical sub-disciplines compiled so far, either as a branch of the philosophy of art (usually called 'aesthetics') or as an independent field of enquiry. Both art and literature figure prominently among those philosophical studies that are both current and traditional (see 1.2.3), a series of outstanding thinkers having reflected on both, notably on poetry and tragedy, from Plato and Aristotle to Hegel and Heidegger. Still, art and literature are not among the perennial subjects of philosophical debate in the sense specified earlier: questions that arise out of the universal human condition, answers to which provide the outer framework of the moral and intellectual basis of human life. On the other hand, such questions are often addressed in great works of art and literature, and this is especially true of myth in the centuries before philosophy.

Just as Greek civilization is older than philosophy by more than half a millennium, so too is the attempt to address the perennial issues of human existence; philosophy may be the chief way in which these questions have been pursued in the west for 2500 years now, but before philosophy, both in ancient Greece and in the still older civilizations of the Near East—not to mention India and China—mankind's search for answers to the perennial questions took the form of myth or religion. Even today pre- and extra-philosophical ways of posing and answering the enduring questions are still very much alive in the great world religions, that is, in the authoritative myths of contemporary European and non-European cultures, the stories retold in sacred books like the Old and New Testaments, the Koran, and others. But the quest for philosophical understanding is different in important respects from mythico-religious thought, and if we are to get some inkling of the new pattern of rationality that emerged with philosophy, we have to consider at least briefly what there was before philosophy made its appearance on the scene.

5.3 Before philosophy

Part of the answer to the question, What was there before philosophy? is to be found in the great epic and didactic poems of Homer (*Iliad*, *Odyssey*) and Hesiod (*Theogony*), and in lesser works of the same genre. Homer is usually situated around the beginning of the eighth century, Hesiod toward the end, that is, around 700 BC. These great poems record what were for the Indo-European peoples who migrated into the Greek peninsula around 1200 BC sacred stories of a kind not altogether unlike the Bible. Yet they differed from other sacred books in a way that may help us to understand why philosophy first arose and took root among the Greeks rather than elsewhere (see 5.3.2 below). In any case, the stories themselves were much older than Homer—assuming there was a single bard of that name—who presumably only carried out, or carried on, the work of compiling them, giving an age-old oral tradition the written form in which it has come down to us.

5.3.1 Early Greek religion and morality

These poems furnish us with most of our knowledge of traditional Greek religion and morality, including (a) a story of the creation of the world in the beginning (a cosmogony) and (b) a description of the cosmos as it now is (a cosmology), though these two, cosmogony and cosmology, were not sharply distinguished. Nor is the way things *are* distinguished from how they *should* and *must* be owing to (c) quasi-personal moral forces or laws operating throughout the universe, Justice, Necessity, Destiny, and Fate, as the poets variously called them. The poems contain, moreover, (d) a tale about the origin or genealogy of the gods (theogony) and of man (anthropogony) as well as (e) an imaginative pre-history of the world going right back to the dawn of civilization, when heroes spoke face to face with gods and demi-gods, and the outcome of actions on the human stage was decided by a greater drama playing itself out among personified deities on Mount Olympus. The feudal society depicted in epic poetry also provides us with a picture of the old aristocratic (f) ideal of human virtue or excellence, in the persons of its war-like heroes and potentates. Finally, the poems contain (g) stories relating to the origins of immemorial rites and festivals and sacred places, like the aforementioned oracle at the shrine to the god Apollo at Delphi, about which more will be said later.

In the terms introduced earlier, these great epic and didactic poems embody the early Greek understanding of the totality of what is, was, will, and must be; they represent the moral and intellectual basis of Greek life throughout the archaic period and long after the birth of philosophy. In recognition of this fact, Plato called Homer, in all solemnity, the educator of all the Greeks. Unlike naive legend and folktale, mytho-poetic *thought* is not just storytelling, fiction, imaginative invention for purposes of entertainment—'myth' in the sense usually given the term today. Nor is it on a par with sacred hymns invoking the presence of a deity at a holy ritual or religious festival. Mythico-religious thought is rather a way of making sense of the world as a whole, of man's place in it, of the relation of man to man and to the divine. In the world and time to which they belonged, the Homeric and Hesiodic myths were accepted unquestioningly as literal historical truth. To those who belong to its thought world, any myth-based religion is nothing short of truth; at the very least, mytho-poetic thought must be acknowledged as a way of *pursuing* truth. Not only is this way of furnishing ourselves with an intellectual and moral basis for life still practised today in the great world religions; it is still thought to be the best way to do so by the vast majority of mankind, that is, by the more or less orthodox practitioners of those creeds world-wide.

Among the early Greeks, then, myths were neither just stories nor the basis of cult—religion in a narrow sense; they represented the communal wisdom of a civilization, its way of seeing itself, its history, the universe as a whole, including the supersensible divine. Human life, as we have said, is never without such a basis, so that we can be sure that the cosmological, cosmogonic, theogonic, and moral ideas of the Homeric and Hesiodic poems supplanted earlier forms of religious worship, in relation to which they represented a first step on the road to furnishing a more rational basis for life. The next great step was philosophy.

5.3.2 From religion to philosophy

In most civilizations, ancient as well as modern, the established moral and intellectual basis of life is regarded as something not to be tampered with by individuals who think they know better, but to be preserved unchanged and interpreted authoritatively, usually by a priestly caste expressly created for the purpose. Of this attitude the Greeks were remarkably free. Homer and Hesiod claimed the authority of divine revelation for their sometimes lurid tales of sexual union and struggle for dominion among the divine beings whom they conceived, now as visible cosmic constituents like Earth, Sky, and Sea, now as fully personified deities—Zeus and the other Olympians. But what one inspired poet claimed to have recorded at the dictation of a muse, another could alter or deny on the authority of his own revelation; and, in fact, the Greek poets and dramatists, right down through the classical age, took the greatest liberties with the stories handed on to them—even to the point of openly doubting the very existence of the Olympian deities. Greek religion was not a religion "of the Book," nor was the temple the chief centre of intellectual life, as in most other ancient civilizations; the priestly class had other duties, chiefly prophecy or augury and the performance of sacred rites and sacrifices to honour and propitiate the gods.

The intellectual climate in Greece was thus one in which criticism and dissent were tolerated to a remarkable extent. Such a climate naturally spawned new theories, including those philosophical cosmogonies and cosmologies that dispensed with the anthropomorphic gods of mythology altogether. True, some early Greek philosophers still wrote in verse or oracular prose, claiming more-than-human authority for a vision of man, the world, and the divine that differed starkly from the half-rational, half-mythological cosmogonies and cosmologies of Homer and Hesiod. Yet the whole process can be regarded as one of gradual *rationalization* or intellectualization of the older theologies, cosmogonies, and cosmologies, these having themselves been a very significant advance from lore to logic by comparison with still older forms of worship of local spirits or daimons—the fertility cults of various kinds about which we know very little, unfortunately, since no writings older than the Homeric poems survive.

The idea of three successive phases in the rationalization of early religious thought seems well suited to bring out the continuity between (1) mythico-religious, (2) philosophical, and (3) scientific thought without minimizing the importance of the discontinuities involved. Of course, from early Greek philosophy it is a very long way to anything recognizably similar to science in our sense of the word. In the nineteenth century the rise of natural philosophy among the Greeks was touted as the first step on the road to a genuine science of nature some two millennia later. In the light of the quarrel between religion and science that had by then been brewing for centuries, there could be no question about the superiority of science. Or so it seemed to the majority, who sided with the Enlightenment; Romantics, for their part, were partisans of older mytho-poetic modes of thinking and their claim to a truth different and more profound than any science can discover. As for the emergence of a novel conception of divinity among the same Greek thinkers, both parties viewed the new speculative rational theology as progress from the naive polydaemonism and polytheism (literally: 'many daimons' or divine beings and 'many gods,' respectively) of earlier times toward the more sophisticated, monotheistic ('one god') conceptions of deity found in the Judeo-Christian tradition.

Whether philosophy is indeed superior to the mythico-religious thought, yet inferior to full-fledged science, or whether something is lost as well as gained in each transition, is a question seldom asked. Under the influence of the Enlightenment idea of human progress, the nineteenth-century French thinker Auguste Comte (1798–1857) was quick to construe these three as successive stages in the intellectual maturation of mankind. On any such view, myth represents the childhood of man, roughly on par with the naive fairytales and bogeymen of the nursery. However, it is worth pondering the respective contributions of myth or religion, philosophy, and modern science to genuine human flourishing. There is no doubt about the pre-eminence of science in virtually all spheres of modern life, or that modern science, whatever destructive forces it may have unleashed, has bettered the lives of countless millions of human beings immeasurably. Nevertheless, we should perhaps not just take the authority of science for granted, equating the fruits of scientific rationality with truth. 'Scientism' is the term applied to the view memorably expressed by the British philosopher Bertrand Russell (see 1.4): "Whatever knowledge is obtainable, must be obtained by scientific methods; and what science cannot discover, mankind cannot know." For Russell, some metaphysical theories are just 'not-yet-science' (see 6.4.3), while others belong together with mythico-religious thought under the headings 'mysticism' or 'fantasy.' In the great explanatory truth sweepstakes, of course, science is the clear winner, lining up a stunning array of truths having both great predictive and immense manipulative power; but if another yardstick is applied, the outcome may be different. What yardstick? is an interesting question, but sheer numbers of truths and practical benefits seem doubtful candidates—unless a strong connection can be established between such knowledge and genuine human thriving.

The whole topic of myth and its significance belongs not just to the philosophy of literature, but to the philosophical reflection upon the phases and forms of religion as well. Hence, the philosophy of religion may be added to the tentative list of philosophical sub-disciplines that already includes philosophical psychology, philosophical cosmology, philosophy of biology, philosophy of education, philosophical anthropology, and the philosophy of literature and art. To these the philosophy of physics will be added soon. In the next two chapters we shall have occasion to add the philosophy of science and logic as well. The reflections there should be helpful in understanding the question of the relationship between truth, rationality, and scientific method. For, as Russell's remark makes abundantly clear, scientific method is frequently regarded as the only reliable means of discovering truth and therefore simply identified with rational procedure; whereas, on a more cautious view, it is only one pattern or texture of rationality, philosophy and even Olympian theology being others.

5.4 The birth of philosophy

The comprehensive religious or mythological world-view discussed above provides the setting in which Presocratic philosophy arose during the last phase of the archaic or pre-classical period. The earliest philosophers came, not from mainland Greece, but from the eastern colonies on the coast of Asia Minor—Ionia, as modern-day Turkey was called—and from the colonies of southern Italy and Sicily in the west. The latter, known in antiquity as 'Great Greece,' was the land in which the mythical pre-historic figure of Orpheus had been worshiped as a divine poet and prophet. Certain Orphic beliefs concerning (i) the purification of the soul and (ii) its survival of the death of the body through rebirth in other bodies had a lasting effect on the philosophy that flourished there. The latter in turn influenced Plato, who visited that part of the world in the early decades of the fourth century. As for (iii) the cosmological and cosmogonic writings ascribed to the legendary figures of Orpheus, Musaeus, and Epimenides, it is uncertain whether any Orphic teachings of the kind are old enough to have influenced philosophy in the western colonies. Anyway, our knowledge of Orphism is extremely limited, being based largely on later sources of doubtful reliability. Indeed, our knowledge of most of the early Greek thinkers is sketchy, confined in some cases to a very few (a) isolated fragments of their writings quoted verbatim (the literal fragments) and (b) scanty references in the writings of later philosophers, theologians, and historians of ideas (indirect fragments or *testimonia*), sometimes as much as a millennium later. Only in a few cases do we have (c) a substantial portion of their work in direct quotation (see 1.5), and even then the interpretive problems are daunting.

Uncontroversial is perhaps only a general interpretive framework that includes a division, along geographical lines, between the eastern (Ionian) and western (Italian) beginnings—*two* beginnings of philosophy, in other words, and two characteristic patterns of thinking. What they share is the tendency to substitute logic for lore, to transform older religious into new philosophical patterns of explanation through the process referred to above as 'intellectualization' and 'rationalization'—through "rational catharsis," as one authority has aptly put it (Werner Jaeger). Yet the one beginning had its roots in the Orphic tradition, giving rise to philosophies at least tinged with magic, mysticism, and myth; the other sprang from the already highly rationalized Olympian theology and cosmology of the Homeric and Hesiodic poems. Out of the latter evolved, by slow stages, philosophies that prefigured the mathematical, mechanical, and materialistic tendencies of modern science.

Such a contrast can be overdone, as it was, regularly, in the so-called successions of master and pupil devised by late-Greek historians of thought; but restrained versions have found wide acceptance among scholars. If nothing else, (1) magic, mysticism, and myth can be set over against (2) mathematical, mechanical, and materialistic tendencies as endpoints of a spectrum on which to locate individual thinkers. Ionian thinkers will figure more prominently at the one end, Italian at the other, though most combine both tendencies to some extent. Indeed, there are Ionians who manifest marked mystical or religious tendencies, as there are Italians who show a strong logical, mathematical, or scientific bent. This, however, is no reason to reject the geographical division outright. Historically, it is exactly what one would expect, the philosophic centres in Italy and Sicily having been founded by immigrants from Ionia fleeing before the Persians who were invading from the east. As we shall see in the course of this book, the rivalry between scientifically-minded philosophers and those of a more religious or traditional bent has never abated and is still very much in evidence today.

Beyond this, it is advisable to distinguish an early phase, in both Ionia and Italy, dominated by (a) rational or natural theology and (b) philosophy of nature (cosmology and cosmogony), from a later phase whose principal focus is (c) the philosophy of being. The latter sets the stage for the classical period, in which questions of ontology or the order of being figure centrally, though it is uncertain whether one can read any particular ontology back into the first such philosophy of being. It is just possible that the very first reflection on being was confined to the abstract *concept* 'being'; that it posited neither the actual existence of anything nor any order of being, as in ontology proper. That is the view to be taken here, though the matter is disputed (see 20.10.2). Not so the fact that, alongside this new concept, 'being,' certain older concepts continue to play an important role, notably 'one' and 'many,' 'motion' ('change'), and 'rest' ('permanence'). These remain central in the classical period as well, not least in the problem of universals discussed earlier (see 4.7.1–4); for there is one universal for many particulars. Once again, the talk of *two* beginnings, one in the early sixth, the other around the turn of the fifth century, is helpful only as long as it is not pressed too far.

5.5 Eastern beginnings

Among the Ionians are the earliest of those philosophers mentioned in Plato's *Apology* (19a–d), men like Thales, Anaximander, and Anaximenes, all of the city of Miletus (hence: 'the Milesians'). Whatever Milesian thought may owe to the myth-making of the preceding centuries, it clearly represents a departure from the older cosmogonic and theogonic genealogies of Homer and Hesiod. Unlike those picturesque but obscure and often confusing stories of the ancestry of the world and the human race, the Milesians proposed coherent, reasoned explanations of the origin and order of the universe in terms of *one* ultimate originative and governing *principle* or *beginning* (*archē*—pronounced 'arshay'—in Greek). They are therefore often called 'monists,' from the Greek word *monas*, 'unity.' Thales described his ultimate principle as water or the moist, Anaximenes as air or wind, while Anaximander avoided all such definite descriptions, calling the first principle underlying all quantitative and qualitative differentiation and change in the world 'the indefinite' or 'undifferentiated' (*apeiron*). For present purposes these differences are less important than what sets all the Milesians apart from the older, mythological tradition.

5.5.1 The archē concept

As a *governing* principle the *archē* was understood as *immanent* in all things, an imperishable, life-bestowing and -sustaining force pervading and controlling the entire universe, including those things that we today should regard as non-living. Though actually *present in* all things, the *archē* was not simply the basic 'stuff' of which they are made, a permanent material substrate found throughout the world in many different forms or states, as Aristotle and the Peripatetic tradition supposed. For one thing, the *originative* principle is *transcendent* as well: like the higher moral forces regarded by the poets as holding sway over the personified Olympian deities of sky (Zeus), sea (Poseidon), and underworld (Hades), the principles of the Milesians are of a higher order than the cosmic constituents, the great elemental masses existing separately, each in its own region—earth (the dry) at the centre, then water (the moist), then air in the upper atmosphere (the cold), and, finally, fiery aether (the hot) in the outermost heavens. Explanatorily, the principles of the Milesians are *prior* to the elemental masses through whose disposition in space an ordered cosmos exists. That is the first sense in which they underlie the cosmos: not as material substrates but as explanatory ultimates.

Within the established spatial order, the elements, with their antagonistic powers, commingle over time in a continuous cycle of regulated interchange—analogous to that going on within the living human body—between the forces of hot, cold, moist, and dry; for the Milesians characteristically couched their explanations of astronomical cycles and the meteorological phenomena in terms of *vital* as well as *mechanical* forces. The greatest of them, Anaximander, clearly conceived the process *morally* as well: as unlawful encroachment by one element upon another, followed inevitably by retribution or restoration of the cosmic balance in the fullness of time. It is tempting to see in all this an aesthetic, perhaps even a social, dimension as well; for this idea of balance, measure, harmony, or proportion—to use a later Greek term, 'form' (see 4.9)—exerted a powerful shaping influence on Greek artistic creation and political life as well as on cosmology and cosmogony. That is the second sense in which the *archē* underlies the universe, then: not as 'stuff,' but as the governing, controlling law or principle of change over time.

Though explanatorily prior both (1) as *transcending* the elemental masses and forces, and (2) as governing the whole cosmic process of flux or change *immanently*, it is questionable whether the *archē* of the Milesians was conceived (3) as *temporally* prior in any sense. Temporal priority suggests a pre-existing entity or pre-cosmic state from which another arose, as in the old theogonies and cosmogonies. Yet, arguably, the first principles of the Milesians were not only impersonal or non-anthropomorphic, that is, devoid of purposive intelligence and desire; for despite anthropomorphic traces, this is largely true even of the basic elements and antagonistic forces at work in the universe. The *archē* itself may not have been conceived as an *entity* of any kind at all—neither primeval 'stuff' nor 'substance' nor 'element' nor primal 'force' nor pre-cosmic 'state.' Or, if it is an entity or state in some sense, as most interpreters suppose, it is at least one of an entirely different sort than the irreducible elements, composite things, and cosmic processes it explains: an entity that itself did not come into being at all. That is more than can be said even of the gods of Greek mythology, who, though undying, are born into an already existing world. Hesiod, one is tempted to say, brought everything forth from a primal *chaos*, a Greek word with connotations of 'yawning' and 'gap,' as in our word 'chasm'; within that *primeval opening*, which itself came into being first, Mother Earth was sundered from Father Heaven before reuniting with him to beget through procreation all manner of living things, starting with the immortal gods. The Milesians, for their part, opened a new gap between entities and originative, governing principles, which, if they are entities, at least did not come into being, though they may not be entities at all.

5.5.2 Other distinctive marks of Milesian thought

The novelty of the *archē* concept of the Milesians may still not be fully appreciated. For talk of a 'material principle' persists to this day, as do efforts to assimilate Milesian to earlier religious patterns of thought. That said, it must be acknowledged that the idea of a cause of the being of entities that is not itself an entity—a cause that is 'beyond being,' in Plato's apt phrase—does not emerge explicitly until well into the fourth century; to suggest that it was present, even implicitly, in Thales or Anaximander is heretical—though just possibly true, and in any case a useful corrective to the interpretive tendencies just mentioned. If the suggestion is correct, then the 'gap' opened by the Milesians is the first instance of what Heidegger has called the 'ontological difference' between being (a 'cause' or explanatory principle that is not itself *a* being, *an* entity) and being*s* (the things or entities whose being is explained by means of that principle). At this early stage, of course, one would scarcely expect the difference to be clear-cut. Nor would it be surprising if later thinkers tended to close the gap again. According to Heidegger, the tendency to 'entitize' the non-entitative is strong in all metaphysical thinking, and there is a good deal of evidence to support his contention.

Apart from (1) the *archē* concept, certain other features distinguish the fledgling philosophical pattern of rationality from the older mythological way of thinking. In taking this bold leap beyond the mythological world-view of the past, the Milesians (2) appealed to no higher authority than human reason itself. Carefully devised explanations in terms of (a) natural powers, (b) basic elements, and (c) a single originating principle or governing law are obviously a very far cry from sacred stories about the designs and deeds of divine beings, whether handed down from time immemorial or revealed to inspired poets and seers by the muses. The Milesians were doing their own thinking; they put their theories forward as the product of their own reflection for others to examine and criticize, hoping to carry conviction by the sheer reasonableness of their conjectures. Though not 'science' in our sense, there is at least something unmistakably rational about the new reliance on discussion, criticism, and debate.

The opposition between the findings of human reason and the promptings of divine illumination is a familiar one in the Judeo-Christian context, where philosophical theology (reason) is customarily opposed to the interpretation of sacred scripture (revelation); but it can be applied, with a certain qualification, to the sixth-century BC confrontation between myth and philosophy as well. The qualification concerns the notion of *faith* in a higher truth that is above, or even contrary to, human reason; for the Greeks display no tendency to countenance the acceptance of incompatible answers to the same questions in religion on the one hand and philosophy or science on the other. That idea arose with Christianity. The Greek word that comes closest to 'faith,' *pistis*, usually translated 'conviction' or 'belief,' is the very word used for rational insight by Parmenides.

In devising their naturalistic explanations of observable phenomena, moreover, the Milesians (3) based themselves on a wide range of facts gathered through careful observation. Self-observation is the likely source of their conception of the whole universe as a single living entity, while ordinary sense experience played a key role in their rational explanations of meteorological and astronomical processes formerly regarded as supernatural. It is not that such things as the cycles of day and night, the seasons, growth and decay, or the revolutions of the heavens had not been carefully observed before; obviously, no agricultural society that ignored them could have survived long. But it took a more penetrating gaze to detect in the daily transmutation of elements in processes like evaporation and condensation a clue to a large-scale cosmological theory. From the data of inner and outer experience, however, the Milesians extrapolated bold, highly speculative theories that few today would consider even a rudimentary form of science. One should be wary, therefore, of efforts to find anticipations of modern molecular theory or crude versions of the principles of the conservation of energy or matter in Milesian thought. Nor, however, is theirs just a further rationalized version of the very mode of representation characteristic of Olympian religion either. 'Philosophy or metaphysics of nature' is the customary designation for such untested and untestable theories—though the Milesians understood nature herself as both living and divine, so that, at this stage at least, *philosophy of nature* and *philosophical theology* cannot be separated. For that reason Aristotle's description of the Milesians as *physiologoi*, 'physicists' or 'physiologists,' is doubly misleading: for one thing, 'physics' today is the basic *science* of nature; for another, Aristotle opposes 'the physicists' to earlier *theologoi*, 'theologians' (chiefly Hesiod, but also Homer), whereas in fact the early Greek thinkers were themselves engaged in theology, though theology of a new kind.

A further innovation is apparent in (4) the contrast between the moral dimension of the transcendent-originating and immanent-governing principle of the Milesians, on the one hand, and the legislative moral decrees of the anthropomorphic gods of the poets on the other. Gone, too, are the vestiges of naive personification that still clung to those higher moral forces in the universe, Destiny, Justice, Necessity, and Fate. In their place we have an *im*personal moral law of measure or balance among powers or spheres of dominion; it is operative throughout the universe, yet without anything resembling motives or intentions. The expression 'demythologization' is often used for the kind of rationalization that consists in partially or completely eliminating the anthropomorphic and purposive patterns of explanation typical of mytho-poetic thinking. It has been suggested that the demythologizing efforts of the Milesians were aimed at countering the tendency, found in later Olympian religion, to make the will of the gods the supreme legislative authority. If this is correct, then a certain development within Olympian religion itself fostered the challenge that came from philosophy. There were no doubt also socio-economic reasons why a mytho-poetic tradition reflecting a much older feudal society and its humanized gods could no longer engage the minds or hearts of the powerful merchant class of a successful trading colony in sixth-century BC Asia Minor; but that part of the story of the birth of philosophy would lead too far afield.

5.5.3 Some technical terms

Many of the ideas introduced so far have technical terms attached to them. 'Animism' (from the Latin *anima* 'soul') is the name usually applied to the tendency to endow inert matter with life. 'Panpsychism' (from the Greek *pan* 'all' or 'everything' and *psychē* 'soul') is used of the tendency to so regard absolutely everything. The conception of the whole universe as not only living but divine is commonly referred to as 'pantheism' (from the Greek words *pan* and *theos* 'god'). Thales is supposed to have said that "all things are full of gods," a view typical of Milesian thought. Construing the whole material universe as a *single* living organism is referred to as 'hylozoism' (from the Greek *hylē* 'stuff' or 'matter' and *zōon* 'living thing' or 'animal'). All three 'isms' are usually treated somewhat condescendingly as typical of so-called primitive thought, although Greek pantheism clearly represents a very significant advance on earlier conceptions of divinity.

The *mythological* conception of the gods as (1) born, like men, into an existing world, yet, unlike men, immortal and very powerful (though still not *all*-powerful or above the moral law), is the predecessor of three *philosophical* conceptions of divinity bequeathed to the west by the pagan Greeks. Of the three, (2) pantheism is the oldest. Pantheism is often alleged to be a form of atheism rather than theism, and rightly so if by 'theism' we mean belief in a *transcendent and personal* god. But there seems to be no compelling reason for understanding 'theism' so narrowly. An example of a pantheist in the modern period is Spinoza. Medieval German mysticism provides further examples of such a religious outlook, all owing something to late-Greek thought, particularly Plotinus (205–270 AD). The other philosophical conceptions of divinity derived from the Greeks are (3) the Platonic notion of a divine craftsman or artificer of the universe (see 16.2, 25.8, and 35.2.2) and (4) Aristotle's idea of god as Unmoved Mover: the divine that neither orders nor acts upon the world in any way except that in which an object of desire moves a living organism to strive toward it (see 20.5.1–2). As we shall see, the philosophy of nature and rational theology were to remain intertwined as (2) gave way to (3) and then (4). Even in Christian metaphysics, with its bold new (5) idea of a sheerly omnipotent

God who creates the world (unlike a craftsman) *out of nothing*, the understanding of nature is shaped by that of divinity, and vice versa. And so too throughout the subsequent history of metaphysics. The very term 'metaphysics' is still widely used either for natural philosophy as distinct from empirical science, or for rational as distinct from revealed theology, or for the two together. Historically, this usage is well anchored in tradition.

So much for 'animism,' 'panpsychism,' 'pantheism,' 'hylozoism,' and 'metaphysics.' Next, a word on the talk of naturalistic, mechanistic, and vitalistic explanations employing powers, elements, and a governing law of change. Though the term *archē* may well have been coined by Anaximander himself, the Greek words corresponding to 'power' (as distinct from 'hot,' 'cold,' and so forth) and 'element' (as distinct from 'earth,' 'water,' etc.) are borrowed from later Greek sources. Both are still in scientific use today. Owing to the altered senses of these terms in later Greek and modern scientific parlance, misunderstandings can easily arise.

Generally speaking, a 'naturalistic explanation' is an explanation in terms of ordinary, familiar processes, without the action or conscious intervention of *super*natural causes or powers. Accordingly, mechanical or mechanistic explanation in terms of the size, shape, position, speed, and direction of moving parts of matter, their collisions and rebounds, is one—some would say the only—type of naturalistic explanation. Examples of such change are close at hand and readily observable; even when put forward as a speculative hypothesis about particles too small to be observed, the ideas involved are still perfectly familiar from everyday experience of middle-sized objects.

Another type of naturalistic explanation is explanation in terms of vital processes like growth and motion in plants and animals or in terms of intelligent goal-directed behaviour in human beings. These are 'vitalistic' (from the Latin *vita* 'life') or 'teleological' explanations (from the Greek word *telos*, meaning 'goal,' 'end,' or 'purpose'). We can get a sense of the relevant differences among types of explanations by considering two senses of 'acting for a reason,' namely (a) acting from a cause, as when a billiard ball begins to move on being struck by another, and (b) acting for a purpose. Such purposive action (in a broad sense) can again be subdivided into (i) functional and (ii) intentional modalities. Thus, when the root system of a plant absorbs water, or its leaves shade its fruit, the purpose is to sustain and optimize life, growth, and reproduction; while when a human community organizes itself in order to grow food for consumption, the end is consciously envisaged and the actions are intentional. Both sorts of purposiveness are immediately and constantly observed in an immense variety of forms every day, from the lowly acorn that becomes a mighty oak, to the complex social arrangements that regulate human cooperative undertakings. In everyday life a great many why-questions are answered in terms of (b), functions and intentions; yet there are those who maintain that, at the scientific level, there is only one model of rational explanation, namely (a), acting from a cause. However, at a time when the conception of matter as inert, lifeless, and purposeless was not yet dominant, it would not have seemed, as it does to scientists and scientifically minded philosophers today, that vitalistic or teleological modes of explanation constitute a less natural or less rational approach to physics than mechanicism; and even today it may not seem so to philosophers whose highest authority is immediate, ordinary experience.

In designating naturalistic explanations 'rational' and distinguishing them from the supernatural explanations of mythology, the intent is not to suggest that before philosophy men did not employ all their faculties, including reason, in an effort to provide themselves with a moral and intellectual basis for living; on the contrary, one might as well suggest that modern science does not engage the creative imagination (see 6.2.3). That would be foolish. Yet where the causes belong to the realm of ordinary everyday experience, the mode of explanation is both more natural and more rational than one that appeals to supernatural factors entirely beyond our ken and reckoning. In this sense, even the theology of the Homeric and Hesiodic poems is more rational or naturalistic than earlier religious systems of representation in which spell, ritual magic, and sacred taboo play a large part. Of course, if one's conception of rationality is based on the abstract intellectual processes involved in mathematical reasoning alone, then one will have to say that *theologoi* like Hesiod are not rational at all, while the *physikoi* are so only to the very limited extent that they were groping their way towards purely mechanical explanations expressible in mathematical terms. Once again we are confronted with competing views of rationality, and not for the last time.

So much for 'mechanism,' 'vitalism,' and 'teleology.' As for 'power,' this is the best term available for what the Milesians designated as 'the hot,' 'the dry,' and so forth. These they understood much less as transient properties of things than as active forces or even substances having their own proper sphere of dominion. 'Power' comes much closer to capturing this idea than 'quality,' the term now usually applied to heat, cold, and the rest. Finally, 'element' may be roughly defined as 'an irreducible form of matter.' While the periodic table of modern chemistry contains (at last count) some 112 such elements, the early Greek thinkers generally recognized four. Thus, water, for them, was an element, though blood was not, while neither is an element to our way of thinking, water being a collection of H_2O molecules, that is, reducible to hydrogen and oxygen. However, the term 'element' can be used loosely for any *relatively* basic form of matter, as well as strictly for any form of matter that is *absolutely* basic. The former is the way the Milesians thought of earth, water, air, and fire. In the absolute sense, some of them may have recognized only one element, water in the case of Thales or air in that of Anaximenes. The Peripatetic tradition confused the *archē* with such an element in the strict sense, even (remarkably) in the case of Anaximander's *apeiron*. But enough has been said already about this mistake.

5.5.4 Later Ionian thinkers

Apart from the Milesians, others who may be called 'Ionians,' at least geographically, include Xenophanes of Colophon and Heracleitus of Ephesus. Both retained the monism, pantheism, and hylozoism of their Ionian predecessors. Yet in their *archē* thinking (if we may so call it, since neither actually used the term) they struck out in new directions. First, in cosmology (a) Xenophanes gave special prominence to earth (perhaps to earth *and* water—the matter is controversial), Heracleitus to fire. Yet both (b) rejected the idea of a divine *originative* principle, reasoning that if the cosmos is divine, it must be eternal, that is, incapable either of coming to be or perishing; what remained of the earlier *archē* concept, therefore, was only an *immanent* governing principle. Finally, both (c) shifted the focus from natural philosophy to rational theology, delivering a caustic indictment of the anthropomorphic polytheism of Homer and Hesiod along with a philosophical critique of the theology of their Milesian forebears.

Though naturalistic explanations of meteorological and astronomical phenomena figure prominently in Xenophanes, they may just be intended to explode naive popular notions that such phenomena were gods or manifestations of an anthropomorphically conceived divine will. Xenophanes's theology is almost entirely negative. Striking is the way he analyzes the abstract *concept* of god, deducing *negative* attributes in accordance with his idea of what is *fitting* or unfitting for the divine. Thus, god is one, motionless, limited (this against the theology of Anaximander), everywhere present and uniformly the same. These characteristics are arrived at by denying manyness, motion, and so forth as unfitting. For the same reason god has no organs or limbs, certainly no human shape, perhaps no definite form at all; he acts without the slightest 'toil' or effort in effecting his will, and so forth. In view of god's oneness, Xenophanes has been regarded as the first monotheist (literally, 'believer in one god'); this is a misnomer if, as seems likely, Xenophanes's god is identical with the whole universe, or if he recognized inferior gods as well, as it seems he did. Anyhow, the word 'monotheism' suggests an idea of divinity like that listed under (5) in the last sub-section, a creator god, whereas Xenophanes's god clearly has its roots in (2), Ionian pantheism. In his negative theology elaborated through analysis of the *concept* of the divine, however, Xenophanes is a precursor of the philosophy of being as described above. His thinking represents a remarkable advance towards the type of abstract conceptual analysis associated with the Italians and Parmenides in particular. It is not surprising, therefore, to learn that Xenophanes left Ionia for Italy, probably when Colophon was captured by the Persians in 546/5 BC. Among the ancients he was widely regarded as belonging to the Italian tradition, even (by Aristotle) as the teacher of Parmenides.

To the extent that it turns on a comparison between human and *divine* knowledge, even Xenophanes's alleged scepticism (see 3.3.1) is just an adjunct to his theology.

Heracleitus followed suit, suggesting in one fragment that true judgment or knowledge belongs solely to the divine nature. His naturalistic explanations of heavenly and other phenomena serve chiefly to illustrate a general theory of the permanent measure or balance preserved in both large- and small-scale cosmological change. Moreover, the moral and theological dimensions of Heracleitus's governing law, or *logos* as he called it, tend to overshadow the natural philosophical aspect. The *logos* (also translated as 'ratio,' 'proportion,' 'measure,' even 'reason') is likened to fiery aether, to be sure, but also to Zeus, the ruler of the gods. Heracleitus even calls it 'Justice,' the name given by the poets to the quasi-personal moral principle to which the Olympians themselves are subject. Whatever his *logos* concept may owe to earlier *archē* thinking, Heracleitus dramatically enhanced the role of conflicting powers, stressing the balance achieved and preserved through tension or strife. This he illustrated through a whole series of evocative images of the cosmic order, like the strung bow, for example. Such metaphors mark him as an early Greek thinker and writer of remarkable visionary and expressive powers. He seems to have been the first to assert the importance of philosophy for human life, identifying understanding of the *logos* with the attainment of wisdom. In so doing he gave vent to his aristocratic prejudices, abusing the common herd of men who neither grasp nor wish to understand the unity of all things—not even when it is explained to them by a Heracleitus! In praising wisdom as the epitome of human virtue, he was again following Xenophanes. Theirs is the antithesis of the old aristocratic ideal of martial virtue captured in the feudal world of the Homeric poems. Despite the sceptical-sounding fragment referred to above, Heracleitus does not doubt men's native ability to understand the *logos* or reason of the universe since, being immanent in all things, it is immanent in men too, as human reason. He claimed to have 'searched himself' in attaining this wisdom, yet assigned outer observation by the senses an indispensable role in the discovery of truth: the very discord or conflict of opposites that seems at first sight to be nothing but strife or warfare exhibits for philosophical understanding the same balance or unity of opposites that it possesses in the eyes of god. The philosopher who grasps this accordingly becomes god-like. We shall have more to say about Heracleitus later in this work (see 20.10.1).

With the decline of Ionia and the destruction of Miletus by the Persians in 494 BC, the traditions that had flourished there were transplanted to Athens by Anaxagoras of the Ionian city of Clazomenae (c. 534–428 on one dating, 500–428 BC on another). He settled in Miletus during the lifetime of Anaximenes, leaving at its fall for Athens, where he taught for some thirty years before being put on trial, convicted, and driven into exile for alleged impiety, maybe also for harbouring Persian sympathies. He concerned himself with cosmology and cosmogony as well as astronomical and meteorological phenomena. In cosmological and cosmogonic thought his main innovations concern the concepts (1) of matter and (2) of mind. We must postpone discussion of the doctrines of Anaxagoras and the Greek atomists until we have traced the Italian tradition down to their time. For both were strongly influenced by the western beginnings to be discussed in the next section.

Among Anaxagoras's students was the great Athenian statesman, Pericles, who was instrumental in saving his life. Anaxagoras's name comes up in Plato's *Apology* too, no doubt because of the striking parallel between his plight and that of Socrates. How his prosecution and eventual banishment—or, for that matter, the trial and execution of Socrates—could have come about in a society as free from religious dogma as Athens is a question we shall consider later (see 9.1.2.1). Here that absence of enforced acceptance of religious dogma is important only as explaining, in part, how and why philosophy arose at all among the Greeks.

5.6 Western beginnings

With Anaxagoras we stand on the threshold of the classical age on the eastern side. The other major figures and movements of the pre-classical age belong geographically to the Italian tradition. The towering personalities of this region are Pythagoras, a rough contemporary of Anaximenes, the last of the Milesians, and Parmenides, a contemporary of Heracleitus.

Pythagoras emigrated from his native Samos in Ionia to Croton in southern Italy, founding a religious community that flourished there throughout the latter half of the sixth century. Pythagorean brotherhoods were also formed elsewhere in Italy, some of them surviving down through the fifth and into the fourth century BC, when Plato came in contact with them. Their teachings exerted considerable influence even on Neoplatonism. Though Pythagoras himself left no writings, his teachings, to judge by later sources, combined mathematical studies with religious devotions and mystical lore. On the basis of his mathematical studies Pythagoras developed a natural philosophy (cosmogony and cosmology) founded on numbers. However, it is difficult to determine whether the Pythagoreans believed that real things actually were numbers, or that they imitated numbers, or that their essences or natures, insofar as they are knowable at all, were expressible as numbers. The difficulties are compounded by the presence of different and opposed tendencies of thought within the school in its early and later phases of development. In any case, Pythagoreanism can be credited with having anticipated that mathematical conception of the universe that was to be profoundly influential in the development of early modern mathematical physics almost two millennia later. In Part Two on Plato we shall consider the Pythagorean doctrines concerning the soul, its temporary imprisonment in the body, and eventual release from a cycle of reincarnations after purification. While their exact relationship to earlier Orphic teachings is obscure, it is probably safe to describe them as a rationalization of the latter, in which mathematical contemplation and natural philosophical speculation supplant the ecstatic rites and devotions of Orphism. As we shall see, Plato's teachings concerning the soul and its relation to the body in the *Phaedo* represent a further intellectualization of the Pythagorean doctrine of the soul, sparked by the rational outlook of his teacher, Socrates.

Parmenides came from the city of Elea on Italy's western coast, a colony founded around 540 BC by refugees from the Ionian city of Phocea. By culture an Ionian, he is supposed to have been a follower of a Pythagorean philosopher named Ameinias. This leads one to expect a confluence of traditions in Parmenides's work, much of which is preserved in literal fragments. He probably owed something to the negative theology of the Ionian Xenophanes (who may have had a hand in the founding of Elea) and to the Heracleitean conception of human reason; yet Parmenides is a watershed in the history of early Greek thought, having been the first to tackle certain abstruse puzzles concerning being and non-being. More than anyone else, he shaped the subsequent course of Greek philosophy right down to the post-classical age, as much through the new, stricter methods of reasoning he pioneered as through the novel conclusions he reached concerning oneness, manyness, permanence, and change.

Both methods and conclusions result from considerations bearing on the use and misuse of the concepts 'is,' 'to be,' and 'being.' Not only were the conclusions themselves, the denial of manyness and change, not based on any observation and experience; they were plainly antithetical to both. Among his Ionian predecessors, even Heraclitus, however disdainful of the ignorant multitude, assigned a key role to ordinary sense experience in making knowledge of the *logos* possible. Parmenides, by contrast, based himself exclusively on abstract reasoning, deducing by a rigorous logic never before seen the sheer impossibility of many changing things. This left the world as we know it a mere illusion. If such conclusions were at odds with everyday experience and sound common sense, so much the worse for the latter! We shall have a closer look at Parmenides's arguments and conclusions later (see 20.10.2). But it should at least be mentioned here that, having elaborated these arguments in the first part of his great poem ("The Way of Truth"), Parmenides appended a cosmology of a kind not altogether unlike those of the Milesians ("The Way of Seeming"). Its status is controversial, but it seems to have been regarded by Parmenides as the most plausible account possible for anyone who relies on sense experience—though fiction, nonetheless, without a word of truth in it.

Even more than their teacher, Parmenides's disciples Zeno of Elea and Melissus of Samos were instrumental in developing the argumentative style of defending provocative philosophical conclusions—including, but not limited to, those reached by Parmenides himself—through exposing the absurdities latent in the opposing commonsense point of view. This came to be called 'dialectic' later on. It was to become the stock-in-trade of the sophists, who employed it to shocking effect in the domains of ethics and politics. It led indirectly, via the refinements of Socratic and Platonic method, to the emergence of a rigorous science of logic in the writings of

Aristotle. The idea of logic as a universal scientific method, common to all fields of enquiry, is one that has generally *not* found favour with the major thinkers of the western tradition, not even with the father of logic, Aristotle himself. As for Zeno and Melissus, they plied their logical or dialectical trade largely within the confines of the philosophy of being inaugurated by their revered teacher, broadening it to include problems of space and time in particular. Conceptual problems concerning space, time, matter, force, and law have come to be the stock-in-trade of natural philosophy ever since. As noted earlier (5.5.3), natural philosophy conjoined with rational theology is what most philosophers nowadays understand by 'metaphysics.' Metaphysics of nature, on its own, often bills itself as the philosophy of physics or of the physical sciences—a further sub-discipline of philosophy to add to our list. One starting point for all this is later Eleaticism.

5.7 Later developments

Doctrinally, the thought of Empedocles, from the city of Acragas on the southern coast of Sicily, spans the continuum stretching from magic, myth, and mysticism (in a popular religious work, *The Purifications*) to elemental physics (in a cosmological work, *On Nature*). Imagine an Orphic or Pythagorean doctrine of the soul, its fall, purification, and eventual release from the wheel of successive births, combined with an Ionian rather than Pythagorean cosmology: such is, very roughly, the philosophy of Empedocles. Like the Milesians he sought the ultimate originating and governing principle of the living universe, opting for two cosmogonic and cosmological principles, Love and Strife, rather than one. The elemental masses—earth, water, fire and air—he redesignated 'the four roots.' These he understood as conscious or sentient as well as divine, unchanging, and imperishable, so that one can speak here, not just of pantheism, but of panpsychism (see 5.5.3). Ionian, too, is the very concrete manner in which Empedocles conceives, not just the material masses of the elements, but the dynamic principles responsible for their combination and separation, Love and Strife. The cosmic principle of Love is particularly novel; for Strife among warring opposites was already pivotal in Heracleitus's conception of cosmic balance or proportion. Stripped of its anthropomorphic and mythological trappings, Love reflects the new importance assigned physical *combination* or union, the coming together of elements and elemental forces. Among the Milesians, *separation* was the key thing; at the very least, separation was just as important as combination; in Empedocles's system the principle of Love predominates. What cannot be stripped away from it is the profound moral significance Empedocles assigns Love and union (the good) as opposed to Strife and separation (evil). This is the prototype of all later interpretations of the cosmos in terms of warring forces of Good and Evil (or God and the Devil). Accordingly, the Heracleitean equipoise or steady state that results from conflicting forces gives way to a constantly repeated history of fall and redemption: upon perfect union of the elements under the rule of Love follows their complete dissolution under Strife; then, through gradual reintegration of the elements by Love, the cosmos comes into being; the complete victory of Love over Strife ultimately destroys the cosmos and restores the primal unity, after which the cycle begins again.

Behind this modified Ionian cosmogony lurk purely abstract considerations about being and non-being stemming from Parmenides and the Eleatic tradition. Nothing can come to be or perish, Parmenides maintained: change or becoming is therefore an illusion. Empedocles accepts the principle while rejecting its alleged consequence: becoming is no coming into being of something new, but a cyclical mixing (and separating) of indestructible elements, the four roots; the imperishability of the elements and the permanence of the process itself are the sops Empedocles gives Parmenides. Even the description of the pre-cosmic state of undifferentiated unity under the rule of Love (called 'the Sphere' by Empedocles) borrows something from Parmenides's description of true being. And like Parmenides, Empedocles comes forward as an inspired poet, his words the supernatural revelation of a muse. The whole poem is arguably just an attempt to give a more rational (Ionian) expression at a macrocosmic level to a vision of the destiny of the human soul that Empedocles acquired as an initiate of Pythagorean mystery religion. At any rate, the *Purifications* develop a story of the soul's fall, reincarnation, purification, and eventual release that parallels the stages of the cosmic cycle, though the influence probably worked both ways: Empedocles modifies the Pythagorean story of the soul in accordance with his physical theory, too. Ultimately, what men call their 'lives,' their physical, embodied existence in this world, is just a temporary state of mixture of the pure immortal soul with tainted bodily elements alien and inimical to it. One key difference between this and Pythagorean teaching is that the soul's journey, for Empedocles, starts and ends in this world; Plato, as we shall see, returns to the original Pythagorean conception of a divine soul that falls into this world from another.

Though older than Empedocles, Anaxagoras published his views later, according to Aristotle. In his cosmology and theory of matter, Anaxagoras did away with the (a) four basic elements in all compound things and with (b) quasi-living powers, their conflict subject to a moral law of balance. The latter were still too anthropomorphic for him, while the former seemed to Anaxagoras still to violate the Parmenidean prohibition on the coming into being of anything new. This will become clearer if we consider how Anaxagoras's own theory accords with the Parmenidean principle.

Matter, for Anaxagoras, consists of infinitely divisible 'seeds,' each containing within itself (i) portions of earth, water, fire, and air; (ii) portions of all other natural substances, such as flesh, bone, hair, and so on, their parts homogeneous with each other and with the whole of which they are parts, though heterogeneous with the parts of other natural substances; and, finally, (iii) portions of the traditional opposites 'hot,' 'cold,' 'moist,' 'dry' as well as every other observable quality, including shapes, colours, tastes, rarity, density, and so forth. Anaxagoras was apt to express this compendiously by saying: "in everything there is a portion of everything." This holds, in the first instance, of the original pre-cosmic mixture in which "everything was together" (the other famous saying of Anaxagoras) and out of which all things came to be; but it is true also of all individual things in the present state of the cosmos.

From this it follows that when, as a result of rotary motion of the original mixture, the seeds separated out of the primal 'everything together' to form the great variety of living and non-living things in the world, nothing really new came into being; for portions of everything already existed in the seeds of the original mixture. That is how Anaxagoras got round the prohibition violated by the doctrine of elements. It did not seem to him that nothing new arose when the four elements of Empedocles combined to form, say, bone or flesh. The problem is solved by his own theory, however, since it is just the predominance of a certain sort of seed over every other, all of them present in a given seed-aggregate or existing thing, that warrants our speaking of this or that as (having come to be) flesh or bone or a man. And so at the level of the seeds, too, the predominance of a certain ratio among the portions makes this a flesh-seed rather than a bone-seed, though in reality it contains portions of everything. Below the level of seeds the same holds true again of its parts, right down to the level of the infinitely small parts of matter.

The details of the theory are disputed, but Anaxagoras's doctrine of matter was clearly a step in the direction of a non-anthropomorphic, quasi-mechanistic, perhaps even mathematical world-picture; for he explained the manifest image of the world in terms of (admittedly unknown) mathematical ratios obtaining among an infinitude of infinitely divisible portions in a mixture. Contrary to the basic tendency of his thought, the later atomists posited an infinitude of *in*divisible particles (atoms), all *homo*geneous and distinguished only by size, shape, position, and motion, thus *reducing* all the differences under (i), (ii), and (iii) to these few basic ones. Nevertheless, without Anaxagoras this culminating development of Ionian science—reductive materialism—would be more difficult to comprehend.

Anaxagoras's theory of matter prefigures not just ancient and modern atomism, but also Descartes's account of the material world as an extended, infinitely divisible, homogeneous material continuum in space (see chap. 24). Note that in his cosmogony the role of mind (or Mind, since life and intelligence is owing to the presence in all composite things of a cosmic Mind) is to initiate and sustain the rotational motion whereby the seeds separate out of the original mixture to form natural kinds of entities, including animals and men. Does Anaxagoras's general theory of mind represent a step towards the later distinction between immaterial souls and material bodies? He himself laid great stress on the fact that mind alone of all things is unmixed—though he also characterized it as pure and fine and powerful, crediting it with perfect foreknowledge of the effects it brings about in 'arranging' all things (his word is cognate with 'cosmos') rather than acting blindly without forethought. From foreknowledge and foreordination, however, it is still a long way to the distinction between soul and body that we shall encounter in Plato, and even further to that of Descartes; yet this aspect of mind qualifies significantly the mechanistic tendency noted in connection with his general theory of matter. Or does it?

Despite clear indications that mind foreknows and foreordains the cosmological process, once the motion begins, mechanical (apparently centrifugal) forces appear to take over; there is no developed theory of intelligent, purposive gathering and ordering of materials in the creative process. One can well understand, therefore, Socrates's disappointment as described toward the end of the *Phaedo*. He relates how, on first getting wind of Anaxagoras's book, he was excited to learn that the chief role in cosmogony was assigned to mind. Yet when he got and read the book (or papyrus scroll, as it was), he was astonished to find so little to indicate that mind acted to produce the best possible arrangement of things. Nevertheless, others, notably Plato, may have been inspired by Anaxagoras's broad hints to develop the notion of a purposive ordering activity aimed at producing the good or best, much in the way a craftsman produces his artefacts. Even if the tendency of Anaxagoras's thought is predominantly mechanistic rather than teleological, as was suggested earlier, he nonetheless comes up well short of blindly operating forces that bring a cosmos about by sheer chance.

Like Empedocles and Anaxagoras, Leucippus of Miletus and Democritus of Abdera, the founders of ancient atomism, stand on the threshold of the classical period and in the shadow of Parmenides and his pupils. It is hardly surprising that some ancient sources take Leucippus to be of Elea and a renegade pupil of Zeno. For the earliest explanation of the natural world in terms of indivisible atoms and the void emanated from a doctrine of being and non-being intended to overthrow the Parmenidean theory, providing an account of manyness and change that gave their due to experience and common sense. At the same time, however, it appealed to the higher authority of the intellect in positing unobserved and unobservable atoms as the ultimate reality. Like Empedocles and Anaxagoras before them, the founders of ancient atomism were attempting to restore the world to mankind after Parmenides had relegated it to the scrapheap of illusion. They did so, not by rejecting, but rather by accepting and modifying, Parmenidean principles. Once again, Parmenides must have his sop: atoms, at least, possess the characteristics of Parmenidean true being (permanent, unchanging, homogeneous, indivisible, etc.), though they make real change possible at the level of the observable. Like Empedocles and Anaxagoras, Leucippus and Democritus borrow liberally from the Ionian tradition as well. Both debts are glossed over by advocates of the popular idea that they (and later Epicurus and Lucretius) were above all scientific thinkers, early ancestors of modern atomic physics. That may be so in the very limited sense in which the Pythagoreans anticipated mathematical astronomy or the Milesians mechanical patterns of explanation; but, historically, the metaphysical, ethical, and religious dimensions of ancient atomism are at least as important as anything that modern scientific hindsight can tell us about them.

5.8 Core concepts

Even from this brief sketch it appears that there are important affinities as well as points of contrast between the philosophies that grew up in the eastern and western halves of the Greek world prior to the classical age of Athens. Their common goal can be described as understanding manyness and change, the succession of opposite states and conditions immediately manifest in the cosmic process, in terms of an originating cause and/or governing principle of primal unity, permanence, and harmony—or, in the case of Parmenides and his followers, explaining manyness and change away as illusion.

In this common pursuit, the Ionians were, on the whole, less influenced by the mysterious side of religion than the Italians, more firmly anchored in the observation of nature, and accordingly more concrete. To the extent that they left writings at all, they were chiefly prose authors. That seems to be in keeping with their general way of philosophizing. The Italians wrote predominantly in verse, often with deliberate mythological echoes and strong spiritualist overtones. Their thought is marked by a higher, in Parmenides's case, the very highest, level of philosophical abstraction. Where the earlier Ionians show a marked preference for *a* first principle (whence the title 'monists'), the Italians, on the whole, went in for two or many, even infinitely many, causes or basic principles ('dualism' or 'pluralism,' as the case may be), some regarding such a pluralistic account as true, like Anaxagoras and Empedocles, others as plausible but at bottom quite false, like Parmenides in his "Way of Seeming."

These titles, like most 'isms,' are fraught with ambiguities that make them very crude tools of analysis. In modern thought, 'monism' is used of philosophies that recognize only a single *kind* of entity, for example, reductive materialism; the prime example of 'dualism,' by contrast, is Descartes's system, which recognizes bodies and minds as two irreducibly different kinds of entities. In an early Greek context, however, the question concerns either (a) the number of entities in existence (one for monists, many for pluralists) or (b) the number of *ultimate* explanatory principles (one, two, many, or an infinite number in the atomists' and Anaxagoras's case). 'Dualism' has various other uses as well. This should serve as a warning that extreme caution is necessary in applying such labels to the Presocratic thinkers. The disparities between the Ionian and the Italian may be more reliably conveyed by certain differences in their core concepts. Most of these were included already in the list given earlier (see 4.9), though it may be worth itemizing them here.

Chapter 5: Philosophy and Mythico-Religious Thought

The very first Ionians established the ideas of (1) *oneness* and *manyness*, and (2) *permanence* and *change*, as *the* fundamental concepts of Greek thought. Similarly, questions regarding (3) the disposition of the great elemental masses and analysis in terms of (4) warring opposites (hot and cold, moist and dry) were to remained central, even though the opposites themselves and the operative principles of their combination and separation varied widely. The characteristic mode of thought of the Pythagoreans and Eleatics, on the other hand, shifts the focus of discussion to a different set of concepts. The new ideas of the Pythagorean school are the highly abstract (5) mathematical notions of indefinitely divisible quantity, number, and harmony or numerical proportion, as well as the religious (6) doctrine (probably derived from Orphism) of the soul's survival of the death of the body and its reincarnation in other bodies in a cycle of births and rebirths. For primary philosophy or metaphysics, however, nothing was so decisive as the new (7) concept of *being* (and non-being) pioneered by Parmenides and developed in later Eleaticism. Such reflection on the meaning of 'being,' 'to be,' or 'is' as Parmenides engaged in represents a level of philosophical abstraction unexampled before or—with the possible exception of Heidegger—since. Once introduced, it had a profound influence even on the course of later Ionian developments, as is seen in Anaxagoras. Nevertheless, there is something very Italian about it.

It was suggested earlier that it is possible to detect behind this juxtaposition of Ionian and Italian a more basic contrariety between scientifically minded thinkers and those more traditional philosophers with affinities for religious rather than scientific thought. Beyond this, it may be tempting to look here for the source of that metaphysical opposition between reductive or non-reductive materialism and ontological idealism described in chapter 4. Yet Plato himself did not go this far when, in the dialogue *Sophist* (246a), he spoke of the "battle of the gods [idealists] and giants [materialists]." He seems rather to have had his own idealism in mind, that is, transcendent realism, on the one hand, and the teachings of the atomists, on the other. Where he alludes expressly to the Ionians and Eleatics, it is not in these terms at all. Nevertheless it may not be altogether far-fetched to see in the divergence of Ionian and Eleatic thought two basic philosophical tendencies that were later to develop into the various species of metaphysical materialism and ontological idealism, even if all the evidence points to the conclusion that modern idealism, of the sort found in Berkeley, Leibniz, and Kant, is among the very few philosophical outlooks *not* actually met with in the Greeks.

5.9 The classical period

The expression 'pre-classical era' covers both (a) the age before philosophy, the age of myth, and (b) early Greek philosophy before Socrates. With Socrates, the so-called classical age of ancient philosophy begins, ending only with the death of

Aristotle in 322 BC. This is the period of the flowering of Greek art, literature, and intellectual contemplation. A short list of authors and titles of works will have to suffice to give some idea of the remarkable heights attained by Greek culture around the time that the greatest works of Greek philosophy were produced.

In politics, the classical period is the age of Pericles, the greatest of Greek statesmen, and the high tide of Athenian democracy. In the field of tragedy it was the time of Aeschylus (525–426 BC), author of the *Oresteia* trilogy, Sophocles (496–404 BC), author of *Antigone* and the *Oedipus* tragedies, and Euripides (480–406 BC), the dramatist who gave us the plays *Medea* and *Hippolytus*. Turning to comedy, it was the time in which Aristophanes (448–388 BC) produced his greatest works, *Clouds*, *Birds*, *Frogs*, *Wasps*, *Lysistrata*. The first of these great comedies will be mentioned later, in the part devoted to Socrates, who figures as a character in it. Aristophanes's widely known burlesque of Socrates's life and teaching may have played a direct role in his condemnation on charges of religious innovation and corruption of the youth in 399 BC. This is also the period of the birth of history. Here we can only mention in passing the so-called Father of History Herodotus (484–425 BC), author of *The Persian Wars*, and Thucydides (c. 460–400 BC), the chronicler of the Peloponnesian war between Sparta and Athens from 427 to 404 BC, a war that ended in Athens's defeat and the temporary overthrow of Greek democracy. It was in the aftermath of this struggle, after the restoration of democracy, that the trial of Socrates, the event that inspired Plato's *Apology*, took place.

Cognate with the word 'classical' is 'classicism,' the term applied to the mistaken notion, long prevalent among admirers of Greek culture, that the age of Pericles, Socrates, Plato, Aristotle, Sophocles, Euripides and the great sculptors and painters who were their contemporaries just sprang up, more or less unheralded, as a timeless ideal for all subsequent art, literature, and philosophy to emulate. Today we understand better than did the Renaissance or the nineteenth century that the classical age, for all its uniqueness and indisputable greatness, had its antecedents too, without which that remarkable burst of creativity in the fifth and fourth centuries would not have been possible. Still, no amount of uncovering of precedents and beginnings can ever explain so unique a phenomenon or render it any less astonishing. The same is true of the rise of early Greek philosophy. Pre-historic traditions, the works of poets and lawgivers, foreign contacts, particularly with Egypt and Babylonia, may all have furnished influences; but they can hardly *explain* an event so momentous and so unparalleled in human history.

5.10 The post-classical age

As for the post-classical period of Greek civilization, we have already mentioned a couple of the philosophical schools founded during this period. To (1) Epicureanism, founded by Epicurus, and (2) Stoicism, founded by Zeno of Citium, we may now add

(3) the Cynics (followers of Diogenes of Sinope who lived from around 400 to around 325 BC), and finally (4) the ancient Sceptics (followers of Pyrrho of Elis, 365–275 BC, and Arcesilaus, 316–242 BC, who was the fourth head of Plato's Academy after the founder).

More will be said about scepticism in particular in 9.1.4. As for Epicureanism, we shall touch on the moral philosophy of Epicurus and on that of the Stoics and Cynics in 12.9.1. Epicurus's naturalism will be discussed in greater detail in the part devoted to Hume (see 31.5.2). The importance and historical influence of these schools is entirely disproportionate to the cursory treatment to be given them here; yet on the whole it is probably fair to say that they produced little that was not largely derivative from the seminal thinkers of the classical age.

The same can perhaps be said of the second or Neoplatonic phase of the post-classical period, which, as the name implies, looked to Plato's writings for its chief inspiration, although it drew heavily on virtually all non-materialist and religious sources in earlier antiquity, including (in varying degrees) Peripateticism, Neopythagoreanism, and Stoicism. A return to classicism is the hallmark of this revival of Plato's thought, the towering figure of the movement being Plotinus, whose name is almost synonymous with Neoplatonic philosophy. He founded an influential school in Rome where he was succeeded by his pupil Porphyry (232-after 300 AD), but there were also important Neoplatonic schools at Athens and Alexandria. The school at Athens was just the old Platonic academy turned Plotinian. One of the last heads of that school was the Proclus from whose *Elements of Theology* Bishop Berkeley quoted in a passage cited earlier (see 4.6). The end of the movement came gradually, recognizable and definitive endpoints being the closing of the school at Athens in 529 AD and the Arab conquest of Alexandria in 642.

6

Philosophy and Science

6.1 Introductory

Earlier (see 2.8) two reasons were given why academic philosophy is often confused with popular treatments of the subject as a personal quest for meaning. The first had to do with the sheer breadth of scope of primary philosophy: if there can be no definitive answers to the big questions, then one's philosophy, it seems, must be a matter of personal taste or preference.

This misconception was cleared up in chapters 3 and 4. Yet its underlying assumption was granted: issues of the scope of the order of knowing and being are in fact unsettleable in principle. The very concept of experience (see 3.3.2) and the guiding idea of being (see 4.9) on which they rest both evolve from one era to the next. Nor is there much reason to believe in gradual progress toward more satisfactory and universally acceptable answers. On the contrary, the marked trend toward subjectivism, scepticism, and relativism over the past several centuries may be indicative of philosophical decline. Even granting all this, however, the striving to secure, through philosophical discussion and debate, a shared intellectual framework for life, including a moral basis for human coexistence, is obviously a very different matter from developing a personal world-view and some set of values to live by, even when the latter, like philosophy, borrows nothing either from science or religion.

The second reason given was that philosophy does not fit any pattern of rationality to be met with in science proper. Even where the scientific enterprise is regarded as inevitably open-ended, it still falls short of the wide-open texture of philosophical controversy concerning the perennial issues. Is the latter then not a texture of rationality at all? Is philosophy perhaps just a mode of individual or collective self-expression after all? Or is the correct inference rather that there are other textures of rationality besides those exemplified in mathematical, social, natural, and biological sciences? We have already encountered what appear to be different patterns of rationality in philosophy and mythico-religious thought, and the same may be true of philosophy and science, even of different types of philosophy. To quote a contemporary writer on scientific methodology (William Newton-Smith): "science is not the only form of activity governable by reason. Scientific inquiry is a particular form of rational inquiry and there is simply no reason to think that it is the only form of inquiry that so qualifies ... It is trite but true to say that all forms of investigation should be examined on their merits to see what insights they embody and what understanding they provide."

The present chapter undertakes a rapid sketch of three patterns of scientific rationality (see 6.2.1–3). Included are those models of rational procedure—in a word, method—widely regarded as typifying the different families of sciences mentioned in the last paragraph. All such considerations belong to a sub-discipline of philosophy known as the philosophy of science. As in our brief foray into the philosophies of literature and religion in the previous chapter, we shall confine ourselves to rudiments. Upon the initial sketch follows a brief examination of the question, What makes these models of enquiry rational, such that it would be irrational to reject any one of them (see 6.3.1–3)? Although the past half-century has witnessed a number of interesting challenges to the rationality of science, these radical trends in the philosophy of science need not be considered here. It is enough that theories having the same logical structure as the mathematical or empirical sciences possess the sort of rationality recognized by the scientific community.

Even should primary philosophy be found to fit none of the familiar patterns of scientific rationality, the case may be very different for certain philosophical sub-disciplines, like formal logic or cognitive science, for example, both of which are well represented in philosophy departments today. Where such sub-disciplines do fit the familiar patterns, the fact will be noted in passing. The main questions at issue, however, are whether primary philosophy as described above (1) fits any of the familiar paradigms of scientific rationality, and, if not, whether it (2) exhibits a pattern of philosophical rationality of its own—failing which it may not be defensible as a rational enterprise at all and the point about academic as distinct from popular philosophy remains moot (see 6.4.1–3).

6.2 Three patterns of rationality

The patterns of rationality referred to above are the (1) deductive, (2) inductive, and (3) hypothetico-deductive methods. These are not the only models of the logical structure of scientific theories, but they are the main ones and the ones that have, at various times in the past, been thought to shed light on the method of philosophy itself. We may therefore confine ourselves to these three.

94   Introduction: What Philosophy Is

6.2.1 Deductive method

The first method is that of the non-empirical mathematical and other formal sciences. Examples are arithmetic, geometry, algebra, calculus, and mathematical or symbolic logic. In all these fields deductive method has been employed with ever-increasing success, starting in some cases from modest beginnings in ancient times, so that today there exists a large body of secure knowledge set out in formal axiomatized systems by mathematicians and logicians. The findings of these disciplines are not just true; they possess that highest attainable degree of certainty or evidence known as 'absolute certainty' or 'apodicticity.' Such strict rational certainty (another synonym for 'apodicticity') can be distinguished from reasonable certainty, or what has been called, misleadingly enough, 'moral certainty.' Moral certainty has nothing to do with ethical issues or morals proper, but corresponds to what we would nowadays call 'a very high degree of probability,' one sufficient for all *practical* purposes (hence 'moral certainty,' since the moral is one branch of the practical).

In the mathematical sciences we start from definitions, axioms, and postulates that are not derived from experience, proceeding by means of some set of known and uncontroversial rules of logical inference to conclusions or theorems. The findings of this particular family of sciences are apodictically certain since to say that a given theorem is true is, on the most widely held interpretation, not to say that it corresponds to any state of affairs or object, but that it follows in logic from the definitions, axioms, and postulates of the system. The latter are nowadays often regarded as (a) a matter of convention or agreement ('By the term x let us understand ... etc.'); but in former times definitions were frequently understood as self-evident truths about the natures of the things to which the definition applied, and axioms as basic truths or dictates of universal human reason. However that may be, it seems plain enough that the social, biological, and natural sciences cannot employ this procedure. For they *are* concerned precisely with the accurate description of objective states of affairs in the world and the causal laws that explain them. The latter plainly cannot be discovered without consulting experience. This difference is something practitioners of these sciences, even those most deeply imbued with the spirit of quantitative or mathematical methods, have always understood. Empirical science, accordingly, looks to one of the other two models for its logical paradigm.

6.2.2 Inductive method

In contrast to the *de*ductive procedure followed in mathematics and logic, the method of the empirical sciences is widely, though not universally, regarded as *in*ductive. Typically, induction starts with observation, a digest of observed regularities among events of certain kinds; these initial findings are then generalized, and the results formulated as universal laws of nature. Inductive method, so understood, is the scientific counterpart of a strategy used all the time in pre-scientific experience when we make generalizations from what we have encountered in a certain number of instances to other cases of the same or a similar kind, past, present, or future. While the starting point is always observation or experience, what the scientist seeks to discover are exceptionless laws that go beyond that limited set of instances actually experienced, allowing him to make accurate predictions and retrodictions concerning *all* cases of the same sort.

The fact that universal laws of nature inductively arrived at *go beyond* the actually observed is just a non-technical way of saying that their content is *theoretical*, usually very highly so, no matter how extensive their *observational* basis. All interesting scientific laws and theories, those that are truly explanatory, go beyond actual experience rather than just epitomizing or summarizing (that is, redescribing in the form of a general statement) a vast number of particular observations. From this it follows that we can never hope to obtain more than moral certainty for our scientific laws, that is, at most a very high degree of probability. For one thing, the observations on which the laws are based are themselves no more than reasonably, never rationally or apodictically, certain; and, for another, there is nothing but past experience to warrant our supposition that unobserved cases will continue to resemble the observed; and even perfectly uniform or exceptionless experience of this kind can never make this supposition more than very highly probable.

A further consequence worth mentioning is that the conclusions of inductive arguments must be confined to the realm of the experience*able*. It seems obvious on a little reflection that inductive procedure cannot be used to make out anything about objects or events presumed to be of an entirely different kind or order than any that actually have been, or ever could be, given in experience (for example, God, the human soul, the secret and inaccessible structure of matter, the hidden powers that may underlie even the most primitive of observable forces of nature). *Hypotheses non fingo* ('I frame no hypotheses'), wrote Newton, giving expression to this limitation of scientific method as he understood it. It was this same Sir Isaac, incidentally, who famously maintained that the three fundamental "Axioms, or Laws of Motion" of his monumental *Mathematical Principles of Natural Philosophy* were derived "from [observed] phenomena and made general by induction." The curious thing is that certain philosophical advocates of induction, notably Locke, have been less wary than Newton, purporting to reach by inductive means conclusions about objects of a completely different nature than those, observation of which formed the basis of their inferences.

The key thing about the inductive procedure, then, is its starting point in experience and observation, from which it advances by means of an intellectual operation known as 'generalizing induction' to laws and theories whose claim to universal validity can be no more than probable. It is worth noting this pair of assumptions, however: (1) that observation precedes theory and (2) that theories are based upon observation. For these are precisely the points at issue between this second and a third paradigm of scientific rationality known as 'hypothetico-deductive method.'

6.2.3 Hypothetico-deductive method

Nowadays most philosophers and scientists tend to regard the hypothetico-deductive method as more typical of the so-called hard natural sciences, modern physics in particular, than inductive generalization. The same may be true, with certain qualifications, of the 'soft' biological and social sciences as well. Hypothetico-deductive method is related in interesting ways both to the method of construction of mathematical models, on the one hand, and to inductive procedure on the other. Like induction, it relies on experience and observation, though not as the *source* of its theoretical claims; experience is rather the *test* or touchstone of scientific hypotheses. Advocates of the hypothetico-deductive model maintain that there is no such thing as an observed fact in complete isolation from theory; what counts as a fact depends upon a background theory, either the particular theory one is intent on testing or a field of competing theories among which one is attempting to decide. 'Facts are theory-laden' is a handy formula for remembering this key point. This being so, the way is open for the free elaboration of mathematical and other theoretical models that go beyond or even run counter to the known data and challenge scientific orthodoxy. For if new theories bring new, sometimes important facts to light, there is a strictly scientific motive to flout the consensus within the scientific community by elaborating new theories to challenge those already found to square well with the known facts.

According to this third model of scientific enquiry, then, theory precedes observation, and facts are dependent upon theories, not vice versa. The empirical character of natural science resides solely in this: that experiment and observation are the *arbiters* of truth; the principal *source* of scientific theories is not so much observation as creative flights of scientific fancy. Accordingly, the scientist must *not* say, in the manner of Newton, *hypotheses non fingo*, but rather precisely *hypotheses fingo*. Scientific procedure is above all a matter of exercising our ingenuity in devising bold hypotheses and theories and putting them to the test in carefully designed experiments, refining and improving them wherever they fail to pass the tests, or abandoning them altogether when competing theories square better with observation and experiment than a given theory can hope to do even with revisions.

From this it follows that we must be wary of theories that are so vague and general as to square with any and all experience, or that are so plastic as to admit of endless *ad hoc* revisions to make them virtually unfalsifiable by any observed facts. (The Latin expression *ad hoc* means, roughly, 'pertaining to' or 'as required by the case in hand.') What distinguishes empirical sciences like chemistry and astronomy from much metaphysics, on the one hand, and from pseudo-scientific theories like alchemy and astrology, on the other, is the fact that any genuinely scientific theory is testable, that is, falsifiable *in principle* by drawing out its empirical consequences using deductive logic and putting them to the test of observations and experiments designed to show that these consequences, and hence the theories from which they are derived, are false. If the theories and their consequences are mathematically exact, so that testing is a matter of precise measurement, so much the better. In general we may say that every time a theory successfully passes such a test it becomes more worthy of acceptance; and the more stringent or exact the test, the more worthy of credence the theory is.

The method of science consists, then, in critical testing of hypotheses and theories—in "conjecture and refutation" (Popper) to use a simple mnemonic formula that is also the title of a famous essay in the philosophy of science. No inductive or deductive reasoning can ever justify this attempt to go boldly and imaginatively beyond the actually observed; and no such justification is required if hypothetico-deductive method is a separate and autonomous pattern of rational enquiry, irreducible to either of the other two.

As for the certainty of science, if the logic of scientific discovery is indeed hypothetico-deductive, then it is impossible ever to be absolutely certain that any particular theoretical claim is true—rather than just particularly worthy of credence given the field of competing theories and the known evidence. For no matter how well corroborated a theory may be, further testing may yet show it to be mistaken. On the other hand, it is possible, on this model, to demonstrate quite conclusively that a given theoretical claim is false (and its denial therefore true), and to do so by a single decisive test or experiment. This fact should give pause to those who are tempted to maintain that truth (like beauty, allegedly) is just 'in the eye of the beholder.' In any case, the advocate of hypothetico-deductive method typically takes the discovery of explanatory truths to be the goal of science, despite a certain scepticism about our ability to be certain that we have discovered such truths even when we have.

6.3 The question of rationality

So much for the three paradigms. The deductive method is a fruitful source of new knowledge in mathematics and logic, though a certain amount of deductive reasoning goes on in all forms of enquiry, perhaps even in all rational discourse. Only in mathematics does it actually extend our knowledge, and even then only if the definitions, axioms, and postulates are basic truths rather than just conventionally adopted starting points; otherwise deductive procedures serve only to clarify the logical implications of, and the logical relations among, our theoretical assumptions. The inductive method boils down to something very like learning from experience.

98   Introduction: What Philosophy Is

While it is obvious that induction is used in common life all the time—indeed we would not survive very long without it—some philosophers and scientists, including great scientists of the past, have regarded induction as the method of empirical scientific investigation as well. Over the last century or so, complex mathematical accounts of probability have been developed in support of this contention. Nevertheless, a more widely held view of science has it that the method of the empirical social, natural, and biological sciences is hypothetico-deductive. If this twentieth-century account of the procedure successfully employed in science since about the turn of the seventeenth century is correct, it is interesting to note how much slower scientists have been to realize just how they have unlocked the secrets of nature than to hit on the key and put it to use. Newton's misunderstanding of scientific method is a case in point.

Now that all three models of rational procedure have been mapped out, we must say something about why it would be irrational on anyone's part to reject any of them outright.

6.3.1 The rationality of deductive method

It was noted earlier that deductive arguments turn on one important criterion of rationality: internal coherence or logical consistency. If a certain theorem follows in logic from certain definitions, axioms, and postulates, then the denial of that theorem is logically inconsistent with those definitions, axioms, and postulates; hence to accept the latter and deny the former is to contradict oneself. Anybody who does this is behaving irrationally. Why, though, should we care about consistency?

This question may not even be answerable except by making certain assumptions. However, assuming that the same question (Why should I care about ...?) does not arise again if 'truth' is substituted for 'rationality,' something of an answer can be given. The proviso is important. If those who profess indifference to consistency claim not to care about truth either, no satisfactory answer can be given. Otherwise, the following response seems very much to the point.

Anyone who contradicts himself is asserting something that is false as well as something else—its contradictory—that is true. That is made explicit in the definition of 'contradiction' to be given later (see 7.10). So if we care about making *only* true statements, we must take pains to avoid contradicting ourselves.

But the danger goes beyond enshrining a single falsehood in one's belief system. As the seventeenth-century German philosopher Leibniz was perhaps the first to point out, from a single contradiction one can derive the truth of *any* statement whatever *and its contradictory*. Hence, embrace any contradiction, and you must admit that all statements (and their denials!) are true. In other words, admit any contradiction and—quite literally—*anything goes*.

Leibniz's reasoning is very simple. Start with the contradiction (1) 'p and not-p,' where 'p' stands for any proposition and 'not-p' for its contradictory. It follows that (2) 'p or x' ('x' being some other proposition) is true. This is so because the force of the logical particle 'or' in (2) is that 'p or x' is true only if either (a) 'p' is true or (b) 'x' is true or (c) both are true; and we know from (1) that 'p' is true. So (2), 'p or x,' follows from (1). Now since the force of the logical particle 'and' in (1) is that 'p' and 'not-p' are *both* true, we can go on to deduce (3) 'not-p' directly from (1). But (2), 'p or x' and (3), 'not-p,' together entail (4) 'x.'

Thus, we have deductively derived an arbitrary proposition, 'x,' from our contradictory premise 'p and not-p' and the premise 'p or x.' And, obviously, we can now go on to use (5) 'p or not-x' in the same way as (2), deducing (7) 'not-x' directly from (5) and (3). Finally, we can draw the conclusion, (7) 'x and not-x,' from (4) and (6)—that is, we can infer any other contradiction 'x and not-x' from our original contradiction 'p and not-p' using only the tools of logic. Here is the entire argument in summary form:

(1) p and not-p;   (the reduced logical form of any contradiction)
(2) p or x;   (from 1: if 'p' is true, as 1 says it is, then so is 'p or x')
(3) not-p;   (this also from 1, which states that 'not-p' is true)
(4) Therefore x.   (from 2 and 3)
(5) p or not-x;   (from 1 again: if 'p' is true, then so is 'p or not-x')
(6) Hence, not-x;   (from 5 and 3)
(7) Hence, x and not-x. (from 4 and 6)

In short, from a given contradiction, you can deduce any proposition you like *and its denial*. Embrace a contradiction, therefore, and you are logically committed to accepting everything and anything as true, both 'There is a book on the desk in front of me right now' and its denial, 'There is no book ...' And that, of course, makes nonsense of the attempt to discern the true from the false—just as does the claim of the out-and-out relativist (see 3.3.1) that there simply is no such thing as truth to be found.

In fact, there may be very little difference between maintaining, as does our relativist, that there is no such thing as absolute truth, so that 'nothing goes,' and saying, with the champion of contradiction, that any and every statement is true, that is, 'anything goes.' For one thing, the relativist typically holds that since there is no such thing as absolute truth, all truth is relative, and anything may be regarded as (relatively) true for someone or some group at some time and place. But, more importantly, the consequences for rational enquiry are exactly the same whether anything or nothing 'goes': there can be no such thing. Thus, if we believe in and care about truth, we shall take pains to avoid accepting contradictory statements or embracing relativism. But as noted at the outset, the 'if' is important. The question, Why care about truth? like the question, Why be rational? is hard to answer satisfactorily. We shall see why in the next chapter (see 7.7.2), where we shall also consider what makes it so difficult to either defend or refute relativism.

So logical consistency is part and parcel of rationality; yet avoidance of contradiction (or inconsistency) can hardly be the whole story about being rational. To see that it is not, we have only to consider the second pattern of rational procedure, induction.

6.3.2 The rationality of inductive method

It has been noted already that inductive arguments are perfectly familiar to us under the name 'generalizations.' Starting from the observed fact that *many or most A*s are *B*s (where, for example, *A*s are some class of entity and *B* some property all or most members of that class happen to possess), they typically draw the conclusion that this or that *A* is likewise *B*; or from the known fact that *all* known or observed *A*s are *B*s, they infer that all *A*s without exception (the known as well as the unknown) are *B*s. Colloquially, we often say: 'you can't generalize'; and, of course, that is true. But it only means that *it is logically possible* to have true starting points and for the conclusion inductively arrived at to turn out false nevertheless. An exception to the rule is always possible.

Still, inductive argument represents a pattern of rationality in its own right, such that it would be quite unreasonable *not* to generalize sometimes. What could be more unreasonable, on the face of it, than for someone to believe that some *A*s are not *B*s if every *A* he or anybody else had ever encountered were a *B*? He could be right, of course; but his belief would be reasonable only if he had good reason to suspect that the sample known to him directly (through observation) and indirectly (through the reports of others) was not representative of the total population of *A*s; otherwise, it would be quite unreasonable to demur. And yet doing so would not involve contradiction, since there is no logical reason why the cases of which one has no experience must resemble in every respect those of which one has had extensive experience.

A famous example of a reasonable expectation that proved wrong is provided by the black swans of Australia. Before Captain Cook had discovered the Australian continent, a textbook example of an inductive generalization was 'All swans are white.' (An even older example from Greek times is 'All ravens are black.') Subsequently, Cook and his party encountered birds that were like swans in every respect except for the pigment of their feathers. No one hesitated to acknowledge that the birds were members of the species 'swan.' So while all *until-then-observed* swans had been white, and while it seemed perfectly reasonable to infer that *all* swans were white, the conclusion nevertheless proved false. Nor can we say that it would have been unreasonable for someone to refuse to draw such a conclusion prior to Cook's voyages, given that a large part of the then-known world was as yet unexplored. But suppose today, with the entire globe explored and its flora and fauna thoroughly and exhaustively catalogued, someone were to refuse to accept the inductively well-supported conclusion 'All ravens are black.' That would surely be unreasonable. Yet this conclusion *could* (logically) be false, while all the observations on which it is based are correct, since it covers not only past and present but future members of the species. And so too with the conclusion of any other inductive generalization, no matter how well supported: it may prove false. Nevertheless, rational people learn from experience; for one thing, they learn not to be too hasty in making generalizations; only fools go on stubbornly expecting what is contrary to all or most experience.

6.3.3 The rationality of hypothetico-deductive method

The hypothetico-deductive method is so called because a theory or *hypothesis* is checked by *deducing* observational consequences from it and observing whether or not they square with the facts. Science, on this model, is much like detective work: first, a hypothesis is devised in order to test a theory; this is then checked against actual experience. For example, a detective may reasonably expect a certain suspect to show some emotion when confronted with the murder weapon dredged up from the bottom of the river; if nothing of the kind occurs, there must be something wrong with the hypothesis that this suspect is the culprit or that this blunt instrument is the murder weapon, and so on. Of course, the suspect may have extraordinary powers of self-control. But that too may be investigated. The scientist's procedure is analogous. On scientific theory A, if I do this (say, create these initial conditions in the laboratory), then that will be observed to happen. If that does not happen (for example, the solution does not change colour), and there was no mistake about the initial conditions, then there is something wrong with the theory on which my hypothesis is based. It may not be entirely worthless; it may just be incomplete or hold less generally than I believed; or it may be in need of more or less extensive revisions.

This is (simplifying, of course) pretty much how general theories and individual hypotheses are tested and revised in science. It is a simple matter of logic that no set of true propositions can have logical implications that are false. So to hold a theory true having reliably discovered its observational consequences to be false would be inconsistent. Faced with results that are inconsistent with his theory, the scientist has various strategies open to him, including finding error in the observational data, explaining them by means of a supplementary hypothesis identifying other factors that skewed the results, and so forth. But he cannot rationally embrace contradictory statements.

As with deductive method, then, logical consistency is at least part of the story regarding the rationality of the hypothetico-deductive method. There is, however, this difference, that the deductive method concerns internal consistency among the parts of the theory: to deny any theorem while granting the definitions, axioms, and postulates from which it is logically derived is to contradict oneself; and we now know why we must avoid contradiction if we care about truth. In the empirical sciences, however, internal consistency among the theoretical components is only a minimal requirement; in addition, the theory must square with all reliably ascertainable data or matters of observed fact. Beyond this, theories are assessed on the basis of their ability to predict observations, especially unfamiliar ones. We can call this aspect of theory evaluation 'observational success.' True, observed facts are always interpreted in the light of theories according to the hypothetico-deductive model, so that there really are no facts in an absolute sense; but there are nevertheless factual propositions of a relatively low theoretical and high observational or empirical content; and these can quite reasonably be regarded as *tests* of more highly theoretical knowledge claims, even though they are nothing like infallible tests of truth, but only a fairly reliable method of refutation by which to eliminate some theories and compare and evaluate others.

In addition to the internal consistency test, then, the hypothetico-deductive model purports to provide us with fairly reliable criteria both for distinguishing scientific from non-scientific theories and for distinguishing 'good' or 'strong' from 'bad' or 'weak' scientific theories, largely on the basis of observational success. 'Testability' is the criterion of the scientific status of theories; and their ability to withstand rigorous testing is the measure of the rationality of accepting them. At the same time, this model does a good job of explaining why accepting a scientific theory without much corroboration through testing, or rejecting as false one that has been thoroughly tested and has stood up to intense scrutiny better than any competing theory, can be regarded as irrational or unreasonable, scientifically speaking, even though not inconsistent from a logical point of view.

Of course, there are other constraints on theories besides consistency and observational success that can make it, all things considered, much more reasonable to accept one theory rather than another. For example, there are often certain purely theoretical considerations that can make one theory preferable to another that is likewise consistent with the data and otherwise displays similar predictive power. For one theory may avoid certain theoretical puzzles or paradoxes to which another is prone; or it may be more elegant, simpler, more highly unified with other theories; or it may be more encompassing in scope or more fruitful of new and interesting research programmes or findings. On the basis of considerations like these, along with those mentioned already, we may say with good reason that one theory is better than its competitors and at least conjecture that it is true or has greater truth content overall.

That, however, is *all* we can do; we cannot be *absolutely sure* that we have discovered the truth and so cut short further enquiry. The history of science is strewn with the remains of discarded theories once held to be unassailable truth. This gives us strong inductive reasons to be cautious about our current favourites, which will probably meet the same fate. About the relative merits of theories, moreover, there will always be controversy, and no matter how long the debate goes on, there will always be some important disagreements. This is the simple consequence of what we earlier designated 'critical rationalism' (see 3.3.1). But that consequence is surely all to the good. Dogmatic and authoritarian proclamations of definitive theories or truths are a sure-fire formula for intellectual stagnation in the domain of science or philosophy.

6.4 The rationality of philosophical enquiry

Some of what has been said concerning the rationality of science may apply to philosophical theories as well. Certainly, eminent philosophers, past and present, have defended the rationality of philosophy by reference to one or the other of these models; and although this may be perfectly correct for some methods and sub-disciplines, the main question here is whether anything of the kind holds for the problems of primary philosophy as described in the preceding chapters.

6.4.1 Philosophy and deductive method

Historically, the deductive method has been used—most would say 'misused'—a good deal in philosophy, notably to develop apodictic proofs for such metaphysical conclusions as the existence of God and the immortality of the human soul. We shall examine famous examples in Parts Two and Three. While the purely deductive structure of formal axiomatized systems of logic and mathematics may strike us as obviously beyond the reach of primary philosophy, the mathematical paradigm has exercised an almost irresistible pull on eminent metaphysicians of the past. Spinoza attempted to cast his whole system of thought in the form of deductive, geometrical proofs; and both Descartes and Leibniz are widely regarded as advocates of a model of metaphysical enquiry that starts from apodictically certain non-conventional definitions, axioms, and postulates, deducing from them conclusions about the existence of God and the immortality of the human soul. The story does not begin in the seventeenth century either: while Plato came eventually to distinguish the mathematical and philosophical methods, the arguments for immortality to be examined in Part Two are clearly constructed on something very like the geometrical model of proof. Thus, the mathematical model took hold of philosophy quite early.

Although some philosophical sub-disciplines, like symbolic logic, for example, may conform to the mathematical paradigm over the whole extent of their field of investigation, the rigour and apodictic certainty of the mathematical method are now generally regarded as beyond the reach of most branches of philosophy. This much, however, remains true even of primary philosophy: the minimal requirement of logical consistency and correct deductive reasoning must be met, especially wherever logical methods are employed in spelling out presuppositions and consequences. Yet, in other respects, primary philosophy and mathematics seem almost polar opposites. Metaphysical doctrines concerning God and the soul are notoriously controversial, while the conclusions of mathematical demonstrations are apodictically certain. There are no 'schools of thought' regarding the value of x in the solution to a differential equation or any other mathematical problem of the same order; nor is there Catholic geometry or Protestant calculus, as there are Catholic, Protestant, Jewish, or Muslim positions in matters of rational (philosophical) theology. There are no doubt solutions that have yet to be discovered to a few very difficult mathematical problems; and there may be solutions to some problems that are simpler, more elegant, more fruitful, and so on, than others. Furthermore, there are all sorts of complex and hotly debated issues of mathematical *theory* still unresolved. The most general of these belong to a sub-discipline of philosophy entitled the philosophy of mathematics. Yet *within* any developed mathematical *system* there are only theorems that have been demonstrated, perhaps others for which a demonstration is still sought, but no issues in the philosophical sense.

In primary philosophy, by contrast, almost *everything* is open to discussion and debate, almost all is theory. Once we get beyond the informational level, philosophy is apparently nothing but dialogue arising from the clash of ideas, interpretations, assumptions, methods, and theories. Here the notion of deductive proof or demonstration seems entirely out of place—at least in discussions of what is *proper to* philosophy. For *all* disciplines, no matter how different their proper procedures, employ deductive arguments sometimes, simply as a means of determining what follows from what—that is, what certain claims actually mean and what they commit us to *logically*, should we decide to accept them. To this rule philosophy is no exception. But deduction is no more the proper method of primary philosophy than it is of the empirical natural or social sciences.

In philosophy, then, there are a great many issues on which fully informed, highly competent professionals may, after due consideration of one another's points of view and arguments, find themselves in fundamental disagreement and without any means of resolving their differences. The thing about primary philosophy is that the range of such issues is much more extensive because of the highly theoretical character of the discipline and its unparalleled universality of scope. However, just as there are many fundamental philosophical issues on which competent, reasonable, thoroughly academically trained philosophers have always disagreed, and will probably continue to disagree, largely because of differences in their starting points, so there are matters about which it is safe to say that no reasonable member of the philosophical community would disagree. Such is, for example, the claim that the method by which philosophy seeks to provide a framework for the examination of the moral and intellectual basis for human life is in some sense rational. If it is no longer tempting to liken philosophical procedures to the apodictic reasonings of the mathematical sciences, the conclusion to be drawn is that some other way of understanding their rationality must be sought; giving up on reason should be a last resort.

6.4.2 Philosophy and inductive method

Once the many deductively elaborated systems of metaphysics collapsed under the weight of their own ponderous proofs and refutations of one another's conclusions, philosophers quite naturally turned to the empirically proceeding physical sciences in search of a model of the rationality of their own discipline. Unlike metaphysics, science had made great strides forward throughout the seventeenth century. It was Hume who, at the beginning of the eighteenth century, first analyzed the logic or method of modern science in a way that was relatively (though not entirely) unencumbered by the mathematical model. Hume hoped to carry out in philosophy a revolution like that recently brought about in physical science by Newton (see 30.5.1). This legacy is still very much in evidence in contemporary efforts to 'naturalize' philosophy, that is, to elevate it to the status of empirical science by, for example, reducing the theory of knowledge to a branch of stimulus–response psychology. This appears to have been the project of the Harvard philosopher Willard van Orman Quine (1908–2001), about whom we shall have more to say later.

Hume held that philosophy—or, at least, legitimate philosophical enquiry—was an *empirical science* like the sciences of nature in most respects except that philosophy investigated *human* nature, specifically, the human mind, rather than physical phenomena. It is for natural science to investigate, with all the empirical means at its disposal, matters of fact and existence, determining as best it can what sorts of events precede, go together with, or follow upon what other sorts of events, and to generalize its findings as invariable natural laws; philosophy, for Hume, investigates the psychological mechanisms governing belief formation in the human mind, both the formation of beliefs about the natural world (natural science) and about the human world (man and society). Philosophy is accordingly indistinguishable from what later became the independent field of empirical psychology. (See 1.2.1 on the process of 'fission' by which various special sciences split off from philosophy, the one universal science.) The mechanism that Hume believed he had discovered is now familiar as the so-called association of ideas, though something like the stimulus–response mechanism plays a large part in Hume's theory as well. So understood, philosophy is the highest empirical science only in the sense that it is more universal than any other; for all beliefs of whatever kind have their ultimate foundation in certain very general laws of human nature governing belief formation. Accordingly, Hume called his associationist psychological theory 'metaphysics,' although metaphysics as an empirical science would have made little sense to any philosopher before him or since; even his most ardent modern admirers have not followed his usage, 'metaphysics' having become pejorative nowadays anyway.

Now care must be taken not to confound (1) the philosophical investigation of the order of knowing and the order of being with (2) the psychological (perhaps also sociological) investigation of the conditions under which warranted and unwarranted conclusions are reached in (1). Obviously, our question concerning the rationality of primary philosophy concerns whether and how theories or beliefs about the order of knowing and being can be said to be rationally warranted by the arguments and evidence for them. Whatever that pattern of rationality may be (assuming there is one), it is difficult to see how it could resemble the inductive model. Other reasons aside, primary philosophy theorizes about the unobserved and unobserv*able* to an extent that could never be deemed rational on this model. For as we saw, it is an inherent limitation of the inductive method that it is confined to objects that are experienceable (see 6.2.2). Nevertheless, a different and lesser strand of Hume's conception of philosophical method sheds some light on the rationality of philosophical procedure generally, and hence on primary philosophy, too, though still not on what is proper to the latter.

Apart from his associationist genetic psychology, Hume was very much concerned with the rational assessment of evidence and arguments. As a rule, only once he had established that the logical pedigree of certain beliefs was bogus did he proceed to the psychological account of why they are almost universally held anyway. The former is a prominent, for many philosophers, *the* distinctive feature of philosophical method. The sciences acquire knowledge of the objects that make up some particular object domain (be it plants, animals, minerals, the past, the emotions, or markets); philosophy occupies itself with the description of the logical structure and evaluation of the status of the theories so developed, that is, their claim to be rational and to furnish objective knowledge.

Although philosophy, on this showing, is not just an empirical science among others, it still has nothing to do with *increasing* our knowledge by logical analysis or deductive reasoning. That, as Hume saw correctly, is the peculiar prerogative of the mathematical sciences. Philosophy merely brings to light the logical structure of beliefs and theories, including metaphysical ones, scrutinizing the logical relationship between evidence and conclusions. Many philosophers nowadays would nod enthusiastic assent to this estimate of what makes philosophy rational. And we shall find that much of the content of the present volume fits this general description. Nevertheless, there is more to the rationality of primary philosophy than this.

6.4.3 Philosophy and hypothetico-deductive method

According to the previous sub-section, two widely held contemporary views of philosophical enquiry hail directly from Hume. The first, philosophy as an empirical, inductive science of the mind, is of no use at all in assessing the rationality of primary philosophy, while the other, philosophy as logical analysis, is relevant, as is the deductive model considered first, yet fails to get at what is distinctive about primary philosophy.

While the hypothetico-deductive model, too, has been used to defend the rationality of philosophical enquiry, it has more often been employed to attack it. The model, it will be recalled, provides a criterion of the scientific status of theories: testability. By any such standard metaphysics is not a science; for most large-scale metaphysical theories transcend the limits of experience and are not empirically testable at all. Nevertheless, metaphysics is not therefore automatically on the same footing as such pseudo-sciences as alchemy or astrology; much less is it a string of meaningless pseudo-statements, as others of its detractors have alleged (see 7.5.1 below). A rather more positive estimate of its rationality, based loosely on the hypothetico-deductive model, takes metaphysics as pushing back the frontiers of science itself. Gradually, through technological and theoretical advances, perhaps also through serendipity, theories that were originally not testable become so, passing from the domain of speculative natural philosophy into that of empirical natural science—much in the manner of those philosophical issues depicted in chapter 1 as traditional but not current. The sphere of the non-scientific thus comprises (a) the pseudo-scientific (and never-to-become-scientific) as well as (b) *not-yet*-scientific theories that may some day pass, as have many before them, into the domain of science. Exactly which theories these are, may be hard to say. In any case, this is roughly how a philosopher as influential as Bertrand Russell saw metaphysics (see 5.3.2). Despite his deeply ingrained scientism, Russell hailed at least some forms of metaphysical speculation as contributing significantly to the growth of scientific knowledge.

Of course, the metaphysics that Russell defends is above all that speculative philosophy of nature that pushes back the frontiers of empirical natural science; it is hard to see how a similar case could be made for the investigation of the order of being or knowing. Is it even conceivable that the problems ranged under these two heads, including matters belonging to rational theology, might pass into the domain of science proper? On the other hand, is there any need for them to do so?

Suppose we were correct in maintaining that creatures such as ourselves require a moral and intellectual as well as a material basis for life if they are to flourish as human beings, and that the history of thought in its mythico-religious, metaphysical, and scientific phases is just the story of mankind's quest for a more rational basis for living. If we equate metaphysical and scientific rationality in the manner of Russell, eliding the difference between the metaphysical and scientific phases, the outcome is just a thoroughgoing scientism. Yet it seems quite possible that metaphysics or primary philosophy, while furnishing the outer framework and foundation for a moral and intellectual outlook large parts of which possess scientific character, might itself have a different rational structure from both the empirical and mathematical sciences. In fact, it can be argued that this must be so if there is to be any real grounding of knowledge in first principles. The foundation, one might argue, cannot belong to exactly the same order of ideas as that which it grounds; for in that case we must again ask, What is it grounded in? and so on, indefinitely, until we come to something of which the same question cannot be asked, at least not in the same way. Only then have we furnished an explanation that is truly based on explanatory *ultimates*.

While not—or, in the case of some parts of the metaphysics of nature, not yet—empirically testable, speculative metaphysical theories must at least square with ordinary experience if they are to be worthy of credence. This holds for the questions regarding the orders of being and knowing, too. There may be more to squaring with experience, however, than just having empirical consequences of the sort that make a theory amenable to testing by observation and experiment. For there is also the capacity of speculative thought to illumine ordinary pre-philosophical and pre-scientific experience *from the ground up*, as it were, making it more perspicuous, more intelligible than at first glance. By hewing close to the way we experience and understand things ordinarily in our day-to-day living, primary philosophy may furnish a conceptual scheme or framework, an order of knowing and order of being, that deepens our pre-theoretical understanding of things, bringing into a clearer light what, in a way, we already knew, though without knowing that we knew it. While nothing like a decisive test by which we can gradually but inexorably narrow down the field of competing metaphysical theories, this at least provides a standard of *rational* preference for one such theory over another.

Metaphysical theories must also be free of internal inconsistencies, of course; and one theory may be preferable to another because it makes fewer or less-questionable assumptions or is immune to certain puzzles and problems to which that other gives rise. One may be richer in content than another that is very vague, or more fruitful of special investigations that illumine ordinary experience in new ways. Moreover, a metaphysical theory may recommend itself as shedding more light than others on the actual history of thought. Given these parameters of theory choice, it appears that even those metaphysical theories that are *in principle* immune to empirical testing, and so can never become science, are nevertheless subject to a variety of rational constraints, that is, *governed by reason*. The debate, in other words, is subject to rational standards, even if not susceptible of the kind of consensus found in the sciences. For this there are many reasons, not the least of which is that what is meant by 'experience' is itself a matter of philosophical dispute. So the issues here may be less tractable than in the domain of science (where, some would say, they are not very straightforward either); but the similarities or parallels as well as the differences so far pointed out provide ample reason for scepticism about attempts to relegate primary philosophy to the realm of feeling, imagination, and personal world-view, let alone to the status of alchemy and astrology or of meaningless gibberish.

The question of the rationality of philosophy is far from settled—or definitively settleable. We shall return to it from time to time in each of the five parts of this book. For whether it be Socrates, Plato, Descartes, Hume, or Sartre, each, as we shall see, has his own views on what it is to be clear-sighted, intellectually rigorous, and philosophically rational.

7

Philosophy and Logic

7.1 Introductory

The present chapter develops some of the logical tools necessary for understanding and appraising philosophical arguments. Most of what follows falls squarely into the category of information (see 2.5.2), though it is vital information for purposes of interpreting and evaluating the philosophical arguments and theories to be considered in the five main parts of this book. Our principle of selection in determining which topics from logic to include is their relevance to what comes later in this work. That would be an intolerably *ad hoc* way of proceeding were the aim to learn logic for its own sake, but it at least has the merit of ensuring that the logic introduced here will have some relevance to the problems of primary philosophy described above.

It was remarked earlier (see 5.6), with reference to Aristotle, the father of logic, that deductive logical procedures have little to do with the methods of discovery actually employed by the great thinkers of the past. Thus, for Hume (see 6.4.2), logical analysis is only a prelude to the empirical scientific task of explaining logically unwarranted conclusions in terms of the psychological mechanisms underlying belief-formation. And so too with other seminal figures of the tradition: formal logical techniques are only a lesser strand in the methods of discovery employed by Descartes and Kant, for instance, although Descartes is still widely regarded as having embraced a single, purely deductive model of scientific method. We shall see in Part Three of this work that this is quite mistaken. Spinoza may seem a hard case at first glance, but if we distinguish between the method by which the starting points of new systems of thought are discovered, on the one hand, and the literary form in which their fruits are presented to the philosophical public, on the other, even Spinoza may be no exception to the rule. Nevertheless, plenty of philosophers in recent times have been sufficiently impressed by the lesser strand in

Chapter 7: Philosophy and Logic   111

Hume to maintain that philosophical problems are 'conceptual' or 'logical' rather than empirical. The contents of this volume will confirm that logical analysis is a very important part of the business of the philosopher. Hence, we cannot do without a little logical theory to complete this Introduction. Still, the information covered here is designed to shed some fresh light on the nature of primary philosophy, too (see 7.5.1–2), although that is more in the way of a bonus than the primary objective of the chapter.

7.2 Terminological preliminaries

We begin with a series of definitions or clarifications of key logical terms: sentence, utterance, assertion, affirmation, negation, statement, and so forth. These are building blocks for all that follows.

A *sentence* is a grammatical unit of speech. It involves no reference to any particular utterer or occasion of utterance. Thus, different people can utter the same sentence at different times, or at the same time (if they speak in unison, for example), and the same person can utter the same sentence at different times, that is, exactly the same grammatically correct sequence of words.

A sentence is accordingly not the same thing as an *utterance*. The latter is a kind of event, namely a speech-act, an overt verbal performance. (For present purposes, we can omit consideration of mental and written verbal performances.) An utterance is complete if the words form a sentence. A complete utterance can be described in all important respects by indicating three things: (1) the sentence uttered; (2) the utterer; and (3) the unique occasion on which the utterance took place.

A grammatically correct unit of speech may be a *wish* ('If only I had been there!'), a *command* ('Be on time!'), a *question* ('Were you on time?'), an *exclamation* or *interjection* ('Ouch!'). Or, alternatively, it may *state a fact*, whether correctly or incorrectly ('You are late, sir.'). All these are just so many kinds of sentences. To this logical classification of sentences correspond the grammatical terms 'optative' for wish sentences, 'imperative' for commands, 'interrogative' for questions, 'exclamatory' for exclamations, and 'declarative' or 'indicative,' both of which are used for ordinary sentences expressing what is alleged to be the case, whether the sentences are in fact true or false.

Apart from these types of sentences, there are also *expressions of praise or blame*, *appeals, suggestions, prayers, exhortations*, and other types of grammatically correct sentences that are used every day, as well as many sentences that are 'hybrids' of two or more of these types. Take, for example, the sentence: 'Can't you be on time for once?' This combines elements of reproof or blame with indicative and even interrogative elements in a way that is not at all easy to sort out. Or the emphatic sentence: '*I* will be punctual.' More often than not, this simple declarative statement is just a disguised imperative: 'Be on time yourself!'

112   Introduction: What Philosophy Is

Declarative or indicative sentences are usually called 'statements.' A slightly better way of putting it is to say that an indicative or declarative sentence *expresses* a statement, either affirmative or negative. If the sentence is grammatically affirmative, then what is expressed, the statement, is an *assertion* or *affirmation*; if, on the other hand, the statement is expressed in an indicative or declarative sentence that is, grammatically speaking, negative, the statement is a *negation* or *denial*. So while all statements are sentences, not all sentences are statements; only declarative or indicative statements, both affirmative and negative, are.

Utterances *of statements* (as opposed to uttering other kinds of sentences, for example, threats) can be called *declarative utterances*. Like statements, they may be either affirmative (assertions) or negative (denials).

All well-formed sentences—indicative, interrogative, exclamatory, and so forth—must be distinguished from strings of words that do not form proper or complete sentences at all since they violate the rules of either (a) grammatical or (b) logical syntax. Take, as examples, 'The is and not!' and 'Caesar is a prime number.' The first of these is formed counter-syntactically; there is no grammatical subject or predicate. It is not a sentence. The second is formed in accordance with the rules of grammatical syntax and is therefore a sentence; but *logically* the only sort of thing of which '… is a prime number' can be said is an integer or numeral, never a person, a human being, or anything else for that matter. So what this sentence expresses is not a statement, not sense, a meaning, but nonsense—just as it is meaningless gibberish to say or write 'The is and not!' However, this time the fact that it is nonsense turns on semantic rather than syntactical considerations, that is, on word meanings rather than grammatical sentence structure. One can also say, as was said above, that it turns on the *logical* syntax of our language (which is a complex affair involving semantic as well as structural considerations) rather than straightforward *grammatical* syntax.

All these ways of describing the difference between 'Caesar is a prime number' and 'The is and not!' come down to the same thing. In a moment, we shall consider a further criterion of meaning or sense that some philosophers insist on adding to the preceding two, namely (c) verifiability, that is, the ability of sentences to be confirmed or disconfirmed, shown to be true or false, in one or the other of two recognized ways. The question is whether sentences that satisfy the conditions of grammatical and logical syntax laid out in (a) and (b) yet fail to satisfy condition (c) are really statements, as they appear to be, or just meaningless pseudo-statements. But first, something must be said about truth and falsity.

7.3 Propositions and truth functions

Only indicative or declarative sentences having a meaning are statements in the sense defined above, and only statements can sensibly be said to be *true or false*. Insofar as a statement must be one or the other, but cannot be *both* true *and* false, it is also called 'a proposition.' Should one and the same declarative sentence be true in one situation and false in another, then it is just a matter of the same grammatically correct form of words (the same sentence) being used to express propositions having different meanings, that is, to express different propositions. This happens frequently enough. The sentence "She's a competitive swimmer" may be true of Melissa and false of Melanie. But, of course, it is not the same proposition that is being asserted in the one case and the other. In the first, it means "Melissa is a competitive swimmer," in the other, "Melanie is a competitive swimmer." Where we are dealing with one and the same proposition, it is *by definition* impossible that it be both true and false or that it be neither true nor false. For the term 'proposition' is usually *defined* in just this way: 'for any p (any particular sentence that is or expresses a proposition), either p (p is true) or not-p (p is false and not-p is true).' 'Proposition,' then, is just another word for what was initially labelled a 'statement.' The two terms will be used interchangeably throughout this work.

By the criterion just specified, strings of words that fail to meet the requirements of grammatical or logical syntax are not statements or propositions, since they are not even sentences; nor are wishes, commands, exclamations, and the like. Unlike the former, these latter are at least sentences, even perfectly meaningful sentences; they just do not state propositions. For a command or wish is just not the sort of thing that can be either true or false, any more than can an exclamation. To call commands, expressions of hopes and fears, or exclamations 'true' or 'false' would be just like saying 'Caesar is a prime number.' For just as 'prime number' can be predicated only of numerals, so 'true' and 'false' can be predicated *only* of simple indicative sentences *or* complex sentences built up out of them by putting them together in certain ways. In the case of complex sentences, there are logical rules for determining the truth value of the whole complex proposition as a function of (a) the truth values of the simple statements comprised within it and (b) the meanings of the logical particles like 'if ... then,' 'and,' 'or,' and so forth, used to connect the latter. Such simple and complex sentences are therefore called 'truth functions' as well as 'statements' and 'propositions.' All three terms are interchangeable.

Note that what we normally call 'propositions' in extra-logical parlance, namely proposals, are precisely *not* propositions in the logical sense but, rather, more or less polite forms of the imperative: 'Let's do the following' or 'How about this?' or 'Why not do so?' Thus, we speak of 'business propositions' and 'political propositions' of various kinds; such propositions (in the non-logical sense) may be interesting, advantageous, appealing, brilliant, foolish, obscene, and a variety of other things—but never true or false. By contrast, the logician's propositions include all and only those sentences of which it would not only make sense to say that they are either true or false, but which *are* and indeed must be either true or false (whether or not we can tell which), yet cannot be both. So it is crucially important not to confuse propositions with proposals, or, in general, the logical meanings of terms with their more familiar extra-logical use.

7.4 Factual and conceptual matters

Now propositions, as defined and explained above, may state either *factual* or *conceptual* truths and falsehoods. Thus (to take the standard textbook example), 'All bachelors are unmarried' is a conceptual truth, while 'Some mothers are males' is a conceptual falsehood, that is, something known to be false without recourse to experience, just on the basis of the meanings of the words or concepts involved. Semantic and logical considerations suffice to make clear the truth of 'All bachelors are unmarried'; there is no need to consult experience since to deny this statement would (given the clear meanings of the words involved) be to contradict oneself. After all, 'bachelor' just means 'an unmarried adult male.' So saying 'All bachelors are unmarried' is tantamount to saying 'All unmarried adult males are unmarried.' And this *must* be true, since 'Some unmarried adult males are married' is patently self-contradictory and false. Such conceptual or *necessary* truths are usually regarded as trivial, however, and rightly so. At most, they clarify our language, namely the meanings of the words used. When the word meanings are vague, of course, even conceptual truths may be of some interest. Nevertheless, they tell us nothing about the extra-linguistic world in which bachelors are found, and supply no new information about the class of people to which the word 'bachelor' actually applies. They are perfectly meaningful and true, indeed necessarily and apodictically true, yet not factual in this sense: they tell us nothing we do not already know just in virtue of understanding the meaning of words like 'bachelor.'

By contrast, 'all bachelors are carefree' or 'all mothers are loving' are factual rather than conceptual propositions. If either were true—presumably, neither is—it would not be true in virtue of the meanings of the words used and ordinary logic. Either *could* be affirmed or denied without contradiction, and this is the mark of a factual as distinct from a conceptual statement. There is, after all, no contradiction or absurdity involved in the notion of a care-worn bachelor, as there is in that of a married bachelor. Factual truths, then, tell us something about the way things are rather than about meanings and the logic of our language. In this sense, they are informative or substantive rather than completely trivial. And that, as we must now make clear, is *all* it means to say that they are 'factual.'

In the previous section the logical had to be distinguished from the everyday sense of 'proposition.' It is vital to understand that 'factual,' when opposed to 'conceptual,' does not mean 'true,' although this is exactly what it means in everyday speech, where 'factual' is correctly opposed to 'false' or 'fabricated,' 'fictitious,' and the like. Thus, a 'factual' newspaper account is contrasted with those that are 'inaccurate,' 'biased,' and so on. The former is true, we say, while the latter contain some statements that are false. But this *everyday* sense is quite different from the *logical* meaning of 'factual.' The latter means, roughly, 'pertaining to matters of fact.' In this sense, even the biased account is perfectly factual: it misdescribes, distorts, misreports the matters of fact to which it pertains.

If it does not even mean the same as 'true,' then obviously this logical sense of 'factual' cannot mean 'known to be true,' that is, 'true, and known to be so.' It refers rather to the sort of statement which, *if* true (something we may not know), just happens to be so, and *could* (logically) have been false instead, if matters stood otherwise. Put differently, 'factual' in the logical sense means 'having to do with *contingent* matters of fact' rather than necessities of logic or language. The shape of the earth is one such matter of fact. It happens to be more or less round, but it could have had another shape. There is certainly no logical absurdity (contradiction) in the notion of a flat earth, however ridiculous it may sound to us. Hence the various statements making up the geophysical view sometimes jocularly referred to as 'the flat earth theory' are all factual statements in our sense, the *logical* sense, even though they happen to be false, that is, non-factual in the everyday sense.

Factual and conceptual truths have also been called (1) 'synthetic' and 'analytic,' respectively. This usage goes back to Kant, although Kant himself did not employ 'synthetic' in quite the way we have explained 'factual,' as we shall see in the next section. His countryman and predecessor Leibniz called them (2) 'truths of fact' and 'truths of reason.' The latter Leibniz also called 'eternal truths,' following Descartes and others, though by Kant's day the expression 'eternal truth' was already outmoded. Writing after Leibniz but before Kant, Hume distinguished between (3) statements about 'matter of fact and existence' (factual truths) and statements expressing 'relations of ideas' (conceptual truths). And, as we have seen, the two are sometimes also called (4) 'contingent' and 'necessary' truths, respectively; for while statements of the latter type *must* be true, the former, if true, *just happen* to be so. That is what 'necessary' and 'contingent' mean. Hence all conceptual eternal truths are necessarily true, all factual truths contingently so for Hume. And as with necessary and contingent propositions, so with their negations: there are necessarily and contingently false as well as necessarily and contingently true statements.

Before we proceed, it may be worth summarizing the points made thus far in a simple list. A sequence of words, we have seen, may be any of the following:

1 not even a grammatically correct *sentence*;
2 a grammatically correct sentence, but not a *statement or proposition*, since it is not declarative or indicative but optative, interrogative, exclamatory, etc.;
3 a *grammatically* correct indicative or declarative sentence, but still without meaning, still not a statement or proposition, since it fails to meet the further requirements of *logical* syntax;
4 a grammatically correct indicative sentence that meets all the requirements of logical

syntax, that is, a statement or proposition having or expressing a meaning.

As far as we know so far, all true propositions belonging to the last rubric are either truths of fact or truths of reason (eternal truths) of a conceptual nature, that is,

4.1 factual, contingent, synthetic, and informative (confirmed by experience);
4.2 conceptual, necessary, analytic, and trivial (based on logic and language alone).

Where Hume differed from Kant (the case of Leibniz is a little more complex) is with respect to the words at the beginning of the previous sentence, 'as far as we know so far.' For Hume took the simple bipartition to be a complete and exhaustive classification of all propositions, while Kant insisted on a third sub-class under 4, a further type of necessary truth that is synthetic and informative, like factual truths, rather than analytic or conceptual, and yet not only necessarily true but demonstrably so. For Kant, all genuine metaphysical knowledge belongs to this third sub-class. It is worth pausing to look into this controversy concerning the logical classification of propositions for the additional light it will shed on primary philosophy as described in the preceding chapters.

7.5 Metaphysical sentences

As the nominal word meaning (see 1.2.3) suggests, metaphysical theories typically include claims regarding the existence of unobservable entities either in the universe or outside it; for example, about (1) the existence of a transcendent being, God; or about (2) the existence of an immaterial entity designated 'the human soul'; or about (3) essences alleged to belong necessarily to all entities of a certain kind and to exist either immanently only or both immanently and transcendently (see 4.7). They also involve claims about the order of dependence, independence, interdependence, or inter-independence (see 4.2) among existing things, for example, that the existence of the world depends upon God; or that the existence of the human soul does *not* depend upon the human body, so that the death of the body need not bring with it the extinction of the soul; or that sensible things depend for their being on immanent or transcendent essences.

Moreover, in traditional metaphysical contexts these claims are typically advanced as *necessarily* true and *demonstrable*. Yet they are certainly neither *logically* necessary nor trivial conceptual matters; that is, one can deny without contradiction the very things they assert, and what they assert is not uninformative, should it be true. Still, since experience and observation can only tell us what *is in fact*, never what *must* be, the case, these theories have no empirical consequences that might serve to verify or falsify them. They consist, in other words, of claims that could *in principle* never gain adequate support from, or, for that matter, be conclusively

Chapter 7: Philosophy and Logic   117

disconfirmed by, experience or observation, no matter how extensive.

7.5.1 Metaphysics as meaningless

As just described, the sentences making up traditional metaphysical theories fit neither 4.1 (contingent matters of fact) nor 4.2 (conceptual eternal truths). One way to avoid having to expand 4 to include a third sub-class of statements is to introduce this further requirement: to be a meaningful statement a sentence must not only be (a) grammatically correct and (b) fulfil the requirements of logical syntax; it must also (c) admit of some form of (dis)confirmation, either by empirical means (for factual truths) or on the basis of logical considerations (for conceptual truths). If the first requirement is grammatical and the second logical, this third requirement is empirical; and indeed those who have argued for it have done so in the name of a thoroughgoing anti-metaphysical empiricism. To put the empirical requirement a little more pointedly: any declarative sentence that is *not* merely a conceptual truth or falsehood, must be empirically verifiable or falsifiable, at least in principle.

Accordingly, a declarative sentence has meaning precisely to the extent that it has empirical consequences; lacking them entirely, it lacks all meaning and is not really a proposition or statement at all. This is the case with metaphysical sentences according to some critics. If not under 4, then where do metaphysical sentences belong in the above classification? Here two responses can be distinguished.

Though not meaningful *statements*, metaphysical statements are still meaningful *sentences*. After all, an optative or exclamatory sentence expresses a wish or a feeling and so has a meaning, though it does not state a proposition, a sentence of the sort that must be either true or false. Another way of putting this first response is to say that metaphysical sentences have no *cognitive* meaning; they merely express in misleading statement form what are in fact perfectly meaningful expressions of wishes, hopes, or emotions—regarding the afterlife, for example, or regarding an intelligent artificer of the universe, or regarding the elusive natures of sensible things that we long to understand in the same apodictically certain way in which we understand the properties of a triangle, for example. Since hopes and other feelings are not the sort of thing that can be true or false, metaphysical sentences belong under 2 in the earlier classification scheme (grammatically correct sentences, but not statements or propositions).

This is moderate by comparison with the radical response that metaphysical statements are utterly meaningless gibberish, completely nonsensical pseudo-statements, similar to those under 3 in the earlier classification. That is, they resemble 'Caesar is a prime number' and sentences of that ilk, yet with this difference: though grammatically *and* syntactically correct, even from the point of view of logical syntax, they fail to satisfy the further empirical requirement of (c) verifiability or falsifiabilty, and are accordingly not genuine declarative statements at all but utterly meaningless pseudo-propositions or nonsense.

7.5.2 Metaphysics as apodictically certain knowledge

Whether the alleged necessary truths in which traditional metaphysics abounds are assigned to 2 or 3, the implications for metaphysics as a form of rational enquiry and a search for truth are exactly the same: there can be no such thing. This devastating verdict of the *logical* empiricism of the twentieth century ('logical' because concerned primarily with the analysis of meaning) is clearly prefigured in the earlier psychological or psycho-genetic empiricism of Hume (so called because it is concerned primarily with the origins of psychological processes like concept- and belief-formation). For Hume, too, metaphysical statements involving concepts like 'necessary being' and 'necessary dependence of this on that' are either meaningful expressions of subjective feeling (his official position) or utterly meaningless pseudo-statements (an alternative he at least considers). This devastating critique of metaphysics was accordingly not unfamiliar to Kant, whose response to Hume was to introduce a third sub-class under 4 to accommodate metaphysical statements generally, arguing that at least *some* such statements are as certain and apodictically provable as the theorems of mathematics. While this is obviously a very bold defence (or counter-offensive), Kant made certain concessions as well.

Proof or demonstration of the necessary truth of metaphysical statements is impossible, Kant conceded, where supersensible objects like God and the immortality of the soul are concerned. So to the question (see 1.2.4), What can I know? the answer is: nothing about God and immortality. However, when it comes to Kant's other two questions, What ought I to do? and What may I hope? this loss can be made good. For in the domain of ethics or moral philosophy—what Kant called 'the metaphysics of morals'—those very statements about God and the afterlife can be demonstrated as *practically* necessary. As for metaphysical statements or principles regarding the nature or essence of the sensible things investigated by natural science, however, these are strictly and apodictically provable, according to Kant. Such theoretical claims belong to what Kant called 'the metaphysics of nature' as distinct from both the metaphysics of morals and the empirical *science* of nature (physics); they are both informative or substantive (since they assert something about the nature of all material things) and yet necessary—not logically necessary, to be sure (they can be denied without contradiction), but rather metaphysically necessary and perfectly amenable to apodictic demonstration.

So Kant expanded the classification of propositions to include not just two, but three sub-classes under 4:

4.1 synthetic and contingent truths of fact ('judgments of experience' in Kant's terms);
4.2 analytic and necessary truths of reason ('analytic judgments'); and

4.3 synthetic but necessary truths.

Under 4.3 Kant ranged, in addition to metaphysical knowledge of sensible things, the whole of mathematical knowledge (arithmetic, geometry, and algebra). Most philosophers nowadays subsume the branches of mathematics under 4.2, conceptual or analytic necessary truths, as far as their conventionally adopted definitions and axioms are concerned, the theorems being logically deduced from the definitions, axioms, and postulates of the system. Whether Kant was right about mathematics, the particular proof-strategy he devised for demonstrating metaphysical truths apodictically is not at all like the method employed in mathematics; that is, metaphysical knowledge does not conform to the mathematical paradigm of rationality at all. It has a unique pattern of rationality all its own, yet one that is no less stringent or apodictic than mathematics. The debate about metaphysics, and to a lesser extent, about mathematics, rages on to this day.

7.5.3 Remarks on this controversy

Whether there is a legitimate place for a further class of statements or propositions is one of the principal points at issue between those anti-metaphysical philosophers who call themselves 'empiricists' and the pro-metaphysical thinkers generally known as 'rationalists,' including Kant (see especially 3.3.2 above and 26.2 below). On the face of it, Kant's claim that metaphysics is as rigorous as the exact mathematical sciences seems almost as preposterous as the charge that it is utterly meaningless gibberish. Here we shall outline a more moderate defence of metaphysics or primary philosophy, abandoning the pretence that the propositions making up large-scale metaphysical theories are necessary truths capable of apodictic proof, but not the claim staked out in the last chapter, and reiterated in a much stronger form by Kant, that metaphysics has its own distinctive pattern of rationality.

First, a remark on the empiricist critique. On the face of it, 'God exists' or 'the soul is immortal' do not appear to have much in common with 'Caesar is a prime number'; nor are they much like expressions of some pious hope for personal salvation or some ultimate plan and purpose in the universe. In fact, on what seems the most reasonable interpretation, things stand quite otherwise: such statements may be false; that is, there may be no God, and we may face total extinction upon dying. But surely these sentences, and their denials, are meaningful statements that *might* at least be true, whether or not we can ever *know* their truth or falsity reliably.

We should perhaps add one slight qualification regarding 'God exists.' We shall see later that if taken to mean 'a necessary and eternal being (God) exists,' this may indeed be quite meaningless, a logical and metaphysical muddle; but since 'a necessary being' is neither what we usually mean by 'God,' nor the only thing the word 'God' can mean (nor the only thing it does mean in metaphysical contexts),

'God exists' apparently has a meaning. And as with this, so with other metaphysical claims: they pretty clearly are genuine statements, in some contexts at least, and neither meaningless pseudo-statements nor expressions of feeling.

A more promising line of defence than that boldly adopted by Kant is suggested by those champions of hypothetico-deductive method who insist that (c) verifiability (or falsifiability) is not a criterion of meaningfulness at all but of the scientific character of statements and theories. Following their lead, we can first sub-divide 4.1, statements that are factual, contingent, synthetic, and informative, into two classes:

4.1.1 observational statements (which are at least somewhat theory-laden); and
4.1.2 highly theoretical statements (with very little empirical content).

The latter can be divided again into:

4.1.2.1 scientific theories and
4.1.2.2 non-scientific theories.

The non-scientific may be pseudo-scientific, and certain of its detractors would no doubt want to place metaphysics here; yet it makes better sense to reserve a separate rubric for metaphysical statements and theories about the order of knowing and the order of being, sub-dividing as follows:

4.1.2.2.1 pseudo-scientific (alchemy, astrology, etc.);
4.1.2.2.2 metaphysical (theories concerning the order of knowing and being).

Even where metaphysical statements are pretty clearly incapable of ever becoming scientific, as when the whole order of knowing or being is in question, this may signify no more than that they belong to a revisable and controversial rather than apodictically necessary or empirically verifiable outer framework of very highly theoretical statements. Theories of this kind have played, and still play, an important role in mankind's gradual evolution toward a more rational basis for living; they sparked a progressive rationalization of religion itself, both in early Greek thought and in the encounter between the Christian religion and later Greek philosophy; and they have influenced, and continue to influence, the evolution of the modern scientific understanding of the world as well. Beyond this, they may have a completely autonomous role to fulfil in making ordinary experience more intelligible and transparent. If they fall outside the framework of both the exact mathematical and the empirical natural sciences, they may nonetheless have a distinctive rationality all their own, as Kant believed. That is the question that was addressed in the last chapter, and it will crop up again and again as we proceed.

7.6 Arguments and inferences

We revert now to strictly logical matters. Having dealt at length with propositions, which are the building blocks of arguments and inferences, we pass next to the consideration of arguments and inferences themselves. We begin again with some terminological matters.

7.6.1 Argument, inference, syllogism, and enthymeme

What is called a (logical) 'inference' in the context of discovery (discovering further truths on the basis of those already known) is also called an 'argument' in the context of proof (that is, attempting to demonstrate to others the truth of what one has discovered for oneself). So arguments and inferences are really the same thing looked at in two different ways.

An argument or inference consists of two or more propositions. Those consisting of only two propositions, a single premise and a conclusion drawn immediately from it, are *direct* inferences. For example, from (1) 'No Canadians are members' one can infer (2) 'No members are Canadians,' (3) 'All members are non-Canadians,' (4) 'All Canadians are non-members,' and so on. Or from 'p and x' ('p is true and x is true') we can infer p ('p is true') immediately (see 6.3.1). An inference that consists of two (or more) premises and a conclusion is an *indirect* inference. Both may be called 'deductions' or 'deductive' inferences (or reasonings). The immediate are sometimes described as 'discursive,' the mediate 'ratiocinative' (from the Latin *ratiocinare* 'to reason'). This distinction will prove important when we come to Descartes.

One variety of indirect inference that was exhaustively studied by Aristotle over 2000 years ago is called by the technical name 'syllogism.' Put very simply, a syllogism is an indirect inference involving three terms, one of which (the 'middle term') is employed in each of the two premises (the 'major' premise and the 'minor' premise), while the two others (the 'extremes') occur separately in the premises and together in the conclusion. Thus, in the time-hallowed textbook example of a syllogism,

P1 All men (that is, human beings) are mortal,
P2 All Greeks are men,
C Hence, all Greeks are mortal,

the middle term is 'men,' the extremes 'Greeks' and 'mortal,' while P1 and P2 are the major and minor premises, respectively.

As for direct inference, Aristotle catalogued the valid forms of such inference in what has come to be known as 'the 'traditional square of opposition' in a work entitled *de Interpretatione*. It is worth noting, though, that sometimes what looks like a direct inference may really be indirect because a further, tacit or unstated, premise is involved and necessary in order to make the argument go through. An argument that is stated incompletely, one or more premises being 'understood' rather than stated, is called an 'enthymeme' or an 'enthymematic argument.' For example, if someone argues that abortion is murder since murder is the taking of a human life and abortion is the taking of a human life, the suppressed premise is that a foetus is already a human being. This argument is really an enthymeme.

7.6.2 Validity and invalidity

Arguments are not true or false; it is rather the premises of arguments that are true or false. Arguments themselves are either good or bad arguments according as they are (a) either formally *valid* or *invalid* and (if valid) according as they are (b) either *sound* or *unsound*. Formally valid arguments may be rendered invalid owing to an informal flaw. We shall discuss four informal fallacies in 7.7, using our *ad hoc* selection criterion (see 7.1), though there are many other types of informal blunder. But first we must consider formal validity and soundness.

What formal validity is can be seen from the above example of a syllogism:

P1 All men are mortal.
P2 All Greeks are men.
C Hence, all Greeks are mortal.

'Validity' means that there is a *necessary logical connection* between the premises (P1 and P2) and the conclusion (C), such that *if* the premises are true, then the conclusion must be true too. This way of putting it makes it clear that *validity* does not depend on the *truth* of the constituent propositions. Another argument of the same form having false premises and a false conclusion is equally valid, for example:

P1 All birds are four-footed.
P2 All men are birds.
C Hence, all men are four-footed.

What is valid, then, is the *form*, irrespective of the truth or falsity of the constituent propositions ('the matter'). Hence the expression 'formal logic.' Even if one were ignorant of the meanings of the words 'Greek' 'men,' 'mortal,' 'bird,' 'four-footed,' and therefore in no position to judge whether the constituent propositions or premises of the argument are true, one could still see that the argument is valid by considering the form of the constituent propositions and the meaning of logical terms like 'all':

P1 All such-and-suches are so-and-so.

P2 All these are such-and-suches.
C Hence, all these are so-and-so.

Accordingly, one can have a valid argument whose premises are false and whose conclusion is true, for example:

P1 All cows are bipeds.
P2 All birds are cows.
C All birds are bipeds.

Or one can have an invalid argument all of whose premises and conclusion are perfectly true:

P1 All cows are quadrupeds
P2 All Holsteins are cows
C All Holsteins are black and white.

The point about the last example is that there is *no logical connection* between C and P1 and P2. That is what it means to say that this argument is invalid. In the example beginning with 'All birds are four-footed,' the argument is valid because *if* the premises were true (as they are not), then the conclusion would be true as well (as it is not).

In the light of the foregoing it appears that a valid deductive argument may be defined in any of several ways. For example, (1) a valid deductive argument is one in which the conclusion is implicitly contained in the premises. Or (2) a valid deductive argument is one in which the conclusion is logically connected with the premises in such a way that it cannot be false if they are true. Alternatively, we may say: (3) in the case of a valid deductive argument, to affirm the premises and deny the conclusion is to *contradict* oneself, that is, to both assert and deny the same thing. These are just different ways of describing the same feature of arguments.

7.6.3 Soundness and proof

An argument is 'sound' if and only if (a) it is (formally and informally) valid and (b) its premises are true. If either condition is not met, the argument fails to *prove* or establish its conclusion (it is 'non-probative,' as philosophers sometimes say).

Since anything less than soundness means that the argument is non-probative, it is above all soundness that counts in the context of proof. This means that arguments that claim to prove something must be examined both for the truth of their premises and for the validity of the inference involved, since only true premises together with a logically valid inference constitute proof.

7.7 Informal fallacies

As already noted, sometimes an argument that is formally valid can be rendered invalid by what is called an *in*formal fallacy. It is worth noting four such logical blunders, all of which are important for purposes of this book. Three of them go by Latin names: (1) *ad hominem* and *ad verecundiam* arguments, (2) circular arguments or *petitio principii*, (3) equivocations, and (4) *obscurum per obscurius*.

7.7.1 Ad hominem *and* ad verecundiam *arguments*

The Latin phrase *ad hominem* means literally addressed 'to' or 'against the man.' Instead of speaking to the issue, that is, rebutting the argument put forward by one's opponent, or criticizing the position he is defending, the disputant guilty of this blunder engages in irrelevant personal attack upon the individual advancing the argument or defending the position. Basically, the fault here is irrelevancy. The character or other attributes of a person has no bearing whatever on the truth of his premises or the validity of his argument.

An example of this fallacy occurs in the *Apology* where Socrates attacks Meletus personally for not caring about the youth of Athens instead of responding to the charge that he, Socrates, is corrupting the youth. (He does, of course, respond to it afterwards, so the aberration is temporary.)

In one respect the so-called argument from authority—Locke calls it an *argumentum ad verecundiam* (literally, 'an appeal to venerableness')—is just an *ad hominem* argument in reverse. As the latter sort of argument alleges deficiencies of intellect or character on the part of the speaker or writer, so the other appeals to the personal or intellectual eminence of those who hold a certain view. ('This view is held by many great philosophers' or 'by all the saints of the Church' or 'by Marx and Engels themselves,' and so on.) At bottom, however, both are just instances of the same irrelevancy. Presumably, the greatest fools and scoundrels may just happen to have hit upon the truth or devised a valid argument, much as the greatest geniuses and paragons of virtue can go wrong—sometimes very badly wrong—in their counsels and reasonings.

Before leaving this subject it is worth noting that one kind of *ad hominem* argument is not fallacious at all. We shall refer to this as 'an *ad hominem* argument in the good sense.' This sort of argument shows, not that a certain claim is false, but only that it has consequences that must be unwelcome for the particular individual who advances it (whence *ad hominem*). Provided the one who argues in this way does not think he has refuted the claim made rather than just confronted a specific advocate of the claim with a difficulty, there is nothing wrong with this; in fact, it is generally very useful.

7.7.2 Circular arguments

Circularity (also called 'begging the question' or by the Latin name *petitio principii*) is an interesting informal fallacy. The basic idea is that the argument assumes the very thing it is trying to establish. The underlying principle is the same in a number of different cases, namely: 'you cannot use x to establish x.' According as 'x' is either (1) a *faculty of the mind*, or (2) a particular *truth*, or (3) a *form of proof*, the specific charge of circularity differs.

The fallacy is most obvious in (1) attempts to establish the reliability of some faculty of the mind using that very faculty. Thus, it would be futile to try to establish the reliability of sense perception by means of observation, as it would be pointless to try to establish the reliability of reason by any process of reasoning.

The most common form of the fallacy, however, is (2) the attempt to establish the truth of a proposition by means of an argument in which that very proposition figures as a suppressed premise or assumption. To return to an earlier example, suppose I am arguing that abortion is murder, and suppose I make tacit use of the premise that the foetus is a human being (in embryonic form). If this is precisely the point that my opponent disputes, holding, for example, that it makes no sense to refer to a few clusters of cells attached to the uterus (the foetus shortly after conception) as 'a human being,' I am begging the question or arguing circularly.

Less common is (3) the attempt to establish the validity of a certain form of proof or principle of argument by means of an argument or proof that has that form or uses that principle. For example, to give a deductive proof that deduction is a valid way of deriving one truth from another would be circular. Similarly, to argue that generalizing induction from past experiences is reliable because it has always worked in the past would be using induction to validate induction. And that is circular.

Now that something has been said about circularity and logical consistency, it is possible to expand on the earlier observation (see 6.3.1) that it is hard to answer the question 'Why be rational?' The fact is that it is impossible to argue for or against rationality without falling into either inconsistency or circularity. Suppose one denies that people ought to be rational because, say, it interferes with spontaneity or with having a rich emotional life, or for some other reason. If one defends this position by giving *reasons* to accept it, then what one does (reasoning, giving reasons) is inconsistent with what one says (rejecting reasoning or the giving of reasons). Hence, we have a contradiction. Suppose, however, one takes the view that everyone ought to strive to be rational as far as possible. Then if one actually defends this view by giving reasons or rational arguments in support of it, one is taking for granted the very thing one's opponent denies and thus is arguing circularly. There is a striking example of exactly this problem at the heart of the philosophy of Descartes, as will be seen in Part Three (see chap. 25).

Another instance of arguing in a circle is the attempt to refute the complete sceptical relativist (see 6.3.1). How is one to argue that the relativist's view is false without taking for granted the very notion of non-relative truth that one's opponent denies? On the other hand, how is the relativist to argue that he is correct in thinking that there simply is no such thing as truth without taking for granted the very thing he denies, that is, contradicting himself?

Sometimes arguments that lead to an infinite regress, that is, a reiteration of the same problem at the next level, and so on, level after level, are called 'circular.' They keep confronting us with the same problem over and over again, getting us nowhere, or rather, getting us right back where we started from. This is circular, although this is a distinctive type of circularity for which the designation 'infinite regress' is probably better, since it avoids confusion with the other types just considered.

Explanations, too, can be circular. Any explanation that identifies a cause belonging to the same order of events as the effect it explains just pushes the causal explanation back one step, leaving us with the same type of question from which we began. This, too, is sometimes called an infinite regress—unless we can arrive at a cause that is of an entirely different order such that it no longer makes sense to ask, What caused it? Here we see an important consideration behind all arguments to the existence of a 'first cause' belonging to an entirely different order of being. Without such a cause, no genuine (non-circular) or complete explanation is possible.

A related though different intellectual misdemeanour worth mentioning here is circularity in definitions rather than arguments or explanations: defining a term using in the definition the very term being defined. This obviously gets us nowhere, since unless we already understand the term being defined, we cannot understand the definition itself. We shall see a stunning example of this fallacy in the Platonic dialogue *Meno*. Definitions are the subject of section 7.13.

7.7.3 The 'hermeneutical circle'

In contexts other than those of *argument and proof*—and this may include many types of analysis and understanding—it is not always a flaw to start out from the point we want to end up at. Sometimes, in fact, it is unavoidable, and we may return to our starting point with a deepened understanding of the truth we started out from. If so, something has been accomplished, real progress has been made, and there is nothing 'vicious' or 'vitiating' about our choice of a starting point. (*Vitium* is a Latin word meaning 'defect' or 'flaw,' even 'sin' in some contexts.)

An example of this might be reading a text—whether a philosophical text or a literary work—with a certain interpretation in mind, certain assumptions or preconceptions, that is, about what the author is trying to say. This, it has been argued, is not an obstacle to, but a necessary prerequisite for, successful understanding and interpretation. Provided we are willing to revise our assumptions in the light of what we actually encounter in the text itself, there is nothing vicious about this procedure. The notion of a non-vicious circle may be applicable to the hypothetico-deductive method itself. After all, on this view of science, the enquirer must take for granted certain things, make various theoretical assumptions, in other words, in order to test his theories against the facts afterwards. But as was noted earlier (see 6.2.3), there may just be no such thing as facts, absolutely speaking—that is, facts independent of the theories being tested. So there is a kind of circularity here. But is it vicious? Apparently not, if this is indeed the procedure to which progress in science is owing.

The circularity of interpretation, incidentally, is sometimes referred to as 'the hermeneutical circle' (from the Greek *hermeneuein*, to understand, make understandable). If we move from the context of analysis, understanding, and interpretation to that of *argument* or *definition*, however, circularity becomes *vicious* (a fallacy or flaw). An argument or definition really proves or accomplishes nothing when it *assumes* the very thing at issue.

7.7.4 Fallacy of equivocation

So far we have dealt with irrelevancy and circularity. The fallacy of equivocation is a third type of informal fallacy. It consists in using the same term in different senses in different premises of the argument. This invalidates (or vitiates) the argument. Consider the following textbook example:

P1   The end of a thing is its perfection.
P2   The end of life is death.
C   Therefore death is the perfection of life.

Obviously, this is a formally valid argument of the form

P1   All e's are p's.
P2   d is an e.
C   Therefore d is a p.

But 'end' in P1 means 'goal,' while in P2 it means 'last event.' There is an equivocation that makes the argument worthless. And so too with any deductive argument in which either the middle term or the extremes occur in different senses.

7.7.5 Obscurum per obscurius

The last sort of informal fallacy to be considered is a fault met with in certain theories or explanations rather than arguments, so it is not often included among informal fallacies in treatments of the subject in logic textbooks. Still, since it shows a proposed explanation to be worthless on informal grounds, it may be included here, not least because we shall later encounter a few arguments of this very sort.

The basic idea of this reproach is somewhat like the charge of circularity brought against definitions and arguments. If one takes for granted the point to be proved, or the intelligibility of the term to be defined, one's proof or definition is worthless. Now the same is true of an explanation in which the *explanans*, the part that does the explanatory work, is harder to understand than the original phenomenon one is trying to explain, the *explanandum*, as it is called. Proceeding thus, one explains something that we understand only inadequately by means of something that we understand *even less*, perhaps *not at all*.

For example, to explain all manner of extraordinary occurrences through the intervention of supernatural powers in the course of human affairs or in the sequence of natural events is to explain something that is obscure by reference to something that is even more obscure: *obscurum per obscurius* ('the obscure through the more obscure') in Latin. At the level of definitions, a parallel would be defining a word whose meaning is difficult to grasp in terms of others that are more difficult still. This explains nothing.

7.7.6 Fallacy and falsity

Not every intellectual error is a fallacy, though we often say 'that's a fallacy' when we mean 'that's not true.' Strictly, only formally or informally invalid inferences or arguments are fallacies ('formal fallacies' and 'informal fallacies,' respectively).'That's false,' or 'a falsehood' can be correctly said, not of an argument, but at most of a *premise* in an argument, that is, *a proposition*. As we saw earlier, if the argument contains a false premise, then, although valid, it is unsound. So we must add 'fallacy' to the list of words, including 'proposition' and 'factual,' whose meanings differ in logic and ordinary usage (see 7.3–4).

7.8 Implication, entailment, and consistency

Logic is concerned with arguments and so with the *relations* among *propositions*, that is, with what is consistent or inconsistent with what; what entails or implies what; what follows from or is presupposed by what. Thus, when we say of any set of propositions that one entails or is inconsistent with (entails the negation of) another, or that two together, if true, entail the truth (or falsity) of a third, we are engaging in logical analysis, that is, clarifying the logic of the situation. This is a different matter from determining which propositions are in fact true or false. Logical analysis is concerned with matters like: *if p is true, then q* must be true, or must be false, or may still be either true or false (since p and q are logically unrelated), and so on. *Whether p is in fact true* is not a matter of logic; even if p is a logical truism, that particular feature of *p* is not relevant to the consideration of what exactly *follows* from its truth—though if it is a necessary truth, then so is anything that follows from it in logic.

Alternatively, we can describe logic as concerned with the relations of *implication or entailment or consistency* among propositions, or as concerned with the forms of valid logical derivation. This underscores an important point noted earlier, namely, that logic as a formal discipline concerns itself only with the forms of propositions, that is, with laws according to which a proposition or propositions having a certain *form* determine(s) the truth of a proposition or propositions having a certain other form, *no matter what the content of the propositions*. For this reason, as was pointed out earlier, we speak of 'formal logic.'

Given that logic is concerned with relations of entailment, consistency, and inconsistency among propositions having certain forms, and given that there are other conditions of truth and other paradigms of rationality besides consistency, logic cannot be the ultimate arbiter of either truth or rationality (reasonableness). Nevertheless, anything that does not satisfy the demand for logical consistency may be regarded as containing a falsehood and its acceptance as irrational. So logical consistency is a minimal requirement, a necessary condition of truth and rational acceptance, but not sufficient in and of itself. Kant hit this point off nicely when he maintained that the laws or principles of logic provide only a "negative condition of all truth," that is, the necessary conditions of thought in general, the conditions of logical consistency in thinking about anything whatever. Since all representing or thinking is necessarily thinking *of something*, an object, if we distinguish (1) representing an object in some manner or other from (2) representing or thinking an object in a logically consistent manner and (3) representing an object truly, as it really is, then the principles of logic form no more than a negative criterion of truth understood as the *agreement* of thought with its object. To represent an object truly, we must at least represent it and represent it consistently, but that is not enough; more is required for truth. That is Kant's point. And, we may add, more is required for rational acceptance of an alleged truth.

7.8.1 Circularity of valid deductive arguments and vicious circularity

Since *by definition* its conclusion is contained in its premises, a valid deductive argument tells us no more than we already know. (See the first of the definitions of 'valid deductive argument' given at the end of 7.6.2 above.) Take, for example, the following valid deductive argument:

P1 All men are mortal.
P2 Socrates is a man.
C Therefore Socrates is mortal.

One might object that in order to assert the major premise, '*All* men are mortal,' one would have to know the conclusion, that *Socrates* is mortal, already; for Socrates is a man and one cannot assert that *all* men are mortal without taking Socrates's mortality for granted. So the whole argument is circular.

This is clearly correct: all deductive arguments are circular. Still, deductive arguments do help to make clear the implications of the propositions we assert, implications not always seen at first glance. Their use in mathematics, in a context of discovery, helps us to see implications of our definitions and axioms that one could not easily recognize without such (sometimes long and complicated) reasoning processes. Using those definitions and axioms, together with such propositions or theorems as we have already been able to derive from them, we carry on deducing more and more theorems. This is circular in one sense, but not vicious circularity, since it really leads to the discovery of genuinely *new* knowledge. (A vicious circle occurs, when instead of establishing the conclusion by inference from *agreed upon* or *self-evident* premises, as in mathematics, we take for granted something that is contested, thus begging the question. See 7.7.2 above.) Even outside mathematics, deductive reasoning may serve to bring out the order and connections among items of knowledge whose logical relations we were not aware of. Its usefulness *in the context of discovery* is not impaired by the charge of circularity to which it is open *in the context of proof*. So it is perhaps not entirely fair to say, as has one contemporary philosopher, that the "appearance of genuine novelty in deductive inference is only psychological, because it is due to our incapacity to comprehend in one flash of insight the implications of more complicated sets of premises."

7.8.2 *The reversibility of valid deductive arguments*

As noted earlier, hypothetico-deductive method is essentially a method of theory testing. It allows us to assert that a given theoretical statement, t, is false if we accept the truth of certain uncontroversial statements q and r, along with that of certain simple observation statements, o^1, o^2, and so on, garnered, say, from experiments. For if t together with these uncontroversial statements entails the negation of any of those observation statements, then the truth of the latter logically entails the falsity of t (or of one of those other statements uncontroversially assumed to be true).

This inference is possible because deduction itself is reversible. One usually argues from the truth of the premises of a valid deductive argument to the truth of its conclusion; but one can just as well argue from the manifest falsity of the conclusion to the falsity of at least one of the premises (since, by definition, it cannot be the case for any valid deductive argument that the premises are true and the conclusion is false). Take, as an example, what has been called 'the detective's syllogism':

P1   The robbery was not an 'inside job' (that is, nobody let the robbers in).

P2 The doors and windows are the only means of access.
C   Either a door or a window will be found to have been forced open.

If, upon examining the doors and windows, it is found that they have not been forced, one may validly infer that either P1 or P2 is false, that is, that somebody on the inside helped (say, provided a key or left a window unlocked) *or* that there is another way of getting in. These 'hypotheses' ('it was an inside job,' 'there's another way in') must then be examined to determine which is the correct explanation.

This should help to explain why we said in the last chapter that the scientist who employs the hypothetico-deductive method is like a detective (see 6.3.3).

7.9 *Modus ponens* and *modus tollens*

Several arguments to be considered in this work, particularly in the parts on Plato and Descartes, can be formalized as deductive arguments with simple premises. Yet some deductive arguments are not syllogisms but have complex premises called 'hypotheticals' or 'conditionals,' that is, 'if ... then' sentences. Here are two forms of argument that we shall encounter in our study of Plato:

modus ponens ('positing mode')   *modus tollens* ('taking-away mode')

P1 If p, then q.   P1 If p, then q.
P2 p.   P2 not q.
C   Therefore q.   C   Therefore not p.

The hypothetical proposition forming P1 consists of an antecedent, p, and a consequent, q. In P2 of *modus ponens* the antecedent is affirmed as true. In P2 of *modus tollens* the consequent is denied. These are formally valid arguments, that is, the conclusion, C, follows from the premises.

Examples are, first: If Socrates is a man, then he is mortal. But Socrates is a man. Therefore, Socrates is mortal. This is just our earlier example of a valid deductive argument cast in *modus ponens* form. As an example of *modus tollens*, take the following argument: If it was not an inside job, then either the doors or the windows will have been forced. But neither the doors nor the windows have been forced. Therefore, it was an inside job.

Corresponding to these valid forms of argument are two formally invalid or logically fallacious arguments (or simply: 'fallacies') called 'the fallacy of denying the antecedent' and 'the fallacy of affirming the consequent,' respectively. For example:

P1 If p, then q.   P1 If p, then q.

P2 But not *p*. P2 But *q*.
C Therefore not *q*. C Therefore *p*.

Consider the following concrete examples. First, the fallacy of denying the antecedent: If the Minotaur is a man, then he is mortal. But the Minotaur is not a man. Therefore, he is not mortal. Obviously the Minotaur could perfectly well be mortal without being a man since men are not the only living things that die. So the argument is invalid. Next, an example of affirming the consequent: If it is not an inside job, then either the doors or the windows will have been forced. But the door has been forced. Therefore, it wasn't an inside job. Obviously, the detective who reasons this way may have been given a false scent by the insider who pulled the job. Both arguments or argument patterns are obviously fallacious. To see exactly why these are fallacies, we have only to consider the meaning of P1, which is the same in both cases.

P1 states a relation between *p* and *q*. This relation, called 'logical implication' or 'entailment,' can be put this way: '*If p* is true, then *q* is true' just *means* 'It is logically impossible that *p* is true *and q* false.' So P1 tells us something about the truth-value of *q* (that it must be true) *if p* is true. P1 further tells us something about the truth-value of *p* (namely, that it cannot be true) *if q* is false. But P1 tells us *nothing* whatever about the truth-value of *q* if *p* is *false*, or about the truth-value of *p* if *q* is *true*. So nothing can be *validly* inferred from P1 and the falsity of *p*, or from P1 and the truth of *q*.

If someone were to ask why these argument forms are valid, or how we know they are, it would be difficult to provide an answer. The question seems to require an answer in terms of something simpler than inference itself. But what could be simpler than this: 'If *p* (is true), and if *p* cannot be true and *q* false, then *q* (is true too)'? Or: 'If not *q* (*q* is not true), and if *p* cannot be true while *q* is false, then not *p* (*p* is not true) either'? There just is no more rational procedure than reasoning in this way—unless it is simply avoiding contradiction (avoiding saying anything that could be formalized as '*p* and not-*p*'). Clearly, we are very close to a *basic* rational procedure here, as in the other forms of deductive inference.

7.10 Contraries and contradictories

We have repeatedly mentioned contradictions and avoidance of contradiction (that is, of asserting and denying the very same thing). By definition, two propositions or statements are contradictories if and only if their meaning is such that exactly one is true and one is false (that is, they cannot both be true and they cannot both be false). But not only propositions or statements may be contradictories; terms or concepts may be contradictories as well, so that both in philosophy and in everyday speech it is not uncommon to speak of 'a contradiction in terms.' Examples of this are 'a round square' or 'a female brother.' Such terms or concepts are considered as predicates designating properties. But whether we have in view an opposition between propositions, on the one hand, or between terms, concepts, predicates, or properties, on the other, we must distinguish two kinds of opposites: contradictories and contraries. (There are other kinds of opposites, but these are the most important for our purposes.)

We have already defined *contradictory opposites* (or 'contradictories') in the case of propositions; as for terms or concepts, contradictories are, for example, 'large' and 'not large,' 'red' and 'not red,' or, generally, 'x' and 'not-x' (where x stands for any term). The distinctive thing about contradictories, when speaking of predicates, is again that while they cannot both be truthfully asserted of the same thing, both assertions cannot be false either. Speaking of its properties, we cannot say that a thing is both red and not red (both these properties cannot belong to it at the same time and in the same way), nor can it be said to be neither red nor not red.

By contrast, *contrary opposites* (or 'contraries') are terms like 'large' and 'small,' 'beautiful' and 'ugly,' 'red' and 'blue,' or generally, x and y. While such opposites as these cannot both be true of the same thing (at the same time and in the same respect), they *can* both be false, that is, a thing can be neither red nor blue—for example, a yellow thing is neither red nor blue: *both* contraries are accordingly falsely asserted of the thing. Similarly, a person may be neither beautiful nor ugly but, say, 'average looking'; or an object can be neither 'large' nor 'small' but 'middle-sized.'

These, then, are contrary opposites, while 'beautiful' and 'not-beautiful' are contradictory opposites, since an average-looking person is still 'not-beautiful.' Likewise, moral and non-moral are contradictory opposites, since every deed must (logically) be one or the other, the pair covering good, bad, and indifferent actions alike; on the other hand, not every deed is moral or *im*moral, since some are morally indifferent.

As we distinguish contraries from contradictories in speaking of opposites on the level of terms or concepts, so too in the case of propositions. A pair of contrary propositions cannot both be true, but unlike contradictory propositions, they *can* both be false. For example, 'all things are red' and 'no things are red' are contraries, not contradictories: they cannot both be true, but they can be (and are) both false.

7.11 The logic of ordinary language

Not all logic deals with artificial languages constructed with invented symbolisms like p and q (any propositions), and logical operators like v (or), • (and), ⊃ (entails), ~ (not), and so on. (There are other logical symbols in use, even for the same operations; these are only illustrations.) The language we speak every day has its own logic. That is, certain things logically entail, presuppose, are logically consistent or inconsistent with certain others in our ordinary use of English, and so too in the case of all other languages.

For example, if I say: (1) 'Vanessa is divorced,' this logically entails the proposition: (2) 'Vanessa was in the past married.' In other words, to assert (1) and deny (2) is to *contradict oneself*; it is *logically* inconsistent. It is part of the *logic* of the word 'divorced' that (1) entails (2) for any person 'A.' Similarly, saying: (1) 'A remembers (or recollects, is reminded of) x by y' logically entails certain things, for example, that what A now recollects was known to him before, but also that he forgot about it, and so on. Otherwise 'remember' or 'recollect' would not be the right word. Plato provides a remarkable example of such logical analysis in his Recollection Argument for the immortality of the soul in the dialogue *Phaedo* (see 18.2).

7.12 Meaning

The connection of questions of meaning or semantics with what has been said already about inference and argument is this: working out the logical implications of the use of a certain word in ordinary language is the same as spelling out all that the word actually means. Of course, there is also the other question: not what a given statement means exactly, but whether it has any meaning at all. That question arose in the context of the classification of sentences above. But 'meaning' is an elusive concept, and we must now try to disengage some of the many meanings of 'meaning.'

7.12.1 Preliminary note on single quotation marks

In the immediately preceding sentence the word 'meaning' occurs twice with single quotation marks around it and once without. Why?

Single quotation marks are sometimes used as so-called scare quotes to mark an unusual or a borrowed expression, a hackneyed phrase (cliché), a buzzword, a colloquialism, or the like. For example, philosophy is not 'relevant' or 'with it.' In the first case, the single quotation marks indicate that the speaker is aware that 'relevant' is an expression that is thoughtlessly overused nowadays; in the second, he indicates that the expression used is slang, too colloquial for the context. The expression 'disclaimer quotes' is sometimes used as well. The idea is that the author wants to alert the reader to his own misgivings about a particular use of a word, to disclaim belief that it is entirely—or at all—suitable.

Sometimes single quotation marks are used as what are called 'sneer quotes,' for example: he is very 'successful' but totally unprincipled. Here the single quotes indicate that the speaker has low regard for success achieved by unscrupulous means. Sometimes sneer quotes are downright nasty. For example, if a reviewer writes that the 'intellectuals' will like a certain 'arty' film that he himself considers rubbish, he is just taking a swipe at the intelligentsia or the university crowd.

But in philosophy single quotes are used mainly to signify that we are talking about *words* rather than *things*. Compare, for example, these two sentences:

(1) Horses are four-legged animals.
(2) 'Horses' is a six-letter word.

Clearly, the first is about horses, those noble four-legged beasts, while the second is about the English word applied to them. The distinction in question is sometimes referred to as 'the use-mention distinction.' In the first sentence, the word 'horses' is being used to say something about horses; in the second, it is not used at all but only mentioned.

The distinction is an important one. Throughout this work, terms that are mentioned will be (and have been up to this point) enclosed within single quotation marks. Double quotation marks indicate quoted material. There will also be plenty of disclaimer quotes.

7.12.2 Meaning: sense and reference

The word 'meaning' is ambiguous in English. The meaning of a word may be: (1) the (set of) object(s) to which it may be correctly applied, for example, the general term 'planet' means (in this first sense): Mercury, Venus, Saturn, Jupiter, Earth, and so on; or (2) the property, or set of properties, common to all the objects to which a term is correctly applied, that is, the relevant class-defining characteristics. For example, 'planet' means (in this second sense) 'any body in interstellar space, having a certain size, a certain type of orbit,' and so on. That is what all planets have in common and what distinguishes them from stars and other heavenly bodies.

(1) is called the 'extension,' 'extensional meaning,' 'reference,' or the 'denotation' of the general term (the set of things it can be applied to, which may contain only one member or be an empty set); in the case of a proper name that applies to only a single thing, logicians speak of the 'referent' or 'nominatum' or 'designatum' (the entity designated). (2) is called the 'intension,' 'intensional meaning,' 'sense,' or 'connotation(s)' of the general or abstract term. All words that do not name and are not simply gibberish have some connotations, though their *exact* connotations may be hard to determine. Instead of 'denoting' or 'referring,' philosophers may speak of 'signifying' or 'naming.' Since too many different ways of drawing the same distinction can become confusing, it may be best to stick to sense and reference wherever possible.

Now (1) and (2) correspond roughly to the distinction between *giving examples* (from among the things belonging to the extension of a term) and *giving a definition* (of the term itself, that is, its key connotations). Socrates, as we shall see, was always on the lookout for definitions, for the intensional meaning of the specifically moral terms he asked about. He could not be put off with examples of things these words are correctly applied to.

More will be said about Socratic definitions, and about the other kinds of definitions distinguished by philosophers, in the immediately following section. Right now it is worth noting four points concerning the two meanings of 'meaning' just distinguished, 'sense' and 'reference.' First,

(a) a term may have a sense, but no referent.

Examples are 'unicorn,' 'satyr,' 'golden mountain,' 'ghosts,' 'goblins,' 'gremlins,' and, some would say, 'God.' I understand perfectly well what 'ghost' means (the sense of the word), yet I am convinced that there are just no such things. So 'ghosts' has a sense but no referent. Furthermore,

(b) terms that have different referents must also have different senses.

If two words really refer to different sets of things, then this fact can only be accounted for by some difference, however slight, in their senses. Thus, if someone refuses to go along with your inclusion of a certain female rock star in a list of divas, it is quite possible that the two of you agree about the meaning of 'diva' but disagree about that female rock star's talents. In that case the sense is not in dispute, only the reference is. But the disagreement may be owing to a disagreement about the sense of the word 'diva' too. For your friend the term may include the connotation of a certain classical repertoire—which rather lets our lovely rock star out. In any case, if your way of using the term includes and his excludes her, the two uses must involve different senses of the same term. And so too with the use of different words: if their referents really are different, so must their senses be. In addition,

(c) terms that have the same sense must also have exactly the same referent(s) (if any).

This, too, is obvious. If two words are perfectly synonymous, they will be applicable to exactly the same class of things. Take synonyms like 'man' (in the generic sense) and 'human being,' 'engine' and 'motor,' 'automobile' and 'car,' for example. These are just different words for exactly the same objects. Finally,

(d) terms may have different senses but the same referent.

There are two famous examples of (d) as applied to proper names, furnished by two equally famous twentieth-century logicians, Gottlob Frege (1848–1925) and Bertrand Russell. The first is 'the morning star' and 'the evening star,' the second 'Scott' and 'the author of the Waverley novels.' The two names cited by Frege obviously have quite different senses, but both refer to the planet Venus, just as Russell's two expressions both refer to the same Sir Walter. Yet it is not enough simply to understand the meanings of the two expressions 'morning star' and 'evening star' in order to know that they refer to one and the same entity; one needs some knowledge of astronomy as well. In Russell's famous example, some knowledge of literary history is required.

Or take, as a further example, a general term designating a class of abstract entities, 'a figure bounded by three straight lines' and 'a plane figure whose internal angles equal two right angles.' These expressions have exactly the same referents (namely, the set of all triangles), yet different senses. You need to know a little geometry to recognize that their referents are the same. Or consider another pair of names: 'the city adjacent to Hull' and 'the seat of the Canadian Parliament.' It is not sufficient to understand the senses of these two expressions to know that they have the same referent, the city of Ottawa; some geopolitical knowledge of Canada is required as well. One final example goes back to Aristotle. Take two general expressions for a class of concrete entities: 'creature with a heart' and 'creature with kidneys.' These expressions apply to exactly the same set of animals, though it takes a little knowledge of biology to grasp that this is so. Just knowing what the expressions mean (their connotations) is not enough. After all, it is no more difficult to conceive of creatures with hearts but without kidneys than of creatures (like fish) with hearts but without lungs. On the other hand, it *is* enough to understand what the expressions 'mother' and 'female parent' mean in standard English to know that they denote or refer to precisely the same set of individuals. Similarly, it is enough to know the meaning of 'triangular figure' and 'trilateral figure' to know that they apply to exactly the same set of geometrical figures—you need a certain command of language, but no knowledge of geometry.

Thus we can say that in the case of all words having the identical referent, if the sameness of referent *cannot* be determined just on the basis of their connotations, on the basis of word meanings alone, then their connotations or senses are *different*, even though their referents are *the same*.

Based on these considerations we can formulate some possible rules of inference from one kind of meaning to another and assess their validity:

1 Same sense, therefore same referent.

This inference is valid. As we saw under (c), if two words have exactly the same connotations, they must both be applicable to exactly the same set of things (if any).

2 Different referents, therefore different senses.

This too is valid for the reasons given under (b) above.

3 Same referent, therefore same sense.

This inference is *not* valid. As we saw in connection with (d), words with quite different senses may refer to the same thing(s), for example, 'morning star' and 'evening star,' or they may not; so we cannot validly infer sameness of sense from sameness of reference.

4 Different sense, therefore different referent(s).

As we also saw under (d) above, we cannot infer difference of reference from difference of sense either. This is again invalid.

These rules will prove useful when we come to examine one of Plato's arguments for the existence of entities called 'Forms' in chapter 20.

7.13 Definitions

One further bit of logical theory will stand us in good stead later, an outline of the theory of definitions. Traditionally, definitions are regarded as of two kinds, verbal or real. The verbal have only to do with words, the real with non-linguistic reality (things, Latin *res*) as well. What we define are, of course, words, not things; but real definitions express in words the essence or nature of possibly or actually existing things. Not all philosophers are satisfied with this traditional division, and we shall consider later the means by which some attempt to eliminate real essences and real definitions altogether (see 21.3.2).

Verbal definitions are either lexical, stipulative, or operational, while the real are either ostensive or essential definitions. More will be said of real definitions in a moment. We begin with verbal definitions, distinguishing the three different kinds just mentioned.

7.13.1 Verbal definitions

Those verbal definitions called 'lexical' (sometimes also 'reportive') are just our ordinary dictionary definitions as compiled by groups of social scientists called 'lexicographers.' Definitions of this kind merely record the actual (or preferred or correct) usage of words by providing a list of acceptable synonyms or defining phrases.

Sometimes, however, we introduce new terms or symbols into our language, or use already existing terms or symbols in new or special ways. These are called 'stipulative definitions.' They typically begin: 'Let (the word or symbol) x mean (stand for) ...' or 'By x I (we) mean ...' Here there is no question of right or wrong, as in the case of reportive definitions; the writer simply lays it down by fiat that a certain word or expression will be used in a certain way, that is, *stipulates* how it is to be understood (regardless of how it is ordinarily understood). About this the writer obviously cannot be mistaken. The new term (or new use of an old term) introduced in a stipulative definition may be selected (1) more or less arbitrarily, that is, for no particular reason at all, or (2) as a matter of personal preference. Alternatively, it may be introduced (3) for the sake of convenience, say, for purposes of abbreviation or avoidance of cumbersome locutions. Finally, (4) it may *have* to be introduced owing to some lack in the existing language, which offers us no ready-made means of expressing what the writer wishes to say—for example, when scientific or technological advances lead to the positing of a new type of entity or the invention of a new sort of device, for example, 'quark,' 'laptop,' and technical terms of that sort.

Operational definitions form a third class of verbal definitions. The speed of a moving object may be determinable (at least very roughly) using a yardstick and a stopwatch. (There are obviously more accurate measuring devices, but that is unimportant in the present context.) The intelligence quotient of a child can be determined by means of testing procedures (for example, the Stanford-Binet test). Here a simple arithmetical operation (distance divided by time, intellectual age divided by chronological age) is used to define the physical concept 'speed' or the psychological concept 'intelligence.' These definitions specify certain *mensurational and mathematical operations* to be performed. Similarly, the linear expansion of a mercury column in a glass tube forms the basis of an operational definition of temperature. What is temperature? Well, it is just the value that an observer reads on a correctly calibrated tube of mercury or on the dial attached to a certain sort of device. That is an operational definition of 'temperature.'

Scientists are very fond of operational definitions. Ask a physicist what an electron is, or what the word 'electron' means, and he will likely tell you how to measure the energy an electron emits, adding something to the effect that the word 'electron' just means 'whatever it is that produces a measurable quantity of energy in those circumstances.' As to *what* exactly it is that does so, the scientist will probably say he neither knows nor cares so long he knows how to measure it, that is, as long as he can define his terms *operationally*. Thus, the scientist is perfectly aware that in defining his terms operationally he is giving a merely *verbal* definition. He probably prides himself on avoiding metaphysical statements about what electrons 'really' are, their essence. This sort of anti-metaphysical attitude is very common nowadays, both among scientists and scientifically minded philosophers. It is probably fair to say that it is a widespread bias.

7.13.2 Real definitions

The preceding are varieties of verbal definition. The two types of definition to be discussed next are both non-verbal or real: ostensive and essential definitions. Again, to say that they are 'non-verbal' is just to say that they involve a reference to non-linguistic reality, to real things in the world, actual or possible.

We define words ostensively (from the Latin *ostendere* 'to point') by pointing out the thing or things to which they apply. The correct use of a proper name is defined ostensively by confronting the learner with (a picture of) the thing or person to which or to whom it applies. In the case of general names, a certain amount of practice may be required. In science, words like 'red,' 'light,' 'heat,' or 'pleasure,' for example, may be defined operationally, but the usual way of explaining their meaning is by calling attention to something within the hearer's inner or outer experience. How else would one bring a foreigner or a child to use 'red' in a way that discriminates between, say, 'red,' 'burgundy,' 'ochre,' 'magenta,' 'scarlet,' and the like? If someone were in doubt as to whether this burgundy belt is red, the only way to make the difference clear is by using examples. This is the way children first learn the meanings of colour words, and they can hardly be explained satisfactorily any other way. One could not explain them at all to a person blind from birth.

The word 'red,' then, is a case of definition where the giving of examples is entirely appropriate. This type of definition is important because it is by this means that we give a host of ordinary words reference to the real or extra-linguistic world. We might define one word, say, 'apple,' in terms of other simpler or more general terms (including 'fruit,' 'reddish,' and 'roundish'), but ultimately the simple terms of our definition would have to be defined ostensively in order to make our language 'connect' either with *outer* experience of things in the world, in the case of words like 'red,' for example, or with *inner* experience of psychic states for all such words as 'anger,' 'love,' 'hate,' 'perception,' and so on.

Verbal—lexical, stipulative, and operational—definitions (from the Latin *verbum* 'word') can also be called 'word' or 'nominal' definitions (from the Latin *nomen* 'word' or 'noun'). Opposed to these are not only ostensive but also another variety of real definitions that we shall dub 'Socratic definitions.' When Socrates asks for the definition of a term ('What is x'?), he is asking neither how most or all people habitually use it (that is, for a lexical definition), nor how a particular individual wishes it to be understood (a stipulative definition), nor for an example (an ostensive definition). The last point is particularly clear from the treatment given those who proffer examples in response to the request for a definition. Socrates applies a gentle therapy designed to cure them of the misconception that examples are wanted. For Socrates, the correct definition of a term reveals something about non-linguistic reality, about the nature or essence of all those real things to which the word is correctly applied.

Of course, Socratic definitions, like all definitions, employ a form of words or a defining formula. Are Socratic definitions therefore only verbal definitions after all? To avoid confusion on this point, we have to distinguish *what* is defined from the *means by which* it is defined. Like lexical and stipulative nominal definitions, Socratic definitions employ a linguistic formula (rather than, say, pointing or performing a certain operation) as a *device* of defining a word. But unlike verbal definitions properly so called, *what* they define is not *only* a word or term; the definition describes in words *the essence or nature* of a class of things, something that belongs to those things as they exist in the real world—or at least would belong to them necessarily if they did exist in the real world. So the real definitions in question are descriptions *in words* of the *essence* of a certain class of actual or possible things or persons or actions.

The essence can be understood provisionally as a property (or set of properties) that (i) is *distinctive* of a certain class of things, belonging to that class alone, and that (ii) *makes* those things the very sort of things they are. As already noted, a lot of philosophers as well as scientists nowadays are very wary of Socratic definitions and essences. That is a debate that cannot be pursued any further here, though we have already taken it up in chapter 3 and shall do so again in chapter 21.

7.14 Predicates and predication

To conclude this survey, one last bit of logical theory will prepare us for our study of Socrates and Descartes. The notion of a predicate—'*Y*' in the sentence '*X* is *Y*'—is familiar enough from English grammar, but there are certain types of predicate and predication that are of interest primarily to logicians rather than grammarians. The relevant distinctions are, first of all, between accidental and essential predication, and then among various types of essential predication, particularly the distinction between a defining characteristic and a mere *proprium*. For when Socrates does not get mere examples in lieu of the sought-after real definitions of moral virtues, it is a *proprium* that he gets instead—or so at least on one occasion that will occupy us in chapter 11. Still, some interpreters take that *proprium* for a universal accident, and not without reason, as we shall see, if we pause to consider the differences between (a) definition, (b) genus, (c) *proprium*, and (d) accident. For sometimes a *proprium* is hard to distinguish from what has been called (by the British philosopher William Kneale) "an accident on a cosmic scale."

According to a doctrine of classification dating from the third century AD, with roots in Aristotle's *Topics*, a proposition of the form '*X* is *Y*' that states (a) the definition of something must be distinguished from one that merely states (b) the genus to which *X* belongs. Let us assume, for purposes of illustration, that the classic scholastic formula *animal rationale*, 'a rational animal,' is the correct definition of 'man.' (We shall return to this famous scholastic definition in a number of later contexts. See 18.2 and 24.6.1.) If this is the correct definition, then 'man is an animal' does no more than indicate the genus to which all men belong, and is not a definition. Of course, 'man is an animal' is not only true but *necessarily and universally* true, like the definition. So it too is a kind of essential predication, possessing what is called 'strict' (universal *and necessary*) as opposed to merely 'comparative' universality (more or less general or universal, but not necessarily so). However, the specific type of universality in (b) is different from that of (a). For while the predicate belongs universally and necessarily to the subject in both cases, the converse is true only of definitions: all men are rational animals *and* all rational animals are men; whereas *not* all animals are men, even though all men are animals. So the predicate of a definition has a special kind of universality that is lacking in the other type of '*X* is *Y*' statement under consideration, a statement of the genus. (a) sets out something that not only (i) applies to all men, but (ii) is distinctive of them alone; (b) applies just as universally, but is not distinctive.

Both types of '*X* is *Y*' statements considered so far differ from a third type of essential predication in which *Y* is what (on the doctrine under consideration) is called (c) a 'property' or, technically, a *proprium*, the Latin word for 'property.' Take, for example, the stock illustrations 'Man is a featherless biped' or 'Man is capable of learning grammar,' or 'Man is capable of laughter.' Here the predicate *Y* is again *universal*. It may or may not belong *necessarily* to the subject, however; it is hard to tell in such cases. We are inclined to say that it depends on what one means by 'man.'

As soon as we turn from examples such as 'man' to exact mathematical concepts like 'triangle' ('a closed plane figure bounded by three straight lines'), it is easy to find *propria* that are perfectly uncontroversial, as in the geometrical theorem: 'The internal angles of a triangle are equal to two right angles.' 'Having all internal angles equal to two right angles' is a property that can be demonstrated as belonging necessarily to all triangles and *only* to triangles. That is, the converse is universally and necessarily true as well: any closed plane figure having all internal angles equal to two right angles is a triangle. Without being the definition of a triangle, this too has the very kind of strict universality that belongs to a definition. There is, however, this difference between a *proprium* and the definition, that the *proprium* does not specify (ii) what *makes* the subject the sort of thing it is; it does not single out that very thing, the essence, in virtue of which triangles are triangles or men are men, as does the real or essential definition. (Recall our provisional characterization of a Socratic definition as a description in words of a property or set of properties that (i) is *distinctive* of a certain class of things, belonging to that class alone, and that (ii) *makes* those things the very sort of things they are.)

All three cases of predication considered thus far differ from a fourth in which a certain property or characteristic is ascribed to a subject as (d) an accident, for example: 'Some men are timid' or 'All men are gullible.' In the first case the very form of predication is not universal ('some' rather than 'all'), while in the second the predicate is not universal in the strict sense. *If* it applies to members of the species, or even if, by sheer chance, it applies to all members of the species, it just *happens* to do so; it is purely accidental that it does so. 'Timidity' and 'gullibility' are thus accidents of the species 'man.' These are instances of accidental rather than essential predication. If exceptionless, they would be 'accidents on a cosmic scale,' as in the statement 'All ravens are black' (see 6.3.2).

If mathematical examples are wanted, take the following. A particular triangle may just *happen* to be scalene or larger in area than a certain square, but a figure may well be neither of these things and still be a triangle. These, then, are plainly accidental to triangularity. Still, it may be worth pointing out again that a property belonging necessarily to all triangles and only to triangles may still not be the essence. It is true that among closed rectilinear figures *all and only* triangles possess internal angles equal to two right angles; but unless this is the very thing that *makes* them triangles this is not the essence but what was just termed a *proprium*. Similarly, being a featherless biped holds true of every human being; and, conversely, every featherless biped in nature is a human being; but unless having only two feet and lacking feathers is what *makes* men human, this is only a *proprium* rather than the essence of man. Now how do we distinguish such *propria* from what Kneale calls "accidents on a cosmic scale"?

The answer is that outside mathematics it is difficult to do so reliably, which is why, in the Platonic dialogue referred to above, doubts arise as to whether Socrates gets a *proprium* or a universal accident in lieu of a definition. Some accidents clearly belong to *all* members of a certain class or species without exception, but not to them alone. Here there is no difficulty. All ravens are black, but since blackness does not belong *only* to ravens, this is clearly not a *proprium*, let alone a defining feature of the species. However, there would be a certain imprecision in the distinction drawn between accidents and *propria* if an accident could ever belong to all and only members of a certain species. Suppose there were some other characteristic, 'q,' that did in fact belong to all and only to members of the species 'raven.' It would then be *at least* an accident on a cosmic scale, but it might also be a *proprium*. Without some discoverable necessary or logical connection between the characteristic in question and the definition (like that which the geometer discovers between 'having internal angles equal to two right angles' and 'a figure bounded by three straight lines'), we just could not know whether to call it an accident or a *proprium*. That is a problem we run into with inexact (non-mathematical) concepts. Earlier we encountered a similar difficulty in drawing a sharp distinction between *proprium* and essence in the case of a concept like 'man.' As soon as we move on to exact mathematical concepts, both problems disappear.

Now the Platonic dialogue mentioned above has to do with the definition of an inexact moral concept, so it is not surprising that some commentators maintain that what Socrates gets instead of a definition is a universal accident. We shall call it a *proprium* (see 11.8), but given the non-mathematical subject of the dialogue it is impossible to be sure. The distinctions drawn in this section between (a) definition,

(b) genus, (c) proprium, and (d) accident will also be helpful to us when we come to Descartes's famous Wax Example in the Second Meditation (see 24.7.3). But since both interpretive problems presuppose the requisite background knowledge of traditional logical doctrine, we have treated the key distinctions in advance here.

Recommended readings and references

Armstrong, A.H. 1983. *An Introduction to Ancient Philosophy*. Totawa, New Jersey: Rowan and Allenfield (Helix Books).

Cornford, F.M.. 1957. *From Religion to Philosophy. A Study of the Origins of Western Speculation*. New York: Harper Torchbook.

Cornford, F.M.. 1965. *Principium Sapientiae. A Study of the Origins of Greek Philosophical Thought*. New York: Harper Torchbook.

Ferguson, W.K. and Bruun, G. 1936. *A Survey of European Civilization*. Boston: Houghton Mifflin. Vol. I, Chapter 2. (A good, brief overview of the civilization of ancient Greece.)

Morford, M.P.O and Lenardon, R. J. 1971. *Classical Mythology*. London: Longmans. (A useful reference work on Greek and Roman myth.)

Flew, Antony 1977. *Thinking Straight*. Buffalo, N.Y.: Prometheus Books. (Among logic textbooks, this stands out as one that pursues the practical objective of enabling the student to spot logical flaws and illegitimate moves in philosophical texts.)

Heidegger, Martin. 1984. *Early Greek Thinking*. Translated by David Farrell Krell and Frank A Capuzzi. San Francisco: Harper-Collins Publishers.

Jaeger, Werner. 1967. *The Theology of the Early Greek Philosophers*. Oxford: Oxford University Press.

Koyré, Alexandre. 1957. *From the Closed World to the Infinite Universe*. Baltimore and London: The Johns Hopkins Press.

Miles, Murray. 1997. "Philosophy and Liberal Learning." *Queen's Quarterly*. Vol. 104, No. 1 (Spring 1997).

Newton-Smith, William H. 1981. *The Rationality of Science*. London: Routledge. (A quick way to get up to date on philosophy of science over the last half-century.)

Owens, Joseph. 1959. *A History of Ancient Western Philosophy*. Englewood Cliffs, New Jersey: Prentice-Hall, Inc.

Popper, K.R. 1962. "Towards a Rational Theory of Tradition." In *Conjectures and Refutations*. New York and London: Basic Books. (A philosopher of science's perspective on the transition from mythico-religious to philosophical thought.)

Price, B.B. 1992. *Medieval Thought. An Introduction*. Oxford and Cambridge, Mass.: Basil Blackwell. (Contains, among other things, a good introductory survey of the development of the universities and the curriculum in medieval times.)

Questions for reflection, discussion, and review

1. Consider your own prior education it in terms of the distinction between the (1) indoctrinational, (2) informational, and (3) interpretational dimensions of the educational experience. Does the distinction hold up? How useful is it in distinguishing the primary, secondary, and tertiary levels of education?
2. What sense does it make to speak of 'the good life for man'? Doesn't this presuppose that there is such a thing as *the* good life? Don't we know for a fact that what is a good life for one person is not necessarily good for another and that there can be no one good life for everyone?
3. Distinguish five questions at issue in determining the correct order of knowing.
4. What are the key points of difference between the realist and idealist approaches to the five questions referred to in 3 above?
5. Define and compare (a) scepticism (b) relativism and (c) critical rationalism.
6. Protagoras maintained that "Man is the measure of all things." Which, if any, of the positions mentioned in the previous question does this statement represent? Do you agree with Protagoras? Explain your answer.
7. Without going into specific problems, distinguish in general terms the problem of the order of being from that of the order of knowing.
8. Identify the specific problems subsumed under the general headings 'the order of knowing' and 'the order of being.'
9. Berkeley maintained that "to be is to be perceived." How would you go about responding to the claim that if a tree falls deep in the forest and no sentient creature is around, there is no sound? Does the tree exist, but not the sound? Do both exist? Neither? Defend your position with arguments.
10. We say that 'seeing is believing.' Is 'to be' the same as 'to be visible and/or tangible'? In other words, is to be something the same as to be something material? If so, why? If not, why not?
11. We speak, by extension of the meaning of the term 'literacy,' of 'computer literacy.' Can you think of other 'literacies'? Would 'philosophical literacy' be among them, and if so, what might it involve?
12. We live in an age of specialization. What point might there still be, if any, in attempting, as in metaphysics, to encompass the whole of what is in thought?
13. How would you assess the relative importance of (1) the material and (2) the intellectual and moral basis of human life for genuine human thriving? How important is each in your own personal estimate?

PART ONE

SOCRATES AND THE ROAD TO WISDOM

I say that it is the greatest good for man to discuss virtue every day and those other things about which you hear me conversing and testing myself and others, for the unexamined life is not worth living.

Socrates of Athens, *Apology*

8

Sources and Outline

8.1 Introductory

If Socrates was an oral philosopher who wrote nothing at all (see 1.5), how are we to make out anything concerning his philosophy? One answer to this question has it that there is only a slender basis on which to do so; that despite the written testimonies of several fourth-century writers, only a single work or two of Plato, presumably his very first literary efforts, furnish historically reliable information concerning the thought of the historical Socrates. Unfortunately, even they do not tell us much—certainly much less than scholars are accustomed to infer from some ten or so early Platonic dialogues, supplemented by a few observations of Aristotle and the Socratic works of Xenophon (see 1.5). Regarding the character of the man Socrates and his way of life, the situation is better; but in all that concerns Socrates's philosophical method and teachings, our situation is largely one of irremediable ignorance.

As a rule it is a mark of sound scholarship to be as scrupulous as possible about one's sources. Yet the sheer restraint of this "minimalist account" (as it calls itself) involves a risk. For in this particular case the price of erring on the side of caution is high. We risk finding ourselves with a string of reliably attested, remarkably lofty ethico-religious pronouncements made by one of the chief spokesmen of the fifth-century Greek Enlightenment, yet without the means to weave them into a rationally coherent philosophical outlook such as might be expected of "the father of Western rationalism" (E.R. Dodds). Such coherence as the pronouncements have in the early Platonic dialogues is alleged to be Plato's doing; moreover, the outlook itself is Plato's, not that of the historical Socrates. In the eight or so dialogues after the first two, Plato provided successive *partial* accounts of a unified philosophical vision that was only to be elaborated as a whole in the great dialogues of his so-called middle period. Furthermore, his position on most matters remained relatively static over the course of his long literary career. That is why the minimalist approach calls itself 'unitarian': it seeks to do justice to the unity of Plato's thought, rejecting the dominant 'developmental' approach, according to which Plato first (a) gave written expression to the oral teachings of the historical Socrates, subsequently (b) developing markedly different views of his own, and finally (c) modifying certain of these in the last phase of a philosophical career that spanned more than forty years.

In the present chapter, we shall first review and briefly assess the sources of our knowledge of the philosophy of the historical Socrates. Having clarified the basis on which a reconstruction of Socrates's thought is to be attempted, we shall propose a test. Even if the approach selected passes the test, the interpretive issues will hardly be settled. This is all to the good, since the minimalist challenge helps keep before our eyes the wide range of possible approaches to Plato's dialogues. The chapter concludes with a brief outline of the stages of the exposition in the remaining chapters of Part One.

8.2 Sources of the philosophy of Socrates

Our chief source of knowledge of the philosophy of Socrates is, by all accounts, (1) some or all of the early dialogues of Plato. In addition, there are (2) various passages in the writings of Aristotle in which the latter reviews the teachings of his predecessors, including Socrates, before setting out his own views on the subject in hand. While Aristotle is usually more concerned to present his own ingenious solutions to knotty problems than to do justice to the ideas of his predecessors, it is probably significant that in some of these contexts he distinguishes sharply between Socrates and Plato. Finally, there are (3) some works dealing with Socrates by the contemporary historian, Xenophon. In addition, the fifth-century poet and contemporary of Socrates, Aristophanes, provides a comic caricature of the latter as a sort of philosophical freak, part sophist, part natural philosopher, part buffoon. Since we have reliable knowledge that Aristophanes ascribed to Socrates views of which others were the originators, it is best to discount him altogether as a source of Socrates's philosophy and to read his play *Clouds* for the sheer fun of it.

We begin our consideration of the sources of the philosophy of Socrates with a brief look at Xenophon and Aristotle before returning to Plato.

8.2.1 Xenophon and Aristotle

Xenophon is generally considered an unreliable source. Unlike Plato, he probably did not belong to the inner circle of Socrates's followers. He left Athens two years before Socrates's death, and was subsequently banished from the city for some thirty years. While Socrates figures in four of his works, Xenophon may have drawn his portrait largely from others' writings, including Plato's. Above all, he was no philosopher devoted to the search for truth and the right way of living, but a soldier-historian and adventurer, as different from Socrates in both character and temperament as can be imagined. This probably precluded him from understanding either the man or his thought on any but a superficial level.

Aristotle, who first came to Athens more than thirty years after the death of Socrates, is certainly without the limitations of character or intellect that impeded Xenophon, who at least knew the man personally. Yet his writings are a sketchy source at best, references to Socrates being relatively few and far between. Of only four or five philosophical beliefs or practices ascribed to the historical Socrates, most could have been drawn from Plato's dialogues. Since they provide no extensive elaboration, Aristotle's remarks furnish no independent corroboration of Plato's portrait either. And yet there are two points that Aristotle must have had from sources other than Plato's writings, probably reliably: (a) Socrates inaugurated the search for universal definitions that eventually led Plato and his followers to posit transcendent Forms; and (b) Socrates was exclusively a moral philosopher. For in the dialogues of Plato, it is one and the same Socrates who (a) espouses both immanent and transcendent realism concerning universals (see 4.7) and (b) discourses on matters of mathematics and metaphysics as well as morals.

Regarding (a), Aristotle took the What is ...? questions (see 7.13.2) found in seven early Platonic dialogues for typically Socratic requests for real definitions circumscribing immanent essences; as for transcendent essences or Forms, these he regarded as an innovation of Plato and his followers. Now, of course, Aristotle himself provided the fuller theoretical elaboration and justification for the type of essentialism he ascribed to Socrates, partly in his logical theory of definitions, but mainly in his metaphysical controversy with the Platonists concerning universals (see 4.7); and Aristotle frequently distorted his predecessors' views by casting them in a light in which they appear as scattered elements of his own unified system of thought. We saw a stunning example of this in the Peripatetic treatment of the Milesian *archē* concept (see 5.5.1–2). But the description of the relative positions of Plato and Socrates concerning universals is unlikely to be a distortion of this sort. True, the interpretation adopts a *metaphysical* point of view that was not Socrates's own; for according to (b) Socrates concerned himself exclusively with moral matters. Still, on the whole, it makes good historical sense to see Aristotle as defending the moderate metaphysical position on universals that was recklessly abandoned by Plato. Such a position is clearly stated in some early dialogues, employing an explicit distinction between essence and *proprium* (see 7.14), and while the metaphysical vocabulary may be Plato's, we should probably accept Aristotle's testimony that something very like this was already taken for granted by Socrates.

On this particular point there is something like scholarly consensus despite general agreement on Aristotle's shortcomings as a historian of ideas. Those shortcomings may only attest to the fact that certain types of intellectual eminence can be as great an obstacle to successful historical understanding as the intellectual deficiencies of a Xenophon. For Aristotle set out to synthesize in a single comprehensive system of thought all that was of lasting value in the prior history of Greek intellectual contemplation. Being, like Socrates, an eminently sensible, middle-of-the-road thinker, he excluded the transcendent Forms of the Platonists, along with much else that belonged to the extremes of the spectrum opposing magic, myth, and mysticism to mathematical, mechanical, and materialistic tendencies (see 5.4). In the Middle Ages, St Thomas carried out a similarly ambitious synthesis of Aristotelian and Christian thought, while in the nineteenth century Hegel attempted much the same thing for the whole of Greek, medieval, and modern metaphysical thinking. Like Aristotle, Aquinas and Hegel are frequently accused of having cast the history of thought in a distorting mould to suit their synthetic or systematic aims. Heidegger's synoptic view of the history of thought has come in for similar criticism. The first requirement of philosophical scholarship is that the right balance be struck between philosophy and scholarship. It is hardly surprising that great thinkers frequently err on the side of philosophy, or that critics without an original philosophical idea to bless themselves with relentlessly beat the drum of scholarship.

8.2.2 Plato

Given the unreliability of Xenophon's portrait and the scantiness of Aristotle's testimony, our main, if not our only, source of knowledge of the moral philosophy of Socrates is Plato. There are twenty-six dialogues whose authorship is undisputed, while several more, along with a series of letters, are doubtfully genuine. Although Socrates figures as *a* (usually *the*) central character in all but one of the dialogues considered authentic, these are nothing remotely like reports of actual conversations, though similar conversations may have taken place, for all we know, in a few cases. The fact is that the writing of Socratic dialogues was already an established genre of literary *fiction* well before Plato turned his hand to it in middle age, taking it to new philosophical heights. His mastery of the dialogue form has been imitated, but never equalled, let alone surpassed, in the twenty-three centuries since.

In one particular case Plato tells us he was actually present at the scene of a dialogue: the trial of Socrates, whose defence speech is reported in the *Apology* (see the references to Plato's presence at 34a and 38b). But even here he does not claim to report the speech word for word. Nevertheless, since Plato published the *Apology* not long after Socrates's death, and since many contemporary readers of the dialogue would have heard the speech as well, it probably bears a significant resemblance to what Socrates actually said in the Athenian courtroom. For this and other reasons, even the minimalist approach takes the *Apology* as a historically reliable document.

On the other hand, in the *Phaedo* it is specifically mentioned that Plato was not personally present at the scene of Socrates's death (see 59b), and this is obvious from the private settings of the *Crito* and the *Euthyphro* as well, the only other dialogues directly concerned with the trial and death of Socrates. Some other dialogues, for example, the *Protagoras* and the *Parmenides*, are set in a time when Socrates was a young man and Plato was not even born! So here there can be no claim to what is called 'historicity' (historical accuracy), although for all we know some parts of some dialogues may in fact be fairly accurate depictions of things actually said by Socrates in conversations witnessed by Plato. Parts of the *Protagoras*, for example, are sufficiently different from Plato's later views to have suggested to both Aristotle and modern scholars that they are authentic Socratic teachings. Minimalists dispute the point, treating, apart from the *Apology*, only the *Crito* as in some measure historical.

8.3 The chronology of Plato's dialogues

Before making any specific conjectures about Plato's dialogues as a source of the philosophy of Socrates, we had best set out an overall chronology, identifying the early dialogues of Plato in particular. That is done in the table below. Various points of dating and chronology are in dispute among scholars, but the ordering of the table has the virtue of relative simplicity and, if wrong, is at least not very far wrong. It can be accepted as a likely story, no more. The three groups of the table *may* correspond to historical phases in the development of Plato's thought, but, as we have seen, the developmental approach is controversial. Dialogues marked with an asterisk (*) will be examined in whole or in part in the first two Parts of the present work.

Group I (Early Dialogues)
a. Socratic Dialogues
(in alphabetical order) *Apology,* *Charmides, Crito,* *Euthyphro,* *Gorgias, Hippies Minor, Ion, Laches, Protagoras, Republic I*
b. Transitional Dialogues
(in alphabetical order) *Euthydemus, Hippias Major, Lysis, Menexenes, Meno**

Group II (Middle Dialogues)
(in probable chronological order) *Cratylus, Phaedo,* *Symposium, Republic II–X, Phaedrus, Parmenides, Theaetetus.*

Group III (Late Dialogues)
(in probable chronological order) *Timaeus, Critias, Sophist, Statesman, Philebus, Laws*

There is no need to go into the evidence for or against any particular matter of date or chronology that is controversial, much less to review the supporting evidence for those matters on which virtually all scholars agree. It should be noted, though, that the chronological ordering of the Group I dialogues is, on the whole, more doubtful than either of the other groups. That is why we have resorted to an alphabetical listing. Nevertheless, that the *Apology* is the very first, and that the *Crito* may be the second published work of Plato, would probably not be contested by many scholars, even those who entertain doubts about the *Crito*.

8.4 Historicity of the early Socratic dialogues of Plato

One reason that has been given for privileging the *Crito* along with *Apology* is its close connection with the trial of Socrates. A similar argument might be made for the *Euthyphro*, whose fictional setting is the day before the trial, and for the death scene of the *Phaedo*, where Socrates's sentence is carried out. Both the *Euthyphro* and the first half of the *Meno* are, moreover, dialogues in which definitions of moral terms are sought. Since we have accepted Aristotle's testimony concerning the Socratic search for definitions, we shall want to exploit the relevant portions of these (or other, similar) dialogues for possible insights into the philosophic practices of the historical Socrates. Such is the rationale for putting an asterisk beside these five dialogues in the above table.

The approach described stops well short of the sort of maximal interpretation that treats the dialogues of Group I(a) as collectively furnishing a wealth of historically dependable information, not just about the life and character of Socrates, but about his philosophical convictions and the methods and arguments used to support them. We shall take instead a middle road, confining ourselves to a few that are closely related to the *Apology*. The upshot is nevertheless a developmental view that is akin to a maximal approach in spirit, but more restrained. The test of its correctness will come in Part Two, where we shall consider the *Phaedo*, a key dialogue of Plato's middle period. If a close examination of several early dialogues in Part One brings to light a complex and intricately wrought moral theory that hangs together as a whole and yet is *strikingly at odds* with the moral theory and the general philosophical outlook of the Socrates of the *Phaedo*, then we shall consider ourselves justified in treating the teachings and methods of the early dialogues as roughly those of Socrates, perhaps tidied up and systematized by Plato, yet without serious distortion of his teacher's thought. The crux lies in the words "strikingly at odds." For our approach to pass the test, it must be manifestly harder to make good sense of the Group I and Group II dialogues as a unified whole, gradually unveiled, than to posit development and even a reversal of perspective, starting from an initial position that Plato accepted in his apprentice years but rejected in his philosophical maturity. Obviously, agreement on this point will be hard to achieve. In any case, the decision must be postponed to the end of Part Two, and even there it will simply be left to the reader to decide for himself or herself on the basis of the evidence presented. As for the Group III dialogues, the middle road just described does not involve any stand on question of doctrinal continuity or change between Plato's second and last periods.

8.5 Socrates and Plato

The approach just described rests on certain reasonable conjectures concerning the relationship between Plato and the historical Socrates that are by no means the only ones one can make.

On the competing minimalist view, the dialogues of Group I(a) are, with two exceptions, works of philosophic fiction. In the eight or so dialogues that followed his very first literary productions, the young Plato was still learning his craft as a writer of Socratic dialogues. Accordingly, he furnished only partial insights and partially worked out supporting arguments for a total metaphysical, epistemological, moral, and political vision that was already before his mind, in the essentials, almost from the start. That vision went well beyond anything he could have heard from the lips of his revered teacher, though in ways he probably believed would have met with Socrates's approval had the latter not confined himself to moral philosophy. Using the fictional character 'Socrates' much in the manner of other writers of Socratic dialogues, Plato thus prepared his audience by stages for his own teachings before actually elaborating these comprehensively in the masterworks of Group II. (It has even been suggested that he was recruiting students for the Academy he hoped to open—drumming up business, to put it crassly.) The portrait of the man Socrates is a good likeness, even in the works of Group III; and some few doctrines can reasonably be ascribed to the historical Socrates himself on the basis of the two earliest dialogues. Nevertheless, most of the philosophical content is Platonic. In particular, Plato provided the metaphysical and epistemological underpinnings for an attitude toward morality and moral education not unlike that of Socrates, since without such foundations, he believed, the legacy of Socrates lacked the rational justification required for it to prevail against the teachings of the sophists.

What is certainly correct in this sketch is the last point concerning metaphysical and epistemological underpinnings. Otherwise, our preferred picture looks very different. The young Plato was Socrates's most gifted pupil, a member of the inner circle, and a born philosopher persuaded of the truth of Socrates's teachings as he had heard them set forth in conversations over the course of many years. But this same Plato was also a talented dramatic writer, having, according to some reports, composed dramas before becoming a pupil of Socrates. After his teacher's death, he undertook to preserve the latter's teachings in the form of imaginary dramatic encounters between Socrates and other (often well-known) historical figures. It is not hard to understand his motives for trying to present both the man and his philosophy more faithfully than others who had written in the same genre. For we know from a letter that is probably authentic that Plato's friendship with Socrates was a turning point in his life—as it had been in the lives of other prominent young men of his generation. What could be more natural, then, than to wish others to experience, through the medium of literature, the beneficent influence of the conversation of Socrates? For the success of the venture we have the testimony in a lost dialogue of Aristotle concerning a Corinthian farmer, who, on reading one of the early dialogues of Plato, "left his farmland and his vineyard to pledge his soul to Plato and to plant and cultivate Platonic fields." Of course, in addition to leaving a more accurate historical record of the thought of his great teacher, the young Plato wished to erect a lasting monument to the personality of this unique individual. The two aims were probably inseparable in his mind.

With advancing years, however, Plato began to develop a philosophy of his own, one very different from that of Socrates. He nevertheless continued to set down his ideas in the form of dialogues whose principal character is a fictional 'Socrates.' He probably never saw his own as a repudiation so much as a continuation of Socrates's philosophy, though in this he was sorely mistaken. The transformation of Socrates's thought begins already in the dialogues designated 'transitional' above. These works—including the latter half of the *Meno*—are no longer a reliable historical source, while the middle dialogues are Plato's own philosophy and not that of Socrates, even antithetical to the latter in many respects. One difference is the prominence given metaphysical and mathematical interests quite foreign to Socrates. Yet even in the middle and later dialogues there are a few passages which help complete the historical portrait of Socrates, the man—for example, the opening passages and the death scene in the *Phaedo*, the speech of Alcibiades in a middle-period dialogue called the *Symposium*, and the description of Socrates's midwifery in another entitled *Theaetetus*.

8.6 Outline of the part on Socrates

If the picture just sketched is even roughly accurate, then the teachings of the Platonic Socrates correspond (perhaps with slight departures and some elaboration) to those of the historical Socrates only in the case of certain dialogues of Group I(a)—the exact number is debatable—though the personality of Socrates, even as depicted in the middle and late dialogues, retains important traces of the character of the man. We shall begin our study with a chapter on the life and character of Socrates (see chap. 9). This is a departure from the practice to be followed later, where biography will be treated very cursorily. That is because our chief concern is neither with the whole system of thought of certain historical figures, nor with the "life and times" of any of them, but with understanding certain key works that altered the course of the history of thought. For this we may need to know something about the men and their times, but the focus is to remain upon understanding some eight or so philosophical texts. The reason for the exception made in this case is the extraordinary interest of the man from the point of view of the beginner. For Socrates has always been regarded as something like the embodiment of philosophy itself, partly because he was its first great martyr.

Our main concern in the following chapters is the interpretation of a few dialogues concerning virtue and happiness or the good life for man (chaps. 10 to 13). The following is a schematic outline of the topics and works to be dealt with in the following chapters:

I. The Life and Character of Socrates

1 Gadfly (Socratic wisdom in the *Apology*)
2 Stingray (Socratic method in the *Meno*)
3 Silenus (Alcibiades's speech in the *Symposium*)
4 Midwife (a passage from the *Theaetetus*)
5 Ironist

II. The Moral Philosophy of Socrates

1 Defence of the Philosophic Life (in the *Apology*)
2 Socratic Piety (in the *Euthyphro*)
3 Virtue and Happiness (in the *Crito*)
4 Concluding Appraisal

9

Life and Character

9.1 Gadfly: Socratic wisdom

At 30e the Socrates of the *Apology* describes his mission in life this way:

> I was attached to this city by the god—though it seems a ridiculous thing to say—as upon a great and noble horse which was somewhat sluggish because of its size and needed to be stirred up by a kind of gadfly. It is to fulfill some such function that I believe the god has placed me in the city. I never cease to rouse each and every one of you, to persuade and reproach you all day long everywhere I find myself in your company.

This is Socrates's own description of the life he has led—that of a gadfly. To understand it is to understand the nature of Socratic wisdom.

9.1.1 The structure of the Apology

While the overall structure of the *Apology* is fairly transparent—the three main parts are usually separated by a gap in the printed text—the structure of the individual parts themselves is less clear. The three-part structure is: I. Socrates's Defence Speech (17a–35d), II. Socrates's Assessment of a Penalty after the Verdict (35d–38b), and III. Socrates's Prophecy and Farewell (38c–end). The Greek word translated as 'defence speech,' *apologia*, is a technical forensic term (a term of the law courts). It refers to that portion of the trial in which the accused responds to the charges, and has nothing do with our modern word 'apology' (which is nevertheless derived from it). Socrates, it hardly needs pointing out, expressed absolutely no regret about anything.

Part I, Socrates's defence speech, has two distinct themes or sections, to be

Chapter 9: Life and Character   159

labelled A and B in what follows. Section A explains what exactly Socrates's actions were, such that he was brought to trial on charges of corrupting the youth and of atheism or irreligion. In other words, it describes how he has lived (18a to 28b). Section B shows that he has not only never wronged anyone by his actions, but that it would have been morally wrong for him *not* to act and live as he had (28b to the end).

Section A, the description of the life led, again has two sub-sections: A-1 contains a reply to his "first accusers" (18a), that is, to the misleading rumours about his activities that have been circulating in Athens for years (18e–24b), while A-2 is a reply to the recent or "later accusers" (18b), Meletus, Anytus, and Lycon, who have brought the indictment (24b–28b). The cross-examination of Meletus is a good example of Socratic method but adds nothing to the portrayal of Socratic wisdom in the *Apology*; it will be left for the later consideration of Socrates's method in connection with Meno's characterization of the man as a stingray (see 9.2.2). A-1 must be examined here for the light it sheds on the nature of Socrates's wisdom.

9.1.2 Reply to the earlier accusers

A-1 contains three central claims regarding the life Socrates has led. First of all, Socrates insists that he is not "a student of all things in the sky and below the earth" (18b–c). He repeats the point later, stressing that he is not one who "busies himself studying things in the sky and below the earth" (19b). In short, he is (1) *not a natural philosopher* of the sort met with in the Ionian tradition from Thales to Anaxagoras (see chap. 5). Second, Socrates is equally insistent on the fact that he is (2) *not a sophist* who takes payment to teach people how to "make the worse argument [appear] the stronger" (18b) or who "makes the worse into the stronger argument, and teaches these same things to others" (19b). Or, as he puts it elsewhere, he is not one who "undertakes to teach people and charge a fee for it" (19d). Finally, (3) Socrates comments on the source of these misconceptions about him, telling the story of Chairephon's visit to Delphi and the oracle's pronouncement (20c–24b). For once he has rebutted the rumours about him as without basis in fact, he owes his audience an explanation of how they have arisen.

It is in connection with the story about Chairephon that the *problem* of Socratic wisdom arises (see 9.1.3–5 below). This in turn sheds an interesting light on Socrates's role as *gadfly* of Athens (see 9.1.6). However, we shall begin with a brief consideration of the first two points regarding Socrates's life.

9.1.2.1 Socrates and the physiologists

The need for repeated disavowals of any interest in natural philosophical speculation, be it astronomical, meteorological, or cosmological, was probably occasioned by

Aristophanes's widely known burlesque, *Clouds* (see 8.2). Aristotle, as was noted earlier (5.5.2), rather misleadingly dubbed the earliest Greek philosophers *physikoi* or *physiologoi*, 'physicists' or 'physiologists,' since they devised theories (*logoi*) about astronomy (the sun, moon, stars, planets, comets, eclipses, and so on), meteorology (the phenomena in the upper regions like thunder and lightning, clouds, rain and rainbows, snow, winds, hail, frost, and ice), and subterranean phenomena (earthquakes, volcanic eruptions, and so forth) in the context of a general cosmogony and cosmology. The epithet was intended to distinguish men like Anaximander, Xenophanes, and Heracleitus from the poets or *theologoi* ('theologians'), who provided mythological accounts of many of the same natural phenomena. Apart from dreams and waking visions, meteoric and subterranean phenomena were widely held to be the principal means by which the gods communicated their will to men. Thus, anyone who offered purely naturalistic explanations (see 5.5.3) of such phenomena easily laid himself open to charges of impiety or atheism.

Coming as he did after the *theologoi* and the *physikoi*, Socrates (to paraphrase Cicero) brought philosophy down to earth, giving it an entirely new focus upon *man and moral issues*, above all on the question of the good life. With the possible exception of Democritus, he was the first full-fledged moral philosopher, even if, as Aristotle maintains, the turn toward "political science and the virtues" was a general trend in his generation. Unlike Democritus, however, Socrates confined himself exclusively to questions of this latter sort. So in his defence speech he is quite right to protest being lumped together with those earlier natural philosophers, many of whom, he says, almost incredulously, "do not even believe in the gods" (18c). Why he should say this of his predecessors is not hard to see; for in devising explanations of meteoric and subterranean phenomena without recourse to the divine, the Greek physiologists were, as noted above, kicking away one of the main props of popular belief in the existence of gods.

Although the error is laid squarely at the doorstep of his "earlier accusers," this confusion of Socrates with earlier thinkers who were engaged in physical enquiries is Meletus's blunder too. There is every reason to think it is deliberate on his part. Meletus was no doubt aware of the popular Athenian prejudice against philosophers who meddled with traditional religion; and he would certainly have known of the widespread confusion of the astronomers and natural philosophers with the sophists as well. It was no trifling matter, then, for him to insinuate or maintain that Socrates taught "that the sun is a stone and the moon earth" (26d). In traditional Greek myth, of course, the sun, moon, sky, and earth were all personified deities. The sun god, whether Hyperion or his son Helios, rises daily from the earth-encircling river Okeanos in the east and crosses the sky in a chariot, returning from west to east either under the earth or upon the waters of Okeanos in a golden bowl; while the moon goddess, Selene, daughter of Hyperion and sister of Helius, drives her chariot by night. In rejecting Meletus's charge, then, Socrates is defending himself against the imputation of disbelieving in the existence of all such deities.

Why, however, does he claim that Meletus is confusing him with Anaxagoras? Anaxagoras indeed taught that the sun was an incandescent stone, somewhat larger than the Peloponnese, and that the moon was made of earth, and so on. He is supposed to have become persuaded of these things after the fall of a meteorite at Aegospotami in 467 BC. But long before the meteorite, Anaximenes, another Ionian, was led to similar conclusions by purely theoretical considerations. Xenophanes, writes the distinguished Greek scholar John Burnet, "seems to have taken the gods of mythology one by one and reduced them to meteorological phenomena, and especially to clouds." Empedocles, too, developed naturalistic explanations of sun, moon, and stars. Anaxagoras, however, was a recent example well known to the Athenians; for he was the first philosopher ever to have been tried and condemned at Athens on charges of heresy or impiety. This must have made the choice obvious for Plato (or for Socrates, if Plato is here reporting something actually said in his teacher's defence speech). But it raises another problem concerning something said earlier.

In chapter 5 we remarked on the great latitude permitted poets and philosophers in the treatment of traditional myths and stories handed down from Homer and Hesiod. Yet late in the fifth century, a Greek seer named Diopeithes succeeded in having a decree enacted at Athens authorizing the indictment of those who "disbelieve in divine things or teach theories about what goes on the sky." This patriotic defender of the state religion was no doubt shrewd enough to see that purely naturalistic explanations of astronomical phenomena posed a threat to his and his fellow seers' authority and livelihood. The offence was regarded as a crime against the state and made punishable by death. In the ensuing decades there may have been many trials on charges of atheism involving individuals less famous than Socrates and Anaxagoras. Of these we understandably have no record. Protagoras is sometimes mentioned as a famous defendant who escaped by flight, as Socrates refused to do. Anaxagoras fared better than Socrates at least; thanks to the intervention of his friend, the great Athenian statesman Pericles, he had only to go into exile. The fact that the dates of this dark period of persecution correspond to those of the Peloponnesian war is probably no accident. In times of war, thought critical of the state or its religion easily comes to be regarded as subversive or sympathetic to the enemy cause.

The confusion fostered by Meletus raises another question that is not so easily answered. Even if Meletus is disingenuously playing to the ignorant and resentful crowd by lumping Socrates together with Ionian *physiologoi*, does Socrates, in repudiating the charge, really mean to say that he actually believes the traditional mythological accounts of the sun and moon gods? Does he sincerely believe even in the existence of the Olympian gods? We shall return to this question of the nature of Socratic piety when we consider the *Euthyphro* (see 11.12.1).

9.1.2.2 Socrates and the sophists

So much for the confusion of Socrates with those earlier Greek thinkers interested in natural philosophy. The second confusion concerns another group of thinkers known collectively as the sophists. This muddle too was fostered in the public mind by Aristophanes's burlesque. Like Socrates, the sophists were primarily interested in moral rather than physical matters, especially moral education; and like him they were free-thinkers whose views were frequently at odds with popular morality and religion. There the resemblance ends, however. Who were these sophists, then, and what did they teach?

Perhaps the most famous sophist was Protagoras, the man who coined the dictum 'Man is the measure' (see 3.3.1 and 3.5 above). In the Platonic dialogue named for him, Protagoras explains to Socrates exactly what it is that he teaches. The sophist, he says, teaches three things chiefly: *prudence* in the management of one's affairs and how to speak persuasively in the law courts and the public assembly, this being what makes men good at the art of politics and useful citizens; *moral virtue*, that is, nobility of character and goodness; and, finally, *skill in poetry*, that is, knowing which sayings of the poets are true and which are not, in other words, how to read the poets *critically*. Certain prominent sophists apparently published expository works on the poets, particularly Homer and Hesiod. Supplementing the *Protagoras* with the description of the sophist Gorgias in the *Meno*, we can perhaps sketch the likeness of the fifth-century sophist as follows.

First, (a) the sophist is typically an itinerant 'educationist' who goes about from town to town offering to 'associate' (this being the sense of the Greek word *synousia*, literally 'being together') with the youth of the place and to make them better. What 'making better' means will be explained in the last two points. Second, (b) the sophist takes a fee for his services (see *Meno* 91b). What he claims to teach is (c) the art of rhetoric, that is, in the words of the *Meno* (95c), to "make people clever speakers." 'Rhetoric,' incidentally, covers what we would call public speaking, argument, and debating skills, all of which go to make up our idea of oratorical skill. The main aim of the rhetorical art is victory over one's opponents, that is, swaying the jurors or the assemblymen, not the discovery of truth. As mentioned already, it also covers a form of 'literary criticism,' that is, assessing critically the educational benefit of the works of poets. With these skills one would naturally be effective in furthering one's private interests in the law courts and influencing the legislative assembly. Finally, (d) the sophist claims to make those with whom he associates better in a moral sense, that is, more virtuous, not just better able to look after their own and the state's interests. According to Meno, the sophist Gorgias was a great exception in claiming to make men "clever speakers" but *not* to make them better in the sense of 'more virtuous' (see 95c). If this is true, then the majority of the sophists clearly laid considerable stress upon (d) in particular.

Socrates, on the other hand, (a) hardly ever left Athens, except on military campaigns. For this we have the testimony of the *Crito* (52b): "You have never left the city, even to see a festival, nor for any other reason except military service; you have never gone to stay in any other city, as people do; you have had no desire to know another city or other laws." The point is reiterated at *Crito* 53a: "You have been away from Athens less than the lame or the blind or other handicapped people. It is clear that the city has been outstandingly more congenial to you than to other Athenians." Moreover, Socrates (b) never took money from anyone for associating with them. This fact is attested by the following passage of the *Apology*:

now if I profited from this [persuading people to care for virtue] by charging a fee for my advice, there would be some sense to it, but you can see for yourselves that, for all their shameless accusations, my accusers have not been able in their impudence to bring forward a single witness to say that I have ever received a fee or ever asked for one. (31c)

The same point is made again later in the work: "I do not converse when I receive a fee and not when I do not" (33a). And it is emphatically underscored in the *Euthyphro*: "I pour out to anybody anything I have to say, not only without charging a fee but even glad to reward anyone who is willing to listen" (3d). From his dogged insistence on this point, we may infer that this difference between Socrates's complete disinterestedness and the profit motive of the sophists had great weight with Plato.

As for teaching people to speak well, Socrates (c) states at the beginning of the *Apology* that he does not himself know how to speak well, at least not in the usual sense—that is, unless speaking *the truth* is speaking well. Argument, as Socrates employs it, is a means of discovering truth and detecting error, both in himself and others. It is employed, if not to discover, then at least to get us closer to, the truth of the matter in hand, or to rid us of errors at the very least, not to give us the upper hand over others in public and private disputes. Finally, Socrates (d) claims that he has no knowledge to teach others. Here are some typical passages in which this claim is repeated over and over again:

Certainly, I would pride and preen myself if I had this knowledge [expertise in human excellence, moral and non-moral], but I do not have it, gentlemen. (20c)

I am very conscious that I am not wise at all. (21b)

[H]e thinks he knows something when he does not, whereas when I do not know, neither do I think I know. (21d)

I have never been anyone's teacher. (33a)

So the confusion of Socrates with the sophists, like his identification with the so-called physiologists, is just a muddle, though it was probably a widely shared misconception at Athens in Socrates's own lifetime, one that Meletus was happy to play upon for his own disreputable ends.

9.1.2.3 Chairephon and the oracle of Delphi

After denying that (a) he has ever engaged in speculation about nature and the universe as a whole and that (b) he has ever claimed to be able to teach virtue and prudence to the young for a fee, Socrates concludes his reply to his first accusers with the story of Chairephon's visit to the Oracle at Delphi. The purpose of this story is threefold.

First and foremost, Socrates feels he owes the jurors some (1) explanation of how these stories about him have arisen if they are totally untrue. His reputation for wisdom, together with the failure of others to distinguish his merely "human" from that more-than-human wisdom to which physiologists and sophists lay claim, has led to his being confounded with one or both of these classes of men. That the purpose of the anecdote about Chairephon is to clear up the *source* of this confusion is stated repeatedly. For example, Socrates asks: "From where have these slanders come?" (20c), answering immediately that "[w]hat has caused my reputation is none other than a certain kind of wisdom" (20d). Or again: "Consider that I tell you this [story about Chairephon] because I would inform you about the origin of the slander" (21b).

The second purpose is (2) to shed further *positive* light on the exact nature of his activities and on the kind of wisdom he in fact has as well as on the kind he does not claim to possess. As just noted, his wisdom is very different from that to which the physiologists and the sophists pretend.

What kind of wisdom? Human wisdom, perhaps. It may be that I really possess this, while those whom I mentioned just now [the sophists, Evenus, Gorgias, Prodicus, Hippias] are wise with a wisdom more than human. (20d)

Third and finally, Socrates wishes (3) to explain the hostility toward him on the part of the poets, politicians, craftsmen, and others in the city. Not only did Socrates publicly humiliate all these men by showing them to be ignorant of the very things they pretended to know best; he did so before the youth of the city, who enjoyed following him about and listening to him, thus setting a bad example that some of the latter would follow. (On this point, see the passages at 23c to 24b.)

The most important thing in all this, from our point of view, is the nature of Socratic wisdom. For apart from the helpful light it sheds on Socrates's character and role as the gadfly of Athens, the nature of this wisdom is profoundly puzzling.

9.1.3 The problem of Socratic wisdom

In the course of the last phase of his reply to his earlier accusers, the account of Chairephon's visit to the oracle, Socrates makes a couple of apparently conflicting statements concerning wisdom. To begin with, he says (1) "I am very conscious that I am not wise at all" (21b); or, as he puts it later, "they ... will say that I am wise, even if I am not" (38c). Yet at the same time, he claims to possess a kind of wisdom, as was just seen: (2) "What kind of wisdom? Human wisdom, perhaps. It may be that I really possess this, while those whom I mentioned just now [sophists, physiologists] are wise with a wisdom more than human" (20d).

Now there are three obvious problems with asserting (1) and (2). In the first place, it seems clear that, in the words of the later *Theaetetus* (145e), "knowledge and wisdom are the same thing." That this is so for the Socrates of the *Apology* is evident from the way in which he passes from the expression "things of which I *know* nothing at all" (19c) to—in the very next line—"if someone is *wise* in these [same] things" (e.a.). Given that 'wisdom' and 'knowledge' are used interchangeably, when Socrates says, in effect, 'I know that I have no wisdom,' he is saying 'I know that I know nothing.' But if so, he is contradicting himself. For 'I know that I know nothing' means as much as: 'I know something, namely that I know nothing at all'; that is, 'I know one thing' and 'I do not know anything at all.' And this is flatly *self-contradictory*.

Second, Socrates could easily avoid this contradiction by saying that all he really meant was that he knows only *one* thing and nothing else. He might have said: "*All* I know is that I know nothing (else)." This is not inconsistent. But he would then fall into a pretty *radical form of scepticism*, limiting all his knowledge to a single item, to one truth. Yet in his conversations Socrates invariably assumes that he and his interlocutors are in search of truth. Far from despairing of the possibility of discovering truth (other than the truth that we are incapable of discovering any further truths), he says things like: 'We've now clarified what your opinion is. Let's see if it is *true*.' (See for example *Meno*, 78c.) So Socrates is not such a sceptic as it might seem from his saying: 'I know one thing only, namely that I know nothing besides this one thing.' Far from it. Hence, he cannot really mean anything like this when he contradicts himself in (1).

Finally, statement (1) above seems to be logically inconsistent with statement (2). Socrates can claim *either* to have *no* wisdom at all *or* to have only *a kind of* wisdom, but he cannot *consistently* claim *both* to have no wisdom *and* to have a kind of, that is, some, wisdom.

9.1.4 Types of scepticism

While we are on the subject of scepticism, and before attempting to see whether there is any way out of these difficulties, it may be worth pausing to distinguish two later varieties of ancient scepticism, Academic and Pyrrhonian. (A third, Cyrenaic scepticism, will be omitted.) These are relevant to the problem of Socratic wisdom, especially as the Academic sceptics claimed Socrates as their intellectual ancestor; but it will also be useful later on, when we encounter the very different scepticisms of Descartes and Hume. The opposite of scepticism (diffidence about, or mistrust of, our cognitive faculties), incidentally, is dogmatism (confidence—or over-confidence—about the extent of our knowledge or about some particular item or items of knowledge). Descartes, as we shall see, is only a sceptic for starters; his final position on a wide variety of issues is thoroughly dogmatic (see chap. 23 below). Hume, by contrast, is a sceptic first and last (see chap. 28 below).

Scepticism as a developed philosophical posture dates from the Hellenistic period (see 1.3.1), when certain observations and criticisms of earlier Greek thinkers were fashioned into a battery of stock arguments designed to show either (a) that no knowledge is possible (apart from the knowledge of our own ignorance) or (b) that it is impossible to determine *whether* we have any knowledge at all (and thus even to know for certain that we are ignorant).

(a) is called 'Academic' scepticism, having been formulated in the Platonic Academy in the third century BC by Arcesilaus (c. 315–241 BC) and Carneades (c. 213–129 BC). The main source of our knowledge of academic scepticism is a work on the subject (aptly entitled *Academica*) by Cicero. The Academic sceptics developed a whole arsenal of arguments to prove that (i) the information derived from the senses is not reliable; that (ii) even the results of our reasoning (say, in mathematics) are paradoxical in some cases and therefore not absolutely certain; and that (iii) there is no reliable criterion for distinguishing true from false perceptions or conclusions. Consequently, everything is mere opinion, not knowledge. This type of scepticism dominated the Platonic Academy right down to the first century BC, at which time it began to give way to what is called Neoplatonism (see .13.1) and a return to doctrine or dogmatism.

(b) is called 'Pyrrhonian' scepticism. This movement stems from the legendary figure Pyrrho of Elis and his student Timon of Phleius (c. 315–225 BC). Pyrrho's best-known disciple is Sextus Empiricus, a Greek physician and philosopher of uncertain dates (possibly around 200 AD) who wrote an *Outline of Pyrrhonism*, to which we owe most of our knowledge of Pyrrhonism, and much of what we know about Presocratic philosophy as well. According to legend, Pyrrho was a complete doubter who was content to follow the appearances of things, or common sense, but refused to commit himself to the *truth* of any judgment whatsoever. His followers criticized the Academic sceptics, on the one hand, for saying that nothing can be known, and dogmatists, on the other, for holding that a great deal can be known. As an alternative, they proposed a third posture: complete suspension of judgment on all questions—including the question whether or not anything can be known. The

Pyrrhonians may even have suspended judgment as to whether their own arguments furnished any knowledge! At least one late sceptic, Metrodoros of Chios, drew this conclusion. It is difficult not to admire such consistency, even if it is hard to accept conclusions so extreme and counter-intuitive.

9.1.5 A solution to these problems

Scepticism was the second of three problems or puzzles occasioned by Socrates's statements concerning his wisdom. Having digressed briefly to consider some varieties of scepticism, we return now to our three problems. All can be dispelled by the following considerations.

First, all that Socrates in fact says in (1), if one retranslates the passage literally, is that *he is not aware, he is not conscious*, that he is wise. There is a great difference between (i) 'I am not conscious that I *am* wise' and (ii) 'I am conscious that I am *not* wise' or 'I know that I know nothing.' Only (ii) invites the charge of self-contradiction. If close attention is paid to the actual wording of the Greek text, however, it turns out that Socrates actually asserts (i), that he is not aware ('I am not conscious ...') or sure that he in fact knows anything that would count as wisdom ('that I am wise'). In other words, he does not know with complete certainty that he actually knows anything, *although he may.*

So the first problem can be taken care of without attributing any sort of scepticism to Socrates, thus eliminating the second problem as well. For (i) is perfectly consistent with Socrates's having in fact quite a bit of knowledge, both about trivial matters and even about rather important matters. Socrates is just not *certain* that his beliefs really amount to knowledge, that is, whether they are true or not. So he neither flatly contradicts himself (first problem) nor espouses an uncharacteristic scepticism (second problem); it is only a mild and reasonable scepticism to which he is giving voice here, one very like that described as 'critical rationalism' above (see 3.3.1). We might put the point of (1) this way. Socrates acknowledges that while human beings *may* well be able to obtain knowledge, and while he himself *may* have attained to some, no human being can ever be absolutely *sure* that his convictions really constitute knowledge. This is a moderate and plausible position that boils down to this: all human knowledge-claims are *fallible*; and that is the essence of the critical rationalism first formulated by Xenophanes and renewed in our time by Popper (ibid.).

In dealing with the first two problems we said nothing of the nature of the 'important matters' referred to. Would knowledge of right and wrong and of the good life for man figure here? Surely not, since there is no reason to believe that Socrates thought these beyond the scope of fallible human knowledge; quite the contrary. The great German classicist Bruno Snell once remarked that the difference between human and divine knowledge is that "[t]he gods know the meaning and the end of their existence as human beings can never hope to do." This, including the meaning of death, is probably among the important matters Socrates frankly acknowledges to be beyond his grasp. That seems likely from the whole tenor of the *Apology*. What else Socrates might mean by 'important matters' is difficult to say with any degree of confidence.

We notice also that in (2) Socrates draws an explicit distinction between human and more-than-human or superhuman wisdom or knowledge. That is the solution to the apparent contradiction between (1) and (2). For suppose Socrates means by 'superhuman wisdom' perfect knowledge or complete certainty about the most important matters; and suppose that by 'human wisdom' he means knowing certain other things in the fallible way we humans can know them, including that one does not have knowledge of the infallible superhuman kind and that all human knowledge is worth little by comparison with it. This suffices to reconcile Socrates's statements that he both (2) has (human) and (1) lacks (superhuman) wisdom. That this is indeed the correct solution is borne out by the statement Socrates makes concerning those who purport to have a more-than-human-wisdom: "he thinks he knows something when he does not, whereas when I do not know, neither do I think I know" (21d). The crux of Socratic wisdom is knowing, in the fallible manner proper to human knowledge, what we do and do not know.

All this seems perfectly consistent, if still somewhat—though perhaps not unduly—sceptical.

9.1.6 Socrates, gadfly of Athens

A gadfly is a largish insect like our horsefly that settles on men and beasts and stings them painfully. Here is how Socrates describes his own activities in the streets, porticoes, marketplaces, and gymnasia of Athens:

So I go around seeking out anyone, citizen or stranger, whom I think wise. Then if I do not think he is, I come to the assistance of the god and show him that he is not wise. Because of this occupation I do not have the leisure to engage in public affairs to any extent, nor indeed to look after my own, but I live in great poverty because of my service to the god. (23b)

I shall not cease to practise philosophy, to exhort you and in my usual way to point out to any one of you whom I happen to meet: Good Sir, you are an Athenian, a citizen of the greatest city with the greatest reputation for both wisdom and power; are you not ashamed of your eagerness to possess as much wealth, reputation and honours as possible, while you do not care for nor give thought to wisdom or truth, or the best possible state of your soul? Then if one of you disputes this and says he does care, I shall not let him go at once or leave him, but I shall question him, examine him and test him, and if I do not think he has attained the goodness that he says he has, I shall reproach him because he attaches little importance to the most important things and greater importance to inferior things. I shall treat in this way anyone I happen to meet, young or old, citizen or stranger, and more so the citizens because you are more kindred to me. Be sure that this is what the god orders me to do. (29d–30a)

For I go around doing nothing but persuading both young and old among you not to care for your body or your wealth in preference to or as strongly as for the best possible state of your soul. (30a)

I went to each of you privately and conferred upon him what I say is the greatest benefit, by trying to persuade him not to care for any of his belongings before caring that he himself should be as good and as wise as possible, not to care for the city's possessions more than for the city itself, and to care for other things in the same way. (36c–d)

I was attached to this city by the god—though it seems a ridiculous thing to say—as upon a great and noble horse which was somewhat sluggish because of its size and needed to be stirred up by a kind of gadfly. It is to fulfill some such function that I believe the god has placed me in the city. I never cease to rouse each and every one of you, to persuade and reproach you all day long everywhere I find myself in your company. (30e)

To be such a gadfly was Socrates's mission in life, assigned him (he firmly believed) by the God Apollo. We shall return to Socrates's mission later.

9.2 Stingray

9.2.1 *The subject of the* Meno

The *Meno* is one of the transitional dialogues (see above 8.3) that begin to set out doctrines of Plato's own not held by Socrates. (Here it is above all the so-called theory of Recollection, which we shall get to know in our study of the *Phaedo*, that is Platonic rather than Socratic. It occurs first in the *Meno*, beginning at 80d.) Nevertheless, the first part of the *Meno*, up to 80d, offers some reliable insights into the activities and character of Socrates, particularly his philosophical method.

The question with which the *Meno* begins is: Can virtue be taught? Right at the outset, four possibilities are envisioned: (1) virtue is acquired by learning (as is anything that can correctly be called 'knowledge'); (2) virtue is not so much knowledge as a disposition to behave in a certain way owing to practice and repetition; (3) virtue is inborn, innate, exists "by nature" (70a) in some people (and not in others), is a "natural gift" (86d), an "inborn quality" (99e); (4) 'some other way' (e.g., virtue is a gift or dispensation of the gods, akin to the gift of poetry or prophecy).

But Socrates characteristically insists that it is not possible to answer a question about a *quality* of virtue ('teachability') without knowing what *virtue itself* is. And so the discussion of this question actually begins with the prior question, 'What is virtue?' The dialogue ends with Socrates conjecturing that the answer to the original question is (4), but that particular question will not concern us here. Even the question 'What is virtue?' is secondary from our point of view. For we want to know what the *Meno* can add to our understanding of the life and character of Socrates as described in the *Apology*.

9.2.2 Meno's definition of virtue and Socrates's refutation

The Thessalian Meno, who was deeply impressed by the sophist Gorgias when the latter visited Thessaly, is surprised (71b–c) to hear Socrates profess ignorance of what virtue is. He is eager to answer the question in the manner of Gorgias, and comes up with the following 'definition' (D1):

D1 First, if you want the virtue of a man, it is easy to say that a man's virtue consists of being able to manage public affairs and in so doing to benefit his friends and harm his enemies and to be careful that no harm comes to himself; if you want the virtue of a woman, it is not difficult to describe: she must manage the home well, preserve its possessions, be submissive to her husband; the virtue of a child, whether male or female, is different again, and so is that of an elderly man if you want that or if you want that of a free man or a slave. And there are many other virtues, so that one is not at a loss to say what virtue is. There is a virtue for every action and every age, for every task of ours and every one of us—and Socrates, the same is true of wickedness. (71e–72a)

This, of course, is not a Socratic definition of 'virtue' at all, but a catalogue of examples. Socrates is at some pains to explain this to Meno:

Even if they are many and various, all of them have one and the same form which makes them virtues and it is right to look to this when one is asked to make clear what virtue is. (72c)

Once Socrates has made clear what he is after in asking 'What is virtue?' using both homely examples like bees and strict mathematical definitions ('a shape is the limit of a solid'), Meno advances a general definition of virtue ('P' stands for 'premise,' 'C' for 'conclusion, and 'D' again for 'definition'):

D2 Virtue is to desire beautiful [or good] things and to have the power to provide them. (77b)

Hearing this, Socrates easily persuades Meno (see 77c) that

P1 All men *always* desire what is (or seems to them) good for them, what they believe will make them happy (Or simply: 'All men strive for happiness.')

P1 is a very simple statement of a doctrine known as eudaemonism, from the Greek word *eudaimonia*, often translated 'happiness.' It seems from others of the early dialogues of Plato that the historical Socrates held a doctrine of this general type, as did most Greek moralists. The doctrine asserts, at a first rough approximation, that every rational agent seeks his own happiness; or, negatively, that no rational human being acts in such a way as to harm himself or impair his own happiness or chances of happiness—at least not insofar as he is governed by reason. Now from P1 it follows immediately that desiring good things cannot be what distinguishes virtuous from vicious characters, since *all* men, both virtuous and wicked, desire good things. Accordingly, the source of the difficulty, desiring good things, must be dropped from the definition. Meno understands this.

More will be said of eudaemonism later. Right now it is worth mentioning that, unlike our word 'happiness,' *eudaimonia* means neither some more or less transitory sense of pleasure, nor an intense feeling of joy or elation, whether fleeting or lasting, nor yet just plain 'feeling jolly' most of the time. The merely nominal word meaning is roughly 'a state or condition that is owing to the good (*eu*) will or influence of a supernatural being' (*daimōn*). In pre-philosophical Greek, it was hardly ever used of a state of mind, and almost always of material wealth or high standing and honour, both thought of as a man's divinely apportioned lot in life. In philosophical Greek, by contrast, it signifies something more like what we mean by a person's long-term well-being—having a good life, thriving and flourishing as a human being, rather than as a beast might thrive and flourish by giving full vent to its appetites and desires. To be 'happy' in the Greek sense, then, is to have a life that is both human and well worth living, one that is rich rather than poor in those things that make a life a worthwhile *human* existence. This may include wealth and standing, but need not do so, unless those things are really essential to a good human life. Happiness in this sense will also include episodes of 'happiness' in our modern-day sense, perhaps a great many of them; but it is certainly not to be identified with such states, or with some rate of frequency in their occurrence. Perhaps the expression used in the Introduction, 'human flourishing,' is the best translation, though the prosaic expression 'quality of life' would be the closest equivalent in present-day speech. More will be said about *eudaimonia* later.

Since it follows from P1 that desiring good things cannot be what distinguishes virtuous from vicious characters, Meno simply drops it from his definition, which, in its revised form, runs:

D3 Virtue is "the power of securing good things.' (78b)

Meno also clarifies what he means by 'good things': health, wealth, honour, and political success. At this point Socrates has succeeded in clarifying Meno's definition, and proposes to "see then whether what you say is true" (78c). And so the refutation begins.

To a question from Socrates, Meno responds that

P2 The ability to provide good things unjustly would not be virtuous but vicious.

So the definition has to be reformulated as follows:

D4 Virtue "is to be able to secure good things with justice." (79b)

But now Socrates has to remind Meno that justice was admitted earlier to be *a part* of virtue (78e, 79b). So Meno has defined virtue using virtue in the definition:

D4 'Virtue is being able to provide good things virtuously.'

Such definitions are *circular* (see the end of 7.7.2): they make the very thing to be explained part of the explanation itself—which explains nothing, gets us nowhere, leads us right back where we started from. Socrates reminds Meno that "we rejected the kind of answer that tried to answer in terms still being the subject of enquiry"—like 'virtue.' He is referring to the passage at 75d, where he laid it down that "the answer must not only be true, but in terms admittedly known to the questioner," that is, terms that do not themselves again require definition. Hence the conclusion:

C This cannot be the definition of virtue, and Meno must start all over again. (79c–d)

Reduced to perplexity, Meno remarks:

Socrates, even before I met you I used to hear that you are always in a state of perplexity and that you bring others to the same state, and now I think you are bewitching and beguiling me, simply putting me under a spell, so that I am quite perplexed. Indeed, if a joke is in order, you seem in appearance [Socrates was snub-nosed with protruding eyes] and in every other way, to be like a broad torpedo fish [the stingray], for it too makes anyone who comes close and touches it feel numb, and you now seem to have had that kind of effect on me, for both my mind and my tongue are numb, and I have no answer to give you. Yet I have made many speeches about virtue before large audiences on a thousand occasions ... [B]ut now I cannot even say what it is. I think you are wise not to sail away from Athens to go and stay elsewhere, for if you were to behave like this as a foreigner in any other city, you would be driven away for practising sorcery. (80a–b)

This passage confirms two things said in the *Apology* about Socrates's manner of examining those claiming to know something about important matters like virtue. First, Socrates himself has no positive teaching. His aim is mainly negative: the *testing* of others' views to see whether they are knowledge or merely the pretence of knowledge. Meno apparently recognizes this fact, whereas those to whom Socrates refers in the *Apology* thought he believed himself to have knowledge of the matters about which he questioned them. Second, cross-examination by Socrates induces a state of perplexity (numbness, befuddlement) in the cross-examined. This, to judge by Meno, is often felt to be extremely unpleasant.

Hence Meno's advice to Socrates at 80b: Don't try this sort of thing in a city less tolerant than Athens. Of course, from the *Apology* we know that Meno (who was a foreigner) overestimated the tolerance of the Athenians!

9.2.3 Aporia

The word translated as 'perplexity' is cognate with the Greek noun *aporia*. The syllable 'a-' is a negative prefix in Greek, called 'the alpha-*privativum*.' Certain English words follow this Greek model, for example, 'atemporal' (see 16.5.1), 'amoral' (see 32.4.1), 'atypical,' 'asymmetrical,' 'atheism,' and so on. It does the same work as the syllables 'un-' (for example, 'unending') and 'in-' (as in 'indefinite') or 'im-' (as in 'impersonal') in many Latin and English words. Having two such means of negation at our disposal, the one drawn from Greek, the other from Latin, we can employ them in order to draw certain technical distinctions, for example, that between 'amoral' and 'immoral' (ibid.). This can be handy at times.

Poros is the ordinary Greek word for a path or passage or way. So *aporia* means literally 'lack of passage,' 'impasse,' 'no way out,' or 'no way onward.' The term was used in ordinary Greek for a lack of monetary means, that is, poverty. By extension, it came to be applied to the mental state of being at a loss, puzzlement, disorientation, or befuddlement, even (as Meno suggests) being benumbed, stupefied, dumbfounded, dazed. This is the typical result of Socrates's cross-examinations. It may be a matter of not knowing a way out of a quandary or, alternatively, coming to an impasse, not being able to proceed onward toward a satisfactory conclusion or resolution. All this is covered by the single Greek word *aporia*.

Nevertheless, discussion that results in perplexity or *aporia* can represent positive progress toward the discovery of truth (always Socrates's aim!) in a number of ways. First, even where Socrates does not propose any positive answer of his own, but only tests and rejects another's, a range of important matters pertaining to the problem in hand may be cleared up in the process. Thus, after a number of false starts, Meno finally grasps the meaning of the general type of question, 'What is x?' and how answering such a question differs from merely giving examples. Something similar occurs in the *Euthyphro*, where the question is 'What is piety?' Like Meno,

Euthyphro tries to answer by giving an example: 'Piety is doing what I'm doing right now ...' He too gets a lesson concerning the difference between definition and examples. But there is a further benefit as well.

Second, perplexity can knock the smugness out of us, making us realize our ignorance about the point at issue and bringing the question to life by enhancing our understanding of the *problem*. Numbness may subside, leaving us in a better frame of mind to pursue the question *modestly* and *intelligently*. This is what the Socrates of the *Meno* suggests:

Have we done him any harm by making him perplexed and numb? ... Indeed we have probably achieved something relevant to finding out how matters stand, for now, as he does not know, he would be glad to find out, whereas before he thought he could easily make many fine speeches to large audiences. (84b)

But there is a further type of progress as well.

Third, the debate may provide an opportunity to examine other beliefs that both Socrates and his interlocutor accept, like P1: 'All men always desire what is (or seems to them) good for them, what they believe will make them happy.' After examining them together, they may be confirmed in these beliefs or they may abandon them, regardless of whether they are able to make any headway with the main question occupying them. And that too can represent progress.

So Socrates is telling the truth when, at *Apology* 28e, he states as his aim "to examine *myself* and others" (e.a.). The premises he gets Meno to agree to in order to show the latter's definition of virtue to be unsatisfactory are premises like P1 (see previous paragraph), which Socrates himself accepts.

9.2.4 *Socratic* elenchus

The Greek word Socrates uses for his practice of cross-examining people is *elenchos*, often Latinized as *elenchus*. His method is accordingly called 'elenctic,' this being the adjectival form of the word. In ordinary Greek, the verb *elenchein* means 'to examine critically,' 'to cross-examine,' 'to censure' or 'find fault' with someone or something.

We have an example of *elenchus* in the cross-examination of Meletus in the *Apology*. This is probably typical of the type of public humiliation to which Socrates subjected people. It addresses in turn each of the two charges in the indictment (corruption of the youth and 'neologism,' that is, religious innovation or non-conformism, even heresy: not believing in the gods of the city but in other, new gods). Regarding the first of these charges, corrupting the youth, Socrates's response is threefold.

First, Socrates shows that Meletus, while accusing him of being the corrupter, is

Chapter 9: Life and Character 175

unable to say who improves the youth, which surely suggests that he has never been seriously interested in the welfare of the youth of Athens at all. This, of course, is not much of an argument, since it is directed against the person rather than the claim, an *ad hominem* argument (see above 7.7.1). Two other arguments that are not strictly *ad hominem* follow, although Socrates unfortunately uses them, too, to bolster his *ad hominem* attack.

In the second argument Socrates shows how improbable it is that he alone of all the Athenians corrupts the youth, as Meletus claims, while practically everyone else in Athens makes them better. For in no known case of training (physical training, horse training, and so on) is it true that one person alone corrupts or spoils, while many or all others improve the subject or trainee. This is a kind of *inductive argument* (see 6.2.2) or argument from parallel cases. It is designed to show that Meletus's claim is grossly at odds with the course of ordinary experience. For in the other cases mentioned (horse training and athletic training) it is not at all true that the many make the subject better; on the contrary, only the few experts do. How likely is it, then, that the reverse is the case with the youth of Athens? Aristotle tells us that Socrates was the first to use this type of argument, and his testimony is confirmed by other authors of Socratic dialogues apart from Plato. Such arguments are not strictly refutative, in the sense of proving the falsity of his opponent's claim, but they certainly can raise a strong presumption against its truth.

So much for the second argument. Finally, Socrates gets Meletus to make his charge more specific: not just 'Socrates corrupts the youth,' but 'Socrates corrupts the youth *intentionally*.' Having done this, he elicits certain premises, starting with this one:

P1   To live among good people is beneficial and among bad ones harmful to oneself;

From this it follows immediately that

P2   To make others around one worse is (indirectly) to harm oneself.

But according to popular belief (and Meletus is a firm adherent of popular wisdom),

P3   no one deliberately harms himself.

This is just a restatement of the principle of eudaemonism found in the *Meno*: that all men, insofar as they behave rationally, desire and pursue what is (or seems) good for themselves. Since Socrates is no exception to this rule, the conclusion from these premises is that

C   Either (a) Socrates does not make the young people worse at all or (b) he does so unintentionally.

In either case, (a) or (b), the claim 'Socrates corrupts the youth intentionally' is false.

Notice how Socrates refutes Meletus using the latter's own beliefs (e.g., P1, P2). Aristotle also tells us that this type of refutation was typical of Socrates, who did not claim to know or teach or prove anything himself, but only showed that others' views must be mistaken since the views under examination, or other collateral views they held, led to false (or contradictory) consequences.

That takes care of the charge of corrupting the youth. Regarding the second charge, believing in "other" gods than those of the city (26b–28b), Socrates first gets Meletus to accuse him of complete atheism and then points out the *logical inconsistency* of alleging *both* (1) that he believes in "other" gods than those of the city *and* (2) that he believes in no gods whatever. For (1) entails logically that Socrates believes in some gods, which is the negation of (2).

This practice of using the answerer's true beliefs to refute his false claims is typical of Socratic *elenchus*. Schematically, p must be false (where p stands for any proposition) because it logically contradicts q and q is what the answerer himself *and Socrates* both accept as true. Sometimes instead of q there may be a whole string of premises, q, r, s, and so on, that jointly contradict p (even though they may be consistent with it individually). Of course, this only shows that p is false *if* q is true. Socrates's interlocutor could abandon q and continue to maintain p—although this is exactly what never seems to happen. Instead, p is agreed to have been refuted, sometimes rather grudgingly.

9.2.5 Peirastic, dialectical, and apodictic arguments

Socrates's elenctic arguments test the claims of others, usually resulting in their rejection. Following Aristotle, we can also call such arguments 'peirastic,' from the Greek word for 'test' or 'put to the test,' *peirao*. Indeed, 'to test' or 'make trial of' is a further meaning of the Greek verb *elenchein* itself.

In a work entitled *On Sophistical Refutations*, Aristotle opposes *peirastic* to *dialectical* and to *apodictic* proofs. *Apodictic* arguments are *positive*: they are used to establish one's own conclusions. Moreover, they employ as premises only propositions which are self-evident, that is, known to be true without any proof. If valid, apodictic arguments establish their conclusion with the *highest degree of certainty* possible. Such arguments are typical of mathematics, for example, geometry, which uses as its premises axioms and definitions that require no proof, axioms like 'things equal to the same thing are equal to each other' and definitions like 'a triangle is a figure bounded by three straight lines' (see 6.2.1.).

Dialectical arguments, on the other hand, are *negative*: they refute an opponent's views by showing that they contradict others that "commend themselves to all or to the majority or to the wise," as Aristotle puts it in his *Topics*. The latter are embodied in premises that are not self-evident, even though accepted by the majority or by the wisest as true. Since the premises of such counter-arguments are at best only very highly probable, their conclusions, too, are *less than perfectly certain*. Dialectical arguments are appropriate in ethical enquiries according to Aristotle, who makes extensive use of them there.

Finally, *peirastic* arguments are, like dialectical arguments, *negative* in force, or refutations; yet they differ from the dialectical in that they use as their premises beliefs accepted by the answerer himself (and the questioner) as true, not by "the majority or ... the wise." Hence their conclusions, too, which are always negative, are quite *uncertain*.

Socrates, according to Aristotle, used *only* peirastic arguments in his moral enquiries. There are several reasons why neither apodictic nor dialectical arguments were available to him. For one thing, (1) the historical Socrates was interested only in moral questions, questions like 'What is virtue?' or 'What is justice?' or 'What is piety?' The answers to moral questions do not admit of mathematically exact proof. On the other hand, (2) Socrates did not claim to know the answers to these questions himself, but only examined others' answers. So only a *negative* form of argumentation would do for his purposes. Finally, (3) Socrates repeatedly asserts that what 'the many' think is completely irrelevant in moral deliberations. For this we have the testimony of the *Crito*: "My good Crito, why should we care so much for what the majority think?" (44c). Or again at 47c of the same work: "So with other matters, not to enumerate them all, and certainly with actions just and unjust, shameful and beautiful, good and bad, about which we are now deliberating, should we follow the opinion of the many and fear it, or that of the one, if there is one who has knowledge of these things." Thus, of the two negative forms of argument, only the peirastic, not the dialectical, can be used to administer the sting of *elenchus*.

9.3 Silenus

We turn now to a third source of insight into the life and character of the man Socrates, the description of Socrates given by Alcibiades in the dialogue entitled the *Symposium*.

9.3.1 Alcibiades's speech in the Symposium

The *Symposium* is a third-hand narration of speeches given in praise of the god of Love at a drinking party (Greek: *symposion*) held at the house of the tragic poet Agathon to celebrate the victory of his tragedy in the festival competition. Alcibiades, who arrives late and inebriated, insists on delivering a speech in praise of Socrates. In the speech, he likens Socrates to a silenus. Sileni (plural of Silenus) are little figures of satyrs (half man, half goat), usually depicted as playing flutes or Pan pipes, and quite repulsive to look at: flat-nosed, pointy-eared, in a word, animal-like. Quite common in statuary shops in Athens in the fifth century, they were made so as to open, revealing beautiful little golden images of gods inside.

In his speech, Alcibiades stresses three features of these sileni as hitting off facets of the character of Socrates. First, (a) satyrs were supposed to be spell-binding musicians or flute players. According to Aristotle, the melodies of the satyr Olympus (whom Alcibiades mentions) produced in the hearer a trance-like state of possession, exercising a kind of supernatural force. Socrates, according to Alcibiades, has the power to bind a spell on people with words or argument rather than with the flute. The relevant passage is found at 215e–216a (the translation is Benjamin Jowett's):

I have heard Pericles and other great orators, and I thought that they spoke well, but I never had any similar feeling; my soul was not stirred by them, nor was I angry at the thought of my own slavish state. But this Marsyas [a legendary satyr to whom Alcibiades is likening Socrates] has often brought me to such a pass that I have felt as if I could hardly endure the life which I am leading ... For he makes me confess that I ought not to live as I do, neglecting the wants of my own soul, and busying myself with the concerns of the Athenians.

That is the first parallel. In addition, (b) satyrs were associated with excessive eroticism or sexual appetite. Alcibiades remarks at 216d "how fond [literally: amorously inclined, erotically disposed] he [Socrates] is of the fair. He is always with them and is always being smitten by them." And at 223a he comments: "where Socrates is, no one else has any chance with the fair." In the *Charmides* (154b–c) Socrates remarks on his own susceptibility in this regard (see also 155d), poking fun at it at *Meno* 76b–c, where he suggests that the handsome Meno is taking advantage of him and that he only answers Meno's questions because he cannot resist the fair. Finally, (c) while ugly or bestial on the outside, sileni contained something beautiful or divine on the inside.

Now Socrates fits this description in three ways, according to Alcibiades. First, while outwardly the most erotically inclined of men, he is *really* the most temperate or self-controlled. Beauty, like wealth and honour, are really of "no account with him ... he regards not at all the persons who are gifted with them" (216e). This is fully borne out by the story of Alcibiades's unsuccessful attempts to seduce Socrates with his beauty, beginning at 217a. Secondly, while Socrates's words appear laughable on the surface ("he talks of pack-asses, and smiths and cobblers"), they have hidden depths of meaning:

he who opens the bust and sees what is within will find that they are the only words which have a meaning in them, and also the most divine, abounding in fair images of virtue, and of the widest comprehension, or rather extending to the whole duty of a good and honourable man. (221e–222a)

Finally, while outwardly claiming to know nothing and be ignorant of all things, Socrates is in fact wise.

9.3.2 Further features of Socrates's character

It is worth noting in passing some other features of Socrates's personality mentioned in Alcibiades's speech. We can simply list them without elaborate comment, since they speak pretty much for themselves.

First, there is Socrates's remarkable drinking ability, alluded to both at 214a and at 220a. This is obviously intended to underscore his complete and utter self-mastery, the point made already by the story of his resistance to the charms of the handsome young Alcibiades. No matter how much this Socrates fellow has drunk, it seems, there is no effect whatever on his outward demeanour. Next, there is Socrates's physical endurance (219e–220b) and his stalwart courage in battle (220e–221c). He is a man of extraordinary physical as well as moral courage. This historical fact is attested also in the dialogue *Laches* (181b). Moreover, we learn here of Socrates's strange tendency to go into a 'trance' of thought (220c -d), a 'brown study' as we say, becoming completely oblivious of his surroundings as he ponders some profound philosophical problem with extraordinary intellectual concentration. Finally, there is Socrates's piety, as evidenced by his offering up prayers (ibid.). This last feature of the man's character is borne out by many details in the dialogues that we shall be studying; indeed, apart from his piety and the religious duties he regards as incumbent upon him, it may not be possible to understand fully the life that Socrates led. We shall return to this theme in chapters 11 and 13.

These details complete Alcibiades's portrait of the man Socrates. We shall return to Alcibiades for our final summation at the end of the chapter.

9.4 Midwife

9.4.1 Theme and structure of the Theaetetus

The Platonic dialogue *Theaetetus* is devoted to the question, 'What is knowledge?' Although this looks like a Socratic 'What is ...?' question, the historical Socrates probably did not possess an explicit theory of knowledge, any more than he had an explicit metaphysical theory of universals. The dialogue belongs clearly to Plato's own middle period (see 8.3 above). Nevertheless, it casts an interesting sidelight on the character of the historical Socrates.

The *Theaetetus* as a whole falls into an introduction and three parts, with the section that interests us figuring as an interlude between them. We can set out its structure schematically as follows:

180   Part One: Socrates and the Road to Wisdom

Introduction: The Question, 'What is knowledge?' and its Clarification (142a–148d).
       First Interlude: Socratic Midwifery (148e–151e)
Part I.   First definition: Knowledge is perception (151e–187a).
       Second Interlude: Lawyers and Philosophers (172c–177c).
Part II.   Second definition: Knowledge is true belief (187a–201c).
Part III. Third definition: Knowledge is true belief together with (the ability to give) an account or justification of that belief (201c–end).

For our purposes here, only the first interlude, that dealing with midwifery, is relevant.

9.4.2 The midwife's (maieutic) art and Socratic elenchus

In the course of the interlude the six alleged aspects of the midwife's art emerge. To begin with, we can simply list them without elaborate comment:

(1) Midwives deliver women of the babies their bodies have conceived.
(2) Midwives are usually too old to conceive and bear children themselves.
(3) Midwives are best able to determine who is pregnant and who is not.
(4) Midwives are the best matchmakers.
(5) Midwives are best able to induce labour in one who is pregnant.
(6) Midwives are best able to decide which children should be delivered and given life and which should be "smothered in the womb" or, if born, exposed and allowed to die.

Of the six, only (4) strikes one immediately as odd, and may have so struck Plato's contemporaries as well. This detail must be pure invention for the purposes of the contrast to follow. As for (6), it may seem odd to us, but the idea that the head of the household might decide on his own authority (perhaps with the advice of a midwife) to expose a weak or deformed infant would not have seemed strange to Greeks, who would have known of the practice in the archaic period.

If we now compare the Socratic *elenchus* with the midwife's art (*maieutikē technē* in Greek), we find that Socrates (1) delivers *men* of the ideas which their minds or *souls* have conceived, yet (2) is himself 'barren,' just like the midwife: "I ask questions of others and have not the wit to answer them myself" (150c), he remarks. Or again: "[N]one of these theories comes from me; they all come from him who talks with me. I only know just enough to extract them" (161b). Furthermore, Socrates (3) recognizes which of the young men who come to him are pregnant and which are not, (4) making matches for those who are not pregnant by 'marrying them off' to the sophists. Moreover, Socrates (5) is able to "arouse and allay" birth pangs in those who consort with him, that is, to induce perplexity or *aporia* (151a). Finally, he (6) takes the offspring away if he finds that the idea of which he delivers someone is a "folly" (151c) or a "wind-egg" (161a), as he calls also it.

So much, in rapid overview, for the formal parallels drawn in the dialogue. Attempting to interpret them now, we find that (1) and (2) seem to have to do with the nature of *intellectual creation*, while (3) and (4) concern *education*, opposing the Socratic and sophistic ideals of education to one another. Finally (5) and (6) concern *self-knowledge* as the chief benefit of elenctic refutation. All this needs to be spelled out somewhat.

In the first place, then, parallels are developed between all the phases of childbirth, on the one hand, and intellectual or artistic creativity, on the other: conception, pregnancy, labour, midwife-assisted birth, rearing of offspring are the phases common to both. There is no reason to believe that this parallel is really Socratic rather than something that interested Plato in his middle period. Of course, the analogy that Plato invented has since become a tedious commonplace in descriptions of artistic creation. That, however, cannot be blamed on its inventor. In Plato's own day it must have seemed fresh and illuminating. Whether for good or ill, its effect on the theory of art has proved lasting.

The next two parallels with midwifery bring into focus two radically different conceptions of education: (a) transfer of skills and information from the teacher to the pupil, that is, putting something into the (presumably empty) heads of the students; (b) drawing out of the minds of the young the truth or knowledge that is already there, 'leading forth' (*educere* in Latin) what is already latent in the pupil but needs to be 'delivered' through the pains of labour. (a) is at least alluded to in (4), (b) in (3).

Now (a) is pretty clearly education as the sophists understood it, whence Socrates sends those who are *not* pregnant to Prodicus to get 'filled up' with knowledge of the sort the sophist deals in. Even if the historical Socrates never actually described himself as a midwife, it is clear enough that he at least subscribed to an ideal of education that corresponds closely to (b). For implicit in (b) or (3) is the conviction that even though there is just *one* truth to be discovered, about moral as about other matters, one truth that is the same for all men, not subjective nor culturally relative, nevertheless *everyone still has to discover it for himself*. All a teacher can ever do is to recognize the pupil who is 'pregnant' and point him in the right direction. This ideal of learning by working things out for oneself is, as already noted (see 2.6), the vital thing in higher education, the ideal of education pioneered by Socrates in opposition to the 'discipleship' model of the sophists. It was remarked above that this Socratic ideal was taken up into the thought of the eighteenth-century Enlightenment, through which it has continued to shape the contemporary notion of higher education. The heart of the matter lies in the idea that one can possess fully only what one has acquired through one's own intellectual effort. It was this that was to find a profound echo in the Enlightenment ideal of individual liberty as *autonomy*. We shall see how this is so later, when Socrates's moral theory will be briefly compared and contrasted with that of Kant (see 12.8.5), a leading figure of the European Enlightenment. In the next section we shall see how this ideal of intellectual autonomy features in Socrates's use of irony as well.

Finally, from the last two parallels with midwifery we see that the positive value of elenctic refutation consists in the self-knowledge it furnishes. *Elenchus* (a) induces (painful) labour: "Dire are the pangs which my art is able to arouse and to allay in those who consort with me" (151a). The *first degree of self-knowledge* is discovering what one actually believes, what views one holds about a certain matter. By questioning, Socrates is able to elicit opinions and so to help the answerer discover what his own beliefs are, beliefs he perhaps did not know he held. But elenctic refutation also (b) deprives us of our non-viable brainchildren, demonstrating our ignorance, which is also painful: "For I have actually known some who were ready to bite me when I deprived them of a darling folly" (151c). The *second degree of self-knowledge*, then, consists in the realization that one's belief about a certain matter is untenable and has to be abandoned or revised: the realization of ignorance or *aporia* (see above 9.2.3). Third, and finally, elenctic refutation (c) shows us how to rear the viable offspring. "Many," says Socrates, "have gone away too soon; and have not only lost the children of whom I had previously delivered them by an ill bringing up, but have stifled whatever else they had in them by evil communication" (150e). This *third degree of self-knowledge* consists in recognizing those beliefs or ideas that are worthy of retention, the positive discovery of such truth as one does possess.

These three degrees of self-knowledge amount to wisdom in the authentic Socratic sense: the knowledge of what we do and do not know. In this connection, consider the passage at 210c, at which point Socrates and Theaetetus have rejected all of the latter's definitions of knowledge:

But if, Theaetetus, you should ever conceive afresh, you will be all the better for the present investigation, and if not, you will be soberer and humbler and gentler toward other men, and you will be too modest to fancy that you know what you do not know. These are the limits of my art.

The maieutic art described in the *Theaetetus* is almost certainly the creature of Plato's artistic imagination, fashioned by embroidering upon the elenctic method invented by his great teacher. But that there is a kernel of historical truth in the embellishments seems plain enough. For the elenctic examination *of others* requires that those others first put forward an opinion for examination, and very often Socrates must 'worm it out of them,' or, as Plato has it, deliver them of their soul's offspring. This phase of the process undoubtedly preserves a genuine trace of the philosophic method of Socrates.

9.5 Ironist

9.5.1 Some definitions of irony

Irony is a figure of speech or a rhetorical (literary) device. Others figures are, for example, hyperbole (exaggeration), metonymy (using the part for the whole, for example, 'a sail' to mean 'a ship'), synecdoche (using the whole or the genus for the part or species, for example 'the French' for 'the French government'), metaphor, simile, antithesis, hendiadys (literally 'one through two,' for example, 'law and order' for law), and so on. Oxymoron is a favourite, as when the game of rugby is described as 'ordered chaos,' for example.

Irony, then, belongs to this family of figures of speech, which could be extended considerably. Cicero (1st century BC) defines it as a figure of speech in which "what you say is quite other than what you understand." This Quintillian (1st century AD) alters to "in which something contrary to what is said is to be understood." They differ only in that the former definition takes the speaker's, the latter the hearer's point of view. Dr Johnson's famous dictionary (1755) defines 'irony' as "a mode of speech in which the meaning is contrary to the words." Finally, Webster's Dictionary offers the following definition: "Irony is the use of words to express something other than, and especially the opposite of, [their] literal meaning."

Of course, we use the words 'irony' and 'ironic' fairly loosely nowadays to describe situations in which the intent and the outcome of an action are at odds. Thus, it would be 'ironic' in something like the now customary sense if, intending to avoid lunch with that old bore, Jack, I deliberately chose a restaurant other than his usual spot and ran smack into—Jack, of course. Similarly, we might call it ironic that the ill-considered Treaty of Versailles that brought peace to Europe was largely responsible for plunging it into war again twenty years later; that certainly was not the intent of the treaty-makers. But if (1) the contemporary sense of irony differs from (2) the classical definitions cited above, the latter, as we shall see presently, differ in an important respect from (3) the original Greek sense of the term.

9.5.2 Examples of irony

We say the opposite of what we mean for a variety of purposes, but mainly when either (a) jesting, (b) mocking, or (c) propounding a riddle. Thus, suppose you are bedridden and obviously very ill. A friend nevertheless asks how you are. You reply in a deadpan tone: "Never felt better!" meaning just the opposite. This is jesting irony. Again, somebody commits a particularly gross social blunder, and you comment, in flattering tones: "Always the perfect gentleman (lady), aren't you?" meaning to say: "How tactless!" This is mocking irony. Finally, somebody gives you a bit of unsolicited advice on a matter that is none of his business. You neither agree nor disagree but say (perhaps with a certain emphasis): "I'll certainly take that under advisement." Literally, this expresses something like regard for the advice given, when, in fact, you intend to leave the other person guessing at what you think of the suggestion. The irony is of the riddling variety.

Note that the key thing about irony in all these forms is that there be *no intention to deceive*. If there were, if the speaker really wanted the hearer to take his words literally and believe something false, it would be incorrect to speak of irony.

9.5.3 Socrates's use of irony

The Greek word for irony occurs in connection with Socrates in Plato's early dialogues *both* in the uses just described *and* in a different sense: as a term that connotes deliberate deception. Some speakers think that Socrates is trying to deceive them, just *pretending* not to have any answers to the questions he asks, when in fact he has (or thinks he has). In other words, they take him to be *posing* as an enquiring pupil, feigning or dissembling, when in fact he thinks himself superior to (say) the sophist whom he is questioning. According to these characters, Socrates uses this ploy because he prefers to refute others rather than risk being refuted himself.

From these passages we can infer that in Plato's time, 'irony' and 'ironical' *could* also have the sense of deliberately misleading one's hearer by saying (and trying to make him believe) something untrue, even if it has no such sense today. Did Socrates sometimes *dissemble* in the way his opponents allege? Relevant here is this passage from the dialogue *Gorgias* (458a–b):

As for me, I would be pleased to cross-question you, provided you are the same sort of human being as I; if not, I would let you go. What sort is that? One of those who would be pleased to be refuted if I say something untrue, and pleased to refute another if he says something untrue, but more pleased to be refuted than refute—as much more as being rid oneself of the greatest evil is better than ridding another of it; for I do not believe that anything could be as evil for a human being as to harbour false beliefs about the things we are now discussing [that is, virtue and whether it is profitable or not].

In a similar vein, Socrates remarks in the *Protagoras*: "My object is to test the validity of the argument; and yet the result may be that I who ask and you who answer may both be put on our trial" (333c); and later (348a) he speaks of "putting one another to the proof [or test] in conversation."

If these passages are a true reflection of the attitude of the historical Socrates, then he is certainly no dissembler. The uses of 'ironical' that can be and are correctly applied to Socrates are thus only those in which 'speaking ironically' is inconsistent with 'wanting to deceive.' That means: (a) jesting, (b) mocking, and (c) riddling irony. The 'irony' that he was frequently accused of by his contemporaries—(d) wilful deception—was almost certainly alien to him.

9.5.4 Socrates's most characteristic irony

Socrates's most famous irony—his self-effacing manner—combines all three types of irony just mentioned. For at one level, Socrates's mock humility and deference to others, his way of cajoling them into submitting to his *elenchus*, are the expression of a fun-loving, playful personality. While deeply serious about the issues under discussion, he prefers to be light and entertaining rather than sombre and earnest, and his jests are indeed sometimes very funny. At another level, however, Socrates's deference is intended to make fun of others. He will call famous sophists "admirable" or "wise"; not infrequently, he begs them not to be stingy with their wisdom and to share it with him; he tells Euthyphro he wants to become his disciple, and so forth. This mockery evokes different responses. Sometimes the victim is so vain as to take Socrates literally and be flattered, though Socrates has dropped plenty of hints that he is poking fun at him. Sometimes he thinks Socrates is practising deceit in order to avoid being refuted himself and becomes abusive. Sometimes the victim recognizes that Socrates is mocking him and rebukes him for it. So the range of responses to this mockery is quite varied.

However, the deepest level of Socratic irony is the riddling aspect. Beyond jest and mockery (including self-mockery), Socrates's serious intent is to help his answerers toward virtue, that is, *self*-knowledge as the wisdom that consists in knowing what one knows and does not know. Education, for him, is not a matter of transferring skills from one person to another, as the sophists believed; genuine education is rather *discovering the truth for oneself*. In this we see the depth of Socrates's respect for the autonomy of the individual human being ('autonomy' means roughly: being self-governing and also answerable to and for oneself). In this respect for individual autonomy we can distinguish a number of different aspects, including Socrates's belief (1) that *every* human being has within himself the wherewithal for attaining whatever wisdom is within the reach of mankind; (2) that it is *up to each one of us* to exercise his powers in scrupulous self-examination; and (3) that *no one else can do so for us*. These are the ideals that make Socrates indeed "the father of Western rationalism" (see 8.1) and the precursor of the European Enlightenment of the eighteenth century.

Even when Socrates believes he knows something to be true or false (not, of course, with perfect certainty—only the gods are capable of that), he still wants his answerer to discover it for himself. His work is the midwife's art of leading it forth, teasing it out, coaxing the other's beliefs out into the open so that they can be examined. He has to ask the right questions, point his interlocutor in the right direction, provoke him with riddles, sting or numb him, press him onwards to the realization of the consequences of his beliefs and of their consistency or inconsistency with each other; but truth is something that each much discover for himself.

9.6 Conclusion

This concludes our sketch of the character of the man Socrates, the gadfly, stingray, silenus, midwife, and ironist of the Athenian marketplace. There is a remarkable consistency running through these various characterizations of the man within the dialogues. To what extent it is the consistency of Plato's unified fictional portrait, or of historical fact, is impossible to say with complete confidence. Rather than attempting a summary, the last word on the subject of the man Socrates may fittingly go to the Alcibiades of Plato's *Symposium* (221c), for it is both perceptive and just:

Most of his ways might perhaps be paralleled in another man, but his absolute unlikeness to any human being that is or ever has been is perfectly astonishing.

10

Defence of the Philosophic Life

10.1 Introductory

In the account given earlier of the subject matter of perennial philosophy (see 3.2) attention was confined largely to metaphysics or primary philosophy; detailed discussion of moral philosophy, the other chief domain of perennial philosophical problems, was postponed until later. It has been noted several times already that Socrates, the first moral philosopher, was interested *only* in ethical matters; it is time now to describe the various problems making up the domain of moral philosophy or ethics.

As in the discussion of logic, the principle of selection is again that of relevance to the texts to be interpreted, in the first instance to the *Apology*; later, when we come to the moral philosophy of Sartre, we shall have to supplement this initial account, though much that is said here will be applicable there as well. Having completed our survey of ethics and applied the results to the *Apology*, we shall be in a position to pose the main question to be pursued in Part One: What sort of moral theory did Socrates hold? Three possible answers will be proposed, although it will not be possible to decide among them on the basis of the *Apology* alone; an answer will be found only after we have completed our study of the *Euthyphro* and the *Crito* in the next two chapters.

10.2 Basic concepts of moral philosophy

Moral philosophy or ethics is that branch of philosophy concerned with (1) moral rules, principles, or maxims; (2) their application to particular moral problems; and (3) the meanings of moral concepts as well as the nature of moral value judgments in general.

The attempt to establish some basic norms or rules of moral conduct is called 'normative ethics' or 'normative ethical theory.' The application of such rules to particular moral problems makes up applied ethics. The current but non-traditional problems mentioned in chapter 1 belong to applied ethics, problems like abortion, euthanasia, civil disobedience, capital punishment, and so on. Finally, reflection upon the status of moral knowledge or value judgments in general—asking, for example, whether they can be objective, and just what kind of objectivity they are capable of, if any—is called 'meta-ethics.' The latter also includes reflection on the meanings of moral terms like 'good,' 'right,' 'just,' 'duty,' 'freedom,' 'responsibility,' and so on.

Our question, What sort of moral theory does Socrates hold? is about the normative ethical theory to which he subscribed. The way in which he applies it in considering the question of civil disobedience in the *Crito* will be our best guide in reconstructing the theory itself. To begin with, however, we must distinguish normative from meta-ethical theories.

10.2.1 Normative ethical theories

A normative ethical theory will be either (a) a theory of obligation (or duty) or (b) a theory of virtue (or the virtues). The former sets out the basic rules or duties the observance of which is required of us by morality, and from which all our other duties may be derived. For example, according to one theory of obligation that we shall consider in detail later (see 11.11), our basic duty is to obey God's commands. Our derivative duties might then be: not to steal, not to kill, not to lie, not to commit adultery, and so forth, since God (according to the Old Testament) has revealed to mankind commandments proscribing these behaviours. A theory of virtue, on the other hand, sets out the basic character traits or personal qualities which belong to a morally good or even excellent human being and from which the virtuousness of other traits may be derived. To illustrate the point by reference to the same normative ethical theory, obedience to the divine will (being 'god-fearing') would be a basic virtue, while truthfulness, honesty, forbearance, marital fidelity, and so on would be derivative virtues.

Obviously, any moral theory of obligation could be 'translated' into an equivalent theory of virtue, or vice versa, since to any actions that may be duties there corresponds a character trait or disposition toward acting in just that way always or for the most part, this being the relevant virtue. Later, when we come to Sartre, we shall examine in detail the two main types of modern normative ethical theory, deontological and consequentialist or teleological theories (see 38.2–3). In this part we shall focus on the eudaemonist theories of the ancients, making only brief mention of Kant's deontological and the utilitarian consequentialist theory for purposes of contrast.

10.2.2 Meta-ethics

Theories are usually about something other than theories. Take, for example, theories about the physical universe. If we ask what the so-called Big Bang theory is about, the answer is: the origin of the material universe. Similarly, theories may be about the human mind, for example, psychological theories like those of Freud, Jung, Adler, and so on. Or they may be about morality, for example, the normative ethical theory according to which our first and most basic duty is to obey God's commands. By contrast with these, a *theory that is about another theory* is called a 'second-order theory' or a 'meta-theory.' Such a theory comes 'after' (Greek, *meta*) the theory it is about in the order of learning, but is often considered higher in dignity and so 'beyond' (*meta*) it as well. Accordingly, theoretical reflection on the status of propositions making up normative ethics (the second-order theory about first-order moral theories) is called 'meta-ethics.'

The example of a meta-ethical issue given above was: Are ethical values objective? or, equivalently: Can moral value judgments be objectively justified? Another is: What does the word 'wrong' mean when applied to some particular action or type of action? Does it mean 'God forbids it'? Or does it rather mean: 'Most people (in a given society) disapprove of it?' Or is it not a question of numbers or majorities at all, but of power, so that calling something 'wrong' really means: 'The powerful people in society (who are in a position to impose their preferences on others) disapprove of it'? Or, finally, does it simply mean that the individual speaker who is using the word dislikes or disapproves of the action in question? Or might it mean something else altogether? This is a meta-ethical question.

Later we shall take a closer look at a type of meta-ethical theory that questions whether ethical value judgments can be objective in any sense at all (see 32.4.2). While we have already said a good deal about relativism concerning truth (see 3.3.1), it remains to consider relativism concerning right and wrong, or 'moral relativism,' as it is called.

10.2.3 Descriptive and prescriptive enquiries

The foregoing may suffice as an outline of the three main branches of ethics or moral theory: normative ethics, applied ethics, and meta-ethics. However, philosophers are not the only ones who speak and write about morality. Morality can be studied by historians, sociologists, anthropologists, psychologists, and other social scientists in order to determine what people *in fact* believe (or believed in the past) and how people behave (or behaved in the past), as well as to explain why they do or did accept and follow just those rules or norms of conduct. We can say, then, that this type of social scientific study of morality aims at description on the one hand and explanation on the other.

Yet morality is also studied with a view to *assessing* some moral belief system, present or past, that is, *criticizing or justifying* it. The point here is *not* merely to describe or explain what people do or did *in fact* believe or do, but to determine whether certain beliefs or actions *ought* to be approved and acted upon *and why*. This type of study is called 'normative' or 'prescriptive' or 'evaluative' as opposed to 'factual' or 'descriptive.' It aims at justification (or showing something to be unjustifiable, that is, criticism) of some set of moral norms. Only the latter belongs to ethics or moral *philosophy*, though factual knowledge about the results of social scientific enquiries may be highly relevant to the philosopher's activity, especially in meta-ethics.

10.2.4 Facts and values

Having distinguished two types of questions or enquiries concerning morals, the factual and the normative, we must now consider the corresponding types of *propositions* or statements: (1) descriptive or factual propositions or statements, by which we simply assert (accurately or mistakenly) that something is true, that is, describe (correctly or incorrectly) what *is* the case, perhaps also explaining it, yet without evaluating it as 'good' or 'bad,' without expressing approval or disapproval; and (2) prescriptive or normative propositions or statements that assert something to be *good or bad,* prescribe or prohibit it, justify or condemn it, that is, express approval or disapproval of some kind and some degree. The most obvious examples of normative statements are moral commandments in the imperative mood ("Thou shalt ..." or "Thou shalt not ..."), but there are many other ways in which to express positive or negative norms of conduct, including some fairly subtle ones that imply rather than state moral approval and disapproval while appearing, on the face of it, merely factual. Take, for example: "The bloodshed was necessary in order to preserve freedom." This is obviously not a factual statement or causal explanation of the bloodshed, though it may look like one; it is a normative proposition, an attempt to justify the bloodshed. Normative statements are more familiar under the everyday name 'value judgments.'

It should perhaps be added that the intent of the foregoing is not to suggest that all statements fall neatly into one or the other of two exhaustive categories, 'normative' or 'descriptive.' This is frequently not the case. The point is rather that any statement will be completely *analyzable* in terms of this dichotomy. The outcome will very often be that the statement in question is neither wholly one nor the other, but combines elements of both. We saw something analogous in the case of the apparently indicative statement '*I* will be punctual,' which was found to have imperative force as well (see 7.2). Consider this sentence: 'The twentieth century was marked by world wars of unprecedented brutality.' Is it a descriptive or a value judgment or both?

10.2.5 Moral and non-moral value

Now that we have distinguished facts and values at the level of statements and theories, the next step is a distinction between two kinds of values.

When discussing questions, statements, or theories of value, we have to separate those concerned with (A) non-moral values from those concerned with (B) moral values. Some things or actions are called 'good' or 'bad' only in a non-moral sense, while some are so called strictly in a moral sense, and some in *both* senses. Thus, for example, we might speak of a good book (that is, one that is enjoyable to read), a good bookcase (solidly built, pleasing to look at), a good car (well-designed, reliable, economical, responsive, safe, and so on), or a good meal (tasty and ample). Obviously, these things are all good in a *non-moral* sense. Constructing a bookcase or car so that it is good is the right way to construct it—again, in the *non-moral* sense of 'right.' Other things good in the non-moral sense are: physical beauty, intelligence, health, wealth, career success, reputation or honour, life itself, and anything that is a means of acquiring or preserving these.

We may divide these non-moral goods into two very broad classes, (1) the private or personal and (2) the public or social. Under (1) we can subsume (a) bodily goods like beauty, health, and the sensual pleasures of food, drink, and sexual gratification, the enjoyment of wealth, comfort, luxury, and property, even life itself, the goodness of which is apparent from the extraordinary lengths to which people will go to preserve it. Further, we can include (b) intellectual goods like extending our knowledge and developing our capacities to think, analyze, and solve problems. Most people find these things rewarding, and when what is grasped or understood is something as important as the right way to live, the satisfaction must be very great indeed. To the private or personal category belong also friendship, affection, love, and all such (c) emotional goods. Although not everyone rates (b) and (c) as highly as (a), these are still generally acknowledged to be good things of a very high order. Given the choice, most people would want to have them, and some would even prefer them to fame and fortune, though not everyone would be willing to make the requisite effort to acquire a much larger share in intellectually good things, for example.

Under (2), social or public goods, we should certainly include such things as influence, prestige, fame, popularity, political success, all of which accrue to individuals, and benefits like peace, stable government, and economic prosperity that are in some measure common to the members of a collectivity. This may suffice for (A) *non*-morally good things. On the other hand, actions like telling the truth or honesty, keeping promises, tolerance, and respecting others' dignity, liberty, and property are (B) good in a *moral* sense. Here it is a matter of realizing our moral potential, developing or displaying what we call 'character' or 'integrity.' Acting in these ways is 'right,' the right way to act, in the distinctively moral sense of the word 'right'—or so most of us believe. The person who behaves in this way possesses moral uprightness or probity; we speak of his having 'character' or being 'of good character.' For convenience, this classification of different kinds of goodness or value can be set out in a simple diagram as follows:

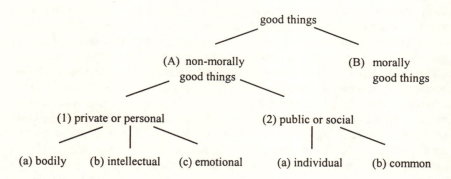

Now, of course, just as non-moral goods may straddle categories, so the behaviours under (B) may be good in a non-moral as well as a moral sense. This is the case for truth-telling, for example, if (as we say) 'honesty is the best policy,' that is, if it is in our best interests to be honest, as well as being the morally right thing to do. Supposing that one may reasonably expect to derive benefits or rewards from honesty—for example, respect, cooperation, business opportunities, and so on—the moral virtue of honesty is 'good' in the non-moral sense as well. As Kant once put it, honesty is not just the best policy, it is "better than policy." This means that moral goodness is intrinsically superior to non-moral goodness, so that the significance of the benefits derived from honesty pales beside the inherent worth accruing to the individual who possesses this moral attribute.

So at least some morally good things are also non-morally good, honesty being Kant's example. By the same token, a certain form of government or a certain economic system may be 'good' or 'better' than another in the moral sense, in the non-moral sense, or indeed in both senses. For example, a market economy such as our own may be better than a so-called command economy such as existed until recently in most Eastern European countries in the moral sense, because it is more just; in the non-moral sense, because it generates greater wealth; or in both these senses because it *both* generates more wealth *and* distributes it more equitably—if that is indeed the case, which some would no doubt contest.

10.2.6 Obligatoriness and permissibility

Where neither the performance nor non-performance (omission) of a certain action is a duty, that action is 'right' in the sense of 'permissible.' Where, however, omission is morally wrong, performing the action in question is 'right' in the much stronger sense of 'obligatory': it is our *duty* to so act. Thus, saying that a certain action is morally 'right' may just mean that it is not wrong (it is permissible); but it *can* mean that it would be wrong *not* to do it (it is obligatory or a duty). Accordingly, when Socrates says that he was right to live as he did, it will be worth considering which of these two things is meant: (1) that there was nothing wrong in what he did (it was permissible); or (2) that it would have been wrong to do otherwise (it was his duty to live as he did).

Here it is important to distinguish two quite different types of obligatoriness and permissibility as well. For purposes of understanding Socrates's defence speech, we must take account of the difference between what morality and what religious piety requires or permits. Those who hold that our basic moral duty is to obey God's commands may be inclined to deny any difference between moral and religious duties; but, on the face of it, there does seem to be a wide gulf between the rites and practices (for example dietary practices) that, say, Christian or Jewish or Muslim piety requires of the believer, and those standards of conduct that morality requires of *all* human beings, regardless of their religious convictions. It seems to be distinctive of morality that its rules are binding on all men in relevantly similar circumstances, whereas religious duties, like abstaining from drinking alcohol or from eating meat or covering or uncovering one's head at worship, are incumbent only on the faithful. In a Greek context the distinction seems to have run along the dividing line between duties toward men and duties toward gods. Thus the demands of morality in dealings with one's fellow men were a very different matter from the rites and observances owed the gods by the state religion.

10.2.7 Moral and non-moral excellence

From the foregoing it should be clear that persons, too, can be 'good' or 'excellent' in a moral or in a non-moral sense, according as they have the habit of doing the right thing in the moral or in the non-moral sense of 'right.' Thus, the habit of acting rightly in the moral sense makes a person or agent morally virtuous, commendable, praiseworthy or, as we say nowadays, an 'ethical person.' But doing things in the right or best way (taking 'right,' 'better,' and 'best' in a non-moral sense) involves a different kind of excellence—skill, for example, or know-how, prowess, dexterity, flair, patience, methodicalness, perseverance, resourcefulness, sound judgment, and so on. These too can be called 'virtues,' but they are non-moral virtues. To avoid ambiguity, we shall adopt the practice of reserving the term 'virtue' for moral goodness. Non-morally good character traits like those listed above will be referred to as forms of 'excellence.' Both translate a single word in Greek, *aretē*, which is derived from the superlative of 'good' (literally: 'bestness').

10.2.8 Intellectual excellence as a variety of non-moral excellence

One kind of non-moral excellence (among others) is intellectual excellence. There are several aspects to this, but chief among them are (1) the possession of knowledge, that is, being well informed about relevant factual matters, and (2) being rational, that is, willing and able to think for oneself and to follow appropriate problem-solving procedures in a competent manner. Both aspects may involve such things as being fair-minded, having good judgment, being clear-sighted, free of irrational superstitions, prejudices, intellectual dishonesty, 'tunnel' or 'blinkered' vision, as we say, and so forth.

Now to our way of thinking it would seem that intellectual excellence is as different from moral excellence or virtue as it is from physical excellence (say, beauty, strength, or athletic ability). It appears, in other words, that a person can be smart but morally wicked, or more than a little dull-witted and yet morally good (the 'salt of the earth,' as we say). Examples from history, or from one's own experience, are not hard to find. However, Socrates did not think that intellectual excellence and moral virtue were to be found separate in this way, and we shall soon discover why he denied this possibility (see 12.9.2). Still, on the face of it, intellectual and moral excellence or virtue do appear to be quite separate and distinct things such that one of them could easily be found, even in a high degree, in a particular individual in whom the other was notably absent. Neither would seem to be any more closely associated with the other than with athletic prowess, for example.

10.2.9 Intrinsic and instrumental non-moral value

Some things that are good in the non-moral sense are (1) good in themselves but not as a means to anything else; some are (2) good as a means to something else but not good in themselves; and some are (3) *both* good in themselves *and* as a means to something else.

When something is good in itself and desired for its own sake it is called 'intrinsically good' or 'an intrinsic good'; if it is desired for the sake of something else to which it is a means or instrument, it is called 'instrumentally good' or 'an instrumental good.' And if our threefold distinction is correct, some things are both intrinsically and instrumentally good.

Pleasure, satisfaction of desire, or happiness is something (1) good in itself: other things may be the means to pleasure, satisfaction, or happiness, but pleasure and happiness are not themselves a means to anything else: we desire them *for their own sake*, as an integral part of a happy or good life. So too health. We desire other things in order to recover or preserve our health, but we do not normally desire health as a means to any further end. The enjoyment of good health is just part of, rather than a means to, the happiness we human beings seek in life.

Money or wealth, on the other hand, is (2) an instrumental good, good as a means of procuring all sorts of other things, some of which are again just a means to pleasure or happiness, while others form part of the pleasant or happy life itself. But money is not an intrinsic good (except for a deranged person, for example, a miser who hoards money and refuses to put it to the use for which it is intended). Similarly, medical procedures are only instrumentally good, good as a means to health. They are not an intrinsic good (except, perhaps, for a hypochondriac, who actually enjoys medical treatment).

Finally, the acquisition of knowledge is (3) both an instrumental and an intrinsic good. With knowledge one can acquire many other desirable things, including money and power or influence, so it is an instrumental good; but for most human beings learning is not just a means to pleasure and happiness; it is a *part* of happiness or the good life itself. Life without the experience of learning would be poorer, less worth living, since learning is an intrinsically valuable experience for most if not all people. It is useful, to be sure, but even if it were not useful it would remain valuable as one of those things that are above use (see 2.7).

In this connection, consider the opening sentence of Aristotle's *Metaphysics*: "All men desire by nature to know." To paraphrase: understanding the true causes of things ("to know," in Aristotle's sense) is something human beings desire simply for its own sake; it is part of, and not just a means to, the good life for rational creatures such as ourselves ("by nature"). Like health, prosperity, social bonds, affection, episodes of sensual and other sorts of pleasure, knowledge is an intrinsic part of the best sort of human life, of human flourishing, as we called it earlier. Not surprisingly, Aristotle believed it was a very big part of the good life for man, probably overemphasizing its importance in the end. There is something very Greek about this prejudice in favour of contemplative living, just as there is something quite typical about the anti-intellectualism of our own age.

A final point to conclude this section: One can ask oneself whether leading a morally good life is also good in the non-moral sense, that is, whether a morally good person is apt to be happier or unhappier than a morally bad one (even a morally bad one who suffers no pangs of conscience), other things—like health, fortune, social circumstances, personal relationships, and so on—being equal. If so, then one can further ask whether moral goodness or virtue is intrinsically good or instrumentally good or both. Does moral virtue enhance happiness only as a means of getting other good things (like wealth, status, friendship, love, and so on); or is virtue, as the saying goes, 'its own reward,' that is, an intrinsic good, a part of, rather than a means to, happiness or human flourishing? Or is virtue both instrumentally *and* intrinsically good?

These questions, as we shall see, have a great deal to do with the moral philosophy of Socrates and the defence put forth in the *Apology* in particular. And so do the various distinctions leading up to them, as we shall now try to show.

10.3 Moral distinctions employed in the *Apology*

The preceding distinctions between facts and values, moral and non-moral goodness, rightness as obligatoriness and rightness as permissibility, between intellectual excellence and other non-moral virtues or excellences, and, finally, between intrinsic and instrumental non-moral goodness can all be applied to the *Apology*, and arguably must be so applied if we are to understand Socrates's defence speech correctly.

To begin with facts and values, Socrates's defence speech has two distinct themes or strands. These he announces at the very beginning when he mentions "truth" and "justice" (17b–c). The first of these refers to the question of (1) what his actions were, such that he has been brought to trial on charges of corrupting the youth and of atheism, that is, how he has lived. This is a descriptive matter of *fact*: what he in truth did and did not do—though it is asked with explanatory intent, in order to clear up the source of certain rumours. The other theme, justice, refers to his claim (2) that he has never wronged anyone by his actions, and that, indeed, it would have been morally wrong for him not to act and live as he had. This is a prescriptive matter or question or *value*, of right and wrong in the strong moral sense of obligation.

These, as we have seen, are two quite different types of question. Even where both are involved in a single line of enquiry, it is important to separate them for purposes of analysis or understanding, even when they are not so separated by those whose thought we are trying to understand. The importance of distinguishing them can be illustrated with reference to the refutation of Meletus in the *Apology*, the key premise of which was (paraphrasing 25d):

No rational person deliberately harms himself (insofar as he is rational).

Or, in the words of the *Meno*:

All men *always* desire what is (or seems to them) good for them, what they believe will make them happy. (77c)

This we described (see 9.2.2) as the basic principle of eudaemonist moral theories. It looks like a *factual belief* about human behaviour and motivation, about the end at which all rational human action *in fact* aims. But the Greek moral theorists probably did not distinguish this descriptive generalization from a basic *normative* rule or action guide: you *ought* (*normative!*) never to do what you know to be harmful to yourself, what impairs or destroys your happiness or chances of happiness, or even what produces more harm than good for you, since such behaviour would be irrational. Only by distinguishing these two strands of the principle can we understand its role in eudaemonist moral theories like that of Socrates. This in turn allows us to grasp the difference between two normative questions: (a) Why (*ought* one to) be moral? and (b) What (sort of behaviour) is moral? This distinction will turn out to be the key to understanding the moral philosophy of Socrates, though it has consistently been overlooked by scholars.

Understood simply as a descriptive statement about how all or most people behave, the principle of eudaemonism may or may not be true. Perhaps human beings behave irrationally sometimes, choosing things that impair their chances of happiness in the long run, even when they understand the long-term consequences of their actions. Or are they always persuaded that the consequences of their choices are good for them? It is hard to say. Yet in its normative signification the principle figures fairly uncontroversially in argument the intent of which is to provide an answer to the question, Why (*should* one) be moral? The argument runs something like this. If (P1) being moral is somehow indispensable to happiness; and if (P2) every rational being strives (that is, *ought* to strive) for happiness; then (C) every rational human being ought to choose to be moral. This can be called 'the basic argument of eudaemonism.' Controversial among the Greek moralists was only P1. For as we shall see later, different eudaemonist theorists saw the indispensability of moral virtue to happiness in quite a different light (see 12.9.1). And as there was disagreement about the question, (1) Why be moral? so too about what sort of behaviour morality requires of us, that is, the question, (2) What is moral? So even where the factual and normative dimensions of the principle are not sharply distinguished, it is important that *we* distinguish them for purposes of analysis and evaluation.

As for the distinction between moral and non-moral goodness, this too can be nicely illustrated from the *Apology*. For Socrates repeatedly states that he was never concerned for his own safety and the preservation of his own life (a significant non-moral good!), nor for position and power, nor for wealth, but only for justice and doing his duty or fulfilling the 'mission' imposed upon him as a duty by the god Apollo. In other words, he valued moral goodness over non-morally good things throughout his life. Indeed, this is the key theme running through the entire defence speech.

Next, as regards the distinction between right as permissible and as obligatory, we note again that Socrates claims to have been *right* to live the life he led, not just in the sense that everything he did was *permissible* (that is, that he did not do anything wrong) but in the strong sense of obligatory: he *would have done wrong not to live as he did*. It was his duty to fulfil his mission since the god Apollo imposed it on him. Less clear is whether the duty in question is a moral or a religious duty. That is a matter that we cannot decide until we have determined to what sort of moral theory Socrates subscribes.

As for intellectual excellence as distinct from other non-morally good qualities or characteristics, Socrates describes himself as urging others to "care for ... the best possible state of your soul" (30a). This means, in the first instance, striving for moral virtue. But it also means striving for intellectual excellence, caring for truth as well as justice. Socrates mentions both these things separately, though he personally regards them as inseparable, as noted above. Why he did so will become clearer in due course.

Finally, with regard to intrinsic and instrumental goods, consider Socrates's remark at 30a: "Wealth does not bring about excellence (*aretē*), but excellence brings about wealth and all other public and private blessings for men." From this it appears that virtue, for Socrates, falls into that category of goods that are both intrinsic and instrumental. Later we shall see that Socrates means something more than this: that without moral virtue money and other non-moral goods, public and private, are not really goods at all!

10.4 Normative ethical theory in the *Apology*

Even the brief survey of the preceding section should be sufficient to make it clear that the defence speech of the *Apology* makes tacit use of most if not all the now-standard moral distinctions set out in the last section but one. If Socrates is doing more than just describing the life he has led, if he is evaluating it, as he must, if he is to *defend* the life he has led, then some moral standard or yardstick is required. The question, then, is, What sort of moral theory does Socrates presuppose in his defence speech?

10.4.1 Service to the god

Socrates argues for the justice (moral goodness) of the life he has led by appealing over and over again to a single principle of right action: *obedience to the god Apollo*. Whether this is really the sole or even the chief basis of his conduct and deliberations is the question that we have been leading up to throughout this chapter. A negative answer to this question will be given in the next chapter. At this stage we can only clarify the question and set out some possible alternatives.

At first glance, the evidence *for* this single principle of right action may seem overwhelming. After all, Socrates states the key precept repeatedly, for example at 29b ("it is wicked and shameful to ... disobey one's superior, be he god or man") and at 29d ("I will obey the god rather than you, and as long as I draw breath and am able, I shall not cease to practise philosophy"). And again at 30a he remarks: "Be sure that this is what the god orders me to do, and I think that there is no greater blessing for the city than my service to the god."

In addition to these direct statements, Socrates cites a series of five indirect proofs that all his actions since Chaerephon's unauthorized visit to the oracle have been governed by the precept of obedience to the god. The first is (1) his willingness to face banishment, disfranchisement, and even death rather than abandon his mission:

"whether you acquit me or not, do so on the understanding that this is my course of action, even if I am to face death many times" (30b). The second proof is (2) his poverty:

That I am the kind of person to be a gift of the god to the city you might realize from the fact that it does not seem like human nature for me to have neglected all my own affairs and to have tolerated this neglect for so many years while I was always concerned with you, approaching each one of you like a father or an elder brother to persuade you to care for virtue. Now if I profited from this by charging a fee for my advice there would be some sense to it, but you can see for yourselves that, for all their shameless accusations, my accusers have not been able in their impudence to bring forward a witness to say that I have ever received a fee or ever asked for one. I, on the other hand, have a convincing witness that I speak the truth, my poverty. (31a–c)

It is not from any motive of gain, then, but as the willing instrument of the god that Socrates has neglected his own affairs and his family in the performance of his duty.

The third proof is (3) the fact that he has remained a private citizen (in obedience to a divine sign) rather than entering public life:

It may seem strange that while I go around and give this advice privately and interfere in private affairs, I do not venture to go to the assembly and there advise the city. You have heard me give the reason for this in many places. I have a divine sign from the god which Meletus has ridiculed in his deposition. This began when I was a child. It is a voice, and whenever it speaks it turns me away from doing something I am about to do, but it never encourages me to do anything. This is what has prevented me from taking part in public affairs, and I think it was right to prevent me. Be sure, gentlemen of the jury, that if I had long ago attempted to take part in politics, I should have died long ago, and benefited neither you nor myself. (31c–32a)

According to this, the claim that his basic principle of action is obedience to divine command is borne out by the well-known fact that he has never engaged in politics. He has not done so (a) because he was commanded by the oracle to carry out a mission, and his own judgment told him that if he entered politics he would perish and so be unable to do as commanded. Moreover, he has not done so (b) because he was specifically forbidden to enter politics by a divine sign or voice, Socrates's *daimonion* (roughly, 'supernatural power'), as it is called. While (a) may be an over-interpretation of what Socrates actually says, note that he cannot be saying simply that he stayed out of politics because to do otherwise might have cost him his life. That would be very surprising from one who displays so little concern about the loss of life in the performance of his duty. His point is surely that he would have been unable to carry out his mission had he engaged in actions that he knew might cost him his life, so that to do so would have been tantamount to disobedience.

The fourth proof is even more oblique but points nonetheless to the same conclusion. Socrates insists (4) the fact that neither the young nor their elders accuse him of ever having harmed anyone:

> If I corrupt some young men and have corrupted others, then surely some of them who have grown older and realized that I gave them bad advice when they were young should now themselves come up here to accuse me and avenge themselves. If they were unwilling to do so themselves, then some of their kindred, their fathers or brothers or other relations should recall it now if their family had been harmed by me. (33d)

This may be simply a direct reply to the charge of corrupting the youth, but it may also be intended as evidence of blamelessness owing to god-fearingness. The final proof is (5) that he has not begged nor made pathetic appeals by dragging his family into court. This he has not done, not only out of respect for the city the god has commanded him to serve, but also out of respect for the sanctity of the judges' oath (see 34b), that is, out of respect for an oath sworn before god and therefore binding on all who take it.

All these proofs, as he calls them, appear to establish one thing: the fundamental rule or motive guiding of all Socrates's actions throughout the period of his life discussed in the *Apology* is obedience to the god Apollo.

10.4.2 Service to the city

The key role played by piety, god-fearingness, or obedience to god in Socrates's defence suggests that he has only one basic moral rule: service to the god Apollo. If so, his working morality might be summed up this way. Basic is the principle: I ought always to obey the commands of god (as transmitted "by oracles and dreams and in every other way that a divine manifestation has ever ordered a man to do anything" (33c). From this, and from the fact that (as he thinks) the oracle has commanded him to spend his life examining himself and others, Socrates could then infer: (1) I ought to go about urging my fellow citizens to care for the (non-moral and moral) goodness of their souls (truth and justice) rather than worldly non-moral goods like wealth, reputation, and power, since that is what the god's riddle (in effect: 'No man is wiser than Socrates') enjoined on me. Furthermore, Socrates could also infer from his basic duty of obedience to the god: (2) I ought not to enter politics (since a divine sign has commanded me not to and since, if I did, I would perish and no longer be able to carry out the task imposed on me as my moral duty by the god Apollo).

However, it is difficult to see how certain of Socrates's *other rules of conduct* could be derived from this basic rule. What about (3), for example: it is wrong to deliver an innocent man (Leon of Salamis) up to the authorities to be put to death, especially when the authorities have seized power by unlawful force? And what of (4): it is wrong to put generals on trial jointly when the law prescribes separate trials for each? Socrates nowhere says that Apollo (or the divine sign) commanded him *not* to do either (3) or (4). So how could he know that they are wrong if obedience to god were his *only* moral principle?

The solution may be that Socrates really has two moral rules or action guides. The first, Rule I, as we may call it, is: I ought always to obey the commands of god (or the divine sign), while the second, Rule II, is: I ought never to harm anyone (least of all my own city-state, for that harms all my fellow citizens). We may call the basic moral duty in Rule II 'Service to the City.' Socrates, after all, mentions both service to the god and service to the city of Athens among the justifying reasons for his actions. One thinks here chiefly of Socrates's repeated description of himself as "god's gift to you" (30e; also 31a) and his refusal to do anything that might "bring shame upon the city" (35a). The underlying principle, however, is, according to the solution now being proposed, Rule II: not harming others, *especially* not acting in a way that would harm *all* others, the collectivity or city. This can be called 'the principle of non-maleficence.' ('Maleficence' just means 'doing harm'; hence 'non-maleficence' means 'not harming.')

Now from Rule II we *can* derive (3), I ought not to be a party to the killing of an innocent opponent of the regime. For it would be bad for the city if Socrates or others were to act in this way, since it would lead to lawlessness and terror. And we can similarly derive (4), I ought not to go along with an unlawful manner of putting the generals on trial. For it was illegal to do so and lawlessness leads to the breakdown of civic order and harm to all in the city. So it looks as though Socrates's actions may be guided by Rule I *and* Rule II after all.

10.4.3 Two rules or one?

The question arises, Does Socrates have one basic rule (Rule I) from which the other (Rule II) is derived ? Let us call this 'Option A.' Or is his one basic rule in fact Rule II, from which Rule I is derived? This may be called 'Option B.' Or, finally, does he have two separate and independent rules, neither of which is derivable from the other, though one overrides the other in cases of conflict? This we can call 'Option C.'

On the first option, Socrates's *basic moral rule* is: Obey god's commands. Right is what god orders, wrong what he forbids. Now supposing Apollo to be truly benevolent, that is, favourably disposed to all mankind or all Athenians, he would no doubt command men not to harm others, especially not *all* their fellow citizens, that is, the city as a whole. Socrates would have to rely on his own judgment in deciding what actions were beneficial or harmful to others or the city; but there is no *basic* duty not to harm anyone. It is just that one of the god's commands, one of the *derivative* duties stemming from the *primitive* or primary duty of obedience to god, is to do no harm, especially to the city. If the correct option is A, then Socrates's moral theory is a variety of what is called 'the Divine Command Theory,' after its basic principle.

On Option B, Socrates's *basic or primary moral duty* would be: Never harm anyone. Obedience to the divine command would then be a secondary rule derived from this basic duty rather than a separate duty. Since (let us again suppose) god is good and wants the good of mankind, to obey his commandments will always be to act in the best interests of mankind, even if we human beings are unable to see exactly how this is so. So on Option B obedience to god is not a basic duty but derivative from the duty to refrain from harm. After all, it is hard to know what god might want us to do in a particular situation. But we can usually make out how to avoid harm, and if we know god wants us to avoid harm, then in so acting we shall also be obeying him.

If this second is the correct answer to the question, What is moral? then it seems likely that Socrates held a version of that type of normative ethical theory that has been called 'eudaemonism.' As noted earlier, the theory is so called, not after its basic principle, non-maleficence, which answers the question, What is moral (and immoral)? but after the answer it gives to the different question, Why be moral? That answer is: Never harm anyone else because to do so is wrong and to engage in wrongdoing is always to harm yourself, whereas no rational human being would ever harm himself willingly (that is, destroy his own happiness).

On Option C, finally, Socrates recognizes two separate moral duties, neither of which is derived from the other (both of which are basic) and which *could* in principle conflict at times *if* god commanded something that was harmful to another or to the city. Of course, if in this merely hypothetical case of conflict, Rule I overrides Rule II, then we still have a form of the Divine Command Theory or Option A. On the other hand, if Rule II overrides Rule I in case of conflict, that is, if we have to avoid harming anyone even if it means disobeying the gods, then the theory boils down to Option B: non-maleficence based on eudaemonism. Finally, if neither of these two principles overrides the other, if they are both basic, we are left with Option C, a mixed theory.

10.4.4 Preview of the solution

Now to what sort of moral theory did Socrates actually subscribe? In order to decide this question we shall have to examine the *Euthyphro* and the *Crito*, since the *Apology* itself provides no clear-cut answer, only a number of options. The *Euthyphro* will shed valuable light on Socrates's attitude toward religious tradition, making it quite clear that he cannot have held the Divine Command Theory of morality. Probably, in fact, no Greek ever did. When Euthyphro is invited to consider this option, he categorically rejects it without so much as an argument. And indeed, it would have seemed very far-fetched to any Greek that the Olympian deities might *create* right and wrong. For one thing, their gods were not thought of as *creators* at all. That is a Judeo-Christian innovation (see 5.5.3–4). Far from deciding right and wrong by their own arbitrary decrees, the Greek gods were themselves subject to the quasi-personified moral principles Destiny, Justice, Necessity, and Fate that governed the whole cosmos.

This is what we saw earlier, in chapter 5. In fact, it was suggested there that the earliest philosophical theories may have arisen partly in order to reverse a recent trend among the poets. In the oldest myths there can be no question of the gods making or ordaining the moral any more than the natural order of the universe; the personified Olympian deities preside over their assigned portions of the cosmos, and here their power is very great; but they rule in strict subordination to a higher moral law, a higher dispensation or apportionment of lots that is not their own doing and against which they transgress only at the price of certain retribution. In some late parts of the Homeric poems, however, and to an even greater extent in Hesiod, there is a tendency to characterize the gods as lawgivers; and the speculations of the earliest Greek philosophers may have aimed at restoring something akin to earlier mythological ways of thinking about the physical and moral order of the universe. Euthyphro, as we shall see, is quite as untouched by these later developments in epic and didactic poetry as he is by philosophy itself; for him, the idea that gods make the moral law is apparently unthinkable. It is perhaps safe to say that something of the sort would have been the instinctive reaction of most Greeks.

The examination of the *Euthyphro* will serve to eliminate Option A, the Divine Command Theory. We shall next turn to the *Crito* for the valuable light it sheds on Socrates's conception of the relation between virtue and happiness. This will make it clear that Socrates's moral theory is indeed a form of Option B, non-maleficence based on eudaemonism, rather than a mixed theory. Socrates's answers to both the central questions of moral philosophy, What is moral? and Why be moral? will be reviewed critically in the concluding appraisal of chapter 13.

11

Socratic Piety

11.1 Introductory

The *Euthyphro* takes us back in time to the day before the *Apology* outside the court of the King Archon, one of nine chief magistrates prescribed by Athenian law, and the one charged with overseeing religious affairs, including legal cases involving murder and impiety. Unlike the rather fanciful charge of corrupting the youth, impiety was expressly proscribed by Athenian law as an offence against the state religion punishable by death. It was prosecuted by a public indictment or *graphē* (translated "indictment" at 2a), since impious behaviour was believed to pose a serious threat to the public good if allowed to go unpunished. There was, however, nothing like a crown attorney's office at Athens; private citizens brought indictments on behalf of the state. (Accordingly, Meletus, a private citizen, prosecuted Socrates in the *Apology*, seconded by Anytus and Lycon.) Impiety was only vaguely defined in law, it being left largely to the courts to decide what constituted impious conduct; but atheism certainly would have been so designated, so that Socrates's presence at the Court of the King Archon is not surprising.

What business Euthyphro had there is less obvious. At Athens murder was treated as a private wrong against the family of the slain person. It was dealt with in a civil prosecution (*dikē*, translated "prosecution" at 2a) for damage wilfully or negligently inflicted. Under Athenian law only a near relative of the victim could prosecute for murder on behalf of a freeman, while only the owner could prosecute the killer of a slave. In initiating proceedings against his own father on behalf of a day labourer or servant who had killed his father's slave, Euthyphro is on very shaky ground indeed. In this particular case, the father's victim was a foreigner (a Naxian, we are told), so no Athenian plaintiff could come forward to prosecute; it may be that Euthyphro hoped to convince the King Archon that allowing the murderer to go unpunished on that account would result in blood guilt and religious pollution affecting the whole community. That would certainly be in character. There is some evidence that the action did not go to trial, either because Euthyphro decided to abandon it after his conversation with Socrates (if there ever was such a conversation!) or because the King Archon rejected the suit at the preliminary hearing. A trial with 501 paid jurors was, after all, a costly affair; the King Archon had to determine whether the evidence warranted the expense before allowing the plaintiff to proceed.

While the *Euthyphro* takes us back a day, the action of the *Crito* takes us forward in time to a fictional scene in Socrates's prison cell about a month after the trial. The *Phaedo* is set in the same place on the following day, shortly before Socrates's execution. So the three dialogues we shall be interpreting in this and the next part form a dramatic unit of sorts. While the *Crito* is probably earlier and a more reliable source of information concerning the thought of the historical Socrates, the *Euthyphro* is a typical dialogue of definition. If Aristotle is correct about the Socratic search for definitions, then it too is important for purposes of reconstructing Socrates's philosophical method and teaching.

11.2 The structure of the *Euthyphro*

From a consideration of the setting, we move next to a schematic overview of the structure of the *Euthyphro*. This, incidentally, is how we shall approach each of the works to be studied. The approach may have been less schematic in dealing with the *Apology*, but it was at bottom no different: we begin always with an overview and then specify those parts of the work that will occupy us in particular:

A. Introduction: The dramatic situation and the Character of the Man Euthyphro (2a–5c)
B. The Search for a Definition of Piety (5c–end)
1 Example of a pious action rather than a definition of 'piety'(5c–6c)
2 First definition: "that which is dear to [or is loved by] the gods is pious, what is not [what is hated by the gods] is impious" (7a)
3 Second definition and its refutation: "the pious what *all* the gods love, and the opposite, what all the gods hate, is the impious" (9e)
4 Third definition: "the godly and the pious is the part of the just that is concerned with the care of the gods" (12e)
5 Fourth definition: piety is "that part of the just that is concerned with the care of the gods" (12e)," that is, with "service to the gods" (13d)
6 Fourth definition = first (or second) definition (14b–15b)

In the first half of this chapter, we shall focus our attention on the first three sections of B., the search for a definition of piety. This will suffice to settle the main question concerning the type of moral theory held by Socrates, providing us with a much clearer picture of the search for definitions that we have taken to be a genuine feature of the philosophical activity of the historical Socrates.

11.3 The good, the just, and the pious

Since the ostensible theme of the *Euthyphro* is the search for a definition of *piety* or *holiness*, we may well ask how this religious subject can help us to grasp the nature of Socrates's normative ethical theory.

It is worth noting at the start that in Greek (1) 'the holy' or 'the pious' (*to hosion*) is not sharply distinguished from (2) 'the right' or 'the good' in the moral sense (*to kalon*). Nor is (2) 'the good' clearly separated from (3) 'the just' (*to dikaion*), the Greeks apparently having made no such distinction between the latter two as is common nowadays. *We* might be inclined say that moral goodness is a matter of having the right moral principles and acting on them, while justice is a matter of applying those principles fairly and equitably in one's dealings with everyone, without discriminating between friend and foe, countryman and foreigner, freeman and slave, men and women, and so forth. But this is clearly not so for Socrates. Consider his remark to the jury in the *Apology*: "Do not deem it right for me, gentlemen of the jury, that I should act towards you in a way that I do not consider to be good or just or pious" (35c–d). We encounter the comparatives of the same adjectives in the *Crito*, "better, or more just, or more pious" (54b), and in other contexts as well. It is unlikely, then, that Socrates (or any Greek) saw a difference between justice and goodness or holiness.

The lack of a clearly demarcated concept of the holy is evident also from the fact that Plato sometimes (a) includes holiness as a fifth among the standard *cardinal* virtues (justice, courage, wisdom, and temperance), as in the *Protagoras* (349b), at other times (b) subsuming it under justice, as in the latter portion of the *Euthyphro*, while on still other occasions he (c) does not consider holiness at all in discussing the virtues, as though it were really nothing over and above, or specifically different from, the other virtues just listed.

While piety, moral goodness, and justice appear to be different expressions for the same thing, in the fourth and fifth sections of the search for a definition of 'holy' in the *Euthyphro* (see the outline above) a distinction crops up between right conduct (1) in one's dealings with the gods and (2) in one's dealings with men. It is Euthyphro who says: "I think, Socrates, that the godly and the pious is the part of the just that is concerned with the care of the gods, while that concerned with the care of men is the remaining part of justice" (12e). Even though given up later, some such distinction between 'the pious' and 'the just' suggested itself quite naturally to the Greeks, *to hosion* having for them the connotation of behaviour (especially prayers and sacrifices) sanctioned by *divine* law. Thus, at the very end of the *Euthyphro*, Socrates himself describes piety as "wisdom in divine matters" (16a); and a little before this Euthyphro responds affirmatively to his suggestion that piety and the pious are "a knowledge of how to sacrifice and pray" (14c). The Greeks must have distinguished, therefore, between moral and religious duties, or rather between the demands of morality in dealings with one's fellow men and the rites and observances owed the gods by the state religion (see 10.2.6). And insofar as moral and religious duties are largely a matter of giving others (Gods or men), *what is due* to them, some of the connotations of justice are closely allied to both (namely, returning good for good, bad for bad, like for like). Of course, it is not an *egalitarian* notion of justice like ours that is in play here, since popular Greek morality has it that what is due to a friend is very different from what is due to an enemy (on this see 12.8.1). Interestingly, Euthyphro may be championing some such egalitarian ideal when he says: "It is ridiculous, Socrates, for you to think that it makes any difference whether the victim is a stranger or a relative. One should only watch whether the killer acted justly [rightly] or not; if he acted justly, then let him go, but if not, one should prosecute, even if the killer shares your hearth and table" (4b). And later (6a) he accuses his critics of inconsistency for approving certain actions on the part of the gods which they yet condemn in him. *We* today feel a natural sympathy for this point of view, though Plato's original readers would certainly have found it shocking, as, presumably, he did himself.

The upshot, then, is this. Although the question in the *Euthyphro* concerns piety in particular, it is perfectly legitimate to treat 'the pious' as synonymous with 'the right' or 'the good' (in the moral sense), mining the *Euthyphro* for insights into the type of normative ethical theory held by Socrates.

11.4 Characters, theme, and first stage

11.4.1 The character of the man Euthyphro

The dialogue begins with an introductory conversation designed to shed light on the character of Socrates's interlocutor and to introduce the theme, holiness, by way of a specific problem. We learn that Euthyphro is a religious innovator and self-styled prophet (3b) who feels called to the office of moral innovator as well on the basis of his religious insights (4d–e). This Euthyphro is in fact a rather pompous know-it-all. Consider his remark about his earlier prophecies: "[A]nd yet I have foretold nothing that did not happen. Nevertheless, they envy all of us who do this" (3b). Or the bit of dialogue in which Socrates remarks, with heavy irony: "It is not the part of anyone to do this [prosecute one's own father for murder under these doubtful circumstances], but of one who is far advanced in wisdom." With this poor Euthyphro agrees enthusiastically: "Yes, by Zeus, Socrates, that is so" (4a–b).

Finally, it should be noted that Euthyphro is intellectually rather slow on the uptake. He completely misses the irony (with mocking intent) of the previous quotation. He still misses it when Socrates continues: "It is indeed most important, my admirable Euthyphro, that I should become your pupil" (5a). And so on, in much the same vein, right through the dialogue. In this regard, Euthyphro differs from Meno, who, while displaying the vanity of the amateur intellectual, is much sharper. Euthyphro is so conceited that even Socrates's questioning will not succeed in deflating him, reducing him to a knowledge of his own ignorance, as it did Meno. Indeed, he is so slow-witted that Socrates will hardly succeed in helping him discover any important truth for himself. At the end of the dialogue, he departs, quite unaltered as far as we can tell.

11.4.2 Theme and first stage of the dialogue

For a man like Euthyphro to display such brazen self-confidence would have seemed surprising to Plato's readers. For the moral aspects of the situation in which Euthyphro finds himself are anything but clear. After all, the man being prosecuted for murder is Euthyphro's own father; in patriarchal Greek society, the strict duty of respect and obedience to one's father went well beyond ties of natural affection. Moreover, the death in question was not the result of premeditation; in our terms, it was accidental homicide, or manslaughter. Finally, the hired man who was killed was himself a murderer, probably caught in the act by Euthyphro's father. So the moral situation with which the reader is presented at the outset of the dialogue is anything but clear-cut.

That is surely deliberate on Plato's part. The intention is to bring home to the reader the need for a criterion or standard—in this case, a definition of 'holiness'—by which to judge Euthyphro's course of action. That is one of the most important features of the sort of definition that Socrates is after: it must be able to serve as a standard such that, understanding both it and all the morally relevant facts of the case, one would be able to judge reliably whether or not some particular course of action is an instance of holiness or its opposite, unholiness, or neither. Just how far Euthyphro himself is from understanding what Socrates is after is plain from his first answer to the question, What is holiness?

Euthyphro's answer is: "I say the pious is to do what I am doing now, to prosecute the wrongdoer, be it about murder or temple robbery or anything else, whether the wrongdoer is your father or your mother or anyone else; not to prosecute is impious" (5d–e). This is an example, an ostensive definition (see 7.13.2), where none is wanted. We are reminded of the *Meno*. True, it is not a whole swarm of examples, such as Meno gave, but it boils down nevertheless to two things: first, a concrete instance, what Euthyphro himself is doing at the time, and, second, a somewhat more general statement that serves to illustrate the characteristic enquired after, namely 'prosecuting murderers and temple robbers and the like, regardless of who they are.' To see why neither answer will do, we must consider carefully what the *Euthyphro* has to teach us about the nature of Socratic definitions.

11.5 Socratic definitions

Apart from (1) the search for universal definitions, we have Aristotle's word for it that (2) the use of so-called inductive arguments or arguments based on analogy was typical of Socrates's manner of philosophizing. The latter point is confirmed by other writers of Socratic conversations before Plato. An argument from analogous cases was employed in the cross-examination of Meletus (see 9.2.4), and we shall soon see another in the *Euthyphro* (see 11.9 below). What interests us just now is the Socratic search for universal definitions.

A good deal has been said about Socratic definitions already (see 4.7.1–2; also 7.13.2). The point of our earlier remarks was to introduce the problem of universals that separates metaphysical realists from conceptualists and nominalists, while setting transcendent realists like Plato and his followers apart from immanent realists like Socrates, Aristotle, and the Peripatetic tradition generally. In the present context, two questions are of prime importance, namely (1) What sort of definitions was Socrates after? and (2) Why? that is, What did he hope to accomplish by discovering the correct definitions of those moral terms that appear to be the only ones that concerned him? We shall take the second question, the uses of definitions, first. The nature of Socratic definitions will be touched upon briefly here and given prolonged consideration in the next section.

11.5.1 The uses of definitions

To the latter question part of the answer is certainly that Socrates regarded correct definitions as (a) necessary for unravelling complex moral problems like that faced by Euthyphro. Indeed, in the absence of any but vague, popular ideas of justice or piety, how could one determine reliably whether any particular action is just or unjust, pious or impious? About such matters there is, after all, a great divergence of opinion among people in different places, among citizens of the same country at different times, and even among fellow citizens and contemporaries.

Agreement with others aside, we are quite frequently at a loss ourselves to identify the right course of action in a particular set of circumstances. For the Socrates of the early dialogues, it has been said, correct definitions are to moral deliberation and action roughly as scales and yardsticks are to the arts of weighing and measuring: we need an agreed-upon standard to refer to in order to resolve for ourselves any moral quandaries that may arise and to settle any differences we may have with others in regard to moral matters. Definitions provide that standard, a kind of 'moral compass' by which to chart our course of living.

This, however, is only part of the answer to the Why? question. Another is that (b) unless we know exactly *what* something is, such that we are able to provide a Socratic definition of it, we cannot answer reliably other questions concerning it that may be of great practical importance. Suppose, for example, that what is at issue is virtue. Unless we know what virtue is, Socrates held, we cannot answer such questions as: How can virtue (or any particular virtue) be acquired? How can we best instil it in others, especially the young? Is it teachable at all? Are all the virtues in some sense one? Is virtue profitable, that is, conducive, or an impediment, to human happiness, to a truly good life? Such questions may be of very great practical importance. Attempts to devise the best system of moral education will depend on them. On the last of them turns the whole question, How ought I to live? And yet we need to be in a position to give correct definitions in order to answer these pressing practical questions satisfactorily. Or so the Socrates of the early dialogues steadfastly believed.

11.5.2 The nature of definitions

Before proceeding further it may be worth quoting a passage from the *Euthyphro* that sums up admirably Socrates's own answer to both questions asked above, What? and Why?

> Bear in mind then that I did not bid you tell me one or two of the many pious actions but that form itself that makes all pious actions pious, for you agreed that all impious actions are impious and all actions pious through one form, or don't you remember? ... Tell me then what this form is, so that I may look upon it, and using it as a model, say that any action of yours or another's that is of that kind is pious, and if it is not that it is not. (6d–e)

The language here may be Plato's, but if Aristotle is right, the 'form' referred to here is the essential character or property described in the correct Socratic definition of piety. That, in a nutshell, is *what* Socrates is after. And *why* he seeks it is at least partly explained too: as a model by which to judge particular cases, a pattern that they either do or do not 'fit.' Of course, what the word 'form' covers is in need of clarification. We must specify one by one the conditions that must be fulfilled for anything to count as an adequate Socratic definition. That will be the focus of the next section. But first, a preliminary point regarding terminology, and another concerning punctuation.

Of the various types of definitions distinguished in 7.10 (verbal, real, reportive, stipulative, operational, ostensive, essential), all but the ostensive consist of two elements: (a) a *definiendum* ('the term to be defined'), 'x,' and (b) a *definiens* ('the defining formula'), 'y.' Thus, for example, 'piety' (*definiendum*) might be defined as 'obedience to God's commands' (*definiens*) or 'a triangle' (*definiendum*) as 'a figure bounded by three straight lines' (*definiens*), or 'speed' (*definiendum*) as 'distance over time' (*definiens*). Whether these are correct definitions does not matter; the point is merely to illustrate the meaning of *definiens* and *definiendum*.

A further point worth mentioning has to do with the use of quotation marks. Recall that in the case of Socratic or essential definitions, it is not just a *word* that is defined, but the essence of the thing or things (*res*) to which the word refers. That is why Socratic definitions are called 'real' definitions. Strictly, therefore, one should speak of the definition of (say) virtue rather than the definition [of the word] 'virtue.' (See 7.12.1 on the use of single quotation marks.) Nevertheless, if virtue itself is correctly defined in terms of y, then the expression involving 'y' is the only adequate verbal definition of the word 'virtue.' So there is no reason to be too fussy about the use of single quotation marks in what follows, or to be puzzled by the talk of defining a thing rather than a word.

11.6 Adequacy conditions for Socratic definitions

The question, What sort of definitions is Socrates after? is only too succinctly answered by Plato's reference to a 'form' common to many things to which the same name applies; a fuller answer must specify exactly what conditions any proposed definition must satisfy.

In order to be adequate a Socratic definition must satisfy *two formal conditions* and *one* further condition that can be regarded as *material* since it has to do with the content rather than the form of the *definiens*. Simply stated, the formal conditions of adequacy are: (1) coextensiveness of *definiens* and *definiendum*—that is, both expressions must apply to exactly the same set of things, thus guaranteeing the strict universality of the definition; and (2) the *definiens* must fully *explain*, clearly and without circularity, what *makes* the things defined the sort of things they are. The material condition of adequacy is (3) truth: the formally adequate definition given must be the *correct* one.

For convenience, we can refer to these three conditions as 'universality,' 'explanatoriness,' and 'truth,' respectively. Implicit in the second formal requirement are three demands, namely that the definition be (a) full, (b) clear, and (c) non-circular. These are simply part of the meaning of (2), 'explanatoriness,' rather than additional requirements. We must now explain all three adequacy conditions with the help of examples.

11.6.1 First adequacy condition

According to the first, *definiens* and *definiendum* must be coextensive. This means that the defining formula must apply to *all and only* those things to which the word being defined applies. Thus, in the simplest terms, if 'x' is to be correctly defined as 'y' (if y is to be the correct definition of x), then *all* things to which the term 'x'

(*definiendum*) applies must also be things to which '*y*' (*definiens*) applies, and vice versa: *all* things that are correctly called '*y*' must be correctly called '*x*' too. For example, if a whale is properly defined as 'a very large fish-like marine mammal,' then *all* whales must be very large fish-like marine mammals and all very large fish-like marine mammals must be whales. (Here the admittedly vague term 'very large' is intended to exclude dolphins and porpoises from the class of whales.) Or, to take an example from the *Euthyphro* itself, if 'god-beloved' is proposed as the *definition* of 'pious,' the first condition of adequacy is that *all* pious things be god-beloved *and* that *all* god-beloved things be pious; or, as we say, combining both conditions: *all and only* things which are pious are god-beloved. To put the same point slightly differently: something is pious (*x*) *if and only if* it is god-beloved (*y*).

Mathematical examples may help here since, as noted earlier (see 7.14), mathematics employs only exact concepts as distinct from what are called 'concepts of natural kinds,' like 'whale,' or 'fish' in our examples. It is clear from what has been said already that 'a figure bounded by three straight lines of equal length' is *not* the correct definition of a triangle, since all such figures (equilateral triangles) are indeed triangles, but not *only* such figures are triangles. Triangles can be isosceles (only two sides equal) or scalene (all sides unequal) as well as equilateral. So, in this case, 'if,' to be sure, but not '*only* if.' The proposed definition fails the test since it includes too much in the *definiens* and is therefore too narrow in the range of things to which it applies.

On the other hand, 'a figure bounded by straight lines' is not the correct definition of a triangle either, since all triangles are indeed figures bounded by straight lines, but not all figures bounded by straight lines are triangles. Obviously, squares are bounded by straight lines, as are octagons, and yet no rectilinear plane figure that encloses a space and has more than three sides is a triangle. So, in this case, 'only if,' certainly, but not 'if.' The proposed definition again fails, this time because it does not include enough in the *definiens* and is consequently too wide in its application. The same point could be illustrated by leaving the words 'very large' out of the earlier definition of 'whale.'

So the first formal adequacy condition is (in a handy mnemonic formula): *if and only if*. Terms that are coextensive are also called 'convertible,' so instead of 'coextensiveness' we might have used 'convertibility' as shorthand for the first adequacy condition. Both amount to universality in the strict sense specified above (*all and only*), and this, all things considered, is perhaps the simplest designation to remember. So in calling the first adequacy condition 'universality,' it is important to bear in mind the *strict* nature of the universality sought.

11.6.2 Second adequacy condition

A second formal adequacy condition is this: the *definiens* or defining formula must specify the very reason *why* the things defined share a common name; or, rather, it must pick out that *by which* or *because of which* they are such as they are, all the same *kind* of thing, to which therefore the same name applies. In addition to universality, this is a key part of what the Platonic Socrates, in the passage cited earlier, referred to as 'form.' As an example, take 'god-beloved,' proposed by Euthyphro as a definition of 'pious.' The second adequacy condition is that god-belovedness is precisely what *makes* all pious things pious and the *only* thing that makes them so. Or in general terms: All things which are *x* (pious) are *x because and only because* they are *y* (god-beloved). In a mnemonic formula: 'because *and only because.*'

It was noted above that the *definiens* must explain (a) *fully* and (b) *clearly* what makes all things of a certain kind the sort of things they are. The first part of this, *fully*, is clarified by the words '*and only* because' in our mnemonic formula. As for *clearly*, it is a necessary condition of explanatoriness that the *definiens* be simpler and more perspicuous than the *definiendum*. It is no good giving someone a definition of something that he is having difficulty understanding in terms that he understands just as little or even less! That is why, at *Meno* 75d, Socrates states explicitly that in responding to requests for definitions "the answers must not only be true, but in terms admittedly known to the questioner." Clarity, like fullness, is an implicit requirement already built into the second adequacy condition, explanatoriness, although the *Meno* mentions it in the same breath with the third adequacy condition, truth. A further implicit requirement of the second condition is that the definition cannot employ the very *same* term that is to be defined. At 79d Socrates reminds Meno that in defining 'shape' they had "rejected the kind of answer that tried to answer in terms still being the subject of enquiry and not yet agreed upon." To do otherwise is circular (see above 7.7.2). Thus, in addition to being fully explanatory and clear, Socratic definitions must be (c) non-circular.

11.6.3 Third adequacy condition

Taking the first two (the formal) adequacy conditions together, we may say:

For '*y*' to be a *formally* adequate *definiens* of the *definiendum* '*x*,' (1) all and only *x*'s must be *y*'s, and (2) their being *y*'s must be precisely what makes them *x*'s, and the only thing that makes them *x*'s.

Or, to put the whole thing in a simple mnemonic formula: '*if and only if, because and only because.*'

So much for the formal adequacy conditions of definitions. As for the material condition, (3) truth, this is absolutely crucial, since more than one formally adequate definition is possible. In other words, a *definiens* could be formally *the right sort of formula* to provide a correct Socratic definition, since it satisfies conditions (1) and (2); but so could a different formula. In addition, then, it must be *the correct* formula. So defining piety as god-belovedness may fulfil adequacy conditions (1) and (2); but if the moral theory known as the Divine Command Theory (which defines 'right' and 'wrong' in terms of what God commands and prohibits) is mistaken, then condition (3) is not satisfied.

A corollary of the third or material adequacy condition is that any definition which can be shown to have contradictory consequences fails to satisfy it. For of two logically contradictory consequences exactly one must be true and one false (see 7.10); and any proposition that logically entails something false must itself be false (see 6.3.3). Euthyphro's first definition, "what is dear to the gods is pious, what is not is impious" (7a), is refuted in just this way. For the definition entails that one and the same thing, provided it is loved by one god and hated by another, is both pious and impious (see 8a). This is not really a separate condition, but rather a technique by which falsity can be detected; hence we speak of *three* adequacy conditions: (1) convertibility or coextension, (2) explanatoriness (including clarity and non-circularity), and (3) truth (including consistency, although more than just consistency is required, since a perfectly consistent answer may still be false).

11.7 Socrates's own statement of these adequacy conditions

Where, if at all, does Socrates actually lay out adequacy conditions (1), (2), and (3)?

Condition (1) has two parts: (a) *all* and (b) *only*. We find the first in this passage:

[I]s the pious not the same and alike in *every* action and the impious the opposite of all that is pious and like itself, and *everything* that is to be impious presents us with one form or appearance in so far as it is impious? (5d e.a.)

This means: for piety to be definable at all, *all* pious actions must possess the property or feature(s) named in the defining formula. That is why, when Socrates rejects Euthyphro's initial example, he says: "You agree, however, that there are many other pious actions" (6d). So whether Euthyphro gives one example ("what I am doing now"), or a job lot of examples (prosecuting for murder, for temple robbery, and so on), he still has to admit that these are not *all* the things to which piety belongs.

As for the second part, 'only,' it is spelled out in this later passage:

And is then all that is just pious? Or is that which is pious just, but not all that is just pious, but some of it is and some is not? (11e)

In other words: all pious actions are just, but *not* all just actions are pious. Socrates illustrates the same point using 'fear' and 'reverence': all reverence is fear, but not all fear is reverence. Therefore, to offer 'fear' as a definition of 'reverence' is to fail to meet the first adequacy condition, just as 'a figure bounded by straight lines' is not a formally adequate definition of 'triangle.' The general point behind these examples is that where x and y (piety and justice, reverence and fear) are *not* coextensive, that is, where the first includes *more* under it than the second, the latter *cannot* be the complete definition of the former.

Condition (2), explanatoriness, again has two parts: (a) *because* and (b) *only because*, with (b) bringing out the requirement of completeness or fullness that is implicit in explanatoriness, along with clarity and non-circularity. We might again ask where (a) and (b) are stated in the text. It has to be admitted that Socrates nowhere explicitly states (b), although (a) is found in passages like these:

I did not bid you tell me one or two of the many pious actions but that form itself that *makes* all pious actions pious, for you agreed that all impious actions are impious and all pious actions pious *through* one form. (6d e.a.)

Is the pious loved by the gods *because* it is pious, or is it pious because it is loved by the gods? (10a e.a.)

Condition (3) is material rather than formal, and it too is stated in a couple of places:

Splendid, Euthyphro! You have now answered in the way I wanted [that is, the answer seems to satisfy the formal conditions of a definition]. Whether your answer is *true* I do not know yet. (7a e.a.)

Then let us examine whether that [definition] is a sound statement, or do we let it pass, and if one us, or someone else, merely says something is so, do we accept that it is so? Or do we examine what the speaker means? (9e)

11.8 The Euthyphro dilemma

The passage at 10a, to be quoted again in a moment, is famous as 'the Euthyphro dilemma.' A dilemma is roughly an 'either/or situation,' where neither alternative is very appealing or satisfactory. 'He is in a real dilemma' means, roughly: 'He has two and only two choices, both of which are unattractive.' That is why we speak of being on the 'horns' of a dilemma: it is rather like trying to manoeuvre one's way round an unfriendly bull. If successful, the manoeuvre is called 'slipping' or 'escaping between the horns of a dilemma.' Thus, we are at present in the process of trying to escape between the horns of the dilemma posed by minimal and maximal interpretations of the early dialogues of Plato.

Now the philosophical dilemma with which Socrates confronts Euthyphro is this:

Is [Alternative 1] the pious loved by the gods because it is pious, or [Alternative 2] is it pious because it is loved by the gods? (10a)

On the *first alternative*, all pious things are loved by the gods, but they are loved by the gods because they are pious or holy, not vice versa. In other words, the gods indeed love all and only pious things, but this is not what makes those things pious. Something else, some other characteristic, makes them pious; it just so happens that the gods love all things that possess this pious-making feature.

As a clarification of the definition, "the pious is what all the gods love" (9e), this first horn satisfies the first *formal condition* of adequacy: (1) pious if and only if loved by the gods. Or, somewhat differently put: (1) all pious things are god-beloved and all god-beloved things are pious. But it fails to satisfy the second formal condition: (2) pious *because and only because* loved by the gods. Like the giving of examples, then, this alternative falls short of a Socratic definition. It does not state the essence or real definition of piety, but names instead a *proprium* ('god-belovedness') that *all* pious acts have in common (on *proprium*, see 7.14).

On the *second alternative*, the definition means that the pious is pious because [and only because], the gods love it. Now this alternative clearly satisfies both formal conditions of adequacy: if and only if, because and only because. But it is unclear whether this Divine Command Theory of morality satisfies the *material condition*, (3) truth. It results in *a* real definition all right, a Socratic definition or theory of the *essence* or nature of piety. But is it the *correct* real definition or theory? We never find out, since Euthyphro goes (for reasons indicated at the end of the previous chapter) straight for the *first alternative* and is refuted for offering a definition that fails to satisfy formal condition (2). We never learn whether the other alternative, which fully satisfies(2), also satisfies (3). Later, we shall consider this second alternative, the Divine Command Theory, on our own. But first we must examine Socrates's refutation of the alternative Euthyphro in fact opts for.

11.9 Refutation of the first alternative

At 10d–e Euthyphro rejects the second while embracing the first horn of the dilemma, stating clearly that the pious is *not* pious because the gods love it (rejection of the second horn) but that the gods love it because it is pious (acceptance of first horn). How does the refutation (*elenchus*) proceed?

It turns on a logical principle that is nowhere stated, but which can be labelled, in modern terms, the 'Principle of Substitutivity without Change in Truth Value,' or, less grandly, the 'Principle of Inter-substitutivity.' The principle can be spelled out roughly as follows:

If two words have exactly the same intensional meaning (as they must if they are to be *definiens* and *definiendum*, respectively), then it must be possible to substitute one for the other in any proposition without *changing the truth-value of that proposition* (that is, if it is true, it will remain so, and if it is false, it will remain so).

The Platonic Socrates seems to understand this principle, even if he did not formulate it, for he clearly *uses* it to defeat Euthyphro's proposed definition. The principle entails that if substitution *changes* the truth value, even in a single proposition, then the term substituted was not precisely equivalent to (an exact synonym of) that for which it was substituted. So we have something of a test here that can be applied to any proposed definition of 'piety.'

Now by rejecting the second horn, Euthyphro maintains in effect that (P1) the love of the gods *does not* make pious things pious. But when questioned he also maintains that (P2) the love of the gods *does* make god-beloved things god-beloved. Socrates secures his agreement to P2 by citing a series of parallel cases and inviting him to reason inductively from the examples to the case in hand: being carried and carrying, being led and leading, being seen and seeing, and, finally, being loved and loving. That which is carried is carried because someone carries it; it is not true that someone carries it because it is carried. By analogy with the first three cases, that which is loved is loved because someone loves it. This Euthyphro freely acknowledges: "[what is loved] is not loved by those who love it because it is being loved, but it is... loved because they love it" (10c). Since this is presumably true both for the things that men love and for those that the gods love, it follows that (P2) the love of the gods makes god-beloved things god-beloved, in other words, that which is god-beloved is god-beloved because the gods love it.

The conclusion that follows from P1, P2, and the Principle of Intersubstitutivity is that (C) 'god-beloved' cannot mean the same as 'pious.' For substituting 'god-beloved' for 'pious' in the true statement P1, we get: the love of the gods does *not* make god-beloved things god-beloved. But this, according to P2, is false. And substituting 'pious' for 'god-beloved' at both places in P2, we get: the love the gods *does* make pious things pious. But this according to P1 is false. In other words, these two true propositions, P1 and P2, become false after substitution! If Euthyphro himself *will not say* that the pious is pious because the gods love it, but is *fully prepared to say* that the god-beloved is god-beloved because the gods love it, how can 'pious' and 'god-beloved' be identical in meaning? They cannot, and this is exactly the consequence drawn in Socrates's rather confusing statement of the outcome of the *elenchus* at (10e–11b). He begins this way:

But if the god-beloved and the pious were the same ... [that is, if 'god-beloved' were the correct definition of 'pious'], and [if (P1) the pious] were loved because it was pious, then the god-beloved would [also] be loved because it was god-beloved.

In other words, if their meanings were exactly the same, then 'god-beloved' could be substituted for 'pious' at both places in P1, 'the pious is loved because it is pious,' without change in the truth-value of the proposition. Socrates continues:

and if [P2] the god-beloved was god-beloved because it was loved by the gods, then the pious would also be pious because it was loved by the gods.

In other words, if the two words meant the same, 'pious' would be substitutable for 'god-beloved' in P2, 'the god-beloved is loved because the gods love it,' without changing its truth-value. But this is again precisely what Euthyphro himself will not allow, as Socrates points out, taking this second case first:

but now you see that they are in opposite cases as being altogether different from each other: the one [the god-beloved] is of a nature to be loved because it is loved [by the gods], the other [the pious] is loved because it is of a nature to be loved [because it is pious]. I'm afraid, Euthyphro, that when you were asked what piety is, you did not wish to make its nature clear to me, but you told me an affect or quality of it [a *proprium*, namely], that the pious has the quality of being loved by all the gods, but you have not yet told me what the pious is [that is, given me a definition, stated its essence].

Only repeated, careful reading of this tricky passage (10e–11b) can make sense of it. The point of the final sentence is this: Euthyphro cannot have given the right definition or described the essence of piety because *he has not given a definition or specified the essence of anything at all*. He has not said what *makes* pious things pious, that is, identified the essence (Greek: *ousia*), thus satisfying the second adequacy condition as well as the first; he has at best only pointed to a *proprium* of all pious things (Greek: *pathos ti*, a universal property of the pious), at worst only to an "accident on a cosmic scale" that all pious things just happen to possess: god-belovedness. (On these differing interpretations of *pathos ti*, see 7.14.) Thus, there is no need to go on to see whether the third adequacy condition is satisfied, since the supposed definition is not really a definition at all.

11.10 Second alternative: theological voluntarism

Had Euthyphro selected the *other* alternative, 'piety' would have been defined in the manner of the Divine Command Theory. According to this theory, 'morally good' just means 'commanded (or loved) by a god, the gods, or God,' while 'morally bad' is definable as 'prohibited (or hated) by a god etc.' (For convenience, we shall ignore the Greek context and simply use 'God' from now on.) But since this was not Euthyphro's choice, this theory is not examined in the *Euthyphro* at all. Nevertheless, it will be worth our while to consider its strengths and weaknesses briefly in order to determine whether Socrates might have held a moral theory along these lines. For that is the question that was posed at the end of the previous chapter.

The Divine Command Theory is also called 'theological voluntarism' (from the Latin *voluntas* 'will'). Its central tenet (see 10.2.1) is that our *basic* moral duty is to obey God's commands or will; all our *derivative* moral duties are just the specific commands or wishes of God. So all and only those things are morally good and right which God wills, loves, or commands, while all and only those are wrong which God prohibits. Furthermore, the *only* thing that makes those actions right or wrong is the fact that God commands or forbids them. In the language used earlier, all morally good things are morally good *if and only if* and *because* and *only* because God commands them. So had Euthyphro selected the other horn of the dilemma, he would at least have given a Socratic definition of 'piety'—though a mistaken one, as we shall see in a moment.

According to theological voluntarism God does not command us to do or omit certain things because they are *intrinsically* good or bad; they are intrinsically neutral and become good or bad because *and only because* he commands them; his commands *make* certain things good or bad, and they are *the only thing* that makes those things good or bad. This means that unless and until commanded by God, acts like (refraining from) murder, theft, and so on are neither good nor bad. God's commands are the *only* and *ultimate* standard of right and wrong. This, to be exact, is the normative ethical theory known as 'theological voluntarism'; as a meta-ethical theory (see above 10.2.2) about the meaning of the ethical terms 'right' and 'wrong,' 'good' and 'bad,' the Divine Command Theory has it that 'good' may be defined as 'commanded by God,' while 'bad' may be defined as 'forbidden by God.'

11.11 Evaluation of theological voluntarism

Before we consider whether Socrates's frequent references to obedience and service to the god Apollo point to his having held such a theory, a quick appraisal may be in order.

On the credit side of the balance sheet, the Divine Command Theory overcomes all varieties of moral scepticism, making short work of the claim that moral values are purely personal and moral value judgments therefore merely subjective. If subjective, then of course relative, perhaps not to the individual ('in the eye of the beholder'), but at least to the community or the particular historical epoch in which just these moral values are cherished. To moral relativism and scepticism the Divine Command Theory is a powerful antidote. For it provides us with a whole range of moral absolutes, namely whatever *God himself* approves or disapproves of. These values are entirely independent of what different individuals in the same society, or different societies, or even all individuals in all societies may think about moral goodness and evil. Thus, contrary to the claim of the moral relativist, even the parties to a perfect consensus can be wrong, indeed *absolutely* wrong. More will be said about moral relativism and scepticism later, when we come to the part on Sartre (see 32.3.2). The point we take for granted now is not that they are false, but only that it would be an asset for a theory to provide non-relative values and standards of conduct.

Second, and still on the positive side, the Divine Command Theory answers the question, Why be moral? Suppose that being moral is indeed a matter of obeying God's commands. That is apparently only the answer to the question, What is moral? But since God knows all our actions and judges us for them (at the Last Judgment, for example), it is obviously in our best interests to be moral as well. If you know what is good for you, you had better lead a morally good life! This is a plus for the Divine Command Theory, since other theories about what is moral may have no such ready-made answer to the question, Why be moral? A critic might agree that a certain theory correctly describes what is in fact moral and immoral, that is, what sort of behaviour morality requires of us or prohibits, and still say: 'Well, I prefer to do as I please, ignoring my duty whenever it suits me, since that is easier, or in my best interests, while morality requires me to think of others.' What morality requires of us and what rational self-interest recommends may, on other theories, be two different things, but not on the Divine Command Theory. It could not possibly be in anyone's best interests to disobey the moral edicts of an all-powerful, all-knowing, and vengeful God.

As for the drawbacks of the Divine Command Theory, one consideration is the fact that atheists and doubters cannot take it seriously. A moral theory that assumes something as controversial as the existence of God cannot expect to win the adherence of the hordes of people who entertain doubts on the subject. It *could* be true nevertheless, but as an attempt to explain to people what their duties are it cannot be expected to carry conviction with any but the faithful. This is an undesirable consequence rather than an argument against the correctness of the theory; but the point deserves careful consideration anyway: if we base something as important as morality on something as controversial as theism, even a particular version of theism, we may not be helping the cause of morality at all.

More important, though perhaps still not decisive, is the difficulty of determining *what* God commands. That is, there are problems about deriving specific duties from the general one of obedience to God. If we go by the Judeo-Christian Bible, then once we get beyond the so-called Decalogue we may find passages that seem to contradict one another, or whose intent is unclear. Questions of interpretation of God's revealed will arise and may prove next to insoluble. Consensus will be very hard to achieve in some cases, even among those who accept the same authoritative body of scripture. For among readers of the same Bible there are both 'fundamentalists' or 'literalists' and those who insist on the 'spirit' rather than the 'letter' of the law. Of course, consensus becomes even harder to achieve when there are differences of opinion about what in fact is the revealed word of God, or how different sources of revelation are to be ranked in importance.

Presumably, nothing said so far will shake the committed theist's confidence in his divinely ordained morality. But what if it can be shown that the Divine Command Theory makes nonsense of traditional religious conceptions of God's wisdom and goodness? As for divine wisdom, theological voluntarism has the consequence that all God's commands are *arbitrary*. For if things are good because God wills or commands them and for no other reason, then he clearly does not command them because they are intrinsically good and because he knows them to be such. In other words, God *cannot have any reason* for commanding this rather than that; that is what was meant by saying that his commands are entirely arbitrary or whimsical, even irrational. If he had commanded or permitted the most heinous crimes, they would not be crimes at all but either permissible or our moral duty. But if God does not act rationally, from insight into the good, in commanding this rather than that, what sense are we to make of the traditional notion of divine wisdom?

Finally, this meta-ethical theory similarly empties the theological doctrine of divine goodness of all content as well. According to the meta-ethical version of the Divine Command Theory, the proposition 'God commands the good' is equivalent to 'God commands what he commands' since 'the good' is defined as 'what God commands.' As the latter statement is completely empty (a 'tautology,' that is, literally, saying the same thing over again), so is the former; its vacuousness is just not immediately obvious in the former case. The vacuity of the concept means that the notion of divine goodness lacks the specific content 'good' has when we apply it to human behaviour. Thus, we say a person is good when he or she consistently chooses good over evil or the lesser among moral evils. Obviously, we cannot say that God is good in this sense, since anything he chooses would be good just in virtue of his choosing it. It is difficult to see why a God who is not good in this (or, for that matter, in any other non-vacuous) sense should be an object of worship. The consequences of the Divine Command Theory for religion are, in short, disastrous.

11.12 Socratic piety and the Divine Command Theory

So much for theological voluntarism itself. Given the outcome, we may want to consider briefly the nature of Socratic piety before returning to the question, Did Socrates hold any such theory?

11.12.1 Socratic piety

Socrates expresses surprise and disbelief at Euthyphro's suggestion that the gods are literally capable of fighting, murder, and revenge. He balks in particular at Euthyphro's literal acceptance of stories of such behaviour on the part of a son toward his father: "I find it hard to accept things like that being said about the gods, and it is likely to be the reason why I shall be told I do wrong [in the indictment]" (6a). This attitude toward popular religion was by no means original with Socrates. A century earlier Xenophanes had complained that "Homer and Hesiod have ascribed to the gods all things that are a shame and a disgrace among mortals, stealing and adulteries and deceivings of one another" (see 5.3.4). Now, is Socrates echoing Xenophanes, Heracleitus, and Anaxagoras here, that is, (1) doubting the very existence of the gods of Olympian theology; or is he only saying (2) that he cannot accept those particular stories about them that attribute *negative human emotions and vices* (anger, lust, revenge, mutilation, murder, adultery, lying, perjury—or all of the above) to divine beings?

The idea that Socrates might have gone as far as, or even further than, earlier Greek thinkers is by no means far-fetched. For there were both agnostic and atheistic unbelievers in Greek times. Of course, the *word* 'agnostic' was only coined in the nineteenth century, by the British philosopher C.K. Clifford. It comes from the Greek *agnoein*, meaning 'not to know' or 'to be ignorant of'. 'Nescience' is perhaps the English word that comes closest. Although the Greeks lacked the word, they were perfectly familiar with the anti-religious outlook to which the term 'agnosticism' is applied. Protagoras began a treatise *On the Gods* with the sentence: "On the subject of gods, I cannot know either that they exist or that they do not, nor what kind of beings they might be; there are many obstacles to knowledge, both the obscurity of the subject and the shortness of man's life." As for atheism, Diagoras of Melos and Theodorus of Cyrene are cited by Cicero (first century AD) as noted atheists of the fourth century BC.

Nevertheless, only (2) is clearly supported by the texts; as for (1) atheism, most of the evidence seems to be *against* it. First, in the *Apology*, Socrates expressly distances himself from both the naturalism or rational enlightenment of Anaxagoras and those earlier so-called physiologists who make nature itself divine, insisting that he believes in the *super*natural divine. True, in saying that he believes that the sun and the moon are gods, not lifeless stone or earth, as Anaxagoras held, he does not say whether he actually believes in the *anthropomorphic* or *personified* deities of the Greek myths. However, Socrates clearly ascribes personal character traits to Apollo, benevolence, for example, the desire to benefit the city of Athens by assigning Socrates his mission as gadfly; and he plainly believes that a benevolent god sometimes sends him signs in order to warn him that he is about to do wrong. From this it seems certain that Socrates believes in *personal* supernatural divinities. Moreover, in the last part of the *Euthyphro*, Socrates reiterates his scepticism about Euthyphro's suggestion that piety is a sort of 'commerce' or trade between men and gods: men make sacrifices to the gods in return for favours for themselves and ill luck for their enemies. Socrates fails to see how beings such as gods can either need or obtain any benefit from men, or how they can intervene in human affairs in order to *harm* men, if they are indeed good. From this, too, it is clear that he attributes moral, and hence personal, attributes to divinity. The point is well borne out by that passage in the *Apology* where Socrates, perplexed by Apollo's oracle, reflects: "For surely he does not lie; it is not legitimate [or right, that is, morally right] to do so." Of course, the traditional gods of Homer, the Olympians, lie all the time; it is this and all other moral failings that Socrates refuses to ascribe to the divinities in whose existence and personal nature he clearly believes.

From all we know about him, then, it appears that Socrates holds a fairly traditional belief in the gods of his ancestors, but that there are certain things he is just unwilling to accept as being contrary to reason. He refuses to believe that (a) the gods have human passions and vices; that (b) the gods want or need honours or offerings from men, that is, that human beings can curry favour with the gods; or that (c) the gods confer benefit on the supplicant *and harm* on the supplicant's enemies in response to entreaties and offerings. What all three suggestions have in common is a clear tendency to demean or debase the divine, to bring the gods down, not just to the human level, but to the level of the basest human motives and actions. And this Socrates would not hear of.

Summing up, we can perhaps say this about Socratic piety: In matters of religion, Socrates's attitude was as different from that of the orthodox, doctrinaire believer as it was from the religious innovator and self-styled prophet of the gods, Euthyphro. Here as elsewhere he took human reason to be the final arbiter of truth, not scriptural sources or ancestral tradition. He was respectful of religious tradition *where it did not conflict with reason*; but if reason and tradition clashed, Socrates insisted unequivocally on following the dictates of reason. Although primarily a moral philosopher who did not speculate about the divine, Socrates at least had a *moral* theology. That is, he held reasoned philosophical views about the *moral* attributes of the divine, even if his focus on morality made him reluctant to use reason to discern any of the other attributes of divinity. And that moral theology included the goodness of the gods in an apparently non-vacuous sense, indeed their clear superiority in this regard to mankind.

11.12.2 Socrates and theological voluntarism

More will be said in chapter 13 about Socratic piety and its crucial importance in understanding the life Socrates led. As for to the Divine Command Theory, it seems reasonably clear, all things considered, that Socrates believed that Apollo commanded him to live as he has lived because it was good; it was not good simply because Apollo commanded it. Similarly, the divine sign warned him against certain things because they were wrong; they were not wrong because the divine sign warned him against them. In short, it is not divine prohibition but something else that *makes* these things wrong. If so, then Socrates was no adherent of the Divine Command

Theory. And, as noted already, it is entirely unlikely that any Greek ever seriously espoused it. The belief in an absolute moral law, a justice inherent in the very fabric of the cosmos, was just too deep-seated among the Greeks. It is present in Anaximander's law of encroachment and redress, and in the Heracleitean *logos*; whatever men *or gods* may do, in the fullness of time Justice will prevail. It is just as little subject to the will of the gods, even the highest of them, as it is the product of merely human legislation. True, there were among the sophists of the fifth and fourth centuries BC those who were prepared to deny that right and wrong have any objective existence, making the moral quality of actions dependent on the will of the most powerful group within the community. This is voluntarism all right, but not *theological* voluntarism. It should not surprise us that Euthyphro failed to select the second alternative, even though no reasons are given or even hinted at in the dialogue itself. Neither should it come as a surprise that Socrates's remarks about the gods, both there and in the *Apology*, show no trace of his having held such a theory.

Is then perhaps the avoidance of harm Socrates's basic action guide? Recall the alternatives considered earlier: either (Option A) Socrates is a proponent of the Divine Command Theory, whose sole basic principle is obedience to God's commands; or else (Option B) his basic principle is 'Never harm others' (least of all, the collectivity or the state), since to wrong others by harming them is harmful to oneself, and no rational human being would harm himself. This type of moral theory was called 'eudaemonism.' Or, finally, (Option C) Socrates might hold a mixed theory. We have now eliminated Option A on the basis of our examination of the *Euthyphro*. Left are two options. To choose between them we must consider the relationship between virtue and happiness in the *Crito*.

12

Virtue and Happiness

12.1 Introductory

It is in the *Crito*, a dialogue probably written earlier than the *Euthyphro*, that we find definitive Socratic answers to the questions, What is moral? and Why be moral? By following the stages in which this dialogue unfolds, we shall be able to identify Socrates's basic moral principle as the principle of non-maleficence (see 12.7). His general theory of morals can then be shown to be of the eudaemonistic type discussed above (see 9.2.2 and 10.3), but different in important respects from the eudaemonistic theories of other prominent Greek moralists and a radical departure from popular Greek morality in his day. To get the full measure of the theory, it may not be enough to contrast it with popular and philosophical Greek views. Accordingly, in the second half of the chapter we shall briefly juxtapose the morality of Socrates with that of Jesus, Hobbes, and Kant as well (see 12.8.3–5). A critical evaluation of the theory will be attempted in the next chapter.

The stages in which the *Crito* unfolds are:

1 The Setting of the Scene in Prison (43a–44b)
2 Crito's Attempt to Persuade Socrates to Escape (44b–46a)
3 Socrates's Two Ground Rules for the Examination of the Question (46b–48d)
4 Socrates's Three Moral Principles (49a–51c)
5 Application of the Moral Principles to the Question in Hand (51c–53a)
6 Concluding Examination of Crito's Initial Arguments (53a–end)

In this chapter, we shall consider all these stages in succession, though stages 3 through 6 are deserving of special attention since they offer an instructive example of Socrates's manner of applying his moral principles to a particular problem of applied ethics usually designated that of civil disobedience (see 1.2.3 and 10.2).

12.2 The setting of the scene and Crito's arguments

The first two stages can be rapidly summarized. The chief thing to note with respect to the portion of the dialogue devoted to laying the scene is the implicit faith Socrates places in the dream which tells him he will depart this world "on the third day" (44b). This is further evidence of his pious acceptance of the supernatural and testifies to his sincerity in the passage of the *Apology* where he states: "To do this has, as I say, been enjoined upon me by the god, by means of oracles and dreams, and in every other way that a divine manifestation has ever ordered a man to do anything" (33c). Apart from this, the only other noteworthy dramatic touches are, on the one hand, the serenity of Socrates—Crito marvels at his capacity to sleep so peacefully in such circumstances—and, on the other, the deep bonds of affection and loyalty that unite these two old friends. This is all relevant to the portrait of Socrates that Plato paints in these early dialogues; but the *Crito* is important above all for the light it sheds on the thought of Socrates.

With the scene set, the philosophical portion of the dialogue gets under way almost immediately. To begin with, Crito advances seven arguments intended to persuade Socrates to escape. They can be presented in summary fashion as follows: (1) If Socrates does not escape, Crito will lose a valued and irreplaceable friend. (2) Furthermore, Crito's reputation will be tarnished, since "the many" will not believe that he tried to persuade Socrates to escape and the latter refused, but that Crito was unwilling to part with his money to help a friend. (3) If he does escape, Socrates need not fear that the friends who helped him will suffer any confiscation of property; bribes will ensure against this. (4) Moreover, a good life awaits him among Crito's friends in Thessaly. (5) If he does not escape, he will gratify those enemies who desire his death. (6) In addition, he will abandon his children to the fate of orphans and (7) the reputation of all his friends will suffer.

The conclusion (46a) of all these arguments is: "Consider, Socrates, whether this is not only evil, but shameful, both for you and for us."

12.3 Socrates's ground rules

Socrates is quite prepared to consider Crito's proposal. Having listened patiently to his old friend, he now invites Crito to consider the matter together with him, laying down two important ground rules for the ensuing discussion (46b–49b).

12.3.1 First ground rule: the supremacy of reason

The first ground rule concerns the method to be followed in determining what course of action to take. At bottom, it opposes reason to (1) emotion, (2) authority, and (3) tradition or custom, asserting that in cases of conflict one's own reasoning must prevail over feelings like fear, over the authority of one's contemporaries (whose good opinion one naturally desires as a civilized person), and regard for the opinions of one's ancestors—or for that matter, regard for the opinion of posterity—though this last point is not actually spelled out. Here is the way Socrates puts it:

> We must therefore examine whether we should act in this way or not, as not only now but at all times I am the kind of man who listens only to the argument that on reflection seems best to me. I cannot, now that this fate has come upon me, discard the arguments used ... and if we have no better arguments to bring up at this moment, be sure that I shall not agree with you, not even if the power of the majority were to frighten us with more bogeys, as if we were children, with threats of incarcerations and executions and confiscation of property. (46b)

The question of the right course of action is to be decided, then, by a process of *moral reasoning*, that is, dialectical reasoning, the Socratic method of enquiry. So the first ground rule is to think for oneself and follow the best reasoning, the best arguments. As Socrates put it the *Euthyphro*, "the lover of enquiry must follow his beloved wherever it may lead him" (14c), to which we can add, on the strength of both the *Crito* and the *Apology*, 'even should it lead him to his death.'

12.3.2 Second ground rule: the supremacy of moral reasons

As the first ground rule opposed emotion, authority, and tradition to reason, so the second opposes different kinds of reasons to one another. That is, it opposes moral goodness to all sorts of non-morally good things (for example, safety, security, the esteem of others, the welfare of one's friends and family, the preservation of one's life and those of others), asserting that in deliberations about what course of action to take, the concern for *moral* goodness must always be paramount, overriding the desire for non-morally good things should there be a conflict. Thus, we should always do our moral duty, no matter what the apparently bad consequences for ourselves or others, be they our dearest friends or our own children. Once it has been decided what is morally right, *that* shall be done, *no matter what*. Here is how Socrates himself formulates the second ground rule:

> [W]e must examine next whether it is right for me to try to get out of here when the Athenians have not acquitted me. If it is seen to be right, we will try to do so; if it is not, we will abandon the idea. As for those questions you raise about money, reputation, the upbringing of children, Crito, those considerations in truth belong to those people who easily put men to death and would bring them back to life if they could, without thinking; I mean the majority of men. (48c–d)

The passage is reminiscent of two others from the *Apology* that are worth quoting here, since they were not examined earlier:

> Someone might say: "Are you not ashamed, Socrates, to have followed the kind of occupation that has led to your being now in danger of death?" However, I should be right to reply to him: "You are wrong, sir, if you think that a man who is any good at all should take into account the risk of life or death; he should look to this only in his actions, whether what he does is right or wrong, whether he is acting like a good or a bad man." (28b)

> [W]herever a man has taken a position that he believes to be best, or has been placed by his commander, there he must, I think, remain and face danger without a thought for death or anything else, rather than disgrace. It would have been a dreadful way to behave, gentlemen of the jury, if at Potidaea, Amphipolis and Delium, I had, at the risk of death, like anyone else, remained at my post where those you had elected to command had ordered me, and then, when the god ordered me, as I thought and believed, to live the life of philosophy, to examine myself and others, I had abandoned my post for fear of death or anything else. (28d–29a)

Both passages anticipate the second ground rule of the *Crito*, and in particularly memorable form.

12.4 Socrates's three moral principles

Once the ground rules have been established in the third stage, the discussion of the moral dilemma can begin. Socrates now lays down three moral principles or maxims for Crito's consideration (49b–51c), securing (without argument) his agreement to each. The first is:

(1) We ought never to injure or harm anyone, even when the other has harmed us first.

In Socrates's own words: "One should never do wrong in return, nor injure any man, whatever the injury one has suffered at his hands" (49d). This can be labelled, for ease of reference, the *principle of non-maleficence and non-retaliation*.

The second principle can be put this way:

(2) We ought never to break agreements entered into without deceit or compulsion.

Or, again, in Socrates's words: "when one has come to an agreement that is just with someone, should one fulfill it or cheat on it? ... [Crito answers:] One should fulfill it" (49e).

The meaning of the qualifying phrase "that is just" is explained at 52e, where the personified laws of Athens tell Socrates that he entered into certain agreements "without compulsion or deceit, and under no pressure of time for deliberation." This makes perfect sense. It is even enshrined in law today. If, for example, a salesman bullies, tricks, or rushes a customer into signing a contract, using threats, or lies, or persuading him not to read the fine print, no competent judge would declare the signatory bound by the contract. Otherwise, however, the contract is binding; and so too when one gives one's word, even without a written contract: one's word is at least morally, if not legally, binding, if Socrates's principle is a sound one. This second principle can be conveniently referred to as the *principle of fidelity*. 'Fidelity' here just means: 'keeping faith,' 'keeping one's agreements.'

The third maxim is:

(3) We ought never to disobey our parents or guardians.

In Socrates's words again: "It is impious to bring violence to bear against your mother or father, it is much more so to use it against your country" (51c). This can be called the *principle of filial piety*. 'Filial' means 'of a son (or daughter),' while 'piety' in this context has no religious connotations, but refers to the kind of respect owed a parent. What this principle means is self-explanatory, though the correctness of principle is much less obvious, to our way of thinking, than in the case of the previous principle or even the first. As we shall see, not very much turns on it.

12.5 Application of the principles

The fifth stage of the dialogue contains the application of these principles to the case in hand. In each instance, the application is perfectly straightforward. First, as to the principle of non-maleficence/non-retaliation, the reasoning is, very simply, this: If I escape, I will injure the city by destroying its laws. That Socrates would indeed harm the city were he to escape is plain from the words of the personified laws: "you pay no heed to us, the laws, as you plan to destroy us" (52c–d). They also call him "destroyer of the laws" (53b) and warn: "you depart, if you depart ... after shamefully returning wrong for wrong and injury for injury ... after injuring those whom you should injure least—yourself, your friends, your country and us" (54c).

As for the principle of fidelity, the reasoning is just as simple: If I escape, I will be breaking my agreement with the city. The personified laws are perfectly clear on this point. It is they who speak in these passages:

[W]hoever of you remains [in the city when he could go elsewhere], when he sees how we conduct our trials and manage the city in other ways, has in fact come to an agreement with us to obey our instructions. We say that the one who disobeys does wrong ... because in spite of his agreement, he neither obeys us nor, if we do something wrong, does he try to persuade us to do better. (51e–52a)

[Y]ou are breaking the undertakings and agreements that you made with us without compulsion or deceit and under no pressure of time for deliberation. You have had seventy years during which you could have gone away. (52e)

3. Finally, as regards the application of the principle of filial piety in Socrates's present circumstances, the argument is the same. If I escape, I will be disobeying my 'parent,' the state: "the one who disobeys does wrong," say the laws, "first because in us he disobeys his parents, also those who brought him up" (51e).

The outcome of these deliberations is perfectly straightforward, since there is *no conflict* among these moral duties; all three principles, when applied to the case in hand, yield exactly the same conclusion: 'I ought not to escape.' Alternatively, principles (1), (2), and (3) could be used to establish a further principle:

(4) We ought never to break the law.

In other words, civil disobedience is always wrong, from which the same conclusion follows. For Socrates could have reasoned:

P1 We ought never to break the law (4).
P2 If I escape, I will break the law.
C   I ought not to escape.

This way of viewing the argument would explain clearly why Socrates refused to go along with the proposal to try the generals jointly for their actions at Arginusae, when the law specified they should be tried separately. Since it was unlawful, it was also morally wrong from his perspective. But the same thing follows from the principle of filial piety on its own, given that Socrates regards the relationship of city to citizen as that of parent to offspring.

12.6 Rebuttal of Crito's arguments

Now that it has been determined, unambiguously, that it *would not be morally right* to escape, Socrates's course of action is clear: he will stay in prison and face execution. This is in accordance with the second ground rule set out in the third stage. Nevertheless, the sixth and final stage of the dialogue is devoted to rebutting Crito's initial claims that it would be best *in the non-moral sense*, that is, it would be in Socrates's best interests, and that of his family and friends, for him to escape.

Again, the personified laws provide the rejoinders. The replies to Crito's initial arguments are, very briefly, as follows. (1) As for the effect upon *his friends*, it is fairly certain, contrary to what Crito claims, that they will be stripped of their citizenship, exiled, and expropriated for their part in Socrates's escape. (2) As for

Socrates himself, (i) if he flees to a well-governed state virtuous men will shun him as a subverter of laws (and hence as one who corrupts the youth), while (ii) if he flees to Crito's friends in ill-governed Thessaly, he will crown a dignified life spent in the serious pursuit of philosophy by escaping in the undignified manner of a runaway slave and by leading a bovine existence unworthy of a man, since no one would take him seriously were he to talk about justice or any other philosophical matter. (3) As for *Socrates's own children,* (i) if he flees and takes them with him to Thessaly, they will lose their Athenian citizenship and forfeit an Athenian upbringing or education; while (ii) if they stay at Athens, his friends will see to their education, whether he flees or dies. In the first case his sons will be worse off, while in the second they will be no better off whether Socrates escapes or not.

12.7 Socrates's basic moral principle and working ethics

So far we have enumerated three moral principles. From these we have also inferred a fourth maxim that is not mentioned, but is at least implicit, in the *Crito*:

(4) Always obey the commands of the state.

Neither mentioned *nor implicit* is the moral principle that figures so prominently in the *Apology*:

(5) Always obey the commands of god.

Its absence from the *Crito* would certainly tell against ascribing the Divine Command Theory to Socrates, had that not already become reasonably clear from the *Euthyphro*. Yet in the *Apology*, Socrates said that (5) is more important than (4):

> if you said to me ... 'Socrates, we do not believe Anytus now; we acquit you, but only on condition that you spend no more time on this investigation and do not practise philosophy, and if you are caught doing so you will die'; if, as I say, you were to acquit me on those terms, I would say to you: 'Gentlemen of the jury, I am grateful and I am your friend, but I will obey the god rather than you.' (29c–d)

On this basis we can add a second-order principle to Socrates's working ethics, that is, a principle that governs the use of other principles, a meta-principle, as we can say, much in the same sense that meta-ethics was termed a 'meta-theory' (see 10.2.2):

(6) In case of conflict between principles (4) and (5), (5) ought to take precedence over (4).

But we have already seen that neither Socrates nor, presumably, any other Greek

232   Part One: Socrates and the Road to Wisdom

intellectual would have regarded (5), obedience to divine commands, as the foundation or basic rule of morality. The question, then, is: Which of the other moral principles enunciated by Socrates is his *basic* principle, the foundation of his morality? Is it,

(1)   Never deliberately harm anyone (even if that person has harmed you)?

Or is it:

(2)   Never break promises or undertakings of any kind (provided they have been entered into without haste, compulsion, or deception)?

Or, finally, could it be:

(3)   Never disobey parents and teachers?

On reflection, it looks very much as though (1) non-maleficence/non-retaliation is basic in relation to (2) promise keeping, (3) obeying parents and guardians, and (4) respecting the laws, since promise breaking, disobedience, and lawlessness all cause one kind of harm or another, even if (in the case of promise breaking) only by disappointing a reasonable expectation that one has oneself raised.

Non-maleficence, then, seems the best candidate for Socrates's basic moral principle and foundation of his working ethics. For all the important secondary principles can be derived from it alone. What this shows beyond a shadow of a doubt is that, in the context of the popular Greek morality of the day, Socrates was a radical moral innovator.

12.8 The Socratic principle of non-maleficence and non-retaliation

12.8.1 Popular Greek morality

The first of Socrates's three maxims is by far the most interesting, precisely because it flies in the face of most Greek moral thinking. Indeed, it would have shocked most Greeks, since at the heart of their traditional moral code was the so-called *lex talionis* (the law of retaliation), that is, roughly: Return harm for harm. Thus, in Euripides's play *Ion* (1046–7) an elderly slave and trusted servant remarks: "But when we wish to harm our enemies, there is no law that can prevent." This, however, is only part of a broader principle famously formulated this way in Plato's *Republic* (332c): Benefit your friends ('friends' meaning 'those who confer distinct benefits on you,' but also your neighbours, fellow citizens, comrades-in-arms, kinsmen, loved ones, and so forth) and harm your enemies (those who harm you or damage your interests, your name, your group, etc.). The two parts of this are just corollaries of the maxim, ascribed to the lyric and elegiac poet Simonides (c. 556–468 BC), that justice consists in "giving to each what is owed" or what is "due" to him. An even older source is the Athenian poet and lawgiver, Solon, who prays for wealth and authority "that I may thus be pleasant to my friends and bitter to my enemies." So where friends are concerned, what is due is something good or pleasant; in the case of enemies, however, it is something bad or "bitter." The first half is nicely captured by Xenophon in one of his historical works: "All men, I think, regard it as right to show goodwill to him from whom one has received gifts." Elsewhere in the same work Xenophon, too, puts both parts of the code together: "[T]he virtue of a man is to surpass his friends in benefactions and his enemies in harm." This sounds just like Meno: "First, if you want the virtue of a man, it is easy to say that a man's virtue consists of being able to manage public affairs and in so doing to benefit his friends and harm his enemies" (71e).

The *lex talionis* is the underlying principle of the morality of the Greek gods and heroes in the works of Hesiod and Homer, and it is to be found, in one form or another, throughout the philosophy and literature of the fifth century BC as well. The harm in question may even lie in the past wrongs of one family against another. While popular Greek morality in the time of Socrates, Plato, and Aristotle is a complex affair, certain passages from Plato's dialogues and Greek literature show that the traditional *lex talionis* retained its full force in Socrates's day. Indeed, for a Greek of that time, retaliation against enemies is one of the greatest of legitimate pleasures. Thus, a speaker in Thucydides's history of the Peloponnesian war exhorts his countrymen "to engage in anger, convinced that, as between adversaries, nothing is more legitimate than to claim to sate the whole wrath of one's soul in punishing the aggressor, and nothing more sweet, as the proverb has it, than vengeance upon an enemy." This is a very far cry indeed from the rule most of us learned at our mother's knee, "two wrongs don't make a right." For a Greek of the fifth century, two wrongs did make a right: if another injures me or my interests, then in returning harm for harm I am simply restoring the legitimate boundary between us which the other has overstepped. Nothing could be more just or (if we are perfectly honest about it) more agreeable!

This bleak picture of Greek popular morality as fierce and unforgiving is somewhat mitigated by the respect the Greeks apparently had for magnanimity, that (translating literally) 'greatness of soul' that could lead a man to forbear even when in a position to exact retribution. To be the sort of person who did not bear a grudge when no lasting harm was done, who overlooked minor provocations or settled for something less than full satisfaction according to the letter of the law was regarded as a mark of character and nobility, though admiration for this quality of mind stopped well short of the idea that enmity actually deserved forgiveness, let alone good, in return.

12.8.2 Old Testament morality

Obviously, this rule of traditional Greek morality is very like the more familiar Old Testament creed of the ancient Hebrews,

> thou shalt give life for life, eye for eye, tooth for tooth, hand for hand, foot for foot, burning for burning, stripe for stripe" (Exodus 21:23–25)

usually shortened to: 'an eye for an eye, a tooth for a tooth.' The idea conveyed by the sequence of illustrations is obviously that the retaliatory act should be *the same as or equivalent to* the wrong inflicted. Concrete examples can be found at many places throughout the Hebrew Bible. Thus, at Genesis 9:6 we read: "Who so sheddeth man's blood, by man shall his blood be shed." Of course, in the case of some forms of wrongdoing (rape, bearing false witness, and so on), it would make no sense to inflict the *same* harm on the guilty party; and yet as soon as the rule is taken to mean that the retaliation should 'fit' the wrong done, all sorts of problems concerning what harm is most fitting can arise.

Socrates's morality of unilateral and unconditional non-maleficence and non-retaliation, by contrast, comes down to something like this: Never inflict *any* harm on anyone, not even your worst enemies, and not even when you have been harmed—even very severely harmed—first.

Obviously, this moral principle stands in stark contrast both to popular Greek morality and to the Old Testament creed. If it seems that the contrast could not be starker, we have only to consider for a moment the moral teaching of Jesus.

12.8.3 The morality of Jesus

The moral teaching of the New Testament is encapsulated in what is sometimes called 'the Golden Rule.' The rule that most of us learned at mother's knee ('Do unto others as you would have them do unto you') is just the last part of this more elaborate principle:

> But I say unto you which hear, Love your enemies, do good to them which hate you, bless them that curse you, and pray for them which despitefully use you. And unto him that smiteth thee on the one cheek offer also the other; and him that taketh away thy cloke forbid not to take thy coat also. Give to every man that asketh of thee; and of him that taketh away thy goods, ask them not again. And as ye would that men should do to you, do ye also to them likewise. (Luke 6:27–31)

In another of the gospels the same thing is put more simply:

Therefore all things whatsoever ye would that men should do to you, do ye even so to them: for this is the law of the prophets. (Matthew 7:12)

This can be described as the *theory of unconditional unilateral beneficence*—as well as non-maleficence, of course. It may be what Jesus means by his "second commandment" when he says (Mark 12:29–31):

The first of all the commandments is, Hear O Israel: The Lord our God is one Lord; and thou shalt love the Lord thy God with all thy heart, and with all thy soul, and with all thy mind, and with all thy strength: this is the first commandment. And the second is like, namely this: Thou shalt love thy neighbour as thyself.

Loving one's neighbour as oneself presumably means bestowing on him, insofar as lies in one's power, all the good things that one would wish for oneself, not just refraining from inflicting on him anything one would not want to undergo or suffer oneself.

These passages convey the positive side of Jesus's moral teaching, though it has to be admitted that there are other things in the New Testament (particularly about hell and eternal punishment) that may be difficult to reconcile with it. That question can be left aside here. There is no need to dwell on the difference between (1) Jesus's positive injunction to return *good* for harm, *not even seeking to avoid harm* when others mean us ill, and (2) Socrates's teaching that we should simply avoid harming others at all costs, even when they have harmed us first, though we may certainly do everything in our power to avoid being harmed so long as our efforts do not involve inflicting harm on others (even our assailants). It is clear enough that the so-called 'Golden Rule' enjoins positive beneficence, even towards one's worst enemies, that is, *unconditional* beneficent love; it means, therefore, not just 'Love thy neighbour,' but 'Love thy enemy' (as thyself). If Socrates was a great moral revolutionary in relation to the popular Greek morality of his day, Jesus was an even greater innovator in relation to the Old Testament morality of his contemporaries. It is hard for us to imagine what it must have been like for an Ancient Hebrew to be confronted with a moral gospel that set the standard of conduct so high. This, of course, is not intended to suggest that Jesus was the first ever to propound a moral code of such loftiness; that distinction probably belongs to the sages of the Eastern tradition, Buddha and Lao-tse, who lived five to six hundred years earlier.

12.8.4 The morality of Hobbes

As Socrates's teaching differs from that of traditional Greek, Hebrew, and New Testament morality, so it differs from the moral theory of mutual or reciprocal non-maleficence that was to be espoused almost two millennia later by Thomas Hobbes. Hobbes's teaching is encapsulated in the following dictum:

be sociable with them that will be sociable, and formidable with them that will not. (*Elements of Law*, I, xvii, 15)

Depending on how one interprets it, this may be quite a different maxim from any considered so far. At first blush, it bears a family resemblance to the traditional Greek dictum: "Help your friends and harm your enemies." Nevertheless, in its first part it stresses *non*-maleficence (being sociable) rather than beneficence (helping your friends). Moreover, being sociable is a duty *only* towards those who neither mean nor have done us any harm. So the first part enjoins *conditional* rather than unconditional non-maleficence. Accordingly, the initial bit of Hobbes's dictum appears to fall somewhere *between* traditional Greek morality (conditional beneficence and maleficence) and the morality of Socrates (*un*conditional non-maleficence), enjoining *conditional* non-maleficence towards all.

The latter part of the maxim, however, enjoins us to do whatever we can to ensure that others cannot harm us, to make ourselves "formidable," in other words, chiefly by increasing our own power so as to instil in others a well-justified fear of reprisal should they venture to harm us. On the face of it, 'being formidable' seems to come up short of actually harming others. Yet the maxim appears to divide those who are not friends (the 'unsociable') into two camps: those who have, and those who have not as yet, harmed us. 'Being formidable' no doubt includes retaliation against the former class of 'enemies' for harm already inflicted upon us; as for those who have not yet harmed us, the maxim seems to urge *deterrence* rather than harm.

Just how far this goes is not clear, however. It is doubtful, for example, whether it would be wrong to harm those whom we have reasonable grounds to *suspect* of *meaning* us serious harm, even before they have actually given offence. On the whole, it seems likely that the pre-emptive strike figures as morally legitimate in Hobbes's notion of being formidable. If so, then a corollary of Hobbes's principle could (without gross exaggeration) be put this way: 'Do unto others *before* they do unto you.' This is not the whole story, of course, but it appears that Hobbes might endorse some such consequence as this corollary as well.

12.8.5 Kantian morality

So much for Hobbes. A very different, but comparably influential moral outlook is that of Kant, whose basic moral principle is known as 'the categorical imperative.' The name sounds less forbidding if we gloss it as 'the unconditional ('categorical' as opposed to 'hypothetical') moral law or command' ('imperative'). Now, at bottom, there is no more danger of confusing (1) Socratic unconditional non-maleficence with (2) Kant's categorical imperative than with (3) Hobbes's conditional non-maleficence or (4) Jesus's unconditional beneficence; still, the contrast may again prove instructive. For it helps one to situate Socrates on a continuum or spectrum of moral outlooks, so that one can ask whether, in the final analysis, Socrates sets the standard of morality too high and, if so, whether any other major philosopher got significantly nearer the mark.

Kant's categorical imperative is given various formulations in his writings, not all of them obviously equivalent, although Kant himself apparently took them to be so. The most famous is: Act in such a way that you always treat humanity, whether in your own person or in the person of any other, never simply as a means, but always at the same time as an end. We can paraphrase as follows: treat others as autonomous (self-governing) beings with their own ends, not simply as means to *your* ends. The key thing here is what Kant elsewhere characterizes as *respect for the dignity of persons*: recognizing that every human being possesses a special dignity as a rational agent capable of governing his own life and actions and directing them toward ends of his own choosing. This is what distinguishes persons from things. Only inanimate things may be treated simply as means to our ends. We can leave aside questions about animals and whether they may be used for our purposes; as for persons, Kant's teaching is unequivocally that we simply have no right to use them *ever*, not even in order to further *un*selfish ends of our own like the good of society at large. To usurp another's autonomy, even when convinced that what we are doing is for his or her own good, or for the good of the majority, or for the good of all mankind, is, from the Kantian perspective, an affront to the dignity of the person.

Contrasting this with the other maxims considered so far, we can say that the Kantian categorical imperative enjoins neither non-maleficence nor active beneficence, whether conditional or unconditional; that is, it instructs us neither to refrain from harming others (Socrates), nor always to benefit others regardless of the harm they may have done us (Jesus), nor to refrain from harm conditionally (Hobbes). Instead, it directs us *not* to consider the consequences of our actions for our own or for others' non-moral good (happiness) *at all*. In commanding us simply to respect the dignity of persons, the Kantian maxim shifts the focus away from acting for certain *ends* to acting from a certain *motive*. Thus, in all its various formulations, the categorical imperative commands us to act from the motive of obedience to the categorical imperative, or from reverence for the moral law, or from respect for persons, these formulations being equivalent according to Kant.

Behind this *shift in focus from consequences to motives* lies the following consideration. If moral goodness were only a means to certain non-morally good ends, it would have only extrinsic value; whereas if moral goodness depends on the motive involved, the goodness of an action is intrinsic to the action itself. *Moral goodness, Kant assumes, must be intrinsic goodness*; it cannot depend on non-morally good consequences, real or intended, and still concern *morality*. We may and do approve of a great many things that produce, or at least show a tendency toward, the non-morally good, the satisfaction of human needs or desires; but this, Kant holds, is not enough for *moral* approval, at least not if moral goodness is intrinsic goodness. Moral approval depends *exclusively* upon the moral goodness of the *will* or motive from which the action springs. Whether or not *any* non-moral good is actually brought about or even intended, is entirely irrelevant, morally speaking.

From this point of view theories like that of Socrates, Jesus, or Hobbes are not really *moral* theories at all. Now Kant was certainly right to think that Socratic eudaemonism, like all forms of eudaemonism developed by the Greek moralists, is just a form of enlightened self-interest or self-love, and further, that Christian benevolence is at bottom nothing but *active* (beneficent) love of others. The interesting question is whether or not they are genuinely moral attitudes, even though they make rightness dependent upon the non-moral goodness of consequences rather than the motive of reverence for the moral law. They certainly look like genuinely moral attitudes. We shall postpone the critical examination of Kant's theory until the part on Sartre (see 38.2). The point just now is to present Kant's view as a foil to the moral theory of Socrates. Even from the preceding sketch it is clear that Kant's moral theory, whatever its faults, gave new prominence to the notion of the rational autonomy of the individual that underlay the Socratic ideal of education. Partly for this reason, Kant played a key role in the eighteenth-century European Enlightenment, almost as pivotal as that of Socrates in the Greek Enlightenment of the classical period.

12.8.6 How high should the standard of morality be?

In terms of the loftiness of its moral ideal, Socrates's teaching falls somewhere between the others we have considered—demanding less than Jesus but more than either Hobbes, popular Greek morality, or the Old Testament creed.

Just how much does morality require of us, then? How far must we go in order to lead a morally acceptable life? Clearly, Jesus's injunction sets the bar too high. Unilateral beneficence towards all, even those who persecute us, willingness to bear, not just without resentment or hatred, but with beneficent love, whatever harm others may wilfully inflict upon us, is no doubt admirable in the extreme; but it is also far more than simple morality requires. It is a recipe for sainthood (and probably for martyrdom!) rather than for moral goodness. Nietzsche, incidentally, refused to allow that such a morality was even admirable; to him Jesus seemed the epitome of the religious zealot, eager to die rather than live for what he believed in. Nietzsche took a mischievous pleasure in asserting that, had Jesus not died so young (at thirty-three, by the usual reckoning), he would almost certainly have recanted his teaching! However outrageous this may seem to Christians—and it was meant to be shocking—about one thing, at least, Nietzsche was right: from a moral point of view, universal, unconditional, and unilateral beneficence is 'supererogatory' ('more than can reasonably be demanded'), as philosophers say. It may be a religious duty for those who follow Christ, but it is not a moral one.

As for Hobbes's moral standard, this is arguably too low and apt to provide a licence for some pretty nasty pre-emptive strikes against presumed enemies who have as yet done nothing to harm anyone. Historically, it seems that Hobbes's principle has been the 'morality of choice' among the modern nations of the world—with what results, a slight acquaintance with the last few centuries of history suffices to show.

Does Kant, too, set the standard of moral conduct too high? In a way, yes. In practical terms, the sort of conduct Kantian morality requires—treating others as ends rather than means—is certainly within the reach of most anyone and probably sufficient to guarantee a morally acceptable life; too high is Kant's theoretical standard of what makes such conduct morally right, what gives it moral worth: complete unconcern about consequences, that is, about the happiness or unhappiness (as opposed to the autonomy and rationality) of individuals and mankind. By this standard, as we have just seen, the maxims of the ancient Hebrews, Greeks, Socrates, Jesus, and Hobbes are not *moral* rules at all. Later we shall argue that Kant was mistaken about this (see 38.2).

Falling, as it does, somewhere *between* Jesus and Hobbes, Socratic morality is probably closer to the mark, although there is reason to believe that it is still somewhat too high. Like the Kantian theory, the moral theory that goes by the name 'utilitarianism' (see 38.2) lowers the bar somewhat vis-à-vis Socrates, while still keeping it above the level prescribed by Hobbes. Perhaps, as some moral philosophers have suggested, the best theory is a so-called mixed theory combining elements of both Kantian and utilitarian morality (ibid.). Interesting though the question is, we cannot stop to consider in detail what a morality that is right on the mark might look like. For there are still some very important features of Socrates's moral theory to be sketched.

12.9 Socrates's eudaemonism

In describing the moral theory of Socrates, we have repeatedly distinguished two questions: (a) What is moral? and (b) Why be moral?

We have now answered the first question. Since being harm-producing is the basic wrong-making feature of all wrong actions, and since it is *the only thing* that renders such actions and the characters of those who perform them morally bad, to refrain from harm, and from returning harm for harm, is to live a morally good life. This is our basic moral duty, and from it all others derive.

The second question is more complex. The answer is implicit in Socrates's second ground rule, the supremacy of *moral virtue* over *happiness*. It states that the concern for *moral goodness* must be paramount, overriding the desire for other non-morally good things for ourselves or others. But what exactly is *the relationship between moral virtue and happiness* according to Socrates's second ground rule? Is he perhaps saying something like the following:

(1) Moral goodness has nothing to do with happiness at all. When we have to choose between moral goodness and other good things (things we think will make us happy), we should always choose the morally good, no matter how damaging to our happiness.

Probably no Greek moralist ever held this view or anything like it. Nor did anyone else before Kant, who was the first to insist that questions of morality (duty) and questions of personal happiness have absolutely nothing to do with each other (see above 1.2.4 and 12.8.5). In doing so, he was reacting, not just to the Greek, but to all those eighteenth-century moralists who made the non-morally good and bad consequences of actions the *sole* determinants of their moral quality. This includes British moralists like Bishop (Joseph) Butler (1692–1752), Francis Hutcheson (1694–1746), Hume, and Thomas Reid (1710–1796). For Hume the tendency of a certain (kind of) action to produce good or harm in society is its sole good- or bad-making feature, whence Hume is an important ancestor of later utilitarian theories. Kant went to the opposite extreme. His point was not merely that there are, *in addition to consequences*, other good-and bad-making features; nor was it that certain actions may also be *intrinsically* morally good or morally bad, regardless of their non-morally good or bad consequences. Rather, Kant insisted that non-moral goodness and badness—that is, considerations of benefit and harm, happiness and suffering—are *completely irrelevant* from a moral point of view. If you do not choose morality for its own sake—regardless of considerations of your own or others' happiness—then your choice is not a moral one at all.

If Socrates, as a Greek, could not possibly have been espousing this Kantian point of view, (1), then perhaps he is saying something like the following instead:

(2) Being morally good is *indispensable* to happiness itself. There can be no real happiness without moral goodness, for a life is just not a good life, not really worth living, without moral probity. Since the end of all rational action is to be happy, and since moral goodness is indispensable to happiness, no rational human being would knowingly sacrifice moral goodness for non-moral benefits, no matter how enticing. Faced with a choice between moral virtue and other non-morally good things, a rational individual can never hesitate to take the morally right course of action.

In fact, almost all Greek moralists held one version or another of (2), and Socrates was no exception. As evidence of this, consider his remark in the *Crito*:

[T]he most important thing is not life [biological survival as opposed to death], but a good [that is, happy, satisfied, fulfilled] life ... And ... the good life, the beautiful life, and the just [morally good] life are the same. (48b)

In other words, the goal of life is not simply staying alive but having a good—a happy, fulfilled—life; the goal, in other words, is human flourishing, as we called it earlier (and as the Greek *eudaimonia* has been aptly translated). Having such a life and leading a morally good life are just "the same" according to the passage just cited.

If this is correct, then Socrates's moral theory is a form of eudaemonism. Now the point of all eudaemonist moral theories is that *leading* a good life (moral virtue) is either (a) identical with, (b) a significant part of, or (c) an *indispensable* part of *having* a good life or *eudaimonia*. Minimally, it is (d) the most important means to such a life. The question now is, Which version of eudaemonism did Socrates hold: (a), (b), (c), or (d)? He states that the good life and the happy life are "the same," which certainly suggests (a). But we shall see that this is not really his view of the matter at all—that (c) is in fact the correct answer. So let us turn now to the question of the exact form of eudaemonism espoused by Socrates.

12.9.1 Some eudaemonist theories

In what follows we sketch briefly four different theories of the relation between virtue and happiness that were widely discussed in antiquity. They are contrasted, first, in respect of (i) whether moral virtue is regarded as an intrinsic or as an instrumental good. For some eudaemonists hold that happiness is an end in itself precisely because it is composed of other ends that are desirable for their own sakes; the latter (including moral virtue) are parts of, rather than just means to, happiness. For other eudaemonists other good things (including morality) are only means to happiness or a good life, either the best means (though not indispensable) or else necessary means.

Eudaemonist theories differ, secondly, in respect of (ii) the place assigned moral virtue in the good life. Is the moral life not even a necessary condition of the happy life, such that one could have a good life without leading a good life? Or is it in fact necessary, yet without being sufficient in the absence of non-morally good things? Or is morality both necessary and sufficient for a truly good life, even in the absence of all the other good things of life? Or, finally, is the moral life simply identical with the happy life?

That is the second respect in which different eudaemonist theories can be compared and contrasted. Third and finally, each such theory involves (iii) a certain attitude toward other non-morally good things and their sufficiency or insufficiency in rendering a life good or happy (if not 'the best of all possible lives').

With these points of comparison in mind, we begin our consideration of eudaemonistic moral theories with (1) a view that owes something to Aristippus (a pupil of Socrates of about Plato's age) but was more coherently developed by Epicurus, the founder of Epicureanism. Identifying happiness with pleasure (Greek: *hēdonē*) and the absence of pain (hence: 'hedonism'), the Epicureans argued that a rational man will prefer moral virtue to vice because, and only because, it is the best *means* to securing the greatest hedonic benefits (especially friendship and tranquillity of mind). So (i) moral virtue is an instrumental rather than an intrinsic good according to Epicureanism, a means to lasting and secure pleasure or the good (happy) life, while pleasure is the only thing that is good in itself or intrinsically good. Hence, moral goodness (ii) plays a big part in happiness; it is the best though not the only means to it (sufficient, but not necessary), certainly not identical with it. As for the third point, (iii) other things, particularly non-morally good things, are good precisely to the extent that they are instruments of lasting pleasure and do not become impediments thereto, as is often the case with the pursuit of bodily pleasures. In this Epicurean form the doctrine is very remote from pure sensualism, that is, maximizing one's opportunities for sensual pleasure; this refinement was apparently absent in the original doctrine of Aristippus himself, who was by all accounts a *bon vivant* devoted to good food, wine, and women.

On (2) the view of the mature Plato and of Aristotle, virtue is (i) not so much a means to happiness as a constitutive part or ingredient of the happy life itself. In other words, morality is intrinsically good, good in itself, or good for its own sake rather than just as a means to something else. However, virtue is *not the only thing* constitutive of happiness. Other things which are parts of, rather than means to, happiness are: honour, pleasure (and absence of pain), and the exercise of intelligence, that is, theoretical contemplation. All these, like moral virtue, are desirable for their own sakes. Whether a life is happy or not depends above all on achieving the right balance of all these morally and non-morally good things. So virtue on its own is again (ii) not sufficient to make a human life happy, humanly worth living; on the whole the 'mixed life' that includes such goods as pleasure, honour, theoretical knowledge, as well as moral virtue, all in the proper proportions, is the best life for man. But is moral goodness, just on its own, necessary for human happiness according to Plato and Aristotle? The answer to this question is far less clear, mainly because of the extraordinary value placed on intellectual contemplation by both Plato and Aristotle. This tends to suggest at times that theoretical contemplation is sufficient on its own; and in that case, moral virtue cannot be necessary for a good life. However, on balance, it seems that moral virtue is *probably* necessary for the happy life as Plato and Aristotle conceive it. As for (iii) things other than virtue, many of these, as has been pointed out already, are good, even intrinsically so.

Next, there is (3) the form of eudaemonism shared by Antisthenes (another of Socrates's younger friends, probably around 445to 365 BC), the Cynics (followers of Diogenes of Sinope, an older contemporary of Aristotle), and the Stoics, followers of Zeno of Citium, whose world-view was later espoused by Cicero and many prominent Romans, including the Emperor Marcus Aurelius Antoninus (121–80). According to all these thinkers, (i) virtue is again not a means to happiness, but constitutive of, or an ingredient in, happiness (as for Plato and Aristotle); but contrary to what Plato and Aristotle supposed, (ii) it is in fact the *only* thing that is constitutive of happiness, the only thing that makes a life non-morally good, that is, happy, satisfying, fulfilled, well worth living. Here, then, the morally virtuous life and the happy life are really "the same," as Socrates put it. For the Cynics, moreover, (iii) other things usually considered to be good are in fact bad, hindrances to 'true' happiness. (Either Diogenes himself or else the proto-cynic Antisthenes is supposed to have said: 'I would rather go mad than experience pleasure.' He lived in some sort of tub and carried all his worldly possessions around with him in a sack. Legend has it that when Alexander the Great rode up to the aged Diogenes and offered to grant him any favour he asked, the old Cynic, who was warming himself in the sun, asked the great Emperor to stand aside and stop blocking the sunlight.) The later Stoics moved away from this extreme position. While sticking to the view that no external things could *strictly* be pronounced "goods," they were not all to be despised either: some they considered "preferable," others just "indifferent" rather than positively evil.

This brings us, finally, to (4) the view of Socrates, for whom (i) virtue is again not just a means to happiness (as for Aristippus and Epicurus) but rather a part, constituent, or ingredient of happiness, good for its own sake. However, (ii) it is neither just one part of happiness among others, as in (2), nor is it simply "the same" as happiness, as in (3), that is, the *whole* of it. Socrates's position is rather that moral virtue is both *necessary and sufficient on its own to render a life happy*, even in the absence of all non-morally good things and in the presence of all sorts of non-morally bad things, for example, extreme poverty, dishonour, sickness, imprisonment, even untimely death. This is not true of any other constituent of happiness: though they are indeed goods rather than evils or merely indifferent, neither wealth, nor social standing, nor bodily nor intellectual pleasures suffice for happiness on their own or all together, while moral virtue *does* so suffice. Yet while necessary and sufficient for happiness, moral goodness is not the *whole* of happiness either, since there are other good things that may enhance one's happiness. This brings us to the final point, namely (iii) all the other good things are conducive to human happiness *only if* combined with moral virtue; without it they bring *no increase* in a person's share of happiness or the good life. That is the point of Socrates's rather misleading remark at 30a that "[w]ealth does not bring about [moral] excellence, but excellence brings about wealth and all other public and private blessings for men." This might be mistaken for a rather crass recommendation of moral goodness as a means to wealth and pleasure—hardly what one would expect from Socrates. More literally translated, however, the passage states that moral virtue or excellence is what makes all these other good things good; it is an indispensable condition of their contributing to the overall goodness of one's life. And this is perfectly consonant with Socrates's character, even if he himself cared relatively little for the acquisition of these other good things, even along *with* virtue.

12.9.2 The Socratic paradoxes

In order to test the above interpretation of Socrates's moral outlook, let us consider whether it clears up some well-known but very paradoxical things that Socrates says in the *Apology*. Afterwards, we shall examine some even more famous paradoxes from other dialogues.

According to the nominal word meaning, a paradox is (1) any assertion that runs counter (*para*) to most people's opinion (*doxa*). Apart from this non-technical sense, the term also has two technical uses. According to the first, a paradox is (2) a statement whose truth entails its falsehood. Thus (to cite a famous ancient paradox), when the Cretan Epimenides says 'All Cretans are liars,' meaning that they always lie, then if what he says is true, it follows (since he is a Cretan and hence lying) that it is false. But if what he says is false, that is, if even one Cretan does not always lie, then nothing at all follows. In the second technical sense, a paradox is (3) a statement whose truth entails its falsehood *and* whose falsehood entails its truth. Thus, if I say: 'Everything I say today is false,' and I say nothing further the rest of the day, then if what I have said is true, it is false, as in the case of Epimenides; but unlike the case of Epimenides, if what I have said is false, then it is true.

Only the first or non-technical sense of 'paradox' is relevant to the Socratic paradoxes, of which we shall consider first those that occur in the *Apology*. For understanding the way in which moral virtue is *indispensable* to happiness (that is, necessary *and* sufficient), without just being the same thing as happiness (identical with it), permits us to make good sense of certain otherwise baffling passages in Socrates's defence speech.

For example, Socrates maintains that, contrary to what most people think,

(1) the good or well-being of the soul (moral virtue) is a much greater good than material and social goods.

This is admittedly a fairly minor paradox, though it plainly runs counter to what most people think, especially if we judge their convictions by their pursuits or actions. It finds clear expression in the *Apology* at 29d–e:

[A]s long as I draw breath and am able, I shall not cease to practise philosophy, to exhort you and in my usual way to point out to any one of you whom I happen to meet: Good Sir, you are an Athenian, a citizen of the greatest city with the greatest reputation for both wisdom and power; are you not ashamed of your eagerness to possess as much wealth, reputation and honours as possible, while you do not care for nor give thought to wisdom or truth, or the best possible state of your soul? Then, if one of you disputes this and says he does care, I shall not let him go at once or leave him, but I shall question him, examine him and test him, and if I do not think he has attained the goodness that the says he has, I shall reproach him because he attaches little importance to the most important things and greater importance to inferior things.

However at odds with most people's opinion about what is worth pursuing, from Socrates's moral perspective this makes perfect sense; for money, honours, reputation are not goods at all except when their possessor has moral virtue as well. They *are* good things from Socrates's perspective, but only because he possesses moral virtue as well; otherwise they could contribute nothing at all to his 'quality of life.' Though indisputably good things, therefore, they are relatively insignificant in comparison with virtue. That is what Socrates means in saying that the goods of the soul are vastly superior to those of the body.

The next two pronouncements are far more paradoxical. To begin with, Socrates repeatedly espouses the rather bizarre view that

(2) the only really serious harm a person can come to is harm to the soul (loss of moral and/or intellectual excellence).

There is clear evidence for this in the *Apology* at 41d, for example:

[A] good man cannot be harmed either in life or in death ... So I am certainly not angry with those who convicted me, or with my accusers. Of course ... they thought they were hurting me, and for this they deserve blame.

Here Socrates is deliberately overstating the case. It is not that his accusers have done him *no* harm at all, but that they have done him no *serious* harm; the harm they have actually inflicted on him pales to insignificance alongside the harm they have done themselves in forfeiting their own moral integrity—the prime requisite for a good life—by harming an innocent man.

Both paradoxes considered thus far make good sense in light of Socrates's moral theory as interpreted above. Now for a further paradox:

(3) To do harm to others is always to harm one's own soul more than one harms the other; that is, to do harm is always worse for the doer than the victim (since the doer's soul is made worse, while the victim's soul is not affected).

To put the point more succinctly still: it is worse to inflict harm than to suffer it. That this is Socrates's view is clearly attested by the *Apology* at 30c–d:

Be sure that if you kill the sort of man I say I am, you will not harm me more than yourselves. Neither Meletus nor Anytus can harm me in any way; he could not harm me for I do not think that it is permitted that a better man be harmed by a worse; certainly he might kill me, or perhaps banish or disfranchise me, which he and maybe others think to be great harm, but I do not think so. I think he is doing himself much greater harm doing what he is doing now, attempting to have a man executed unjustly.

Notice that this time Socrates does not say that the evildoer cannot do the good man *any* harm, but only that he cannot do him *serious* harm, that is, harm as great as that which he inflicts on himself. This is more accurate than the formulation at 41d, and expresses the meaning of that passage as well.

This third paradox comes very close to that at the heart of the later dialogue *Gorgias*: it is better to suffer injustice at the hands of another than to inflict it oneself; and if one does commit an injustice, it is better to undergo punishment for one's misdeeds than to escape retribution. It is a riveting spectacle to see the Socrates of the *Gorgias* defend this pair of tenets, undeterred by the sneers of the most cynical sophists of his day. What his opponents cannot grasp is his unwavering conviction that loss of moral integrity spells ruin, while preserving it intact, or recovering it through paying for one's mistakes, must suffice for a truly good human life even in the absence of all non-morally good things. It was the reading of the *Gorgias*, incidentally, that sparked the conversion experience of that Corinthian farmer mentioned earlier (see 8.5).

So much for the paradoxes encountered in the *Apology*. The most famous of the Socratic paradoxes are not these, however, but the joint claims that (4) no man desires (non-morally) bad things, in other words, that all those who pursue things actually harmful to themselves do so involuntarily; and that (5) no man ever does moral evil knowingly and voluntarily but always unwittingly and therefore unwillingly. These are known in the scholarly literature as the prudential and the moral paradox, respectively. In the simplest terms, the *prudential paradox* is that one cannot both *know* that something is bad for one (an imprudent choice) and still pursue it, the *moral paradox* that one cannot both know that something is morally wrong and still do it. Both statements seem manifestly false because they are at odds not just with most people's beliefs but with what appears to happen all the time. The solution of these paradoxes is the ultimate test of any understanding of Socrates's moral theory.

Unfortunately, we cannot stop to explain these paradoxes fully, but this much, at least, should be noted. For Socrates, no man who truly *knew* what role moral virtue and the desire for morally good things play in the conquest of happiness (*eudaimonia*) would either do or desire to do wrong; for to do wrong, he would recognize, is to forfeit any chance of happiness, and no rational human being desires or would willingly bring about the destruction of his own happiness. Consequently, when men do wrong, they may know exactly what they are doing in the ordinary sense of 'know'; but they lack *full* knowledge of the importance of virtue in achieving happiness. In that sense, they act unknowingly, unwittingly, contrary to their wish or will to be happy. If they had such knowledge, they would neither desire nor ever do what is morally wrong. In that sense, *virtue is knowledge* for Socrates. There is no separation possible between moral and intellectual virtue; the man who has knowledge cannot but be virtuous, while the one who is wicked shows his ignorance thereby. We shall return to Socratic intellectualism (as it is called), the doctrine that virtue is knowledge, in a later context (see 19.3.2).

12.9.3 The autonomy of the individual

The absolutely astounding thing about these Socratic paradoxes is the perfectly uncompromising way in which they make each individual human being solely responsible for his or her own life; the quality of *my* life is dependent on me alone, on my character and actions; no one else can destroy or even impair *my* moral virtue, which is not just necessary for happiness, but sufficient even on its own, in the absence of every non-moral good and even under conditions of extreme deprivation. Since no one, no adversity, and no misfortune can prevent me from *leading* a good life, it follows that nothing can stand in the way of my *having* a truly good life either. This is a moral theory that puts the onus squarely on the autonomous individual; external factors hardly enter into it at all. In other words, there are no excuses; our lives will be as good or as worthless as we make them. We shall encounter a similar point of view later, in Sartre (see 37.2), the last figure to be examined in this work, although Sartre reaches this conclusion by a path as remote as possible from that of ancient eudaemonism.

It is worth remarking, in conclusion, that Socrates's views on the moral autonomy of the individual are the exact antithesis of those developed later by his wayward disciple Plato, according to whom the individual can only achieve the pinnacle of moral goodness and the humanly best life in community with others, indeed in a perfect society. The whole of one of Plato's longest and best-known works, the *Republic*, is devoted to expounding this theory and describing—in sometimes lurid and repulsive detail—the organization of such a society. He returns to the theme in a late work called the *Laws*. This, however, is not the strand of Plato's thought that we shall pursue in Part Two. Instead, we shall turn our attention to metaphysics, omitting consideration of the moral and political consequences Plato himself drew from his metaphysical theory.

13

Concluding Appraisal

13.1 Introductory

We conclude our examination of Socrates's moral theory with a brief critical appraisal of his answers to the two central questions, What is moral? and Why be moral? (see 13.2–3). Such critical reflections add little to the exposition and can be omitted by those concerned primarily with understanding what is being said in the dialogues themselves. However, a little reflection on the martyrdom of Socrates raises a further question that may provide a more fitting conclusion to Part One. Why does Socrates apparently *go further* than is strictly required by the standard of conduct laid down in his moral theory? Non-maleficence and non-retaliation may suffice to explain his refusal to escape from prison; but a different and higher conception of duty is behind his service to the city, a positive *beneficence* toward others, toward *all* his Athenian fellow citizens in fact. This, as we have seen, forms no part of his moral theory. To understand the life and death of Socrates as depicted in the dialogues we must consider Socratic piety once more (see 13.4). For it is a religious duty that, in the end, provides the vital clue to what Socrates lived and died for.

13.2 Socrates on what is moral

While Socrates's moral theory represents a remarkable step forward, setting a far higher standard of conduct than popular Greek morality, the question we are still not done with is whether that standard is too high. On the face of it, a morality that considers consequences for others as vital in discerning right from wrong, but treats consequences for the agent himself as totally irrelevant, is probably asking more of us than common decency demands. Why, after all, should I not consider myself, provided I consider the happiness and well-being of every other individual as at least equally as important as my own? That proviso seems sufficient to guarantee the level of disinterestedness and impartiality requisite for a genuinely moral point of view; for Socrates, however, my own interests only come into play when faced with the question, Why be moral? As far as What is moral? is concerned, I am to consider only the consequences of my actions for others: I must avoid doing harm to them no matter what the cost or sacrifice for me. That is surely setting the bar too high. A more balanced view would consider the consequences for all concerned.

If consequences for others are not the whole story, it seems nevertheless that they are an extremely important part of it. That is why something very like non-maleficence still figures as *a* basic moral duty in a number of influential moral theories today. It will be difficult to deny that being harm producing is at least *one* 'bad-making feature' of morally bad things. If so, then at least something of Socrates's remarkable achievement in ethics still stands. On the other hand, it seems equally clear that consequences, even for all concerned, are not the sole determinants of right and wrong. Here Kant can provide a further corrective to Socrates's theory. For consider some clandestine act of cowardice or cheating that, as a matter of fact, has absolutely no negative effect on anyone's happiness. Should we say that such an action is not morally bad or wrong? Of course, if a certain type of action is harm producing, or even just potentially so, that seems a good *moral* reason for refraining from it ourselves and condemning it in others. But there is more to the moral quality of actions than this. On reflection it seems that certain things may be just *inherently* wrong or base or mean-spirited, quite apart from their direct and indirect, actual or potential, consequences. This is where Kant was right after all. Acts of dishonesty or moral cowardice, it seems, are just *intrinsically* bad. If so, then even a consideration of all the consequences, harmful and beneficial, for the agent and for others, is still only one part of the story; intrinsic goodness and badness are another. Kant's mistake was to take the latter for the whole story.

A third interesting line of criticism is this. Socrates's great achievement was to extend the principle of non-maleficence even to enemies, that is, even to those who have done one harm. Yet there is no evidence that he advocated its impartial application to *all* human beings, male and female, freeman and slave, citizen and alien. Historically, there is just no record of Socrates's having objected to the subjugation of women or to the institution of slavery or to the imperialism of the Athenian state in its dealings with smaller and weaker Greek states. Here Socrates seems to have had what has been called a 'moral blind spot,' one shared by most Athenians. It would be different, no doubt, if no one at the time had defended egalitarian or abolitionist ideas; we might then draw solace from the fact that such moral ideals were simply beyond the intellectual horizon of that remote age. But the fact is that there were outstanding men among Socrates's contemporaries and friends who espoused something very like the ideal of universal human rights associated with the European Enlightenment of the eighteenth century.

From this criticism it appears that there is another bad-making feature of actions that has nothing to do with either inherent badness or consequences (harm), namely *injustice* in the modern sense, that is, not applying the principle of non-maleficence (or any other moral principle) *evenhandedly* to all human beings alike, regardless of age, birth, sex, nationality, and the like. To make Socrates's moral theory more acceptable, then, apart from bringing in the interests of the agent and some notion of inherent goodness and badness, an additional principle of distributive justice would have to be added. (On the difference between rightness and justice in the modern sense see above 11.3.) These are not just cavils, but serious flaws in the theory. To attempt to explain exactly how they are to be remedied would be to expound a better theory. That is obviously not our purpose here.

13.3 Socrates on why be moral

The second point in the appraisal of Socrates's moral theory is his answer to the question, Why be moral? Here it seems that Socrates's version of eudaemonism goes decidedly too far. It is scarcely credible that a life in which there were none of the so-called external or material goods, but instead extreme deprivation, hardship, agonizing suffering, and premature death, could be called 'happy,' 'good,' 'worth living,' merely because the individual's moral virtue was preserved intact. On the whole, the mixed life espoused by Plato and Aristotle (see 12.9.1) seems closer to the right conception of human thriving than the Socratic doctrine of the supremacy of virtue, especially if we tone down the somewhat self-serving emphasis that philosophers are apt to place on intellectual contemplation.

Nevertheless, Socrates pioneered the eudaemonistic theory that his successors were to refine and perfect. And a very remarkable and thought-provoking theory it is, too, even from a contemporary vantage point, precisely because it is so alien to the popular wisdom of today. It is very hard for us even to imagine that there can be an answer to the question, What is the good life *for man*? Our rejection of the question itself is almost immediate. What makes one 'feel good about oneself,' we want to say, varies greatly from individual to individual; each of us must judge for himself what makes life richer or poorer, more or less worth living. There is just no answer that holds universally for all mankind and therefore no point in searching for one!

As plausible as this way round the problem seems today, to the Greek moralists it was no less evident that the question makes perfect sense, for all its generality, and that it is capable of being answered in a manner that at least ought to be acceptable to all reasonable human beings. To answer it is, of course, not to say that everyone ought to be a merchant or an artist, lead an urban or a rural existence, go into public or remain in private life, marry or stay single, and so on; such choices are indeed a matter of individual preference. Nevertheless, there are, so the Greek moralists believed, certain things that *any* life must contain if it is to be genuinely worth living; and the accounts of the eudaemonist theorists included morality among these things, though many a sophist demurred. This fact underlines an important point: the correct answer to a question must not be confused with an answer that everyone accepts. One could perfectly well claim to have found the right answer to a question despite the fact that it is hotly contested in some quarters, provided what one means is that it is an answer that at least *would* find universal acceptance if everyone were clear-sighted enough, adequately informed, sufficiently disinterested, and perfectly rational—as most, in fact, are not. So when someone makes a claim to truth, it is never to the point to retort: "Not everyone will accept that!" If the truth in question is somewhat profound and out of the way, that is precisely what one ought to expect.

To understand the Greek moralists' outlook concerning the good life for man we must rid ourselves of another misconception as well. Apart from thinking in terms of matters of individual choice or 'lifestyles,' we are apt to put the question of happiness in terms of what makes one 'feel good about oneself'—as though this had anything to do with the Greek concept of *eudaimonia*! Misled, no doubt, in part by the translation of *eudaimonia* by 'happiness,' we may *think* we are adopting the outlook of the Greek moralist if we say something like the following: "I could never live a life of selfish exploitation of others because, even if I managed to do so without getting caught, amassing riches and power and the means of procuring pleasure beyond my wildest dreams, I would never really feel good about myself knowing I had acquired these things by cruel and immoral means. My conscience would prevent me from being happy." To see just how completely this misses the point, we have only to consider for a moment an individual who is devoid of conscience, who takes unalloyed delight in his ill-gotten gains and in the suffering he has inflicted upon others. The pertinent question is, Is *this* a life worth living? Is this the good life (for a human being as opposed to a beast of prey)? Once the question is put in these terms, we have entered into the characteristic perspective of the Greek moralists. Some sophists apart, they had complete confidence that the answer to this question could only be 'No.' Even those sophists who answered it in the affirmative at least regarded the question as answerable. Whichever side one comes down on in the end, it seems clear that the initial difficulty, for us today, is to appreciate the question. We are very quick to say that the perennial question of the good life for man (and with it the question, Why be moral?) is unanswerable. But is that really so? It is enough for the present if this examination of the moral theory of Socrates has at least raised a doubt on that score.

13.4 Moral and religious duties

If the principle of non-maleficence sets the standard of right conduct too high, it nevertheless sets it *lower* than the actual conduct of Socrates would suggest. That is the surprising thing. True, Socrates's theoretical emphasis is entirely on avoiding actions *harmful* to others; nothing suggests that he is under any obligation to *benefit* others in any way. Universal non-maleficence is, after all, perfectly consistent with a hard-hearted indifference to the well-being *or* suffering of others *so long as one does not inflict or add to it oneself.* In his *Groundwork of the Metaphysics of Morals*, Kant painted a striking portrait of a man

cold in temperament and indifferent to the sufferings of others—perhaps because, being endowed with the special gift of patience and robust endurance in his own sufferings, he assumed the like in others, or even demanded it; if such a man (who would in truth not be the worst product of nature) were not exactly fashioned by her to be a philanthropist, would he not still feel in himself a source from which he might draw a worth far higher than any that a good-natured temperament can have?

Assuredly he would, concludes Kant. "And it is precisely in this that the [moral] worth of character begins to show—a moral worth and beyond all comparison the highest—namely that he does good, not from inclination, but from duty."

With this we may disagree on the grounds that an active concern for the betterment of the lot of others, or at least the alleviation of suffering and unhappiness, is a big part of what morality requires of us. However that may be, one thing is clear: the above is hardly the portrait of Socrates. It is not just that Socrates (a) does his duty gladly, with wit, grace, and unfailing good will towards others, even his enemies and the very jury that unjustly condemns him. Nor is it simply the fact that he (b) does so from self-interest, believing that doing one's duty is the key to a happy life and a necessary condition of all other happiness-enhancing things. In fact, Socrates not only refrains from harming others, he (c) strives to confer on them the greatest of benefits: "for I go around doing nothing but persuading both young and old among you not to care for your body or your wealth in preference to or as strongly as for the best possible state of your soul" (*Apology*, 30a–b). This he does at great personal sacrifice: "Because of this occupation, I do not have the leisure to engage in public affairs to any extent, nor indeed to look after my own, but I live in great poverty" (23b). And he does so at great personal risk: ultimately, it costs him his life. Yet he pays the price cheerfully, without the slightest hesitation: "this is my course of action, even if I am to face death many times" (30c).

Now these passages simply cannot be understood in the light of Socrates's moral theory as interpreted in the preceding chapters. The Socrates of the early dialogues is a philanthropist; by his own account, he is the greatest benefactor that the city of Athens has ever had: "there is no greater blessing for the city than my service to the god" (30a) Yet, just as clearly, his personal code of conduct does not make it incumbent upon him to benefit anyone. Why, then, does he live as he does? It is no good answering 'from rational self-interest,' since that is the reason why he is moral rather than immoral. What he considers moral is neither benevolence nor active beneficence, let alone self-sacrifice for others' sakes, but rather refraining from harm and retaliation.

The answer to the question of Socrates's service to the city must be sought outside the confines of his moral theory. This much seems obvious. The short answer is: 'Socratic piety,' that is, "service to the god," obedience to the divine will. We have seen how Socrates's theory of non-maleficence and non-retaliation revolutionized the Greek conception of moral duty, and just how far it accounts for the life he led; to understand what the moral theory leaves unexplained, we must consider Socrates's equally novel conception of religious duty.

It was remarked at the outset of chapter 11 (see 11.3) that the Greeks distinguished between moral and religious duty. The latter meant, roughly, giving the gods their due, namely prayer and sacrifice, and the former, giving men what is owed them, that is, benefit to friends and harm to enemies. Thus, Euthyphro, that paragon of scrupulosity in religious matters, wished to define piety as "that part of the just that is concerned with the care of the gods" (12e). This is perfectly in keeping with conventional wisdom. Socrates even compliments him on a good start, drawing him out eagerly until Euthyphro acknowledges that piety is "a kind of service to the gods" (13d)—Socrates's own view, in fact. But to his dismay, Euthyphro lapses into a purely conventional, even platitudinous, account of what "service" consists of, namely "to say and do what is pleasing to the gods at prayer and sacrifice" (14b). Socrates replies almost wistfully: "you are not keen to teach me [what piety is], that is clear. You were on the point of doing so [when you said it was service to the gods], but you turned away" (14c). In the last phase of the dialogue, Euthyphro's disappointing rejoinder is reduced to the very definition examined and rejected earlier, "what is dear to the gods" (15b).

For Socrates himself, by contrast, piety or service to the gods means an obligation toward one's fellow men over and above what morality requires of us. After all, if the gods are superior to us, they must be our *moral* betters as well. That was implicit in Socrates's remark early in the *Euthyphro*: "I find it hard to accept things like that being said about the gods" (6a). The idea is a very old one: "As the heavens are higher than the earth, so my ways are higher than your ways, and my thought than your thoughts," says the God of the Old Testament to the prophet Isaiah (55:8). Gods do no such harm as is depicted in the Homeric tales of them wreaking horrible vengeance on one another or persecuting mortals by arbitrary and cruel punishment of those who have not honoured them appropriately. Non-maleficence is the core of *human* virtue; and as divine wisdom is "more than human" (20e), so too divine virtue: it involves, as human virtue does not, positive benevolence toward all mankind. The gods are even the source of *all* good things for men. Yet the supreme good they wish to confer on mankind, according to Socrates's moral theology, and the condition of all other good things, according to his moral philosophy, is a good that cannot be bestowed except with the aid of men like Socrates. Men's chief obligation toward the gods is to make the lives of their fellows as good as possible. Since morality is both the chief part of the good life for man and the indispensable condition of all other good things, the aid of the philosopher is indispensable to the divine purpose. Such is Socrates's divinely imposed mission, taken up in all humility and consciousness of his own inadequacies, yet elevating him, not just above the common morality and his own, higher morality, but seemingly even above human nature. As he puts it to the Athenian jury:

That I am the kind of person to be a gift of the god to the city you might realize from the fact that it does not seem like human nature for me to have neglected all my own affairs and to have tolerated this neglect now for so many years while I was always concerned with you, approaching each one of you like a father or an elder brother to persuade you to care for virtue. (31b)

13.5 Conclusion

So much for Socratic piety and the duty it imposes on the philosopher. Without it we cannot completely understand the life and death of Socrates.

One final question about that life, to conclude Part One. We know that Socrates *led* a good life, that in his devotion to the god Apollo he served the city of Athens above and beyond the call of moral duty, even laying down his life for his beliefs. Did he also *have* a good life? Given his own convictions regarding moral virtue and happiness, this would be difficult to deny. If we apply a different standard from Socrates's own, the question becomes more debatable, but the outcome, on any *reasonable* standard we might choose, is apt to be the much the same. There is something very Greek about the idea that the road to wisdom is also the road to happiness. In fact, the latter might have been a better title for Part One.

Recommended readings and references

Benson, Hugh, ed. 1992. *Essays on the Philosophy of Socrates*. Oxford and New York: Oxford University Press.

Burnyeat, Myles. 1976. "Socratic Midwifery, Platonic Inspiration." *Bulletin of the Institute of Classical Studies* (University of London), 24. (An interesting scholarly study that carefully separates Platonic and Socratic elements in the *Theaetetus*.) Reprinted in Benson.

Dover, Kenneth. 1974. *Greek Popular Morality*. Oxford: Basil Blackwell. (The definitive treatment of the subject. Particularly relevant are pp. 180–4.)

Flew, Antony, ed. 1964. *Mind, Body, and Death*. London: Collier Macmillan Publishers. (An excellent introduction to the questions about the mind–body relation, and their bearing on immortality, in the western tradition.)

Flew, Antony. 1979. *A Dictionary of Philosophy*. Second Revised Edition. New York: St Martin's Press.

Frankena, William. 1963. *Ethics*. The Foundations of Philosophy Series. Englewood Cliffs, New Jersey: Prentice-Hall. (The introduction deals with the *Crito*.)

Kahn, Charles. 1996. *Plato and the Socratic Dialogue. The Philosophical Use of Literary Form*. Cambridge: Cambridge University Press. (An important 'minimalist' challenge to the developmental approach taken here.)

Popkin, Richard. 1979. *The History of Scepticism: from Erasmus to Spinoza*. Berkeley: University of California Press. (Deals with the later history of Academic and Pyrrhonian scepticism.)

Rachels, James. 1986. *The Elements of Moral Philosophy*. New York: Random House. (A good discussion of the Divine Command Theory.)

Santas, G.X. 1979. *Socrates. Philosophy in Plato's Early Dialogues*. Boston and London: Routledge & Kegan Paul.

Snell, Bruno. 1982. "Human Knowledge and Divine Knowledge among the Early Greeks." Chapter 7 of *The Discovery of the Mind*. New York: Dover Publications.

Vander Waerdt, P., ed. 1994. *The Socratic Movement*. Ithaca: Cornell University Press.

Vlastos, Gregory. 1993. *Socrates. Ironist and Moral Philosopher*. Ithaca: Cornell University Press. (The definitive work on the moral philosophy of Socrates and the source of many of the ideas of the preceding chapter.)

Vlastos, Gregory. 1994. *Socratic Studies*. Edited by Myles Burnyeat. Cambridge: Cambridge University Press.

Questions for reflection, discussion, and review

1. How would you describe the character of the man Socrates in your own words?
2. Socrates describes himself as possessing "a kind of wisdom." Was it folly on his part to speak this way before his Athenian jurors? What does he mean?
3. What do *aporia* and *elenchus* mean? What do they have to do with the story of Chairephon's visit to the oracle at Delphi?
4. "Honesty is the best policy" (Anonymous). Discuss.
5. "The unexamined life is not worth living" (Socrates). Discuss.
6. "Wealth does not bring about virtue, but virtue brings about wealth and all other public and private blessings for men" (Socrates). Discuss.
7. How important is it to define the terms being used in any debate? Are clear definitions the starting point or the goal of discussion? Does the situation differ significantly in different disciplines, say, mathematics and philosophy?
8. It has been said that the ability to understand the significance of 'the Euthyphro dilemma' is a good test of a student's aptitude for philosophy. Do you agree?
9. What do you think of Socrates's ground rules in the *Crito*? Is it realistic to expect people to deliberate in accordance with these rules?
10. How would you describe your own working ethics? Which, if any, of Socrates's three moral principles (non-maleficence and non-retaliation, fidelity, filial piety) would you be likeliest to accept as part of your own working ethics? Why?
11. Do you think Socrates, having been unjustly condemned, should have taken up Crito's offer of help in escaping? Why, or why not?
12. Explain the concept 'paradox.' The text tries to make sense of three paradoxes in the *Apology*. Can you make sense of the so-called prudential paradox? What about the moral paradox?
13. In terms of his own moral outlook, does it make sense for Socrates to consider death preferable to wrongdoing?
14. Do you think actions can be inherently bad, even if they are not harm producing and not the sort of action that *could* reasonably be expected to cause harm?
15. Reflecting on the moral philosophy of Socrates and other eudaemonist theorists examined, do you now think that the question of 'the good life for man' makes sense? Or is it just a matter of personal preference?
16. Given the manner in which he ended his life, convicted of a capital offence of which he was not guilty, do you think that Socrates had a good life?

PART TWO

PLATO AND THE ROAD TO REALITY

There is likely to be something such as a path to guide us out of our confusion, because as long as we have a body and our soul is fused with such an evil we shall never adequately attain what we desire, which we affirm to be the truth [or reality].

Plato of Athens, *Phaedo*

14

Doctrines and Influences

14.1 Introductory

The great British Plato scholar F.M. Cornford once spoke of two metaphysical doctrines as the "twin pillars" of Platonism: (1) the theory of Forms or Ideas and (2) the immortality of the soul. The architectural metaphor was expanded (by R.E. Allen) to include (3) Plato's theory of recollection as the "architrave" sitting atop the twin pillars. All three elements form a single, unified structure. For genuine knowledge, according to Plato, is knowledge of universal entities or Forms existing in a realm beyond the sensible world; and the acquisition of such knowledge is a matter of recollecting those transcendent universals that the disembodied and immortal human soul was acquainted with before birth but has since forgotten.

These three theories form the principal objects of our study of Plato's *Phaedo*. Regarding the first, we should note that the words translated 'Form' and 'Idea' (*eidos* and *idea*) both derive from the same Greek word meaning 'to see.' 'Idea' is in fact just a transliteration rather than a translation of one of the two words coined by Plato for his transcendent universals. Nevertheless, we shall use 'Form' rather than 'Idea' in what follows, since the latter, even capitalized, naturally suggests either a psychological event or a mental content. This is the last thing we should think of. As was shown in the Introduction (see 4.7), Plato's transcendently real universals exist (a) in their own right, independently of the human mind; to the extent that traces or copies of the otherworldly originals exist in us as well, either unnoticed or explicitly recollected, the Forms may be said to exist *both* in their own right *and* (b) in the human mind. And they exist, furthermore, (c) in all those particular things to which the same universal term is correctly applied. So they are not at all like the universals of the conceptualist (see 4.8), whose nature it is to exist only in the mind, either as mental occurrences or as contents. In other words, they are not 'ideas' in anything like the modern sense in which we are apt to understand the term today.

14.2 A snapshot of Plato's philosophy

In chapter 8 we noted that Plato's views on many subjects underwent radical change in the course of a long and extraordinarily fruitful philosophical career, largely, we may conjecture, under the pressure of criticisms from within the Academy itself. The study on which we are embarking can therefore provide no more than a "snapshot" of Plato's core metaphysical doctrines at the beginning of the so-called middle period (see 8.3). This particular snapshot is, however, a privileged one, for the metaphysical outlook expressed in the *Phaedo* underlies what has popularly been understood by 'Platonism' down through the ages, particularly during medieval times, when most of Plato's other writings were not available in Latin translation. Of course, our discussion of the *Phaedo* will be confined to only about one-half of the dialogue, so even the snapshot will be severely cropped to fit the available space.

As Plato's core metaphysical doctrines underwent change and development, so too his views on that other perennial issue of philosophy, the good life for man. The ideal of the 'mixed life' sketched in our earlier survey of eudaemonist theories (see 12.9.1) was largely the fruit of the last phase of Plato's thought; the moral outlook of the *Phaedo*, by contrast, is a highly intellectualized version of the extreme asceticism practised by certain religious communities existing in Plato's day, and exemplified in the eudaemonism of the earlier Cynics and later Stoics as well. So our study of the *Phaedo* will again furnish only a snapshot, this one of Plato's moral outlook at the very beginning of the middle period.

Asceticism may be provisionally described as the practice of abstention from bodily pleasures (enjoyment of food, drink, sex) as positive evils, together with an active striving for the purification of the soul, whether through ritual devotions and prayer, or through mortification of the flesh, or through intellectual and spiritual contemplation, or by all these means. Puritanism, the ideal of a pure life, has been a powerful undercurrent in religious thought down through the ages, taking root in mainstream Christian theology and ethics at the beginning of the Middle Ages owing to the influence of the Church Fathers, particularly St Augustine, who was himself powerfully influenced by those late-Greek thinkers known as the Neoplatonists (see 1.3.1 and 5.10). Plato, for his part, was profoundly influenced by the contemporary religious sect of the Pythagoreans while still a relatively young man. His remarkable intellectualization or "rational catharsis" of the more primitive ascetic tendencies of that sect owes much to the influence of his teacher, Socrates. Socrates, it hardly needs pointing out, was no ascetic, even if he preached moral and intellectual development as the greatest goods for man, greater by far than either bodily pleasures or social goods. Whether the result is, as Aristotle suggests, Pythagoreanism Socraticized, or whether it is better described as Socraticism Pythagoreanized, is not a question that need detain us; both answers may correctly describe different phases of Plato's development, the latter being perhaps marginally more apt in the case of the *Phaedo*.

14.3 Structure of the dialogue and outline of the part on Plato

We begin, as usual, by identifying those elements within the overall structure of the dialogue that will occupy us in what follows. The *Phaedo* can be divided into ten parts or stages as follows:

1 Introduction (57a–59c)
2 Opening Conversation on Suicide (59c–63a)
   (a) Pleasure and Pain
   (b) Socrates's Dream
   (c) Suicide
3 Socrates's Defence of the Philosophic Life (63b–69e)
4 First Argument for Immortality: Cyclical Argument (69e–72e)
5 Second Argument for Immortality: Recollection Argument (72e–78b)
6 Third Argument for Immortality: Affinity Argument (78b–84b)
7 Simmias's and Cebes's Objections and Socrates on Misology (84c–91c)
8 Reply to Simmias (91c–95a)
9 Reply to Cebes: Socrates's Story and the Final (Causal) Argument (95a–107c)
10 Concluding Myth and the Death of Socrates (107c–end)

We shall cover only stages 3–6 in any detail, though the whole dialogue is well worth reading. The death scene in particular (stage 10) sheds valuable light on the life and character of Socrates.

The portion of the dialogue devoted to a new defence of the philosophic life (stage 3) has a direct bearing on the proposed test of our approach to the dialogues (see 8.4). For assuming the *Apology* is a reasonable facsimile of the actual defence speech delivered by the historical Socrates (as even minimalists allow), and comparing it with the very different defence speech placed in the mouth of the fictional Socrates of the *Phaedo*, we shall find the whole moral outlook, not to mention the conception of philosophy and of death itself, so radically altered that it would be difficult indeed to accommodate both speeches in a single, relatively static framework of thought. To that extent, the analysis of the defence speech confirms the developmental approach being taken here (see chap. 15).

To get a clearer sense of what has changed and why, we must examine the Pythagorean background of Plato's *Phaedo*. That will be done later in the present chapter, after some preliminary remarks on the dramatic setting of the dialogue and the manner in which its main subject is introduced. Before interpreting stages 4 through 6, we must acquaint ourselves with some traditional conceptions of soul, death, and immortality (see chap. 16). The main focus of our textual exegesis, however, will be the first three arguments for immortality (see chaps. 17 to 19). On this follows a systematic and historical consideration of Plato's theory of Forms in the context of the Greek metaphysics of form as it developed from Socrates to Aristotle (see chap. 20). The concluding appraisal might have been entitled, 'Why study Plato?' (see chap. 21). For there is not a single argument for immortality in the *Phaedo* that is not riddled with ambiguities and/or logical blunders, so that the question naturally arises, Why bother? The last chapter explains why the study of the "twin pillars," and indeed of Plato's theory of recollection, is well worth the effort for anyone who cares about philosophy.

14.4 Setting and theme

The *Phaedo* opens with a brief narrative that sets the scene in Socrates's prison cell, sketching a memorable portrait of Socrates on the morning of the day of his execution. The opening vignette reinforces the lessons concerning Socratic piety already learned from the *Apology* and *Euthyphro*, specifically his (1) acceptance of dreams as divine portents and his (2) scruples about disobeying divine commands, even unwittingly.

In this connection it is worth noting the ambiguity of the injunction to "[p]ractise and cultivate the arts" (60e) issued by the different dream figures that have appeared to Socrates in the course of his life (presumably just different guises of the god Apollo). The Greek word translated as 'the arts' is *mousikē*, from which our word 'music' is derived. It comes from the Greek word for 'muse,' so that *mousikē*, in Greek, covers all those activities (including, for example, history and astronomy) presided over by one of the traditional muses, not just singing, playing the lyre or flute, and the like. Philosophy is counted as one of these arts only in a rather loose sense; it is sometimes included, along with astronomy, under the arts presided over by the muse Urania. Socrates accordingly assumed that he had been obeying the visions all his life by engaging in philosophy. But in prison it occurred to him that 'the arts' might have been meant in the narrower, popular Greek sense of 'music,' that is, 'poetry' or 'verse making,' so he turned his hand to writing poetic hymns to Apollo and versifying Aesop's fables just to be sure he was not guilty of disobeying the god. Note that even this narrower Greek sense of 'music' still does not coincide with our sense of the word today.

Next the main theme of the *Phaedo*, death and immortality, is introduced by way of a discussion of suicide. The topic of suicide is first broached in Socrates's reply to an enquiry of the poet Evenus (see 60d), who had asked, through Cebes, about Socrates's reasons for writing poetry while in prison. Socrates answers by recounting his dream, but ends by urging Evenus "if he is wise [that is, if he is a philosopher], to follow me [into death] as soon as possible" (61b). (Evenus, incidentally, is the sophist mentioned in the *Apology* at 20b–c as charging five minae to associate with the young.) Having implied (rather than stated) the paradoxical view that

(1) the wise or wisest man (the philosopher) is willing (or eager) to die,

which is, of course, directly contrary to what most people believe, Socrates next cites, apparently approvingly, the common belief that:

(2) no man ought (it is 'unlawful' that is, contrary to *divine* law) to commit suicide.

So Socrates advises Evenus to die soon, but not to take his own life. The way from here to the theme of death and immortality is short. For Cebes immediately gets on the scent of a contradiction in what Socrates has said (62a). After various attempts to state his difficulty, Cebes launches into an argument against (1) that runs as follows:

P1 "God is our protector and we are his possessions" (62d), that is, he is our master, we his servants.
P2 "It is not logical that the wisest of men should not resent leaving this service in which they are governed by the best of masters, the gods." (62d)
C "[T]he sensible man would always want to remain with [be the servant of] one better than himself [the god]"; that is, "the wise man would resent dying, whereas the foolish would rejoice at it." (62e)

By this argument Socrates is challenged to mount a defence of (1): it is best for some men (philosophers) to die. For just this was presupposed, without supporting argument, in his advice to Evenus. The next stage of the dialogue, the defence of the philosophic life, is accordingly devoted to an elaborate philosophical argument for the paradoxical view stated in (1). The problem with that argument, according to Cebes, is that it takes for granted that the soul of the philosopher continues to exist after the death of the body. This, too, ought to be established by argument rather than simply taken for granted, Cebes avers. And so we come to the part of the dialogue devoted to the three arguments that will occupy us later.

In conclusion it is worth noting the way in which (2) is introduced. Socrates backs up the prohibition on suicide with nothing more than an "explanation that is put in the language of the mysteries, that we men are in a kind of prison, and that one must not free oneself or run away" (62b). It may be the same mystery religion that is behind (1) as well. To what does the Platonic Socrates refer here?

14.5 Plato's encounter with Pythagoreanism

While (1) is, on the face of it, a bizarre claim for anyone to make, it is especially odd coming from Socrates, who, in the *Apology*, repeatedly disavows any knowledge of whether death is a good or a bad thing (see 29a, 35a, 37b, 40a, and 42a). Both (1) and (2) become comprehensible, however, in the light of a personal encounter with Pythagoreanism that transformed Plato's life and thought for the second time. As we know, the first such transformation came about as a result of his friendship with Socrates. Then, some ten years after Socrates's death, a new encounter set Plato on a course that was to result in convictions quite remote from, and inconsistent with, the teachings of Socrates, including (1) and (2).

The "explanation ... in the language of the mysteries" to which Socrates refers is one that any contemporary reader of Plato would immediately associate with the religious sect of the Pythagoreans that still flourished in Greece around this time. One of these Pythagoreans was Philolaus, whom Socrates mentions at 61d as the man from whom Cebes may have already heard that the philosopher is willing and eager to die. In fact, the shadow of Pythagoreanism hangs over the entire *Phaedo*. It is apparent from a number of features of the dialogue. Apart from (a) the mention of Philolaus, a noted Pythagorean who settled at Thebes after the expulsion of the sect from southern Italy in the mid-fifth century, there is (b) the circumstance that the dialogue is set in Phlius (or Phleius), a community in the northeastern part of the Peloponnese where a Pythagorean society was still in existence around the time of Socrates's execution (399 BC). Moreover, there is (c) the fact that Echecrates, to whom Phaedo tells the story of Socrates's death, is known (according to Diogenes Laertius, a source from the early third century AD) to have been a Pythagorean. These cues would have been hard for any contemporary reader of Plato to miss.

Not very much is known about Pythagoreanism, however, nor about how it differed from another, related mystic or religious sect, Orphism (see 5.4). Yet we do know that Plato came into contact with Pythagoreanism and for a while fell completely under its spell. Specifically, we have reliable knowledge that, in 388–87 (or 389–88) BC, at the age of about forty, Plato travelled to Italy and Sicily on the first of three voyages to the west. According to Cicero, "he devoted himself to Pythagorean men and studies" there, "spending much time with Archytas of Tarentum [a noted Pythagorean mathematician and philosopher] and Timaeus of Locri." On returning to Athens, Plato founded the Academy and began writing the great dialogues of the middle period, including the *Phaedo* and the *Republic*. These dialogues, which are Plato's own philosophy (see chap. 8), combine (a) the legacy of Socrates with (b) certain elements of Pythagoreanism and (c) key ideas of the Presocratic philosophers, chiefly Heracleitus and Parmenides.

We already know something about (a) from our study of Socrates. To understand the defence of the philosophic life in the *Phaedo*, we must now examine (b) briefly. (c) is relevant mainly to the emergence of the theory of Forms in Plato's middle period. The consideration of the theory of Forms, and the influence of Heracleitus and Parmenides upon it, will be postponed until chapter 20.

14.6 Pythagorean themes in the *Phaedo*

The so-called Pythagoreans were followers of Pythagoras (see 5.6), a Greek from the island of Samos (off the Ionian coast) who, fleeing tyranny at home, settled in the Greek colony of Croton on the southern coast of Italy. There he founded a religious society that flourished in the latter half of the 500s BC, but was almost totally destroyed a century later, around the time Plato was born. Some survivors fled to Thebes and Phlius, where they founded new societies that were still prospering around the time of Plato's birth (c. 427 BC), dying out gradually toward the end of the fifth century.

While their exact teachings are largely a matter of conjecture, the Pythagoreans, so far as we can make out from later sources, held doctrines of the following sort:

(1) The soul of a person is a *fallen divinity* confined or imprisoned within the mortal human body and condemned to a cycle of reincarnations as man, animal, and plant, from which it can win release only by achieving *purification*.

This echoes the supposed teaching of the much older Orphic sect that the body is base or evil (see 62b: "we men are in a kind of prison"), while the soul is the divine part of man. In accordance with this doctrine, a strict discipline of purity was observed in Pythagorean communities, including silence, self-examination, abstention from sensual pleasure, and performance of religious purification rites. Members also devoted themselves to mathematical study and contemplation as activities that purified the soul by turning it away from gross bodily things toward higher, immaterial objects. This way of life had a parallel in the Orphic practices of abstaining from killing animals and eating their flesh, which had as much to do with the belief that human souls dwelt in animal bodies (reincarnation) as with a belief in the inherent uncleanness of the body itself.

For convenience, we can label the following four further doctrines 'Pythagorean-Orphic,' since we cannot be sure of the exact differences between the two sects:

(2) metempsychosis, transmigration of souls, their reincarnation in other bodies, particularly the bodies of animals;
(3) pollution or corruption of the soul by the body;
(4) a corresponding notion of purification, of ridding the soul of the taint of the body;
(5) the notion of the soul's ultimate release from the cycle of rebirth and its disembodied existence once it has become pure.

All these doctrines are echoed in the *Phaedo* at some point, though only (1), (3), and (4) are directly in evidence in Socrates's defence of the philosophic life, the subject of the next chapter. Both (2) and (5) will be discussed further in the context of the third argument for immortality in chapter 19. As we shall see, very little in the *Phaedo* is comprehensible apart from the Orphic-Pythagorean cloud that hovers over Plato's entire middle period and was to have a lasting effect on his thought. It is an element that is conspicuously absent from the dialogues of the first period, most (if not all) of which were written before Plato's first journey west.

15

New Defence of the Philosophic Life

15.1 Introductory

Socrates begins his defence of the philosophic life in the *Phaedo* by casting everything he is about to say in the form of an *apologia*, that is, a defence speech delivered by the accused as part of the formal proceedings in a court of law (see 9.1.1). On the day of his execution, Cebes has accused him of being altogether too ready to depart this world, and Socrates playfully suggests that he must respond to this new indictment or *graphē* (see 11.1) much as he did to that brought against him by Meletus, Anytus, and Lycon. Thus, at 63b he says: "I must make a defence against this [Cebes's new challenge] as if I were in a court." And: "Come then ... let me try to make my defence to you more convincing than it was to the jury (63b)." A little further on he repeats the macabre jest: "I want to make my argument before you, my judges, as to why I think that a man who has truly spent his life in philosophy is probably right to be of good cheer in the face of death and to be very hopeful that after death he will attain the greatest blessings yonder" (63e). Socrates even wishes himself better success in persuading the present company than he had with the Athenian jurors. And as he comes to the end of his speech he reinforces the comparison once more: "If my defence is more convincing to you than the Athenian jury, it will be well" (69e).

In the present chapter, we shall take a close look at this mock defence speech, comparing it detail for detail with the actual speech as imaginatively reported by Plato in the *Apology*. Surely Plato would not have harped so on the *apologia* theme had he not wished the reader to undertake some such comparison. It is almost as though he were deliberately setting up signposts to guide us from the old to the new philosophic outlook. It was certainly open to him to introduce the main theme of the *Phaedo*, death and immortality, in any number of other ways; that he chose to do so by a

268   Part Two: Plato and the Road to Reality

defence speech reminiscent of the *Apology* must be significant.

15.2 The *probandum*

As noted in the previous chapter, the defence of the philosophic life in the *Phaedo* elaborates an argument *for* the contention:

(1)   The wise or wisest man (the philosopher) is willing (or eager) to die.

At the outset, however, Socrates himself puts what appears to be the claim or conclusion to be established this way:

that [a] some future awaits men after death, as we have been told for years, [b] a much better future for the good than the wicked. (63c)

In this formulation, (a) is equivalent to life after death, while (b) refers to reward and punishment in the afterlife. However, this is not so much the *probandum* (literally: 'that which is to be proved') of the defence of the philosophic life itself, as of the *whole* of the *Phaedo*, and in particular of the four arguments that follow upon the defence speech. In fact, the existence of an afterlife with reward for the good and punishment for the wicked is simply *taken for granted rather than proved* at this stage of the dialogue, as Cebes will object explicitly at 69e–70b. That objection leads into the four 'proofs' of immortality in the later stages of the dialogue.

Thus, the whole defence of the philosophic life is predicated on the *assumptions* that (a) the soul survives the death of the body and (b) that it is rewarded. But there is a further important assumption as well, namely (c) that *the person* is therefore rewarded, that is, that the man, person, or human being is identical with the soul. In examining the defence speech here, we postpone consideration of these assumptions to the following chapters.

15.3 The argument in defence of the philosophic life

How does Socrates's argument for (1) run? If we 'formalize' it (recast it in the form of a deductive argument with premises and conclusion), the argument looks like this:

P1   Definition of 'the philosopher': "the one aim of those who practice philosophy in the proper manner is to practice for dying and death." (64a) "[T]he philosopher more than other men frees the soul from association with the body as much as possible." (64e–65a)
P2   Definition of 'death': "we believe that death is this, namely, that the body comes to be separated by itself apart from the soul, and the soul comes to be separated by itself apart from the body." (64c)

Notice that the definitions of 'philosophy' or 'the philosopher' and 'death' are couched in very nearly the same terms. As a consequence, if someone were to pursue philosophy, that is, seek to live as a philosopher, and yet shun death, he would be pursuing and shunning the same thing, that is, behaving in a manner that is inconsistent. And that is precisely the conclusion drawn:

C "I am likely to be right [that is, *consistent*, as one who has spent his life in philosophy] to leave you and my masters here without resentment or complaint, believing that there, as here, I shall find good masters and good friends" (69d–e). "[I]t would be ridiculous [inconsistent] for a man to train himself in life to live in a state as close to death as possible, and then to resent it when it comes." (67d–e)

Given that it is inconsistent or unreasonable to *both* pursue *and* shun the same end, the separation of the soul from the body, the argument is formally valid. Yet one has only to reject either definition in the premises and the whole argument immediately falls to the ground.

In point of fact, neither definition is rejected or even queried by those present. Simmias, who answers at this stage, is completely docile, agreeing like a true disciple of the Pythagorean philosopher Philolaus (see 14.5) to all the strange new ideas proposed here regarding virtue and knowledge. The argument is allowed to pass as a successful defence until Cebes brings out the tacit assumption in the very definition of death: that the soul survives the destruction of the body. This calls Socrates's definition of death into question after all, though only belatedly. Nevertheless, given the fact that the definition finally comes under scrutiny, it would be unfair to suggest that Plato simply has it his own way, making matters easy for himself by defining his terms to suit his purposes. Moreover, it has to be acknowledged that an attempt is made to furnish support for the definition of philosophy by a series of questions about the pursuits and attitudes of the "true philosophers" (66b).

From this formally valid but, for reasons Cebes will later point out, extremely vulnerable argument arise the two questions that will occupy us throughout the remainder of this and the next chapter. First, how does *this* conception of philosophy and the philosophic life square with that in the Socratic dialogues, especially the *Apology*? And second, how does this definition of 'death' differ from *our* conception of death? How does *this* notion of the 'survival of death' differ from the Christian conception of immortality? The first question will be dealt with in the remainder of this chapter, the second in the next.

15.4 Comparison of the defence speeches in the *Apology* and *Phaedo*

We can answer the first question by considering (i) what philosophy is according to the *Apology* and the *Phaedo* (15.4.1) and (ii) the very different conceptions of moral virtue presented in the two dialogues (15.4.2). In addition, we shall have to give some thought to (iii) the philosopher's attitude toward death as described in each dialogue, for here too very striking dissimilarities are apparent (15.4.3).

15.4.1 Philosophy in the Apology and the Phaedo

Regarding (i), we have to consider knowledge, certainty, or wisdom as portrayed in the two dialogues. This is a complex topic, but a few general points seem fairly uncontroversial.

To begin with the *Apology*, the activity of philosophy as portrayed there can be aptly described as the *love* of wisdom, the *striving after* truth; philosophy, moreover, is the pursuit of truth *in the spirit of intellectual modesty*, that is, without vain pretensions or illusions about one's own powers or knowledge. What most characterizes Socrates as a philosopher is precisely his dogged determination to reduce those who harbour such illusions to the beneficial state of *aporia*. The aim of philosophy is the *search for* truth, although perfect certainty (divine wisdom), as the Socrates of the *Apology* insists, is not for us, being rather the prerogative of the gods.

By contrast, philosophy in the *Phaedo* is neither the halting and ever-renewed search for truth, nor the partial and tenuous grasp of it; it is rather the rational discovery and proud possession of perfect, unqualified wisdom, something very like the high road to reality:

> Is it not in reasoning if anywhere that any reality becomes clear to the soul? (65c) ... [W]hoever of us prepares himself best and most accurately to grasp the thing itself which he is investigating will come closest to the knowledge of it (65e) ... [He] will do this most perfectly who approaches the object with thought alone, without associating any sight with his thought, or dragging in any sense perception with his reasoning, but who, using pure thought alone, tries to track down each reality pure and by itself. (65e–66a)

True, this may not be possible in *this* life, since the complete separation of the soul from the impeding influence of the bodily senses is impossible so long as we live; but it *is* possible *even for human souls* after death (separation from the body):

> [I]f we are ever to have pure knowledge, we must escape from the body and observe matters in themselves with the soul by itself. It seems likely that we shall, only then, when we are dead, attain that which we desire and of which we claim to be lovers, namely wisdom ... not while we live; for if it is impossible to attain any pure knowledge with the body, then one of two things is true: either we can never attain knowledge or we can do so after death. Then and not before, the soul is by itself apart from the body. (66d–e)

The correct alternative is, of course, the second: that we can attain such knowledge after death and only then. Accordingly, Socrates concludes:

> Will then a true lover of wisdom, who ... knows that he will never find it [wisdom or knowledge] ... except in Hades [in the afterlife], be resentful of dying and not gladly undertake the journey thither? One must surely think so, my friend, if he is a true philosopher, for he is firmly convinced that he will not find pure knowledge anywhere except there. (68a–b)

That said, it must be acknowledged that there are still many echoes of the intellectual modesty of the Socrates of the *Apology*, for example, in the following passage:

> I should be wrong not to resent dying if I did not believe that I should go first to other wise and good gods, and then to men who have died and are better than men are here. Be assured that, as it is, I expect to join the company of good men. *This last I would not altogether insist on.* (63b–c e.a.)

But no longer is there the unbridgeable gulf between *human* and *more-than-human* wisdom that we know from the *Apology*. That much seems clear. Whether human wisdom is in effect reducible to disdain for the body and the deliverances of the senses is a question we must consider in the context of morality.

15.4.2 Morality in the Apology *and* Phaedo

So much for the first point of comparison, the nature of philosophy in the *Apology* and the *Phaedo*. Turning now to morality, we recall that the good life for man is a matter of enlightened self-interest according to the Socrates of the *Apology*. The preference for the *good things of the soul* (especially virtue) over the *goods of the body* and *social goods* is just a matter of rational choice; it is a question of preferring the greater to the lesser good, that is, a good that *on its own* guarantees a happy life, as does virtue, to a good that only contributes to happiness if accompanied by virtue. But the *non-moral goods of the body* (for example, health, strength, beauty, sensual pleasure, life itself) and *non-moral goods of the social kind* (like prestige, social connections, good reputation, success in politics or war) are still good things, according to the *Apology*, even if lesser goods in themselves and entirely worthless in the absence of moral goodness. The key to having a truly good life is to be able to *moderate* our perfectly natural desires for these things in order to put "first things first," that is, *moral goodness* ahead of all else.

Now compare this eudaemonistic doctrine with the asceticism of the *Phaedo*. The so-called non-moral goods of the body are suddenly regarded as *inherently evil*: "as long as we have a body and our soul is fused with such an evil we shall never adequately attain what we desire, which we affirm to be the truth" (66b). Here we encounter an out-and-out *puritan ethic* of self-denial, abstinence from bodily pleasure, in short, an ethic of *renunciation rather than moderation*. Philosophy itself is a means, even the chief means, of "purification" of the soul from the taint of the body (67c). This is clearly the import of the following passages, which can be quoted without elaborate commentary:

Do you think it is the part of a philosopher to be concerned with such so-called pleasures as those of food and drink? ... What about the pleasures of sex? ... What of the other pleasures concerned with the service of the body? (64c–d)

The body keeps us busy in a thousand ways because of its need for nurture ... It fills us with wants, desires, fears, all sorts of illusions and much nonsense, so that, as it is said, in truth and in fact no thought of any kind every comes to us from the body. Only the body and its desires cause war, civil discord and battles, for all wars are due to the desire to acquire wealth, and it is the body and the care of it, to which we are enslaved, which compel us to acquire wealth, and all this makes us too busy to practise philosophy. Worst of all, if we do get some respite from it and turn to some investigations, everywhere in our investigations the body is present and makes for confusion and fear, so that it prevents us from seeing the truth. (66b–d)

any man whom you see resenting death was not a lover of wisdom but a lover of the body, and also a lover of wealth and honours, either or both. (68b)

Furthermore, in the last part of this section of the dialogue (68c–69d), all the cardinal virtues of the Greeks (see 11.3 above), including wisdom, are apparently reduced to purification of the soul from the bodily stain, that is, contempt for the body and bodily pleasure.

The virtue of courage is considered first. Socrates remarks on something "strange" (68d), even "illogical" (ibid.), about the way in which it is ordinarily understood. For the brave are normally thought to "face death, when they do [face death rather than run away], for fear of greater evils" (68d)—for instance, for fear of loss of honour or of possible harm to one's loved ones or fatherland. Accordingly, they are "brave through fear," which seems "illogical" to Socrates. Similarly, the moderate restrain their appetite for pleasure through fear that licentiousness may deprive them of other pleasures—health, for example, or reputation. So they are moderate through "a kind of licence" (69a), which is again branded "strange." To be perfectly consistent one must understand these virtues differently; and Socrates immediately goes on to boil "true virtue" (69c) down to despising the body and bodily pleasures. Thus, on a consistent view of the matter, the virtuous man displays neither fear in battle nor immoderation in his appetites nor injustice toward his fellow citizens because and only because he has purged away boldness and fear, pleasure and pain through the cultivation of wisdom or knowledge; and this is nothing other than the "cleansing or purification" (69c) of the soul by separating it as far as possible from the body in detached intellectual contemplation of the truth.

Thus, virtue is still knowledge, as in genuine Socratic intellectualism (see 12.9.2); but behind the sameness of the formula lurks a very different and strikingly un-Socratic ethic that owes considerably more to "those concerned with the [Orphic-Pythagorean] mysteries" (69c) than to the moral gospel of Plato's teacher. Nevertheless, it is worth noticing that the puritanism or asceticism of Pythagorean-Orphic religion has been *intellectualized* through a marked emphasis on the exercise of reason and the denigration of the senses as sources of moral and every other kind of knowledge:

[D]oes purification not turn out to be what we mentioned in our argument some time ago, namely, to separate the soul as far as possible from the body and accustom it to gather itself and collect itself out of every part of the body and to dwell by itself as far as it can both now and in the future, freed, as it were, from the bonds of the body? (67c–d)

This is *Orphic-Pythagorean moral virtue intellectualized*, transposed to the epistemological plane. One might almost say that the moral outlook of the Plato of the *Phaedo* amounts to a reversal of the Socratic formula 'virtue is knowledge.' For here 'knowledge is virtue.' A powerful strain of Orphic-Pythagorean–style religious purification of the soul is behind the reversal, except that now the purification is not through performance of any rites (fasting, mortification of the flesh) or ceremonies, but through philosophizing alone, exercising reason, thought, intelligence *without the senses* in the pursuit of the 'absolutes,' the eternal objects (see chap. 20 below). The inherent evil ascribed to the body derives primarily from its role as an obstacle to the exercise of reason and acquisition of knowledge, not so much as an impediment to moral virtue—although that is, of course, true as well. Still, this moral epistemology of Plato, as we might call it, is something new.

15.4.3 Death according to the Apology *and the* Phaedo

The final question regarding the defence of the philosophic life in the *Apology* and the *Phaedo* has to do with the philosopher's attitude toward death.

In the *Apology* Socrates expresses *agnosticism* about whether death is a good or a bad thing. The main passages in support of this were listed earlier (14.5), but it may be worth quoting a few of them here:

[T]o fear death, gentlemen, is no other than to think oneself wise when one is not, to think one knows what one does not know. No one knows whether death may not be the greatest of all blessings for men, yet men fear it as if they knew that it is the greatest of all evils. (29a)

Yet I have often seen them ... men who are thought to be somebody, doing amazing things as if they thought it a terrible thing to die. (35a)

[T]he penalty Meletus has assessed against me [that is, death], of which I say I do not know whether it is good or bad. (37b)

Now the hour to part has come. I go to die, you go to live. Which of us goes to the better lot is known to no one except God. (42a)

In the *Phaedo*, by contrast, death is an unmitigated good, even among the "greatest blessings" (64a) the philosopher can obtain, the highest fulfilment of his striving. Consider Plato's definition of 'death' again:

[W]e believe that death is this, namely, that the body comes to be separated by itself apart from the soul, and the soul comes to be separated by itself apart from the body. (64c)

According to this, soul and body are two distinct "substances" or "things" capable of existing in their own right apart from one another (see 4.2–3 on 'substance'). The soul can and does continue to exist after the corruption of the body; in the case of the philosopher's soul, the separation from the body is the consummation of all its striving.

15.5 Conclusion

This concludes our comparison of the *Apology* and the *Phaedo*. In the light of the stunning differences noted, it is probably futile to resist the standard view that the earliest dialogues reflect the thought of Socrates, from whose shadow Plato began to emerge in the transitional dialogues, reaching a fully independent and, in crucial respects, opposed standpoint of his own in the *Phaedo*. Still, once we get beyond the dialogues dealing with the trial and imprisonment of Socrates, caution is called for in discerning Socratic from Platonic elements. To that extent, the minimalist challenge is a salutary one.

16

Soul, Death, Immortality

16.1 Introductory

The second of the two questions raised in connection with the defence of the philosophic life in the *Phaedo* (see 15.3) was: How does Plato's concept of death differ from our own? How is his notion of the survival of death different from the more familiar Christian concept of immortality?

To answer this question we must first consider what Plato means by 'soul.' There is in fact no *one* concept of soul in play in the *Phaedo*'s first three arguments. As we shall see presently, the ambiguities of 'soul' are responsible both for the initial plausibility and for the fundamental weakness of the proofs of immortality. At bottom, Plato is still grappling with an intractable philosophical and religious inheritance regarding the soul, struggling to harmonize discordant strands of meaning. Whatever the defects of the arguments, however, his is the signal achievement of having brought the whole question of the nature of the soul into the forefront of philosophical debate—where it has remained ever since.

Apart from a historical reflection on the concept 'soul' in the next section, the preliminaries must also include a consideration of the differing conceptions of the relationship between (1) the soul, (2) the body, and (3) the person or human being in (a) Platonic and (b) Christian thought. The differences are profound, for despite a very marked influence of Platonism on Christian theology, it was essentially the very different, Aristotelian conception of the person (see 27.9.2) that won out in the Middle Ages, shaping the orthodox Christian idea of immortality in all decisive respects. That, of course, does not mean that Plato's lasting contribution is not of great significance in its own right. Just the opposite is the case. Here it is above all the differences that are important.

16.2 Plato's conception of the soul

Plato operates with three distinct concepts of the soul (Greek: *psychē*) in the *Phaedo*. The first is soul as the

1 intellectual, cognitive, or rational faculty, the faculty of discerning truth from falsehood.

This is the conception that predominates throughout the dialogue, not only in the defence of the philosophic life, but also in the second and third arguments for immortality, the so-called Recollection and Affinity Arguments. It is prefigured in the *Apology*, where Socrates admonishes his fellow citizens to "give thought to wisdom or truth, or the best possible state of your soul" (29e) rather than wealth, reputation, and honours; for to the extent that the two can be separated at all (see 12.9.2 on Socratic intellectualism), the emphasis here is clearly on cognitive or intellectual rather than moral development. Looking back to Presocratic and Homeric times, we may label this 'the noetic soul,' from the Greek word *nous* (or *noos*), usually translated 'intellect' or 'understanding.' The term has a complex history before, in, and after Plato, but the connotation that is decisive for the *Phaedo* is something like 'grasping the truth intuitively.' In Homeric times *nous* meant various things besides immediate insight, this meaning having come to the fore in Presocratic philosophy, notably in Parmenides. It is the only sense of *nous* not also ascribed to animals in the Homeric poems.

Unfortunately, intelligence itself is conceived in a confusing variety of ways by Plato. For transcendent realism recognizes an intermediate mode of existence between (a) particular sensible things and (b) universal Forms, namely (c) universal essences existing in particular things (see 4.7.1). Consequently, intelligence may be conceived (i) concretely, as rational *activity* in an individual mind; (ii) less concretely, as the intellect or cognitive *capacity* of an individual human being; (iii) abstractly, as (or as *like*) a universal Form; (iv) less abstractly, as a universal property existing in, and constituting the essence of, every individual man; even (v) cosmically, as the Mind or Intelligence of the whole universe (see what is referred to as Socrates's Story in stage 9 of the dialogue). The latter three are obviously *im*personal notions of soul, while the first two describe the soul of a particular person. In exactly which way soul is to be understood in each context of the *Phaedo* is not always easy to determine.

In addition, soul is the

2 moral faculty of deliberation and rational choice, the faculty of discerning moral good from bad or evil.

This too figures prominently in the defence of the philosophic life, specifically in the discussion of the virtues at 68c–69d. In the *Crito* it is referred to as "that part of us, whatever it is, that is concerned with justice and injustice" (47e). The emphasis this time is on volition, will, or choice rather than the cognitive faculty. In the Affinity Argument, the soul as moral or deliberative faculty features in the passage in which different types of human life and afterlife are contrasted (81d–82d). Pythagoras seems to have been the first to think about the individual human soul in moral terms, and not surprisingly the Affinity Argument is the most overtly Pythagorean of the trio of arguments to be examined later.

Finally, soul is the

3 vital or life-giving force, the biological principle in living things.

Soul in this sense is obviously not confined to human beings. It is the only one in play in the first argument for immortality, the so-called Cyclical Argument. Yet its meaning there is highly ambiguous. Concretely understood, it is (a) the particular life-force in the individual living being. Yet the Cyclical Argument also makes use of a conception of a *cosmic* life-force or soul-stuff, namely the total quantity of vital energy existing in the universe throughout all time. From this impersonal 'reservoir of life,' to which nothing can be added, and no part of which can be destroyed, the individual human soul separates itself at birth, when it occupies a particular organic body, returning to its origin upon separation from the body at the time of death, before undergoing a new incarnation. In the Final Argument of the *Phaedo*, however, the life-giving force in living things is expressly assigned (b) the intermediate status accorded *immanent* Forms. For there "soul" is the answer to the question, "what is it that, present in a body, makes it living?" (105b), and we are immediately given to understand that as fire is the Hot and disease the Sick existing in particular things, so soul is Life existing in an individual living entity. Some scholars even take the soul of the Final Argument to be (c) a Form. Of (a), (b), and (c), only the first is personal.

The question of the relationship of the cosmic life-force just described to the cosmic Mind or Intelligence alluded to above is by no means easy. Does Plato simply identify the two, and if so, is this not problematic? Moreover, the relationship of this cosmic soul of the *Phaedo* (whether understood as Mind or Life or both) to the World Soul of Plato's great dialogue on cosmogony and cosmology, the *Timaeus*, is a separate puzzle. Plato, we recall, was the originator of that conception of god as artificer or craftsman of the universe that supplanted Ionian pantheism and prepared the way for the *creator ex nihilo* of Christian theology (see 5.5.3). While the idea of the universe as a living animal was already well established in Greek thought, only in the *Timaeus* was the universe understood as possessing a soul endowed with reason and an organic body, both fashioned separately by the divine craftsman who brought forth a living cosmos from the primal chaos of disorderly matter. The *Republic* contains a couple of tantalizing references to the "maker of our senses" (507c) and to the "workmanship" of the "maker of the sky" (530a), but whether the *Timaeus* doctrine of cosmic soul is already prefigured in the *Phaedo* is impossible to say with any confidence.

16.3 Inherited soul lore

These diverse strands of meaning originate in attempts to understand life and death that go back to archaic and even pre-historic times. The very richness of those religious traditions that Gilbert Murray once dubbed "the Inherited Conglomerate" led E.R. Dodds to remark that "the psychological vocabulary of the ordinary man was in the fifth century in a state of great confusion, as indeed it usually is." The same might be said, with appropriate qualifications, of the conception of soul in philosophy in the fourth century BC—not to mention our own hazy notions of mind, soul, and spirit today.

Two conceptions of soul are widely prevalent in primitive cultures, and, judging by Homer, the earliest Greek peoples were no exception. For Homer used *psychē* for both (1) the life-soul and (2) the death-soul, that is, the ghost, spirit, or shade of the dead person existing in Hades. (1) refers to the animating principle in man, the purely physical basis of life in human beings. This is obviously a remote ancestor of Plato's third conception of soul.

The word *psychē* itself is cognate with various other Greek words denoting breathing and exhalation in particular. Scholars accordingly surmise that the Homeric life-soul, which is breathed out and flutters forth at death, is derived from an even earlier idea of soul in popular language and imagery, the (3) breath-soul. This mediating pre-Homeric notion may go some way toward explaining how (1) and (2) came to be designated by the same word.

As for perceiving and knowing, deliberating and willing, feeling or emotion—all that is included in Plato's first and second conceptions of soul—these were not assigned to *psychē* at all, but either to what Homer calls (a) *thumos* (the seat of appetite and emotion) or to (b) *noos* (the seat of intelligence, yet with a strong sensory component). Moreover, this nomenclature covers *both* what we should regard as a concrete mental or psychic act *and* the bodily organ that forms its physical basis. The two are simply not distinguished at this stage.

Indeed, none of the rigid dualisms that seem so obvious to us were known to primitive or archaic man: soul and body, inner and outer, thought and action, living and non-living, human and animal, natural (profane or secular) and supernatural (sacred or holy). In Homer one and the same word may refer to (i) a perception, or decision, or feeling that *we* should call 'inner' and to (ii) the organ that is its seat in the body (in the head, heart, or midriff), even to (iii) the overt action that ensues—say, the act of fleeing in the case of fear felt in the *thumos*. Lifeless matter is still unknown. So-called animism (see 5.5.3) can accordingly have nothing to do with a tendency of early man to project his own inner life onto the surrounding environment; for he has no 'inner life,' no conscious soul, to project. All bodies, including his own, are inhabited by more or less mysterious forces, sacred and profane. When a man is said to fight 'like a lion,' this is no mere metaphor; the characteristic indwelling power of the lion is really present in him; and when he experiences an unwonted accession of strength, or succumbs to an overwhelming passion, bringing either glory or ruin upon himself, he and everyone else naturally takes it that a divine power is responsible for the action and its consequences.

As for the death-soul, that shadowy image or ghostly double of the living man or person, it is apparently just the life-soul *as it exists in the world below* after departing the living body and this world through the mouth or an open wound. The Homeric death-soul is neither a supernatural nor even an incorporeal phenomenon: it is visible, a spectral image of the living person now dead, though less solid and intangible than he or she. The individual human being or person is not identified with this death soul any more than with the life-soul. Rather, during his lifetime the man is associated primarily with the perishable *thumos*, after death with the corpse that remains behind when the *psychē* withdraws. As there is no conception of a single soul uniting all the various functions assigned to *psychē*, *noos*, and *thumos*, so there is none of a single organic body as distinct from an assemblage of limbs, chest, head, and organs.

So much for the pre-historic and Homeric background. Conspicuously absent from all this is any conception of the soul as (a) divine or of divine origin, and as (b) an immaterial substance capable of existing without a material body. Nor does the notion of *psychē* include as yet (c) the mental functions and equipment associated with the conscious life and the moral character of an individual man. Yet these missing elements form the indispensable basis of the mystical Orphic and Pythagorean doctrines of metempsychosis or transmigration discussed briefly in chapter 14. It is among Orphics and Pythagoreans of the sixth century BC that we first encounter doctrines of the passage of the identical moral and intellectual self, a being both immaterial and divine, through a series of lives or bodily existences back to that other world from which it came. From them it passed to Plato, who, stripping it of its vestiges of material imagery, attempted to furnish this mystical religious vision with a rational philosophical justification in his arguments for immorality.

16.4 Some conceptions of death and survival of death

Careful attention to the ambiguities of 'soul' will repay the effort as we go through the arguments in the *Phaedo*. They have a direct bearing on the concepts 'death' and 'immortality,' to which we turn now.

All the usual ways of conceiving the death of a living animal or human being boil down to variants of two root conceptions: death is either (A) an alteration, that is, a change of state undergone by a living being, or (B) sheer obliteration, its extinction, the perishing or ceasing to exist altogether of a living being. If (B), then there is no room for any notion of survival of that which dies; its coming back into existence, if it did, would be tantamount to creation of a new being. Not so, however, on alternative (A), which opens up a wide range of possibilities.

Given (A), death is either (1) an alteration in which no part perishes *permanently*, as for example in the Christian doctrine of resurrection, understood as reincarnation of the human soul in *the same* body it occupied during its earthly existence; or it is (2) an alteration in which only a part perishes permanently, the living body, while a part survives, the soul. Here there are again at least three possibilities. First, the soul may (a) migrate to *another* body, that is, it may survive as the *same* person with a *different* body, reincarnation in a body *different* from that in which it was last born being what is meant by the terms 'transmigration' and 'metempsychosis' (see 14.6). Second, the soul may (b) exist without any body at all, yet as the same person. This may be described as disembodied *personal* existence. Finally, the soul may (c) exist without a body as (i) part of a completely *im*personal life-force animating the universe, while the person perishes. This we may call simply 'disembodied existence.' Another variant of (c) has the soul continuing to exist as a quantum, not of vital force, but of (ii) spiritual *intelligence*, reabsorbed at death into the boundless "sea of divinity," as Leibniz once put it. Leibniz suspected the so-called Quietists of the seventeenth century (see 34.2) of holding an unorthodox doctrine like this. A similar teaching was inaugurated, as we shall see presently, by certain thirteenth-century Christian followers of the Arabic philosopher Averroës (1126–1198).

Before these variants of (2)(a)–(c) are described in a little more detail, it may be helpful to summarize the foregoing in a chart of the main ways of conceiving death and the survival of death. Note that what is being conceptualized in each case is the death of a person. Nevertheless, the ways in which this all-too-familiar event is conceived vary radically, as the diagram on the next page shows.

Of the differing ways of thinking of death depicted there, (B) is (alas!) the most straightforward and that most consonant with ordinary experience of the death of living organisms. After all, we normally say of someone who has died that he or she simply is no more. This conception of death was vigorously defended in later Greek times by Epicurus, who urged that men had no reason to fear death "since as long as we exist, death is not with us, but when death comes, then we do not exist." Before concluding that this is cold comfort, consider: Fear of punishment after death is, Epicurus believed, the greatest single obstacle to human happiness or tranquillity of mind, greater even than the likewise groundless fear that the gods intervene for good and ill in the course of human affairs. Both fears are allayed by Epicurus's atomistic conception of the soul as a perishable composite, of which the simple parts are imperishable, together with his conception of the gods as utterly blessed beings who lack, and therefore desire, nothing, taking not the slightest interest in the affairs of men. (This is partly traceable to Xenophanes. See 5.5.4.) We shall discuss Epicurean naturalism later (see 31.5.2), but only as a foil to the related naturalism of Hume.

Chapter 16: Soul, Death, Immortality 281

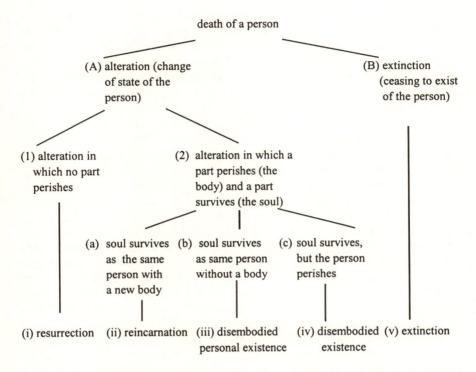

Of (2)(a), reincarnation, something has been said already, and more will be said below. (2)(b) is familiar enough from the popular representations of spirits associated with mediumistic seances, and the like. Television and film frequently portray the dead as present among the living, their bodies completely invisible to the other characters, yet perceptible to us, the viewers, as a translucent ectoplasm, that is, a barely visible filmy tissue. The prototype for this portrayal of the dead is found in Homer, in Book XI of the *Odyssey*. Odysseus descends alive to the underworld and describes the dead, some of whom he recognizes (his mother, for instance), as ghostly spectres or phantoms, souls occupying shadowy, insubstantial bodies, condemned to dwell in the realm of Hades. Their mode of existence suggests that they are aware that being dead is not nearly so agreeable as being alive in the world above. In the *Phaedo* (see 81c–e), Plato himself predicts something not unlike this as the fate of souls that are impure at the death of their bodies: they haunt graveyards, longing to be reunited with their bodies. In speaking of death as an opportunity to meet and to converse agreeably with great men of the past now living in the underworld (*Apology*, 41a–b), Socrates may be evoking Odysseus's picture in the minds of his audience, though he paints it in much brighter colours; the lugubrious tonalities are restored in the *Phaedo*

passage just mentioned. In Hesiod's didactic poem *Works and Days* we find a race of dead who become disembodied daimons or demi-gods, serving almost as what we should call 'guardian angels' of the living. This picture of disembodied personal existence *for some* in the afterlife is apparently taken up by Heracleitus (fragment 63). Yet the same Heracleitus warns (fragment 119) that "[a] man's character is his daimon," shifting the responsibility for good or ill fortune squarely from the traditional daimon to the individual himself.

Of the above conceptions of death, (2)(c) is perhaps the most difficult to comprehend. Mention was made earlier of a cosmic soul that animates the whole universe much as human and animal souls animate organic bodies. In the context of this picture of the universe, as a macrocosm of the human microcosm, a picture that was quite common in Greek and Roman antiquity, death and the survival of death are the return to its cosmic source of that quantum of vital energy that quickens our bodies during our brief human existence here on earth. A related view of life or *psychē* as a single mass, parts of which are strewn through the universe in various impure forms, only to be reunited with the source after undergoing purification, may have been held by Pythagoras, though his doctrine of immortality is essentially one of type (2)(a), metempsychosis or reincarnation of souls. The same is true of Empedocles; some features of his thought no doubt suggest reabsorption of the individual soul into a common reservoir of life, with loss of personal identity, though he too has an elaborate and explicit doctrine of transmigration.

Another related version of (2)(c) is that associated with the thirteenth-century Christian followers of the Arabic philosopher Averroës. It asserts the survival of the intellectual rather than the vital portion of the soul. This was, of course, a very far cry from the individual survival of *the person* required by Catholic doctrine. It was the more threatening as some basis for it can be found in the fifth chapter of the third book of Aristotle's work *On the Soul*. The heresy was important enough to have prompted a polemical attack by St Thomas Aquinas, that paragon of Church orthodoxy (as he was to become). Naturally, the idea that my rational or intellectual powers—the powers I exercise whenever I reason logically from premises to conclusions in philosophy and mathematics—might survive the destruction of my body, or that they might even be altogether indestructible, takes it for granted that those same powers are quite unlike sensation and imagination in this respect: they do not depend on any corresponding operations in the body and brain. Implausible as this sounds, it was not this that St Thomas objected to in the Averroist doctrine. On the contrary, his own proofs of the soul's immortality turn crucially on the allegedly self-evident principle that what can *operate* separately, without the body, can also *be or exist* separately, and that the intellectual functions of the rational soul are in fact thus independent of the body. No, Aquinas's worry regarding the Averroist doctrine was rather that no individual person is identifiable with his intellectual powers alone; on the contrary, these seem to be something common, shared in to some degree by all humanity. So survival of the intellectual powers, even their survival forever, is not the survival of the person, not *personal* immortality. This point needs to be spelled out more fully in the next section. The purpose of the foregoing was just to facilitate an understanding of the above chart.

16.5 The concept of immortality

'Immortality' (in the sense in which it matters to human beings) means: *personal* survival of death forever. Obviously, each of us lives on in the memories of acquaintances, friends, and loved ones for a while; and through exceptional works and deeds some people may live on for a very long time in the thoughts of posterity, millennia in fact. But this is not what we are talking about when we speak *literally* about 'immortality.' As the American humorist Woody Allen once put it: "I don't want to achieve immortality through my work. I want to achieve immortality by not dying." Unfortunately, this is not what is meant by 'immortality' either, although it hits off amusingly one thing that is *not* meant, by philosophers at least. The full-bodied concept of 'immortality,' philosophically understood, involves the three key notions mentioned above. It can accordingly be given a preliminary clarification by considering in turn the meanings of the words (1) 'forever,' (2) 'survival,' and (3) 'personal.'

16.5.1 The word 'forever'

The adverb 'forever' is ambiguous. It can mean either (a) 'everlastingly' or (b) 'eternally' or (c) have some third, hybrid meaning that overlaps with (a) and/or (b) but coincides with neither. Historically, (a) and (b) correspond to earlier and later Greek philosophical usage of the word *aiōn*. Plato is at the watershed between them (see below). The two hybrid uses to be noted in what follows come from Greek mythology and Christian theology, respectively.

The root sense of (a) is 'perpetual existence,' 'existence throughout all time'; in other words, existence *in* time rather than outside it, but without a *temporal* ceasing to be, whether or not it has a beginning. This concept first emerged among the early Greek philosophers, who applied it to the world's lifetime. Should the everlastingly existent have a beginning, as did the cosmos in the eyes of the Milesians (see 5.5.1), for example, though not for Xenophanes or Heracleitus (see 5.5.4), then it begins *with* rather than *in* time. By the same token, it can have no end except with time itself. The successive phases of its duration, past, present, and future, coincide exactly with those of time itself. This is the sense of 'everlasting.'

In English, the abstract noun used to express a duration coextensive with that of time itself is 'sempiternity' (from the Latin *semper* 'always'). For reasons to be considered later (see 18.8), sempiternal existence appears to be the *most* that can be intended in the first or Cyclical Argument for the immortality of the individual human soul. Whether human souls are 'born' *with* the world, at the beginning of time, or into an already existing world, is simply not clear from that argument. By contrast, the case of the Olympian gods of Greek mythology is perfectly clear. Born into a temporal world that existed before them, they are indeed exempt from ageing and death, existing throughout all time subsequent to their birth; but their deathlessness or immortality is clearly something less even than the sempiternal existence that the early Greek philosophers assigned the cosmos that begins to be with time itself. Hence the need for an additional rubric, (c).

As for (b), to exist eternally is to exist outside of time and the temporal order of change altogether, to be literally time*less* or *a*temporal (on the alpha-*privativum* see 9.2.3). Anything the parts or phases of whose existence are all coexistent or simultaneous rather than successive may be called 'eternal' in this second sense. Of such a hypothetical entity it would indeed be correct to say that it *is or exists*, but not that it *was* or *will be*; whatever exists in this way (if anything does) remains immutably frozen in an 'eternal present,' a 'permanent now,' as it was called (*nunc stans*). This is what Plato made of the early Greek philosophers' concept of 'forever,' deliberately transforming it, without however eliminating the earlier usage. He develops a notion like (b) in the dialogue *Timaeus* (37d–38a), though it is already prefigured in the discussion of the Forms and the soul in the Affinity Argument of the *Phaedo*. An even earlier source on which Plato is quite clearly drawing here is Parmenides (see 20.10.2). Plato actually shifts from (a) to (b) as he moves between the Cyclical and Affinity Arguments for the immortality of the individual soul. And this poses a problem for the validity of his arguments, as we shall see soon enough.

Being eternal in the sense just explained entails existing necessarily: the eternal cannot not exist. So not only can that which exists eternally have neither beginning nor end *in* time; it can have neither a beginning nor an end nor a duration that coincide *with* those of time either. It is in the strict sense 'ungenerated and imperishable.' The sempiternally existent, by contrast, *may* not in fact perish, but it is nonetheless perish*able*, as it is gener*able*. Eternal existence is clearly the sense of 'existing forever' ascribed to the Forms in the Affinity Argument; and the implication of the whole argument is that this sense of 'forever' applies to the individual human soul as well. As for the Christian doctrine of resurrection of the body and its reunion with the soul "at the end of days" or the end of time, this is again a hybrid notion that at least borrows something from (b). Here too our rubric (c) comes in handy.

Whether existence forever in sense (b) is an intelligible notion in itself, or an inherently confused pseudo-concept, is hard to say. It is just such eternal and necessary existence that, in later Christian theology, is ascribed to God the creator, and to God alone. All created beings have the reason or cause of their existence in something else outside them—immediately in the last member of some chain of secondary causes, and ultimately in the first cause, God. God alone has the reason for his being in himself. That is what it means to say that God is a necessary and eternal being. We shall see in Part Four that Hume mounted a powerful attack upon theistic arguments based on this particular notion of divine existence, arguing that they involved a conceptual muddle that renders their conclusions, not so much false, or invalidly derived from the premises, as sheer unintelligible nonsense (see 26.9.3). For Hume, it is not the Judeo-Christian idea that there exists a divine being, the creator and sustainer of the universe, that is meaningless or incoherent; it is rather the philosopher's conception of God as a necessary being or eternal existent that makes no sense according to his philosophical principles.

As was seen earlier, certain contemporary philosophers, no doubt inspired by Hume's attack, extended the charge of meaninglessness, not just to *all* talk of God's existence and attributes, but to all metaphysical theorizing whose conclusions admit of no empirical corroboration or test (see 7.5.1). That would seem to be taking matters too far. It is very difficult to believe that to affirm God's existence *in any sense at all* is to say nothing meaningful; but as regards a necessary or eternal being in the sense described in (b), Hume's worries are real enough. It would be rash to wish to go to the wall defending this notion. Fortunately for religion, no non-dogmatic believer need do so.

The perplexities here are compounded by others concerning an existent all the phases of whose being are simultaneous. Kant, for one, took it to be self-evident that the parts or segments of time (or duration) are successive, while the parts of space are simultaneous. We grasp this in the same evident manner in which we know that time is inherently one-dimensional, flowing as if in a single line from future to past through the present moment, while space is three-dimensional, extended in length, depth, and breadth. If this is correct, then the notion of a being all the parts of whose existence are simultaneous is as muddled as that of a being who exists necessarily.

16.5.2 The word 'survival'

So much for 'forever.' Normally, 'to survive' means 'to escape death,' 'not to die at all' (as Woody Allen quite rightly saw). Hence, to say of one and the same thing, for example, a human being, that he or she died *and* survived is flatly self-contradictory. But it is no contradiction to say that *one part* of a human being dies (the material body), while *another part* survives (for example, the immaterial soul). This is how Plato gets round the difficulty of both dying and surviving. According to him, the soul survives, while the body perishes. This is made explicit toward the end of the *Phaedo*: "When death comes to man, the mortal part of him [the body] dies, it seems, but his deathless part goes away safe and indestructible, yielding the place to death" (106e).

Another way of avoiding contradiction here is the path taken by the Judeo-Christian resurrection doctrine: one and the same thing (the human person) *first* dies (does not survive) and *then*, after an interval, 'rises from the dead,' brought back to life, as the same flesh-and-blood person he or she was before, through a miracle of divine omnipotence. For a reference from the Old Testament, bearing out the claim that resurrection is resurrection of the body, see Job 19:26: "though worms destroy this body, yet *in the flesh* shall I see God" (e.a.). Or Isaiah 26:19: "Thy dead men shall live, together with my dead body shall they arise." (See also 66:22–3 and Daniel 12:2.) And in the New Testament, there is I Corinthians 15:42–4: "So also is the resurrection of the dead. It is sown in corruption; it is raised in incorruption ... It is sown an animal [natural or biological] body (*psychikos*) and it is raised a spiritual (*pneumatikos*) body." The relation of this animal body to the spiritual body is mysterious, that is, beyond human understanding; but that the same body survives, not just the soul, as in Plato, is clear enough from passages like these.

16.5.3 The word 'personal'

We come, finally, to the third element in the notion of immortality. Personal survival means surviving as the *same persons* we are in our lifetimes. There are two important consequences of this. The first is that (1) unless *I* am my soul, my soul's survival is not *my* survival *as the very person I am now*. The second is that (2) if *I* am in part a body, then, if my body does not survive, *I* do not survive.

Plato recognizes (1) and simply equates the soul with the human being, denying that the body forms an essential part of the person at all. Hence the soul's survival of the body's death is *personal* survival, the survival of one and the same person. By contrast, the Christian doctrine of resurrection is predicated on the truth of (2). Since on the Christian conception of personhood, deriving from Aristotle and Aquinas, embodiment is essential to the human person (as distinct from purely spiritual natures like angels), Christian theology posits the *reconstitution* of the body by an act of divine omnipotence. As already noted, however, though it is the same flesh-and-blood person who lives on after the resurrection, the exact relationship between the biological body that dies and the spiritual body that is resurrected is mysterious.

17

Cyclical Argument

17.1 The *probandum*

With Plato's conception of the soul now clearer, and with his concept of immortality sharply distinguished from the more familiar Christian notion, we are in a good position to understand exactly what is at issue in the first argument for immortality.

The *probandum* is only item (a) of that which was described earlier (see 15.2) as the *probandum* of the whole dialogue, namely "that [a] some future awaits men after death, as we have been told for years, [b] a much better future for the good than the wicked (63c)." In other words, the argument is intended to show that "our souls exist in the underworld" (71e); the question of reward and punishment is not even mooted until the third argument.

It might appear that the *probandum* of all three arguments is succinctly stated when Cebes brings Socrates up short by remarking that the entire defence of the philosophic life simply takes for granted the soul's survival of death. Most men, Cebes points out, find it hard to believe what Socrates has said about the soul. "They think that after it has left the body it no longer exists anywhere, but that it is destroyed and dissolved on the day the man dies, as soon as it leaves the body; and that, on leaving it, it is dispersed like breath and smoke, has flown away and is gone and is no longer anything anywhere" (69e–70a). Accordingly, Cebes asks Socrates to furnish grounds for believing "[a] that the soul still exists after a man has died and [b´] that it still possesses some capability and intelligence" (70b).

While (a) coincides with that of the *probandum* at 63c, (b´), having intelligence, is unmistakably different from (b), reward and punishment. While (b) is addressed only in the Affinity Argument, (b´) having conscious awareness or "intelligence" after death is to be established by the Recollection Argument.

Since the Cyclical Argument is restricted to (a), commentators have taken it merely

288   Part Two: Plato and the Road to Reality

as an opening gambit, a first attempt to circumscribe logical, metaphysical, and religious dimensions of the problem and to bring into play key concepts and ideas that will figure in its ultimate solution. In examining this and the following arguments, we should keep that possibility in mind.

17.2 The argument formalized

"Fallacious and misleading arguments," Kant once remarked, "are most easily detected if set out in correct syllogistic form." The first or Cyclical argument for immortality can be formalized as follows:

P1   All *becoming* is a becoming of opposites from their opposites; for example, the stronger comes to be from the weaker, the smaller from the larger, the worse from the better, the juster from the more unjust.

The relevant text passages for this innocuous-sounding premise are: "those [things which come to be] that have an opposite must necessarily come to be from their opposite and from nowhere else" (70e) and "all things come to be in this way, opposites from opposites" (71a). Exactly what this premise means, or rather the various things it might mean, will become clearer later on. For the moment, it will suffice to point out that the word for 'becoming' or 'genesis' covers 'change' of any kind, and that 'change' comprises (1) the coming-into-being of a non-living thing like an artefact as well as (2) the birth of a living organism, and (3) any change of state or properties in either a living being or an artefact.

The second premise can be put this way:

P2   Moreover, there is a corresponding process back again, from the second opposite back to its (the first) opposite.

This premise is formulated in the following terms: "between each of those pairs of opposites there are two processes: from the one to the other and then again from the other to the first; between the larger and the smaller there is increase and decrease" (71b). Note that a separate argument is given for this premise, to be called 'the supplementary argument' when we consider it in 17.3 below. Now for the third premise:

P3   Being alive (having been born) and being dead (having died) are opposites.

In Plato's own words: "is there an opposite to living, as sleeping is the opposite to being awake? Quite so ... What is it? Being dead ... Do you not say that to be dead is the opposite of being alive?" (71c–d). On the strength of these premises, Plato draws an initial conclusion that may be put this way:

C1 Therefore living things are born again from those which have died (that is, incarnation or *re*incarnation or birth = *re*incarnation), just as dead things are observed to come from those that were living.

Plato draws this first conclusion as follows: "Therefore if these are opposites, they come to be from one another and there are two processes of generation between the two ... Then ... living creatures come to be from the dead ... Then in this case one of the two processes of becoming is clear, for dying is clear enough ... Shall we not supply the opposite process of becoming? ... Is nature to be lame in this case? Or must we provide a process of becoming opposite to dying? ... Coming to live again" (71c–e). This formulation of the initial conclusion is obviously somewhat strung out, but it boils down to C1 above.

However, the argument does not end here. Next comes a further premise that can be formulated this way:

P4 If the living come from the dead, then our souls must exist in the underworld.

That is, in Plato's words, "if that is so ['that the living come from the dead in this way no less than the dead from the living'] it seems to be a sufficient proof that the souls of the dead must be somewhere whence they can come back again" (72a). With the aid of this premise, a second, the final, conclusion can now be drawn:

C2 The souls of the dead exist in the underworld.

This follows from C1 and P4. It is put in several ways in the course of the argument, for example: "Then our souls exist in the underworld" (71e). Or again: "the souls of the dead must be somewhere whence they can come back again" (72a). Also: "the souls of the dead exist" (72d–e). It is clearly recognizable as (a) of the *probandum* stated in 17.1.

17.3 The supplementary argument

So much for Plato's main argument. It concludes with a supplementary argument for P2, namely that the process described in P1 must be *two-way, bi-directional*, or *cyclical*. The whole first argument for immortality is usually called 'The Cyclical Argument' after P2, though it is sometimes also referred to as 'The Argument from Opposition' after P1.

The form of the supplementary argument is *modus tollens* (see 7.9). Starting from a conditional statement ('if ... then'), the consequent (or then-clause) is denied, the conclusion being that the antecedent (if-clause) must therefore also be false. Thus, the first premise of the supplementary argument is:

P5 *If* the generation of the states of things from their opposites were linear rather than cyclical (p), *then* everything would eventually end up in the same state (q).

Or, as it is stated in the text: "If the two processes of becoming did not always balance each other as if they were going round in a circle, but generation proceeded from one point to its opposite in a straight line and it did not turn back again to the other opposite or take any turning, do you realize that all things would ultimately have the same form, be affected in the same way, and cease to become?" (72b). This general p and q are then replaced with specific ones:

P6 *If* the process from living to dying were linear rather than cyclical (p), *then* everything would end up dead (p).

Again, in the words of the text: "If everything that partakes of life were to die and remain in that state and not come to life again [p], would not everything ultimately have to be dead and nothing alive [q]?" (72c–d). Now for the minor premise of the hypothetical or conditional syllogism:

P6 But generation and life are unceasing.

This premise, 'not q,' is not explicitly stated in the text, but it is clearly 'understood' or taken for granted. And so the conclusion follows:

C3 Therefore the process of generation is not linear [not p] (from life to death only) but cyclical (from living to dead and from dead back to living),

which is the only proof offered of P2 of the main argument.

17.4 Synopsis of the main and supplementary arguments

Since this is a rather long argument, it may be useful to present the whole train of thought synoptically. In the synopsis that follows, the last part of the main argument is presented in *modus ponens* and the supplementary argument in *modus tollens* form.

Main Argument, first part

P1 All becoming is becoming of opposites from their opposites.
P2 This process of becoming is two-way or 'cyclical.'

Chapter 17: Cyclical Argument   291

P3   The living and the dead are opposites.
C1   Hence, (dead things come from the living and) living things come from the dead.

Main Argument, last part (in *modus ponens*):

P4   If C1 (*p*), then the souls of the living exist after death (*q*).
      [But C1 (*p*) has already been proved]
C2   Therefore (*q*) the souls of the living exist after death.

Supplementary Argument for P2 (in *modus tollens*):

P5   If the process were not cyclical (*p*), generation would cease (*q*).
P6   Generation is unceasing (not *q*).
C3   = P2 Therefore the process is cyclical (not *p*).

17.5 Critical examination of the cyclical argument

Is this a good argument? In other words: Is it valid? Is it sound? (On validity and soundness, see 7.6.2–3.) Formalization suggests that the argument is a formally valid deductive argument: its premises, *if true*, would logically entail the truth of its conclusion (C2). But are its premises true—or even *probably* true? The key premises are clearly the following:

P1   All *becoming* (production of artefacts, change of state, birth of a living thing) is a becoming of opposites from their opposites.
P3   Being alive (having been born) and being dead (having died) are opposites.

17.5.1 Examination of the first premise

Why should we accept P1? Here is Socrates's evidence for it:

Let us examine whether those that have an opposite must necessarily come to be from their opposite and from nowhere else, as for example when something comes to be larger it must necessarily become larger from having been smaller before ... [and] if something smaller comes to be, it will come from something larger before, which became smaller? ... And the weaker comes to be from the stronger, and the swifter from the slower? ... Further, if something worse comes to be, does it not come from the better, and the juster from the more unjust? ... So we have sufficiently established that all things come to be in this way, opposites from opposites? (70e–71a)

Four points are worth noting in regard to this passage. First, all the examples are relations: not great, but great*er*, not swift, but swift*er*, and so on. Now it is true (in fact, necessarily true as a matter of logic, namely the logic of ordinary language) that for something to *become more x* (whatever *x* stands for), it must have previously been *less x* than it is now; to say that it is now bigg*er* logically entails that it was formerly smaller than it is now. And so with all relations. So Socrates's point holds good for all opposites that are *relational* terms.

The second thing to note is that P1 is true (again, as a matter of logical necessity) of *contradictory* opposites: if something 'becomes red' it follows that it was 'not red' before; otherwise it would not be correct to speak of its *becoming* (rather than just being) red. So red necessarily 'comes from its opposite,' not-red. But P1 does *not* hold for *contrary* opposites: if something 'becomes red' it does *not* follow in logic that it was 'blue' (or any other contrary opposite of red) before, though it *may* have been. So red does not necessarily come from any of its contrary opposites. (On contradictory and contrary opposites, see 7.10.)

Now for a third point. The first two points establish between them that P1 is universally true *both* of relational *and* contradictory, *but not* of contrary opposites. It is therefore of the utmost importance for the assessment of this argument that we determine whether 'living' and 'dead' are indeed either (i) relational or (ii) contradictory opposites.

As for (i), it seems clear enough on the face of it that 'living' and 'dead' do not admit of degrees of intensity. Something cannot become 'more living' or 'deader' in the way it can become faster or slower. 'Alive' and 'dead' (so long as we take them literally) admit of no comparative or superlative, even though we may speak metaphorically of feeling 'more alive' and the like. So 'living' and 'dead' are not relational opposites.

As for (ii), the contradictory opposite of 'living' is 'non-living,' while 'dead' is only the contrary opposite of 'living.' Everything is either living or non-living; both cannot be true *or* false of one and the same thing. That is the unmistakable mark of contradictories as opposed to contraries. By contrast, 'dead' (in the sense of 'having died') is not the contradictory but only the contrary opposite of 'living.' For while it cannot be true of anything that it is both living and dead (in the relevant sense), both statements can of course be false. 'Cannot both be true but may both be false' is the distinguishing mark of contraries as opposed to contradictories. For example, a table is neither living nor dead—where 'dead' means 'having died'—since it was never alive in the first place. Thus, if something 'becomes living' or 'comes to life,' it follows that it was previously non-living; but it does *not* follow, as Socrates implies, that it was 'dead' ('had died'), so that its coming-to-life is really a coming-*back*-to-life, a coming-to-life-*again*. The upshot of our consideration of (ii), then, is that 'living' and 'dead' are contrary rather than contradictory opposites. And according to (i), they are not relational opposites either.

That was the third thing to be established. Our conclusion from these three points is that P1 is true of *some*, not *all* opposites, and, moreover, that the opposites specified in P3, 'living' and 'dead,' are a case to which P1 does *not* apply. So the argument is already in serious trouble.

The fourth and final consideration suggests that the argument might still be saved. The suggestion might be made that P1 is not a *logical principle* (a rule about what logically entails what) governing the use of terms in propositions at all. It may be a causal principle (a rule about what causes what), that is, a cosmic principle or natural law governing what happens in the physical universe. (The likelihood is that Plato did not distinguish these sharply—if indeed he distinguished them at all.) In that case, however, P1 is just false: though it may hold for some cases of generation and change in the physical universe, it certainly does not hold for all or even most cases. For example, the generation of children is by parents who are *like* them, not their opposites in any sense; and the generation of certain properties is not by their opposites but by their 'likes' (for instance, hot things make other things hot, and so forth.) So any attempt along these lines to save the argument is itself doomed to failure.

Summarizing the four points regarding P1, we may say that P1 is either (a) a logical principle and necessarily true as well as strictly universal for all cases of relations and contradictory opposites, but (unfortunately) inapplicable to contraries, of which 'living' and 'dead' are examples; or P1 is (b) not a logical principle at all, but a cosmic law, in which case it is simply false, as can be easily demonstrated by counter-examples such as that given above.

17.5.2 Examination of the third premise

We turn now to P3: Being alive (having been born) and being dead (having died) are opposites.

Now if 'opposites' means 'contradictories,' P3 is false and the argument is, though formally valid, unsound (it contains a false premise). On the other hand, if 'opposites' means 'contraries,' P3 is true, and the argument, though formally valid, commits the informal fallacy of *equivocation* (see 7.7.4). How so?

In order for *both* P3 and P1 to be true (as they must be for the argument to be sound, that is, contain *only* true premises), 'opposites' must mean 'contraries' in P3 and 'contradictories' in P1. But the fallacy of equivocation (see 7.7.4 above) consists precisely in using the same term (here: 'opposites') in different senses in different premises of the argument: first in the sense of 'contradictories' in P1, then in the sense of 'contraries' in P3. Thus, *either* 'opposites' is used in different senses in P1 and P3, so that both premises are true; but then there is an equivocation. *Or* 'opposites' is used in the same way in both premises, in which case one of the two (either P1 or P3) must be false and the argument, while both valid and free of equivocation, is simply unsound since it contains a false premise.

17.5.3 Examination of the supplementary argument

It is worth noting that the supplementary argument presupposes (in its first premise) that there is only a fixed quantity of 'the living,' so that if the process were one-way, from living to dead, but not back from dead to living, that fixed quantity would at length be exhausted, used up. If we reject this unargued assumption on the grounds that new life can be (and is being) generated all the time, the whole supplementary argument collapses.

We conclude, then, that the Cyclical Argument is deeply flawed and, even on the most sympathetic interpretation, patently unsound. Three further arguments remain, however, the first two of which will be considered in the following chapters.

18

Recollection Argument

18.1 The *probandum* and manner of proof

As noted in the previous chapter (see 17.1), the *probandum* stated at the outset of the Cyclical Argument has two parts—"[a] that the soul still exists after a man has died and [b] that it still possesses some capability and intelligence" (70b)—the second of which is not even touched on in that argument. This defect (along with certain other inadequacies) of the first of Plato's arguments for immortality is to be remedied by the second.

The *probandum* of the second argument for immortality involves three claims that can be strung together in a single thesis as follows: (1) All knowledge is a form of recollection of concepts and truths (2) first acquired by the soul before birth, (3) at which time the soul must have existed apart from the body. Of these, (3), the soul's pre-existence (existence before birth), is the main point to be established by inference from (2). Still, the main burden of the argument is to show that (2) itself follows from (1). (3) is then inferred immediately from (2) by taking for granted a certain conception of 'birth' (the becoming-incarnate of a discarnate soul).

As for (1), it is not merely assumed without analysis or argument. On the contrary, it is based *in part* on a very careful logical analysis of the meaning of the word 'recollection.' Still, the model of recollection is more or less *imposed* on cognition or knowing, so that (1) may have to be said to be taken for granted after all. This is not the only occasion on which an inappropriate model leads Plato seriously astray. We shall consider other instances of the same mistake in 18.10.2 and 20.12.2 below. But even apart from the blatant inappropriateness of the model, Plato's conception of cognition as recollection involves a number of unargued metaphysical and epistemological assumptions that we shall have to examine closely.

296   Part Two: Plato and the Road to Reality

18.2 The logical analysis of recollection talk

The first part of the argument (73c–74a) consists in a logical analysis of the meaning of 'recollecting.' Here Plato is concerned—although he would certainly not have put it this way—with the *logic of recollection talk*. Is there any warrant for describing his intentions in this blatantly twentieth-century idiom?

Consider a parallel case. Alluding to the difference between the Scholastic-Aristotelian definition of 'man' as a 'rational animal' and the *proprium* 'featherless biped'(see above 7.14), Locke once remarked that God did not create man simply a featherless biped, leaving it to Aristotle (the founder of logic) to make him rational. His point was that men reasoned correctly long before Aristotle took it into his head to produce a systematic compilation of the correct forms of logical inference. So too with the logic of recollection talk: Plato and others were perfectly capable of analyzing the logic of ordinary language long before anything like twentieth-century 'ordinary language philosophy' appeared on the scene. So there is nothing wrong with characterizing the first part of the argument in terms of ordinary language analysis.

As was pointed out earlier (see 7.11), the language we speak everyday has its own logic. Certain statements logically entail, presuppose, or are logically consistent or inconsistent with, others. The example given earlier was 'Vanessa is divorced,' which logically entails 'Vanessa was married.' Or, to recall the example of the Cyclical Argument, if I say 'This has become bigger,' my saying so logically entails the proposition 'This was at some time in the past smaller (than it is now).' To assert the first and deny the second proposition (which it entails, logically) is accordingly to contradict oneself; it is *logically* inconsistent. It is part of the *logic* of 'divorced' and 'become' and relational terms like 'bigger' that the one proposition logically implies or entails the other.

Now let us, following Plato, apply these lessons to recollection talk. To say:

(1)   'A is reminded of x by y' or 'A recollects (remembers) x on seeing y'

logically entails a number of things. Take Plato's example of a lover who sees the lyre or garment of his beloved and 'recollects,' 'is reminded of' or 'remembers' the beloved (73d), or one who, "seeing a picture of Simmias, recollect[s] Simmias himself" (73e). In a first phase of the preliminary analysis, Plato spells out three things logically entailed by this use of 'recollects,' beginning with:

(2)   'A thinks of y at some point in time, $t1$.'

Thus, for example, a lover (A) sees the lyre (y) belonging to his beloved (x), or he sees his beloved's picture (another value of y). Some proposition of the form of (2) is the first thing entailed by (1). In addition, however, (1) entails a proposition like:

(3) 'A thinks of x at some point in time, t2, after t1.'

This much is perfectly clear. If I am reminded of someone by something, I first perceive the thing, whereupon the person I am reminded of comes to mind. So seeing the lyre or picture (y) makes the lover think of his beloved (x) *in the next instant or later*. But something else besides (2) is entailed as well, namely:

(4) 'A has already thought of x *before* t2 and t1 (call this time 't1-n').'

Thus, in our example, the lover would have to have seen his beloved playing this lyre *prior* to seeing the lyre on the present occasion in order to be correctly described as 'recollecting' or 'remembering' the beloved upon seeing the lyre again; or, to take the other case, the lover would have to have seen the beloved himself at an *earlier* point in time (and already have been acquainted with him) in order to be correctly said to be 'reminded' of him on seeing the picture for the first time. In (4) we have generalized 'seen' to 'thought of' in order to cover cases where there is no first-hand acquaintance with the person recalled, as when, for example, I see a picture of the Queen (whom I have never met). I still recall the Queen. Even at that, there are still further entailments. The first is:

(5) 'A has *forgotten* or ceased to think about x at some time between t1-n and t1.'

This particular entailment of (1) one is spelled out clearly when Plato writes: "Is this kind of thing not recollection of a kind ... especially so when one experiences it about things that one has forgotten, because one has not seen them for some time" (73d–e). That is exactly the point captured in (5). If at the very moment of seeing x the lover were already thinking of his beloved, it would not be correct to speak of his 'being reminded' of him. But (1) entails something further still:

(6) y (the lyre or the picture) and x (the beloved) are somehow *associated* in A's mind, whether (a) by 'likeness,' either perfect or imperfect; or (b) by some other principle of association.

Thus, the picture is more or less *like* the person pictured, while the lyre, on the other hand, is *unlike* the person it belongs to, though in the latter case the relation of 'belonging to' or 'ownership' serves as the principle of association uniting x and y in A's mind.

The upshot of the entire analysis, then, is that (1), 'A recollects x on seeing y,' entails (2) through (6). This is Plato's exacting logical analysis of the concept of recollection or recollection talk. And it is a very impressive example of ordinary language analysis, even by twentieth-century standards.

18.3 The imposition of the model of recollection on human knowledge

The next step is to interpret knowledge or cognition on the model of recollection so that knowledge appears to be nothing but a form of recollection. This will ensure that 'A knows x' carries important logical implications of 'A recollects x,' including A's (the soul's) having existed prior to birth.

In question, incidentally, is not *all* knowledge, or rather, not everything that *we* would call 'knowledge' nowadays. Empirical matters of fact regarding past, present, or future states of affairs in the world are not 'recollected' and are therefore not 'knowledge' in Plato's sense; they are either reported or observed or conjectured on the basis of reports and observations. Such would be opinion, not knowledge, for Plato, though it certainly is 'knowledge' in *our* sense of the word. (We shall return to this epistemological assumption in a moment.)

So Plato's analysis of knowledge on the model of recollection is restricted to the soul's acquisition of certain concepts only, namely mathematical concepts like those of shapes and numbers, moral concepts like justice and virtue, as well as any other concepts that correspond to what Plato calls 'Forms.' The exact extent of such knowledge, a question with which Plato seems to have wrestled, need not be fixed for the moment; it is enough that it clearly includes mathematical and moral concepts.

Obviously, the business of construing knowledge as recollection involves *more* than just logical analysis of the way in which a term is ordinarily used. It *imposes* the logical features of recollection talk, as ordinarily engaged in, on knowledge talk as well. The result is something very remote from knowledge talk as we know it. Furthermore, it brings into play certain *metaphysical* assumptions about what is real (that is, that Forms exist) as well as certain *epistemological* assumptions about what constitutes *genuine* knowledge (as noted above). These metaphysical and epistemological assumptions will be examined later, in chapter 20, when we come to the theory of Forms and the dubious model on which Plato construes the difference between knowledge and opinion.

No argument is given here in the *Phaedo* for the metaphysical assumption that Forms exist or for the epistemological assumption that they are the only objects of genuine knowledge, since Simmias and Cebes say at the outset (74a) that they accept these assumptions. So we too must simply go along with them for the time being.

18.4 The argument

Now we are ready to tackle the main body of the Argument from Recollection. It can be formalized as follows. (Once again, as in the case of the Cyclical Argument, the text passages corresponding to the individual premises and conclusions are appended after the formalized version.) The first premise is:

Chapter 18: Recollection Argument 299

P1 There exists such a thing as X itself, the Form or essence of all x's.

In the words of the text: "there is something that is equal. I do not mean a stick equal to a stick or a stone to a stone, or anything of that kind, but something else beyond all these, the Equal itself. Shall we say that this exists or not" (74a).

The Equal is, of course, a concrete instance of the general type of existent (a Form) referred to in P1. The specific example selected is of no importance for the argument. This is even made explicit: "our present argument is no more about the Equal than about the Beautiful itself, the Good itself, the Just, the Pious and, as I say, about all those things to which we can attach the world 'itself'" (75c–d). Any of these entities to which 'itself' is correctly attached—that is, any Form—could be used to illustrate and support the general claim in P1 about what there is in the universe as a whole (or, rather, what there is *outside* the *sensible* portion of the universe as a whole, in addition to the equals, beautiful things, just things, and so on, that are met with in it).

The next premise concerns, not the existence of such entities, but our knowledge of them.

P2 It is by perceiving x-like things that one comes to think of X itself.

To establish this, Socrates asks: "Whence have we acquired the knowledge of it [of Equality]? Is it not from the things we mentioned just now, from seeing sticks or stones or some other things that are equal [that] we come to think of that other which is different from them [absolute Equality]?" (74b). Or at another place: "These equal things and the Equal itself are therefore not the same? ... But it is definitely from the equal things, though they are different from that Equal, that you have derived and grasped the knowledge of Equality?" (74c).

It is worth noting that the sensory experiences mentioned here are merely *occasions* of our becoming consciously aware of the knowledge in question, not *sources* of such knowledge; for the doctrine is that the Form of Equality itself is already present in the mind, though we are unaware of it until the appropriate sensory experiences 'trigger' such awareness. Then, we not only 'have' the concept of equality in us, but also know what Equality is. So the occasioning cause of our awareness of what we already have in us must not be confused with the source or cause of something's beginning to exist in us, entering the soul, in the first place, or with the source of our knowledge of it. For the process of becoming aware of it is a rational, not a sensory, one, even if dependent on a sensory occasion or stimulus. All this will be borne out by later parts of the *Phaedo*.

The next premise can be put this way:

P3 x-like things are *imperfect* likenesses of X itself.

This is, after all, the gist of Socrates's questions: "do we experience something like this in the case of equal sticks and the other equal objects we just mentioned? Do they seem to us to be equal in the same sense as what is Equal itself? Is there some deficiency in their being such as the Equal, or is there not?" (74d). The relationship between the copies or instances observed by means of the bodily senses and the originals of which they are copies is that of 'falling short' of the perfection of the original.

There are at least three things, one or more of which Socrates could mean by 'deficiency,' and the Greek text (which is uncertain) makes it hard to determine just what he has in mind. On the one hand, (1) equal objects (like our two sticks) may appear equal to the naked eye and yet fall short of the absolute or perfect equality that belongs to the Form 'Equality itself.' For if one were to take a ruler to them, one would find that the two sticks are in fact slightly unequal; there may be a thirty-second of an inch difference, or there will be some smaller difference that a more accurate measuring device than a ruler could easily detect. But there always will be some (in principle) detectable difference. In the same way, lines drawn on paper or on a blackboard that appear uniformly straight to the naked eye, would, on closer inspection or under sufficient magnification, reveal curvature and irregularity. By contrast, the Straight itself (compare: the Equal itself) is perfectly straight.

Something of this sort Socrates *may* have in mind here, though he does not say so. What he does say is: "Look at it this way: do not equal stones and sticks sometimes, while remaining the same, appear to one person to be equal and to another to be unequal" (74b). So Socrates *at least* means that (2) a pair of sticks considered equal in length by one observer may not appear equal to another; and perhaps even that they may not appear equal to the same observer under different observation conditions (though this additional point is not spelled out in the text). The same is not so, however, for Equality itself. It always appears equal, never unequal, to everyone who grasps it at all.

So (2) is at least part of Socrates's meaning here. But he may also mean that (3) our two sticks, though in fact equal to each other, are not equal in length to *all* other things. Hence, they are in one respect equal, namely to each other, and in some respects unequal, depending on what else they are compared with. Thus, a woman may be beautiful compared with other women, but not compared with a goddess. By contrast, the Equal itself is not unequal by comparison with anything, nor is the Beautiful ugly in any respect; rather, the Equal itself and the Beautiful itself are perfectly equal or beautiful in *all* respects at all times and never more or less so. This is the way Plato draws the contrast between Forms and particulars in *Republic* 479a–b and 523a–524c. He couples (3) and (2) at *Symposium* 211a–b. For the purposes of this argument in the *Phaedo*, however, it does not matter much which precise point (or points) he has in mind.

Now for the next premise:

P4 Acquaintance with the perfect X (X itself) must be *prior in time* to perceiving the imperfect x-like things which resemble it.

Two passages reflect this premise clearly: "Whenever someone, on seeing something, realizes that that which he now sees wants to be like some other reality but falls short and cannot be like that other since it is inferior, do we agree that the one who thinks this must have prior knowledge of that to which he says it is like, but deficiently so?" (74d–e). The other passage reads: "We must then possess knowledge of the Equal before that time when we first saw the equal objects and realized that all these objects strive to be like the Equal but are deficient in this" (74e–75a).

There remains now only one more premise before the initial conclusion can be drawn, namely:

P5 The perception of x-like things begins immediately after birth.

This is the purport of the answer given the question, "But we began to see and hear and otherwise perceive right after birth?" (75b). From these premises the conclusion follows:

C1 Hence, either (a) we are born with the knowledge of X itself and retain it throughout life; or (b) we acquire it before birth and forget it at birth; or (c) we acquire and forget it at birth.

Here is how Socrates himself puts the initial conclusion: "One of two things follows, as I say: either [a] we were born with the knowledge of it, and all of us know it throughout life, or [b] those who later, we say, are learning, are only recollecting and learning would be recollection" (76a). This covers two options. Yet Simmias replies to the above later on: "Unless [c] we acquire the knowledge at the moment of birth, Socrates, for that time is still left to us" (76c). This is the third possibility.

Next, a further premise is introduced in order to eliminate (a):

P6 But not (a), since men are not able to give a satisfactory account of X itself, which they would be able to do if they really had this knowledge from birth onwards.

The content of this premise is implied by Socrates's questions: "A man who has knowledge would be able to give an account of what he knows, would he not? ... And do you think everybody can give an account of the things we were mentioning just now?" (76b), for example, what Equality itself is. The answer to these questions is clearly 'no.' So option (a) drops out. So does (c), the final possibility, since if (c) were true we would have to both acquire and lose this knowledge at birth (which, it is suggested, is self-contradictory): "Do we then lose it at the very time [that is, birth] we acquire it?" (76d). With (a) and (c) thus eliminated,

C2 Only (b) remains, and the soul existed before birth, acquired this knowledge, then forgot it at birth, and only *remembers* it during life rather than acquiring it for the first time.

"So then, Simmias, [a] our souls also existed apart from the body before they took on human form, and [b] they had intelligence" (76c). The first part of this is equivalent to (3) in the initial statement of the *probandum* in 18.1. It is inferred directly from (2), the pre-natal acquisition of knowledge, which is in turn the result of (1), the alleged fact that knowledge must be construed as recollection. As for the other part of the conclusion, (b) intelligence, we shall return to it later.

18.5 Synopsis and preliminary assessment of this argument

The Cyclical Argument, though formally valid, collapsed under scrutiny as either involving an informal fallacy (owing to equivocation) or as being unsound (owing to a false premise). What about the Recollection Argument? To begin with, we can synopsize the argument in the following way:

P1 There exists such a thing as X itself, the Form or essence of x or of all x's. (74a)
P2 It is by perceiving x-like things that one comes to think of X itself. (74b–c)
P3 x-like things are imperfect likenesses of X itself. (74d)
P4 Acquaintance with the perfect X (X itself) must be prior in time to perceiving the imperfect x-like things which resemble it. (74d–e)
P5 The perception of x-like things begins immediately after birth. (75b)
C1 Hence either (a) we are born with the knowledge of X itself and retain it throughout life; or (b) we acquire it before birth and lose it at birth; or (c) we both acquire and lose it at birth. (76a–c)
P6 But neither (a) nor (c). (76b–d)
C2 Therefore (b), and the soul existed before birth. (76c)

Like its predecessor, this argument must be regarded as formally valid. But it is only *sound* if the assumption underlying P1, P3, and P4 is true; that is, it is sound only if that metaphysical theory of Forms is true. Are there then Forms like Equality itself, "the Greater and the Smaller" (75c), "the Beautiful itself, the Good itself, the Just, the Pious" (75c–d), and so forth? Are there even Forms like "Size, Health, Strength" (65d), "Oneness" (101c), "Twoness" (ibid.), "Bigness" (100e), "Tallness" (102b–e), "the Cold" (105a), "the Odd" (105b), and their contraries? What about "the Whole" (ibid.) and Life itself (cf. 106d)? Unless such Forms as these are transcendently real (see 4.7), unless they really exist in their own right outside and independent of our minds, it is mistaken to claim that all genuine knowledge is recollection of concepts first acquired through pre-natal acquaintance with Forms.

We shall examine the assumption underlying these key premises more fully later (see chap. 20). At this stage, we want to consider a different difficulty. In the last phase of the Recollection Argument (77a–b), Simmias and Cebes formulate an objection. The argument, they point out, proves that the soul exists *before birth*, but *not* that the soul exists *after death* as well. Socrates has therefore only shown "[h]alf of what needed proof" (77c). In reply Socrates remarks that the Cyclical argument for the soul's *post-existence* and the Recollection Argument for its *pre-existence* can be "put together" to produce the desired result (77c–d). How adequate is this response, given what we understand by 'immortality' or (in Plato's terms) 'deathlessness,' namely: (1) *personal* survival of death (2) *forever*?

18.6 'Soul' in the Cyclical and Recollection Arguments

Regarding (1), *personal* survival, note that Plato just assumes that the soul that survives death is equatable with the person. But, for one thing, 'soul' is taken in two different senses in (a) the Cyclical Argument (soul = life principle) and (b) the Recollection Argument (soul = rational or cognitive principle); and, for another, neither sense, nor yet the combination of the two, seems equatable with what is ordinarily meant by 'the human person.' Let us consider these points in turn.

If that which undergoes the cycle of rebirths were the soul in the sense of the rational or cognitive principle in humans, then the Cyclical argument would hold good only for rational beings. But at the outset of the argument Plato states in no uncertain terms:

Do not ... confine yourself to humanity if you want to understand this more readily, but take all animals and all plants into account, and, in short, for all things which come to be, let us see whether they come to be in this way, that is, from their opposites if they have such. (70d–e)

So the operative conception of soul, in the Cyclical Argument at least, must be: the vital or life-giving force in all living things. In the Recollection Argument, on the other hand, the soul is clearly understood as the cognitive or noetic principle in the *human* soul. That this is so is clear from the second part of the conclusion: "So then, Simmias, [a] our souls also existed apart from the body before they took on human form, [b] *and they had intelligence*" (76c, e.a.).

The Recollection Argument, then, is not just an attempt to prove the same thing as the Cyclical in another way; it takes 'soul' in a different and richer sense: not just life, but living intelligence. As a consequence, any attempt to combine the two arguments involves a fairly gross *equivocation* on 'soul'—much as the Cyclical Argument itself involved an equivocation on 'opposites.' For the soul whose pre-existence is established in the Recollection Argument (the intellect or intelligence) is *not the same soul* whose post-existence was established in the Cyclical Argument (the vital principle in living things).

18.7 Soul and person

This shift in the sense of 'soul' is the first problem with the alleged equivalence of soul and person. Now the shift from soul as life-giving to soul as cognitive principle indeed brings us (i) *closer* to something like *personhood* as we normally understand it, though perhaps still (ii) not close enough. For unless the survival of one and the same soul is the survival of one and the same person, the Recollection Argument fails to establish anything like personal immortality.

We are (i) closer because having intelligence (cognition) is normally taken to be a necessary feature of what we call persons. Recall that for Kant respect for the dignity of *persons* is simply respect for the other as a rational, intelligent being capable of governing his own actions and directing them toward ends of his own choosing (see 12.8.5 above). By contrast, vital functions (nutrition, growth, reproduction) are common to persons *and* non-persons (like the plant and animal organisms to which the Cyclical Argument is supposed to apply.) In fact, the vital functions may not even be necessary features of persons at all. For granted that all the persons whose existence we are sure of do happen to have living bodies, could there not be *disembodied persons* (spirits, angels, God) having no material bodies and hence nothing akin to the vital principle in us? 'Life' in them would presumably just be the same thing as 'intelligence,' whereas in us these two are quite different. On reflection, one finds the idea of persons without bodies, and hence without vital functions, a coherent notion; it is at least not obviously self-contradictory, so the existence of such beings is at least logically *possible*, though their actual existence is questionable.

From the foregoing it seems that having a living body is *not* included in the concept of a person (though it *is* included in the ordinary and the specifically Christian concept of a *human* person, as noted earlier). On the other hand, the suggestion that there might be persons *without any form of intelligence* does seem to be a contradiction in terms. So in the Recollection Argument we are getting a little *closer* to our own, and to the specifically Christian, conception of (human) personhood than in the Cyclical Argument; but equally clearly, we are not there yet.

Unless mere intelligence (cognition as opposed to will, desire, and memory) is not just *necessary*, but also *sufficient* for personhood, even the demonstration of the pre-existence of a soul having intelligence (only) still leaves us far from anything like *personal* existence before birth. At first blush, it would seem that (a) mere intelligence—the intellect or reason—is not enough. What about (b) our emotional dispositions, our loves and hates, fears and longings? What about (c) the will, our characteristic desires and ways of satisfying them? And what about (d) memory of our individual pasts, and (e) the moral attributes acquired during our lives—what we call 'character'? Are these not also necessary for personhood and hence for personal survival of death?

More will be said about the concept of the human person in the context of the mind–body problem in Descartes. In that setting, embodiment is understood as essential to the human person, just as it is in the Christian tradition. The same topic will come up again in connection with Sartre's notion (borrowed from Heidegger) of the self. For Heidegger and Sartre, the individual self or person is essentially rather than just accidentally (f) involved with non-human things and with other selves in a shared environment or world. All this is part of 'personhood' in the very rich sense in which Heidegger and Sartre tacitly reinterpret that concept. Even without having studied Descartes and Sartre, it seems very likely that at least some, if not all, of those things listed under (a) through (f) have a lot to do with our *individual* personhood as we ordinarily understand it. If these characteristics are not preserved, then whether or not my intellectual faculty survives, *I* do not survive as the same person I am in this life. So although the Recollection Argument got us (i) closer to a full-bodied conception of personhood, it still does not get us (ii) close enough.

18.8 Pre-existence, post-existence, immortality

So much for (1) *personal* survival of death. This brings us to survival (2) *forever*.

Even supposing one could just combine them, pre-existence and post-existence would still not add up to 'existence forever,' either in the sense of (a) 'throughout all time' (sempiternity) or (b) 'outside of time' (eternity). Yet 'forever' in the sense of (a) 'sempiternity' seems to be the *only* thing that *could* result from adding together pre-existence and post-existence, since only what is 'in time' can be spoken of as existing 'before' and 'after' some event like birth (incarnation) or death (becoming discarnate again). Nevertheless the soul could enjoy 'pre-existence for a time' and 'post-existence for a time,' after which comes—complete *extinction*. So 'forever' in the sense of 'everlastingly' is the only sense that *could* be proved even by putting the two arguments together—and yet, clearly, even this is not proved.

As for 'forever' in the sense of 'eternally,' it is the special task of the Affinity Argument to establish the existence of the soul 'forever' in this particular sense. Like the first two arguments, it is not just another attempt to prove the same thing (personal survival of death forever) in a different way. Something new is introduced. But since the Affinity Argument attempts to establish 'existence forever' in the sense of 'eternal existence' (like that of the Forms), it introduces a *new equivocation* into the idea of 'deathlessness' or 'immortality.' Recall that the first equivocation concerned the sense of 'soul'; the second concerns the sense of the soul's survival of death 'forever.' When all is said and done, this is rather a lot of equivocation.

18.9 Summary of the criticisms so far

With the talk of 'special tasks' for each argument, it begins indeed to appear that the first three arguments for immortality form part of a complex web of argument within which each individual argument has its own job to do (see 17.1). Yet this approach seems to result in nothing but dubious assumptions and equivocations. So far we have seen that (1) Plato just assumes, without argument, (a) the existence of Forms and (b) that knowledge is, or is like, recollection (after a period of forgetting) of Forms with which we had a prior acquaintance. Moreover, (2) Plato just assumes that the soul is the person, even though neither (a) the vital principle nor (b) the cognitive principle nor (c) both together would seem to square with what we ordinarily mean by a 'person' or 'personhood.' (3) Furthermore, these two senses of 'soul' introduce a first equivocation into the longer train of thought that extends over the first three arguments. In addition, (4) neither of the first two arguments, nor the two taken together, establish 'deathlessness' or 'immortality' *forever* in the sole relevant sense of 'forever' ('everlastingness'). And, finally, (5) when the Affinity Argument tackles the problem of 'forever,' it brings in a new sense of 'forever' ('eternally'), and thus introduces a second equivocation.

18.10 The major flaw in the first two arguments: circularity

But there is another flaw that completely vitiates both the Cyclical and the Recollection Arguments, taken individually or in conjunction. In both arguments the terms 'being alive' or 'being living' and 'being dead' or 'having died' are used in such a way that the very thing to be proved is taken for granted, namely that the souls of living things existed before birth and continue to exist after death. This is the informal fallacy of *circularity*, *begging the question*, or *petitio principii* (see 7.7.2). It will repay close attention.

18.10.1 Three different senses of 'becoming'

Consider these three senses of 'becoming' in English (or of *genesis* in Greek):

1 'Generation' in the sense of 'production': the bringing into being *of a thing*, that is, the coming-into-being, the *beginning to be* of a non-living entity, say a tool which formerly did not exist and which an artisan manufactures out of pre-existing materials.
2 'Generation' as change or alteration, that is, becoming this or that, for example, red: an already existing thing or entity (living or non-living) acquires a certain property, say, redness.
3 'Generation' in the sense of 'procreation' or 'reproduction': birth, that is, the *beginning to be* of a *living thing*, an animal, say.

Now note that 1 and 3 both have the sense of 'beginning to be.' Talk of 'becoming' in either of these senses *logically entails* that that which 'becomes' *did not* exist before. But in 2, that which 'becomes' would *logically* have to exist already, prior to becoming thus-and-so, that is, prior to acquiring a certain property. In other words, the implication is just the opposite: 'becoming' here means, not 'beginning to be,' but 'alteration,' 'change *of state*'; and only something that already existed without property x before could 'become x'—say, red.

18.10.2 The vicious circle

Now Plato blatantly begs the whole question of the soul's existence before birth and after death by construing birth and death as *changes or alterations* (on the model of 2) rather than as the *coming-into-being and extinction* of a living thing (on the model of 3). Alteration, we just saw, presupposes that whatever undergoes alteration existed already before and continues to exist after it. Coming-into-being and ceasing-to-be, on the other hand, *logically* presuppose that what comes into being or ceases to be *did not* or *does not* exist before or after the process in question.

In other words, Plato just assumes 'birth' or 'being born' to be something that happens to *souls*: meant is that the (already existing) soul *acquires the property* of incarnateness, embodiment. Yet most people understand 'birth' and 'being born' as something that happens to *living things*, namely that a living thing (that did not exist before) *begins to* exist. Plato takes it that the soul exists prior to birth because he assumes that birth equals incarnation or reincarnation. Of course, if 'being alive' is taken to mean 'having been born,' and this in turn to mean 'having entered a body,' that is, 'acquired the *property* of being incarnate,' then 'being alive' *logically presupposes* having already existed prior to birth, and the very thing to be proved is presupposed. For that is just part of the 'logic' of the talk of 'being born'—in Plato, namely, though not in ordinary speech.

So only what is *already existent* and *lacks a certain property* can acquire that property at some subsequent point in time; only something which already exists outside the body, can enter the body (go from existing in a discarnate state to existing in an incarnate state), which is what 'being born' is taken to mean here. In the more customary sense of the expression, however, 'being born' is said of the living thing, the whole animal, not just of the soul of the animal. 'Being born' in the *usual* sense thus logically entails *not* having existed previously, since only that which did not exist previously can *begin* to exist or *come into* existence. In blithely ignoring the ordinary and introducing a special sense of 'birth,' Plato begs the question of pre-existence.

A parallel objection can be brought against Plato's definition of 'death' as the 'separation of soul and body.' It begs the question whether the soul exists after death (post-existence), since 'dying,' for Plato, is just a matter of a thing's losing a property: the soul loses the property of being in a particular body and continues to exist without any body (in a disembodied state) or else passes into another body. But the way we ordinarily understand 'death' (say, of animals), 'dying' just means the ceasing to exist altogether of the living animal. And the same *may* be true of persons: the death of the person is usually taken to mean that person's ceasing to exist altogether (extinction). If this is mistaken, that must be *shown*, not just *assumed*, by giving a special sense to the word 'death.'

18.11 Evaluation of the Recollection Argument

In addition to all (1) the special problems associated with combining the two arguments and (2) the general weakness of the Recollection Argument considered in its own right, there is also (3) the fact that its conclusion seems so manifestly false. The argument, in simplified form, is:

P1 There exist Forms.
P2 Knowledge is recollection of pre-natal acquaintance with these Forms.
C Hence we (the soul) must have existed before birth.

But since in any valid deductive argument it is impossible for the premises to be true and the conclusion false, the temptation is very strong to turn the tables and reply: the conclusion, C, is obviously false, since, on the customary interpretation of 'being born,' before I was born I did not exist at all. Therefore one or both of the premises, P1 and/or P2, must also be false (see 7.8.2 above on the reversibility of valid deductive arguments).

This counter-offensive may beg the question too. But at least it does not turn on a special sense of 'birth,' sticking close to ordinary language and common sense—usually a sound practice, unless compelling reasons exist for doing otherwise.

19

Affinity Argument

19.1 The *probandum*

The last argument to be considered is the Affinity Argument. Recall once more what Socrates set out to prove at the beginning of the defence of the philosophic life: "that [a] some future awaits men after death [that is, there is life after death], as we have been told for years, [b] a much better future for the good than the wicked (63c)." The Cyclical Argument sought to establish (a), post-existence. The Recollection introduced a different point, namely "that [b´] it [the soul] still possesses some capability and intelligence" (70b). But neither the Cyclical nor the Recollection Argument even tries to establish (b) reward and punishment after death. That is introduced by the Affinity Argument, which is supposed to bolster something like (1) as well.

We say 'something like (1)' because the Affinity Argument sets out to establish *more* than just (a) that the soul continues to exist *for a time* after the death of the body. This much is assumed by Socrates and his interlocutors to have been shown already, by the Cyclical Argument. The Affinity Argument tries to establish *more* even than (b) that after the death of the body the soul continues to exist throughout *all* time, *everlastingly or sempiternally*. True, at the death of the body some souls, those of non-philosophers, undergo a series of incarnations or rebirths taking place successively in time; while assumed already in the Cyclical, this is only spelled out fully in the Affinity Argument. But in addition to this, the Affinity Argument argues (c) that after the death of the body the soul *of the philosopher* will continue to exist *outside of time, eternally*. And that is something quite new.

However, this is true *only* of the souls of philosophers, which have been 'purified.' For the souls of other men, an unending cycle of reincarnations in other, especially animal, bodies awaits as punishment. So the philosophers do have a better lot after death than the souls of other humans, which is exactly the point referred to under (b).

19.2 The argument

The argument is obviously intended to address, in a way the previous arguments did not, Simmias's and Cebes's fears that the soul may be "dispersed" (77b) or "scattered" (78b) like a vapour exhaled by the body at death (see 17.1). Behind such fears lies a commonsense materialist conception of soul that the preceding arguments have not addressed directly (see 4.3 on non-reductive materialism and 16.3 on Homeric and popular notions of life soul and breath soul).

The whole discussion can be divided into *three parts*, only the first two of which take the form of an *argument*. The third is very largely *unsupported speculation* of a distinctly religious rather than philosophical flavour. The content of each of the three parts can be summarized as follows:

PART A (78b–79a) first recalls that it has been established already that there are "two sorts of existences" (unchanging Forms and changing particulars) and proceeds to set out in detail the different and contradictorily opposed characteristics of each "sort."

PART B (79b–80b) examines the 'affinity' (hence: 'Affinity Argument') of the human soul with the Forms and of the human body with particular things, concluding that the soul possesses all those characteristics (including "deathlessness" and "indissolubility") previously identified as belonging to the Forms, while the body possesses those characteristics (including dissolubility or perishability) previously identified as belonging to particular things. The conclusion (C3) is that it is therefore "unlikely" that the soul is dispersed at the dissolution of the body.

PART C (80c–84b) tries to differentiate, not by argument but by recourse to an intellectualized version of Pythagorean and Orphic purification doctrines, between the fates of two different types of human souls after death: *reincarnation* (in an animal body) is the fate of the non-philosopher's soul, while *disembodied existence for eternity* awaits the soul of the philosopher after death.

19.2.1 Two orders of existence

We can formalize the argument of Part A as follows, appending the key passages in which the premises are actually stated:

P1 It is (logically speaking) only compound or composite things which can break up or dissolve, while uncompounded or simple things are (logically or necessarily) the sorts of things that are indissoluble.

Chapter 19: Affinity Argument 311

The passage on which P1 is based reads: "Is not anything that is composite and a compound by nature liable to be split up into its component parts, and only that which is non-composite, if anything, is not likely to be split up?" (78c). This is hardly controversial. It is just part of the *meaning* of the terms 'composite' (that is, 'put together') and 'non-composite' or 'simple' ('not put together,' 'having no parts') that things to which the former term can be correctly applied can also be broken up into their constituent parts, while those things (if any) to which the latter epithet applies are not divisible into parts. The question whether any things of either kind exist is still open at this stage. And it remains so even after the next premise:

P2 Moreover, composite things are the sorts of things that are constantly changing, while the uncompounded or simple things are the sorts of things which are always unchanging or the same.

Socrates puts this premise in the form of the following question, which is answered in the affirmative: "Are not the things that always remain the same and in the same state most likely not to be composite, whereas those that vary from one time to another and are never the same are composite?" (78c). Notice that this is only "likely," while the preceding premise is a matter of logic and hence strictly necessary. The next premise is:

P3 In the previous discussion reference was made both to particular things, for example, equal things or beautiful things, which are constantly changing, and to simple unchanging Forms (Equality itself, Beauty itself).

The passage of which this particular premise is the upshot is rather long, but worth citing in its entirety:

Let us return to those same things with which we were dealing earlier, to that reality of whose existence we are giving an account in our questions and answers; are they ever the same and in the same state, or do they vary from one time to another; can the Equal itself, the Beautiful itself, each thing in itself, the real, ever be affected by any change whatever? Or does each of them that really is, being simple by itself, remain the same and never in any way tolerate any change whatever? ... What of the many beautiful particulars, be they men, horses, clothes, or other such things, or the many equal particulars, and all those which bear the same name as those others? Do they remain the same or, in total contrast to those other realities, one might say, never in any way remain the same as themselves or in relation to each other? (78c–e)

One more premise is required before the conclusion of Part A can be drawn:

P4 The Forms are the kinds of things which are "invisible" and "perceived with the mind," while the many particulars are the sorts of things which are "visible" and "perceived with the senses."

Here is the exact wording: "These latter you could touch and see and perceive with the other senses, but those that always remain the same can only be grasped by the reasoning power of the mind? They are not seen but are invisible?" (79a). Now for the conclusion:

C1 Hence, it has been assumed in the previous discussion that there are "two sorts of existences": "the seen," which is "changing," and "the unseen," which is "unchanging."

That is, in Socrates's words again: "Do you then want us to assume two kinds of existences, the visible and the invisible?" (79a).

19.2.2 The affinities

So much for Part A of the Affinity Argument. With two separate orders of existence established—Forms and ordinary sensible things—the task of Part B is to make the case for assigning the soul and the body, the former to one, the latter to the other, of these two orders of existence. The argument continues as follows:

P5 The human being consists of two parts, the body and the soul.

This receives very little or no supporting argument. It is simply stated: "Now one part of ourselves is the body, another part is the soul?" (79c). So too the next premise:

P6 The soul is like the invisible and the body like the visible.

In the text: "So the soul is more like the invisible than the body, and the body more like the visible" (79b). The next premise is more complex:

P7 The soul *in the body, using the bodily sense organs*, apprehends changing particular things which are like the body but unlike the soul. Thus, the soul, whose objects are constantly changing, becomes subject to constant change (in beliefs) and error. But when the soul separates itself from the body as far as possible and remains *by itself* alone, it apprehends the unchanging (Forms) and is itself unchanging. (This is wisdom.)

This is the more or less explicit content of the following long but important passage:

Haven't we said some time ago that when the soul makes use of the body to investigate something, be it through hearing or seeing or some other sense—for to investigate something through the senses is to do it through the body—it is dragged by the body to the things that are never the same, and the soul itself strays and is confused and dizzy as if it were drunk, in so far as it is in contact with that kind of thing?

But when the soul investigates by itself it passes into the realm of what is pure, ever existing, immortal and unchanging, and being akin to this, it always stays with it whenever it is by itself and can do so; it ceases to stray and remains in the same state as it is in touch with things of the same kind, and its experience then is what is called wisdom? (79c–d)

A further premise is contained in Socrates's statement: "So the soul is more like the invisible than the body, and the body more like the visible?" (79c), that is:

P8   The soul is "like the unchangeable" and the body "like the changing."

Just one more premise is necessary before the conclusions of Part B can be drawn:

P9   The soul, being the natural ruler, "resembles the divine," the body, being the natural subject, "resembles the mortal."

This is the sense of the passage stating that "nature orders the one to be subject and to be ruled, and the other to rule and be master. Then again, which do you think is like the divine and which like the mortal? Do you not think that the nature of the divine is to rule and to lead, whereas it is that of the mortal to be ruled and be subject?" (80a). Now for the conclusions:

C2   The soul is in all respects considered like the Forms, the body like sensible particulars.

That is the first conclusion. In the text: "the soul is most like the divine, deathless, intelligible, uniform, indissoluble, always the same as itself, whereas the body is most like that which is human, mortal, multiform, unintelligible, soluble, and never consistently the same" (80a–b). The further conclusion that completes Part B is:

C3   It is therefore "not natural" for the soul to be dissolved.

In Socrates's words: "Well then, that being so, is it not natural for the body to dissolve easily, and for the soul to be altogether indissoluble, or nearly so?" (80b). This conclusion is presented as allaying the fears expressed by Cebes at 77b and 78c.

19.3 Pythagorean purification and immortality doctrines intellectualized

So far we have outlined the first two parts of the Affinity Argument. As already noted, Part C does not so much advance the argument as indulge in a quasi–Pythagorean–

Orphic speculation on the fate of 'purified' and "polluted and impure" (81b) souls after the death of the body. It is here that reward and punishment of souls come into the picture, that is, the second point mentioned in the *probandum* (see 19.1): "a much better future for the good than for the wicked" (63c).

This speculative flight of fancy combines (1) key elements of Orphic-Pythagorean religious belief with (2) certain features of Socratic intellectualism (see 12.9.2) and (3) Plato's own theory of Forms, resulting in that un-Socratic, thoroughly Platonic hybrid encountered earlier in the defence of the philosophic life: philosophy conceived as "practice for dying and death" or "training for death" (81a). Let us consider the individual elements of this heady witches' brew.

19.3.1 The Orphic-Pythagorean inheritance

The five key Orphic-Pythagorean elements in the third part of the Affinity Argument are the soul's (1) divinity, (2) transmigration, (3) corruption, (4) purification, and (5) release from the bodily prison (see above 14.6).

As we shall see in a moment, the third argument for immortality contains some pretty striking echoes of the Orphic-Pythagorean doctrine that the soul is a fallen divinity 'imprisoned' in a body. Moreover, a doctrine of metempsychosis or transmigration of souls, their reincarnation in other bodies, particularly animal bodies, is clearly in evidence. So too the notion of pollution or corruption of the soul by the body, together with the corresponding idea of purification, ridding the soul of the taint of the body through intellectual contemplation. Finally, we meet here again with the idea of the soul's ultimate release from the cycle of rebirth and disembodied existence once it has become pure. But all this is filtered through certain Socratic influences and doctrines of Plato's own, which we must now consider in detail. The net effect, as we have said, is to intellectualize the religious doctrine, "rational catharsis," as we have called it, borrowing a phrase from Werner Jaeger.

19.3.2 Socratic intellectualism

What is known as 'Socratic intellectualism' is usually encapsulated in the dictum 'Virtue is knowledge' (see 12.9.2). Like most 'isms,' 'intellectual*ism*' places a special emphasis on one side of a dichotomy. In this case, (a) the intellect or faculty of knowledge is assigned the chief role in the acquisition of moral virtue at the expense of (b) training or practice. The opposing viewpoint (for which no corresponding 'ism' exists) was memorably formulated by Aristotle: "where moral virtue is concerned," he wrote, "the most important thing is not to know what it is [the thesis of intellectualism], but how it arises [that is, how to inculcate it in individuals]; we do not wish to know what courage is, we wish to be courageous." Since, for Aristotle, moral virtue consists in certain ways of acting, the task of the moral teacher is to foster certain habitual behaviours in his pupils—not to enlighten them regarding the nature or meaning (definition) of 'courage,' 'temperance,' 'wisdom,' and so forth, but to make them courageous, temperate, and so on. From this perspective, the Socratic view is tantamount to claiming that once one has learned the principles of medicine or architecture one is already a doctor or an architect, even without practical experience of healing or building. Experience informs us that this is quite wrong in the case of medicine and architecture, and the same, Aristotle contends, is true of morality.

While this seems eminently sensible, it is not hard to see why, for the historical Socrates, the choice of a morally good life is simply a matter of knowing what is in one's own best interests, that is, knowing the answer to the question, Why be moral? As was shown in the previous part, Socrates was convinced that he who practised virtue could not fail to achieve happiness, while without it one could not but lead a life that, however pleasant, was essentially not worth living. To *know* this is simply to achieve practical or moral wisdom—as distinct from the sort of theoretical wisdom that comes of knowing what one knows and does not know or being able to define moral value terms correctly (see 9.1.5 above). On such knowledge all the other moral virtues (courage, temperance, justice, and piety) must follow; for the man who understands wherein true happiness consists will not fear death so much as loss of his moral integrity, will not seek to take advantage of others, but to deal justly with them, and so forth.

Clearly, Plato's conception of virtue as purification from the taint of the body through the exercise of reason in pure (sense-free) *knowledge* owes something to Socratic intellectualism. Indeed, this is just Socratic intellectualism taken to new extremes. Accordingly, it was suggested earlier (see 15.4.2) that Plato turns Socrates's teaching around: 'virtue is knowledge' becomes something very like 'knowledge is virtue'—whereby 'knowledge' now means, roughly, 'the intellectual contemplation of the Forms.' This goes well beyond anything found in Socrates, for whom concrete particular instances form the indispensable starting point and constant touchstone of the process of reasoning that gradually brings us closer to the essence or definition. Moreover, the rewards of virtue or knowledge are altogether different: happiness or fulfilment (*eudaimonia*) in *this* life for Socrates, the return of the purified soul to the realm of Forms after the death of the body for Plato. If this is not an apt description of Plato's moral theory as a whole, it at least describes the moral outlook of the *Phaedo*.

19.3.3 The Platonic synthesis

To see in more detail just how Plato transformed Pythagoreanism in accordance with Socratic intellectualism and his own theory of Forms, we can simply follow the outline of the central Orphic-Pythagorean doctrines given in 14.6 above.

(1) *Fallen Divinities.* In Plato, *reason*, understood as the capacity to grasp the other world of eternal and unchanging essences or Forms, becomes the *divine, the eternal element* in man. Yet the functioning of human reason is impaired by the *body* and the senses, by the *animal or temporal* (that is, mortal) element in man. So man is a being situated somewhere *between* the animal and the divine, striving upward, but always at risk of sinking downward to the sub-human or animal level.

(2) *Transmigration.* Through neglect of the divine element within them, human beings can *actually become animals* after the death of the body: human souls migrate to animal bodies.

(3) *Corruption.* The "greatest and most extreme evil" (83c), as Plato terms it, is the holding of false beliefs about what is truly existent. This is a striking intellectualization or "rational catharsis" of the Pythagorean teaching concerning evil.

(4) *Purification.* The exercise of reason in philosophical enquiry (withdrawing the soul from the bodily senses into rational contemplation of the Forms of things) becomes the chief means of purifying the soul (replacing meditation, austerities, observance of taboos, performance of purification rites, engaging in mathematical contemplation, and so on.)

(5) *Release.* Through such purification the soul can be released, can pass outside of time, into eternity to rejoin its objects, the Eternal Forms.

A single quotation will bear out the first three points regarding imprisonment, the corruption of the human soul by the human body, and the transmigration of souls:

> these [ghosts seen in graveyards] are not the souls of the good but of inferior men, which are forced to wander there, paying the penalty for their previous bad upbringing. They wander until their longing for that which accompanies them, the physical, again imprisons them in a body, and they are then, as is likely, bound to such characters as they have practised in their life ... Those, for example, who have carelessly practised gluttony, violence and drunkenness are likely to join the company of donkeys or of similar animals ... Those who have esteemed injustice highly, and tyranny and plunder, will join the tribes of wolves and hawks and kites ... And clearly, the destination of the others will conform to the way in which they have behaved. (81d–82a)

The meaning of this is plain enough. As for imprisonment and purification, there is the following passage:

> The lovers of learning [philosophers] know that when philosophy gets hold of their soul, it is imprisoned in and clinging to the body, and that it is forced to examine other things through it as through a cage and not by itself, and that it wallows in every kind of ignorance. Philosophy sees that the worst feature of this imprisonment is that it is due to desires, so that the prisoner himself is contributing to his own incarceration most of all. As I say, the lovers of learning know that philosophy gets hold of their soul when it is in that state, then gently encourages it and tries to free it by showing them that investigation through the eyes is full of

deceit, as is that through the ears and the other senses. Philosophy then persuades the soul to withdraw from the senses in so far as it is not compelled to use them and bids the soul to gather itself together by itself, to trust only itself. (82d–83a)

This is as harsh toward the senses as the previous passage was toward donkeys. (No one has ever accused the donkey of being a particularly noble mount, and its stubbornness is legendary. But violence and drunkenness?) In any case, we encounter here the same conception of philosophy as "practise for dying and death" (64a), for release from the body and the senses, first met with in the defence of the philosophic life. Finally, regarding intellectualism and release into the realm of the Forms, consider the following passage:

The soul of the philosopher achieves a calm from such emotions; it follows reason and ever stays with it contemplating the true, the divine, which is not the object of opinion. Nurtured by this, it believes that one should live in this manner as long as one is alive and, after death, arrive at what is akin and of the same kind, and escape from human evils. (84a–b)

19.4 Evaluation of the Affinity Argument

Like the Recollection Argument, the Affinity Argument takes a lot for granted, chiefly (1) that the soul is the person, so that the soul's survival is the survival of the person, and (2) the existence of Forms apart from the sensible particulars of which they are the essences, that is, "two sorts of existence," *two worlds* (see C1). It argues from the fact (see P6, P8, and P9) that the *soul–body relation* resembles the *Form–particulars relation* in *some* respects (for example, both are relations of the invisible to the visible), to the conclusion (C2) that the similarity holds in *all* respects, particularly in respect of (C3) deathlessness or immortality. The argument establishes its conclusions (C2 and C3) as no more than probable or likely (if its premises are true). So it is not a strictly deductive but a probable argument at best, the conclusion of which could (logically) be false even if all the premises were true.

The key prop on which the argument rests is the theory of Forms, the two-world metaphysics taken for granted in Part A. It is this which we must examine in the next chapter before considering, in the final chapter, what, if anything, we have learned from our analysis of Plato's arguments—apart from the fact that none of them actually proves very much at all, certainly not the immortality of the soul.

20

The Metaphysics of Form

20.1 Introductory

Having analyzed three of Plato's arguments for immortality, we must now consider the Forms whose existence is a key premise in the latter two. The full significance of Plato's theory of Forms is likely to become clearer if we examine it in the wider context of the distinctively Greek *metaphysics of form* that evolved during the classical period, culminating in Aristotle's theory. While finite form was the guiding idea of being throughout ancient Greek metaphysics—indeed ancient Greek culture—as a whole (see 4.9), later epochs were to understand being and the metaphysical science of being in fundamentally different ways. Still, the metaphysics of form is a good starting point from which to develop a *working definition of metaphysics* for use in subsequent parts of this work (see 20.7).

20.2 The sources of our knowledge of the origin of the theory of Forms

Relatively little is known about the exact problems and puzzles—whether in logic, mathematics, moral philosophy, or all three—that induced Plato to erect the theory of Forms as the chief pillar of his philosophical system. Lacking decisive testimony on the precise nature of the difficulties the theory was designed to clear up, all we can say with confidence is that considerations *like* those to be presented at the end of this chapter (see 20.11–14) probably played a key role in its formation. However, the whole matter must remain somewhat controversial, rational reconstruction being the best anyone can do.

Aside from (1) Plato's own middle period and late dialogues, our main source is again (2) Aristotle. The first book of the *Metaphysics* lists (and dismisses) five Platonic arguments for the existence of Forms. Elsewhere in the first book, and again in the thirteenth, Aristotle fleshes out the first argument, suggesting some historical influences upon it. In addition, there is (3) a lost Aristotelian treatise entitled *On Ideas*, part of which was paraphrased by an early-third-century AD Peripatetic, Alexander of Aphrodisias, in his commentary on Aristotle's *Metaphysics*. Here all five arguments reappear under the same titles. Much of the detail omitted by Aristotle in the *Metaphysics* (presumably because he had already written on the subject elsewhere) is restored from the lost work, to which Alexander apparently still had access. The Platonic arguments are set out schematically, with Aristotle typically showing, first, (i) that they *do not prove enough* (since they in fact demonstrate the existence only of immanent, not of transcendent universals or Platonic Forms), then (ii) that they *prove too much* (since, if valid, they would establish, along with the desired types of Forms, others that the Platonists do not countenance). In one case, Aristotle shows that an argument for Forms (iii) leads to an infinite regress. Clearly, (ii) is an example of what we earlier called 'a good *ad hominem* argument' (see 7.7.1), while (iii) amounts, as was also noted earlier (see 7.7.2), to a charge of circularity, an infinite regress being circular in a certain way. However, the problems of interpretation to which Alexander's paraphrase gives rise are formidable. Instead of simply following the texts of Aristotle or Alexander, therefore, we shall do better to set out the problems and evaluate Plato's solution in contemporary terms—though always with an eye to the ancient sources.

20.3 Anachronism

Taking this approach, we shall sooner or later have to face the objection that some of the problems identified cannot possibly have been on Plato's mind when he first formulate the theory of Forms, either because he only became interested in such issues later in his career, as can be seen from subsequent dialogues, or because the concepts and distinctions involved only emerged much later in the history of philosophy, perhaps as recently as the twentieth century. The objection, in short, is *anachronism*: reading *back* (Greek: *ana*) into an earlier *time* (*chronos*) or phase of a philosopher's career various concepts, distinctions, and problems that belong to a later stage in the development of the discipline or of that particular thinker.

This is a serious charge. Yet anachronism does not result simply from *applying* our own tools of analysis—say, the distinction between the normative and the descriptive dimensions of the eudaemonist principle (see 10.3)—to the thought of an earlier age, but rather from *attributing* those very concepts, distinctions, and problems to the author or period we are attempting to understand. So we can freely grant that our way of presenting the considerations that led to the theory of Forms is not exactly Plato's, nor yet Aristotle's or Alexander's—and still claim to understand Plato, perhaps better than he understood himself! Kant had some inkling of this possibility when he wrote that "it is by no means unusual, upon comparing the thought which an author has expressed in regard to his subject, whether in ordinary conversation or in writing, to find that we understand him better than he has understood himself." As it happens, Kant was speaking of Plato's theory of Forms in the passage from which this is taken; but his point is a general one that applies to the study of intellectual history as a whole.

Our aim in what follows, then, is to understand Plato better than he understood himself, if possible, employing for the purpose philosophical distinctions and logical tools of analysis, some of later, some of very recent, date, in order to shed light on the partially unstated problems to which the theory of Forms is Plato's brilliant but flawed solution. Many of the relevant logical tools were set out in chapter 7. The intent is *not* to suggest that Plato himself was cognizant of our concepts and distinctions, or that he would have seen any need for them had they been explained to him—although the latter possibility cannot be excluded either. In passing from exposition (always the first step!) to evaluation of the theory of Forms, the approach will be the same. There is no need to worry about objections that run: "Plato is not liable to that criticism since no one in his day drew the distinctions on which it is based." Philosophically, the objection is entirely beside the point, while, historically, there is more to understanding a great dead author than grasping the meaning he intended his writings to convey to contemporary readers. That is a worthwhile task, to be sure, but historical understanding does not stop there.

20.4 The two-world metaphysics

Our starting point is the Affinity Argument of the previous chapter. The upshot of Part A was the contrast between "two sorts of existence" or beings, that is, the existence of another world beyond this, a "place beyond the heavens," as Plato calls it (*Phaedrus*, 247c), populated by separately existing distinct universals or Forms.

20.4.1 Characteristics of Forms

As described in detail in the third argument for immortality, Forms possess the following salient characteristics, all of which are directly traceable to the poem of Parmenides:

1 divine;
2 immortal (literally: 'deathless,' 'undying');
3 intelligible, that is, knowable only by thought or reasoning, not by means of the senses;
4 incorporeal or immaterial;
5 uniform (literally: 'single-formed'), that is, simple, without inner differentiation: they are what they are *in all respects, thoroughly and perfectly* (unadulterated);
6 indissoluble, that is, indestructible, imperishable, not susceptible to corruption or decay;

7 unchangeable, that is, not capable of any form of change or alteration, strictly immutable.

All these characteristics figure at some point in the Affinity Argument. Which are basic, which derivative, is hard to say. Is 2 a consequence of 1, or are divinity and immortality *mutually* entailing properties? If passing away or perishing is just one particular kind of change, then is 6 a consequence of 7? Be that as it may, 3 (non-sensible or intelligible), 4 (incorporeal), and 7 (unchanging) tend to be given pride of place in most scholars' enumerations of the essential properties of the Forms, along with this further characteristic, arguably the most important of all:

8 separateness, existing "by itself" or "itself by itself."

More will be said of 8 in the next sub-section. The first seven characteristics are sometimes referred to as the *essential* (or 'categorial') properties of Forms, meaning that they belong to all Forms simply *as* Forms. However, two *functional* characteristics identified earlier as belonging to Socratic definitions characterize Platonic Forms as well. For one thing, Forms

9 serve as standards or yardsticks,

'paradigms,' as Plato calls them; they allow us to settle definitively any doubts or differences of opinion that may arise about whether this or that is a bona fide instance of (say) justice (see 11.5.1). Yet unlike weights and measures, which are just as tangible or sensible as those things to which they permit us to assign definite weights and dimensions, the Forms are *non*-sensible standards or exemplars. Furthermore, like the real essences captured in Socratic definitions, Forms

10 *make* the individuals, of which they are the Forms, the sorts of things they are.

In speaking of Socratic definitions, this final feature was summed up in the phrase 'because and only because.' It leads Plato to posit a special type of *causal* relationship between Forms and particulars. In view of these functional characteristics, scholars are apt to say (following Plato) that particular things *depend* (causally) on the corresponding Forms for their being and their intelligibility. Or, in the terms of chapters 3 and 4, sensible particulars depend on Forms both in the order of being and in the order of knowing.

These two functional characteristics go a long way toward explaining the epistemological and metaphysical 'work' Plato intended the theory of Forms to do. As for the essential or categorial features, they could quite easily have been 'read off,' so to speak, from Parmenides's great poem, where they already figure as the marks or characteristics of true being.

20.4.2 Forms and particulars

Though listed among the characteristics of the Platonic Forms, separateness (8) is not so much one property among others as that which makes the Forms more than just universal properties of things, namely *universal things* having properties and relations of their own, *substances* existing in their own right. Like the essences described in Socratic definitions, Forms exist (a) immanently in the particular things whose essences they are (so the Final Argument of the *Phaedo*). They are accordingly real properties, or rather the essences, of such things. Yet each Form exists also (b) transcendently, apart from all sensible things, as a separate, universal entity "itself by itself" (Affinity Argument). Aristotle's word for this is *choris* (separate). Moreover, the Forms exist (c) in the human mind, though only traces of them are actually discerned there until such time as the mind turns its attention to the traces within, enlivening them by focusing its rational gaze upon them (Recollection Argument). Still, for Plato, both *mental* existence—the *only* existence assigned universals by conceptualists (see 4.8)—and *real* existence outside the mind in sensible things depend upon the real and *separate* existence of the Forms in a transcendent realm.

In addition to Forms populating this transcendent realm of true or perfect being, there *exists* (in another sense) the world that we ourselves inhabit, the world made up of those particular sensible things that most people believe to be the only things that are. They too can be said to *be*—despite Parmenides's arguments to the contrary (see 5.6 and 20.10.2). Yet they exist only imperfectly and dependently, owing to that functional characteristic of Forms noted in 10 above. Thus, for example, all equal things exist as 'taking part in' the separately existing Form of Equality; and similarly, just actions, men, laws, constitutions, and states exist by 'participating' in the separately existing Form of Justice—much as beautiful robes, temples, statues, and human bodies all depend for their being on the separately existing Form of Beauty itself. These particulars can be described in ways contradictorily opposed to the Forms: (1) not divine, that is, secular or profane; (2) not immortal, in other words, temporal and perishable; (3) non-intelligible, but sensible; (4) corporeal or material (with the exception of particular immaterial souls); (5) not uniform, but multiform and varied; (6) not indissoluble, but dissoluble, capable of breaking up; (7) not immutable, but changeable and constantly changing. They make up a second, immanent realm of being, one that is (8) dependent on the transcendent Forms in two ways: such entities can neither (9) be understood nor (10) be or exist apart from the Forms.

20.4.3 Forms and metaphysics

The exact relationship between universal Forms and sensible particulars proved an intractable problem for Plato, necessitating revisions of the theory that are beyond the scope of the present chapter. The terms used in the previous paragraph, 'participation,' 'taking part in,' and 'depend upon' are vague; Plato recognized their inadequacy and tried to remedy it without ever abandoning the theory of Forms. The question with which we shall be concerned in this chapter is only, What sorts of considerations may have led Plato to embrace this theory so wholeheartedly at the time of the *Phaedo*? The source of the misgivings he was to have later on, and the later stages in the evolution of the theory itself, form a separate topic that can be left aside here.

As we know only too well by now, a theory like that just described, a theory about (1) *what there is, what exists, what is real*, whether perfectly or only imperfectly so, and about (2) what depends upon what for its being and (3) for its being known, is called 'metaphysics.' A good deal was said on the subject already in chapters 3 and 4, although at that stage we focused primarily on (2) the order of being and (3) the order of knowing, neglecting the prior question (1), What is there? What exists? Of course, that question was always implicit, since reductive or eliminative forms of idealism and realism are just efforts to revise our commonsense inventory of the universe, our 'ontology,' as philosophers say.

Before examining the arguments that persuaded Plato of the metaphysical theory of Forms, it may be useful to consider again the nature of metaphysics, this time from a more historical perspective. As far as the theory of Forms goes, the next two sections are dispensable, and anyone eager to get on with the consideration of Plato's doctrine should proceed straight to the working definition of 'metaphysics' in 20.7. The task of these historical remarks is to distinguish as carefully as possible between the original Aristotelian matrix of metaphysics and various subsequent accretions, so that when we mix Aristotelian and later elements, as we must in order to arrive at a suitable working definition of metaphysics, we shall at least not be guilty of having confounded them anachronistically.

20.5 Metaphysics as 'beyond physics'

The exact origins of the word 'metaphysics' are obscure, but the Greek expression from which our word derives may go back as far as the direct pupils of Aristotle, the earliest so-called Peripatetics (see 2.1). Literally, *ta meta ta physika* means 'the things after (or beyond) the physical things.' Given its nominal meaning (see 1.2.3 and 3.2), the expression was quite naturally taken to refer either to (a) the *studies* that come *after* those devoted to changing sensible or material things (*ta physika*), or (b) a *realm* of supersensible entities existing *beyond* place and time, if not (c) both. But at the end of the eighteenth century the idea got started that the name originated in (d) the canonical ordering of Aristotle's works by a first-century BC Peripatetic editor who placed certain writings that seemed to fit nowhere else 'after the physical works.' At a loss to find a descriptive title for their contents, he simply named them for the place he had assigned them in the Aristotelian corpus. This view, which is now no longer defended, became widely influential, partly because the writings in question deal even more with sensible than with supersensible things, but mainly because Aristotle himself never used the expression (1) 'metaphysics,' preferring the following designations: (2) 'first philosophy,' (3) 'theology,' (4) 'wisdom,' and (5) 'the science of being *qua* being.' (The Latin *qua* translates a Greek word meaning 'as' or 'under the aspect of.')

To make sense of this we must review rapidly (i) the astronomical picture of the world and (ii) the account of the causes of the motions of the heavens found in natural, or what Aristotle called 'second,' philosophy, a connected series of treatises that includes his *Physics*. For the conception of divinity described earlier as having originated with Aristotle (see 5.5.3) was embedded in a theological cosmology apart from which the names for this Aristotelian science are not readily understandable.

20.5.1 The universe and the causes of motion

The universe for Aristotle—as indeed for medieval and Renaissance thinkers right down to Copernicus (1473–1543)—was a finite spherical plenum, a bounded material continuum without any void. 'Bounded,' of course, only in space; for the same universe is *un*bounded in time, being in sempiternal regular motion without beginning or end (see 16.5.1 on sempiternity). At its circumference are the celestial bodies, the heavenly spheres of pure aether, as Aristotle called the fifth material element whose nature it is to move in a circle. The rotational motion of the outermost sphere, the *primum mobile* ('first moving thing' or 'first heaven'), causes the daily rotation of all the other heavenly spheres nested concentrically within it. Next to this outermost sphere, in which the fixed stars are set, come the spheres of the planets, one inside the other, beginning with the sphere of the sun. To every basic motion observable in the heavens, there corresponds a sphere—either fifty-five or forty-nine in total according to the best astronomical reckoning of the day. At the centre of the whole universe, perfectly motionless or at rest, is the earth, the terrestrial or sublunar realm composed of the four traditional elements, earth, water, fire, and air. While the whole celestial realm is immune to change or decay, the four sublunar elements are naturally corruptible and constantly destroyed, that is, transmuted into one another.

Such, in simplified terms, is (i) the world picture at which Aristotle arrived by giving a straight physical interpretation to the mathematical model by which others had succeeded in reducing the apparently irregular motions of the sun, moon, and planets to the uniform rotations of multiple spheres. As for (ii) the causes of celestial motion, each heavenly sphere was conceived much in the manner of the first Ionians, as a living, divine animal, its imperishable celestial body conjoined to an immaterial soul or intelligent mover. So—leaving aside the device by which Aristotle prevents the motion of each sphere from carrying through to all those inside it—the whole animated heaven is moved in daily rotation by the conjoined mover of the outermost sphere, while each sphere within moves with its own proper motion owing to a conjoined Intelligence or mover. As for the outermost sphere itself, it must either be moved by a self-moving conjoined mover that is not moved by anything else, like the immanent World Soul of Plato and the Platonists (see 16.2), or else by a transcendent Unmoved First Mover beyond the first heaven, as Aristotle and the Peripatetic tradition held (see 5.3.3).

Now each conjoined mover or divine soul is conceived as separate from the celestial sphere that it moves by intelligent desire; each is, in other words, an incorporeal *substance*, an entity in its own right. Yet the soul of every living substance is the *form* of its body according to Aristotelian natural philosophy (see 27.9.2 on the Aristotelian conception of man). So these separate souls are both substances and forms. Now in Plato, as we have seen, 'form' indeed designates a substance, an absolutely permanent, completely real, unchanging, and indestructible thing. In Aristotle, by contrast, a form—for example the soul of a living being—is *not* normally a thing or substance, but rather a constitutive *principle* of a substance, its immanent principle of actuality or *relative* permanence (its essence), as distinct from its matter, the correlative principle of potentiality for change (see 20.6.4). So what is true of soul as the principle of life, sentience, and intelligence in living plants, animals, and humans manifestly does not hold when it comes to the immaterial souls or Intelligences that move the heavenly spheres: the latter are *pure* forms without matter, that is, *perfectly actual* and immaterial *substances*; lacking all potentiality for change or decay, they are absolutely permanent and immobile. And that, in the context of Aristotle's natural philosophy, is odd, to say the least.

Are the divine soul substances of Aristotle's cosmology just the last remnants of those Platonic Forms to which our human souls are alleged to be akin owing to their divine origin? It is difficult to say with confidence, although Plato's otherworldly tendencies seem to be more in evidence here than anywhere else in Aristotle. This much, though, seems clear: the relation of each mover to its celestial body being roughly analogous to that of the soul of a living and intelligent human being to its organic body, the divine movers are conceived quasi-anthropomorphically, as moving their bodies in sempiternal rotational motion by the knowledge and desire they have of something higher and better toward which they strive, namely the activity of the First Unmoved Mover. However, this final piece of the theory belongs to metaphysics rather than physics.

20.5.2 Physics and metaphysics

The Aristotelian science of *physics* takes as its starting point (a) the observable motions of sensible things, celestial and terrestrial. Through rational reflection on the conceptual difficulties attending the alternative, it establishes that (b) the process of change or motion in the material cosmos must be sempiternal. On this basis it then reasons to (c) the existence of sempiternal causes of such motion. Having established the *existence* of the conjoined movers and the First Unmoved Mover, the task of physics is complete. Consideration of (d) their *mode of operation* belongs to metaphysics. Recapitulating the proof of existence in the *Metaphysics*, Aristotle shows that the First Unmoved Mover moves the others in the manner of an end or goal of intelligent action, a purposive (teleological) rather than what is called an efficient or productive cause of motion. It is as though the eternal rotation of the animated heavens sprang from the intelligent desire to emulate as far as possible the absolute perfection of the sempiternally unchanging activity of the First Unmoved Mover. For not only does the First Mover not 'act' upon anything (except as the goal of its intelligent striving), but nothing can be the object of the activity of this supremely perfect living Intelligence *except itself*. 'Thought thinking itself': that is the baffling—not to say grotesque—way in which Aristotle conceived god.

In the Christian Middle Ages, with the ascendancy of the idea of creation *ex nihilo*, this Aristotelian First Mover was transmuted into the first efficient or productive cause of the existence of all things. Thus, Aristotle's conception of the divine as perfectly actualized or absolutely immutable essence, as completely determinate or *finite form*, yielded to Aquinas's notion of God as *infinite existence*. For Aquinas (see 4.9), God *is* existence and the ultimate cause or source of everything in the universe that merely *has* existence. Finally, the supremely aloof and totally self-absorbed god of Aristotle was merged not just into the Wise Creator of the book of Genesis, but also into the God of Abraham, Isaac, and Jacob, indeed into the Loving Father of the Christian scriptures as well. Whether such a synthesis of the so-called God of the Philosophers with the God of revealed scripture can ever succeed—without serious detriment to both philosophy and religion—is a good question. In any case, the effort resulted in momentous changes that transformed metaphysics itself, as we shall see in the course of the next section.

20.5.3 Names for metaphysics

According to Aristotle, it is in physics that we first reason from observable motion or change in the terrestrial and celestial realms to the existence of the supersensible causes studied in metaphysics. Although metaphysics thus comes 'after physics' *for us*, that is, both in the order of learning and in the actual history of what Aristotle calls 'science,' *in itself*, that is, in Aristotle's ranking of the scientific disciplines, metaphysics is 'higher' or 'prior' to physics and all other theoretical disciplines owing to the special dignity of its object, the supersensible divine. What was later called (1) 'metaphysics' is thus *in itself* the 'first' science of all, (2) 'first philosophy.' Moreover, since the first or ultimate causes of motion are divine, Aristotle calls this science (3) 'theology.' Finally, since the man who seeks wisdom wishes to understand the first causes and principles of things, and since first philosophy alone deals with ultimate causes and reasons for everything, this science is called (4) 'wisdom.' These relations of priority and posteriority were presumably not lost on that Peripatetic editor who placed the writings making up the *Metaphysics* after the physical treatises. And indeed, metaphysics has always been so called chiefly on account of its distinctive content or subject matter. That much is clear. Less clear, as we shall see in the next section, is the precise nature of its subject matter.

20.6 Ontology, theology, and the science of causes and first principles

From the foregoing it might seem almost as though the subject matter of first philosophy were confined to the supersensible substances considered in the late books of Aristotle's *Metaphysics*. But in fact the middle books develop a far more detailed account of the being of changing sensible substances composed of both matter and form. Moreover, the earlier books stress over and over again that this science seeks to understand the constitutive principles or causes of the being of *all* beings, sensible *and* supersensible, of being as such or in totality. Hence the final designation used by Aristotle: (5) 'the science of being *qua* being.' The question of its relationship to 'theology' sheds valuable light on one of the most important developments to occur in the later metaphysical tradition, the separation of general and special metaphysics. For purposes of arriving at a working definition of metaphysics, we shall have to consider a few other post-Aristotelian changes in the conception of the subject matter of metaphysics as well.

20.6.1 Metaphysics as onto-theology

Metaphysics, according to Aristotle, is both (1) the most universal science, the science of *all* being, and (2) the highest science, the one that treats of the *highest domain* of being, the supersensible divine. From the eighteenth century on, (1) was known as 'ontology' and divorced from (2) theology, or 'rational theology' as (2) came to be called in order to distinguish it from revealed theology, the science of sacred scripture.

In favour of this terminological innovation it must be said that metaphysics or first philosophy appears in one light when understood as (1) the all-encompassing *universal science* of being *in general* (as distinct from all those particular sciences that hive off some compartment of reality for separate study), and in a very different light when understood as (2) the *highest science* (as distinct from all those that study some domain of being other than the divine). Against any such distinction between (1) *general* metaphysics, the science of being *qua* being, and (2) *special* metaphysics, the science of supersensible being, stands only the fact that it has no basis in the texts of Aristotle, who used 'theology' and the other designations considered in the previous section for both types of enquiry without distinction.

Consideration of other theoretical sciences may help clarify what is meant by a 'universal' and a 'special' science. In its specialized sub-disciplines Aristotelian *natural philosophy* treats of sensible things or substances, terrestrial and celestial, and those in between, the meteorological phenomena, reasoning from these to the sempiternal existence of the supersensible substances studied in metaphysics. By contrast, *mathematics*, the chief branches of which are arithmetic, geometry, astronomy, optics, harmonics, and mechanics, investigates only the non-sensible, unchanging quantitative attributes and relations of substances (number and dimension), considering them in the abstract, apart from the concrete particular things or substances whose attributes and relations they are. Unlike both these special sciences, first philosophy or *metaphysics* investigates (a) material or sensible and (b) immaterial or supersensible beings, including both (c) those beings that are substances, that is, things capable of existing in their own right, and (d) all those that are not substances, those which can only exist or be 'in' substances, never in their own right. Metaphysics is accordingly (1) the universal science of being *qua* being or ontology, as it was later called. Yet it must be constantly borne in mind that this most universal science is, for Aristotle himself, *at the very same time* the study of those beings that 'are' in the fullest and primary sense, the fully actual, absolutely permanent and unchanging divine beings. Metaphysics, in short, is (2) theology. In studying being in its most perfect or primary instance, one is—somehow—studying being *as* being, the being of *all* beings. The universal science of being *just is* the highest science, for Aristotle, the science that goes beyond (transcends) the temporal, sensible world to the sempiternal, supersensible divine, disclosing the attributes of the separate Intelligences that move the heavenly spheres and of the First Unmoved Mover. For Aristotle and his Greek successors, these two aspects of metaphysics were indissolubly one.

This peculiarity has been a source of puzzlement right down through the history of metaphysics. Heidegger's intent was not so much to dispel as to enshrine the puzzle when he coined the expression "the onto[logical]-theological constitution of metaphysics" to describe the unresolved *problem* of metaphysics that the west inherited from Aristotle. At the very least it is a handy device by which to recall the dual nature of Aristotelian metaphysics; at most, it is an illuminating attempt to understand a thinker better than he understood himself, introducing distinctions that were unknown to, and would probably have been regarded as unhelpful in, his own time.

20.6.2 Metaphysics as the science of axioms or first principles

The distinction between theology or special metaphysics and ontology or general metaphysics is just the first of several post-Aristotelian distinctions that have to be incorporated into the original Aristotelian matrix if we are to arrive at a serviceable working definition of 'metaphysics.' With reference to this first distinction it should be pointed out that while metaphysics always remained (a) the universal science of being *qua* being, concerned with absolutely everything that is, substances and non-substances, sensible and non-sensible beings, there was a marked tendency in modern philosophy to stress special metaphysics, the study of supersensible being, at the expense of general metaphysics. In the period between Descartes and Kant, moreover, (b) rational psychology and (c) rational theology were separated as autonomous sub-disciplines of special metaphysics. For the human soul, too, is a particular non-sensible or supersensible being. Around the same time various problems that Aristotle had treated in the non-empirical portions of natural philosophy came to form a third sub-discipline of special metaphysics, (d) rational cosmology.

This is the fourfold conception of metaphysics inherited by Kant from his immediate predecessors. Like them, he understood all four branches of metaphysics as concerned only with first principles, that is, with basic (underived) truths known independently of the senses. (Thus, for example, rational psychology and physics contain the first principles of empirical psychology and empirical physics.) This idea, too, has an Aristotelian pedigree. For apart from (1) being *qua* being and (2) the divine, Aristotle's first philosophy also investigates (3) axioms or principles, notably the so-called principle of contradiction (roughly, the principle that 'the same thing cannot both be and not be at the same time in the same respect,' later reinterpreted as the principle of *non*-contradiction and formalized as: 'A is not not-A' or 'not [*p* and not-*p*].' See 6.3.1, 7.10, 25.5). Such principles are 'primary,' 'universal,' and 'unchanging'—the hallmarks of the metaphysical for Aristotle, whence (3) is at bottom no more separable from (1) and (2) than these from each other according to Aristotle. This third aspect of metaphysical enquiry was to become the dominant one for Descartes and Kant, and that means for modern philosophy as a whole. As we shall see in Part Four, Hume uses the word 'metaphysics' *exclusively* in the sense of (3) a science of first principles. From his perspective, the first principles of knowledge are basic psychological laws or principles of human nature. Thus, psychological enquiries into the first causes of human knowledge and belief are 'metaphysical' enquiries in Hume's idiosyncratic sense of that term (see 6.4.2 and 28.6). Other modern thinkers retained more of the old Aristotelian conception of metaphysics than did Hume. Thus, Sartre, whom we shall study in Part Five, calls his philosophy an 'ontology,' by which he means a study of the *being* of man as distinct from all the particular sciences that study some aspect of human nature. Still, generally speaking, both (1) ontology and (2) theology recede into the background behind the (3) science of first principles for most moderns, mainly owing to Descartes's having declared his inability to make any sense of a general science of being and Kant's assault on the whole idea of scientific knowledge of the supersensible. At the same time, principles of *being* tended to recede as principles of *knowledge* came to the fore—but that is another story, involving a new guiding idea of being (see 4.9 above on the *ens cognitum*, and 22.2 below).

20.6.3 Existence and essence

In order to arrive at a working definition of 'metaphysics' we must incorporate still further more or less un-Aristotelian distinctions into the original Aristotelian matrix. Apart from the division between a general and a threefold special metaphysics, the distinction between existence and essence—that is, between what there is, what exists, what is real or actual, and the natures or essences of things—was to become increasingly important. While not foreign to Aristotle, it is still only tangential to his conception of first philosophy, which, as we saw, is sharply focused upon finite form or essence in its treatment of both sensible and supersensible things. Still, unless we put this distinction to work, we can hardly understand those developments of the Christian Middle Ages described at the end of the last section; nor, for that matter, can we make sense of the attempts to prove the existence of the external (material) world that abound in the metaphysics of the seventeenth and eighteenth centuries.

In the post-Aristotelian tradition, then, metaphysical discussion focused increasingly on the question, (A) What is there? What exists? What is real? Of course, this too has roots in Aristotle, who, in the physics and again in the metaphysics, reasoned from the sempiternal existence of changing sensible things to that of unchanging supersensible causes, including the First Unmoved Mover. Discussion of proofs of God's existence was to occupy a considerable place in both medieval and modern metaphysics. As for the existence of the external world, this is something it had never occurred to Aristotle or the medievals to demonstrate, though Descartes and Kant devised intricate proofs that became the focus of much metaphysical debate for centuries to come. That is not to say that questions regarding the existence of sensible things are a new feature of metaphysics. As we have seen, Plato laboured to anchor the shadowy being of sensible things in the solid existence of Forms, swelling our commonsense ontology by the addition of a whole realm of supersensible entities; and even before Plato, Parmenides shrank drastically the number of entities of all kinds—to just *one* on most interpretations, to *zero* on the view to be taken later (see 20.10.2). So even though Aristotle himself had no conception of a separate metaphysical discipline concerned with existence and what there is, such questions occupy a very important place in metaphysics before, after, and even *in* Aristotle, especially if we consider his implicit critique of Parmenides and Plato.

20.6.4 The concept of a cause

Apart from the question (A), What is there? What exists? What is real? metaphysics has always concerned itself with the problem (B), What does the reality of the real *depend* upon? This can be rephrased as: What are the *causes* of being, of the real? Yet in the medieval period, 'cause' too began to be understood differently than in Aristotle. Among thinkers for whom it was a matter of faith or divinely revealed truth that God brought the created universe into being 'out of nothing,' the notion of productive or efficient causality could not help but loom much larger than for Aristotle, for whom cosmic change was sempiternal. Thus, 'cause' came to denote *primarily* causes in our sense, that is, *efficient causes*, as when one entity (be it substance or a property) depends on another for its existence, its generation, or coming to be. This is the way in which finite material and thinking things depend on God for their existence according to the creation story accepted by Christian philosophers right down to the eighteenth century; and it is in this way that the key problem of mind–body union and interaction was posed throughout modern philosophy. Mind and body interact so as to produce changes in each other, and the metaphysical problem that stubbornly resisted solution is: How can things so different enter into causal transactions with one another at all? (see 27.10).

For Aristotle, by contrast, 'cause' in its main metaphysical use denotes certain *principles*, the forms of things and their matter. Both formal and material causes are really present *in* sensible things. Though different from one another, these immanent or inherent causes are nevertheless not separate entities, like the parts of a composite thing. They are rather complementary non-entitative principles into which the *being* of such entities is analyzable in thought, though not divisible in fact. The formal cause is just the immanent essence after which Socrates was enquiring, *what* a thing is; its matter or material cause, on the other hand, is the principle of change or becoming, that which accounts for its being capable of receiving and losing its relatively permanent form (as it comes to be or perishes) or various transient forms (in undergoing other kinds of change). 'Cause' in a sense altogether different from either (i) efficient/productive, (ii) formal, or (iii) material cause is the First Unmoved Mover towards which the separate Intelligences strive. This sort of (iv) purposive or final cause occupies a special place in Aristotelian metaphysics. However, it is by no means restricted to those fully actual supersensible Intelligences that are pure form without matter, being found in sensible things as well. In them formal and final cause simply coincide: the same formal principle that makes something an actual, fully determinate entity of this or that kind also makes it a complete entity, fully actualized, and hence good in its kind: a fully grown oak tree, for example, or a wooden table good for eating or writing at. Earlier a science that employs final or purposive causes was called 'teleological' (see 5.5.3). Such are opposed to the so-called mechanical sciences, which rely exclusively on efficient or productive causes. Modern science, of course, consists entirely of the latter. But then its aims are entirely different from those of Greek and medieval metaphysics, which sought to comprehend the causes, not so much of existence or coming to be and change, as of being in the sense of the abiding natures and the inherent goodness of things. The problems began when, in the later Middle Ages, formal and final causes began to be invoked not so much to account for the uniformity, order, and apparent finality observable in nature as a whole, as to provide explanations of motion and change in particular sensible things. This indeed proved an obstacle to scientific progress in the successful provision of mechanical explanations of particular natural phenomena.

20.6.5 Aristotle's four causes

Thus, 'dependence upon a cause,' which Aristotle understood in terms of *four* causes, was gradually whittled down until, in modern metaphysics, efficient causality became the sole admissible sense of 'cause' and 'the study of first causes.' There is no need to comment further on the decisive role of the Christian doctrine of creation and the rise of modern mechanistic science in all this. While the medievals at least retained the other types along with efficient causality, Descartes and the seventeenth century banished formal and final causes altogether, both as unscientific (which they are, in the modern sense of 'scientific') and as a bar to scientific progress (which they had become, through misuse).

Consideration of these developments has brought us to one of Aristotle's most famous doctrines, the so-called four causes. Elaborated in the physical works dealing with the becoming of things, the doctrine is also germane to the account of the causes or principles of being in Aristotelian metaphysics. In conclusion, let us sketch the doctrine as applied to both the being and the becoming of artefacts and natural entities.

First, what did Aristotle mean by a causal account of the being of things, say, an artefact such as a house or a natural entity like an oak tree? In one way, the very notion of a causal account of the *being* of things is alien to us. However, seen in the light of our ordinary way of understanding artefacts and natural entities, Aristotle's analysis is perfectly commonsensical and familiar. Take, for example, a house. Like Aristotle, we understand its being in terms of four factors: (1) the material out of which it is constructed—the beams, bricks, mortar, and so on (material cause); (2) the structure or arrangement of these materials, with foundations supporting the walls, walls the roof, and so on (formal cause); (3) its purpose, what such a thing is good for, namely to serve as shelter (final cause); and, lastly, what brought it into being, the builder who arranges the materials according to a plan (efficient cause). The corresponding analysis of an oak tree is: (1) material constituents (roots, wood, bark, leaves, sap, and so on); (2) its structure, the arrangement of these materials, with roots in the earth, leaves in the sunlight, and so on; (3) its functioning well as a distinctive living entity, a normal, healthy oak tree; and, lastly, (4) its parent oak tree, from which came the acorn out of which the new tree grew.

The causes of being function in the analysis of the coming into being of the house or the oak tree as well. The builder must supply the materials of which the house is to consist and arrange them in the structure it is to have so as to serve its purpose as a shelter. And the parent oak tree must produce an acorn that can differentiate into the material constituents of the new tree, arranged in proper order or structure so as to allow the new oak tree to function well as a healthy normal specimen of its kind. That this commonsensical way of looking at artefacts and natural entities should have been so decried in the seventeenth century is only comprehensible in terms of the misuses to which it had been put outside metaphysics.

20.7 A working definition of 'metaphysics'

Basing our definition loosely on the original sense of 'first philosophy' in the ancient and medieval Aristotelian tradition, but looking back to Plato and Parmenides and ahead to Descartes, Kant and Hume, we can now define metaphysics this way:

The philosophical study of *being* in general (of the *existence* and nature or *essence* of things), that is, the study of the being of *all* beings, but especially of the existence and essence of the *supersensible* or *immaterial* (for example, God and the human soul), and of *first principles*.

According to this working definition, the following are metaphysical questions:

1 Do the essences of things exist independently of the things whose essences they are?

To this question Plato answered 'yes,' even going so far as to claim that these Forms are the *only* perfect entities or true beings, and elaborating a theory as to what their reality or being consists in: oneness, permanence, unchangeableness, intelligibility, uniformity, and so forth. This was a departure from the immanent realism of Socrates, into which Aristotle breathed new life through the introduction of the form–matter couplet and the doctrine of the four causes. And it is even further removed from the negative answer furnished by nominalists and conceptualists, for whom universal essences are nothing real apart from ourselves, neither immanent nor transcendent, but features either of our thought and of our language, or of our language but not our thought (see chapter 4). It is Plato's answer to this question that is to occupy us in the present chapter.

2 Does God exist?

As we have seen, the question of the existence of an extra-mundane First Unmoved Mover was already a central concern in Aristotle. It took on new significance in the Christian Middle Ages, dominating modern philosophy in the seventeenth and eighteenth centuries as well. We shall examine some typical proofs of God's existence when we come to Descartes and Hume.

3 Is there anything in man, in human nature, which is immaterial (an immaterial soul), and if so, is it capable of existing *without* the material body (immortality)?

This is the central issue of the *Phaedo*, and will again figure quite prominently in Descartes's *Meditations*. Out of this question it is possible to unfold the various mind–body problems of modern philosophy. Finally, we may add a further question that looms particularly large in modern metaphysics, beginning with Descartes:

4 Does an external (material) world really exist?

This is the question we encountered first in Berkeley's denial that the object of the physical sciences exists in itself, independently of the human mind. That became the issue in modern philosophy, with idealists like Berkeley, Leibniz, and Kant taking up the metaphysical cudgels against reductive and non-reductive materialists and Cartesian dualists. The whole realism–idealism controversy of the moderns was premised on the Cartesian assumption that the existence of one's own mind is self-evident while that of extra-mental material things requires proof. Among the ancients (if one can speak of a 'problem of the external world' at all) the question would not have been, Do material things exist *independently of the mind*? but, What ontological status is to be assigned them vis-à-vis sensible things in the celestial realm or supersensible things like separate Intelligences or Forms? Can one avoid withholding the epithet 'being' from them, and if so how? While a lower or deficient ontological status for material versus immaterial things is sometimes called 'idealism,' this can lead to confusion with the very different modern controversy just described. What matters for our working definition of 'metaphysics' is taking the final question broadly enough to cover both ancient/medieval and modern metaphysical controversies concerning the being or existence of the material world.

20.8 The theory of Forms as a metaphysical doctrine

In the sense of our working definition, Plato's theory of Forms is a prime example of a metaphysical theory, since it posits the *existence* of immaterial and *supersensible* entities beyond the physical or sensible world while ascribing a lesser degree of reality to the latter. Whether it is a coherent theory is another matter. For these transcendent entities are alleged to be (1) both *universal* in the manner of general concepts, the Forms of *many* things, and yet *particular*, each one an *individual* entity distinct from all the others. Moreover, the Forms (2) *exist separately* in their own right (as 'substances' in the technical philosophical sense introduced in 4.2–3), yet are unaccountably also 'present in' (Plato's expression) particular sensible things. What are 'presence' and 'participation' but convenient metaphors behind which Plato hides his perplexity concerning the exact relationship between Forms and particulars? In addition, the Forms (3) are said to be the *causes* of the many particular things that 'partake of' them, the latter being *what* they are *because and only because* they 'participate in' the Forms. Plato must be referring to what Aristotle was to call 'formal causality'; yet it is hard to know what to make of formal causes that are not immanent. Finally, Forms (4) are themselves more real, that is, both more fully existent and more perfectly what they are, than the many particulars whose causes they are. Does being or reality admit of degrees, of 'more' and 'less,' as do sensible qualities like heat or redness?

The very formulation of the theory of Forms points to problems and puzzles, if not outright contradictions. Not everyone would accept the charge of inconsistency (first brought by Aristotle), but, on the face of it, it seems hard to avoid. No attempt will be made to address these puzzles here. Instead, our question is: What led Plato to the adoption of this theory?

The short answer suggested by the ancient sources is: both certain influences and certain arguments—although the latter are largely a matter of conjecture (see 20.2). We shall look at the arguments for the existence of Forms later. As for influences, according to Aristotle there were two chief ones, Socrates and Heracleitus, to which we must add Parmenides, whom Aristotle omits to mention. Let us consider these three influences in turn.

20.9 Socrates and Plato on definitions.

We know that Socrates asked questions of the form, What is x?—for example, What is piety? To such questions neither (1) an example ('What I'm doing now, prosecuting my father for murder') nor (2) many examples ('The virtue of a man, is ... The virtue of a woman is ...') nor just any (3) property that all x's have in common ('god-belovedness') would do as an answer, much less (4) a characteristic that only *some* x's possess, a mere accident. What Socrates sought was rather a description in words of that feature which all x's possess ('if and only if') because it and it alone *makes* them x's ('because and only because'). This real essence *in* things is, when embodied in a descriptive formula, its correct definition.

Now consider the very different ways in which Socrates and Plato conceive the difference between (a) giving the definition of something or describing its essence and (b) naming one or more of its properties, whether the latter be one (i) that *all x's* have in common, a *proprium*, or (ii) that only *some x's* possess, an accident.

For Socrates, this is a difference between *two ways of talking about the same set of particular objects*—in other words, a difference between two types *of predication* (essential and accidental predication, in later parlance). These different kinds of predicate are, however, applied to one and the same set of things, the ordinary physical or material objects, living and non-living, that we encounter in daily experience.

For Plato, on the other hand, the difference is between *two sets of objects talked about*. In other words, talk about accidental properties is talk about one set of things, the many particulars that populate this world; while talk about essential and defining properties is talk about a completely different set of objects, the Forms of those objects mentioned first. This is a clear but dubious step beyond the teaching of Socrates.

20.10 Presocratic influences

The teaching ascribed to Socrates in the previous section was part of the presuppositional content of his moral theory rather than a separate metaphysical doctrine. Socrates, as we have said repeatedly, was exclusively a moral philosopher. Nevertheless, we can ask, Why did Plato go beyond what was strictly implied in Socrates's search for definitions? One reason has to do with Presocratic influences, namely Heracleitus and Parmenides, Plato's most important predecessors in the domain of epistemological and ontological enquiry.

20.10.1 Heracleitus

We have it (yet again) on Aristotle's authority that Plato, "in his youth," was influenced by one Cratylus, a disciple of Heracleitus. Thus, mercifully, there is no need to delve further into 'Heracleitus the Obscure,' as he was called in antiquity. Besides, scholars have concluded overwhelmingly that those who called themselves disciples of Heracleitus generally misunderstood the master, turning his teachings into a doctrine of universal flux in which there is no stability whatever. This is just the opposite of what Heracleitus taught, though *ever-varying change* is, of course, a necessary complement of that measured balance or *enduring harmony* of opposites in which Heracleitus believed, the *logos*, as he called the *idée mère* of his philosophy (see 5.5.4).

Two Heracleitean motifs are mentioned by Aristotle, and these, as much as anything in the authentic teachings of the master, were probably responsible for planting the seeds of the theory of Forms in Plato's mind: (1) that all sensible things are in a constant state of flux or change, and (2) that all such things are therefore unknowable. The second follows from the first inasmuch as *authentic* knowledge, such as the gods possess (and the god-like philosopher to a lesser degree), must be knowledge of the constant 'measure,' the unchanging pattern that governs all change. Having noted that Plato accepted the twin doctrines of flux and unknowability, Aristotle goes on to say explicitly that this led him to posit other, non-sensible things, his Forms.

From Aristotle's testimony in the *Metaphysics* we can surmise that Plato's reasoning went somewhat as follows:

Chapter 20: Metaphysics of Form   337

P1 Knowledge is knowledge of the permanent, that which is always the same.

Of course, this much might have been derived from the Socratic conception of knowledge as concerned with the permanent or unchanging essence or definition rather than from Heracleitus; and according to Aristotle it was partly so derived. Still, judging by a passage from a late dialogue, to be quoted in a moment, Heracleitus at least reinforced the idea.

P2 Particular sensible things are not permanent but constantly changing.
C   Hence, there can be no knowledge of sensible particulars.

In the dialogue named after Cratylus, the Platonic Socrates states: "Nor can we reasonably say, Cratylus, that there is knowledge at all, if everything is in a state of transition and there is nothing abiding" (*Cratylus*, 440a). This comes at the very end of the dialogue, so there is no subsequent drawing out of the consequences; but one surmises the following *modus tollens* argument at the back of Plato's mind:

P1 If everything is in a state of transition and nothing abiding, then there can be no knowledge.
P2 But there is knowledge.
C   Hence, *not* everything is in a state of transition (there *is* something abiding after all).

According to the same passage in Aristotle, Plato retained views taken over from Cratylus even in later life. But the most telling testimony is another passage, much later in Aristotle's *Metaphysics*. It has to do, not just with Plato's biography, but also with the philosophical considerations that moved *others* in his circle to accept Forms:

The theory of Forms occurred to those who enunciated it because they were convinced as to the true nature of reality by the doctrine of Heracleitus, that all sensible things are always in a state of flux; so that if there is to be any knowledge or thought about anything, there must be certain other entities besides sensible ones which persist. For there can be no knowledge of what is in flux.

This testimony regarding the origins of the doctrine is about as clear and unambiguous as any that one might hope for. Nevertheless, some still doubt Aristotle's testimony owing to his general unreliability as a historian of thought (see 8.2.1) and his rather curious omission of any mention of Parmenides.

20.10.2 Parmenides

From the conclusion that changing particulars were unknowable, neither Heracleitus nor Cratylus apparently inferred that they were *unreal* or less real than anything else, even the *logos*. That conclusion was reached by an altogether different route by Parmenides and his successors.

In the dialogue *Cratylus* a character named Hermogenes appears as a philosophical opponent of Cratylus. According to Diogenes Laertius (an early-third-century BC source), this Hermogenes "held the views of Parmenides." If this is correct, and if Hermogenes indeed belonged to the circle of young men around Socrates, as Diogenes claims, it is possible that Plato acquired from this source an early acquaintance with Parmenides. So here again there is no need to enter into the detail of Parmenides's poem in order to gather what Plato might have derived from it for his own theory. Suffice it to say that it was Parmenides who first developed that conception of what it is to be real outlined above: oneness, permanence, unchangeableness, intelligibility, uniformity, and so on (see 20.4.1); or rather, he transposed it from rational theology, where Xenophanes had already applied it to god, to the philosophy of being (see 5.5.4).

From this guiding idea of being, of what it is for something to be or exist at all, Parmenides concluded that the changing sensible things around us, the many particulars making up the motley world of ordinary sense experience, are not real *at all*. All this is semblance (*doxa* in Greek) or illusion. It fails to meet the criterion of true being. This much seems uncontroversially Parmenidean. But along with (a) change, Parmenides also denied (b) manyness or plurality. The significance of this is more debatable. After all, 'one' is the contrary of 'many' (meaning 'more than one' or 'some'), but also of 'none (at all).' Accordingly, two different interpretations of Parmenides's doctrine suggest themselves.

According to the first and most widely held interpretation, the positive import of the denial of (b) manyness is that everything that exists is *one* being, a single entity that is incapable of change of any sort. For if there were change from x to y, there would have to *be* something (y) that is *not yet* and something else (x) that is *no longer* after the change. And that entails some adulteration or dilution of Parmenides's inflexibly strict conception of what it is to be. So the world is not really made up of many changing particulars at all; it is in itself quite other than it appears to us ordinary mortals in everyday experience; it is really *one* rather than many, *permanent* rather than changing, and so on, right through the whole list of characteristics used to distinguish Platonic Forms from sensible particulars. Moreover, it can be known to be such, even by us, if we rely on our intellect rather than our senses. That is the point of saying that it is intelligible. Accordingly, interpreters sometimes speak of the completely static "block universe" of Parmenides, by analogy with certain recent physical theories, although this way of understanding Parmenidean being ('all-in-one-lump') seems to go right back to the ancient atomist Leucippus, who read Parmenides in very much this way. Plato, too, seems, in the *Sophist*, to have understood Parmenides along these lines, though there is some room for doubt on that score. Let us call this the 'monist' (from the Greek *monas*, 'unity,' 'oneness') interpretation.

According to the other and much less prevalent interpretation, the denial of (b) manyness is meant to affirm that *nothing* is real, that nothing at all exists. For according to the inflexibly strict Parmenidean rule, 'being' and 'real' can no more admit of degrees than can 'living' and 'dead' as ordinarily understood (see 17.5.1). Hence, nothing at all of those things ordinarily believed to exist can meet Parmenides's lofty conception of being or reality. Asked 'What is there (in your ontology)?' Parmenides would reply: 'Nothing,' or rather, 'I have no ontology.' We can designate this the 'meta-ontological' interpretation, using 'meta' in the sense explained earlier in regard to 'meta-ethics,' that is, for a second-order theory dealing with the meaning of the terms employed in the first-order theory *of others*—Parmenides himself, on this interpretation, has no first-order theory. For he has no ontology (except in the oblique sense in which we can say that even the complete atheist has a 'theological' outlook). He does, however, have a criterion, and hence a theory, of the *meaning* of 'being,' of what it is for something to be, but no inventory list of what there is (except a blank one). Asked, 'What then is your philosophy?' Parmenides, on this reading, would have to reply that his philosophy is contained, whole and entire, in the strict sense assigned the single word 'is' or 'being.'

The central question at issue in the Presocratic philosophies of the fifth-century BC is often put this way: 'Is reality many and changing? Or is it one and unchanging?' Heraclitus and his Ionian predecessors are usually regarded as taking the former, Parmenides and his followers as holding the latter view. When the question is put this way (one or many?), the interpretive question mooted above is decided from the start. Is then 'none or one or many' preferable to 'one or many?' as begging fewer questions? To be sure, Parmenides himself includes one (*hen* in Greek) among the characteristics of true being. But that need mean no more than that *if* anything could be properly said to exist, it would have to be one; it need not mean that there is indeed something and that it is one. In fact, the latter way of describing his position may have more to do with later Eleatics like Melissus than with Parmenides himself. Still, it is not only the oldest and most widely accepted view of the matter, it is Plato's view as well. So it cannot be simply dismissed, even if it is legitimate to suspect that Plato may have conflated the pupils with the master.

The key lesson that Plato learned from Parmenides is stated clearly enough in the form of a problem in the *Cratylus*: "how can that be a real thing which is never in the same state?" (439e). The implication is that it is quite impossible for such things to be altogether real. Yet for Plato, as we have seen, sensible particulars, while not perfectly real, are *not* entirely *unreal* either; they are just *less real* than the Forms, which alone are absolutely real and the causes of all other being, even of that inferior grade of being belonging to sensible things. Of sensible things that change and pass away Plato might have said what he in fact says of the changeable opinions of "the many": they are "rolling around between being and non-being" (*Republic* 479d). Such is the realm of *becoming*. All this, of course, amounts to an explicit repudiation of Parmenides on either interpretation considered above.

In sum, then, the conclusion that Plato drew from his philosophical encounter with Parmenides was neither (a) that no being is real, nor (b) that everything is one being, but rather (c) the truth of the two-world metaphysics described earlier.

20.11 Arguments for the theory of Forms

Given these influences, and basing ourselves loosely on Aristotle, Alexander, and a couple of later Platonic texts, we must now attempt to reconstruct the arguments that led Plato to embrace the theory of Forms. They vary according as the Forms are conceived in one or the other of three different ways: (1) as the only genuine objects of knowledge; (2) as perfect models or paradigms of particular things; and (3) as the universal entities to which common names refer. Given these conceptions of Forms, Plato may have thought it necessary to posit the existence of such entities in order to explain (1) how such exact *knowledge* as actually exists is possible; (2) how *relations* of more and less can be grasped by the mind; and (3) how the same concept or common name can be *predicated* of many different things.

Taking Plato to have had at his disposal three main arguments for the separate existence of immaterial Forms, we can, for convenience, label these, following Aristotle, (1) the Argument from the Sciences, (2) the Argument from Relations, and (3) the One-over-Many Argument. Something resembling (1) is found at the end of the fifth book of Plato's *Republic*, while passages in the seventh and tenth books have sometimes been alleged to correspond to (2) and (3), respectively. However, neither really formulates an argument, so the reconstruction of the second and third arguments must be a good deal more conjectural. Two further arguments discussed by Aristotle will not be considered at all, the so-called (4) Argument from Thought and the (5) Third Man Argument. Their bearing on the *Phaedo* is less clear in any case. While the labels are drawn from Greek sources, the terms in which the arguments will be formulated here, and even more certain criticisms, go beyond anything in the ancient sources—yet without anachronism, it is hoped. That must be for the reader to decide.

20.12 Forms as objects of knowledge: the Argument from the Sciences

The closest thing in Plato to the first argument called 'from the sciences' is found at *Republic* 477–80, with some pertinent detail supplied by the immediately following sixth book of the work. This argument is particularly deserving of attention, since we have it both as Plato formulated it *and* as Aristotle criticized it, not just in *On Ideas*, but in the *Metaphysics* as well. What follows is a composite sketch that gives greater

Chapter 20: Metaphysics of Form   341

weight to the Heracleitean strand and to the *Metaphysics* account than the text of the *Republic* would warrant on its own. Some attempt is made to supply the defect arising from Aristotle's puzzling reticence about Parmenides's influence.

20.12.1 The argument

The first premise of the Argument from the Sciences is the conclusion of a preliminary argument that runs roughly as follows (see *Republic* 477c–478b):

P1 The faculty of knowledge is different from the faculty of opinion.
P2 Two faculties differ when they have different objects *and* produce different results.

In support of P2 Plato notes that the faculty of sight produces vision, the objects of which are colours and shapes, while the faculty of hearing produces audition, the objects of which are sounds; that is why we say sight and hearing (which we cannot inspect directly or place alongside one another in order to compare them) are *different* faculties. The innocent-sounding P1 asserts knowledge and opinion to be two different faculties of the mind; the implication that they are entirely on a par with sight and hearing will prove the downfall of the argument. In any case, the conclusion of the preliminary argument is:

C Therefore the objects of knowledge differ from the objects of opinion.

That "the knowable and the opinable cannot be the same" (478b) now becomes P1 of the Argument from the Sciences proper:

P1 The objects of knowledge differ from the objects of opinion.

A second premise derives from (a) the acceptance of the (pseudo-)Heracleitean doctrine that changing sensible particulars are not strictly knowable and (b) the rejection of Parmenides's view that they are not real in *any* sense at all. According to (b), the many changing objects of opinion "lie between what purely is and what completely is not" (478d), that is, between what is "eternally the same in all respects" (479a) and the sheer non-being to which Parmenides rashly consigned them. Like the *Phaedo*, the *Republic* makes a great deal of the contrast between changing particulars that are and appear *both* this *and* that, or *now* this, *then* that, and "the things themselves which are always in every way the same" (479e) and which are apprehended, if they are apprehended at all, as necessarily thus and so. Yet according to (a), only "what fully is, is fully knowable" (477a). So:

P2 The objects of opinion are the less-than-perfectly real changing sensible things.

The straightforward conclusion from the first two premises is:

C1 Therefore the objects of knowledge cannot be the less-than-perfectly real changing sensible things.

A crucial assumption here is that things that *differ in nature or kind* (like the eternal and the ephemeral) also *differ in number*; in other words, that things whose properties are different, or even logically incompatible, are therefore numerically two separate things. We shall return to this point when we come to evaluate the argument.

On the face of it, the next premise seems to be nothing more than the inherited Socratic idea that

P3 The objects of knowledge are the unchanging definitions or essences of things.

And indeed Aristotle, in the *Metaphysics* account of the Argument from the Sciences, makes specific mention of Socratic definitions. There is, of course, an unmistakable continuity between the Socratic quest for real definitions and Plato's restriction of knowledge to that which is always the same, the perfect, complete, unchanging, ungenerable, and incorruptible. But there is equally clearly a sharp discontinuity between relatively permanent immanent natures and absolutely permanent transcendent Forms. We shall return to this point too later on.

At this stage a key premise must be supplied, since it is nowhere stated:

P4 There exists knowledge of the essences of things.

How can this particular premise be justified? If Plato assumes it without argument, then it is probably because he understood it in a sense that made its truth incontestable. This requires removal of the Socratic restriction of the search for definitions to certain *moral value words*. Given the state of *aporia* in which that search is usually abandoned, there is little reason for confident assertion of the existence of such knowledge. While the definition of moral and non-moral value words ('Justice,' 'Moderation,' 'Beauty,' and so forth) remains central to Plato's Argument from the Sciences, it is only definition in the exact mathematical sciences that has any chance of placing the question of the existence of knowledge of essences beyond dispute. And indeed, at the end of book six (see 510d), examples drawn from "geometry and the kindred sciences" ('the square,' 'the diagonal') supplant the valuational terms of the earlier Argument from the Sciences. Even if such knowledge exists, however, the conclusion of the argument is not restricted to it. For the conclusion is:

C2 Therefore Forms exist,

Chapter 20: Metaphysics of Form 343

whereby the Forms are taken to be identical with those perfect, unchanging essences alluded to in the preceding premises and exemplified principally by valuational forms. So the whole argument runs as follows:

P1   The objects of knowledge must be different from the objects of opinion.
P2   The objects of opinion are changing sensible things.
C1   Hence the objects of knowledge cannot be changing sensible things.
P3   The objects of knowledge are the unchanging essential natures or universal essences.
P4   Knowledge exists (witness mathematics).
C2   Hence the objects of knowledge must exist—i.e., Forms exist.

20.12.2 Fatal flaws in the argument

This argument is a good example of how an inappropriate model can lead one into error. Plato assumes that the difference between faculties of sight and hearing is a good model on which to construe that between knowledge and opinion. The former do in fact differ as to their objects; and in the absence of any clear distinction between substance and accident, such as Aristotle was the first to draw, it is easy to suggest that their objects—shapes and colours on the one hand, sounds on the other—are numerically distinct entities or things. But even if these objects did differ numerically and not just in nature, do knowledge and opinion differ as to their objects at all? Or is the decisive difference rather a difference in the *evidence* for our beliefs about one and the same object?

Let us get down to cases. I am *of the opinion* (despite what Holocaust deniers may say) that the Holocaust actually occurred; and I take this to mean that roughly six million European Jews were systematically exterminated by the Nazi regime. But if I go and examine the historical evidence (e.g., the sites and means of the killing, the official documents ordering that it be carried out, the confessions of the perpetrators and their accomplices, the reports of the survivors and their liberators, and so forth), then I say I *know* that the Holocaust occurred, not merely that I believe it or that I am of such-and-such an opinion. But the object is exactly the same in the case of belief and knowledge: the Holocaust as a historical sequence of events.

So 'I know p' and 'I am of the opinion that p' are just two different ways of being cognitively related to the *same*, not to different, objects—in the example, the same sequence of events from the past. And even if the objects themselves were different in nature, it would still have to be shown that they differ in number, that each exists separately in its own right. Thus, Plato's main argument for the existence of Forms collapses with the very first premise.

Suppose, however, that we go along with the first premise, and indeed with the other premises of the Argument from the Sciences, as does Aristotle, who takes the object of so-called demonstrative science to be the complete, determinate, unchanging nature or essence of a thing. Though distinct from its changing accidental properties, the form or nature is, of course, not a substance or separate thing in its own right for Aristotle. In that case, the question is obviously whether the argument establishes the existence of anything more than *immanent* forms such as both Socrates and Aristotle believed in. If not, we immediately grasp the point of Aristotle's main objection: the Argument from the Sciences proves too little; it goes no way at all toward establishing separately existing transcendent Forms, although it is not worthless, since it does establish the existence of forms of the type Aristotle himself accepted. Of this, of course, nominalists and conceptualists will remain unconvinced.

Another fatal flaw is evident from what was said above of P4. Mathematics may be a good example of the kind of knowledge that induced Plato to embrace the theory of Forms; but since the theory is not restricted to transcendent mathematical Forms, the Argument from the Sciences, even if it could be rendered sound, would provide no support for the valuational Forms that feature centrally in it.

20.13 Forms as paradigms: the Argument from Relation

20.13.1 The argument

Whereas in the Argument from the Sciences the Forms provide *objects* for knowledge, in the second argument they provide a non-sensible *standard* for ascribing *more or less* of certain valuational and mathematical properties to sensible objects.

A key premise of the Argument from Relation is hinted at in the *Republic* at 504c: "Nothing which is incomplete [or, as we might also translate, 'imperfect'] is the measure of anything." The word 'measure' can be understood in two ways. It may mean (a) a basic unit of measurement, as in our modern or other systems of weights and measures; or it may mean (b) an 'ideal standard of comparison' by which to determine whether or just how far something 'measures up.' In the quoted passage, the latter sense is the relevant one.

To get from this broad hint to a premise of the sort needed for the Argument from Relation, consider a related passage from the Recollection Argument of the *Phaedo*: "Whenever someone, on seeing something, realizes that that which he now sees wants to be like some other reality but falls short and cannot be like that other since it is inferior, do we agree that the one who thinks this must have prior knowledge of that to which he says it is like, but deficiently so?" (74d–e). With this question Socrates ostensibly invites Simmias to reflect on the perception of differences between sensible particulars where one "falls short" of the other in some respect, say, beauty. Comparison of sensible particulars with non-sensible Forms is not in question, nor yet is comparison of relations between sensible particulars with relational Forms. The transition comes swiftly, however: "We must then possess knowledge of the Equal

Chapter 20: Metaphysics of Form   345

before that time when we first saw the equal objects and realized that all these objects strive to be like the Equal but are deficient in this [Equality]"(74e–75a). 'Equal to' is a relational term, while other properties in respect of which things are compared are relational only in the comparative and superlative forms. So the argument is not restricted to a special class of properties, unless it be those that admit of 'more' and 'less.' Taking as our initial premise the necessity for some measure in the sense of an ideal standard or comparison, we can conjecture, on the basis of the *Phaedo* passage, an Argument from Relations rather different from the very puzzling one that, according to Alexander, Aristotle set out and criticized under that very name in *On Ideas*. While Plato nowhere actually formulates such an argument, he does refer to the Forms as 'paradigms' in many places, including *Euthyphro* 6e, *Republic* 500e, *Parmenides* 132d, and *Timaeus* 28–9.

P1   In order to be able to compare particular things to one another as possessing *more or less* of a certain (mathematical or valuational) property, we must possess an ideal standard or perfect paradigm against which these particulars are measured and in comparison with which they are found to 'fall' more or less 'short.'

P2   Sensible particular things are in fact compared with one another and found to differ in respect of the extent to which they possess certain (mathematical or valuational) properties; that is, they do have relational properties (e.g., bigger, biggest, better, best).

C1   Hence, there must exist a paradigm or perfect model, either among the sensible particulars themselves, or elsewhere.

P3   But the paradigm does not exist among the sensible particulars, none of which is ever found to possess any property perfectly.

C2   Hence there must exist a realm of paradigms or Forms beyond the realm of sensible things.

20.13.2 The doubtful premise in this argument

While Aristotle would not have recognized this as *his* Argument from Relations, it does seem that Plato was led to the theory of Forms in part by considerations of this kind. The premise most open to attack, and on which the whole argument turns, is P1. What this dubious assumption comes down to is the idea that the understanding of *imperfection* (and hence greater or less imperfection) depends upon a prior understanding of *perfection*. In other words, we could not recognize imperfection (that something is more or less imperfect in some respect) when confronted with it, unless we already had an idea of absolute perfection (in that same respect). For example, we could not recognize this as more beautiful than that without the prior idea of perfect Beauty, or these two as more equal (say, in length) than those two, without the prior idea of perfect Equality.

But on reflection this seems quite implausible. Why should I not *first* recognize that

346   Part Two: Plato and the Road to Reality

A is more beautiful than B and B more beautiful than C, and *then* form the idea of a perfect Beauty, an ideal of beauty that exceeds the beauty of A far more—perhaps infinitely more—than A exceeds that of C? Plato simply assumes that it *must* be the other way round: perfection before imperfection. Later an argument of the same general type will be met with in Descartes, who declares that he could not understand himself to be an imperfect being unless he had the prior idea of a perfect being, God, to employ as a standard. Is it even remotely likely that this is how we become aware our own limitations and imperfections?

Another argument in Descartes provides a striking instance of that other fallacy noted in connection with the Argument from the Sciences: the curious idea that a difference in kind or nature warrants our positing a difference in number, two complete entities or substances. From it springs Descartes's central thesis that the human mind is a substance capable of existing without the body—whereas Plato argued both for a separate soul and for separate Forms. It is odd that this idea should have exercised so strong a hold on two of the greatest minds of all time, especially since Aristotle understood perfectly well what both Plato and Descartes failed to grasp. It is one thing for A and B to differ in kind or nature, to be logically distinct, as are mind and body (for all but reductive materialists) or form and matter (in the Peripatetic tradition); it is quite another for that which is thus separable in thought or conception (analyzable into two or more components) to be separate or separable in fact, two or more things or substances. Small wonder, then, that Aristotle insisted on the dependence of the soul upon the body and of forms upon the things whose essences they are.

So the Argument from Relations falters with the very first step. There is no need to consider the further inference from a perfect ideal or paradigm existing in the mind, to one existing separately in a transcendent realm—though that too is hardly credible without granting the truth of the theory that genuine knowledge is recollection of something actually existing outside the mind with which we once had a direct, face-to-face acquaintance.

20.14 Predication: the One-over-Many Argument

In the Argument from the Sciences the problem was: How is it possible to really know anything in the manner of sciences like mathematics? There the Forms provided the appropriate type of *objects* for genuine scientific knowledge, eternal intellectual objects. In the Argument from Relations the problem was: How is it possible to have knowledge of the relational properties of things? There the Forms functioned as *paradigms* for the use of comparatives and superlatives in certain judgments. In the One-over-Many Argument the question is: How can the same name be applied to—'spread over,' as it were—different objects ('one [name] over many' [things])? The problem to which the theory of Forms provides a solution in the present case concerns neither *knowledge* nor *relations* but *predication*. Accordingly, the Forms function this time, not as objects or as paradigms, but as transcendently real *universals*, as *abstract* yet separately existing *entities* to which universal names refer.

The name 'One-over-Many' seems to come indirectly from a passage in the *Republic* (596a) in which the Platonic Socrates remarks that "we have regularly assumed one Form for all the many [many individuals of each kind] to which we apply the same name"—one literally 'around' (Greek: *peri*) many, as Plato writes here, or as Aristotle puts it, one 'alongside' (*para*) many. Yet in discussing the theory of Forms toward the end of the first book of the *Metaphysics*, Aristotle refers to the one *over* (Greek: *epi*) many. This is the locution taken up by Alexander from the lost *On Ideas*, and, for whatever reason, it has stuck.

20.14.1 The argument

In the passage just quoted, the *Republic* records the *fact* of a certain habitual assumption; no attempt is made to incorporate it into an argument for the existence of separate Forms. Nevertheless, we can conjecture a formalized argument along the following lines:

P1 Some terms are names (e.g., 'Socrates,' 'the Parthenon') which refer to one particular person or thing, while other terms are applied as predicates to many things (for example, 'man' and 'building'); that is, there are in our language both proper nouns, the names of individual people and things as well as other, general terms.

P2 Since proper names like 'Socrates' and general terms like 'man' both mean something yet have different meanings, they must refer to different objects.

C1 Hence there must be, in addition to the particular things to which proper names refer, universal entities for the abstract general terms to refer to.

P2 Such universal entities are nowhere to be found among the particular sensible things that populate this world.

C2 Therefore, they must exist elsewhere; that is, there must be another world populated by abstract essences or Forms.

In the preceding, no distinction is drawn between (a) generic nouns that apply to many particulars, like 'building' or 'man,' and (b) abstract nouns, designating properties rather than classes of things, like 'architecture' or 'humanity.' As an argument for Forms, the preceding may be slightly more persuasive if couched in terms of (b) or, better yet, (c) abstract nouns belonging to the domain of mathematics and moral philosophy like 'courage,' 'justice,' 'equality,' and so on. For it is by no means clear that Plato *consistently* believed in the existence of Forms for (a) all generic or even (b) all abstract, rather than just (c) abstract mathematical and valuational terms like those just instanced.

In his middle period Plato no doubt did more than just toy with the possibility of Forms for *everything* for which we have universal names (see the passage from *Republic* 596a quoted above). This would include not just so-called natural kinds, like 'animal' or 'man,' but even artefacts like 'bed' (see *Cratylus* 389a, *Gorgias* 503e). Aristotle describes Plato as having held "that there are as many Forms as there are kinds of natural objects." This, if correct, would include 'animal' and other natural species but *not* artificial things. Yet in the somewhat later *Parmenides* (130b–d), the only Forms of whose existence the young Socrates, who is Plato's spokesman there, will declare himself certain are mathematical and valuational Forms. Still, to formulate the argument in terms of such Forms alone would imply that Plato always drew the relevant distinctions clearly, and that he did not vacillate as to what to include; whereas there is considerable evidence to the contrary on both counts. The Greek words *eidos* and *idea*, by the way, are regularly used by Plato and other writers of the time in the sense of 'sort' or 'kind,' that is, for all kinds or classes of things; so it is not at all far-fetched to suppose that the metaphysical theory grew *in part* out of reflection on the significance of the distinction between particular names and general nouns in the Greek language.

20.14.2 Examination of this argument

The chief problem with this argument is P2, which might be reformulated as follows: 'if two words *mean* different things then they must *refer* to different objects.' In other words, P2 is just another way of saying: 'Different sense, therefore different referent(s).' But as was seen in the context of our examination of the meanings of 'meaning' (see 7.12.2), this inference from different sense to different referent is *invalid*.

Plato reasons: since proper names like 'Socrates' have a quite different *sense* than general terms like 'man,' they must also have different *referents*; and since the referents of proper names are the particular sensible things whose names they are, there must be other, universal, non-sensible, things for the universal names to refer to—Forms. Of course, the terms 'Socrates' and 'man' do have different referents, different extensions; but their referents are arguably related as a member of a set of sensible things is related to the whole set or class of which it is a member, *not* in the manner Plato supposes.

Here it will not be amiss to quote the noted American logician and Harvard philosophy professor mentioned earlier (see 6.4.2), Willard Van Orman Quine: "A felt need for meant entities may derive from an earlier failure to appreciate that meaning and reference are distinct." Quine's remark makes it easy to spot the fallacy in Plato's argument. Of course, a great deal more lurks behind Quine's comment, namely the outright rejection of all varieties of realism or essentialism, immanent and transcendent (see 4.7). Whether this is warranted will be considered in the concluding appraisal of Plato's central doctrines in the next chapter.

One thing, however, is clear: we cannot discount Quine's criticism on the grounds that the distinction of sense and reference is a late-nineteenth-century discovery, any more than we can rule out objections based on distinctions like difference in nature and difference in number, or exact mathematical and inexact moral knowledge, or knowledge and belief as differing 'propositional attitudes' (as they are called nowadays) toward the same objects. Whether or not Plato had any inkling of these distinctions, his arguments are not immune to criticisms based on them. With their aid we understand him differently and perhaps better than he understood himself. What is particularly noteworthy about Quine's objection is that if it is correct, the whole metaphysics of form from Plato to modern times is based on a crude error. Our concluding appraisal will accordingly be a defence of the metaphysics of form rather than the Platonic theory of Forms.

21

Concluding Appraisal

21.1 Introductory

It has been suggested several times already that Plato may have intended the sequence of proofs in the *Phaedo* as a continuous web of argument, each particular stage making its specialized contribution to the overall pattern of proof. If so, it may not be fair to hold the individual arguments up to the light, searching for flaws, as in the preceding chapters. But would the *Phaedo* fare better were all four arguments treated as parts of a complex proof structure? Probably not. Which leaves us with the question, Why study the arguments for immortality at all?

Of course, the soul's immortality is only one of the 'twin pillars' of Platonism, the chief pillar being the theory of Forms. And then there is the so-called architrave, Plato's theory of recollection (see 14.1). Yet in both the latter cases, too, we are confronted with the same troubling state of affairs. While practically everyone who calls himself a philosopher nowadays has some interest in Plato, and while many eminent scholars have devoted their careers to the study and exposition of Plato's thought, few contemporary thinkers, if any, would call themselves 'Platonists' or declare allegiance to Plato's two-world metaphysics or theory of knowledge. Historically, the recollection theory was supplanted first by the doctrine of innate or inborn ideas, and then, starting with Kant, by theories concerning the possibility and limits of a priori knowledge. Why, then, study theories that have long since ceased to be live philosophical options, that are now interesting museum pieces at best?

The contemporary relevance of the Platonic doctrine of immortality will be considered first (see 21.2), followed by some remarks on the enduring significance of the problems lying behind the theories of Forms and recollection (see 21.3). Confined as it is to just three central topics, the following is nothing even remotely like a full-scale treatment of the question, Why study Plato? That would require a book in itself; these reflections are little more than a start.

The present chapter can be left for another occasion by those whose immediate needs are met by the preceding exposition of Plato's thought. Nothing in the following parts of the book turns on them.

21.2 Plato on immortality

To begin with, it is worth remarking that Plato's *Phaedo* is one of those seminal works of philosophy that cast a very long shadow over the entire subsequent history of western thought. It is no doubt a gross exaggeration to say with the British philosopher Alfred North Whitehead (1861–1947) that the history of western philosophy is literally "a series of footnotes to Plato," but, figuratively speaking, the compliment is richly deserved.

Quite apart from philosophy proper, the significance of Plato's thought in the history of religion, literature, and the arts cannot be overestimated. Perhaps the chief way in which it has touched the lives of the philosophically uninitiated is through the Christian religion. It was not without good reason that Nietzsche jeeringly described Christianity as Platonism for the masses. For beginning with St Augustine and the Church fathers, Christian theology imbibed deep draughts of Platonic intellectualism and puritanism. The encounter was to shape the orthodox Christian understanding of God, man, and the world for millennia to come. Whether there is any basis for this in the Christian gospels is a nice question.

Even where Platonic and Platonizing tendencies in Christianity have come under sharp critical scrutiny, as they did under Aristotle's influence in the high Middle Ages, the standard Platonic account of the soul and its relation to the body remained essentially that of the *Phaedo*, with portions of the *Timaeus* doing duty as the standard version of the Platonic cosmology. That is why virtually every subsequent attempt to redefine the concept of the person, from Descartes to Sartre, stakes out its own position in opposition to the classic Platonic doctrine of the *Phaedo*. The same can be said of Plato's own later 'psychology' (as the theory of the soul is often called): Plato advanced to new insights into 'soul' and its relation to the body chiefly by criticizing aspects of his own earlier thought. So, historically speaking, the *Phaedo* encapsulates a crucially important phase in the career of one of the world's most influential thinkers; as with few other pieces of philosophical writing, acquaintance with this work belongs to the first and most important rudiments of philosophical culture (see 2.7).

Historical considerations aside, it is worth noting, secondly, that the Platonic arguments for immortality, for all their faults, repay careful consideration with a wealth of valuable insights of a conceptual nature. Even after minute study of the *Phaedo* we may not find ourselves a jot closer to knowing the answer to this question: Do we survive the death of our bodies, or is death tantamount to annihilation of the persons that we are? But chances are that we shall understand the question better. For we only fully understand what it is that we are asking after careful weighing of the full range of possible answers, of the conceptual difficulties facing them, their underlying assumptions, the type of evidence it might take to establish them rationally, and how close or far we are from possessing such evidence. The conclusion to which this state of affairs points may well be, as Kant believed (see 7.5.2), that theoretical philosophy can provide no answers to questions that exceed the bounds of human experience, or, as Sartre might put it, that such questions are simply beyond the scope of every type of rational reassurance of which we humans are capable—without wishful thinking or self-deception. Still, either conclusion, if well founded, would be a valuable lesson learned. Plato himself appears to have been alive to the possibility of such an outcome; for right after the Affinity Argument he has Socrates say: "There are still many doubtful points and many objections for anyone who wants a thorough discussion of these matters" (84c). And a little later on Simmias remarks:

I believe, as perhaps you do, that precise knowledge on that subject [the fate of the soul] is impossible or extremely difficult in our present life, but that it surely shows a very poor spirit not to examine thoroughly what is said about it, and to desist before one is exhausted by an all-round investigation. One should achieve one of these things: [1] learn the truth about these things [from others who know it] or [2] find it out for oneself, or, if that is impossible, [3] adopt the best and most irrefutable of men's theories, and, borne upon this, sail through the dangers of life as upon a raft, unless someone should make that journey safer and less risky upon [4] a firmer vessel of some divine doctrine. (85c–d)

Though not from the mouth of Socrates, this striking passage may safely be taken for Plato's own sentiment—at least here, in one of his more Socratic moods. In his dogmatic moments, the same Plato apparently chafed under the Socratic legacy, betraying the spirit of intellectual modesty that is so evident in this passage.

If the attitude expressed by Simmias is more cautious and reasonable than the confident assertions of the four arguments of the *Phaedo*, this may tell us something about the nature of philosophy itself. For it suggests that all we can legitimately expect of philosophy at times is a better understanding of the questions. Of course, it would be premature to conclude that philosophy can *never* do more than furnish conceptual clarification or provide the sort of analytical tools that can aid us in the assessment of evidence and arguments; for not all philosophical problems are on the same footing as that of immortality. Many interesting questions may in fact be answerable. Nevertheless, some such conclusion does seem warranted in the case of the perennial metaphysical questions common to philosophy and religious thought. Such questions are truly inexhaustible. That is why philosophy is in little danger of ever dying out, at least as long as human nature remains constant and human beings retain the freedom to think and enquire for themselves.

21.3 Plato on Forms and recollection

Turning now to the second pillar, we shall find that a serious intellectual engagement with Plato's theory of Forms can still provide valuable food for metaphysical thought. For the central issue raised by Aristotle's critique of Plato's transcendent realism is still the focus of an important debate today.

21.3.1 Contemporary anti-realism

At the end of the previous chapter we cited with approval Quine's diagnostic comment that a "felt need for meant entities may derive from an earlier failure to appreciate that meaning and reference are distinct." For Quine is correct in thinking that there is no *need* to posit even (1) immanent essences as "meant entities" really existing in things, much less (2) transcendent Forms really existing apart from them, in order to have something for universal terms to refer to; the difference between proper names and universal predicates is a difference in extension or reference that is perfectly understandable through the logical analysis of language.

Now as a general rule, we shall do well to follow Quine's advice and be wary of confounding facts about language with facts about the universe—as Plato may have done in developing his theory of Forms. We should not expand our inventory of existing things without good reason, and there is certainly no *necessity* to swell our ontology in order to accommodate the facts about (a) scientific knowledge, (b) relations, and (c) predication that sparked Plato's three main arguments for the existence of Forms. But neither should we rush to shrink our ontology, to eliminate real universals in the manner of nominalists and conceptualists, or to eliminate immaterial souls in the manner of the materialists, just for reasons of economy. The same goes for the efforts of idealists to eliminate mind-independent material things. What we want is, obviously enough, an ontology that reflects the way things are; and there is no good reason to believe that either extreme parsimony or extreme prodigality is a fail-safe method of achieving this end.

Besides, the fact that the existence of certain kinds of entities (whether immanent essences or transcendent Forms) cannot be validly inferred from known features of (a) knowledge or (b) relations or (c) language does not prove that they do *not* exist either. We shall have frequent occasion later to dwell on the difference between (1) proving that a certain conclusion is not warranted by the evidence and arguments adduced in its favour and (2) showing that conclusion to be false (see 28.4). For all Hume's criticisms of the traditional proofs of God's existence, they are intended to show only (1) that the proofs fail, not (2) that God does not exist (see 31.2). It is perfectly possible, after all, that God does exist even though all hitherto devised proofs of his existence are notoriously bad. So to distinguish, as we have, between meaning and reference, believing ourselves to have shown thereby that forms (or

Forms) do *not* exist, would be to fall into the same trap as Plato; except that in addition to confounding linguistic and ontological considerations, we should also be mistaking the invalidity of an argument for the falsity of its conclusion.

If granting, as virtually all philosophers do nowadays, that such entities as Platonic Forms do not exist, what are we to say about Socratic essences or their successors, Aristotelian (lower-case) forms? Are we to give up *immanent* realism or essentialism, too, disavowing that long and venerable philosophical tradition according to which it is the special goal of philosophical enquiry to understand, not just the meanings of words and the workings of language, not just the contents and activities of the human mind, but above all the *being* or essence of things? Quine would undoubtedly urge us to do so. For it was he who wrote: "Meaning is what essence becomes when it is divorced from the object of reference and wedded to the word." This probably means more than just that the real existence of essences *cannot be validly inferred* from the fact that certain instances of essential predication are perfectly meaningful (despite an "earlier failure to appreciate" this fact); it presumably means that while there *are* such meanings, there just are no such things as essences, not even immanent ones.

Underlying both this and Quine's earlier remark is a nominalism that rejects the idea of real essences in things. His observations reflect the thinking of a twentieth-century school of Anglo-American philosophy that owes a great deal to the English philosopher Bertrand Russell (see 1.4) and his younger colleague at Cambridge, the Anglo-Austrian thinker Ludwig Wittgenstein (1889–1951). To the progeny of this school—and they are legion—it has seemed that those referring expressions that led earlier philosophers to posit such entities as natures or real essences can be eliminated altogether through the logical analysis of language. By substituting equivalent locutions in ordinary language or, better yet, by employing logical formulae that convey the exact meanings often obscured by ordinary language, it is possible, so these opponents of the metaphysics of form maintain, to dispel even the appearance that there exist such entities as unanalyzed ordinary language leads us to posit. For example, Plato's way of talking about (the essence of) Threeness as containing (the essence of) Oddness (see *Phaedo* 104a) suggests that there exist essences like Threeness and Oddness. This is just the distorting effect of what has been dubbed 'the material mode of speech' (MMS). So suppose we employ the so-called formal mode of speech (FMS) instead. Then we shall say, equivalently, that to affirm there are three of anything and yet deny that there is an odd number of them is to contradict oneself. The essences have now been successfully 'paraphrased away.' Or, to take a different example, suppose that instead of saying that rationality belongs to the essence of man, we say instead that to affirm that x is a man and deny that x is rational is to contradict oneself. By such means the idea that essential predication involves reference to immanent essences is shown to be as unwarranted as the inference to transcendent essences or Forms; it is unmasked as an illusion owing to the imprecision of ordinary language. Through the substitution of equivalent expressions it becomes clear that nothing of the sort is really implied; that what were mistaken for ontological implications by those using the material mode of speech turn out, on substitution of the formal mode, to be logical insights concerning what can and cannot be said consistently.

21.3.2 A tentative defence of immanent realism

The first thing to be said in response to this is that while there may indeed be no necessity to posit the existence of something—be that something God, a Platonic Form, an immaterial soul substance, a real essence, or a sub-atomic particle—it may nevertheless exist! To repeat (for what will not be the last time): to show that the inference from the existence of A to that of B is invalid is not to show that there is no B. Still, if the entity or non-entitative principle in question is not an object of experience (as in the examples just given), then we should be wary of swelling our commonsense ontology by positing the existence of something non-sensible. That much seems a perfectly reasonable restriction to impose on our philosophizing.

The second thing to note is that if these strictures on classical metaphysics are justified, then the traditional search for real definitions must yield to the search for word meanings and the logical analysis of language. So too the investigation of the contents and workings of the human mind that figure so prominently in modern metaphysics. That is exactly what Quine and his cohorts have in mind. Once the error of belief in real essences has been spotted, it appears that the universals sought by the philosophers of the past exist nowhere but in language—or, if the conceptualist is partly right, in *language* and in *thought*—but certainly not in *things* in the world, let alone outside it. Yet this is a conclusion that must give us pause. Before we simply consign two millennia of philosophy to the rubbish heap, along with such pseudo-sciences as alchemy and astrology, we had better be sure that we have pretty compelling reasons for doing so. Reasons of what might be called 'ontological economy' or 'parsimony' are not compelling, since the economy of the world may be different from that of our theories.

Even if the reductive analyses and substitutions of the FMM were entirely successful, such anti-metaphysical conclusions would still seem premature. If Quine and his ilk think otherwise, then it is perhaps because they tacitly take for granted some such principle of economy as is generally attributed to the grandfather of nominalism, William of Ockham (see 4.8). According to 'Ockham's Razor,' as it is called, "entities are not to be multiplied beyond necessity." Now if we substitute the words 'without good and sufficient reason' for 'beyond necessity,' this seems perfectly sensible; but what is to stop us from following the lead of R.E. Allen, who takes Quine's second diagnostic remark and turns the tables on him? Essence, writes Allen, "is what meaning becomes when it is divorced from the word and wedded to the object." Perhaps, as this suggests, entities and principles are not to be *eliminated* beyond necessity either! (Let us call this restorative tonic for the victims of Ockham's Razor 'Allen's Elixir.')

There is something questionable about the whole development of contemporary Anglo-American philosophy that has led from things and essences (in ancient and medieval philosophy) via thought and concepts (in modern philosophy) to language and words (in contemporary Anglo-American thought). The same is true of that trend that has progressively deprived the world we experience in day-to-day living of its most salient features, reducing relational to intrinsic, qualitative to quantitative, vital to mechanistic, purposive and intelligent to blind and random features—leaving us, in the end, with a mathematical-mechanistic world picture as remote as can be from everyday experience. Perhaps what bills itself as scientific progress and Enlightenment, as emancipation from the metaphysical fantasies of the past, is really just a falling away from the vocation of philosophy as it has been understood (with variations) by almost every great thinker of the western tradition for over two millennia. Arguably, the greatest benefit to be reaped from a consideration of Plato's metaphysics is precisely the standing invitation it represents to consider just this question. Of course, we must not be tempted to say that because "almost every great thinker" has maintained such and such, there is a strong presumption that it is true. That would be a form of the illicit *argumentum ad verecundiam* (see 7.7.1). But we can say, without committing any fallacy, that the opinion in question is at least worthy of serious consideration prior to rejection.

This is obviously not the place to try to decide the issue of metaphysical realism. It is enough if the question itself is a little clearer than it was back in chapter 4. It is a question that has to be faced, sooner or later, by anyone bent on a serious study of philosophy; happily, by beginning with Plato we face it sooner rather than later. We shall return to this question of things, thoughts, and language in the Conclusion, with a good deal more philosophy under our belts.

21.3.3 Recollection, innatism, apriorism

Many important issues that only come to the fore in modern philosophy have deep roots in Plato and in Greek thought. The theory of recollection is a good example. It was a constant point of reference, explicitly or implicitly, in the great controversy over innate ideas and a priori concepts and principles that divided British and continental thinkers in the seventeenth and eighteenth centuries and still divides empiricists and anti-empiricists today. True, when it comes to explaining the presence in the mind of exact mathematical or fundamental metaphysical concepts and principles, the doctrine of the soul's pre-existence in the realm of Forms has long since ceased to be a live option. As for its successor, the seventeenth-century theory of inborn or innate ideas, it still gets some play in the contemporary debate concerning language acquisition, but not in the theory of knowledge or philosophy of science. Nevertheless, the underlying problem of the possibility of non-trivial a priori knowledge remains unresolved to this day. Again, it is those of a nominalist persuasion who consider the issue itself as dead as is the theory of recollection.

Nominalists tend to be empiricists, and some, like Quine, have entertained hopes of solving the problem of knowledge through a philosophically sophisticated, empirical stimulus–response psychology. As we have seen, Hume's associationist psychology already envisaged a similar aim. The question, however, is not whether some theory of knowledge can hew closer to sensory experience than Plato's or Descartes's or Kant's—any more than the question discussed above was whether some nominalist ontology is more parsimonious than metaphysical realism. The question is rather whether our way of understanding ourselves and our social and natural environment, our pre- and extra-scientific as well as scientific efforts to orientate ourselves within the totality of what is, are set within a framework of ideas that are themselves just the deliverances of ordinary experience. That they are seems less than obvious, and a thoughtful reading of the Recollection Argument can still serve to engender serious doubts on this score.

21.4 Conclusion

The criticisms of Platonic realism and recollection considered in the preceding section are at bottom criticisms of the metaphysical enterprise itself. If the replies tentatively suggested are not entirely on the wrong track, then the future of metaphysical enquiry is at least open—possibly even bright!

If so, then the rationale for a serious engagement with Plato does not stop at gathering pieces in the puzzle of western intellectual history. It goes beyond tool sharpening and analytical insights as well. There are complex metaphysical and epistemological issues waiting to be confronted here: questions about what is included in the totality of things, about the order of being, the order of knowing, the concept of experience, and the guiding ideas of being that underlie particular metaphysical systems of thought (see chaps. 3 and 4). What accounts for Plato's remarkable longevity as a philosopher is largely the exhilarating spectacle of a great mind wrestling with profound and intractable problems that still have not been resolved nor indeed shown to be pointless. No matter how flawed Plato's own arguments and analyses, there may be no better way of coming to grips with the most important philosophical issues still facing us today.

One final point in closing. It is well to remember that Plato, for all his dogmatism, was his own severest critic. The conception of mind, bodies, and persons met with in the *Phaedo* was radically revised in the *Republic*; and the theory of Forms, too, was to undergo a series of refinements and revisions throughout the remainder of Plato's long career as a thinker and teacher. Even the recollection theory undergoes considerable revision between the *Meno* and the *Phaedo*. In all this there is something exemplary for the beginning philosopher. At a minimum, it may mitigate the effect of the dogmatic and authoritarian tendencies that seem such a stunning betrayal of the legacy of Socrates; at most, it provides the single most striking example of that restless energy of self-criticism that is the mark of a truly great thinker. For all these reasons and more, we continue to read and learn from Plato.

Recommended reading and references

Allen, R.E. 1970. *Plato's Euthyphro and the Earlier Theory of Forms*. London: Routledge and Kegan Paul. (A sensitive interpretation, offering a spirited defence of Socratic essentialism.)
Bremmer, J. 1983. *The Early Greek Concept of the Soul*. Princeton: Princeton University Press.
Coxon, A.H. 1970. "Pythagoras" in *The Oxford Classical Dictionary*. Oxford: Oxford University Press.
Dorter, Kenneth. 1982. *Plato's* Phaedo. *An Interpretation*. Toronto: University of Toronto Press. (Philosophically stimulating commentary on the entire text.)
Fritz, Kurt von. 1943. "*Nous* and *Noein* in the Homeric Poems." *Classical Philology*, Vol. XXXVII. (Like Bremmer and Snell, on the Homeric concept of the soul.)
Gallop, David. 1975. *Plato's* Phaedo. Translated with notes by David Gallop. Oxford: Clarendon Press. (A definitive English text and commentary edition.)
Grube, G.M.A. 1980. *Plato's Thought*. Indianapolis: Hackett Publishing Co. (Still a very useful exposition. Organized by theme rather than chronologically.)
Lloyd, G.E.R. 1968. *Aristotle: The Growth and Structure of His Thought*. Cambridge: Cambridge University Press. (A lucid and simple introduction. Chapter 3 deals with Aristotle as a critic of Plato.)
Miles, Murray. 2001. "Plato on Suicide (*Phaedo* 60c–63c)." *Phoenix*, Vol. 55, 3–4.
Nillson, M.P and Croon, J.H. 1970. "Orphism" in *The Oxford Classical Dictionary*. Oxford: Oxford University Press.
Quine, W.V.O. 1953. *From a Logical Point of View*. New York and Evanston: Harper Torchbook. (Several important essays mount an attack on essentialism.)
Robinson, R. 1953. *Plato's Earlier Dialectic*. Oxford: Oxford University Press. (A standard work. Much criticized since its appearance but still very useful.)
Robinson, T.M. 1970. *Plato's Psychology*. Toronto: University of Toronto Press. (Probably the best discussion of this facet of Plato's thought. Follows the sequence of the dialogues in a developmental perspective.)
Ross, W.D. 1951. *Plato's Theory of Ideas*. Oxford: Oxford University Press. (A classic study.)
Ryle, G. 1967. "Plato" in *The Encyclopedia of Philosophy*. Paul Edwards, Editor-in-Chief. New York: Collier Macmillian.
Snell, Bruno. 1982. "Homer's View of Man." Chapter 1 of *The Discovery of the Mind*. New York: Dover Publications.
Van Peursen, C.A. 1966. *Body, Soul, Spirit: A Survey of the Body–Mind Problem*. London: Oxford University Press. (Includes a useful treatment of Old and New Testament conceptions of soul and spirit.)

Questions for reflection, discussion, and review

1. In what ways does the Socrates of the opening and closing pages of the *Phaedo* resemble or differ from the Socrates of the other dialogues studied?
2. What does the word *probandum* mean? What is the *probandum* of the defence of the philosophic life? And of the *Phaedo* as a whole? Do the other dialogues studied thus far have a *probandum*, or is their objective different from the *Phaedo*'s?
3. What does the word 'soul' suggest to you? Is there a difference in meaning between 'soul,' 'mind,' and 'spirit'? Do human beings possess souls at all, or is the concept of soul a fiction of some sort?
4. What characteristics of your former life would you have to retain (be it after death or after a bout of amnesia) in order to consider yourself *the same person* that you are now? Why these characteristics?
5. What reasons can you suggest why philosophers have always attempted to provide proofs of an afterlife with reward for the good and punishment for the wicked? Is the belief in an afterlife of great personal or social importance?
6. Is there any good reason to suppose that the body (the senses and desires) is the source of all evil in human life and thus a hindrance to achieving the best life, individually and collectively? Or is Plato's denunciation of the body just name-calling without rational argument?
7. Do you think Plato must have been conscious of the logical fallacies that scholars have detected in his arguments for immortality?
8. Granted that all of Plato's arguments fail, is there any way at all that human beings can actually *know* whether there is an afterlife?
9. What point might there be in analyzing arguments for immortality that are unconvincing to begin with and that prove fallacious upon careful dissection? Granted that we do not learn from such arguments whether or not our souls are immortal, do we learn anything at all?
10. Is the Cyclical Argument circular? Are all Plato's arguments ultimately circular? Why?
11. To what extent is the Plato of the *Phaedo* true to the teachings of his revered master Socrates? Could he in fairness be said to have *betrayed* the spirit of Socratic wisdom (pursuit of knowledge in the spirit of intellectual modesty)?

PART THREE

DESCARTES AND THE ROAD TO CERTAINTY

I have always thought that two topics—namely God and the soul—are prime examples of subjects where demonstrative proofs ought to be given with the aid of philosophy rather than theology. For us who are believers, it is enough to accept on faith that the human soul does not die with the body, and that God exists; but in the case of unbelievers, it seems that there is no religion, and practically no moral virtue that they can be persuaded to adopt until these two truths are proved to them by natural reason.

Descartes, Dedicatory Epistle to the *Meditations*

22

Subjectivism and Dualism

22.1 Introductory

According to our earlier periodization of the history of philosophy (see 1.3.1), the modern era dates from the middle of the seventeenth century. As for why scholars are almost unanimous in accepting this dating, recall the working definition of 'metaphysics' given earlier (see 20.7): the philosophical study of being in general, but especially of supersensible or immaterial beings (God and the human soul), and of first principles. Descartes (1596–1650) inaugurated a new era in philosophy by providing novel answers to the questions about first principles, about what there is in the universe, and about the relation between matter and mind, not to mention a new way of proving God's existence.

What is distinctive about Descartes's answers can be brought under two simple heads: subjectivism and dualism. The former concerns the order of knowing, the latter the order of being. Both are central to metaphysics as mankind's attempt to orientate itself within the totality of what is (see chap. 3). The former embodies Descartes's unprecedented attempt to provide a moral and intellectual basis for human life that is *absolutely certain*. For these reasons, the title 'Father of Modern Philosophy' belongs quite properly to Descartes and no one else.

22.2 The metaphysical meditations

It is often alleged that the revolution in philosophy brought about by Descartes consisted in turning away from the traditional concerns of metaphysics. Into their place stepped (1) epistemology, that is, the study of the sources and scope of human *knowledge*. According to some, the order of knowing not only gained in importance, it even supplanted the order of being as the central focus of philosophy. Witness, for example, the testimony of a distinguished contemporary Oxford philosopher (Anthony Kenny): "From Descartes onwards philosophers placed in the centre of their discipline ... epistemology. Epistemology is the branch of philosophy which focuses on the question: how do we know what we know?" A leading French expositor of Descartes (J.-L. Marion) takes a somewhat similar view, except that he treats epistemology as a newfangled ontology: with Descartes the science of being *qua* being became the science of beings *qua* known or knowable (epistemology). It was suggested earlier that this innovation really belongs to the later period of Berkeley and Kant (see 4.9).

According to others, Descartes inaugurated (2) a new conception of metaphysics itself as concerned primarily with the sensible or material world studied in modern science. Metaphysics, on this view, is tantamount to a speculative philosophical physics. It deals with the most basic (non-empirical) concepts and principles underlying the empirical scientific study of the universe. The view that Descartes, like Kant after him, was primarily concerned to lay the groundwork for modern mathematical physics is widely defended by historians of science today (notably Daniel Garber and Stephen Gaukroger).

While certain features of Descartes's philosophical writings speak for these views, there are many decisive considerations against them. Here we can only allude to three. For one, (a) Descartes gave his chief work the title, *Meditations on First Philosophy, in which are demonstrated the existence of God and the distinction between the human soul and the body*. Here the talk is of God, the soul, existence, and First Philosophy (Aristotle's expression for what his students were to call 'metaphysics'; see 20.5). There is nothing at all here about knowledge, and hardly anything about material things. In his private correspondence, too, Descartes always referred to this work as his "metaphysical meditations." Furthermore, (b) the extent of Descartes's preoccupation with the question of being (existence *and* essence) in the *Meditations* is obvious on the most cursory reading. (See the outline of the overall structure of the *Meditations* in 25.3 below.) Finally, (c) Descartes's principal doctrine in the *Meditations*, as he says repeatedly, is the *real distinction between body and soul*, that is, the doctrine that the soul is an immaterial thing capable of existing in its own right, without the material body. This metaphysical doctrine concerning the soul's relation to the body will be examined in detail in chapter 27.

These considerations suggest that the work we are about to study is *primarily* a metaphysics in a fairly standard traditional sense. It is concerned above all with the being of the supersensible, that is, God and the human soul, not with the universe of physical or sensible things. Nevertheless, there is no denying that the question of the order of knowing enjoys new prominence in the metaphysics of Descartes, and that the *Meditations* contain important and original doctrines about the material universe as well. Descartes was, after all, a creative mathematician as well as a working theoretical physicist, as proponents of these other views never tire of pointing out. But his main interest was metaphysics, to which everything else was subordinate. If the epigraph to this part means anything, it means just that.

22.3 A new style of metaphysics

Although his basic conception of metaphysics remained remarkably close to that of the Aristotelian mainstream of philosophy, Descartes nevertheless inaugurated a new style of metaphysics, and it is for this that he is regarded as the Father of Modern Philosophy. The main departures from previous metaphysics can be summed up under two heads: (1) reversal of the traditional order of knowing (Cartesian subjectivism), and (2) change, though not a reversal, in the traditional order of being (Cartesian dualism). Consideration of these two points will provide at least a skeletal outline of Descartes's philosophy, to be fleshed out in the following chapters.

22.3.1 Cartesian subjectivism

As far as the *order of knowing* is concerned, Descartes gave metaphysics/theology a new subject-oriented slant. The main innovation is a new *starting point* for knowledge: not (as in Aristotle and medieval Aristotelianism) the physical cosmos around us, but the human soul or mind within us, the 'human subject,' as we say nowadays. Henceforth this is the point of departure of all philosophical enquiry. In a Cartesian context, 'subjectivism' does not mean resting content with 'merely subjective knowledge,' with 'personal' or 'individual truth,' or the like. It means, rather, that strictly objective knowledge *concerning the human subject* is the basis of all objective knowledge concerning anything else.

The elevation of knowledge of the subject to the status of *the* starting point of philosophy represents a radical break with the past. From the high Middle Ages on, Aristotle's focus on ordinary sensible things had dominated Christian philosophy. This is not to discount the decisive influence of Plato's other-worldly tendencies on Christian theology, especially on the Church Fathers; but as of the thirteenth century the until then lost writings of Aristotle on physics and metaphysics began to make their way into the Christian centres of European intellectual life from the Islamic countries of North Africa, where the great libraries of late antiquity were situated (see 1.3.1). Once absorbed into the philosophy and theology of the Christian Middle Ages, they gradually overrode the Platonic elements. Naturally, the works of Aristotle underwent quite radical revision in the process, particularly at the hands of St Thomas Aquinas. They had to be made to fit the Christian conception of the world as "created out of nothing" and the Christian doctrine of the immortality of the human soul through resurrection. In the end it was this medieval Aristotelianism that supplanted Christian Platonism as the dominant philosophy of the period immediately preceding Descartes's appearance on the scene. With it came the emphatic rejection of Plato's dogma that changing particular things could not be reliably known. Henceforth, precisely the sensible, material things around us were to be regarded as the first and most reliably known objects of science. So Descartes was, in a sense, only switching back, if not to a completely 'other-worldly' starting point like Plato's, at least to an immaterial or spiritual starting point, as in the Platonic tradition. His starting point, however, was not a transcendent realm of immaterial entities (the Forms), nor yet an immanent realm of immaterial essences, but an immanent domain of immaterial being: the human soul and its changing states.

More precisely, the soul *and God—in that order*—are the first entities about which certain knowledge is attainable according to Descartes. Moreover, without such knowledge of them there can be no genuine knowledge about anything else, even in mathematics and the physical sciences. So even geometry and physics (not to mention the objects known in everyday experience) depend for their status as knowledge on metaphysics.

That this represents a complete reversal of the traditional order of knowing is plain enough. Ever since Aristotle's lost writings transformed the thought-world of medieval Christendom, knowledge of the non-sensible—God and the mind—was taken to depend upon the immediately and reliably known existence and nature of sensible things. As for the supersensible divine, knowledge of it is acquired *by inference* from knowledge of the sensible world (see 20.5.1–2). Knowledge of the human mind, on the other hand, is a *concomitant* of (literally 'goes along with') knowledge of ordinary sensible things, on which it therefore depends. For it is in perceiving sensible things that we are concomitantly aware of ourselves *as* perceiving them. So although 'earlier' in the order of being ('in himself') God is 'later' in the order of knowing ('in relation to us'). And the knowledge of the human mind, even though concomitant and therefore simultaneous with the knowledge of material things, is also 'later' in the sense that it depends on that of which it is a concomitant. So Descartes's new order of knowing turned the old one around: first comes mind, then God, and finally the world, whereas according to the old order the material or sensible world came first in the order of knowing.

This aspect of the Cartesian revolution in philosophy can be termed 'the subjective turn' or simply 'subjectivism.' It cannot be stressed enough that such subjectivism has nothing to do with claiming that all knowledge is subjective or relative. The point is rather that the only secure starting point for *exact, objective, certain, absolutely reliable knowledge* is the knowledge of the human soul (the human subject) and of God. All other knowledge that is exact, certain, and so forth, depends on, or is derived from, this.

22.3.2 Cartesian dualism

Like most major thinkers down to the eighteenth-century, Descartes accepted the idea of creation in the Judeo-Christian Bible almost unquestioningly. In other words, he retained the traditional primacy of God, the uncreated being and first cause of everything, within the order of being. All else depends for its existence on God, the infinite and eternal being, who depends for his existence on nothing but himself, since he alone exists *necessarily*, by the necessity of his own nature. (On necessary and eternal existence, see 16.5.1 and the later sections referred to there.) God's infinite nature just *is* existence, to exist; he is the infinite source of the existence of all finite existing things (see 4.9 and 20.5.2). That was at bottom the teaching of the medievals, and it is Descartes's doctrine as well.

Yet in regard to *created* minds and *created* matter, Descartes introduced an important change. For Aristotelian metaphysics, as for everyday common sense, mind or consciousness depends upon the body (or brain) for its existence and for the existence of all its states. Descartes did not turn this relation around, making body dependent on mind, as in the later idealistic philosophies of Berkeley and Kant (see chap. 3 above). Instead, he set up *two separate and independent realms of created beings*, neither of which enjoys priority over the other. Nor did Descartes relegate the material to a lower grade or degree of being and reality, as Plato did. Both mind and matter are real; both are substances to exactly the same extent, each existing independently of the other, though both are dependent on God.

So bodies exist, and are the way they are, regardless of whether or what any mind thinks of them; and minds exist and think, regardless of whether they are united with any material body or whether the material world they think about actually exists outside their thought. This aspect of the Cartesian revolution is far removed from later idealisms, though, like them, it is a reaction against earlier materialism, reductive and non-reductive. It is usually labelled 'dualism' or 'mind–body dualism.'

22.4 Outline of the part on Descartes

Cartesian subjectivism and dualism have set the philosophical agenda for all subsequent philosophy throughout the modern era, right down to the present day. This includes especially efforts to overcome one or both of them, not to mention attempts to overcome or eliminate metaphysics itself. The importance of Descartes's *Meditations* can therefore hardly be overrated. In the succeeding chapters we must attempt to flesh out this skeletal picture of Descartes's philosophical system. We conclude this introductory chapter with a brief outline of the topics to be covered.

Descartes's *Meditations* consist of six successive days of philosophical reflection, of which we shall omit the fourth. The remaining topics (to be dealt with in sequence in the five chapters of this part) are:

1 Doubt and Certainty (First Meditation)
2 Mind and Matter (Second Meditation)

3 Truth and Circularity (Third Meditation)
4 Existence of God (Third and Fifth Meditations)
5 Man and World (Sixth Meditation)

Occasional references will be made to the Replies and Objections to the *Meditations*. Descartes solicited, or had a friend solicit, critical comments on his *Meditations* from the leading philosophers and theologians of Europe. He then provided detailed replies to all the objections he had received. All this material (amounting to several times the bulk of the *Meditations*) he published together with the *Meditations* themselves. They are an invaluable source of insight that we cannot do without entirely.

23

Doubt and Certainty

23.1 Three uses of doubt

In the "Synopsis of the following six Meditations," Descartes describes the "extensive doubt" of the First Meditation as having *three uses*:

> Although the usefulness of such extensive doubt is not apparent at first sight, its greatest benefit lies in [1] freeing us from all our preconceived opinions, and [2] providing the easiest route by which the mind may be led away from the senses. The eventual result of this doubt is [3] to make it impossible for us to have any further doubts about what we subsequently discover to be true. (12)

These three uses—(1) freeing the mind of "preconceived opinion," (2) detaching it from the senses, and (3) making "further doubts" impossible—correspond to three obstacles to the free and unhampered exercise of human reason. They are: (1) prejudice, (2) habit, and (3) scepticism. These can be more fully described as (1) the *non-use of reason* owing to submission to authority, (2) the *misuse of reason* owing to undue reliance on the senses, and, finally, (3) the *mistrust of reason* owing to excessive scepticism. Overcoming these impediments to rationality is tantamount to adopting the *critical attitude*, instilling in oneself, through a carefully followed regimen of doubt, the *critical cast of mind*—much as we aim, through physical exercise, to keep our bodies fit. This, and not the raising of a lot of foolish objections to things no sane person would question, is the purpose of the course of doubt relentlessly pursued in the First Meditation. That said, it can and should still be asked whether Descartes takes doubt too far, whether the attitude he recommends is in fact too critical.

23.2 Prejudice: non-use of reason

Many people refuse to think for themselves. Even in the absence of other obstacles, they decline to exercise their native capacity to inform themselves of the facts and arguments bearing on a given issue, or to engage in rational reflection in an effort to discover the truth of the matter for themselves. Instead of passing an informed, reasoned judgment of their own, they prefer to let others do their thinking for them, even about matters that fall within the province of that universal human reason possessed, in some measure, by all mankind.

Judgments passed *prior* to the critical examination of the relevant facts and arguments can be called 'pre-judgments' or, more idiomatically, 'prejudices.' By "pre-conceived opinions" Descartes means: voluntary subjection to the authority of another. There are, of course, plenty of authorities to whom one can defer: parents, teachers, professors, clergymen, eminent members of the professions (law, medicine, and so on), scientists, social scientists, political leaders or parties, institutions like the church or prominent research organizations, 'think-tanks,' the writings of St Thomas Aquinas, of Marx and Engels, the little red book of Chairman Mao, the Bible, 'the many' (that is, what 'most people nowadays' think), 'progressive thinkers,' 'successful people,' 'people who are "with it",' and so on. And there are just as many individuals, who, in some role or other, are willing to submit to the authority of one or more of the above. As 'good members of the profession,' as 'good citizens,' 'good Christians,' 'good Catholics,' 'good Communists,' as 'the party faithful,' as 'true believers' in 'the cause,' and so forth, we may be only too ready to relinquish the right to think critically and independently, to pass judgment for ourselves after mature consideration of the relevant facts and arguments, simply taking over instead the ready-made opinions prescribed by such authorities as these, that is, in a word: prejudices.

If, on the other hand, we practise the "extensive doubt" of which Descartes speaks in the "Synopsis," there simply are no authorities. If we doubt the existence of *everything*, as Descartes does, then, for us, no authorities exist. We are forced to rely on ourselves, that is, on our own reason.

It is interesting to recall in this context Socrates's words to Crito when the latter expressed concern about what "the many" might think, and to compare it to what Descartes says to someone (Gassendi, in fact) who raises an objection based on the authority of "many great thinkers":

Your argument from authority is, I admit, sound enough, but ... you certainly should not have presented it to a mind so withdrawn from corporeal things that it does not even know whether any people existed before it, and hence is not influenced by their authority.

This certainly pulls the rug out from under appeals to authority (see 7.7.1).

23.3 Habit: misuse of reason

Most people have the deeply ingrained habit of believing the testimony of their senses unquestioningly. We trust ordinary sense perception, as perhaps nothing else, relying on observation as the only really reliable guide to what to believe, what is real, what is true. Some even go so far as to deny the existence of anything that cannot be seen, touched, and so on—for example, the soul or God. As Descartes himself wrote in the *Discourse*, there are many who

> are convinced that there is some difficulty in knowing God, and even in knowing what their own soul is. The reason for this is that they never raise their minds above things which can be perceived by the senses: they are so used to think of things only by imagining [picturing] them ... that whatever is unimaginable seems to them unintelligible.

The "extensive doubt" of the First Meditation is an elaborate *exercise* designed to counteract, and ultimately to overcome, this firmly entrenched habit of misusing reason; by a thorough *critique* of the senses we can divest ourselves once and for all of that habit of *naive* or *uncritical* acceptance of the testimony of ordinary sense experience.

23.3.1 Reason and the senses

This quite naturally brings to mind another attack on the senses, that of Plato in the *Phaedo*. However, there is a different, more likely paradigm for a Christian thinker like Descartes, educated as he was at a strict Jesuit school. In the Christian monastic tradition meditation is a spiritual exercise designed to turn the meditator's attention away from the tangible, sensible things around him ('the world') to what is 'within,' the soul and the divine. Like religious meditation, Descartes's philosophical regimen of doubt seeks to turn us inward, instilling in the mind a profound mistrust of the external senses. By casting doubt on judgments derived from that source (prejudices of the senses), as well as from external authorities (prejudices of authority), it gradually turns us *toward* our sole or ultimate authority in matters of truth and knowledge: the "natural light" of human reason. By the correct use of reason Descartes understands: exclusive reliance on the immediate evidence of rational insight that something is so and cannot be otherwise. The intuition of necessary truth is at the same time the immediate experience of what truth in general is. For anyone who has once had the experience, there can be no higher authority than reason itself; certainly, the testimony of the senses can never bring the dictates of reason into doubt. Thus, just as the vulgar doubt the existence of anything they cannot see with their own eyes, so the philosopher doubts everything he cannot 'see' with 'the mind's eye'—the natural light of reason. This reverses the tendency of the ordinary misuse of reason.

The philosopher, then, will accept that and only that which is confirmed by the immediate experience of self-evidence that we can only have within ourselves, by turning inward, away from the deceptive deliverances of the senses; in short, by *meditating*. Descartes is quite explicit on this point outside the *Meditations*. For example, when Gassendi, faced with Descartes's continual appeals to inner evidence as the touchstone of truth, found it necessary to point out that "my thought is not the standard which determines the truth of things," Descartes replied as follows:

If the claim is that *my* thought must not be the standard *for others*, obliging *them* to believe something just because *I* think it is true, then I entirely agree. But this is quite irrelevant ... since I never wanted to force anyone to follow my authority. On the contrary, I pointed out in several places that one should allow oneself to be convinced only by quite evident reasoning ... I say that the thought of each person—i.e., the [evident] perception or knowledge which he has of something—should be for him the 'standard which determines the truth of the thing.' (e.a.)

23.3.2 The title of the Meditations

In this context, there are a few other things to note about the unusual title of the work we are about to study. For one, 'meditations' had been used once before as the title of a philosophical work, by the Roman emperor-philosopher Marcus Aurelius Antoninus in the second century AD. But, as noted already, the real inspiration for Descartes's choice of title probably came from the Christian monastic tradition. The actual models are likely the *Spiritual Exercises* of Ignatius Loyola (founder of the Jesuit order) and the devotional meditations of St Augustine's *Confessions*.

The single most important thing about the title, however, is the implicit appeal to *one's own* rational insight, to the evident intuition of the lone meditating individual. While we can and must submit to worldly and ecclesiastical authorities in matters of conduct, the dictates of one's own reason are the only authority in the search for truth and knowledge. On account of the obvious parallel with Christian reformers of the sixteenth century (see 1.3.2), Descartes's revolution in philosophy has been called "Protestant individualism secularized." The parallel seems apt. Luther, the father of the Protestant Reformation, stressed that salvation came directly from God through grace, of which each individual could be assured in the immediate experience of faith. No longer was there any need for the Church and its clergy as intermediaries; the very distinction between clergy and laity was collapsed, liberating each individual to work out his own salvation for himself. Similarly, Descartes taught that each man's reason, the inner experience of evidence, is his own touchstone of truth, a truth the same for all and accessible in theory to each, though in practice discoverable only by those prepared to meditate earnestly. Small wonder, then, that Descartes has been regarded by his fellow Catholics as a crypto-Protestant. Harder to understand is the fact that "the Protestants thought he was an atheist, and the atheists have tended to suspect that he was a hypocrite" (Harry Frankfurt). Yet given his devotion to the ideals of the new mechanistic mathematical science, together with his frequent protestations of orthodoxy and obedience to ecclesiastical authority, all this may not be so surprising after all.

The most striking thing about Descartes's title, though, is the way in which it harks back to the individualism of Socrates. For it was Socrates, the midwife and ironist, after all, who insisted that each individual must discover the truth for himself (see 9.4.2 and 9.5.4). Nevertheless, we shall have occasion to notice some key differences between Socrates and Descartes later (see 27.13 and 30.5.2).

23.4 Scepticism: mistrust of reason

The last and greatest deterrent to using one's native reason to discover the truth for oneself, relying neither on authority nor the senses, is the mistrust of reason engendered by sceptical doubts about the capacity of reason to 'know' or 'prove' anything.

Descartes lived in a century in which confidence in human reason remained profoundly shaken by the revival of the ideas of the ancient sceptics in the century before. If anything, the shadow of scepticism looms even larger over the *Meditations* than that of dogmatic Aristotelianism. If we practise doubt *ourselves*, he seems to say, taking it to the extremes of scepticism, even beyond the point to which Academic and Pyrrhonian sceptics took it (see above 9.1.4), then, if anything withstands such doubt, that and that alone may be taken as indubitable, certain, or true.

This can be called Cartesian or *methodological* scepticism in order to distinguish it from the *doctrinal* scepticism of Academic and Pyrrhonian sceptics. Such scepticism is a tool or device whose purpose is to lead us to, rather than show us the impossibility of, genuine certainty. We must bear in mind that Cartesian doubt is not *just* a matter of suspending judgment about everything that seems in the least doubtful, as did previous sceptics; Cartesian doubt is above all a deliberate attempt to generate new grounds for suspending judgment on some matters, while accepting as definitively true all and only that which withstands even the most extravagant efforts to cast doubt upon it. The difference is all-important.

23.5 A fourth use of doubt: a new criterion of certainty

So much for the three uses of doubt mentioned in Descartes's "Synopsis." While helping to overcome the (1) non-use, (2) misuse, and (3) mistrust of reason, this "extensive doubt" also (4) provides a reliable *criterion of truth or certainty*.

This further benefit of systematic doubt arises from the first three. The provision of a secure starting point, just one item of knowledge that is absolutely certain and indubitable, will suffice as a *firm foundation* on which to *reconstruct* the whole system of human knowledge disestablished piecemeal by the regimen of doubt. As noted earlier, the discovery of one such truth is, at the same time, the immediate inner experience of what certainty, what truth itself is. Nevertheless, a workable *criterion, standard, or test* is needed to guarantee that everything that we subsequently build upon this foundation is as secure as the foundation itself. For that, the immediate inner experience of truth may not be enough. What is needed is a *directive* or rule like the following: If I am to assent only to what is certain, thus avoiding error and discovering truth, I must not assent to anything which does not clearly withstand *all three* of the progressively more radical grounds of doubt in the First Meditation. Henceforth, the terms 'certain' and 'true' can be correctly applied, not just to the first truth, but to anything that can be shown to withstand each of the sceptical grounds of doubt considered in the First Meditation.

Notice that even if most beliefs erected on the new foundation are substantially the same as those rejected earlier, there will nevertheless be three distinct *gains*: (1) That which was formerly only *believed*, perhaps naively and uncritically, will, *after* the regimen of doubt, be shown to have met the very highest standards of rational criticism that we can apply, and hence to be worthy (if anything is) of the name of *knowledge*. (2) Although many of the elements of the new system of knowledge may be the same, they will be ordered differently, organized rationally, from foundations to 'rooftop.' The upshot, in other words, is a new order of knowing, even if the items within it are substantially the same. From this second, a third, from Descartes's perspective no doubt the greatest, gain follows as a corollary. For (3) understanding what things come first in the order of knowledge—the immaterial, supersensible things—will permanently change our attitude toward metaphysics and the sciences. Thus, Descartes writes in the concluding passage of the "Synopsis":

> The great benefit of these arguments is not, in my view, that they prove what they establish—namely that there really is a world, and that human beings have bodies and so on—since no sane person ever seriously doubted these things. The point is that in considering these arguments we come to realize that they are not as solid or as transparent as the arguments which lead us to knowledge of our own minds and of God, so that the latter are the most certain and evident of all possible objects of knowledge for the human intellect. Indeed, this is the one thing that I set myself to prove in these Meditations. (15–16)

23.6 Summary: four uses of doubt and the critical cast of mind

Here again are the four uses of doubt discussed in this chapter:

(1) overcoming prejudices due to authority;
(2) overcoming the habit of uncritical reliance on the senses;

(3) overcoming sceptical doubts about our ability to know anything; and
(4) providing ourselves with a critical standard of certainty or truth.

Together they serve to inculcate in the reader the *critical cast of mind*. This, for Descartes, means above all: the deliberate refusal to assent to anything that is not either intuitively or demonstrably certain by the strict standard laid down in the First Meditation; in other words, suspension of judgment on all matters that are less than *absolutely* certain. Note the 'all or nothing' principle at work here: unless some possible item of knowledge can satisfy the very highest standard of certainty conceivable, it is not to be believed or accepted *at all*, to any degree, not even provisionally or temporarily. This rule is introduced as the only sure means, if not of discovering truth, then at least of avoiding falsehood or error.

One is immediately struck by the difference between Descartes's maxim and the first ground rule of Socratic enquiry: 'follow the best argument' (see 12.3.). Behind the latter lies a clear recognition that absolute certainty is not for the likes of us. And when it comes to action or conduct, Descartes would probably have agreed. Later we shall compare Descartes's maxim with Hume's very different formula for the discovery of truth and avoidance of error (see 30.5.2). Hume's is predicated on the essentially Socratic conviction that absolute certainty is not for us. Of this there is no hint at all in Descartes's rigid 'all or nothing' approach.

23.7 Implementation

So much for the procedure to be followed. As for its implementation, Descartes points out that it would be an endless undertaking to examine all our beliefs one by one, accepting or rejecting them on an individual basis. But if we examine the "basic principles" (18) on which they depend and if these are found wanting, then everything that rests on them can be rejected all at once. There are two such "principles," that is, two sources or faculties from which all, or practically all, our knowledge stems: (1) sense perception (first-hand to nth-hand observation, aided by memory); and (2) the intellect or reason.

The difference between first- and nth-hand observation is implicit in the disjunctive expression "from the senses [first-hand] or through the senses [hearsay]" (18). As for the other faculty, reason, it includes, first of all, (a) the 'intuitive' capacity to grasp the meaning of certain concepts and the truth of certain first principles or axioms, whether of logic, metaphysics, or mathematics. Thus, 'all bodies are extended,' 'if equals are added to equals the sums are equal,' 'the shortest distance between two points is a straight line,' 'what is done cannot be made undone,' and 'nothing comes from nothing' are all axioms whose truth is immediately intuited by reason. But reason includes also (b) the 'logical' or (as we say) 'ratiocinative' process of deriving conclusions from premises, for example, theorems from the definitions and axioms in a formal axiomatized system like arithmetic or geometry. We shall return to the distinction between the intuitive and ratiocinative or demonstrative knowledge later, when we consider the force of the 'therefore' in Descartes's famous maxim: 'I think, *therefore* I am.' Right now the point is that, like perception, reason includes indirect as well as direct modes of knowing. This may be an opportune time at which to note that 'reason,' for Descartes, has exactly the same meaning as 'intellect' or 'the understanding.' Kant was the first to treat the intellect and reason as two distinct faculties; for Descartes they are two different names for the same 'higher' capacity of the mind.

Now (1) is the source of our (i) pre-scientific, everyday knowledge. As for the knowledge amassed by the physical sciences, it depends on observation *and* on reasoning, on applying mathematical concepts to the material universe in physics and astronomy, for example. Thus (ii) scientific knowledge depends on (1) and (2) together. As for (iii) knowledge in the so-called 'pure' mathematical sciences (arithmetic, geometry, and algebra as opposed to 'applied' mathematics in physics and astronomy), such knowledge depends on (2) reason alone, though such things as diagrams and illustrations can facilitate the acquisition of this kind of knowledge.

Calling these two "principles" into doubt must therefore result in the complete overthrow of (i), (ii), and (iii), that is, the whole system of human knowledge built up hitherto, the entirety of which rests on one or both of them.

23.8 The stages of First Meditation doubt

The stages of Descartes's systematic doubt are:

1. Paragraphs 3–5: Argument from Illusion or the Deceptiveness of the Senses (undermines ordinary sense perception)
2. Paragraphs 6–9: Dreaming Argument (undermines ordinary sense perception and scientific observation as well as the more theoretical parts of the physical sciences and hence these sciences as a whole)
3. Paragraphs 10–11: Deceiving God Hypothesis (undermines the pure mathematical sciences like arithmetic and geometry)
4. Paragraphs 12–13: The Supposition of a 'Malicious Demon' (device for suspension of judgment until truth can be found)

We shall examine the first three stages in turn, leaving out the short section on the malicious demon, or rather proceeding as though 'malicious demon' were just another designation for 'deceiving God.' This is a widely held view among scholars. For present purposes nothing turns on whether there is indeed a difference between the deceiving God and the malicious demon.

23.9 First stage: the argument from illusion

The first argument, from illusion or the deceptiveness of the senses, is designed to call into question perceptual judgments regarding bodies observed under less than ideal circumstances, for example, "objects which are very small or in the distance" (18). On the other hand, the same argument has no force against observation statements about, say, middle-sized material objects perceived at an ideal distance from the observer under something like optimal conditions, and perhaps confirmed by other sensory faculties:

for example, that I am here, sitting by the fire, wearing a winter dressing-gown, holding this piece of paper in my hands, and so on. Again, how could it be denied that these hands or this whole body are mine [or exist]? (ibid.)

Observation statements like these correct others that prove delusive, hallucinatory, or otherwise non-veridical, but it is unclear how they themselves could both be correctly described as performed under *optimal* conditions and yet require or admit of correction in the course of further observation. Of course, they might be corrected by some *other* faculty of the mind, by the intellect or reason, for example, but that possibility is not raised in the First Meditation.

So while the argument from illusion suffices to render doubtful all

(1) observation statements or perceptual judgments about individual sensible objects observed under less than ideal conditions,

it is *not* sufficient to call into question any

(2) observation statements or perceptual judgments about the individual objects of ordinary pre-scientific sense perception performed under optimal conditions: for example, that I am sitting here by the fire, that these are my hands, and so on.

Descartes suggests that one would have to be *mad* to doubt (2), and most people would agree. But then, rather suddenly, he dismisses the suggestion with derision ("A brilliant piece of reasoning!"), discovering grounds for doubting (2) after all.

23.10 The dreaming argument

The reason given for entertaining doubts about (2) is that "there never are any sure signs by means of which being awake can be distinguished from being asleep" (19). If so, then it is at least not crazy to suppose that when I make statements about objects around me, believing myself to be perceiving them clearly, under good or even optimal conditions, I *may* in fact be sound asleep and only dreaming—vividly perhaps—that I am observing something real.

At first, this argument may well seem unconvincing. After all, there are many cues by which waking and dream experience can be reliably distinguished. Upon waking up, we grasp well enough that we have just been dreaming and that we are now awake. Even if we grant this, though, it would not be incoherent to suppose that we might, at some future time, wake up from this our waking life (during segments of which we dream) and recognize that it too was just a dream, what we formerly called 'dreams' having been dreams within a dream. The whole of 'life,' then, *could* be just one long well-ordered ('lucid') dream, for all we know.

Now, of course, Descartes realizes full well that it is not more *reasonable* to suppose this than the opposite; he merely wants to show that it is not *insane* to entertain a doubt of this sort, not, at least, for someone bent on being as scrupulously critical as possible in order to (a) rid himself of his unexamined beliefs or prejudices, (b) overcome his naive reliance on the senses, and (c) arrive at something that will withstand the most extreme doubt, that is, meet the very highest possible standard of certainty. It is enough, then, that this possibility is not logically incoherent for there to be some doubt about whether he is waking or sleeping. There does not have to be any evidence for it.

So this dreaming argument takes over where the argument from the deceptiveness of the senses left off, at (2). It renders doubtful even observation statements about the *particular* objects of ordinary pre-scientific sense perception performed under ideal conditions. It would also call into question exact scientific observations carried out under controlled, experimental conditions—though Descartes does not mention these. It extends, moreover, to the following:

(3) statements asserting the existence of objects *of the same general kind as* the objects of ordinary pre-scientific experience (not *my* head, *my* hands and so on, but heads, hands *in general*).

For it might be argued that even if those *particular* objects that I think I see are only dream images, existing nowhere but in my mind, at least the originals of our dreams and fantasies must exist somewhere outside the mind, assuming our imagination to be only *re*productive rather than sheerly productive of images unlike anything ever seen. Yet this assumption the dreaming argument implicitly denies. If we are dreaming, those 'general kinds of things' *may* be invented too. After all, who is to say that the imagination is *not* a faculty of pure invention? That is not how we normally think of it, certainly, but who is to say we are not wrong in taking it for a reproductive rather than a productive faculty?

In addition to the foregoing, the dreaming argument also calls into doubt:

(4) statements about the sensory *qualities* belonging to these general types of things (their colours, odours, tastes, sounds, tactile qualities).

For it might be argued that even if these *general* kinds of things do not really exist outside the mind exactly as I picture them to myself, even if my imagination *is* productive after all in the sense that it can form ideas of objects that I have never seen and that do not exist anywhere, at least the ideas of the *qualities* I imagine such objects to possess must have been derived from qualities actually existing in things outside the mind. These qualitative 'parts' of things, then, cannot have been created by the mind; they, at least, must exist. But again the dreaming argument implies that this may be quite wrong, that even these simple qualities could have been 'dreamt up' by the mind rather than borrowed from anything external.

Next the dreaming argument calls into question

(5) scientific theorizing about "simpler and more universal things" (20) or *quantitative properties*, including place, time, extension, number, and size.

These statements about the size, shape, place, duration, and number as properties of material things are all false if no extended things really *exist* outside the mind. If there are no bodies, then statements about their quantitative properties such as are found in applied mathematical sciences like optics, music (harmonics), and mechanics are just as false as statements about their qualitative features.

Finally, the same dreaming argument casts doubt on

(6) the sciences of "physics, astronomy, medicine" themselves, "and all other disciplines which depend on the study of *composite* things." (20)

For if no material bodies, no stars, no organisms exist, then even the propositions making up the empirical portions of the sciences of physics, astronomy, and medicine, each of which presupposes the existence of its objects, are all false.

The dreaming argument does *not*, however, extend beyond the "simpler and more universal things" mentioned under (5) to

(7) the "simplest and most general things" (ibid.) which are the objects of *pure* mathematics, like the simple propositions of geometry and arithmetic, for example, $2 + 3 = 5$, or a square has four sides.

Why not? Because, Descartes holds, the truth of the propositions of pure mathematics *does not depend on the existence of anything in nature*. For example, the propositions 'A square has no more than four sides' and 'All the radii of a circle are equal in length' are true whether or not any squares or circles actually exist. For (a) it is highly doubtful that there are in fact any perfect circles in nature. Things ordinarily taken for round prove to be only roughly so; when looked at under sufficient magnification, their boundaries are found to be irregular or wavy. The same goes for figures bounded by straight lines (squares, triangles, and so on). Whether at the level of micro-particles or crystals there might be anything that conforms exactly to the definitions of geometrical shapes employed in mathematics is again doubtful. On the other hand, (b) it is absolutely certain that all the radii of a circle are equal and that a square has no more than four sides. From (a) and (b) it follows plainly that the truth of mathematical propositions does not depend on the existence of anything. Descartes makes an argument very like this in the *Discourse* (1637):

I noted that there was nothing at all in these [mathematical] demonstrations which assured me of the existence of their object. For example, I saw clearly that the three angles of a given triangle must equal two right angles; yet for all that, I saw nothing which assured me that there existed any triangle in the world.

It is in order to overthrow (7) that Descartes has to resort to his *third* ground of doubt: the deceiving God hypothesis.

23.11 The Deceiving God hypothesis

This is the most radical ground of doubt adduced by Descartes, even more far-fetched than the possibility that I am really dreaming when I think I am wide awake. It presents us with the possibility that reason itself might be not just fallible (capable of misleading my judgment sometimes) but inherently fallacious (prone to mislead my judgment *all the time*), whenever and however I employ it. This might be the case if I had been created, not by the God of the Judeo-Christian Bible, who is perfectly good or benevolent, but by another very powerful or omnipotent 'god' who is wicked and a deceiver.

For suppose that this deceiving God or "malicious demon" takes pleasure in tricking me into believing things that are false. In order to do so, he has so fashioned my mind that I have a *feeling of certainty* about, an *irresistible desire to assent* to, things that are in fact quite false. Thus, even simple mathematical propositions like 'A square has four sides' are open to doubt after all. For how am I to know that this is not false, if an omnipotent deceiver can make even false things seem absolutely self-evident and true to me?

It has been suggested, notably by Hume, that a doubt as "extensive" as this—one that extends to the reliability of reason itself—must be "entirely incurable," or, as modern writers have said, tantamount to "intellectual suicide" (Alan Gewirth). Why?

Their point is very simple and can be put this way. If you go so far as to doubt your own reason, it is futile to try to reason your way out of doubt. It is exactly as if you suspected that you were stark-raving mad and then set about trying to find *reasons* to convince yourself of your sanity. How could you trust your own reasonings, having assumed that your reason *may* be impaired?

Much the same thing applies to the Deceiving God hypothesis. Once you suppose that even the strongest reasons, intuitions, arguments, or proofs may be unreliable (since your reason is inherently defective or fallacious), you cannot thereafter *consistently* accept any *reasons, intuitions, arguments, or proofs* to the effect that your reason is reliable after all—*or*, for that matter, that it is unreliable!

This is not just a piece of clever sophistry, but an interesting point about the limits of rationality. It can be put this way:

You cannot provide reasons for mistrusting reason itself without *inconsistency*; nor can you give reasons for trusting reason without *circularity*.

Why would it be inconsistent to *argue* that reason is *always* unreliable? Because what you are doing—arguing, trying to persuade someone of something by rational argumentation, by giving reasons—implicitly *assumes as true* the very proposition you *deny*: that reason, argument, and the like are sometimes reliable. And that is obviously self-contradictory. Why, on the other hand, would it be *circular* to *argue* that reason is sometimes reliable? Because what you are in fact doing already takes for granted the truth of what you are trying to prove. You *say* and want to prove that reason is reliable. By giving reasons and arguments to show this, you are already taking for granted the very thing to be proved. So you cannot give reasons for the reliability of reason without circularity, just as you cannot give reasons against it without contradiction.

The upshot is that attacks *by reason* on rationality *as such*—rather than on this or that use or misuse of reason—are utterly futile (self-contradictory); but, it should be noted, the defence of rationality *by reason* must be equally futile (circular). It would seem, then, that you have to just *assume* reason is always unreliable, or *assume* that it is sometimes reliable; you cannot *prove or disprove* its reliability without falling into circularity or contradiction.

If so, then the old juxtapositions between Reason and Faith, Reason and the Emotions, Reason and Custom, Reason and Passion, Reason and Instinct may be misleadingly put. Where there really is a conflict, the choice facing us is not between Reason and Faith, for example, but between a faith in reason or a faith in the teachings of some revealed religion. And so with emotion, passion, instinct, tradition, or any of the other guides to belief and action customarily set over against reason. As soon as one begins to give reasons for preferring reason, one is arguing circularly. There is scant solace to be drawn from the fact that attacks on reason using reason are inconsistent.

Faced with this situation, it is tempting to adopt the posture of Hume, who, confronting a paradox not unlike the present one, mused on "the whimsical condition of mankind who must act and reason and believe; though they are not able, by their most diligent enquiry, to satisfy themselves concerning the foundation of these operations, or to remove the objections, which may be raised against them." Hume undoubtedly has a point worth pondering, though not everyone will reflect on the condition of mankind with quite the relish Hume feels.

23.12 Concluding summary of the stages of doubt

We conclude this chapter with a brief schematic summary of the three main stages of doubt and the types of judgment that each is designed to render doubtful:

I. The Argument from Illusion

(1) Perceptual judgments regarding bodies observed under less-than-ideal circumstances.

II. The Dreaming Argument

(2) Judgments based on ordinary pre-scientific sense perception carried out under optimal conditions.
(3) Judgments asserting the existence of objects of the same general kind as the objects of ordinary pre-scientific experience (not this head, my hands, but heads, hands, etc. in general).
(4) Judgments about the sensory qualities belonging to the sorts of things mentioned under (3) (their colours, odours, tastes, smells, tactile qualities).
(5) Judgments expressing scientific hypotheses about "simpler and more universal things" or regarding quantitative properties of things like space, time, place, extension and its modes.
(6) The sciences of physics, astronomy, medicine themselves, "and all other disciplines which depend on the study of composite things."

III. The Deceiving God Hypothesis

(7) Judgments about the "simplest and most general things" which are the objects of pure mathematics—that is, propositions like two and three added together equal five, and a square has no more than four sides—the denials of which are self-contradictory.

24

Mind and Matter

24.1 The structure of the Second Meditation

The Second Meditation falls into three very unequal parts:

1 Paragraphs 1–3: The Existence of the Self, Mind, or Soul (*cogito, ergo sum*)
2 Paragraphs 4–10: The Essence of the Self, Mind, or Soul ('What am I?')
3 Paragraphs 11–17: The 'Mind-better-known-than-body' Doctrine (The Wax Example)

Part 3, the only one concerned with body or matter, is disproportionately long, while 1 and 2, dealing exclusively with mind, are of a historical importance altogether disproportionate to their length. With 1, the main task of the first half of the Cartesian project, the establishment of a new order of knowing (subjectivism), is complete. The place of God and the external world—if there is a God and an external world—remain to be determined, but the starting point of knowledge is firmly fixed. To the extent that the mind is already shown to be a thinking substance, capable of existing in its own right, without the body, the task of establishing a new order of being (dualism) is also well under way. The place of God and material things in the order of knowing and of being will be determined once their existence is established in the Third and Sixth Meditations.

We shall discuss 2 in 24.6 and 3 in 24.7. Sections 24.2–5 are devoted to aspects of 1, Descartes's founding principle, *cogito, ergo sum*.

24.2 The requirements of an 'Archimedean point' or first principle

Descartes gets his Second Meditation under way with a quick backward glance over the previous day's doubts, renewing the search for just "one thing, however slight, that is certain and unshakeable" (24). Archimedes, who discovered the law of the lever, is reputed to have said: "Give me a place to stand [that is, a fixed point, and a lever long enough], and I will lift the world." By analogy, Descartes needs only a fixed and immovable point, an absolutely certain *first principle*, in order to rebuild the system of the sciences overthrown in the previous Meditation. On this *metaphysical* foundation the whole edifice of human knowledge, comprising both pure and applied mathematics and all the particular physical sciences, is to be reconstructed in the succeeding Meditations.

The requirements to be satisfied by any principle that may be considered an 'Archimedean point' are three. As a *metaphysical* first principle it must (1) assert the *existence* of something. Moreover, it must (2) assert the existence of a *substance* or thing rather than a mere property, quality, or accident of a thing. Finally, what it asserts must be (3) absolutely or perfectly *certain*.

The fixed starting point or first principle is found in the third paragraph of the Second Meditation. The relevant portion is worth quoting in full:

Is there not a God, or whatever I may call him, who puts into me [my mind] the thoughts I am now having? But why do I think this, since I myself may perhaps be the author of these thoughts [that is, dreaming]. In that case am not I, at least, something? But I have just said that I have no senses and no body. This is the sticking point: what follows from this? Am I so bound up with a body and with senses that I cannot exist without them? But I have convinced myself that there is absolutely nothing in the world, no sky, no earth, no minds, no bodies. Does it now follow that I too do not exist? No: if I convinced myself of something, then I certainly existed. But there is a deceiver of supreme power and cunning who is deliberately and constantly deceiving me. In that case I too undoubtedly exist, if he is deceiving me; and let him deceive me as much as he can, he will never bring it about that I am nothing so long as I think that I am something. So after considering everything very thoroughly, I must finally conclude that this proposition, *I am, I exist*, is necessarily true whenever it is put forward by me or conceived in my mind. (24–5)

This is the formulation of the *Meditations* (1641). In an earlier work written in French (*Discourse on Method*, 1637) and a later Latin work (*The Principles of Philosophy*, 1644), Descartes had given his first truth the formulations *je pense, donc je suis* and *cogito, ergo sum*, respectively. Both can be translated: 'I (am) think(ing), therefore I am.' This last is the formulation in which Descartes's founding principle has become justly famous. With these three Latin words, modern philosophy begins.

24.3 The meaning and certainty of *cogito*

Let us now consider each of the words in the Latin formulation of Descartes's founding principle, beginning with *cogito*. It was noted in 7.12.2 that 'meaning' is ambiguous. To understand what Descartes means by *cogito*, 'I think,' we must consider both (a) its extensional meaning (what it refers to, names, or designates) and (b) its intensional meaning (its connotations or sense). Having ascertained exactly what it means, we can then consider (c) its alleged certainty.

24.3.1 Extensional meaning of cogito

Descartes provides a couple of definitions of 'thought' in other works, though none in the *Meditations* themselves. Both definitions show that the word had a much broader extension for Descartes than nowadays. "The word 'thought' covers everything that exists in such a way that we are immediately conscious of it. Thus all the operations of the will, the intellect, the imagination and the senses are thoughts." And: "By the term 'thought' I understand everything of which we are conscious as taking place within us insofar as there is a consciousness of it in us. And that is why not only understanding, willing, and imagining but also sensing is the same as thought."

To clarify just how Descartes's use of 'thought' differs from ours extensionally, we can distinguish the following:

(a) just thinking about something in the sense of *imagining* it—for example, picturing that you are now lying on the beach in the Bahamas, imagining you can see the sea, feel the sun, and so on;

(b) *conceiving* something in the sense of *understanding* it, for example, the *thought* occurs to you that a week in the Bahamas involves a half day of travel each way (this kind of thinking usually does not involve any mental pictures or imagery);

(c) *judging*, for example, believing that winter is better in the Bahamas, or not believing this, *thinking* that it is false, that it is in fact worse there than here;

(d) actually *perceiving* something with your senses (seeing, hearing, touching, etc.), for instance, seeing the Bahamas out the window of an airplane, or seeing a photograph of the Bahamas;

(e) *volition* or wanting something, for example, wanting to go to the Bahamas, or the opposite, 'feeling aversion,' wanting not to go to Moose Jaw, for example;

(f) *emotion* or feelings like 'loving,' 'hating,' 'fearing' something, for example, loving the warmth of the Caribbean sun, hating or fearing the cold of the prairie winter.

Now *we* could refer to (a) through (c) as 'thinking' without stretching the limits of standard English. After all, we say 'I am just *thinking* of *x*' to distinguish an object or action being imaginatively contemplated from one now actually observed or carried out; and we say 'I *think* …' in the sense of both 'I understand that …' and 'I believe that …' But for Descartes (a) through (f) are *all* 'thinking.' And that certainly is a stretch for contemporary usage.

If there is a word in standard English that has the same extension as Descartes's word 'thought,' that word is 'consciousness.' We would, without hesitation, call (a) through (f) different 'conscious states,' 'states of mind,' 'mental states,' 'psychic states,' or 'modes of *consciousness*,' but not 'modes of *thinking*.'

24.3.2 Intensional meaning of cogito

Shall we then translate Descartes's Latin and French words for 'thought' by 'consciousness,' taking 'I am conscious' as the closest approximation to the intensional meaning of *cogito*? The trouble is that Descartes himself uses the term 'consciousness'—or rather its Latin and French equivalents—in his definitions of 'thought.' Consider again the second definition: "By the term 'thought' I understand everything of which we are *conscious* as taking place within us insofar as there is a *consciousness* of it in us." If 'consciousness' and 'thought' meant the same for Descartes, this definition would be circular (see 7.7.2 and 9.2.2).

But Descartes is not guilty of circularity here. Whereas *we* use 'consciousness' in a manner that is intensionally and extensionally equivalent to Descartes's word 'thought,' Descartes uses it to refer to that one feature that all those things correctly described as 'thought' have in common: they are all *objects* of immediate *inner* awareness, of *self*-awareness. So the above definition, beyond telling us something about the *extension* of the word 'thought' ("not only understanding, willing, and imagining but also sensing"), clarifies its *intensional meaning* too: 'thinking' is *defined* as the immediate object of *self-conscious awareness* of what is going on inside the mind.

So suppose I am thinking about the Bahamas. What I am *thinking of*, the object of *thought*, is the Bahamas. But what I am *conscious of* (in Descartes's sense!) is not the Bahamas, but rather the fact that I am right now thinking about the Bahamas, for example, imagining them, wishing I were there, and so on. I am conscious of my own imaginings, beliefs, wishes, hopes, fears, in fact, of *all* my mental acts or operations. But I can never be conscious (in Descartes's sense!) of the Bahamas. Why? Because the Bahamas are not thoughts in anyone's mind but islands in the Caribbean. So 'consciousness' in Descartes's sense really is just *self*-consciousness, awareness of *my own* thoughts as now actually occurring in me; whereas 'thought' in his sense is awareness of objects, whether real or imaginary, that do or might exist outside my mind. Thus, we can set up the following helpful equation:

'I am thinking x' = 'I am conscious that I am thinking x,' where x is some (real or imaginary) object that can or does exist outside the mind.

Descartes is always careful to distinguish thought (awareness of objects, real or imaginary) from consciousness (self-awareness, awareness *of my awareness* of such objects). 'Thought' is defined intensionally by this unique 'feature': 'being an immediate object of (self-)consciousness.'

24.3.3 The certainty of the cogito

So *extensionally* the term *cogito* can denote anything I am conscious of, while *intensionally* it connotes just that relational property of all thought that makes it an immediate object of *consciousness*. Such objects are, again: all my perceivings, imaginings, willings, judgings, feelings, conceptions, and so forth, all my mental states or acts, all mental events now actually taking place in my mind. So to say 'I think' (*cogito*) is simply to judge that one of these objects of self-awareness is now actual or *exists* at this very moment. In what sense is this certain?

In the First Meditation, 'certainty' was defined in terms of resistance to three grounds of doubt: illusion, dreaming, and the Deceiving God hypothesis (see 23.5). Now compare the following two statements:

(1) 'The flag over there is red.'
(2) 'It seems to me as though there is a red flag over there.'

Clearly, (1) is a statement about an *extra-mental object*, a red flag. It is true only if the flag (a) exists and (b) is red. By contrast, (2) is a statement of the form *cogito* about my now actually occurring *mental state* of perceiving a red flag. It is true only if I am now in fact in a state of mind that is, to me, indistinguishable from that of perceiving a red flag. In other words, it is true even if in fact there is no red flag over there.

Now which of these two is more certain? (1) is not true if (a) I am the victim of an optical illusion, or if I am a crazed communist (b) lying in bed dreaming of a red flag, or if I am (c) being hoodwinked by a malicious demon who controls my thoughts. However, (2) is still true even under conditions (a), (b), or (c). That is, even if I am hallucinating, dreaming, or if a demon is manipulating my thought processes, it remains true that at this very moment I am in a mental state which, to me, is indistinguishable from actually perceiving a red flag. About this I cannot be mistaken. Thus, (2), or any statement having this form ('I am thinking x'), provided it simply reports one's current mental state accurately, asserting nothing about extra-mental objects, is *perfectly indubitable* or *perfectly certain* (impervious to doubt from each of the three First Meditation grounds of doubt) for as long as the mental event in question is actually taking place.

24.3.4 Concluding summary

We can sum up the present section in three simple points:

1. The expression 'I think' (*cogito*) is a variable, the specific value of which is: some actually occurring mental act or state or event.
2. What 'I think' (*cogito*) asserts is the *existence* of such a state or event; what it does *not* assert is the existence of anything extra-mental, anything outside the mind.
3. What 'I think' (*cogito*) asserts is completely impervious to even the most radical forms of doubt, i.e., perfectly certain (as defined in the previous Meditation).

24.4 The *sum* ('I am')

If the foregoing interpretation is correct, why then is 'I think' or *cogito* not Descartes's Archimedean point, the first truth on which all others depend and the first principle of metaphysics?

As noted in 24.2, a *metaphysical* first principle must fulfil *three* requirements in order to serve as an Archimedean point: (1) assertion of the *existence* of something; (2) assertion of the existence of a *substance* or thing rather than a property or quality of a thing; and (3) perfect *certainty*. Conditions (1) and (3) are clearly met by the 'I think'; but condition (2) is not, since the proposition *cogito* asserts the existence only of a fleeting state or condition or property of my mind, not of the mind itself as a substance. The statement 'I exist' (*sum, existo*), on the other hand, satisfies condition (2) as well as the others. For *sum* means 'I exist *as a substance* or thing' rather than merely as a state, property, attribute, or accident of a thing. It means: my existing mental states are the properties or states *of* something (which is not itself again the property or state of something else), namely of a mind or mental *substance*. Accordingly, the *first principle of metaphysics* is the full principle 'I think, therefore I am.' To avoid confusion, it will be best to distinguish the *cogito* ('I think') from the *cogito*-principle ('I think, therefore I am') in what follows.

Without 'I am,' 'I think' fails to satisfy condition (2), while without 'I think,' 'I am' does not satisfy condition (3), perfect certainty. The first principle of philosophy is thus the *cogito*-principle, not the *cogito*. For 'I am' *derives* its certainty from 'I think,' from which it follows. The only question is: How does it follow? This brings us to the *ergo*.

24.5 'Therefore' (*ergo*)

That 'I am' depends upon 'I think' is indicated by the presence of the little word *ergo*, 'therefore.' This is the word normally used to introduce the conclusion of an inference. *Ergo* is accordingly referred to as 'a logical particle.' Does this mean that 'I am' follows from 'I think' *in logic*?

Let us consider a couple of possibilities. First, *sum* may *follow in logic*, either from the stated premise (*cogito*) alone, or from this together with some unstated premise, according to a logical rule of inference. In the former case, the whole principle *cogito*, *ergo sum* involves a direct inference, a piece of discursive reasoning; in the latter, an indirect inference or syllogism, a ratiocinative process, is involved (see 7.6.1 on direct or discursive and indirect or ratiocinative, including enthymematic, inference). Alternatively, 'I think' may *follow in time*, that is, in the course of *one and the same direct intuition* as it unfolds over time: whenever I think, I *first* become conscious and perfectly certain of the existence of my thinking states, and *then* of myself as a substance the existence of which is equally certain. The *ergo* signalizes that this order is irreversible.

Thus, changing the sequence of the interpretations slightly, we have the following three possibilities to consider: (a) indirect inference, (b) direct inference, and (c) immediate intuition.

24.5.1 Syllogistic inference

As for (a), Descartes himself rejects this interpretation out of hand in a number of different texts outside the *Meditations*. The word 'therefore,' he insists, does *not* indicate the occurrence of a logical inference involving a suppressed premise. A traditional syllogistic inference would be something of this sort:

P1 Whatever thinks, is.
P2 I think.
C   Therefore, I am.

Now such a syllogism is a form of reasoning that proceeds from the *universal* (P1) to the particular (P2, and C). But Descartes expressly denies that he is drawing such an inference (with P1 suppressed) in the *cogito, ergo sum*:

if he [the meditator] were deducing it [his own existence] by means of a syllogism, he would have to have had previous knowledge of the major premiss 'Everything which thinks is, or exists.' Yet in fact he learns it from experiencing in his own [particular] case that it is impossible that he should think without existing. It is in the nature of our mind to construct general propositions on the basis of our knowledge of particular ones.

One might want to get round this by trying the *modus ponens* form of indirect inference. Later, Stoic logicians regarded it as a syllogistic form, even though Aristotle, the inventor of the syllogism, did not. Thus, the syllogistic inference would be:

P1 If I think, then I am.
P2 I think.
C   Therefore, I am.

This at least proceeds from a *particular* hypothetical premise (about me, here and now), to a particular conclusion. In other words, it only concerns one's own particular case from start to finish. Accordingly, it squares with the passage just cited. But it is still a form of inference, whereas Descartes insists that the 'I am' is known *immediately* or directly, by intuition, not inferentially. Take, for example, the following, which occurs just before the passage cited earlier: "When someone says 'I am thinking, therefore I am, or I exist,' he does not deduce existence from thought by means of a syllogism, but recognizes it as something self-evident by a simple intuition of the mind." Furthermore, Descartes claims, with respect to *both* these inference patterns, that P2 and C are grasped *prior* (in time) to P1—at least with respect to the order in which we become *explicitly* aware of them. For example, with regard to the *modus ponens* form, he holds that the categorical (non-hypothetical) minor premise, 'I think,' and the categorical conclusion, 'I am,' are both known *explicitly* at a time when the *relation between them* expressed in the hypothetical major premise, 'If I think, then I am,' is still only known implicitly. So in the order of *explicit* knowledge, P2 and C come *before* P1, even if *implicitly* P1 must be known first.

So although these logical inferences are *sound*, it is only *after* grasping the existence of one's thinking and the existence of one's mind that one comes to the realization of the major premise in order to construct arguments like these. Hence (a), indirect inference, is *not* the way one's existence was discovered with certainty in the first place.

24.5.2 Direct inference or immediate intuition

Two possibilities remain to be considered. Is *cogito, ergo sum* then (b) an immediate logical inference from a single premise? No. The passage quoted last states unequivocally that it is not an inference of any kind but "a simple intuition of the mind." Thus, (c) is the correct answer: it is an intuition, albeit a somewhat complex, not perfectly simple, one. 'I am' *follows* 'I think' in the temporal sequence of one and the same gradually unfolding intuition, as I turn my attention from the *existence of mental properties* (initial stage) to the *existence of a mental thing (mind)* that possesses those properties at successive times (succeeding stage). The order is irreversible. That is because a certain general principle is involved, which Descartes formulates this way: "if we perceive the presence of some attribute, we can infer that there must also be present an existing thing or substance to which it may be attributed." It cannot be the other way around, for "we cannot *initially* become aware of a substance merely through it being an existing thing" (e.a.). We have to perceive an attribute first. The coming into play of this principle, however, does not mean that a logical inference occurs after all. It does not imply a logical inference of the form:

P1   Nothing has no properties (where properties exist, so does a substance).
P2   Certain mental properties exist in me.
C   Therefore, a mental substance (my mind) exists.

For, once again, P1 is something I can only grasp explicitly and in its full generality *after* having first explicitly grasped the particular truth 'I am thinking and therefore exist.' So the whole *cogito*-principle, 'I think, therefore I am,' must be regarded as an *immediate though gradually unfolding insight or intuition* rather than as a logical inference. The insight unfolds over time, during which interval a 'movement in thought' takes place from 'I think' to 'I am.' It is this 'movement' of thought, not any logical inference, to which the 'therefore' points. Understood as a *logical* particle, the *ergo* is therefore misleading.

24.5.3 Conclusion

Although the words *cogito, ergo sum* do not occur in the *Meditations*, the third paragraph of the Second Meditation just re-enacts the revolution in thought announced in the earlier *Discourse on Method* with the words *je pense, donc je suis*. Were it not for the fact that Descartes again used the formula in the Latin *Principles of Philosophy*, one might suspect him of having had misgivings about it. Fortunately, we are spared that worry.

Rightly understood, the principle inaugurates a new starting point for philosophy and a new order of knowing. Henceforth the only things known immediately, reliably, and certainly are the ongoings in one's own mind and the existence of the mind (thinking substance) itself. Given this, together with the new standard of certainty implemented in the regimen of doubt, it is not hard to understand how the task of providing a *proof* of the existence of the external world came to loom so large in modern philosophy. Faced with the doubts of Parmenides and Heraclitus, Plato and Aristotle only had to *make room* for the existence and knowability of the world, which, as Descartes nicely put it, "no sane person ever seriously doubted" (see 23.5). Given Descartes's doubt and his manner of overcoming it, nothing less than a demonstration or proof will do.

24.6 Thought as the essence of mind or soul

If there is one thing about Descartes's founding principle that is even more liable to misunderstanding than the 'therefore,' it is the (in Latin, unexpressed) pronoun 'I.' Accordingly, the next stage of the Second Meditation is devoted to the question, What am I? The answer given at the end of the third paragraph is: I am "a thing that thinks; that is, a mind, or intelligence, or intellect, or reason" (27).

This hardly squares with the ordinary conception of the self. Ask most people what they *are* (as opposed to what they *do*), and the reply will be: 'a man,' or 'a woman,' or 'a human being.' The answer of the Second Meditation, "a mind," is the result of certain *constraints* imposed by the *method* followed there. In the Sixth Meditation, as we shall see (chap. 27), Descartes himself reverts to the customary answer, explaining exactly what it is to be a man or a human being—though in a manner that still cannot be squared with what most of us ordinarily think we are (see 27.12–13).

What constraints, then, and what method? The method can be regarded as a simple matter of subtraction. Starting with (A) what I formerly believed myself to be, I take away (B) all beliefs that cannot withstand (i) the argument from illusion or (ii) the dreaming argument or (iii) the Deceiving God hypothesis. This is the constraint just mentioned: nothing is to be retained that is not absolutely certain by the criterion established in the First Meditation. The remainder is (C) what I now may believe myself to be with perfect certainty.

24.6.1 What I formerly believed myself to be

Implementing this method is just a matter of substituting values for the variables in (A) and (B). Descartes considers two candidates for (A), "what I formerly believed myself to be." The first is (a) the philosophical doctrine, hailing from Aristotle, that man is a rational animal (see 2.3, 7.14, and 18.2). But this scholastic definition by genus ('animal') and specific difference ('rational') leads to puzzling problems about the meanings of 'rational' and 'animal.' It is therefore discarded. The second candidate is (b) the "naturally" (Descartes's word) occurring belief of the average person that he or she is a human being, that is, a living body endowed with a human soul—in other words, something not unlike the answer most of us would be inclined to give to the question, What am I? But this is immediately interpreted in a fairly technical philosophical way that owes as much to the Aristotelian tradition for its interpretation of 'soul' as to the modern scientific tradition for that of 'body.' So it is not a very faithful reflection of the commonsense notion of the self after all.

As regards body, Descartes lists five key features of all those things regarded as bodily in nature, namely: (1) figure (shape), (2) location (place), (3) impenetrability (the passive force by which one body resists the entry of any other into the space it occupies), along with (4) perceptibility by the senses and (5) mobility (ability to change place). This is at bottom the conception of body or matter current in the mechanistic natural science of his day, including Descartes's *own* natural science. Except for (4), it has little to do with common sense, according to which the *human* body is above all a living organism. However, the list includes most of the universally agreed upon characteristics of material bodies according to the best philosophical and scientific theories of the day. Only (4) seems out of place, since, according to the same theories, some bodies are too small to be perceived.

Turning next to "the nature of this soul" (26), Descartes identifies four defining features, all of them capacities, faculties, or powers belonging to the soul: (i) the nutritive faculty (broadly speaking, the ability to take nourishment from the environment, to grow, and to reproduce); (ii) the locomotive faculty (the power of *self*-motion); (iii) the sensitive faculty (the capacity for either seeing, hearing, touching, smelling, tasting, or all of these); (iv) the faculty of thinking, or the intellectual faculty, also called 'reason.'

These four items certainly do not have the look of plain common sense about them. They reflect, in fact, the complex Scholastic-Aristotelian conception of what it is that distinguishes a *human* soul from that of lower animals, and both humans and animals from plants and inanimate things. According to this doctrine, which is traceable to Aristotle's work *On the Soul*, (i) nutrition distinguishes *living from non-living things*, that is, the plant or vegetable and animal kingdoms (members of which all nourish themselves, grow, and reproduce) from the mineral kingdom. As for (ii), locomotion, it distinguishes *living animals from living plants*, that is, the animal from the vegetable kingdom. Animals, after all, are *self*-moving; they change place in search of nutrition and mating opportunities. Plants, on the other hand, merely grow, rooted to one spot. As for (iii), sensation, we know that sight and hearing distinguish the *higher forms of animal life from the lower* animal organisms (a mollusc, for example, which can respond to touch or temperature changes, but lacks the other sensory organs). Having the use of sense organs, having a body equipped with peripheral receptors for visual, auditory, olfactory, gustatory, and tactile stimuli, are marks of the higher forms of animal life. And where there is sensation, there is invariably appetite or desire. Finally, (iv), thinking in the sense of intelligent, rational behaviour distinguishes the *highest form of animal life from the higher*. While sharing with other animals the capacities for self-motion, sensation, growth, reproduction, and so on, man is the sole possessor of the capacity for reasonable behaviour, both theoretical and practical, the only rational animal (*animal rationale*).

This, of course, cannot mean that men always behave rationally. That is obviously not true. It must mean therefore that they alone *can* behave rationally, that they in fact do so *for the most part*, and that it is *always* appropriate to appraise or evaluate human behaviour by the standard of rationality—of which it all too frequently falls short. Conversely, it is never appropriate to so judge animal behaviour. Thus, Jonathan Swift's satirical redefinition of 'man' as an *animal capax rationis* ('an animal capable of reason') misses the point, for that is almost exactly what the older definition means. The scholastics were just as aware as Swift of the extent of human folly and baseness—though they were less inclined to satire than the creator of the Yahoos and author of the *Modest Proposal*. The point of their definition is that certain patterns of behaviour, describable as 'rational,' are typical of human conduct both in practical affairs and theoretical contemplation, and that it belongs to the very nature of man to be able—even disposed—to behave in these ways.

24.6.2 What I now believe myself to be

With (A), "what I formerly believed myself to be" firmly in place, we return to the operation of subtraction in which Descartes is engaged. Clearly, features (1) through (5) of bodies, as well as functions (i) through (iii) of souls, cannot withstand the dreaming and the Deceiving God arguments. For if all is a dream and no bodies really exist, then my body does not exist, nor do the faculties of nutrition, sensation, and locomotion, all of which depend upon the body, its sense organs, and its appendages. So all these items become parts of (B), which is taken away from (A). The remainder, (C), is just (iv): "I am, then, in the strict sense only a thing that thinks; that is, I am a mind, or intelligence, or intellect, or reason" (27).

Before we consider the puzzling equivalence of terms in the remainder, it is worth remarking that Descartes is *not* saying definitively that this is all he *is*; the point, rather, is that this is all he *thus far knows himself to be with absolute certainty*. Unfortunately, critics often overlook this point, faulting Descartes for drawing the completely unwarranted and patently false conclusion that he *is* a mind *and nothing more*. In the Sixth Meditation Descartes will acknowledge the fact that he (or that a man, a human being) is a mind or thinking thing *united to an organic body*; for there the question, What am I? is not subject to the same constraints of the method mentioned above, Descartes having deliberately relaxed the requirement of absolute certainty by the end of the Sixth Meditation. There, accordingly, he is content with *reasonable* rather than *rational* certainty about what he is; in the Second Meditation, however, the question, What am I? means: What do I *know* myself to be *with perfect, absolute, or rational certainty*?

To this the answer is, again: "A thinking thing," "a mind," or, in the expanded form of the sixth paragraph:

A thing that doubts, understands, affirms, denies, is willing, is unwilling and also imagines and has sensory perceptions. (28)

These are just some of the values of the variable *cogito*, 'I think.' It is worth comparing this with the fuller, clearer restatement of the outcome in the quick review of the preceding day's meditation at the outset of the Third Meditation:

I am a thing that thinks: that is, a thing that doubts, affirms, denies, understands a few things, is ignorant of many things, is willing, is unwilling, and also which imagines and has sensory perceptions; for as I have noted before, even though the object of my sensory experience and imagination may have no existence outside me, nonetheless the modes of thinking which I refer to as cases of sensory perception and imagination, in so far as they are simply modes of thinking, do exist within me—of that I am certain. (34–5)

This passage seems an optimal formulation of Descartes's answer to the question, What am I? But we are still left with a puzzle concerning the equivalences in Descartes's first formulation of (C), the remainder: "I am, then, in the strict sense only a thing that thinks; that is, I am a mind, or intelligence, or intellect, or reason" (27). Are these expressions really equivalent? It is worth noting in this regard that the scholastic word for 'soul' (*anima*), which figured in (A), is not just replaced with the various terms in (C); rather it is retained by Descartes and used as a synonym for 'mind' and the other terms in (C)—for example, in the long title of Descartes's *Meditations* (see 22.2).

24.6.3 Thought and reason

It would appear, then, that 'thinking thing,' 'mind,' 'intelligence, or intellect, or reason,' and even 'soul' are just different names for *one and the same thing*. This is a radical departure from the Scholastic-Aristotelian doctrine outlined above. From that perspective one might concede, in a pinch, that 'reason,' 'intelligence,' and 'intellect' are different names for 'mind,' which is what distinguishes human from animal souls. But mind (*mens*) differs from soul (*anima*) precisely as (a) the intellectual or rational capacity in man differs from (b) the sensory and appetitive powers in animals and from (c) the vital principle in all living things, including plants. So the *equation* of reason or mind with soul in Descartes's writings is new. Until now, soul was ascribed to living plants and animals as well as human beings; henceforth it belongs to human beings alone. That is the first innovation.

New too is the equation of mind or reason with that which thinks in Descartes's technical sense of the word. For Descartes, as for the scholastics, men differ from animals by possessing reason; but Descartes ties reason to the capacity for thought in the special sense of that term explained above: the ability to perform mental acts or operations *self-consciously*. This, Descartes believed, even the higher primates are incapable of. If all thinking *necessarily* involves a concomitant awareness of one's own thoughts, then even they cannot be said to think. They can indeed sense and desire, but *their* sensing and desiring are merely *bodily* functions, different in everything but name from *our human* sensing and desiring, which are modes of (self-conscious) thought. As with vital functions like growth, nutrition, and so on, sensation and appetite in animals are, for Descartes, entirely material, indeed purely mechanical, processes.

24.6.4 Man, beast, and machine

It is interesting to compare this with the view of Leibniz, who eagerly endorsed the Cartesian *cogito*-principle, but with a difference. For what Descartes took to be the essential feature of thought as such, Leibniz made the distinctive feature of *human* thought in particular. If *human* thinking is essentially *self-aware object awareness*, then animals (so Leibniz) are best understood as having *object awareness without self-awareness*. The thing that sets animals apart from us is this: even though capable of modes of thinking like sensory perception, desire, memory, and even rudimentary induction, animals lack self-awareness; in the absence of the ability to say (or even to think) 'I,' their behaviour towards things and others of their kind does not forge the identity of a self—as ours evidently does. Descartes, for his part, denied to animals, not just the higher forms of thought, but even simple sensation—unless understood exclusively in terms of mechanical processes in the animal body. Animals simply do not have minds at all for Descartes; they are mere automata or machines (intricately contrived robots, if you will).

Needless to say, this part of Descartes's doctrine is hard to square with observed animal behaviour. But though Descartes's analysis of mind has had little influence on the way we think about animals, it was to have a profound effect on attempts to understand the nature of man in the immediately following centuries and this. For once Descartes had suggested that animals were mere automata, it was not long before his materialist successors attempted to apply the same model to man as well. That, however, is a story that cannot be told here. Suffice it to say that the project (still lingering in contemporary work on so-called artificial intelligence) formed no part of Descartes's intentions. On the contrary, Descartes pioneered that way of understanding the human mind that has become canonical in mainstream philosophical and psychological theories. He laid to rest, once and for all, the hoary conception, going right back to Homer, of mind or soul as the vital principle in living things. As for the materialist conception of mind, his victory was partial and short-lived. In addition to his other achievements, Descartes was the first to forge a clear link between *self*-consciousness (called 'apperception' by Leibniz) and reason. Anyone familiar with Kant and later German idealism will confirm the historical importance of this precedent.

24.6.5 Two supplementary points

Two quick points are worth making regarding the final paragraph of the present part of the Second Meditation.

First, the paragraph stresses the fact that it is self-evident to me as I attend to the succession of my mental acts that they are all acts of *one and the same mind or self*; they *all* belong to me, to *one* 'stream of consciousness.' In other words, *given*, along with the sequence of mental states or properties, is the 'I' or substance who has them and that remains one and the same 'I' through its changing states. Moreover, this 'I' or self that thinks is given with exactly the same degree of evidence or certainty as the thoughts themselves. So the proposition 'I think x' could be 'unpacked' further (see

24.3.2): 'I am conscious that *I* am thinking in manifold ways of various different objects.' Here *three* things are taken to be equally certain: (1) the existence of the 'I' that thinks, (2) the existence of its acts of thinking, and (3) the existence of what is thought about—provided these objects of thought are considered only as existing in the mind, as now actually thought about, *not* as extra-mental existents independent of anyone's thinking about them. For the existence of these latter is precisely *not* certain.

The point regarding (1) is important because it is often alleged that Descartes had no right to assert *cogito*, '*I* think,' to be certain; had he been strictly consistent with the principles of his regimen of doubt, he would have asserted only 'there is thinking,' without helping himself to the existence of something that does the thinking, a substance, mind, or self, *sum*. But this objection misses the point made in the final paragraph; (1) is every bit as certain as (2).

The other thing about the final paragraph is the explicit distinction of two meanings of 'sense perception': (a) using bodily sense organs to receive external stimuli, and (b) being in certain mental states that are exactly like those we ordinarily believe to be caused by our receiving external stimuli using our sensory receptors. Now, of course, if we do not have bodies or sensory receptors, if our bodies do not (or at least may not) exist, it is not absolutely certain that we have sense perception (a). But it is still perfectly certain that we have sense perception (b). This vital difference, which was touched on earlier, is also relevant to Descartes's understanding of animals. Without denying them sense perception (a), he insists that they do not perceive in sense (b).

24.6.6 A revolution in the conception of the self

Descartes's answer to the question 'What am I?' inaugurated a *radically new conception of the human mind or soul as self-consciousness*. This is his most enduringly influential achievement. It is far more important than the scientific conception of material bodies for which Descartes provided a new metaphysical justification. Without it, the science of psychology, to say nothing of the modern idea of the self, of the human moral and cognitive subject, is quite unthinkable.

Descartes broke with a tradition of thought, going right back to early Greek literature and philosophy, according to which the soul (*psychē*) is the vital force in living or 'ensouled' things, while mind, intelligence, or reason (*nous*) is the cognitive faculty. In the very oldest tradition, *nous* was not yet understood as part of soul at all, but as a separate set of capacities, many of them common to men and beasts. Only in Orphic-Pythagorean thought was the moral and intellectual self identified with the transmigrating *psychē* (see 16.3). Plato, as we have seen, followed suit, relegating the lower animal functions in man, including sensation and emotion, to the body, while identifying the soul with reason. This, however, is only one strand within the *Phaedo*, where the older conception of soul as life principle is still very much in evidence. In any case, Plato changed his mind in the *Republic*, making reason just one *part* of the soul, along with separate emotive and appetitive parts. Still, it would be a mistake to see Descartes as reverting to the conception of soul that Plato abandoned after the *Phaedo*, purging it of lingering vitalistic elements. For Descartes's conception of the soul is new in key respects (even if not entirely without Greek antecedents), while the use to which he put it was revolutionary. A word on these two points will bring this section to a close.

Only beings endowed with reason think at all, for Descartes, since all thinking is *self*-aware object awareness, and only rational beings such as ourselves can say or even think 'I.' Moreover, this complex formal structure, '*I* am conscious that *I* am thinking *x*,' is necessarily present in all modalities of thought, including sense perception, imagination, understanding or reason, volition, and emotion. Consequently, an element of reason is present too—a point to which Descartes alludes at various places in his writings. Moreover, as long as I think (sense, imagine, will, etc.), that which I think of exists *in my thought*. This is every bit as certain and evident as the existence of my thoughts or of the 'I,' mind, or soul that thinks. On the other hand, whether anything corresponding to the mental object exists outside my mind is doubtful. So is the existence of any physical organ (say, a brain and a living organic body) as the material basis of my thinking.

This is not to say that there *is no* world or that I *do not have* a body, but rather that neither claim is as certain as the fact that I, a thinking thing or substance, exist. By hiving off (1) the self, (2) its thoughts, and (3) its mental objects from the external world of material things, living and non-living, Descartes was able to circumscribe a sphere of absolute certainty. We may, on reflection, reject the use to which he put his insight into the formal structure of what we now call 'consciousness': the formulation of a new metaphysical first principle and starting point for a new order of knowing. And we may regret the artificially wide rift between self and world that Descartes created—so wide that even he was unable to close it, as we shall see. But it is difficult not to admire the depth of his insight into the formal structure of human consciousness and the startling originality of the use to which he put it.

24.7 The Mind-Better-Known-Than-Body doctrine

We turn now to the final, relatively much longer, segment of the Second Meditation, the Mind-Better-Known-Than-Body doctrine, the centrepiece of which is Descartes's famous Wax Example. We begin with a consideration of the *probandum* and the stages of the argument.

24.7.1 The probandum *and the steps in the argument*

This doctrine is the outcome of a comparison of (1) knowledge of the (i) essence and

Chapter 24: Mind and Matter 399

(ii) existence of mind with (2) knowledge of the (i) essence and (ii) existence of body (material things, matter). As for the first part of the *probandum*, (i) the essence of the mind is "better known" than that of body simply means that it is "more distinct and evident" (33), that *more properties or attributes* of one's own mind are known than are known of any body, even one's own. As Descartes remarks outside the *Meditations*, "the more attributes of a given substance we know, the more perfectly we understand its nature." Or again: "the more attributes we discover in the same thing or substance, the clearer is our knowledge of that substance." In the case of (ii), existence, on the other hand, 'better known' means that the existence of the mind is "truer and more certain" (33), that is, *not open to doubt from any of those sources* that occasion doubts about the existence of bodies.

So much for the *probandum*. As for the steps in the argument, there are four:

1 Formulation of the Problem
2 The Essence of Body (Wax Example)
3 How We Know the Essence of Body
4 Comparison of the Knowledge of the Essence and Existence of Body with Knowledge of the Essence and Existence of Mind

We shall consider each step in turn.

24.7.2 First step: formulation of the problem

The argument begins with a general statement of the problem:

I cannot stop thinking this—that the corporeal things of which images are formed in my thought, and which the senses investigate, are known with much more distinctness than this puzzling 'I' [the mind] which cannot be pictured in the imagination. (29)

So the task at hand is to cure ourselves of the naive belief in a certain order of knowing, to root out the deeply ingrained habit of regarding material bodies as the things we know first, best, and most reliably. This will not be easy, given that something like an instinct is at work. The habit being very deeply rooted, it will require a fairly elaborate therapy to eradicate all trace of a belief that has been inculcated in us almost from birth by our natural, instinctive reliance on the senses. Philosophically, of course, the new order of knowing is already established; the point now is to make the philosophical insight take hold of our thinking.

24.7.3 Second step: the essence of body

The next step, the famous Wax Example, immediately reminds one of Socrates's query in the *Euthyphro*: Is god-belovedness the real essence of piety, such that something is pious if and only if, because and only because, it is god-beloved (see 11.6.1–2)? Descartes too is an essentialist or immanent realist (see 4.7.3 and chap. 21); he takes it for granted that something is a body if and only if it has certain attributes, and because and only because it possesses just those attributes. The question to be answered by examining the wax is: What are the *essential* attributes of any body as such? It is not a question about meaning. Nor is Descartes asking what makes this wax wax (rather than, say, rubber), but what makes this wax, or that piece of rubber, or *any* physical thing, solid, liquid, or gas, *a body*. The wax is only an example; it is, however, a rather nice example for purposes of identifying the essential attributes of body, and we shall soon see why.

As a preliminary, consider various qualitative and quantitative characteristics as falling under one or the other of our three headings, (a) essence, (b) *proprium*, or (c) accident (see 7.14). The properties of body that Descartes identified earlier in the Second Meditation (see 24.6.1) were mostly quantitative: figure or shape, location or place, impenetrability, mobility. Depending on how one takes them, these quantitative characteristics can be considered either as universal or particular; for an individual body not only has shape, it has a particular shape (say, 'round' or 'irregular'); it not only has some location or place, but some particular location ('on the table'), some particular degree of impenetrability and of mobility, and so on.

Now in his search for the essence of body Descartes first considers the *particular* individual properties of the wax, both quantitative and qualitative. Do any of the following items belong to the essence of the wax as a body: its sweet taste, fragrant scent, white colour (all qualitative), round shape, specific size (quantitative), hardness, coldness, or the sound the wax emits when struck (again qualitative)? To answer this question he employs the following *test*. Bringing the wax near a heat source, he observes that all these particular sensible qualities and quantitative characteristics just named either change or cease to exist, while the wax itself continues to exist and remains the same wax, the same body it was before. The conclusion he draws is that none of these particular properties belongs to the *essence* of the wax; all are merely *accidental*.

Why is this test conclusive? Remember that to say that certain attributes, a, b, and c, belong to the *essence* of W, is to say two things: (1) W, if and only if a, b, and c; and (2) W, because and only because a, b, and c. (1) is the weaker of the two conditions. In the Replies to the Fourth Set of Objections Descartes formulates it this way: "if something can exist without some attribute, then it seems to me that that attribute is not included in its essence." However, heating the wax demonstrated that a, b, and c could indeed be absent while the wax retained its bodily nature, indeed remained the same wax. So none of these particular qualitative or quantitative features—not taste, odour, or colour, nor round shape nor a determinate size—can belong to the essence of body. Descartes next considers shape and size *as universal attributes*. Do these quantitative features constitute the essence of body?

By 'size' Descartes now means, not any discrete or definite size (for example, the one-inch diameter of a ball of wax), but quantity, magnitude, greatness, or 'sizeableness' (as we might say) in general. This is what philosophers call *continuous quantity*: extension in length, breadth, and depth, being 'spread out' in three dimensions. We can refer to it as 'spatiality' or (pushing the limits of English a bit) 'spread-out-ness.' Obviously, *all and only* bodies have this feature; minds and their contents do not. But is sizeableness all or part of what *makes* them bodies? Before attempting to answer this question, let us consider shape briefly.

By 'shape' Descartes means, again, not any particular shape ('round,' 'square,' 'irregular,' and so on), but the capacity (a) to be bounded in such a way as to possess a definite (regular or irregular) shape, and (b) to change shape. Again, all and only bodies have this property. Philosophers call it *discrete quantity*. Even the melted and altered wax, despite having changed its *particular* size (since it expanded) and its *particular* shape (since it melted down into a puddle), still possesses *some* size and *some* shape. These cannot be taken away from the wax while it remains the same wax that it was. On the contrary, take these properties away and there would not only be no wax, there would be no body present at all. Hence, not only do all and only bodies possess size and shape, but having these properties is the very thing that *makes* them bodies. Moreover, shape and size are the *only* properties that make things bodies. Accordingly, Descartes concludes: the essence of the wax is just "something extended, flexible, and changeable" (31). The wax, in other words, is *essentially* something that has extension and shape and is able to change its extension and shape by changing the relative positions of its parts. More precisely, it is a 'something,' a substance, that is extended in three dimensions in space and capable of changing position; it is capable of undergoing changes in the position of *one part relative to the others* (that is, of changing shape and size or extension) or *of all the parts relative to other bodies* (that is, change of place, or motion).

24.7.4 Third step: the knowledge of the essence of body

With the question concerning its essence answered, the focus shifts from *body* back to the *mind*. After all, the aim is to *compare* knowledge of bodies with knowledge of minds in order to infix in the mind once and for all the reversal in the order of knowing carried out in the previous stages of the Second Meditation. So the question now is, How do I grasp this "something extended flexible mutable"? In other words: which particular *faculty of the mind* grasps the essence of the wax?

Descartes stands in a long tradition that divides the basic functions or operations of the human mind—'thoughts' in Descartes's parlance—into three types: knowing, willing, and feeling. Thus, (1) cognition or perception in a broad sense is distinct from (2) volition or willing. What Descartes calls (3) 'judgment,' that is, affirming, denying, and doubting or suspending judgment, is included under volition. As for feeling, the (4) emotions or "passions of the soul," as Descartes calls them, they are subsumed under perception. Now, according to the same tradition, (1), the cognitive faculty, is itself threefold, comprising (a) sense perception, that is, perception in the narrow sense; (b) imagination or 'common sense,' as Descartes calls it; and (c) the understanding, intellect, or reason. 'Reason' in this sense refers to the higher, discursive and ratiocinative faculty of the mind in particular; it is not just synonymous with 'mind.' So the question to be answered in this third step is: Which of the latter three faculties—the senses, the imagination, or the intellect (reason)—is responsible for conveying to the mind the idea of "something extended, flexible, changeable," that is, knowledge of the essence of the wax?

The (a) senses have at bottom already been ruled out as a source of this idea, since what they convey to the mind are the *particular* properties of things: *this* big, *thus* shaped, and so on. The idea of "something extended flexible and changeable," on the other hand, is *universal*: magnitude or 'bigness' *in general*, shape or 'figurability' *as such*. Descartes therefore makes no mention of the senses, beginning instead with a consideration of (b) the imagination:

Is it [this "something extended, flexible, and changeable"] what I picture in my imagination: that this piece of wax is capable of changing from a round shape to a square shape, or from a square shape to a triangular shape? Not at all; for I can grasp that the wax is capable of countless changes of this kind, yet I am unable to run through this immeasurable number of changes in my imagination, from which it follows that it is not the imagination that gives me my grasp of the wax as flexible and changeable. (31)

He engages in a similar reflection concerning size: it too can change in all manner of ways, in infinitely more ways, in fact, than I can ever imagine one after another (in a finite amount of time). Thus the idea 'extension,' too, is *more general* than any idea of the imagination.

Having eliminated the senses and the imagination, Descartes concludes:

I must therefore admit that the nature of this piece of wax is in no way revealed by my imagination but is *perceived by the mind* alone. (I am speaking of this particular piece of wax; the point is even clearer with regard to wax in general.) But what is this wax which is perceived by the mind alone? It is the same wax which I see, which I touch, which I picture in my imagination, in short the same wax which I thought it to be from the start. And yet, and here is the point, the perception I have of it is a case not of vision or of touch or imagination—nor has it ever been, despite previous appearances—but a *purely mental scrutiny*. (31)

And in the last paragraph of the Second Meditation he remarks:

I see that without any effort I have now finally got back to where I wanted. I now know that even bodies are not strictly perceived by the senses or the faculty of imagination but by the intellect alone, and that this perception derives not from their being touched or seen but from their being understood. (34)

So the following words and expressions are synonymous: 'mental perception,' 'purely mental scrutiny,' 'intellect,' and 'understanding.' To this list of synonymous locutions must be added what Descartes calls 'the natural light' or 'the natural light of reason.' They all refer to the faculty responsible for the non-sensuous *intuition of the essences of things* (as well as the discursive and ratiocinative processes performed by the mind). It is by this means that we grasp "something extended, flexible, changeable," that is, the *essence* or universal concept *of body*. No other cognitive faculty is capable of forming a notion so unrestrictedly universal: not the senses, and not the imagination.

One might object that, arguing as he does here, Descartes would have to conclude that *any* universal concept—the concept of colour, of a tree, a house, a man, and so forth—is a *mente percipere*, a mental perception, and not derived from the senses or imagination. Such concepts, however, clearly originate in sensory experience. With this Descartes would agree. The relevant difference is that not every body is coloured or a tree or a house, and so on; yet every body as such is *and must be* something extended, flexible, and mutable if it is to be a body at all. That is what the Wax Example was intended to show. Thus, the concepts of extension, shape, and mobility possess a *strict* universality that exceeds the *comparative* universality of the other concepts just mentioned. Kant, from whom the distinction between strict and comparative universality is borrowed, argued in a similar vein: sense experience can only teach us what attributes are present in observed things, never that *all* things (observed and unobserved) *must* possess those attributes. Like Descartes he concluded that strictly universal and necessary predicates cannot be derived from sense experience. The claim is highly controversial, but the alleged difference may be enough to forestall the objection.

Concluding the present stage of the argument, Descartes alerts us to a misunderstanding that is engendered by ordinary language when we use expressions like 'I see the wax' and so forth. This way of speaking suggests that I grasp what the wax is (that it is a body) by vision. But not so: I grasp its essence by a kind of mental intuition or mental vision that is independent of the bodily senses. Similarly, I say, 'I see the man,' although it is the faculty of judgment, not the faculty of vision, that determines that what I see (namely, a certain variously coloured, shaped object) is a man. Descartes's point is this. As the way we speak makes it easy to confuse a complex perceptual judgment with simple sensory perception, so we can easily confuse our purely mental intuition of what body is with sense perception of bodies. We must, accordingly, guard against being misled by ordinary language.

24.7.5 Fourth step: comparison

The final and culminating stage in the Mind-Better-Known-Than-Body doctrine is the *comparison* of what the Wax Example has taught us about the nature of body with what both it and the preceding portion of the Second Meditation have taught us about the nature or essence of the mind. Here the point that the mind is better known than material bodies, the reversal of the commonly accepted order of knowing, is driven home with one last, resounding blow.

About *body* we have just learned that it is "something extended, flexible, changeable." About the *mind* we have learned that we cannot perceive what body is by (a) the senses or (b) the imagination, but only by means of (c) the intellect. We have also learned that we perceive the accidents of body unclearly in the former two ways, and its essence clearly in the latter. So every time I perceive something about a body, I perceive something about my own mind, namely that my mind is perceiving something about a body in a certain way (clearly or unclearly, for example). Thus, I actually perceive *more* about the mind itself than about bodies. Here is how Descartes puts it in replying to the objections of a contemporary of his:

> Now we can distinguish many different attributes in the wax: one that it is white; two, that it is hard; three, that it can be melted; and so on. And there are correspondingly many attributes in the mind: one, that it has the power of knowing the whiteness of the wax; two, that it has the power of knowing its hardness; three that it has the power of knowing that it can lose its hardness (i.e., melt), and so on ... The clear inference from this is that we know more attributes in the case of our mind than we do in the case of anything else. For no matter how many attributes we recognize in a given thing, we can always list a corresponding number of attributes in the mind which it has in virtue of knowing the attributes in the thing; and hence the nature of the mind is the one we know best of all.

So the more attributes of bodies I perceive, the more attributes of my own mind (which perceives them) I know at the same time. Since to know the essence of something *better* is to know more attributes of it (see above 24.7.1), the *essence* of mind is better known than the essence of body. And assuming that to know the existence of something *better* is to be less liable to doubt about its existence, the *existence* of the mind is also better known than that of body, as was shown in the first stage of the Second Meditation. So Descartes concludes, first regarding *existence*:

> Surely my awareness of my own self is not merely much truer and more certain than my awareness of the wax, but also much more distinct and evident. For if I judge that the wax exists from the fact that I see it, clearly this same fact entails much more evidently that I myself also exist. It is possible that what I see is not really the wax; it is possible that I do not even have eyes with which to see anything. But when I see, or think I see (I am not here

distinguishing the two), it is simply not possible that I who am now thinking am not something. (33)

And then regarding *essence*:

Moreover, if my perception of the wax seemed more distinct after it was established not just by sight and touch but by many other considerations, it must be admitted that I now know myself even more distinctly. This is because every consideration whatsoever which contributes to my perception of the wax, or of any other body, cannot but establish even more effectively the nature of my own mind. (ibid.)

With that, Descartes hopes, the reversal of the traditional order of knowing is infixed in the mind so firmly that the force of habit can no longer budge it, allowing us to lapse back into the commonsense belief that the ordinary sensible things are what we know first, best, and most reliably.

25

Truth and Circularity

25.1 Introductory

At the outset of the Third Meditation, Descartes has achieved an absolutely secure starting point, but no more. All the knowledge acquired so far concerns a single object, his own mind. Two items—(1) *that* he exists ("I am") and (2) *what* he is ("I am a thinking thing")—are the only beliefs to have withstood all three grounds of doubt, and even they have done so only after drastic cuts to the ordinary idea of the self. As for (3) the essence of body as something "extended, flexible, and mutable," this cannot be regarded as known unless and until bodies are shown to exist. For unlike the truths of pure mathematics, statements about the mathematically describable properties of bodies entail the existence of their objects (see 23.10). If there *are* no bodies, then such statements are just as false as any regarding qualities like colour, odour, taste, and so on. Yet (4) the existence of bodies is only demonstrated in the Sixth Meditation; the Third is devoted to establishing (5) the existence and (6) the nature of God, the same subject taken up again in the Fifth.

The situation in which Descartes thus finds himself at the start of the Third Meditation is one called 'solipsism,' from the Latin *solus ipse* 'himself alone.' Several varieties of solipsism will be distinguished in the next section. To escape this predicament, one might have expected Descartes to prove the existence of bodies *first*, only then tackling the contentious theological issues of God's existence and nature. And indeed, Descartes does *attempt* a proof of the existence of bodies in the Third Meditation—*only to reject it as inconclusive*. He then launches right into his first and allegedly conclusive proof of the existence of a non-deceiving God. What the abortive, followed immediately by this successful, attempt to escape from solipsism shows is plain. Not only is it mistaken to believe that *material things* are better known than *one's own mind*; mistaken also is the belief that they are more reliably known than *God*. For even the later proof of the existence of bodies possessing all those properties "comprised within the subject-matter of pure mathematics" (80) only succeeds *owing to* the earlier proof that God exists and is no deceiver. The order of the proofs is irreversible, for there can be no certain knowledge about bodies if a deceiving God or "malicious demon" manipulates my thoughts, making things that are in fact false seem perfectly true.

From this it is also clear why, along with (5) God's existence, (6) God's nature must be determined before a proof of the existence of bodies can succeed. The crux is God's veracity or truthfulness. In this regard, consider again our earlier point (see 23.11) about the limits of rationality. One cannot establish the reliability of reasoning by any process of reasoning without arguing in a circle; nor can one impugn the reliability of reasoning by any process of reasoning without contradicting oneself. In employing the Deceiving God hypothesis to cast doubt on reason itself, and then overcoming this doubt by a *reasoned* argument that God exists and is no deceiver, Descartes apparently *assumes* that reason is unreliable, going on to *prove* by reasoning that it is reliable after all. In doing so he proceeds in a manner that is *both* inconsistent with his original assumption *and* circular.

In the present chapter we shall consider whether Descartes is guilty of these gross blunders, postponing to the next a consideration of his proofs of God's existence. The problem of circularity will bring us face to face with a new form of theological voluntarism. We considered the Divine Command Theory already in the context of the *Euthyphro*, where it arose in an ethical context; here we shall encounter it in a different, metaphysical setting, the question being, not goodness, but truth. The problem of circularity will also bring us face to face with Descartes's novel conception of truth itself. This new theory of truth as "clear and distinct perception" may be Descartes's single most important innovation, underlying, as it does, the new order of knowing itself.

25.2 Methodological solipsism and Descartes's new order of knowing

Solipsism can be (a) a metaphysical position or (b) an epistemological posture or (c) a methodological device. As a *metaphysical* position, it entails that I am alone in the world, that apart from me there is nothing else, that I am all there is in the universe or, equivalently, that I *am* the universe (the 'all'). As an *epistemological* posture, solipsism implies that the only thing whose existence I have certain knowledge of is myself, my own mind. It does not deny that there *are* other minds or material things in the universe, but only that anything apart from my own mind can be *known* to exist with perfect certainty. Finally, as a *methodological* device for determining the correct order of knowing, solipsism asserts that I myself am the *first* (but not the only) thing whose existence I can be absolutely certain of, and that this first item of knowledge is the indispensable foundation of the rest.

Now it is doubtful whether anyone has ever seriously defended metaphysical solipsism (roughly: 'I am the universe'), though some people occasionally behave as though they thought it were true. The view that "the existence of objects in space" is "doubtful and indemonstrable" is attributed to Descartes by Kant, who refers to epistemological solipsism as 'problematic idealism.' But Kant is mistaken. Descartes is neither a metaphysical nor an epistemological but a methodological solipsist. Only when God and material things are conclusively demonstrated to exist and assigned their respective places in the order of knowing and being is the metaphysical project of Cartesian subjectivism and dualism complete. Only then is the task of rebuilding the whole system of human knowledge accomplished. Solipsism is just the methodological device Descartes employs in order to fix the starting point of the new order of knowing. In that order, (1) the mental, spiritual, or supersensible comes first. This includes both (a) a *finite spirit*, one's own mind, and (b) an *infinite Spirit*, God, *in that order*. Then follows (2) the physical, corporeal, material, or sensible world. Without knowledge of both the mind and God (metaphysical knowledge), certain knowledge of the material universe (physical knowledge) is not obtainable at all.

This is an astonishing reversal, not just of the point of view of common sense, but of the order of knowing as it was understood in the mainstream of philosophical and scientific thought in Descartes's day. As noted already (see 22.3.1), the dominant schools of philosophy hitherto had been forms of Aristotelianism. It was in this philosophy that Descartes himself was trained at the renowned Jesuit School, La Flèche. The fundamental anti-Platonic tenet of all Aristotelian philosophy is that what we know first and best, the basis of all other knowledge, are the material things around us as given in ordinary sense experience. Knowledge of the non-sensible and supersensible (the mind and God) depends upon cognition of sensible things (see 22.3.1). Descartes's new order of knowing—first self, then God, then world—turns this around. Even the scientists of the day, who held no brief for scholastic philosophy, must have been aghast at Descartes's daring claim that, notwithstanding the remarkable successes of the new mathematical science of nature, the metaphysical knowledge of God was more certain than, and a condition of, knowledge of the physical universe.

25.3 The structure of the Third Meditation and the *Meditations* as a whole

Given this sketch of the new order of knowing, it is not hard to see how the Third and Fifth Meditations fit into the overall structure of the work. If we ignore the Fourth, which is a digression in the chain of argument by which Descartes successively reinstates his beliefs in God and the external world, the main line of metaphysical argument in the *Meditations* is as follows:

Meditation I: Doubt

Meditation II: *Existence* and *Essence* of Mind
Meditation III: *Existence* and *Essence* of God
Meditation V: *Essence* of Body and *Existence* or *Essence* of God again
Meditation VI: *Existence* of Body

The structure of the Third Meditation is itself complex. It is much longer than either of its predecessors and includes a great deal besides the proofs of God's existence and veracity that form the centrepiece of the Meditation. Breaking it down in the usual way, we get the following scheme:

1. Paragraph 1: Introduction (Review of the Previous Meditation)
2. Paragraphs 2–4: The Truth Rule
3. Paragraphs 5–6: Classification of Thoughts or Mental Phenomena and Identification of the Most Common Source of Error
4. Paragraph 7: Classification of Ideas into Innate, Adventitious, and Factitious
5. Paragraphs 8–10: First Attempt to Prove the Existence of Something Outside the Mind Using Adventitious Ideas of Bodies
6. Paragraphs 13–22: Second Attempt: Causal Argument for the Existence of God Using the Innate Idea of God
7. Paragraphs 23–27: Objections to the Causal Proofs and Replies to the Objections
8. Paragraphs 28–36: Second Causal Proof for the Existence of God
9. Paragraphs 37–38: The Innateness of the Idea of God

In the present chapter we shall confine ourselves to that brief portion of the Third Meditation (stage 2) that bears on the problem of truth and circularity, leaving the proof of God's existence (stages 6 and 7) for the next chapter, where it will be considered together with the other proof, found in the Fifth Meditation. As for stages 3, 4, and 5, they will be interpreted in chapter 27 ("Mind and Matter"). For they both pertain to the question of the existence of matter, stage 5 being the abortive proof of the existence of matter mentioned above. Stage 9, the innateness of the idea of God, will be discussed briefly in the next chapter along with the proofs of God's existence (see 26.7.1–2). As we shall see in the present chapter, Descartes's conception of truth is the basis of all his philosophical innovations.

25.4 Descartes's truth rule

Having reviewed the previous day's results in the first paragraph, Descartes begins the Third Meditation proper by asking whether there is anything else of which he is certain. His answer: Yes, if he knows with certainty that he—a thinking thing or mind—exists, he must at least know what certainty is. Reflecting on his first truth, he discovers that its certainty consists in nothing but the clarity and distinctness of his perception (cognition) that he thinks and that he therefore exists. And so he sets up the "general rule": "whatever I perceive very clearly and distinctly is true." This has come to be known as Descartes's 'truth rule,' the English for a Latin expression used by Descartes himself (*regula veritatis*).

Descartes's truth rule can be described as an *inference licence* or *principle* of argument. It states that the inference from (P) 'I perceive x clearly and distinctly' to (C) 'x is true' is a valid one. In other words, it 'licenses' the inference from P to C, which looks like a direct inference, but is in fact an enthymeme (see 7.6.1), with the truth rule as a suppressed major premise:

P1 Whatever I perceive clearly and distinctly is true.
P2 I perceive x clearly and distinctly.
C Therefore, x is true.

25.4.1 The definition of 'clarity' and 'distinctness'

Descartes does not define the terms 'clear' and 'distinct' in the *Meditations*. That is because he holds that anyone who reflects on his knowledge that he is thinking and therefore exists will understand what 'clear and distinct' means far better than any definition could explain it. However, *The Principles of Philosophy* give the following definition of 'clarity': "I call a perception 'clear' when it is present and accessible to the attentive mind—just as we say that we see something clearly when it is present to the eye's gaze and stimulates it with a sufficient degree of strength and accessibility." According to this, an object is perceived somewhat clearly if we are aware of it at all, while the greater the degree of our awareness of it, the more clearly we perceive it. *Just as* an object that is too small or too far away from us does not stimulate our sense organs sufficiently to produce changes in our bodily receptors (eye, optic nerve, brain), *so* there is a threshold of conscious awareness below which we are simply not aware of objects at all. Slightly above that threshold we become aware of something, but only very unclearly; further above it, we have a clearer awareness, and so on, with ever increasing degrees of clarity, all the way up to a very clear awareness, one that floods one's whole consciousness. Relevant examples of these differing degrees of clarity might be (1) a tumour that is impeding the functioning of an organ without producing any conscious feeling of pain; (2) a superficial cut that produces a very dull, almost imperceptible pain. With these we may contrast a large tumour or stab wound causing such acute pain that we can literally think of nothing else. The opposite of 'clear' is 'obscure.' Thus (2) is obscure.

'Distinctness' is defined in the same place as follows: "I call a perception 'distinct,' if, as well as being clear, it is so sharply separated from all other perceptions that it contains within itself only what is clear." According to this, a clear perception is distinct if (a) all of it, all the individual or constituent perceptions making it up, are clear, that is, the objects of conscious awareness; and (b) nothing is presumed to be included in it which is not in fact in it. When these two conditions are satisfied, the perception is sharply *distinguished* from all other perceptions. Thus, for example, on first entering a room, I take in everything within my visual field 'at a glance' and therefore indistinctly. With time I may direct my attention to the contents of the room one by one. These things were seen on first entering, too, but not as clearly as now that each is singled out for attention. The whole impression of the room was initially confused (the opposite of 'distinct'), but is now clear, or at least clearer. Once the individual items in the visual field have been made clear by attending to them one after the other, the whole perception is distinct rather than confused. There is no chance any longer of mistaking this room for the one just like it down the corridor.

From these definitions it follows that "a perception can be clear without being distinct, but not distinct without being clear." Take, for example, a perception of pain in the foot. Why is this perception clear but not distinct? Because in addition to the acute awareness of the sensation of pain now actually occurring in my mind (which may be very clear, depending on the intensity of the pain), I am apt to suppose that there is disturbance in an extra-mental object, my body, specifically my foot, which is the source of this pain. As long as I attend only to the sensation in my mind, I perceive the pain clearly; but when I make a judgment about my foot, which is an extra-mental object, something unclear creeps in. Hence, the perception of pain is not distinct. On the other hand, if I do not make that judgment, if I suspend judgment, the perception of pain *can* be made distinct as well as clear.

Now take a different example, say, the perceptions of a chiliagon (thousand-sided figure) and of a myriagon (ten-thousand-sided figure). According to Descartes (see 72-3), we have clear and distinct perceptions of both chiliagon and myriagon when we *understand* exactly what the words 'chiliagon' and 'myriagon' mean. On the other hand, when we try to picture or *imagine* them, our perception becomes confused. We end up imagining a many-sided figure that could be either of the two, or any of a host of other many-sided polygons. If a clear perception is indistinct in this way, it is, as already noted, 'confused.' So the opposite of 'clear and distinct' is 'obscure and confused.'

Even though sensations can be distinct as well as clear, the example of the chiliagon and myriagon as *understood* and as *imagined* illustrates a point worth keeping in mind: *most* of our clear and distinct ideas belong to the class of conceptions of the *intellect* or *reason* rather than perceptions of the senses. They are chiefly, but not exclusively, mathematical (square, triangle, chiliagon, etc.) and metaphysical ideas (mind, matter, God, truth, etc.) according to Descartes. However, as we have seen, even the perceptions of the senses can be *made* clear and distinct by inhibiting the natural tendency of the mind to judge that objects resembling those sensations or perceptions actually exist outside the mind and produce those sensations in us.

Other 'clear and distinct' perceptions are not ideas (concepts) at all, but 'common notions' or 'axioms,' as Descartes calls them, that is, truths (propositions) or 'eternal truths,' as they were traditionally called. Descartes is sometimes faulted for using the term 'idea' broadly to cover truths or propositions as well as concepts and sensory representations of individual things. However, this usage does not really create any problems. Examples of clearly and distinctly known truths are the mathematical axiom that 'if equals are added to equals the sums are equal' or the metaphysical axioms 'what is done cannot be undone' and 'something cannot come from nothing.' In 25.5 we shall consider several different classes of clearly and distinctly perceived eternal truths or eternal verities, as they are also called. First, we must return to the truth rule that "whatever I perceive clearly and distinctly is true."

25.4.2 The problem of a criterion

With the meaning of 'clear and distinct' now sorted out, we are in a position to consider a first objection to Descartes's truth rule. We noted that the rule was an *inference licence* or *principle of argument*, justifying the inference from (P) 'this (proposition) is clearly and distinctly perceived' to (C) 'this (proposition) is true.' We can therefore also call clarity and distinctness a *criterion of truth*. This is in fact the very criterion of perfect certainty described earlier as the fourth use of Cartesian doubt (see 23.5). There it was characterized as immunity to the three grounds of doubt elaborated in the First Meditation; here it is designated 'clarity and distinctness.' The two are just different formulations of the same criterion. But what good is a criterion of truth, it might be objected, if we can just as easily be mistaken about the criterion as about truth? Unless we can recognize clarity and distinctness *without fail*, *infallibly*, we shall need a criterion of the criterion, and perhaps a criterion of the criterion of the criterion, and so on *ad infinitum*.

This type of 'infinite regress' is sometimes called 'circularity' (see 7.7.2), since the solution to the problem (here: of a criterion) just raises a new problem (of a criterion) of exactly the same type. Now an objection like this is mooted in the third paragraph of the Third Meditation, where it is suggested that we may sometimes be mistaken about whether we perceive something clearly and distinctly. For example, the very things that most people take to be very clear and distinct—the existence of the material universe, including their own bodies—were found to be doubtful, that is, *not* clear and *not* distinct at all. Descartes responds by carefully separating *what is* and *what is not* clearly and distinctly perceived in this case. Clear and distinct is (a) the occurrence *in the mind* of the *ideas of* corporeal bodies; confused and obscure is (b) the existence *outside the mind* of bodies, or of objects that resemble those ideas in the mind and cause them. The immediately obvious difference here, Descartes maintains, is the "strength of my perception" of (a) relative to the "strength of my perception" of (b). This, he implies, is something about which nobody who exercises reasonable care can possibly be mistaken.

So there is no need for a criterion of the criterion, and so on. Whether or not our perceptions are clear and distinct is something about which we cannot be in any doubt as long as we exercise the appropriate degree of care. Thus, if a Euthyphro, for example, claims to perceive clearly and distinctly that what he is doing in prosecuting his father is right, and that to do otherwise would be wicked, the mere strength of his conviction does not suffice to show that what he maintains is clearly and distinctly perceived and therefore true. Many people claim to perceive clearly and distinctly all manner of things about which they are grossly mistaken, however deeply convinced. What is required is again *Cartesian therapy* to determine whether or not what they take to be as clearly and distinctly perceived as the fact of their own existence really is so. About this there can be no mistake once one has reflected adequately on the clarity and distinctness of one's perception of one's own existence. What falls short of this standard or criterion of certainty will be as immediately evident as the criterion itself.

25.5 The Cartesian circle

One charge of circularity (infinite regress) having been successfully dealt with, another springs up in its stead. The second objection to Descartes's truth rule has become famous under the name 'the Cartesian circle.' It can be simply stated in the following way.

The First Meditation laid it down that even those things that I perceive clearly and distinctly might be false should the "author of my being" in fact be a deceiver capable of manipulating my reason so that even things that are false seem true, that is, *seem* maximally clear and distinct. This being so, the truth rule itself is worthless until I have proved that God is no deceiver. But if I *use* the truth rule to prove that God exists and is no deceiver, then I am taking for granted the very thing to be established, the reliability of the truth rule, and that is arguing in a circle. The same is true if I use any particular clearly and distinctly perceived axiom or common notion in order to prove God's existence and veracity. So Descartes must still deal with the threat to the truth rule posed by the Deceiving God hypothesis.

He attempts to do so in the fourth paragraph, by considering a number of statements or propositions that seem to contain nothing obscure and confused—that is, they seem perfectly clear and distinct. As already mentioned, such propositions are called 'eternal truths' or 'eternal verities.' They coincide more or less with what Leibniz called 'truths of reason' (see 7.4). Now Descartes distinguishes various kinds of eternal truths. First, there are what he calls (1) "common notions" and simple truths of mathematics. An earlier example of a self-evident principle or common notion of this type was: 'if equals are added to equals the sums are equal.' Examples of simple truths of mathematics are '2 + 3 = 5' (arithmetic) and 'a square has four sides' (geometry). Second, there are eternal truths like (2) 'what is done cannot be made undone,' the causal principle that 'nothing comes from nothing,' and the alleged suppressed premise of the *cogito* principle 'whatever thinks, exists' (see above 24.5.1). The eternal truths under (1) stand for *all* self-evident principles and simple truths of mathematics, while those under (2) stand for the 'common notions' or 'axioms' of metaphysics, all of which concern existence. It is unclear where the truth rule, 'whatever I perceive clearly and distinctly is true,' belongs. We might subsume it under (2), even though it has nothing to do with existence, on the grounds that the nature of truth is a metaphysical issue. To the axioms or principles mentioned so far, we could add certain (3) axioms of logic, like the principle of contradiction (see 20.6.1) and others. Unlike the universal metaphysical axiom or eternal truth 'whatever thinks, exists,' the *particular* metaphysical truth concerning existence expressed in (4) the *cogito*-principle, 'I think, therefore I am,' is not an eternal truth, although it too is absolutely certain and maximally clear and distinct.

The second objection to Descartes's truth rule, then, is this: Granted that (4) the *cogito*-principle and the eternal truths listed under (1)–(3) are all maximally clearly and distinctly perceived (if anything is), are they therefore absolutely certain and true, given the Deceiving God hypothesis? If so, there is no problem about using them in order to prove God's existence and veracity. But if their certainty depends on first showing that God exists and is *no* deceiver, then neither the truth rule nor any other axioms just mentioned may be used in showing that God exists and is no deceiver—on pain of circularity.

25.6 A welter of problems

Descartes's response to this straightforward challenge is fraught with problems. The numbers (1), (2), and (4) inserted parenthetically in the quotation below refer to the different classes of clearly and distinctly known truths distinguished above; the letters (a) and (b) indicate two incompatible views of the certainty of these truths. The response is as follows:

[W]henever my preconceived belief in the supreme power of God comes to mind, [a] I cannot but admit that it would be easy for him, if he so desired, to bring it about that I go wrong even in those matters which I think I see utterly clearly with my mind's eye. Yet [b] when I turn to the things themselves which I think I perceive very clearly, I am so convinced by them that I spontaneously declare: let whoever can do so deceive me, he will never bring it about [4] that I am nothing so long as I continue to think I am something [*cogito*-principle]; or make it true at some future time [2] that I have never existed, since it is now true that I exist [eternal truth: 'whatever thinks, exists']; or bring it about [1] that two and three added together are more or less than five [simple truth of mathematics], or anything of this kind in which I see a manifest contradiction. And since I have no cause to think that there is a deceiving God, and I do not yet know for sure whether there is a God at all, any reason for doubt is a very slight and, so to speak, metaphysical one. But in order to remove even [a] this slight reason for doubt, as soon as the opportunity arises I must examine whether there is a God, and, if there is, whether he can be a deceiver. For if I do not know this, it seems that I can never be quite certain about *anything* else. (36 e.a.)

Regarding (1), simple mathematical truths, (2), metaphysical axioms or eternal truths, and (4), the *cogito*-principle, Descartes says two things here that are, on the face of it, incompatible. He begins by saying (a) that they *are* rendered doubtful by the Deceiving God hypothesis. Then, however, he reverses himself, remarking: (b) "when I turn to the things themselves" that these sorts of truths are about, none of the truths can be doubted—that is, not even a deceiving God could deceive me. Finally, he concludes by reaffirming that (a) they are after all subject to a "very slight doubt" owing to the Deceiving God hypothesis, so that unless and until even this very slight doubt is removed, none of (1), (2), and (3) is absolutely certain.

In fact, however, this apparent inconsistency is only the proverbial 'tip of the iceberg.' Specifically, *three* charges of inconsistency or contradiction suggest themselves based on a close reading of this passage, as well as *three* different charges of circularity in argument. Let us consider the contradictions first, before turning to the various circularity problems.

25.6.1 Consistency problems

In the Second Meditation Descartes stated that (3) the *cogito*-principle was immune from doubt—even from a doubt occasioned by the Deceiving God hypothesis. Here in the Third Meditation he repeats this in (b)—not even a deceiving God could "bring it about that I am nothing so long as I continue to think I am something"—but says just the opposite *twice* in (a)—there is doubt after all, though a "very slight" one. So (a) is inconsistent with (b) within this passage, and it is also inconsistent with the assertion of the absolute certainty of the *cogito*-principle in the Second Meditation. That is the first apparent contradiction.

Furthermore, in the First Meditation Descartes treated (1) the simple truths of mathematics, for example, 2 + 3 = 5, as doubtful, since a deceiving God might make even falsehoods seem very true to me. Yet in (b) of the above passage he suggests that the truths of mathematics are on the same footing as the *cogito*-principle, that is, that *both* are completely immune from doubt. So (b) is *inconsistent* with the treatment of mathematical truths within the First Meditation, where their status differs from that of the *cogito*-principle, as well as with (a) here.

Finally, (1) the truths of mathematics, (2) the common notions of metaphysics, and (4) the *cogito*-principle are *all deliverances of reason* rather than the senses or imagination. To say under (a) that they are made even slightly doubtful by the Deceiving God hypothesis is therefore to doubt the reliability of reason itself. Yet

Descartes tries to reason his way out of this doubt (by a reasoned proof that God exists and is no deceiver). This procedure assumes the reliability of reason. It is therefore *inconsistent* with (a), the express denial of the reliability of reason. That it is also circular will be shown in the next sub-section.

25.6.2 Circularity problems

The whole passage obviously gives rise to serious worries about Descartes's consistency. As if this were not bad enough, the way in which Descartes reasons his way out of the doubt expressed here is patently *circular*. The general nature of this informal fallacy was described (see 7.7.2) as follows: You cannot use x to prove x. But depending on the value of x (whether it is a faculty of the mind, a proposition, or an argument form), there are different kinds of circular reasoning. Now consider Descartes's proposed manner of eliminating this "slight reason for doubt."

First, he has to take for granted the reliability of logical inference in order to *infer* the reliability of his reason from God's existence and non-deceptiveness (veracity). But *you cannot establish the reliability of a faculty using that very faculty*.

Second, Descartes proves that God exists and is no deceiver using the metaphysical axiom 'nothing comes from nothing' (see chap. 26). But according to (a), axioms or common notions can be known to be true only if it is known that God exists and is no deceiver. But *you cannot establish the truth of a conclusion by means of an argument one of whose premises presupposes the truth of the conclusion*. That is circular.

Finally, Descartes's truth rule, 'everything I perceive clearly and distinctly is true' was called an inference licence or principle of argument. Descartes has to prove that God exists and is no deceiver in order to justify the use of this rule, since a deceiving God could make even false things appear clearly and distinctly true. He does so by inferring 'God can be no deceiver' from 'I clearly and distinctly perceive that God can be no deceiver,' and by inferring 'God exists necessarily' from 'I clearly and distinctly perceive that God exists necessarily.' The proofs themselves have the very logical form they are supposed to justify. But *you cannot justify a principle of argument by means of an argument that uses that principle*; you cannot justify the truth rule by means of an argument that uses the truth rule.

When scholars speak of 'the Cartesian Circle,' they have in mind one or more of these problems. The many solutions been proposed in the scholarly literature cannot be considered here. Instead, we shall simply plump for the one that seems best.

25.7 Solution of these difficulties

Although the situation looks bleak, there is a simple solution to all these problems. It involves distinguishing between (a) two kinds of clear and distinct perception, and (b) two sorts of natures known in clear and distinct perception. The first distinction dispels the contradictions, the second the appearance of circularity. The textual basis for all this is not found in the *Meditations* themselves but in others of Descartes's writings too numerous and far-flung to quote conveniently here.

25.7.1 Two kinds of clear and distinct perceptions

To begin with, then, we must separate (a) two kinds of clear and distinct perceptions: (i) what is *now* actually being clearly and distinctly perceived to be true, that is, what is currently under the direct scrutiny of reason or the intellect, whether as the simple matter of intuition or as the complex matter of (direct or indirect) logical inference or demonstration; and (ii) what is now *no longer* actually being clearly and distinctly perceived in either manner just described but is only *remembered* to have been so at some time in the past. Now suppose that (i) *is not* and that (ii) *is* subject to doubt from the Deceiving God hypothesis. This removes the apparent contradictions. The *cogito*-principle, the truths of mathematics, and the common notions of metaphysics are not subject to the slightest doubt *when actually under our mental scrutiny*, although they are open to at least a "slight" doubt *when only remembered* as having formerly been thus clearly and distinctly perceived.

This solution is actually suggested by Descartes's words "when I turn to the things themselves," which indicates *actual* clear and distinct perception. And it eliminates at one go, so to speak, all three apparent contradictions. For, first, in the Second Meditation the *cogito*-principle is exempted from even the slightest doubt because it is there considered as *current or actual* clear and distinct perception. It is said to be doubtful here in the Third because it is considered as *remembered* clear and distinct perception. Next, in rejecting mathematics in the First Meditation, Descartes was talking about remembered clear and distinct perceptions; he was thinking of all the simple arithmetic sums and theorems of geometry he remembered having once been taught in school. In saying, in the Third Meditation, that simple mathematical truths are not made doubtful even by the deceiving God "when I turn toward the things themselves," he is speaking of his *now actually occurring* clear and distinct perception of the proofs of those truths or theorems. Finally, Descartes never really doubted the reliability of reason altogether. Now actually occurring clear and distinct perception, whether intuition or demonstration, is not open even to the slightest doubt. Only remembered clear and distinct perception can be doubted. So Descartes is not guilty of contradicting himself by implying the unreliability of reason when he doubts clear and distinct perception (remembered) and then implying its reliability (so long as it is actual) by going on to reason his way out of doubt by proving God's existence.

25.7.2 Two sorts of natures

Now for (b) the further distinction between (i) clear and distinct perception of God's nature and existence and (ii) clear and distinct perception of all other natures (simple mathematical truths, metaphysical truths about the nature of body, about the nature of the mind, and the truth of common notions or axioms). According to the previous sub-section, everything under (ii) is immune to the slightest doubt *as long as actually perceived*, yet subject to a slight doubt *when only remembered*. The question is: *Why are these remembered clear and distinct perceptions subject to a doubt raised by the Deceiving God hypothesis?*

The answer is to be found in Descartes's theological voluntarism. Descartes's omnipotent God not only created him, the heavens, the earth, and all existing things, but even the *natures* or essences of things. To some of these natures, like minds and bodies, he gave actual existence in the world; to others, like the ideal natures knowable in mathematics, he gave only possible, not actual existence. Apart from truths about the thinking, corporeal, and ideal mathematical natures, he even decreed the truth of all axioms, none of which would be true had he not decreed them so. And what God made or decreed, he can also change.

So when I am no longer actually intuiting these mathematical and metaphysical natures and axioms, but only recall having intuited them clearly and distinctly in the past, I have no assurance they are still what I formerly intuited them to be, since an omnipotent deceiver could have changed them in the interim. The same does not apply, however, to (i) clearly and distinctly perceived truths about God's own existence and nature. Once I perceive clearly and distinctly that God exists eternally and is no deceiver, I can rest assured that God still exists and is no deceiver even when I am no longer actually intuiting the proofs. This is because the only thing that Descartes's omnipotent God cannot change is *his own nature*; and that is because the only thing that he did not create is himself. Hence, if I intuit anything clearly and distinctly about God *once*, I am certain that it is true *for all time*.

So the second distinction posits two kinds of essences or what Descartes calls "true and immutable natures": those which can only be changed by God or an omnipotent being, and that which cannot be changed even by God. Obviously, the former are not *absolutely* 'immutable,' 'unchangeable,' or 'eternal,' since they can still be changed by God, who created them. They can be called 'eternal truths' nevertheless, since, though they depend on the divine will, they are entirely independent of *my* will (if this is a triangle, it is not up to me to determine whether or not its internal angles are equal to two right angles, though it was up to God, who chose to create it that way). On the other hand, truths about God's existence and attributes are *absolutely* or *strictly* immutable and eternal, not even alterable by him.

It is now possible to acquit Descartes of all three charges of circularity. First, Descartes does not first assume that *reason itself* is inherently unreliable in *all* its intuitive and deductive uses, and then go on to use reason to show that reason is reliable after all. Exempt from all doubt are (1) current clear and distinct perception of "true and immutable natures" as well as axioms of the "natural light" and even (2) remembered clear and distinct perception of God's nature, though *not* (3) remembered clear and distinct perceptions of natures *other* than God's and of non-theological axioms. So there is no circularity in using reason, namely (1) and (2), to justify reason, that is, (3). This is not using x to prove x.

Second, although the proof that 'God exists and is no deceiver' employs the axiom 'nothing comes from nothing' as a premise, this does not mean that the conclusion is taken for granted in order to guarantee the truth of the axiom. For as long as we actually intuit it directly (rather than just remember it), this key premise or axiom can be known to be true independently of the conclusion that a veracious God exists.

Third and finally, the truth rule 'whatever I *now* perceive clearly and distinctly is true' is ambiguous. It can mean: (a) 'whatever I perceive clearly and distinctly is true *as long as I actually perceive it clearly and distinctly*'; or (b) 'whatever I perceive clearly and distinctly is true *as long as I remember having once perceived it clearly and distinctly.*' The proof of God's existence and non-deceptiveness employs (a), but God's existence and veracity are used to justify (b). Hence, there is no circle.

25.8 Descartes's theological voluntarism

What are we to make of this strange metaphysical doctrine of the divine creation, not just of (1) all actually existing things, but of (2) their essences or natures as well, together with (3) the natures of all merely possible things and (4) the axioms of logic, mathematics, and metaphysics? That God created the actual world is standard Christian orthodoxy; but that he created the "true and immutable natures" of things and all other eternal truths is completely heterodox. Ever since the Christian Platonists of the early Middle Ages relocated the Platonic Forms in the infinite mind of God, the essences of things were simply *identified* with God's creative essence. Whereas Plato's divine craftsman (see 5.5.3 and 16.2) brings order out of chaos by looking away to eternal exemplars (the Forms) existing independently of him, the Christian creator God understands the essences of all possible things by reflecting on his own nature, which contains them all; for the perfect being contains within himself all perfection, that is, the positive characteristics or perfections belonging to the natures of all other things. This reflective act of the divine intellect was called God's 'exemplar causality' by the medievals; as the epitome or exemplar of all things, God has no need to direct his understanding upon models existing apart from him. God's exemplar causality, moreover, is distinct from the efficient causality by which he brings the actual world into existence through an act of will. So the eternal truths are (a) uncreated and yet (b) dependent on God; for they form part of his creative essence and are known by his intellect in reflection on its own nature.

This, or something very like it, can be regarded as standard Christian orthodoxy. The implications of Descartes's departure from it become clearer if we think back to our first encounter with theological voluntarism in the *Euthyphro*. The question there was: 'Is the pious pious because the gods love it? Or do the gods love it because it is pious?' On the former alternative, the good does not exist independently of the will of the Olympian gods; they do not love or choose the good because it is good; rather, whatever is good is made so solely by their loving and choosing (willing) it. As a consequence, the gods can have no reason for loving and commanding this rather than that; their preference is entirely arbitrary. In exercising choice, they are *absolutely indifferent*, since no choice is better *before* they opt for it, and whatever they choose is made good or better only *by* their choosing it. We saw that this was a difficulty arising from the Divine Command Theory: it makes nonsense of the standard notion of divine goodness or benevolence (see 11.11).

Now a similar question can be asked about 'the true': Are true things true because God affirms (assents to) them? Or does God affirm them because they are true? In the latter event, truths exist independently of God's grasping and assenting to them. He affirms them because they are true and because he knows everything. But in the former case, there is no truth that is independent of God. What is true is *made* so by his affirming it. He thus creates the natures or essences of things as well as the things themselves. Accordingly, the intellect by which God conceives the essences of things and the will by which he makes them actual are one and the same in God, though intellect and will in us are different faculties. On his intellect/will depend all conceptual (or eternal) as well as all factual truths concerning everything—except himself. Hence, his affirming/willing certain propositions, conceptual or factual, must be entirely arbitrary. He does not affirm/will them because they are true; they are true because he affirms/wills them. Indifference and arbitrariness, which are defects in us, are perfections in God.

So much for the content of Descartes's Divine Command Theory. As far as good and evil are concerned, theological voluntarism found influential advocates in the later Middle Ages, notably John Duns Scotus (1266–1308) and William of Ockham. (Duns Scotus, incidentally, was the notoriously obscure writer whose name is the source of our English word 'dunce.') It was rejected as altogether heterodox by the majority of Christian thinkers. The extension of the theory to the true and false was a radical innovation of Descartes. This, of course, makes nonsense of the theological doctrine of divine omniscience, just as theological voluntarism in ethics makes nonsense of divine goodness. Descartes's voluntarism is thus even more heterodox than anything known to the Middle Ages, and orthodox Christian theologians would have been even more aghast at it than at the heretical teachings of Scotus and Ockham.

Descartes, however, refused to see it that way. The only alternative to his own view, he believed, was pagan anthropomorphism. By this he may well have meant conceiving God in the manner of Plato's divine craftsman, who looks away to independently existing standards in determining what holds necessarily in a rational world order. However, he does not say so. On the other hand, he does make explicit reference to Pre-Platonic Olympian theology at a couple of places in his writings. Thinking primarily of eternal truths concerning good and evil, Descartes warns that to conceive these as (a) uncreated and *therefore* (b) independent of God is to conceive God himself as subject to a higher moral law in the universe, like Jupiter (Zeus's Latin name) to the Fates. This places an unacceptable limitation on God's power. The pagan Greek gods, we recall, are eternal but not omnipotent (see 10.4.4); the Christian God is both.

In applying the doctrine of theological voluntarism not just to good and evil but to truth and falsity as well, Descartes saw himself as the defender of Christian orthodoxy, as ridding the Christian conception of an omnipotent creator God of the last vestiges of pagan Greek anthropomorphism. Yet as we saw at the outset of this section, the orthodox Christian view of this matter is that the eternal truths are (a) *uncreated* yet (b) dependent upon God's creative essence. They depend on God's intellect, being grasped in his reflection on his own creative essence; they do not depend on his will, which is distinct from his intellect and the cause of the existence of things rather than their essences. God is omnipotent because he can will and do anything that is *logically* possible; his intellect ascertains what is possible and impossible for his will. That he cannot defy the principles of logic and do the logically impossible is not a limitation on his power.

Descartes, however, argues as follows: either the eternal truths are (1) both (a) uncreated and (b) independent or else they are (2) both (a) created and (b) dependent, completely overlooking a third possibility, which is the orthodox Christian view, that the eternal truths are (3) both (a) uncreated and (b) dependent. Since (1) limits God's power in the manner of Greek paganism, he opts, as a Christian philosopher, for what he mistakenly thinks is the only alternative, (2), completely overlooking (3). Descartes's God, accordingly, is sheerly omnipotent. Having created even the eternal truths of logic, along with those of mathematics and metaphysics, he can do even the logically impossible. Having willed that p and not-p cannot both be true, that *bodies* and minds have certain natures, that $2 + 3 = 5$, and that a square has four sides, he can not only conceive, as we cannot, that these things might be otherwise, but he can even *make* them otherwise, if he so chooses. That is why clear and distinct perception is open to a "very slight" doubt when only remembered. If God were a deceiver, he could change even the things I formerly perceived clearly and distinctly to be true when I am no longer attending to them.

25.9 The dependence of all other knowledge on the knowledge of God

We now understand better what Descartes means by "true and certain knowledge" that nevertheless depends on knowledge of God's existence and veracity: clear and distinct perception that is *no longer* actual but only *remembered*. In order to have *any* knowledge that is certain when no longer actual, be it of (a) the *cogito*-principle, (b) mathematical truths, (c) logical, mathematical, or metaphysical axioms, even (d) scientific knowledge of the physical universe, we must know that God exists and is no deceiver.

The role of the divine guarantor is made explicit at the end of the Fifth Meditation, where the problem of "true and certain knowledge" is at last resolved:

> Now, however, I have perceived that God exists, and at the same time I have understood that everything else depends on him, and that he is no deceiver; and I have drawn the conclusion that everything which I clearly and distinctly perceive is of necessity true. Accordingly, *even if I am no longer attending to the arguments which led me to judge that this is true as long as I remember that I clearly and distinctly perceived it*, there are no counter-arguments which can be adduced to make me doubt it, but on the contrary I have *true and certain knowledge* of it. And I have knowledge not just of this, but of all matters which I remember ever having demonstrated, in geometry and so on. (70 e.a.)

If there is to be science, there must be a body of interconnected truths or true propositions on which the philosopher and scientist can rely even when no longer actually attending to the evidence for them; for the grounds for their truth, once clearly and distinctly perceived, cannot be kept before the mind's eye at all subsequent times. For that, the human mind is simply too limited. In the order of knowing, therefore, the knowledge of God's existence and non-deceptiveness comes *before* all the varieties of *remembered* clear and distinct perception listed above. It is the first item of *scientific* knowledge in the sense just described. For since God exists eternally, his nature is strictly immutable; clear and distinct perception of his existence and veracity *now* is not open even to a "very slight" doubt at any subsequent time. In this way the scientific knowledge of God makes all other scientific knowledge possible. It even renders the *cogito*-principle (understood as a proposition within the system of true propositions that is science) certain at such times as the grounds for its truth are only remembered.

Nevertheless, the knowledge of God comes *after* now actually occurring clear and distinct perception of the self, mind, 'I,' or subject in the order of knowing. For God's existence and veracity are proved by inference from the idea of God existing in the human mind. So in the order of knowing it is the 'I' or self that is first. Then comes God and then all other scientific knowledge. In the order of being, however, God comes first, while mind and body are both dependent for their existence on God and independent of one another. Ontological subjectivism of the sort that places the mind or 'I' first in the order of being as well (idealism) is a post-Cartesian phenomenon first met with in Kant. The order of being and the difference between idealism and Cartesian dualism will be discussed in chapter 27.

25.10 Conclusion

According to a venerable scholastic definition well known to Descartes, truth consists in (A) the *correspondence* of thought with its object, that is, in the *agreement* between (a) the judgments of the intellect and (b) things outside the mind. The source of this commonsense definition is Aristotle, for whom the truth expressed in judgments is known when the *same form* that exists really or materially in things comes to exist immaterially or cognitively in the human mind that apprehends them. According to the truth rule of the Third Meditation, by contrast, truth is (B) an immediately introspectible and infallibly recognizable feature of (a) judgments of the intellect alone; it consists solely in the clarity and distinctness of the perceptions that underlie certain judgments. As for (b) things outside the mind, there is no need to consult these in order to know whether such judgments are true as long as they are actual; careful attention to thinking itself will suffice to determine whether the underlying perception is clear and distinct.

In modern philosophy after Descartes, the traditional notions of sameness, resemblance, and correspondence were often derided, if not as absurd, then as the surest road to complete scepticism. For how can entities as different as thoughts and material things 'correspond' or 'resemble' one another? And how are thoughts to be 'compared' with things, when all we ever have direct access to are our thoughts of things? These criticisms (which, incidentally, would not have fazed Aristotle in the least) culminated finally in efforts to understand truth in terms of (C) the *coherence* or agreement of thoughts among themselves. This could only succeed if the correspondence relation between thoughts and things were somehow reduced to a relation among thoughts, as in Berkeley and Kant. Small wonder, then, that Descartes's philosophy is often seen as the first step on the path to modern idealism. His pioneering theory of truth is the watershed between (A) and (C); it inaugurated an epistemological idealism (subjectivism in the order of knowing) without which later forms of ontological idealism (subjectivism in the order of being) are quite unthinkable. But Descartes himself never countenanced (C) or anything like it.

Ultimately Descartes's radically new conceptions of the structure of thought, of the nature of the self (soul), and of the order of knowing are all rooted in his revolutionary idea of truth as "clear and distinct perception." In the present chapter it has been argued that Descartes succeeded in overcoming solipsism, as he succeeded in overcoming doubt, without falling into circularity or inconsistency. The issue is still hotly debated among scholars. If the foregoing interpretation is correct, Descartes is at least not guilty of the grossest blunders with which he has been charged. Whether the proofs of God's existence are sound is another question. The proofs are the subject of the next chapter.

26

The Existence of God

26.1 Introductory

The Latin terms 'a priori' and 'a posteriori' mean, literally, 'from the earlier' and 'from the later.' In their earliest use they were applied to *arguments* from cause to effect ('from the earlier') and from effect to cause ('from the later'). This use is still relevant to Descartes's first argument for God's existence. As he himself writes, "there are only two ways of proving the existence of God, one by means of his effects [that is, a posteriori, reasoning from effect to cause], the other by means of his nature or essence; and since I expounded the first method to the best of my ability in the Third Meditation, I thought that I should include the second method later on [in the Fifth Meditation]."

In more recent times, 'a priori' and 'a posteriori' have come to be used, not of *arguments*, but of *propositions* or *truths*, the premises of arguments, if you will. Since Leibniz, but especially since Kant, propositions known to be true (or false) without recourse to actual experience or observation, inner or outer, are considered a priori, while all others are a posteriori. Following this usage, we can classify *arguments*, too, as a priori or a posteriori, depending on whether they employ *only* a priori propositions as premises, or whether they contain *at least one* premise that is derived from observation or experience.

Descartes's second proof of God's existence is a priori in this latter sense alone: its premises are all a priori, though the reasoning is not from cause to effect. The first proof, by contrast, is a posteriori in *both* senses: it reasons from an empirical premise asserting the existence of an effect to the conclusion that God, the only possible cause of that effect, exists. The a posteriori is accordingly called 'the causal proof,' while the a priori is widely known by the time-hallowed name 'the ontological argument.' We shall examine them in turn in the present chapter.

26.2 Rationalism and empiricism

Those who maintain that there are non-trivial or informative truths about the world that can be known independently of inner and outer experience are called 'rationalists,' from the Latin word for 'reason,' *ratio*. Plato's rationalism is an extreme form, since the senses are not acknowledged as a source of knowledge *at all*. For the Plato of the *Phaedo* and the *Republic*, genuine knowledge arises from the exercise of reason alone, which is just a form of recollection; though the senses may provide the *occasions* for such knowledge (as when we see equal things, for example), they do not contribute to it in any way. The senses are in fact inherently fallacious, a positive hindrance in the pursuit of knowledge.

Most rationalists defend the much more moderate view that some, perhaps a vast deal of, knowledge is acquired through experience, though at least some is independent of experience or a priori—for example, the so-called eternal truths of logic, mathematics, and metaphysics distinguished earlier (see 25.5). The inclusion of some axioms or principles of a metaphysical nature is the hallmark of full-bodied rationalism. For the truths of logic do not, and the truths of mathematics may not, provide any new information about the nature of anything actually existing. Any rationalist worth his salt will maintain that, in addition to such eternal truths as these, there are others of a material or substantive nature, truths about what does, must, or cannot exist that are knowable a priori, independently of experience.

Those, on the other hand, who deny that reason is the source of extra-logical and extra-mathematical concepts ('body,' 'mind,' 'God') and of substantive metaphysical principles concerning existence ('what is done cannot be undone,' 'something cannot come from nothing,' 'God exists,' and so forth) are called 'empiricists,' *empeiria* being Greek for 'experience.' Locke is a dyed-in-the-wool empiricist, as is Hume. For both, *all* our simple or basic ideas, whether logical, metaphysical, or mathematical, be they of physical or of mental objects, are derived from inner and/or outer experience; even universal principles like those metaphysical axioms just mentioned are known, if knowable at all, only by a shaky inductive generalization from observation and experience. Instead of 'simple' or 'basic' ideas we can say, equivalently, that all *the materials* of our knowledge are borrowed entirely from inner and/or outer experience; the role of the understanding or natural reason (the so-called higher cognitive faculty) is only (a) to analyze such ideas into their (common) elements or (b) to combine them in new ways; reason makes no material contribution, no a priori addition, to our empirical knowledge, nor does it furnish any substantive truths or a priori knowledge of its own. This, however, is not to deny that we can and do reason a priori, both discursively and ratiocinatively (see 7.6.1), using the materials furnished by experience. Hume denied, not that there is *any* a priori knowledge, but that there is any outside mathematics (and logic), any concerned with "matter of fact and existence." We shall look more closely at Hume's empiricism in

Part Four (especially 29.3.1–3). Only John Stuart Mill (1806–1873) went further than both Locke and Hume, maintaining that even the reasonings of logic and mathematics are at bottom inductive, so that these sciences, too, are empirical. Such ultra-empiricism, like Plato's ultra-rationalism, has found few adherents.

While it is reasonably clear that *much* a priori knowledge is merely formal or trivial, having to do exclusively with what are variously called 'linguistic,' 'logical,' or 'conceptual' matters, and that *all* a posteriori knowledge is factual, that is, more or less informative about the real world, the main bone of contention between rationalist and empiricist philosophers is, once again, whether there is any a priori knowledge *about really existing natures and states of affairs that must or cannot exist in the real world*. Examples are: 'the human soul is necessarily immaterial (or immortal),' 'every event necessarily has a cause,' ('nothing comes from nothing'), 'God exists necessarily,' and so forth.

For his part, Descartes holds that there are many such truths that can be known a priori, not indeed temporally prior to sensory experience of the material world, but not therefore just *through* such experience either. They are known rather *through reflecting on our own thinking*, by intuiting concepts and truths that are already innate in us. This is just a special kind of inner experience, not the same as empirical awareness of our fleeting inner states, yet arising through reflection upon them. In this way, through rational reflection, we acquire clear and distinct ideas, not just of what thinking in general is (the nature of mind), but of what extension or body is (the nature of matter), of what substance in general is, of what truth or knowledge is, as well as many particular truths concerning God's nature and existence and all other non-trivial eternal truths. For all this is implicit in our acts of thinking. This doctrine has made Descartes the principal target of empiricist attacks on rationalism.

26.3 Aquinas's Five Ways

Before Descartes there were already certain well-known a posteriori or causal arguments for God's existence. Yet all of them started from the *fact* of something known to exist on the basis of ordinary observation or *external* sense perception. Thus, all of St Thomas Aquinas's renowned "Five Ways" of proving God's existence by natural reason, that is, without the aid of divine revelation, start from premises taken by Thomas to be "certain and plain to our senses," that is, confirmed by ordinary *outer* experience. Deliberately modifying the arguments for a First Mover that he found in Aristotle (see 20.5.1), Aquinas argued from (a) something known through the senses to have begun to exist to (b) the existence of something eternal, its ultimate cause. As we have seen, Aristotle argued from the *sempiternity* of motion in the universe to a First Unmoved Mover outside it (see 20.5.2). As a Christian philosopher, Aquinas could hardly accept the sempiternity of the cosmos; for him, it is an article of faith that the universe was created in time by God. The question we shall have to ask ourselves is whether his arguments have strictly probative force for anyone willing to entertain the possibility that the world's existence is sempiternal and thus at bottom inexplicable.

26.3.1 The first way

Thomas's Way One starts from the existence of what was still in his day referred to as 'motion,' that is, motion in the 'old' (ancient and medieval) sense of *physical change*. Of this, motion in *our* sense, namely (1) local motion (change of place), is only one type, the others being (2) growth and diminution, (3) qualitative change or alteration, and (4) coming-to-be and passing-away of things or substances. Now it is a matter of observed fact that things in the universe 'move' in the sense that they acquire and lose accidental properties or accidental being; they grow or diminish in size, for example; they may become hotter or colder; they change place, and so on. In so doing they pass from being 'in potency' (as the scholastics said) with respect to this or that new form or accidental property, x (for example, 'round,' 'hot,' 'on the earth') to possessing that form or accident actually—actually being, say, 'hot,' 'on the ground,' and so forth. In other words, through change things become x 'in act' rather than 'in potency.'

From the indisputable, because directly observable, fact of such motion, Thomas reasons in the first stage of the argument to the existence of an *external* (but still sensible) *cause* of change. The cause of a new accidental existent (the new accident or form that is actualized through motion or change) must be external to the thing that receives it, since the latter could not impart it to itself without already possessing it, without being already in act in respect to that which it is only in potency. Yet it is plainly self-contradictory to suggest that something is at the same time in potency and in act with respect to the same property—in other words, that it both is and is not in act with respect to some form.

After reasoning thus to the existence of an external cause of change *within* the sensible world, Thomas notes in the second phase of the argument that the sequence of such causes cannot go on to infinity. This does not mean that the series or chain of sensible or dependent (caused) or secondary causes cannot be infinite. Whether it is actually infinite or finite is strictly irrelevant to Aquinas's argument. The question is rather whether the whole series, be it finite *or* infinite, must originate ultimately in a cause that does *not* itself receive motion from another, that is, in an absolutely independent *extramundane* cause, something *beyond* the sensible order of dependent causes. In other words, the question is whether or not the series of sensible, dependent, secondary causes *within* the sensible world must terminate in a supersensible, independent, primary cause, a cause of *a different order*, namely God, understood as the ultimate, unchanging cause of the *existence* of the whole order of changing, sensible things.

Here we come to the real crux of the argument. Why must there be a First Cause? Aquinas's answer is breathtakingly brief: because if there is no first cause, then there can be no secondary causes. Now the word 'secondary' here is obviously just a synonym for 'dependent' in the equivalent phrase 'dependent causes.' So there can be no question of Thomas's deciding this crucial factual question of God's existence by pointing out that if there were no first independent cause the *talk* of 'secondary' and 'dependent' causes would be pointless. At issue here, from start to finish, is what there is in the world (or rather, outside it), not language or linguistic conventions. St Thomas is certainly not starting from linguistic premises in order to reach a conclusion about what there is, what is real—an obvious fallacy of the sort he himself was always quick to point out. What Aquinas means is that if there were no First Cause, if the ascending order of secondary causes did not terminate in something ultimate, these secondary causes would themselves not *be*, that is, the whole (infinite or finite) series of causes would not amount to a *sufficient or adequate* cause of the observed effect: change or motion in the world. Yet there manifestly *is* motion! Hence, there must be a First Cause, and this is what everyone calls 'God.'

Now it might appear that Thomas is only drawing the conclusion that an indefinitely extended (perhaps infinite) series of causes is inadequate in the sense that it cannot adequately *account* for the existence of anything. A series through which we regress indefinitely from effect to cause without coming to any First Cause certainly would not furnish a *complete causal explanation* of the observed effects, since the same 'why'-question would arise again and again with regard to each new link in the chain, each new cause, with no possibility of ever completing the whole series. If this were Aquinas's point, then the correct conclusion would be *not* that God exists, but that *either* (1) there exists indeed a First Cause of the entire series that we can grasp, *or* (2) the existence of the observed effect is ultimately opaque to the human intellect, that is, unexplained and not rationally explicable, unintelligible, or at least incapable of being rendered *completely* intelligible by us.

It may well be that this *alternative* is all Aquinas is entitled to on the strength of the First Way. Yet his actual conclusion is not this, but the first alternative: a First Cause actually exists. The same puzzle about the exact nature of the conclusion which Thomas is entitled to draw, as opposed to the conclusion he actually draws, arises in regard to each of the other four ways as well. In each case, he seems entitled to say no more than: unless God exists, the existence of the universe is ultimately opaque to the human intellect. Yet he in fact concludes: God exists, and the existence of the created universe is thus rationally comprehensible. Is Aquinas simply taking for granted that the existence of the universe cannot be opaque to the human intellect? If the changing universe exists sempiternally, as Aristotle believed, then there simply is no first cause of *existence*; at this level, at the level of existence, at least, the universe really is opaque to us. For Sartre, too, there is something about existence that is simply unfathomable. Yet as a Christian philosopher, Aquinas could accept neither the sempiternity of motion nor the final unintelligibility of existence. Do his arguments disprove them or beg the question? Having identified the crux, we can leave the question open.

26.3.2 The remaining four ways

Way Two is similar to Way One. It starts from the being or existence of an order of efficient causes among sensible things within the world, none of which can be the efficient cause of itself. In contrast to Way One, however, the kind of being in question this time is substantial being, that is, the being of things or substances, not the accidental being of properties, like place, heat, and size, that result from processes like local motion, friction, growth, and so on. In terms of our distinction among four kinds of motion in the previous sub-section, it is (4) the coming-to-be of a substance or substantial change that is in question in Way Two.

Now the substantial being of one thing, Thomas points out, is produced by another; it is produced through the agency of some external secondary cause. For example, a man (human being) begets a man, a horse a horse. We observe, then, a series or ordered sequence of such efficient causes and their effects; we observe, that is, the coming-into-being of substances owing to the efficient causality of other substances. (Such substantial change is not as immediately evident as accidental change, which is why Thomas calls the First Way the "most evident.") As in the First Way, whether the sequence of such causes—successive generations of human beings produced through procreation, say—is finite or infinite is strictly irrelevant. For Aquinas, as a Christian philosopher, it is finite, going back to the first man, Adam; but that is neither here nor there. From the existence of a sequence of causes, each subordinate to another, Thomas reasons to the existence of an extra-mundane First Cause outside the whole sequence, that is, a Cause that is not itself dependent upon anything else and hence not *part* of the sequence. This is what is called 'God.' Since the reasoning is exactly the same as in Way One, the same problem about the conclusion arises here as well. It may be that all Thomas is justified in concluding is again: *either* (1) there exists such a cause or (2) the existence of substantial things is just not completely intelligible to us. But his actual conclusion is clearly (1).

We can be even briefer about the other three ways. Way Three starts from the existence of things which are generated and corruptible, 'contingent beings,' in the technical vocabulary of philosophy, 'things-that-are-but-might-not-have-been,' as we might say, glossing 'contingent' in non-technical terms. (Incidentally, the unwieldiness of this non-technical expression gives a pretty good idea of why philosophers actually *need* a 'jargon.' Technical terms like 'contingent' actually simplify matters greatly.) 'Contingent' means literally 'touching together.' In the case of things that come into being and pass away, actual existence 'comes together' with their natures, though this might not have happened. From the existence of such contingent things, then, Thomas's Third Way proceeds to the existence of a Necessary Being, God, a being that, as we might say, 'cannot not be.' Here once again it is substantial change that is the starting point, as in Way Two; but, unlike Way Two, this time it is the contingency, the 'might-not-have-been-ness,' of sensible substances that forms the starting point.

There is no need to belabour the point about a posteriori proofs of God's existence before Descartes. Way Four starts from the *outwardly observed* existence of greater and lesser degrees of perfection in things and argues to the existence of God as a Most Perfect Being. Way Five starts from the *outwardly observed* way in which certain natural things in the material universe, namely those that have a principle of change within themselves, tend toward some good or end. It argues that since material things lacking intelligence cannot have purposes of their own, there must be a supernatural 'Purposer' as the first efficient cause of such change.

The point of importance just now is that all Five Ways of Aquinas start from something observable in the material, sensible, external world. Their premises are a posteriori propositions about *external, material* things. Descartes's causal proof or a posteriori argument for God's existence is sometimes thought to be very close to St Thomas's Way Two, perhaps because efficient causality figures so centrally in it. But Descartes's starting point is altogether different. For Descartes spotted an all-important difference in evidence between (1) factual (experiential or a posteriori) statements about the goings-on in our own minds and (2) factual statements about extra-mental reality. To (1) and (2) correspond two senses of 'experience': (i) inner experience of one's own mental states and (ii) outer experience of bodies (including one's own) through use of the five external sense organs. Obviously, at this stage in the *Meditations* only factual premises based on inner experience come into question for Descartes. For he still does not know whether he has a body or bodily sense organs, whether there are any external bodies, or whether the ideas that he naturally takes to come from bodies outside him, via sense organs, are not in fact spontaneously produced (unbeknownst to him) by his own mind. A proof is only as certain as its weakest premise, and Aquinas's proofs, starting as they do from (2), were all rendered uncertain by their starting point. Descartes's proof begins from (1).

26.4 Technical preliminaries

Descartes's own causal or a posteriori argument for God's existence starts—and can only start, given his methodological solipsism—from the fact of the presence *in the mind* of an idea, the idea of God. If this argument is not entirely original with Descartes (St Augustine developed a similar proof), it is at least he who brought it to prominence among proofs of God's existence. Before interpreting the argument itself, we must deal with some technical preliminaries, namely: (a) the distinction between formal and objective reality; (b) Descartes's causal adequacy principle (on which the whole argument turns); (c) the incorporation of (a) into (b). It is a peculiarity of both Descartes's arguments for God's existence that they involve a good deal of technical scholastic terminology, and no one who does not take the trouble to understand their vocabulary has any hope of correctly evaluating the proofs.

26.4.1 Formal and objective reality of things

The formal or actual reality (or being) *of things* has to do with their being actual or, as we say, 'real' rather than just imaginary; with their having actual existence in the real world outside the mind, and not just mental or cognitive existence in the mind that thinks about them. The latter is their objective reality.

'Formal' and 'objective reality' are expressions that Descartes took over from scholastic philosophy. What these designations suggest to us nowadays is in fact just the opposite of the scholastic meaning described above. To us, 'objective reality' naturally suggests something like 'real existence outside the mind.' Greyish or dun-coloured elephants, we might say, exist or are 'objectively,' while pink ones are only 'subjectively' real. The latter are the stuff of hallucinations and dreams, existing in the mind only as long as someone thinks of them; the former roam the African savannah whether or not anyone thinks of them.

Now Cartesian and scholastic usage is just the opposite of this. What exists in the mind, when someone is actually thinking about it, is called 'objective' or 'objectively real,' from the Latin *obicio* 'to throw,' whence *obiecta* are literally 'things thrown over against (the mind's eye),' projected onto the inner screen, as it were. What really exists outside the mind, on the other hand, is said to be formally and not just objectively real. Of course, some things are both. Thus, flesh-and-blood elephants *may* exist both in the mind ('objectively' in the scholastic sense), provided someone is thinking of them; and, of course, they *do* exist outside the mind ('formally' in the scholastic sense) in the real world, whether or not anybody thinks about them. By contrast, pink elephants exist *only* objectively (in the scholastic sense or 'subjectively' in ours), *not* formally (not 'objectively' in *our* sense), and that only as long as someone thinks about them. So we cannot rely on today's sense of what the terms 'objective' and 'subjective' mean if we want to understand Descartes's argument correctly; there is just no substitute for learning the technical scholastic jargon.

So far we have discussed formal and objective reality (or formal and objective being) as it pertains to (1) things or objects existing either (a) only in the mind ('objectively' in Descartes's sense) or (b) in the mind and outside it in the world ('objectively' and 'formally' in Descartes's sense) or (c) only outside the mind in the world ('formally'). But formal and objective reality are also ascribed to (2) ideas, and we must next consider the meaning of the terms when so used.

26.4.2 Formal and objective reality of ideas

As for (a), the formal reality *of an idea* is its actual existence in the mind as a mode of thought (that is, a property or state of the mind) of which we are self-consciously aware. In respect of their formal reality, as Descartes points out (40), there is no difference among our ideas. They all have exactly the same formal reality as transitory modes or states of thinking. The *objective reality of an idea*, on the other hand, is its 'representational content,' *what* it represents, what the idea is an idea *of*.

In respect of their objective reality, ideas differ. The idea of God differs from that of unicorn, the idea of a unicorn from that of a goat, of a man, of the sky, of the sea, and so on. They differ in respect of *what* they represent, their objective reality. Now there are three ways in which ideas can differ in respect of their objective reality: either with respect to (i) *what* they represent or with respect to (ii) *what kind* of object they represent (e.g., a material or an immaterial object) or with respect to (iii) *how much* they represent, 'how great' their object is.

If they differ *only* in respect of (i), they differ in objective reality but not in kind or degree of objective reality; for example, the idea of a dog and the idea of a house have a different objective reality (the one is *of* a dog, the other *of* a house), but both are of the same kind of object, a finite material thing (even though one is living and the other non-living).

If they differ in respect of (i) *and* (ii), they differ in objective reality *and* in kind of objective reality, but still not in degree of objective reality—for example, the idea of a material thing like my body and an immaterial thing like my mind. If they differ in respect of (i), (ii), *and* (iii), they differ in objective reality, in kind of objective reality, and in degree of objective reality—for example, the idea of my body as a finite material thing and the idea of God, an infinite immaterial being or Mind. Of course, (iii), the matter of 'how great' an object is represented, presupposes a hierarchy or order of objects from the lesser to the greater. This hierarchy applies to both formal reality or formal being and objective reality or objective being. Furthermore, it applies to the formal and objective reality of both things and ideas.

26.4.3 Four degrees of formal and objective reality

Regarding (iii), Descartes distinguishes just four degrees of reality (see 44–5). We can set them out in a list:

Degree 0: nothing, an absence or privation
Degree 1: a positive mode, property, or attribute of something
Degree 2: a finite thing or substance having attributes, properties, or modes
Degree 3: infinite substance or thing

The values 0 through 3 are arbitrarily assigned, for purposes of simplification. Descartes is only interested in the *relative* value—*more* reality or *less* reality. The intent, in other words, is *not* to suggest that degree 2 is exactly twice degree 1, or that degree 3 is three times degree 1 and one-and-a-half times degree 2. In fact, the difference between degree 3 and the others is supposed to be infinite, that is, greater than any assignable value. Something of the sort is also true of the difference between degree 1 and degree 2: no number of mere modes taken together would equal the reality of a substance. But this is a point on which Descartes is very chary of details.

We have already noted that the formal or actual reality of ideas, no matter what they are ideas of, is degree 1, that of modes, while different ideas have different degrees of objective reality, depending on what they are ideas *of*. Thus, the idea of a house has *more* objective reality than the idea of its size: for size is only a property or mode of the house (degree 1), while the house is the thing that has that property or mode (degree 2). As for the zero degree, this belongs to all those presumed properties of things (whether minds or bodies) that may not be properties or modes at all but mere privations or negations. Thus, cold, for example, may be nothing in a body but the absence of warmth, darkness only the absence of light, and rest no more than the absence of motion. Similarly, ignorance may be nothing in a mind but the absence of knowledge, or wickedness (sin) nothing but the absence of goodness, or falsity and error the absence of truth. Or again, blindness in a man may, for all we know, be nothing positive, but only the absence of sight. Blindness, wickedness, and error are called 'privations' rather than 'negations' because sight, virtue, and truth are things a human being should have, something of which the blind or wicked or deceived man is *deprived*. In a stone, being sightless or lacking goodness or truth would be a negation rather than a privation. Of course, for all we know, warmth may be the absence of cold, not vice versa, and so on. So of any two 'opposites' among *sensory* qualities, it is just not certain which is positive, which negative. Accordingly, Descartes treats all sensory qualities alike: to the extent that we cannot be sure whether they are modes rather than privations or negations, they all possess the zero degree of reality. In the case of error or wickedness, however, Descartes holds that it is clear that both are privations, while goodness and truth are perfections.

Let us sum up. In this and the preceding sub-section we have distinguished the following: (1) formal reality of ideas; (2) objective reality of ideas; (3) formal reality of things; (4) objective reality of things; (5) three different ways in which ideas can differ in respect of their objective reality—namely, in respect of (i) what objective reality, (ii) what kind of objective reality, and (iii) what degree of objective reality they possess; (6) the same three different ways in which things can differ in respect of their formal reality—namely, (i) what formal reality, (ii) what kind of formal reality, and (iii) what degree of formal reality they possess. Now for the second key element in Descartes's *a posteriori* proof of God's existence, (b) the causal principle.

26.4.4 First two formulations of Descartes's causal adequacy principle

Earlier we introduced the principle 'nothing comes from nothing' as an example of a metaphysical axiom like the one Descartes alludes to at the beginning of the Third Meditation: 'what is done cannot be undone.' It is a further item of that non-trivial a priori knowledge referred to above (see 26.2): things we know about the world 'in advance,' a priori, without recourse to experience. Descartes calls it "manifest by the natural light" (40), that is, by the light of unassisted human reason as opposed to the supernatural light of divine revelation. It is one of the eternal truths belonging to the field of metaphysics rather than logic or mathematics.

The basic form of the principle is:

(1) 'nothing comes from nothing' or "something cannot arise from nothing" (40)

Is this principle really self-evident? And what exactly does it mean? It obviously has to do with the existence of a *cause* for everything that begins to be: 'nothing begins to be *without a cause of its beginning to be or exist.*' However, the word 'arise' tends to obscure the fact that the cause may be a *sustaining* no less than a *creating* efficient cause. Thus, the principle means: 'everything (that begins to be *or continues to exist from moment to moment*) has some cause (of its beginning or continuing to be).'

Descartes goes on (40–1) to reformulate the principle in two further ways. The first reformulation runs:

(2) "There must be at least as much reality in the efficient and total cause as in the effect of that cause." (40)

Is this the same principle? It seems to tell us much more than (1). Yet, at bottom, it only tells us *explicitly* what is *implicit* in (1), so that it is the same principle after all. For one thing, (2) mentions *efficient* causality, the cause of becoming or coming-to-be, which is only implicit in (1). And, furthermore, (2) mentions the *amount or degree of reality* in the cause and the effect. So although they are the same principle, we may say that (1) tells us explicitly that everything which begins to be has a cause, but only implicitly 'how great' the cause must be in relation to the effect; while (2) tells us only implicitly that everything has a cause, but explicitly that the cause must be at least as great as the effect (or greater).

26.4.5 Meaning of the second formulation

We have seen that there are two types of entities having reality (things and ideas), two types of reality (formal and objective), and four degrees of reality, whether formal or objective. These *degrees of reality* or being can also be called *degrees of perfection*.

If we focus for a moment on the *formal* reality of *things*, leaving both objective reality and ideas aside, we can see that the formulation of the causal principle in (2) means the following. Something with a lower degree of formal reality, a mode of a substance, for instance, cannot be the cause of something with a higher degree of reality, for example, a substance. For if a mode were the "efficient and total" that is, the *sole productive* cause of a substance, one degree of reality (in the effect) would have to come to be from nothing (since it cannot come from the cause, which does not have it); that is, something would come from nothing. And formulation (1) says explicitly that this is impossible. A mode could, however, be a *partial* cause of a substance. There is no reason why a mode, m, together with a substance, S_1, could not produce another substance, S_2, or why a mode, m, in substance, S_1, could not produce a mode, n, in substance, S_2. Yet, as already noted, the difference between the 'plateaus' of reality or perfection is conceived by Descartes in such a way that no number of modes together would ever equal the degree of reality of a substance, and no number of finite substances could equal an infinite substance.

Put this way, (2), like (1), is making the point that 'nothing comes from nothing,' but in a way that spells out explicitly not only that everything must have *some* cause (of its beginning to be), but also *what sort of cause* everything must have (namely, one with at least as much reality as itself). In other words, the reformulated principle tells us what characteristics a cause must have in order to be *adequate* to produce a certain effect. On the strength of (2), then, we can call Descartes's principle a 'causal adequacy principle.'

26.4.6 Third formulation

The second formulation of the causal principle was clarified in terms of the formal reality of things. Now for the third and final step, incorporating (b) the causal principle into (a) the distinction between two types of reality, formal and objective. This results in Descartes's third formulation of the causal principle. To understand it, we have to widen our perspective to include the objective reality of ideas as well as the formal reality of things. For the causal principle is now made to 'cross over' from the latter to the former.

(3) [I]n order for a given idea to contain such and such objective reality, it must surely derive it from some cause which contains at least as much formal reality as there is objective reality in the idea. (41)

Paraphrasing this, we might say: There has to be at least as much *formal reality* (or actually existing perfection) in the cause of an idea existing in the mind as there is *objective reality* (merely represented perfection) in the idea itself. Or, as Descartes himself puts it somewhat later:

(3) [I]t is clear to me by the natural light [of reason] that the ideas in me are like pictures or images which can easily fall short of the perfection of the things from which they are taken, but which cannot contain anything greater or more perfect. (42)

Is (3) just a *logical consequence* of the causal principle formulated as (1) and (2)? In other words, was the talk of 'reality' in (2) completely general, so as to cover both formal and objective reality, both the reality of ideas and things? If so, (3) merely spells out something that was implicit in both (1) and (2), and all three formulations have to be accepted or rejected together.

Or is (3) an *extension* of (1) and (2), an *application* of the causal adequacy principle to something to which it *may* not be applicable at all, namely, the *objective* reality of ideas? If so, one could accept (1) and (2) as certain when confined to 'reality' as 'formal reality' but reject Descartes's claim that (3) is a consequence of (1) and (2) rather than a misapplication of an otherwise acceptable causal adequacy principle to the objective reality of ideas. Since (3) is the key a priori premise in the proof of God's existence to which Descartes is leading up, this question is crucial.

26.4.7 Remaining ambiguities

The cause must have "at least as much" reality as its effect. For all our clarifications so far, this statement is still ambiguous. The first ambiguity presents no great difficulty. The expression 'at least as much' might mean either that the cause contains (a) *exactly as much, the same amount of reality*, as its effect, in which case Descartes says that it contains the reality of the effect only *formally*, or that it contains (b) *more reality* than its effect—that is, as Descartes expresses this possibility, it contains the reality of the effect *eminently*. Since we can safely assume that the cause is adequate to produce the effect in *either* case, the ambiguity, while puzzling, poses no threat to Descartes's argument. The principle asserts: at least (a), if not (b).

But apart from this there is still another ambiguity. We distinguished earlier between (1) formal and objective reality. Which of these must the cause possess? Again, we can safely say that the reality in the cause must be *formal reality*, whether or not that in the effect is formal or objective reality. This much seems clear from the third formulation of the principle; but, if there were any doubt, Descartes makes his meaning clear in one of his other writings: "the objective reality of our ideas," he writes, needs a cause which contains this reality not merely objectively but formally or eminently." As was just pointed out, 'eminently' means a greater, while 'formally' means the same, degree of formal reality.

26.5 The causal (a posteriori) proof of God's existence

With all the preliminaries out of the way, we can now proceed to the examination of the causal or a posteriori argument for God's existence. We shall confine ourselves to the first version of the argument (that under stage 6, as opposed to 8, in 25.3 above). The reworked version is just that, another version of the same argument.

26.5.1 Strategy and procedure

The third formulation of the causal principle is the axis on which the causal proof of God's existence turns. Writes Descartes:

If the objective reality of any of my ideas turns out to be so great that I am sure the same reality does not reside in me, either formally or eminently, and hence that I myself cannot be its cause, it will necessarily follow that I am not alone in the world, but that some other thing which is the cause of this idea also exists. (42)

Given this strategy, Descartes can proceed as follows:

Step I: Take an inventory of all the ideas or types of idea found in his mind.
Step II: Go through the ideas or types of ideas one by one in order to determine whether his mind alone could be the efficient cause of them. (If there is none that his mind could not have produced by itself, then, for all he knows, he may be entirely alone in the universe.)
Step III: Employ the positive outcome of Step II *and* the causal principle as premises in the argument for God's existence.

We shall examine these steps in detail. But first here is a formalized version of the proof.

26.5.2 Outline of the argument

In the formalized argument two *factual* or a posteriori premises come first:

P1 There is in my mind the idea of "a substance that is infinite, eternal, immutable, independent, supremely intelligent, supremely powerful, and which created both myself and everything else" (45), an idea whose objective reality corresponds to 'infinite substance.' (degree 3)

P2 My mind itself possesses a degree of formal reality corresponding to 'finite substance.' (degree 2)

Next comes the causal adequacy principle in its third formulation as an a priori premise:

P3 But "in order for a given idea to contain such and such objective reality, it must surely derive it from some cause which contains at least as much formal reality as there is objective reality in the idea." (41)

From P1, P2, and P3, a first, merely negative conclusion follows:

C1 Therefore I myself cannot be the "efficient and total" cause of the idea of God.

However, the positive conclusion from all this is:

C2 Therefore there must exist outside my mind an entity that possesses formally all the reality which my idea contains objectively, that is, an infinite substance, and this is what everyone calls 'God.'

26.5.3 A closer look at steps I and II

The inventory in Step I turns up the following ideas: (1) myself (as mind), (2) God, (3) corporeal inanimate things, (4) angels, (5) animals, and (6) other men (as embodied minds, minds inhabiting living bodies). Or, in rank order: God, angels, minds, men, animals, inanimate things.

Now, as far as (1) is concerned, there can be no problem about the provenance of this idea: my mind is an adequate cause of my idea of my mind. As for (4), (5), and (6), there is no reason why these could not be factitious or 'made-up' ideas, cobbled together out of (1), (2), and (3). For example, the idea of an animal could be compounded out of the idea of lifeless corporeal body plus the corporeal ideas of nutritive, locomotive, sensitive functions of living bodies (see above 24.6.1). Or the idea of an angel could be no more than that of something *between* human mind and God. So it too could be compounded out of two other ideas. Similarly, the idea of a man adds to that of an animal the idea of (rational) thought.

Next comes (3), corporeal inanimate bodies. Here we have to consider (3a) *clear and distinct ideas of body*: size or extension, shape, position, motion, substance, duration and number; and (3b) *confused and obscure ideas of body*: colour, sound, smell, tastes, heat and cold, and other tactile qualities.

Now as for (3b), these ideas may have the very lowest degree of reality (nothingness = 0 degree of reality); but, if not, their degree of reality is in any case "so slight" (44) that there is no reason why I, a mental substance, could not be the cause of them. At best, they are modes having degree 1 of reality; and I, as a thinking substance having degree 2 of reality, could easily be their cause. As far as (3a) is concerned, the ideas of substance, duration, and number could be produced by me simply by examining myself. For I am a substance, I endure, I am one, I have states which are many, and so on. Furthermore, shape, position, motion are all modes having degree 1 of reality. Since I am a finite substance with degree 2 of reality, I could contain the cause of these ideas not just formally but *eminently*.

Hence, at the end of Step II there remains only the idea of God of which I myself *cannot* be the cause, which was (C1) of the formalized argument, and this, together with the causal principle stating that there must be *some* cause and *what sort* of cause it must be, produces the desired conclusion, (C2), God exists.

26.6 Critical assessment of the argument

26.6.1 First line of attack

Formally, the argument looks valid. Technically, it is a tour de force of finely honed scholastic distinctions and principles. But is it sound? That is, are the premises true and known to be so with perfect or even reasonable certainty?

Within this proof, the factual or a posteriori premise P1 seems unobjectionable. It is at least more certain than the a posteriori premises used by St Thomas in the Five Ways. Therein consists what Descartes regarded as the superiority of his argument. As for P2, it invokes a hierarchy of being (mode or accident, then substance, and so on) of a sort that was pretty well universal in the philosophical thought of the time. It is not unassailable, of course, but the real *crux* is:

P3 But "in order for a given idea to contain such and such objective reality, it must surely derive it from some cause which contains at least as much formal reality as there is objective reality in the idea." (41)

This is just (3), the third formulation of the causal adequacy principle, which 'crosses over' (as we said earlier) from formal to objective reality. Even if one were willing to accept the first two formulations of the principle as applied to the formal reality of things and to the formal reality of ideas, one might well balk at Descartes's assumption that the third is merely a *logical consequence* of (2) rather than a *misapplication* of it to the objective reality of ideas. In other words, one might well want to say: if (3) really is just a consequence of (2), then since (3) is counter-intuitive and probably false, so is (2); whereas if (3) is not a consequence, but an extension of (2) from the formal to the objective reality of ideas, what is indeed self-evidently true for *formal* reality seems strongly counter-intuitive, and therefore probably false, for the *objective* reality of ideas.

To see why it is counter-intuitive, just take Descartes's application of (3) to the question of the origin of the idea of God and ask: If there were no God at all, *could* men have fashioned the idea of just such a perfect, infinite, necessarily existing being for themselves? It seems obvious that they *could* have, starting from their own imperfections, limitations, and contingency and negating all three to form the idea of a most perfect being. This is precisely the objection raised by Descartes's contemporaries Pierre Gassendi and Thomas Hobbes. We today think of Freud's and Marx's theories about the origins of religion, or Voltaire's famous quip that "[i]f God did not exist it would be necessary to invent him." Think of all the anthropological evidence about different ideas of divinity in different cultures. Is it plausible to suggest that the human mind is incapable of fashioning such an idea on its own, without the assistance of God? Hardly.

If the above considerations occasion doubts about P3, then what Descartes claims as a self-evident principle of the 'natural light' of reason proves to be not just doubtful, but downright counter-intuitive, as soon as we get down to actual cases—for example, the crucial case of the idea of God. But this is only one line of attack.

26.6.2 Second line of attack

A more radical line of attack would be to reject *all* forms of the causal adequacy principle, not just (3), but even (1) and (2). This is exactly what Hume did. Without denying that (1) every beginning-to-be of something has an efficient cause and that (2) the cause is of a kind adequate to produce the effect, Hume simply denied that these things were either self-evident or capable of proof, with or without the aid of experience. According to him, only those things can be proved a priori (that is, without recourse to experience, using *reason* alone), the denials of which involve contradiction. Now (1) and (2) *can* be denied without contradiction. Moreover, they cannot be logically deduced from any more basic principles whose denial involves contradiction. Therefore, they are neither self-evident nor knowable a priori. And the same goes for (3).

So much for *reason*. As for establishing the causal adequacy principle by *experience*, this is manifestly impossible, since experience can only teach us what is (or has been, perhaps always has been) the case, never what *must* be the case (past, present, and future).

26.6.3 Descartes's response

Descartes anticipates and responds to the first line of attack within the Third Meditation itself:

And I must not think that, just as my conceptions of rest and darkness are arrived at by negating movement and light, so my perception of the infinite is arrived at not by means of a true idea but merely by negating the finite. On the contrary, I clearly understand that there is more reality in an infinite substance than in a finite one, and hence that my perception of the infinite, that is God, is in some way prior to my perception of the finite, that is myself. For how could I understand that I doubted or desired—that is lacked something—and that I was not wholly perfect, unless there were in me some idea of a more perfect being which enabled me to recognize my own defects by comparison? (45–6)

This is qualified elsewhere by a distinction between implicit and explicit knowledge. Explicitly, we become aware of our own imperfection before we become explicitly aware of God's perfection; nevertheless, that *explicit* awareness of our own imperfection presupposes a prior *implicit* knowledge of perfection. Descartes even lays this down as a self-evident principle: "every defect and negation presupposes that of which it falls short and which it negates."

This reply to the first line of attack is an argument out of the same stable as the notorious Platonic sophism that in order to know that A surpasses B in beauty, one has to have first grasped the Idea or Form of Perfect Beauty itself as a standard with which to compare both; one could not form the idea of perfect beauty by comparing A with B and then imagining something that surpasses B to a far greater extent than B surpasses A (see above 20.13.2). In short, it is not very convincing at all. As for the second line of attack, it is devastating, if correct. Descartes's causal axiom "something cannot arise from nothing" is the hinge on which the whole causal argument turns. Undermine it, and the whole argument falls to the ground. The axiom, and Hume's criticism of it, will receive fuller consideration in Part Four. Our tentative conclusion must be, however, that the proof fails.

26.7 The innateness of the idea of God

The last three paragraphs of Meditation Three raise the following puzzling question having nothing to do with whether the proof of God's existence is cogent. Assuming that God himself, existing formally or actually outside the mind, is the cause of the objective reality of the idea of God existing in my mind, as the proof purports to show, how did he communicate the idea of himself to me?

26.7.1 Proof of innateness

The answer is reached by a process of elimination. The idea is not (a) adventitious (acquired through the senses), for "it has never come to me unexpectedly, as usually happens with the ideas of things that are perceivable by the senses, when these things present themselves to the external sense organs" (51). Descartes's point is that ideas acquired through the senses are independent of the will. It is never up to us just what sensory data we are going to receive in the next moment; since the idea of God never just crops up without our deliberately directing our thoughts that way, it seems that it is not just another sensory idea. One might have thought that this much was obvious; after all, we cannot see God. But can we form the idea of God using the imagination?

No, replies Descartes, the idea of God is not (b) fictitious or factitious, the product of the imagination. For "I am plainly unable either to take anything away from it or add anything to it" (51), as I can with my ideas of pink elephants, dragons, mermaids, or unicorns. Such ideas as these can be varied at will. Descartes expresses the key difference at the beginning of the Fifth Meditation, saying that the idea of God is a "true and immutable nature." What the idea of God contains does not depend on the human will, any more than it is up to us whether the internal angles of a triangle equal two right angles or not (see 25.7.2).

So everything turns on an alleged difference between fictional, including the zoologist's or botanist's morphological, 'essences' (for example, 'land animal'), on the one hand, and pure mathematical and metaphysical ideas or exact essences (for example, 'two' and 'triangle,' 'mind' and 'God'), on the other. The former are, like the ideas of pink elephants, unicorns, mermaids, conventional or made up; their content or objective reality is fixed by individual decision or group consensus, and it can be changed. The latter, however, are independent of, and unalterable by, our individual or collective wills.

Here, too, it is possible to have serious misgivings. On one fairly widely held and plausible view of mathematics, mathematical essences are just conventionally formulated definitions within a rigorously axiomatized formal system. As for 'God,' it is at least doubtful whether in addition to the various factitious ideas found in different cultures there is also the one strictly universal idea of God described in P1 of the causal argument, whose "true and immutable" nature is neither made up nor alterable.

The conclusion Descartes himself draws is this. Since neither the actual occurrence of the idea of God (its formal reality) nor its content (objective reality) depends on the will, as with sensory and fictitious ideas, respectively, the idea of God must be (c) innate, that is, a deliverance of reason or the understanding, placed in me "like the mark of a craftsman stamped upon his work" (51). That is the conclusion reached by a process of elimination. Accordingly, the causal proof of God's existence is sometimes called 'the Trademark Argument.'

26.7.2 Meaning of 'innate'

This is not the place to evaluate further Descartes's distinction between factitious and innate ideas. Instead, we ask two questions about the latter that are directly relevant to the text we are trying to understand. First, what does innateness mean? And second, is there a contradiction in Descartes's saying: (a) the idea of God is innate, inborn, springs from the *nature* of my mind, from my *own* nature; and (b) the idea of God is *not* produced by me (as mind) but rather by something actually existing outside of me, God Himself?

To take the latter question first, (a) and (b) are rendered consistent by a further tenet, (c): my nature is given to me by God. Thus, God gives me my nature, my nature gives me the idea of God (like the trademark stamped upon the work), and so God gives (places in) me the idea of himself. There may indeed be something far-fetched, but there is nothing logically inconsistent about this.

As for the first question, Descartes explains 'innateness' in the penultimate paragraph of the Third Meditation as follows:

[T]he mere fact that God created me is a very strong basis for believing that I am somehow made in his image and likeness, and that I perceive that likeness, which includes the idea of God, by the same [non-sensory] faculty which enables me to perceive myself. That is, when I turn my mind's eye upon myself, I understand that I am a thing which is incomplete and dependent on another and which aspires without limit to ever greater and better things; but I also understand at the same time that he on whom I depend has within him all those greater things, not just indefinitely and potentially but actually and infinitely and hence that he is God. (51)

The key points made here can be restated this way: Careful attention to all that is implicit in my thinking discloses that my own nature consists entirely in this, that I am a thing that thinks and is aware of its own thinking. Now in order to have an explicit idea of God *nothing more* is required than is necessary in order to have this explicit idea of my own nature: I must think and pay close attention to all that is implicit in my thinking. For implicit in the thinking of which I am aware, regardless of what I am thinking about, is the idea of infinite perfection, the idea of a thing or substance, and hence the idea of a perfect or infinite substance or being, God. Even if I only become *explicitly* aware of this idea *after* becoming *explicitly* aware of myself as a finite and limited mind, the idea of perfection is nevertheless implicitly understood *prior* to the explicit understanding of imperfection and makes it possible. For I can only understand myself as an imperfect finite substance before the backcloth of the idea of a perfect infinite substance.

We have already expressed misgivings about the blatantly Platonizing tendencies behind this account of the innateness of the idea of God (see 26.6.3). Nevertheless, this passage indicates how Descartes's general theory of innateness differs from Plato's theory of recollection. 'Innate' here has nothing to do with mysterious traces left in the mind by objects with which it was directly acquainted during its pre-natal existence. 'Innate' means, rather, 'implicit in the nature of thinking itself, in *my* nature as a thinking thing, and capable of being made explicit through attention to my own thinking rather than (as with adventitious ideas) to the things outside me.' This, as already noted, is the source of the ideas of thinking, of substance, of truth (clarity and distinctness) as well as 'God' and "countless" (63) other innate ideas. Whether or not it is defensible, it is certainly a new theory and a significant advance on Plato. The next big advance was to come with Kant and the theory of synthetic a priori

444 Part Three: Descartes and the Road to Certainty

propositions. But that is a long story, partly told already (see 7.5.2).

26.8 The ontological (a priori) argument

So much for Descartes's first argument for the existence of God. To be considered next is the so-called ontological argument. Though not particularly apt, this name, invented by Kant, has stuck. While the causal or a posteriori argument starts from a factual premise but turns on an eternal truth, the ontological argument contains *no* factual or a posteriori premises whatsoever. It is thus an a priori argument in the second sense distinguished earlier (see 26.1).

Once again it is a highly technical argument rife with scholastic distinctions. Hence the need for certain terminological preliminaries here too. Once these are completed, we shall be able to grasp the gist of the argument, which was advanced and debated long before Descartes's time. After a brief look at the history of the argument, including some of the most famous criticisms advanced against it, we must then try to decide whether Descartes's version of the argument in the Fifth Meditation fares any better against these devastating criticisms than its predecessor. We begin, as usual, with a word on the overall structure of the Fifth Meditation.

26.8.1 Structure of the Fifth Meditation

The ontological argument is the centrepiece of the Fifth Meditation, which runs through five stages:

1 Paragraph 1: Introduction
2 Paragraphs 2–6: Mathematical Knowledge of the Essence of Material Things
3 Paragraph 7: Ontological Argument for the Existence of God
4 Paragraphs 8–12: Objections to the Ontological Argument and Replies
5 Paragraphs 13–16: Dependence of All Other Knowledge on the Knowledge of God

The opening paragraph announces the *essence* of material objects as the first theme of the Fifth Meditation, postponing consideration of the *existence* of such objects to the Sixth. We shall postpone both these topics until the next chapter. The second stage merely prepares the ground for the ontological argument. We shall omit stages 2 and 4, paying particular attention to 3, the proof of God's existence. As for 5, the place of the knowledge of God in the new order of knowing, it was quoted and discussed in the last chapter (see 25.9).

26.8.2 Technical preliminaries

As noted earlier (see chap. 20), medieval philosophers made a great deal more than had the ancients of the distinction between essence and existence. The distinction itself was not unknown or unimportant in Greek philosophy, but one can readily appreciate how much more significant it was to become in the light of the Christian idea of creation *ex nihilo*. For the ancients, by contrast, being was conceived primarily as finite form, as what the medievals called *essentia*. This word refers to *what* a thing is, its *nature*. Following Plato and Aristotle, the medievals also called it the 'form' or 'the substantial form' of the thing. Accordingly, the concept of its essence, as expressed in the correct real definition, is the *formal concept* of the entity in question. This is its 'being' in the sense of that which is graspable in a simple act of the intellect or understanding. So understood, the medievals considered a thing no more than *capable* of existing. In other words, its being in this sense is *possible existence* or, simply, possibility.

'Existence,' by contrast, refers to the fact *that* a thing is, its *actual existence*, its being really 'there' rather than merely possible. This includes (i) being actually in the human mind (say, as the representational content of an idea); (ii) being actually in the physical universe (as a really existing material thing); and (iii) being actually outside of time and the physical universe in the mind of an extramundane First Cause, God. This last mode of existence is that which belongs to the archetype or timeless model conceived by God in reflecting on his own creative essence: eternal existence in the divine intellect (see 25.8). The former two are different modes of temporal being or existence: in the human mind (called 'cognitional' or 'intentional' or 'objective' existence) or outside the human mind in the world (called 'real' or 'actual' existence).

The question now arises whether the essence and the existence of things, which we have thus distinguished, are really distinct or different in the things themselves, or whether they are just two ways of looking at one and the same thing, the being of entities. In other words, are they only distinct *in thought*, conceptually distinct, or are they distinct *in fact*, really distinct? Now in the case of all *created things*, the orthodox Christian view is that essence and actual existence are really distinct. Essence and the so-called act of existence are quite separate in created beings themselves, such that when these are caused to exist, something new, the act of existence, is added to the essence. Accordingly, existence is only graspable by a complex act of the intellect that supervenes upon the simple act of conceiving the essence, the formal concept.

This, then, is what it means to say that existing things are created: merely possible beings receive actual existence (or the act of existence) from other beings (their secondary causes) and ultimately from the creator of all being, God (the primary cause). And this is what it is to say, in technical scholastic parlance, that the distinction between existence and essence of such things is a 'real distinction': it is not just something introduced by the mind, merely a 'way of looking at things,' but is already there to be discovered. (We shall see later, in 27.8.1, that Descartes uses this technical expression 'really distinct' in a rather different way.) With these distinctions between (a) essence and existence, (b) various modes of existence, and (c) conceptual or real distinctions now clear, we are in a position to understand the gist of the ontological argument.

26.8.3 The gist of the argument

We have seen that the actual existence of any created thing was believed, in the scholastic mainstream at least, to be really distinct from its essence or nature. Things of a certain nature *may*, though they need not, exist; if they exist outside the human mind, the fact remains that they could also *not* have existed (had God not created them, or had any of their secondary causes been absent) and that they will some day cease to exist. Their actual existence outside the mind is accordingly accidental to their natures; or, to put the same point another way, their existence is *contingent*. In completely non-technical language, they are 'just-happen-to-bes' and hence 'might-not-have-beens.'

It is quite otherwise in the case of God, however. Existence and essence are one and the same in God; they are not distinguishable *even in thought*, that is, not even conceptually distinct, as the scholastics put it. God does not receive existence from without; he *is* existence, namely *his own* existence, and thereby the ultimate or uncaused cause of the existence of all other things. In other words, God's very essence is: *to exist*, to be actual. His existence is *logically* necessary, he is the necessary Being, and indeed the *only* such 'must-be-and-cannot-not-be' in the universe (see 20.5.2).

Now the ontological argument simply *makes explicit* this uniquely distinctive relationship between God's essence and existence: it infers God's actual and necessary existence from his nature or essence. That is why Descartes refers to it as the argument for God's existence "by means of his nature or essence" (see 26.1).

26.8.4 History of the argument

The first ontological proof of God's existence was advanced in the eleventh century by St Anselm of Canterbury (1033–1109), in a work entitled *Proslogion*. In the thirteenth century St Thomas Aquinas examined the argument in his *Summa Theologica* and a number of other writings. His attitude toward it can only be described as ambivalent. Overall, one can say that he (1) acknowledged that God's essence logically entails or involves his existence, as the ontological argument maintained, but (2) warned that their logical relationship was beyond the grasp of ordinary human reason; moreover, Aquinas (3) showed that Anselm's manner of proving God's existence was circular.

Both (1) and (3) are acknowledged by Descartes, who claims that his own a priori proof for God's existence is not open to either charge brought by Thomas against

Anselm's celebrated argument. We shall see that Descartes indeed advances a somewhat different argument, though the gist is the same. St Bonaventure (1217–1274), following another great Franciscan, Alexander of Hales, accepted Anselm's argument, as did Richard of St Victor (died 1173) before and Duns Scotus after him. Spinoza and Leibniz, the other two giants of seventeenth-century philosophy, both accepted Descartes's a priori proof (Leibniz with an important qualification). Unfortunately, we lack space to discuss any of these treatments of the argument.

In the eighteenth century first Hume and then Kant mounted powerful attacks on the original version of the a priori or ontological argument. These we shall examine in due course, attempting to determine whether Descartes's version is any more immune to Hume's and Kant's criticisms than Anselm's version is.

Although people still try to revive the ontological argument from time to time, even in our own day, it is mainly of historical interest as a proof of God's existence, even in those contemporary Catholic circles in which Aquinas's Five Ways are considered strictly probative. On the other hand, the consideration of the inadequacies of the ontological argument can teach us some valuable philosophical lessons, while consideration of the differences between Descartes's and Anselm's versions can afford us some interesting insights, if not into the question of whether there is a God, at least into Cartesian philosophy.

26.9 Anselm's proof

In the *Proslogion* Anselm advances his argument in the context of a comment on the words of the Psalmist, "The fool hath said in his heart there is no God." Now let 'GCB' stand for 'greatest conceivable being' or 'a being than which a greater cannot be conceived.' Let 'D' stand for 'definition,' 'P' for 'premise,' 'A' for 'axiom,' and 'C' for 'conclusion.' Finally, let it be noted that 'understanding' is used here in the broad sense of 'the human mind.' We can now formalize Anselm's argument as follows:

First Stage:

D1 Whatever is understood exists in the understanding (that is, 'to be understood' just means 'to exist in the understanding').
P1 When the fool hears of the GCB, he understands what he hears.
C1 Therefore, the GCB exists in the [fool's] understanding.

Second Stage:

A1 That which exists in the understanding can at least be conceived to exist, not just in the understanding alone, but in reality as well, that is, outside the mind, which is greater.

Final Stage:

P2 If GCB existed in the understanding alone (and not outside it, in reality as well), then the GCB is one than which a greater can be conceived after all (from A1).
C2 But the consequent (the then-clause) of P2 is impossible (self-contradictory), that is, necessarily false.
C3 So (by *modus tollens*) the antecedent (if-clause) of P2 must be false and its denial true: the GCB cannot exist in the understanding alone.
C4 Therefore (from C1 and C3) the GCB exists both in reality and in the understanding (and this is God).

The simplified form in which both Aquinas and Descartes recast Anselm's version of the ontological argument is this.

P1 By the word 'God' we understand that than which nothing greater can be conceived.
P2 To exist in reality as well as in the understanding is greater than to exist in the understanding alone.
C   Therefore, when we understand the word 'God,' we understand that God necessarily exists in reality as well as in the understanding.

26.9.1 St Thomas's rejection of Anselm's argument

In his *Summa Theologica*, St Thomas discusses Anselm's argument in the context of a two-stage treatment of the question, Whether God exists? The result, as noted earlier, is highly ambiguous. In the first stage, Thomas considers whether the existence of God is self-evident. He immediately draws a distinction between (a) that which is self-evident *in itself but not to us* and (b) that which is self-evident *in itself and to us*. He concludes that since existence really belongs to the essence of God, that is, since God's existence really is identical with, and so cannot be distinguished from, his essence (since God *is* his own existence), the proposition 'God exists' is indeed self-evident in itself, but not to us. We finite human beings simply do not have an adequate grasp of the immensity of God's nature or essence. Hence, we cannot understand that it includes His existence—although, of course, it does.

This means that the nerve of Anselm's ontological argument is sound from a logical point of view, but, alas, the argument is of no use whatever to us. Yet Thomas does not leave the matter there. In a second stage, he explicitly considers Anselm's version of the ontological argument as an objection to his own claim that God's existence is *not* self-evident to us. After all, Anselm's use of the ontological argument implies that God's existence is indeed self-evident, even to the likes of us humans: *that* God exists is, for Anselm, part of *our* conception of *what* he is. So St Thomas must face a serious objection to his own view, and this he does in the second stage.

The conclusion of Anselm's argument, as Thomas spells it out, is this: 'Therefore when we understand the word "God," we understand *the word to mean* that God exists in reality as well as in the understanding.' To this Thomas simply responds that "it does not follow from this that what is understood by the word exists in reality, only that it exists as thought about," that is, cognitively. In other words, the mere fact that *we understand the word* 'God' to mean (among other connotations) 'an entity that exists in reality' does not entail that such an entity really exists outside the mind. On the contrary, Anselm's argument *takes it for granted* that there exists in reality a being that corresponds to this concept of ours, that is, a being that fits the description 'GCB.' But this is to assume the very thing the fool or atheist denies, that is, the very thing to be established by the argument. The argument, in short, is viciously circular. About this Thomas would seem to be right.

26.9.2 Kant's criticism

St Thomas began by criticizing the first premise:

P1 By 'God' we understand 'that than which nothing greater can be conceived.'

He claimed that the concept of God is simply beyond our comprehension so that this premise, though true, is of no use to us in proving God's existence. Kant, on the other hand, criticizes the second premise:

P2 To exist in reality as well as in the intellect is greater than to exist in the intellect alone.

The memorable and oft-cited form Kant gave his criticism is: "Being is not a real predicate." By this he meant that existence, whether it be actual existence outside the mind or cognitional existence in it, is *not* an attribute, property, or perfection of a thing *in addition to* its other attributes, properties, and perfections, such that one could legitimately say that to be actually existent is to be 'greater,' 'more,' 'more perfect' than to exist possibly. We can confine ourselves to the task of understanding this *negative* thesis of Kant; his own *positive* theory of possible and actual existence need not concern us here.

A 'real' predicate in Kant's sense ('real' is derived from 'reality,' 'whatness,' 'essence') tells one something about *what* a thing is (see 26.8.2). On the other hand, the word 'exists' in the proposition 'This book exists' does not tell anyone anything more about *what* (sort of thing) this book is than one already knows; it tells you *that* whatever you have in mind when you see or think about the book, or merely understand the words 'this book,' exists, not just in your mind, but outside your mind in the public world as well. 'Exists' is therefore a special kind of predicate, not an ordinary or 'real' predicate. However, only 'real' predicates can form part of the essence of something. Therefore to say that existence forms part of the essence of anything—even God—is to fall victim to a confusion.

Kant is almost certainly right that existence is not a predicate or property like the other accidents, modes, or properties of things. Aquinas was perfectly clear about this, too, though Anselm apparently was not. Thus, P2 is not so much false as profoundly muddled.

26.9.3 Hume's radical critique

St Thomas criticized P1 as unknowable, while Kant attacked P2 ('to exist in reality is greater, more perfect') as a muddle. However, both Thomas and Kant believed (as good Christians) that the conclusion of the argument was true; they just argued, each in his own way, that it was not *demonstrated or proved* true by this particular argument. Hume, by contrast, goes straight for the conclusion, C, urging that what it asserts is simply unintelligible nonsense. The conclusion again:

C Therefore when we understand the word 'God,' we understand that God necessarily exists in reality as well as in the understanding.

Hume's is the most radical criticism of all, since he does not attack the argument as either (a) formally invalid or (b) informally flawed (for example, circular); nor, however, does he attempt to show it to be either (c) unsound owing to the falsity of its premises or (d) useless to us owing to the unknowability of some premise. Nor, finally, does Hume simply contend that the conclusion is, as a matter of fact, (e) *false* (although he almost certainly thought so.) Instead he sets out to show that the conclusion as formulated is (f) *nonsensical or unintelligible*.

How does Hume show this? As we shall see later, Hume held that all our sources of knowledge number only four (see 29.6 below): (1) observation, (2) memory, (3) imagination, and (4) reasoning. The word 'reasoning' covers, on the one hand, (i) causal reasoning based on past experience, that is, a posteriori reasoning (inferences from the existence of a cause to that of its usual effect, for example, from fire to heat; from effect to cause, for example, from heat to fire; and from one effect to a collateral effect, for example, from the presence of firelight to the existence of heat). But 'reasoning' also covers (ii) logical or a priori reasoning, including simple conceptual analysis (for example, 'a triangle has three sides') and longer deductive chains of reasoning (for example, the proof of the theorem 'the internal angles of a triangle are equal to two right angles').

Now given that these are the *only* sources of knowledge, Hume argued that all knowledge must be of one of two kinds: either mathematical and derived from source

(4)(ii), or factual and derived from sources (1), (2), (3), and (4)(i). As for *mathematical knowledge* (arithmetic, geometry, algebra), it consists entirely of *necessary truths*, that is, propositions the denials of which involve contradiction. On the other hand, *factual knowledge* consists entirely of contingent truths. For all knowledge of the *existence of anything* in the real world, whether of things or properties of things, is acquired from either (1) actual or (2) remembered observation or from (4)(i) causal reasoning of various kinds. Items of such knowledge are, accordingly, never logically necessary but always contingent truths. So it may be false to deny the existence of something, but it will never be self-contradictory to do so. As Hume famously puts it: "Whatever *is* may *not be*. No negation of a fact can involve a contradiction. The non-existence of any being, without exception, is as clear and distinct an idea [as free of contradiction] as its existence."

If Hume is right about this, then it follows that the talk of 'logically necessary existence' in the conclusion of the ontological argument involves a *confusion* between two kinds of knowledge or truth. The same holds true for statements like the following: 'God's *existence* cannot be denied without contradiction' or 'God's essence or nature is: *to exist*, to be actual' or 'God is a necessary Being.' According to Hume, people who talk this way literally do not know what they are talking about; they are confusing two things. Far from stating a necessary truth, they are asserting what amounts to a contradiction in terms. 'Necessary existence' is just like 'round square' or 'married bachelor.' We can be sure a priori that nothing in the universe can correspond to the self-contradictory concept of a 'necessary Being'—which is not to say that there may not be a God, a *creator, an omnipotent, omniscient, benevolent being*, in some sense, but only that there cannot be *a necessary being* and that the ontological argument for the existence of the God of the Philosophers is nonsense (see 16.5.1).

26.10 The ontological argument in the Fifth Meditation

So much for Anselm's renowned argument and its critics. Descartes's version of the ontological argument is contained in a single short paragraph (the seventh) of the Fifth Meditation. It is worth quoting in full:

But if [P1] the mere fact that I can produce from my thought the idea of something entails that everything which I clearly and distinctly perceive to belong to that thing really belongs to it, is not this a possible basis for another argument to prove the existence of God? Certainly, [P2] the idea of God, or a supremely perfect being, is one which I find within me just as surely as the idea of any shape or number. And [P3] my understanding that it belongs to his nature that he always exists is no less clear and distinct than is the case when I prove of any shape or number that some property belongs to its nature. Hence, [C] even if it turned out that not everything on which I have meditated these past days is true, I ought still to regard the existence of God as having at least the same level of certainty as I have hitherto attributed to the proofs of mathematics. (65–6)

P1 is recognizable as a form of Descartes's truth rule: "everything which I perceive clearly and distinctly [to belong to the idea of an entity] is true," that is, really belongs to that entity, whether it is a merely possible entity, as in the case of mathematical truths, or an actually existent entity. P2, on the other hand, asserts that I have a clear and distinct idea or perception of God, or that the idea of God is an innate idea of a "true and immutable nature" rather than either an idea acquired through sensory experience or a merely fictitious (imagined) idea or a mental abstraction. We considered the grounds for this belief in our earlier discussion of innateness (26.7.1). P3 asserts that eternal (or necessary) rather than contingent or possible existence belongs to my clear and distinct idea or concept of God's true and immutable nature. C asserts that the proposition 'God exists' is at least as certain as 'a square has no more than four sides.'

In analyzing this argument, we must give due consideration to all those features which distinguish it from the classical form of the ontological argument. Then we can ask whether the argument in this form is still subject to the strictures of St Thomas, Hume, and Kant, or whether it is somewhat more, or even altogether, immune to such objections. Finally, we must consider how Descartes might have responded to the criticisms brought forward later by Kant and Hume. For there is good reason to think that he would not have been especially troubled by them.

26.10.1 Descartes's version of the argument

How does Descartes's ontological argument differ from the classical version? In fact, there is something interestingly new in each premise, though it is far from clear that this will save the argument.

Beginning with P1, we find that the distinctively Cartesian truth rule 'whatever I perceive clearly and distinctly is true' is built right into the argument. P1, in short, is that inference licence (see above 25.4) that permits us to conclude 'x is true' from 'x is clearly and distinctly perceived.' The first premise, then, lays down that fundamental *relationship between clear and distinct perception* and *truth or certainty*, according to which the former is necessary and sufficient for the latter (in some contexts, identical with it).

As for P2, this second premise subsumes the idea of God under the truth rule in P1, asserting that the *idea of God* is every bit as clear and distinct as *mathematical ideas of body* (geometrical shapes like triangle, circle, and so on). Note the comparison with mathematical concepts and the insistence on innateness ("I can produce from my thought ...," "bring forth the idea from the treasure house of my mind," and so on). Neither has a parallel in the classical argument of Anselm. So the idea of God, like mathematical ideas, is the idea of a "true and immutable nature"; that is, it is (a) not acquired through the senses, (b) not fictitious, (c) not an intellectual abstraction, but a complete idea that is (d) innate in the human mind. There is already plenty here that is distinctively Cartesian, in particular the truth rule and the new theory of innateness.

The only conclusion that could be drawn from P1 and P2 as just interpreted is: Everything that I clearly and distinctly perceive to belong to God's nature can be truly asserted of God. It remains to be shown that *necessary and eternal existence* is clearly and distinctly perceived to belong to God's nature. This is what P3 asserts. It is therefore the crux of the whole argument.

P3 differs from anything found in the classical ontological argument in that it further develops the comparison of the metaphysical or theological concept of God with mathematical concepts. But whereas P2 pointed out the similarities ("true and immutable nature"), P3 points out this difference: the idea of God *involves necessary or perfect existence*. This innate and complete idea of a "true and immutable nature" is *unique* in that it alone includes the idea of perfect or necessary existence; all others (particularly, mathematical ideas) include only the idea of *possible or contingent* existence. Obviously, this is what we earlier called 'the gist' of the ontological argument, though here it takes the form of a comparison and contrast with mathematical concepts in particular. Traditionally, the contrast was between the concept of God, in which existence and essence are identical, and ordinary sensible things, in which they are really distinct.

Finally, the conclusion of the argument is not a statement about God (an assertion about extra-linguistic reality) but only *about the truth or certainty* of the proposition 'God exists.' In short, it is exactly the type of conclusion that is warranted by the truth rule in P1: 'God exists' is true (certain) each time I attend to his essence. This, of course, entails that it is true always (even when I do not attend to God's essence), owing to the peculiarity of theological knowledge noted earlier (see 25.7.2). But Descartes does not say so here.

So much for the distinctive features of Descartes's version of the ontological argument. The next step is to see how the argument stands up to the criticisms brought against the classical ontological argument of Anselm.

26.10.2 The traditional criticisms of the argument

St Thomas had two criticisms of the ontological argument. As for the first, that the argument is valid but quite useless to us, Descartes concedes that we do not have an *adequate* idea of God, that is, one that encompasses *all* God's attributes; only God himself can have perfectly adequate ideas of anything. Thus far Descartes is in agreement with Aquinas. But he insists that we have nevertheless a clear and distinct idea of God's "true and immutable nature," that is, a *complete* idea, an idea that is in every respect like our ideas of mathematical natures ('three,' 'triangle,' and the like).

The idea of God, in other words, is not just made up at will, nor is it a mere abstraction or partial idea, but the complete idea of a "true and immutable nature." So whereas Thomas assumes that we need an adequate idea of God for purposes of the ontological argument, Descartes claims that a complete idea will suffice for an argument that is as certain as any mathematical demonstration. After all, complete ideas are all we have of mathematical objects, and they suffice for mathematical proofs. Noting, then, that our idea of God is just such a complete idea, he concludes that the ontological argument is as certain as any proof in mathematics. It follows that God's existence *is* self-evident, even for us, just as the truths of mathematics are; St Thomas unfortunately overlooked the key difference between complete and adequate ideas

So Descartes has a plausible reply to Thomas's first criticism. As for his other criticism, Descartes endorses St Thomas's charge that Anselm's version of the ontological or a priori proof of God's existence is circular. As Descartes puts it, the only valid conclusion from Anselm's premises is: "Therefore, once we have understood the meaning of the word 'God,' we *understand* that what is conveyed [by that word] is that God exists in reality as well as in the understanding." Assume that there exists *in reality* something corresponding to this *idea in the understanding*, and you assume the very thing to be proved.

Descartes's own conclusion, however, is: "Hence we can now truly assert of God that he does exist." This means: we can assert God's existence as certainly as we can assert anything in the science of mathematics. This is all the argument claims to prove: parity of reasoning between two types of demonstration, the one metaphysical, the other mathematical. The conclusion of the metaphysical demonstration of God's existence is indeed the very thing denied by the atheist, but the argument, as Descartes conducts it, is not from conceptual truths (as premises) to a conceptual truth (the conclusion), all the while taking for granted the existence of something corresponding to the subject concept of the conclusion. Since Descartes saw clearly the circularity of Anselm's argument, he would have had to be fairly deluded about his own version to have fallen into the same circle. So perhaps he can be acquitted of Aquinas's second charge as well. But there is still Hume as well as Kant to consider.

In the case of Anselm's argument, Thomas's criticisms were directed at P1, Kant's at P2, and Hume's at the conclusion of the argument. As for Descartes's version, Hume's and Kant's criticisms seem to hit home precisely at P3. For there Descartes quite deliberately crosses two 'divides' set up by their respective criticisms, namely (1) the divide between necessary truths about quantity and number and contingent truths about matter of fact and existence (Hume); and (2) the divide between essence (reality, real predicates) and existence (Kant). So even if Descartes successfully evades St Thomas's criticisms of Anselm, including that of circularity, it is just not clear that he can escape the charges of Hume and Kant. Or is it rather Hume and Kant who beg an important question in setting up these divides as exceptionless?

26.10.3 Descartes's best line of defence against these criticisms

Descartes's argument must seem suspect to anyone who posits a sharp divide between conceptual truths that do not entail existence and factual truths that do. Yet he does not just *assume* that the divide is crossable but tries to *prove* it so by arguing that the divide, as ordinarily drawn, is *too* sharp: it may be unbridgeable in mathematics, but not in metaphysics or theology. This suggests a defence having three components: (1) 'dig in' and insist that what is said about the concept 'God' in P3 is simply *self-evident* by the "natural light" of reason (that is, that there is *no* divide between the conceptual and the factual *in this one case*); (2) grant the strict separation posited by the divide in all *other* cases; and (3) offer a plausible explanation of why most philosophers fail to see the exception and the force of the argument, that is, a credible explanation of their error.

Now Descartes himself sketches a defence along these lines in the discussion of objections to his argument (stage 7 in the outline of 25.3). He argues there that *habit* misleads us since the vast majority of our concepts are either (a) acquired through sense perception or (b) made up (fictitious) or (c) inborn mathematical ideas. While the ideas under (a) and (c) do not include existence, those under (b) may include anything we wish, whence they are only figments of our imagination and tell us nothing more about the actual world than we already know from the ideas under (a). Although (d) the idea of God is an *innate* idea of a *true and immutable nature* that includes *necessary existence* (here Descartes 'digs in'), the prevalence of the other three types of ideas blinds us what is unique about (d). Hence, we overlook a key difference owing to habit.

A similar defence could be mounted against all those who insist on a hard-and-fast distinction between real and other predicates, in the manner of Kant: what holds in the vast majority of cases leads us to misjudge the one genuine exception to be met with in metaphysics or rational theology. Still, on the whole, this defence is rather weak. It sounds like special pleading for the concept 'God.' Whatever the fate of the classical version of the ontological argument, Descartes's version, for all its innovations, is likely to share it. And yet the defence is not as weak as all that. For the burden of proof is on Hume and Kant to show that their division of all propositions into two classes is exhaustive. To set up such divisions as exceptionless and then to deploy them against the ontological argument may be question-begging.

Even if, in the final analysis, Descartes can be acquitted of having committed the outright blunders with which Hume and Kant burden the ontological argument, the chief problem remains: the concept of an eternal or necessary Being (see 16.5.1). This idea of an eternal existent having the reason for its existence in itself, all the phases of its existence being coexistent or simultaneous rather than successive, is very hard to swallow. While this is very bad news for the God of the Philosophers (see 20.5.2), the implications for religious belief are negligible.

27

Man and World

27.1 Introductory

Recall the full baroque title of Descartes's chief philosophical work: *Meditations on First Philosophy, in which are demonstrated the existence of God and the distinction between the human soul and the body*. The last chapter was devoted to the existence of the creator God. We turn now to the division within created being between mind and matter. Here we shall examine (A) the existence and the nature of matter (see 27.3–7) and (B) the distinction, union, and interaction of the human mind and body (see 27.8–10).

Under the first heading we can treat excerpts from three different Meditations, starting with (1) the failed attempt to prove the existence of the external world in the Third Meditation. Next comes (2) the description of the essence of material things at the start of the Fifth Meditation (the analysis of matter), and, finally, (3) the successful proof of the existence of material things in the Sixth Meditation.

The second main topic, (B) the mind–body problem or the problem of the person, also comprises three sub-heads: (1) the real distinction between mind and body (Cartesian dualism), (2) mind–body union, and (3) mind–body interaction. These themes are discussed in the Sixth Meditation and belong to Descartes's philosophical anthropology, the Cartesian theory of man or human nature.

27.2 Outline of the Sixth Meditation and the present chapter

The present chapter, then, deals with portions of the Third, Fifth, and Sixth Meditations bearing on matter and its relation to mind. The overall structure of the Third Meditation was outlined in 25.3. It is the fifth stage in that outline ("First Attempt to Prove the Existence of Something Outside the Mind Using Adventitious

Ideas of Bodies") to which we return here, though we shall have to deal with the two preceding stages ("Classification of Thoughts or Mental Phenomena" and "Classification of Ideas into Innate, Adventitious, and Factitious") as well. The structure of the Fifth Meditation was set out in 26.8.1 above. Here it is the second stage ("Mathematical Knowledge of the Essence of Material Things") to which we return briefly. As for the structure of the Sixth Meditation, it looks like this:

1 Paragraph 1: Introduction
2 Paragraphs 2–3: Probable Argument for the Existence of Body Based on the Distinction between Imagination and Intellect
3 Paragraphs 4–10: Certain Proof of the Existence of the Corporeal World Based on the Ideas of the Senses
4 Paragraphs 11–22: The 'Teachings of Nature' Doctrine
5 Paragraph 23: Rehabilitation of the Senses

The title of this last Meditation is: "The existence of materials things, and the real distinction between mind and body." We shall give close attention to stage 3, the certain proof of the existence of body; as for the real distinction and the problems of psycho-physical union and interaction, the relevant material in the *Meditations* is found strewn throughout the Sixth Meditation, but mainly in Descartes's other writings and letters, on which we shall draw freely in setting out the problems in 27.8–10 below. The skeletal outline of the present chapter dealing with the material world and the nature of man is thus:

A The Existence and Nature of Body or Matter
1 Failed proof of the existence of material things
2 Essence of material things
3 Successful proof of the existence of material things

B The Mind–body Problem
1 Real distinction between mind and body
2 Mind–body union
3 Mind–body interaction

Once we have covered these topics, we shall be in a good position to attempt an overall appraisal of Descartes's philosophy by way of conclusion. Here we can be much briefer than in the two preceding parts.

27.3 Descartes's classification of mental phenomena

To begin, we revert briefly to that point in the Third Meditation where thoughts are divided into (a) ideas, (b) volitions, (c) emotions, and (d) judgments (see 24.7.4) and (a) sub-divided into (i) adventitious, (ii) factitious, or (iii) innate ideas (37–8). Ideas are just those thoughts or mental contents that are cognitive (as opposed to volitional or emotional) in nature. 'Adventitious' means 'coming to us' in sensory experience, while 'factitious' or 'fictitious' both mean 'made up by us' or 'invented' and 'innate' means 'inborn.'

This pair of classifications sets the stage for the failed attempt to overcome solipsism using (iii) adventitious ideas in the mind to infer the existence of bodies as their extra-mental causes. For ideas are classified according to their presumed cause. Sensation or sense perception is ostensibly caused by material things outside us. Our imaginings are produced by the activity of the mind itself. Finally, conception or (intellectual) understanding comes about through spontaneous reflection on that which is implicit in all thought and hence innate in the mind itself (see 26.2). Examples of (i) are the colour 'purple,' the sun, the sky, a mountain, a river, an animal, a man, and so forth. As for (ii), stock examples are the ideas of a golden mountain, a satyr, a mermaid, a unicorn, a chimera (part lion, part goat, part serpent). These are formed by putting together adventitious ideas in new ways. As examples of (iii) Descartes mentions (38) 'truth,' 'thought,' 'thing' (or 'substance'), though he might have included idea of God as well.

Summing up the foregoing in a simple diagram, we get the following overall classification of all mental phenomena (with judgment subsumed under volition, as is Descartes's usual practice). This classification has been powerfully influential throughout the history of modern philosophy. The conception of man as a knowing, willing, feeling psycho-physical being was to go largely unchallenged until Heidegger and Sartre.

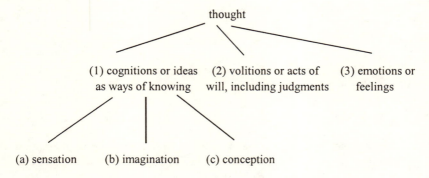

27.4 Causal and representative realism

One further preliminary is necessary before we examine the failed proof of the world's existence. In the Introduction, ontological realism and idealism were distinguished from their epistemological counterparts (chaps. 3 and 4). Now one type of epistemological realism is so-called causal realism. This is the view that *at least some* of the ideas in the mind are *caused* by bodies outside it acting upon the organs of sense. Another is representative realism. The representative realist holds that ideas in the mind *re-present* objects outside it; that things really present in the world are re-presented in the mind just as they are outside it. The relation between the ideas and the things that they represent is variously described as one of 'resemblance,' 'similarity,' or 'sameness' (see 25.10). These two types of realism provide a helpful framework within which to interpret Descartes's proofs of the existence of the external world (the successful no less than the failed attempt) as well as his analysis of the essence of matter.

With that end in view, we can distinguish two varieties of representative realism. 'Qualified representative realism' restricts the thesis that the relation between ideas and things can be one of 'resemblance' to *some* ideas, usually those representing quantitative features like size and shape. It thus excludes ideas of qualitative features like colours, odours, tastes, sounds, and tactile qualities altogether. '*Un*qualified representative realism,' on the other hand, regards the relation of similarity as applicable to *all* ideas: they are one and all capable of being resemblances, copies, or images of something existing outside the mind in the things perceived.

*Un*qualified representative realism, combined with causal realism, is often labelled '*naive* realism' by its philosophical and scientific detractors, who suggest that it could hardly be acceptable to anything but uncritical, pre-philosophical common sense. However, it has had, and still has, many able philosophical proponents, notably in Aristotle and his followers, who might well take exception to the word 'naive.' There is, after all, a good deal to be said for the commonsense view that the things around us really are coloured, odoriferous, hot, cold, and so on, as surely as they are extended in space, so and so large, so and so shaped, mobile, impenetrable, and so forth. A philosophy that aims to provide a clear conceptual framework for understanding ordinary experience need not be, on that account, naive. To dismiss it as such begs important questions about the real being of things and whether it is discovered in ordinary experience or in mathematical natural science.

As for *qualified* representative realism, this, combined with causal realism, may be designated '*scientific* realism.' For the scientific realist, only the quantitative features mathematically described in the exact natural sciences really exist in the things outside the mind. This is precisely the scientific outlook that Descartes pioneered by limiting representative realism to the *clearly and distinctly* perceived (or conceived) among our ideas. Thus, for Descartes, only the quantitative features of things are 'objective' in the modern sense (on this and Descartes's quite different sense of 'objective,' see 26.4.1). It is from this scientific point of view, which coincides with that of metaphysics, that unqualified representative realism is branded 'naive.' Descartes clearly regarded it as such, even if the epithet itself was coined later.

Both causal and representative realism presuppose ontological realism, a realm of mind-independent existing things. Accordingly, we can schematize the two forms of epistemological and ontological realism discussed above as follows:

Causal realism + Unqualified representative realism = Naive realism
Causal realism + Qualified representative realism = Scientific realism

Descartes's treatment of the view here designated 'naive realism' has been every bit as influential as his classification of mental phenomena. True, he was preceded in his scientific realism by Galileo and others, and Locke is responsible for introducing the talk of 'primary and secondary qualities' in terms of which *qualified* representative realism came to be formulated in the eighteenth century and thereafter. (Quantitative features are 'primary,' qualitative 'secondary.') Nevertheless, Descartes's influence cannot be overestimated.

So much for preliminaries. We turn now to the failed Third Meditation attempt to establish the existence of body and the external world.

27.5 Failed attempt to establish causal and representative realism

If causal realism holds true for adventitious ideas known with certainty to exist in the mind, then ontological realism is likewise true and there exist at least some bodies outside the mind. Accordingly, Descartes sets about listing and examining the grounds for his commonsense belief in both causal and representative realism (paragraph 8). He gives three reasons in support of it: (1) he has a *natural tendency* to believe that the adventitious ideas in his mind come from things existing outside it and resemble those things; (2) adventitious ideas *do not depend upon his own will* in the way that his imaginings do, since they come to him whether he likes it or not; and, finally, (3) it seems *self-evident* that what the things outside the mind transmit to it is their own likeness or image. In the next three paragraphs Descartes examines each of these considerations, showing that none is conclusive.

As regards (1), a key distinction is drawn between a spontaneous or *natural impulse* and the *natural light* of reason. As Descartes indicates by calling them 'natural,' both belong to human nature. Yet just as spontaneous (usually selfish) impulses are an unreliable guide to the good, while the natural light of reason is perfectly reliable, so natural inclination is an unreliable guide to truth, often leading us to assent to things that are confused and obscure and therefore possibly false, while the natural light of reason is completely trustworthy, impelling us to assent only to the clearly and distinctly perceived. Accordingly, the natural tendency or impulse to believe that the adventitious ideas in the mind stem from and resemble causes outside it is not to be trusted.

As for (2), Descartes urges that although his adventitious ideas do not depend on his will, they may nonetheless depend on his mind *if* there is, unbeknownst to him, some faculty in him that produces those ideas—just as his mind produces dream images without his wishing or deciding to do so. So one's not choosing to have these ideas does not prove they are not produced by the mind itself, that they come from something outside it.

Finally, with regard to (3), Descartes finds within him two ideas of the sun, one *adventitious*, the other "based on astronomical *reasoning*" (39). According to the one, the sun is a tiny disk, according to the other, it is many times the size of the earth. Now, logically, both cannot resemble the sun, since they do not resemble each other in the relevant respect (size). In point of fact, it is the adventitious idea of sense that does not represent the sun's actual size. So there is nothing self-evident about the conviction that a relationship of resemblance obtains between the contents of my adventitious ideas and extra-mental things.

The conclusion of this examination of the grounds for causal and representative realism is that both are based on "blind impulse" (or instinct), not on the natural light of reason or clear and distinct perception:

All these considerations are enough to establish that it is not reliable judgment but merely some blind impulse that has made me believe up till now that there exist things distinct from myself which transmit to me ideas and images of themselves through the sense organs or in some other way. (40)

27.6 The essence of body

We pass now from the first theme under (A), the failed attempt to establish the *existence* of body in the Third Meditation, to the second, a consideration of the *essence* of body as described at the outset of the Fifth Meditation.

The title of the Fifth Meditation is "The essence of material things, and the existence of God considered a second time"; but the essence of material things is in fact dealt with in two perfunctory paragraphs, the third and fourth. Part of the reason why the essence of body is given such short shrift is that the subject has been discussed already in three places in the Second and Third Meditations: in (1) answering the question 'Who am I?,' (2) in the context of the Mind-better-known-than-Body doctrine (Wax Example), and, finally, in (3) the causal proof of God's existence. It may be useful to recapitulate the earlier findings rapidly, before considering what, if anything, the (4) passage in the Fifth Meditation has to add. For these passages contain the essentials of Descartes's *analysis of matter* insofar as it is found in the *Meditations* at all. The qualifying clause is important. In the *Meditations* Descartes avoided technical philosophical vocabulary wherever possible. Elsewhere he employs a technical attribute–mode–accident schema that owes something to the traditional essence–*propria*–accident schema with which we are already familiar (see

7.14). It may be helpful, in recapitulating, to introduce it here.

In the Second Meditation context, we recall, Descartes is considering what he *formerly* believed himself to be: a mind united with a body. He describes the nature of his body (and body in general) in these terms (see 24.6.1):

> As to body, however, I had no doubts about it, but thought I knew its nature distinctly. If I had tried to describe the mental conception I had of it, I would have expressed it as follows: by a body I understand whatever has a determinable [1] shape and a definable [2] location and can [3] occupy a space in such a way as to exclude any other body; it [4] can be perceived by touch, sight, hearing, taste, or smell, and [5] can be moved in various ways, not by itself but by whatever else comes in contact with it. (26)

As noted earlier, the properties of body listed here are mainly quantitative: shape, place, impenetrability, and mobility. The qualitative aspects are not eliminated, however, since perceptibility by the five bodily senses is included. But the list reflects the scientific realism of Descartes and his contemporaries rather than the naive realism of pre-philosophical common sense. Still, there is no explicit attempt to mark off the essence from *propria* or mere accidents at this stage. Nor does Descartes here construe accidents as properties that bodies possess *only in relation to a mind* rather than *in themselves*. This sort of *reductive or eliminative philosophical analysis of matter*—after the fashion of the ancient atomists—is left for the Wax Example, and even there the technical terminology is omitted, the exception being the term 'essence.'

In the Wax Example the question of the essence or nature of body is answered (see 24.7.3-4) by way of an overtly reductive analysis that leaves only "something extended, flexible and changeable" as a remainder, that is, a set of *quantitative* features found to be constantly present, while the qualitative features of the wax change and even vanish. Flexibility consists in the relative ease or difficulty with which a body changes its shape. This, in turn, is a function of the way in which the parts of a body move or change place relative to one another. Shape, and motion, to which flexibility reduces, are thus the *basic* quantitative features of body. In the traditional terminology familiar to us, they are both *propria* of body, whose essence consists in extension in length, breadth, and depth. All and only those things that are extended in three spatial dimensions change position, that is, undergo changes in the position of one part relative to the others (change shape and size) or of all the parts relative to other bodies (change of place, that is, motion). But what *makes* them bodies is only the fact that they have *some* spatial extension—what, in the Fifth Meditation, Descartes calls "continuous quantity" (63), deigning to use a traditional philosophical term.

Elsewhere, Descartes speaks of extension as the "principal attribute" of body, and of figure and motion as its "modes." These technical terms are substituted for the more traditional 'essence' and *propria*, without, however, meaning anything different. Yet when it comes to the qualitative features of body, Descartes no longer treats these as accidents in the traditional sense, that is, as properties really existing in things and dependent for their existence on the things in which they exist. That, however, roughly, is what accidents were in the Aristotelian tradition. Rather, Descartes treats all such qualitative features of body simply as the effects on the mind of something completely unknown in bodies that somehow produces sensations of colour, odour, taste, and so on in us. Thus, anything that is really present in bodies themselves is describable in terms of extension in three dimensions, shape, and motion; anything not so describable is not really present in bodies at all but arises from the relation between what is thus present in bodies and the human mind. Once we introduce Descartes's technical vocabulary, it becomes clear that the reductive analysis latent in the earlier part of the Second Meditation is relentlessly carried out in the Wax Example. The naive realism of common sense is supplanted by Descartes's scientific realism.

Finally, in the proof of God's existence within the Third Meditation, Descartes classified his various ideas of corporeal things into two kinds: the *clear and distinct* and the *confused and obscure*.

[T]he things which I perceive clearly and distinctly in them [corporeal things] are very few in number. The list comprises size, or extension in length, breadth, and depth; shape, which is a function of the boundaries of this extension; position, which is a relation between various items possessing shape; and motion, or change in position; to these may be added substance, duration, and number. But as for the rest, including light and colours, sounds, smells, tastes, heat and cold and the other tactile qualities, I think of these only in a very confused and obscure way. (43)

Obviously, this classification is not the same as, although it corresponds to, the distinction between essence ("principal attribute") and *propria* ("modes") on the one hand, and mere accidents, on the other; the clearly and distinctly perceived characteristics of body are either essential attributes or *propria*, while all the others are accidental in Descartes's sense, that is, not really found in bodies themselves at all. 'Position' takes the place of 'figure,' but that is just one of the minor variations of the kind found in Descartes's writings. In other places, he will include 'divisibility' along with 'shape' and 'motion' as the modes or *propria* of body. The inclusion here of 'substance,' 'duration,' and 'number' is explained elsewhere in Descartes's writings. The point is that these are attributes of everything that is, whether mental or material, whereas extension is the *principal* attribute of body and thinking the *principal* attribute of mind (the modes of which, as we have seen, are cognition, volition, and emotion). So we can say that Descartes's 'substance–attribute–mode' schema includes a distinction between principal and other attributes.

The three passages considered so far leave very little for the Fifth Meditation to add concerning the essence of body. And, indeed, it is mostly repetition that we encounter here. First, the outcome of the earlier reductive analysis is summarized. Then, the classification into "clear and distinct" and "confused and obscure" ideas is reiterated. But there is something new as well. The *whole of mathematical knowledge is now included under knowledge of the essence of body*. For although the particular truths of arithmetic and geometry do not depend upon the existence of anything outside the mind, mathematical truths, for Descartes, represent knowledge of the "true and immutable" nature of the extended universe as *possibly* existing, whether or not it exists actually outside the mind. But, of course, the world does exist actually outside the mind, and that is to be proved in the Sixth Meditation. We turn now to this, the last of the three themes under heading (A) (see 27.1): the proof of the existence of body or matter.

27.7 The proof of the existence of the external world

Descartes in fact offers two proofs. The first, which we shall omit, is based on a *hypothesis* about the difference between imagination and understanding and is therefore *only probable*. It occupies paragraphs 2 and 3 of the Sixth Meditation. We touched on it earlier (see 25.4.1). Like the proof of God's existence in the Third Meditation, the second proof of the existence of body is a *causal argument* based on the existence of *adventitious* ideas of body in the mind. It is alleged to be not probable but absolutely certain. It is much longer than the merely probable proof, occupying paragraphs 4–11, inclusive. How does this certain argument run?

27.7.1 The probandum

The first thing we must be clear about is the *probandum*. The argument seeks to establish not just the existence of body but *the truth of causal and qualified representative realism*, that is, of scientific realism (see 27.4). Accordingly, the conclusion is formulated this way:

It follows that corporeal things exist [are the true causes of my sensory ideas of them]. They may not all exist in a way that exactly corresponds with my sensory grasp of them, for in many cases the grasp of the senses is very obscure and confused. But at least they possess all the properties which I clearly and distinctly understand, that is, those which, viewed in general terms, are comprised within the subject matter of pure mathematics. (80)

So only the *quantitative* or clear and distinct ideas of bodies, that is, the *non-sensory* ideas of the intellect, 'resemble' anything actually existing in the things themselves.

27.7.2 Outline of the argument

Descartes again proposes an operation of subtraction, not unlike that in the Second Meditation, where he asked, 'What am I?' There, it will be recalled, the operation looked like this: (1) What I formerly believed myself to be, take away (2) all those beliefs which cannot withstand the dreaming argument and Deceiving God hypothesis, leaves (3) What I now may believe myself to be with perfect certainty. The corresponding stages in the Sixth Meditation proof of the existence of body (see paragraph 5) are: (a) "all those things which I previously took to be perceived by the senses, and reckoned to be true" (74), together with "my reasons for thinking this"; (b) "my reasons for calling these things into doubt"; and (c) "What I should now believe about them" (ibid.). Again, (c) is the remainder once the subtraction of (b) from (a) is carried out.

Something in the remainder will then form the starting point of a causal or a posteriori argument proceeding from effect to cause. This is the nub of the argument for the existence of the external world. Let us now look at its stages individually.

27.7.3 First stage: review of former beliefs based on sensory experience

Descartes begins with an enumeration of those former beliefs held to be true on the basis of sense experience. He notes, first, the beliefs that (1) he has a *body of his own* (hands, head, feet, other limbs); that (2) this body is situated among *other bodies* that affect it in favourable and unfavourable ways, causing pleasure and pain; and that in addition to pleasure and pain, which are *internal sensations*, (3) he has other internal sensations (hunger, thirst, and other appetites, cheerfulness, sadness, anger, and similar emotions). Beyond this, he records the formerly held beliefs that (4) he has *external sensations* of extension, shape, movement, light, colours (visual), hardness, heat (tactile), smells (olfactory), tastes (gustatory), and sounds (auditory), and that (5) these external sensations are *caused by bodies outside him*, since they are independent of his will and "more lively and vivid" (75) than his memories and imaginings (causal realism). Furthermore, it was his firm belief that (6) his external sensations *resembled* those bodies outside him which caused them (representative realism), and that (7) *all* the ideas in the mind were acquired in this way through external sensation (empiricism). Finally, he believed himself to be (8) *more intimately joined to his own body* than any of these external bodies since (i) he can never be separated from it and (ii) he feels his internal sensations (pleasure, pain, hunger, thirst, and so on) in parts of it, not in external bodies.

This is a lengthy catalogue of beliefs, but it is not particularly difficult to follow. It is remarkable only in that it neatly sums up the entire belief-system of ordinary common sense under eight heads.

27.7.4 Second stage: grounds for doubt

From this total various items are subtracted on the following grounds. First, there is the fact of the occasional *deception of the external senses* (e.g., judgments about size and shape of bodies seen at a distance). This undermines (4). Then there is the fact of occasional *deceptiveness even of internal sensation* (e.g., the so-called phantom limb phenomenon experienced by amputees). This undermines (1), (3), and also (8). Next, there is the *dreaming argument*. This tells against (1), (2), (4), and (5). Finally, there is the *Deceiving God* hypothesis: as long as I do not know that the "author of my being" (77) is all-powerful and good, I can at least imagine that my faculty of clear and distinct perception (including even my ideas of extension and shape) is inherently deceptive. This undermines (1)–(8). Items (5) and (6) are weakened more particularly by the *distinction between natural light* and *natural impulse* (see above 27.5). Since impulse sometimes misleads me as to the good, perhaps it also does so as to the true. So the natural impulse to believe some form of representative realism is unreliable. This is especially damaging to (6). Finally, there is the *possibility of unknown faculties*: just because I am not conscious of willing certain ideas to occur does not mean that there cannot be some other faculty in me (apart from the will) that is producing them. This undermines the causal realism of (5).

27.7.5 Third stage: what I now believe

When Descartes asks what he *now* believes, he means *now that he knows that there is a God who cannot be a deceiver*. Thus, that particular ground of doubt drops out. What remains, then, of (1) through (8) once the Deceiving God hypothesis is eliminated? Two things. First, that I *probably* have a body, but that I am *certainly* separate and distinct from that body, that is, a thinking thing capable of existing without that body (at least by a miracle). And second, that this thinking thing has certain *faculties* like the *passive faculty* of sensation as contrasted with the *active faculty* of imagination which 'makes things up' out of the materials of sensation. This is certain rather than probable.

27.7.6 The causal argument for qualified causal and representative realism

Now the second of these points becomes the starting point and first premise of a certain argument that runs this way (unstated premises are in square brackets).

P1   Adventitious ideas originating in the *passive* faculty of external sensation exist in the mind as modes of thought.

The existence of these ideas and the passivity of the mind in receiving them are, to repeat, absolutely certain. Next, we supply two unstated a priori premises:

[P2 Every effect has some cause, some *active* power of producing that effect; and
P3 The cause must contain in itself either formally or eminently all the reality, formal and objective, that is contained in its effect.]

From these premises a first conclusion (C1) follows. Two further premises lead to the final conclusion (C2):

C1 There are four, and only four, possible causes of the existence of adventitious ideas of sensation in the mind: (i) myself (as a mind, a mental substance); (ii) bodies (substances) that contain formally (in their modes) as much and the same kind of reality which these ideas contain objectively; (iii) God himself (as an infinite mental or spiritual substance); (iv) something less perfect than God that still contains more reality in itself than the ideas of external bodies contain objectively, that is, contains their reality eminently.
P4 But *not* (i) since I am not conscious of any active faculty of producing these ideas;
P5 And *not* (iii) or (iv) since *in that case God would be a deceiver*, which he is not.
C2 Hence (by process of elimination) (ii): Bodies exist (and qualified representative and causal realism are true).

That is Descartes's argument for the existence of the external world. Note that it turns not just on (1) his causal adequacy principle, but on (2) the knowledge that God exists and is no deceiver as well. Thus, even the knowledge that there exists an external world *depends* on the knowledge of God in the new order of knowing established by Descartes. As noted already, this is a complete reversal of the order of knowing as understood in previous philosophy and by common sense.

We distinguished earlier the division *within* created being, between mind and matter, from the question of the union of mind and matter in the human being or man. We have now concluded our treatment of all three topics pertaining to (A), the existence and essence of matter (see 27.2). The second main head, (B) the mind–body relation, likewise comprises three separate topics: (1) the real distinction between mind and body (Cartesian dualism); (2) mind–body union; and (3) mind–body interaction.

27.8 The real distinction between mind and body: Cartesian dualism

The doctrine of the real distinction between mind and body is the *central doctrine of Descartes's metaphysics*. It is not going too far to say that the *Meditations* as a whole were written for the sake of this central tenet of Cartesian dualism. What exactly does it assert?

'Real' is a technical term. It is not opposed to 'unreal,' 'illusory,' 'imaginary,' or any of its usual antonyms in standard English. The word 'real' (to repeat) comes from the Latin *res*, meaning 'thing'; to say that there is a 'real distinction' between A and B is to say that A and B either are, or belong to, two *res*, two entities of the sort that can exist independently of one another, each in its own right. Or so at least in Descartes, for whom *res* or 'thing' and 'substance' are just interchangeable terms. This use of *res* and 'real distinction' differs from that of St Thomas (see 26.8.2). Still, both Descartes and Thomas oppose 'conceptual' to 'real' distinctions, the former being distinctness in *thought* rather than *fact*, so the correct antonym of 'real' in both philosophical uses is 'ideal' (from 'idea,' thought), 'dependent upon the mind.' The difference between Descartes and Thomas on this point is important enough to warrant a digression on different types of distinctness.

27.8.1 Real distinction in Descartes and St Thomas

For Aquinas, a real distinction is based on a difference in things themselves—for example, essence and existence in created things, or form and matter in sensible things, or substance and accident. These are no doubt distinctions that *we* draw, but they reflect real differences in the things thought about, differences that would continue to exist even were we to analyze things quite differently. We understand essence and existence, form and matter, substance and accident as different because they really *are* so and we have discovered the fact; these distinctions are accordingly real.

A merely conceptual distinction, on the other hand, is one to which no difference corresponds in the things themselves; it exists only in thought. For example, *we* might distinguish between God's existence and essence, although in God (and in God's own conception of himself) there is no difference at all. That is why Aquinas held that Anselm's famous argument was valid from God's perspective but utterly useless to us, since we are unable fully to comprehend the identity of God's nature and existence (see 26.9.1). Between these extremes it is possible to conceive various distinctions with *more or less* basis in fact, and the scholastics developed a rich vocabulary to mark these sometimes subtle differences, which we cannot pursue here.

For Thomas, then, those *res* that are really distinct need neither be nor belong to two substances, two entities capable of existing in their own right. Essence and existence, form and matter, though really distinct, are *res* but *not* substances, not beings having what we earlier designated 'degree two' of reality (see 26.4.3). Yet precisely this holds for Descartes's use of 'real distinction.' Entities that are really distinct need not be substances, but they must at least *belong* to different substances or *res*. Thus, two modes (having only what we have called 'degree one' of reality or perfection) may be really distinct if they belong to two different substances, say, a certain emotion and a certain shape, the former belonging to a mind, the latter to a material thing. Mind and body, on the other hand, are really distinct as two separately existing substances. As for conceptual distinctions, Descartes understands these much as does Thomas; they are distinctions imposed on things by our thought, though we cannot stop to elaborate further Descartes's interesting doctrine of distinctions, which is every bit as subtle as that of his scholastic predecessors.

27.8.2 Difference in number and difference in nature

Applying the foregoing now to the mind–body relation in particular, we find that there are two aspects to Descartes's doctrine of the real distinction between mind and body. First, as already mentioned, (1) mind and body are *two* substances (*numerically* distinct, distinct in number), two things, each capable of existing in its own right; and, furthermore, (2) mind and body are two heterogeneous *kinds* of substances (distinct *in nature*): an unextended thinking thing (mind or soul) and an unthinking extended thing (body or matter). Mind and body, then, are distinct (1) *in number* and (2) *in nature*.

Now Descartes was firmly convinced that (2) logically entailed (1). Any two entities, A and B, are distinct in nature, when their concepts are either (a) logically unrelated or (b) contradictorily opposed. That is, either the clear, distinct, and complete concept of the one contains nothing at all belonging to the clear, distinct, and complete conception of the other, in which case the two are distinct in nature as logically unrelated; or the clear, distinct, and complete concept of the one contains at least one thing that cannot (logically) belong to the other, and the two are distinct in nature as contradictorily opposed. Descartes, then, believed that whenever A and B are distinct in either of these ways, they are also distinct in number, really distinct, two substances rather than just two aspects of one and the same thing or two ways of talking about the same thing.

On the face of it, this inference would appear to be a fallacy, as can be seen from the following considerations. The psychological or mental may indeed be entirely different in nature from the physical or corporeal, talk about minds being logically unrelated, even contradictorily opposed to, talk about material bodies; yet both may just be 'aspects' of one and the same entity or substance talked about: a man, a person, or a human being. Yet Descartes's inference starts from the (2) separate conceivability of two things (mind and body), their distinctness *in thought*, since their clear, distinct, and complete concepts are logically unrelated and even opposed to one another; and from this he infers their (1) separability in fact, in reality, their being two things capable of existing separately, one without the other, in particular the mind's ability to exist separately from the body.

Now it seems clear from the foregoing that if Descartes simply inferred (1) from (2) in this way he would be committing a pretty gross fallacy. There is just no logically valid way of getting from separateness *in thought* (different in nature) to separateness *in reality* (different in number, two things, not one). Earlier we noted just this fallacy in the case of Plato's arguments for the separate existence of Forms (see 20.12.1–2 and 20.13.2). Just because I can have a full and complete conception of one thing as existing without another does not mean that it really can exist without that other thing *except on the assumption of an omnipotent God* who is capable of making actual anything that I can conceive of as possible. Descartes would have regarded the need for this further premise not as a weakness but as the peculiar strength of the proof; for it shows how *all* other knowledge, including the metaphysical knowledge of the real distinction between body and soul, depends upon the knowledge of God. In other words, the modification of the traditional order of being in Cartesian dualism reinforces the reversal of the traditional order of knowing (see 22.3.1–2).

27.8.3 Two senses of 'Cartesian dualism'

Note once again that Descartes does not reverse the traditional realist view that thought depends upon material things for its existence and most of its 'contents'; he does not claim, as would Bishop Berkeley, that, conversely, things depend upon thought (ideas) for their existence. Instead of idealism of this sort (dependence of things on ideas), his position is correctly described as dualism: two separate, independent realms (ideas and extra-mental things), neither of which has priority over the other in the order of being. This is a modification rather than a complete reversal of the traditional realist view. Descartes's position is itself a new form of realism, alongside reductive and non-reductive materialism (see chap. 4). It is not the beginning of idealism concerning the order of being as it is in regard to the order of knowing (see 25.10), where what we know first, best, and most reliably are, for Descartes, precisely thoughts or ideas in the mind.

This brings home an important point. 'Cartesian dualism' understood as a designation for (1) Descartes's philosophical anthropology or theory of man as a composite of two really distinct things or substances, mind and body, is just a *corollary* of Cartesian dualism as a name for (2) Descartes's fundamental metaphysical outlook, his understanding of the whole order of being and man's place within it. Too often the term is used only in sense (1), whereas (2) is the real heart of Descartes's metaphysics.

Renewed reflection on the *cogito*-principle should suffice to make clear the force of (2): the existence of (at least some) thinking does not depend upon the existence of any extra-mental reality—any more than the existence of an extra-mental reality depends upon its being thought of by some mind. Mind and matter, the mental and the physical, are two separate and independent realms, neither of which depends for its existence upon the other.

As the notion that mind and body are *distinct in number* surfaced already in the *cogito*-principle of the Second Meditation, so the doctrine that they are *distinct in nature* arose in the context of the Third: "I conceive myself as a thing that thinks and is not extended, whereas I conceive of the stone as a thing that is extended and does not think" (44). And the point is reiterated not once but twice in the Sixth Meditation:

[O]n the one hand I have a clear and distinct idea of myself, in so far as I am simply a thinking, non-extended thing; and on the other hand I have a distinct idea of body, in so far as this is simply an extended, non-thinking thing. (78)

[T]here is a great difference between the mind and the body, inasmuch as the body by its very nature is always divisible, while the mind is utterly indivisible. (85–6)

This perfect *heterogeneity* or difference in nature between the mind and the body, from which Descartes, using God's omnipotence, derived his dualism in sense (2), is the very source of the most serious problems besetting dualism in sense (1), the Cartesian theory of man or human nature. Those 'heterogeneity problems' (as we shall call them) will be considered under the heading of 'mind–body interaction' in 27.10. But the difference *in number* confronts philosophical anthropology with difficulties almost as insuperable as those arising from the difference *in nature* between mind and body. For having separated mind and body in so radical a fashion, it is unclear how Descartes can ever get them back together in a manner that does justice to our ordinary experience of ourselves as one being, one substance, not a composite of two. This we shall discuss now under the heading 'mind–body union.'

27.9 Mind–body union

27.9.1 Mind and brain

Both before Descartes and since, the most prevalent view of the mind–body relation has always been that thought processes depend upon the material or sensible in at least two ways. First, (1) most thinking is about material objects, whence most of the mind's stock of ideas depends causally upon bodies actually existing outside the mind and acting upon the senses. This is certainly true of those ideas that represent qualitative features, for example colour, odour, taste, and so on; and it is true as well for those quantitative features that are peculiar to this or that individual body, its particular size and shape, for example. Furthermore, (2) all thinking whatsoever depends upon certain physical (electrochemical) processes in the human body, specifically, in the brain.

On this view, every mental act is *irreducibly different from* physical processes in the brain, yet *all* mental processes without exception *depend on* such physical processes for their existence or occurrence, while *many* depend on the existence of physical objects apart from the body and brain as well. This is the position of the Aristotelian mainstream (it was termed 'non-reductive materialism' in chapter 4) and, in a different form, of the psycho-physical dualism of much modern psychology. It is also the opinion of plain common sense. It differs markedly from the so-called spiritualism common to Plato, Aquinas, and Descartes, according to which *some* thinking, namely purely intellectual thought, is utterly independent of matter and the brain. It differs also from the reductive materialism of Democritus, Epicurus, Hobbes, and Gassendi, as well as from that of some contemporary neuro-philosophy or cognitive science, including artificial intelligence, according to which there is just no difference at all between the mental and the physical, the former being reducible without remainder to the latter.

How would Descartes respond to the two theses of non-reductive materialism outlined in the last paragraph but one? His response to (1) can be summed up as follows. No doubt *some* ideas first enter the mind by the action of external bodies on the organs of sense and the central nervous system (sensation). Once stored there, they are capable of being refreshed later and even recombined in new ways (memory, reproductive imagination). However, the mind possesses certain other, purely intellectual ideas (or concepts) and principles (or truths) that are innate rather than derived from anything external. External sensation is only the *occasion* of our becoming explicitly aware of principles we already knew without knowing that we knew them. And so too with the concepts involved in those principles. This is the crux of the doctrine, sometimes called 'nativism' or 'innatism,' discussed earlier with reference to the idea of God (see 26.7.1–2). The thing to bear in mind is that innate ideas, for Descartes, are not actually present to consciousness prior to, and independently of, sensory stimulation; what is in the mind is a certain disposition to form such ideas given the appropriate sensory cues. And even then, reflection on the contents of our own thinking is necessary if we are to conceive these ideas and truths clearly and distinctly. Superficially, the doctrine resembles what Plato has to say about the Idea of Equality and the sense perception of equals, although, for Descartes, (a) the idea of equality (all lower case) exists only in the mind, not also in a transcendent realm of Forms, and (b) there is no fanciful doctrine of the soul's pre-existence. At bottom, therefore, the meaning of 'innate' is different (ibid).

As for (2), it is often thought that Descartes's response is at bottom that of most forms of psycho-physical dualism today, namely, that while thinking or mental activity is irreducibly different from the concomitant states of the human brain, there exist nevertheless brain states for *every* occurrence of mental activity. But that is not so. Pure thought or pure intellection (thinking the innate ideas and truths mentioned above) takes place without any concomitant occurrences in the human brain. Purely intellectual thinking *could* take place, Descartes holds, even if no body, no sense organs, no brain existed at all; but since such thinking would include neither sensation, nor imagination, nor memory, the mind which is thus independent of the body amounts to no more than the pure intellectual faculty of thinking the eternal truths and performing certain logical operations. So even if this *rational soul* survives death, this is still a very far cry from personal immortality as explained in chapter 16 above.

This doctrine of thinking without brain activity is surely as strange and incredible as anything to be found in Plato's teachings concerning the soul. Is it just Platonism revitalized? It is often thought that Cartesian dualism was anticipated in the essentials in the mind–body relation described in the *Phaedo*. As we shall see in the next subsection, this account of their relationship overlooks salient differences between Descartes and Plato.

27.9.2 Platonic, Aristotelian, and Cartesian man

If Descartes follows Plato rather than Aristotle in his conception of the human soul, his position on the nature of the union between mind and body is a curious amalgam of doctrines taken over from both Plato and the Aristotelian tradition. We can sum up the Platonic, Aristotelian, and Cartesian views of man by ascribing to each two theses on the nature of the union between mind and body.

Ignoring for the moment the whole question of the phases in the development of his thought, the Plato's view can be conveniently summed up as the doctrine of *accidental union*: man is an *ens per accidens* (an accidental being), the union with the body being accidental to the human soul. This is the doctrine Descartes alludes to when, in the Sixth Meditation, he writes: "I am not present in my body as a sailor is present in a ship" (81). He rejects the view outright in the *Discourse on Method*:

I showed that it is not sufficient for it [the rational soul] to be lodged in the human body like a helmsman in his ship, except perhaps to move its limbs, but that it must be more closely joined and united with the body in order to have, besides this power of movement, feelings and appetites like ours and so to constitute a real man.

The full Platonic doctrine in fact comprises two claims: (1) that the union with the body is accidental to the soul; and (2) that the soul is the person. As we shall see, Descartes rejects only the latter. This, however, is enough to make the Platonic pilot-and-ship model unacceptable to him.

Key to the Platonic doctrine is the idea that the soul is a substance capable of existing in its own right; the body is only the temporary housing or prison of the soul. The very different Aristotelian conception of man can be summed up as the doctrine that the union of mind and body is a *substantial or essential union*. Man accordingly is an *ens per se* (an essential being). This too can be formulated in a pair of theses: (1) the union with the body is essential to the human soul (this is what distinguishes the human soul from higher intelligences according to St Thomas); and (2) the union of soul and body is the (human) person. Evidently, theses (1) and (2) of Aristotelianism are just the flat denials of the corresponding theses of Platonism.

Behind them lies the Aristotelian conception of living plants, animals, and humans as composites, not of two entities or substances, but of two complementary principles, form and matter. To call them 'principles' is to say that they are not themselves entities or substances, not parts of a composite substance, but non-entitative causal constituents of a single substance, the living thing. In this sense the soul of a living being is its form, while the organic body is its matter. 'Mind is the form of body' (*mens forma corporis*) was the stock scholastic formula for the Christian view of man derived from Aristotle, just as 'mind using a body' (*mens utens corpora*) was a convenient mnemonic device for the Platonic view.

Coming now to the Cartesian conception of man, we encounter a strange *amalgam* of the two classical views. Descartes agrees with the Platonists concerning (1): the union with the body is merely accidental to the soul. Yet he sides with the Aristotelians regarding (2): the person is a union of soul and body, not just a soul. Unfortunately, Descartes calls the upshot a doctrine of 'substantial union,' claiming that man, for him, is an *unum* or *ens per se*, despite a key difference between this and the Aristotelian doctrines summed up in the formulae 'man is a substantial union of body and soul' and 'man is an *ens per se.*' The alleged agreement, in other words, is merely verbal. To call Descartes's a doctrine of substantial unity, as he himself does, is grossly misleading. But though, for Descartes, the union with the body is accidental to the soul, it is *not* accidental to the person, man, or human being. That is just the consequence of his having embraced thesis (2) of Aristotelianism: the union of the soul with the body is the (human) person. So while not a doctrine of substantial union in the Aristotelian sense, Descartes's doctrine is not pure Platonism either. Hence we speak of an 'amalgam' of the two classical views.

The fact is that Descartes developed an original conception of the person or human being, one opposed *both* to Platonism and to Aristotelianism. It is not so radically new as all that, of course, since it merely combines tenets of two older traditions to form a new synthesis. Whether the synthesis is coherent is a question that cannot be pursued here. It is certainly not consistent with either Platonic or Aristotelian principles. So it is clearly a mistake to consider Descartes's view as nothing more than a renewal of the Platonic doctrine in the *Phaedo*. That much is clear.

In conclusion, it may be useful to set out the contrasting positions once again in schematic overview:

The Platonic View of Man:
P1 The union with the body is accidental to the soul.
P2 The soul is the person.

The Aristotelian View of Man:
A1 The union with the body is essential to the human soul.
A2 The union of soul and body is the (human) person.

The Cartesian View of Man:
P1 The union with the body is accidental to the soul.
A2 The union of soul and body is the (human) person.

The question with which Descartes's solution to the problem of mind–body union inevitably leaves us is this: How is this account of man as a composite being consisting of two separate and independent substances to be reconciled with that immediate experience of the intimate union of body and mind which we, after all, have every waking moment of our lives? What Descartes thus put asunder, no one has yet been able to join together satisfactorily without abandoning the new metaphysical posture carved out by Descartes.

27.10 Mind–body interaction

The doctrine of mind–body interaction forms the second element in Descartes's philosophical anthropology. It is not always sharply separated from the problem of mind–body union, though the two, as we shall see, are quite distinct problems subsumable, along with the doctrine of real distinction, under our second topic, (B) the mind–body relation (see 27.1).

As Descartes understands it, mind–body interaction comprises both (a) the action of the soul upon the body in volition and imagination and (b) the action of the body on the soul in sensation and the passions or emotions. In perfect harmony with both science and common sense, Descartes holds that interaction of both kinds (two-way interaction) can and does take place in living human beings all the time. Leibniz, for one, denied this.

The two puzzles regarding mind–body interaction to be considered here arise from the complete heterogeneity of mind and body, their difference in nature. For it is Descartes's teaching that mind and body are not only two things (substances) capable of existing in their own right (although in fact conjoined in the case of every living human being); they are also *utterly disparate in nature*, completely *heterogeneous*. The mind is "a thing that thinks and is not extended," whereas any body is "a thing that is extended but does not think" (44). Mind and body have fundamental properties that are not only different but *contradictorily* opposed. We saw in the previous section that Descartes's theory of man runs into difficulty when it tries to make sense of the intimate union of mind and body, having dwelt so insistently on their substantial duality or real distinction. In a similar manner, Descartes is hard pressed to make sense of the *fact* of mind–body interaction, having maintained the complete heterogeneity of their natures. For convenience, the two puzzles to be set out now may be referred to as 'heterogeneity problems.' There are other mind–body problems in Descartes, particularly about the location of the mind within the body, but the heterogeneity problems are without doubt the principal ones.

Put in the simplest terms, the first problem is this. How can Descartes consistently maintain the following three propositions?

1 Mind and body causally interact in sensation and volition.
2 Mind and body are substances of totally disparate (heterogeneous) natures (the one extended, divisible, and unthinking, the other unextended, indivisible, and thinking).
3 All causal interaction takes place mechanically, by *contact* of the surface of a mover with that of a thing moved.

The inconsistency here may not leap to the eye. The fact is that *any two* of these propositions are perfectly consistent with each other. Yet a little reflection shows that any two together entail the denial of the third. So while 1 and 2, or 1 and 3, or 2 and 3 may be consistently maintained, it is impossible to assert all three propositions without contradiction.

The crux of the problem is obviously 3, that all causal interaction takes place by contact, since it makes absolutely no sense to speak of place, surface, motion, shape, and so on in the case of a thinking, unextended, indivisible entity like the mind. One possible way out of this difficulty is, therefore, to admit, in the unique case of mind–body interaction, the operation of a cause other than mechanical efficient causes. There is evidence in Descartes's writings that this is in fact the solution he opts for; for when pressed he is willing to say that, as the scholastics held, the mind is the substantial form of the body. This is just another way of saying that the human mind is the formal rather than efficient cause of man's being man (see 20.6.5 on Aristotle's four causes). Yet since, for the most part, Descartes is overtly hostile to any type of causality other than efficient, mechanical causality, it seems strange for him to revert to formal causality in dealing with the problems of *psycho-physics*, that is, mind–body interaction. Answering one of his objectors (who challenged him on another issue), he writes: "we have sensory awareness of something only by contact," or again, "sense perception occurs by means of contact." Of course, in the same place he also writes: "all action *between bodies* occurs through contact," thus restricting the principle to physics. Still, there is a difficulty for Descartes in admitting formal causality, even if only in the realm of psycho-physics. It is hard to see how this exception can be made consistent with the general tenor of the Cartesian system as a whole.

That is the first heterogeneity problem. Another, not dissimilar problem is this. It is hard to see how Descartes can consistently maintain 1 and 2 above along with

4 A cause must be *like* its effect in nature or kind.

Yet this seems to be implied in the Third Meditation principle: "there must exist in the efficient and total cause at least as much reality as in the effect of that cause"; that is, there cannot be anything in the effect that was not in the cause, otherwise something would have come from nothing. Again, the logical situation is exactly as before: any two of these propositions, though perfectly consistent with each other, jointly entail the denial of the third.

There is, of course, a possible way out, and that is to deny that Descartes held the view stated under 4. And indeed, there is plenty of scope for interpreting Descartes's causal adequacy principle as something other than a causal likeness principle. It may well mean no more than that the cause must possess, not the same degree and kind of reality as the effect, but *any* kind of reality *provided it is of at least the same degree or greater*. In that case, this particular problem disappears. Even at that, though, Descartes is still not entirely off the hook. For if the mind–body interaction is construed as an instance of efficient causality, a puzzling problem remains about how an immaterial entity like the mind can enter into causal transactions with a material body; whereas if it is a causal relation of a uniquely special kind, it is difficult to see how Descartes can give any positive account of it within the mechanistic parameters of his system of thought. Not just Descartes's critics, but even his disciples, were quick to pick up on this point. Nowhere does Descartes provide what has seemed to scholars to be an adequate reply. Yet he refused to recognize an unresolved problem here. And if he had, it is not even clear whether Descartes himself would have regarded it as a defect of his system. On the contrary, it seems to be precisely what he was aiming at, as the next section will make clearer.

27.11 The amphibious nature of Cartesian man

Consideration of these two heterogeneity problems tells us two apparently conflicting things about human nature as Descartes understands it: (1) man *is part of* nature, of the physical universe governed by exceptionless laws of efficient, mechanical causality; and (2) man *transcends* the natural realm, escaping the jurisdiction of those same scientific laws. There is in fact no contradiction here, any more than in the doctrine of the *Phaedo* that man both dies and survives death. For man is part of nature as a body yet transcends it as a mind or intellect; even as a mind inhabiting a body, man's nature still transcends material nature, since, as we have seen, the very causal transactions that take place between mind and body are not of the same type as those studied in the physical sciences but of an unexplained and, for Descartes, it appears, inexplicable sort.

Cartesian man, in short, is a curiously amphibious creature, undeniably a part of the natural world and yet not strictly subject to its laws. This has been thought to be the fundamental puzzle in which Cartesian philosophy issues. Yet it is not all that different from the doctrine of human life 'here below' as half-divine, half-bestial, already encountered in the *Phaedo*, or from the Christian conception of man's divided nature, destined for a life of blessedness in full communion with the All-highest, yet fallen into baseness and wretchedness through original sin. It would be very surprising if these parallels were simply a matter of chance. After all, the tension between what we are accustomed to call our 'lower' and 'higher' natures comes to light almost as soon as we begin to reflect upon our experience and condition; and it is just this conflict that the Platonic, the Christian, and the Cartesian conceptions of man all take into account, each in its own way.

Of course, to say that Cartesian man is no more puzzling than Platonic or Christian man is to acknowledge that he is no less so either. Although, at one level, we may understand ourselves as an amalgam of two antagonistic natures, at a more immediate level each of us undeniably experiences himself as a single human being, as one entity having one nature, not two, as a unity—in the happiest cases even a unison—of divergent impulses and tendencies. Plato seems to have recognized this after writing the *Phaedo*; for in the *Republic* the idea of harmony plays a great role in his revised account of the human soul. If this, or something like it, accurately reflects our most immediate experience of ourselves, then there is something seriously amiss in the Cartesian or any other picture of man that splits human nature in two. In lieu of the lengthy appraisals with which the two previous parts concluded, we shall end Part Three with a brief consideration of a few reasons for the apparent unsatisfactoriness of Descartes's conception not just of man, but of God, of the material universe, and of experience itself. We begin with a word on the point of view of the appraisal.

27.12 The point of view of the concluding appraisal

Any attempt to assess Descartes's philosophical achievement should start with the positive side of the balance sheet. Here the tally is impressive. A radically new conception of the self, mind, or soul and of the very structure of thought, the soul's principal attribute, provides a new starting point for philosophy, a new order of knowing based on a completely novel conception of truth as clear and distinct perception. In the order of being, moreover, Descartes pioneered a metaphysical dualism that was to supplant all earlier forms of reductive and non-reductive materialism and—partly owing to misunderstandings—usher in the era of modern idealism. His analysis of matter, in particular, provided a metaphysical justification for the methods and basic concepts of the fledgling mathematical physics of his day.

Despite all this, Descartes has been a favourite butt of twentieth-century philosophical critique. A starting point in thought rather than things has seemed to some to be the source of many of the ills to which modern philosophy is heir and of which both ancient and medieval philosophy were comparatively free. Radical doubt, innatism, intuitionism, mind–body dualism have all come under repeated attack from those whose philosophical outlook is essentially that of modern science. Much of this criticism is focused on Descartes's analysis of mind. For by sundering the private sphere of the individual's inner mental life from the public world of outer experience—the only experience whose authority is recognized by modern science—Descartes deliberately set a whole realm of being beyond the reach of the empirically proceeding natural and social sciences. This is the point of the famous gibe that Descartes turned man into "a ghost in a machine": a spirit that eludes, lodged in a body that obeys, empirically established scientific laws.

The British philosopher who coined this phrase, Gilbert Ryle, was concerned to defend the idea of a unified science having unrestricted universality of scope. 'Behaviourism' may be defined as the view that all talk of mental states, events, and processes must be explicable in terms of overt, observable linguistic and other behaviour, failing which it means nothing at all. Ryle's philosophical behaviourism, like the much-better-known psychological behaviourism of B.F. Skinner and his followers, sought to deliver the soul back into the clutches of modern empirical science, much as Descartes himself delivered up material bodies, while keeping both the soul and God as the exclusive preserve of metaphysics.

It is often said that the teachings of any philosophy that is to be acceptable today must at least square with the findings and outlook of modern science. While most contemporary philosophers tend to adopt the scientific outlook (sometimes quite uncritically), it seems clear from the practice of others working within the same western traditions that a fruitful pursuit of philosophy is likewise possible in a Christian faith perspective or, for that matter, in a pagan Greek perspective—even today. Each of these outlooks has produced its characteristic critique of Descartes's philosophy. At least as important as the behaviourist critique, though perhaps not as fashionable, are the many others that fault Descartes for turning his back on the reliable starting point of ancient Greek and medieval Christian philosophy, the things given in ordinary sense experience. This comes of introducing a new concept of experience, namely inner experience. Most telling of all is perhaps the demand, still heard from time to time, that any philosophy that is to be acceptable today must be brought into accord with what Hume called "common life," that is, with ordinary pre-scientific and pre-doctrinal experience—as distinct from those attitudes and beliefs acquired through one's early religious or later scientific training. Forms of this demand, with Descartes as the main target, are found in Heidegger and Sartre as well as Hume. It is when we consider Descartes's system of thought from this perspective, rather than that of scientific or religious orthodoxy, that we are best able to get the measure of the awkward philosophical position into which Cartesianism manoeuvred modern man.

27.13 Concluding appraisal

If we start our appraisal with the analysis of matter (see 27.6), it may seem that Descartes went altogether too far in meeting the demand that philosophy reflect the outlook of modern science. For that scientific image of the world (see 4.4) that

Cornford once epitomized so memorably as "the dance of material particles" is as remote as possible from the motley, noisy, redolent world of everyday sense experience that we inhabit day to day. Descartes deliberately reduced the external world to countless spatially discrete parts of extension in motion, acting upon one another by collision or contact. Accept this doctrine and one finds oneself inhabiting a featureless continuum of matter, a material plenum indefinitely extended in three dimensions in space and indefinitely divisible into more and more parts—a pure construct of mathematical reason, in short. All the rest, everything we believe to belong to this world we inhabit and to which we are so attached, exists only in the mind, not unimportant for practical purposes, but not part of the real being of our natural environment.

When it comes to the self or person, ordinary experience fares little better. Here the metaphysical thrust is *anti*-scientific for a change. In order to place the human soul beyond the reach of mechanistic, materialistic science, Descartes conceives man as a "thinking thing" closely conjoined to "an extended thing," the particular bit of matter that forms its bodily machine. Their union, however, leaves the conscious mind as untainted as possible by the bodily machinery it inhabits during its lifetime. Its *own* in the strict sense are only its thoughts—so much so that even if the whole world, including its body and all other minds, were to perish in the next instant, or to turn out to be an illusion, a strangely coherent dream, the mind would remain perfectly intact, a complete thing or substance existing in its own right, and no less a *human* mind for the loss of its body and its world. What this Cartesian "mind, or intelligence, or intellect, or reason" has to do with *me* as a human being is a good question.

A similar question can perhaps be asked about the God of the Philosophers and religious experience of the holy—if the talk of experience is warranted here. The point, however, is the same. Cartesian rationalism opens a gulf between ordinary human experience and the deliverances of reason that is at least as wide as any familiar to us from Plato. For Descartes, the use of reason opens a new window on ourselves and our world whose authority simply overthrows everything we have hitherto believed we knew. It is not as though Descartes were unaware of what he was doing, either. When some critics put it to him that his world was a mathematical abstraction, the imaginary or ideal product of reason and totally remote from the real physical world investigated in physics, he responded by saying that to accept such a criticism would be to admit

that nothing that we can in any way understand, conceive, or imagine should be accepted as true; in other words we must entirely close the door to reason and content ourselves with being monkeys or parrots rather than men ... For if the things we can conceive [clearly and distinctly] must be regarded as false merely because we can conceive them, all that is left is for us to be obliged to accept as true only things which we do not conceive [clearly and distinctly]. We shall have to construct our doctrines out of these things, imitating others [that is, following *their* authority] without knowing why, like monkeys, and uttering words whose sense we do not in any way [clearly and distinctly] understand, like parrots.

This is a hard saying. No one wants to be a monkey or a parrot. On the other hand, must opening the door to reason—to adapt Descartes's metaphor—entail abandonment of the self and world of everyday experience? Why, after all, should it not be possible, and even expected, that the fruits of rational reflection square with and illumine that ordinary experience that is the common estate of all mankind, not just the Christian or the Muslim, the scientist or the philosopher? As a philosopher, one may wish to deepen that pre-philosophical understanding that one already has of oneself, one's natural and social environment, perhaps even of the supernatural divine. The aim, on this conception of philosophical reason, is not to correct or overthrow that type of knowing and understanding in which we live out our daily lives, but to learn to articulate it in a conceptually more rigorous and transparent manner. This may mean working against the inherited interpretive schemes—prejudices, if you will, whether borrowed from religion or science or from some philosophical system—that tend to impose themselves on our thinking the moment we begin to reflect, distorting the experience that we only seek to understand better. However that may be, it seems clear that reason *need* not be construed as at odds with both experience and tradition in the manner in which the apodictic evidence of mathematical intuition is opposed to the obscure and confused deliverances of the senses and of hearsay. Yet that is unquestionably Descartes's picture.

If rejection of this picture means that we have to forgo a moral and intellectual basis for living that is absolutely certain, or as certain as mathematics, that may be all to the good. Perhaps all we can reasonably aspire to—not as monkeys or parrots, but as men—is to follow the best argument, as Socrates put it, carefully considering all pertinent facts, assumptions, and authorities, weighing in the balance all that we and our kind have learned from experience—along, of course, with anything that may tell against the apparent authority of experience as the great teacher of mankind. Although not by any means Descartes's royal road to certainty, this may be the best road open to the likes of us.

Recommended readings and references

Adam, C. and Tannery, P. 1897–1913. *Oeuvres de Descartes*, 11 vols. Nouvelle présentation par P. Costabel et B. Rochot, Paris, Vrin-CNRS, 1966 sq. Paris: Vrin. (The standard Franco-Latin edition of Descartes's works.)

Ariew, R. and Grene, M. 1995. *Descartes and His Contemporaries*. Edited by Roger Ariew and Marjorie Grene. Chicago: University of Chicago Press. (A recent collection of essays on the Objections and Replies.)

Butler, R.J., ed. 1972. *Cartesian Studies*. Oxford: Basil Blackwell. (Older, but still a very useful anthology of essays.)

Cottingham, John. 1984. *Descartes*. Oxford: Basil Blackwell. (Probably the best short monograph treatment of the subject.)

Cottingham, John. 1992. *The Cambridge Companion to Descartes*. Cambridge: Cambridge University Press. (Recent, highly recommended.)

Cottingham, John. 1993. *A Descartes Dictionary*. Oxford: Blackwell. (A useful glossary of technical terms, ordered alphabetically by concepts.)

Doney, W., ed. 1968: *Descartes. A Collection of Critical Essays*. Notre Dame and London: University of Notre Dame Press. (Still one of the best collections of its kind.)

Garber, D. 1992. *Descartes' Metaphysical Physics*. Chicago and London: University of Chicago Press. (Advanced and focused on the scientific work. Garber is mentioned in chapter 22 as a proponent of the view that Descartes inaugurated a new type of metaphysics.)

Hooker, M., ed. 1978. *Descartes. Critical and Interpretive Essays*. Baltimore and London: The Johns Hopkins University Press. (Contains many useful essays.)

Kenny, Anthony. 1968. *Descartes. A Study of His Philosophy*. New York: Random House. (A very reliable guide to the issues. Proceeds meditation by meditation. Kenny is mentioned in chapter 22 as a proponent of the epistemological interpretation of Descartes.)

Miles, Murray. 1999. *Insight and Inference. Descartes's Founding Principle and Modern Philosophy*. Toronto: University of Toronto Press. (A full-scale scholarly version of the interpretation of Descartes sketched here. Probably too advanced for undergraduates.)

Wilson, Margaret. 1978. *Descartes*. Routledge: London. (A somewhat more advanced monograph than Cottingham's, but still quite readable for undergraduates.)

Questions for reflection, discussion, and review

1. What aspects of metaphysics are captured by each of the following designations: 'theology,' 'ontology,' 'first philosophy'? Can you fit them together into a coherent whole?
2. 'Relativism' is sometimes called 'subjectivism.' How does *Cartesian* subjectivism differ from relativism?
3. Descartes's regimen of doubt is designed to instil in the reader a more critical cast of mind. In your view, are people today generally too critical or too uncritical in the beliefs and attitudes they adopt? What do you see as the benefits and dangers of the critical attitude? Can one ever be *too* critical?
4. Recall the distinction between (1) relativism, (2) scepticism, and (3) critical rationalism described in 3.3.1 above. If we proceed further in the same direction (from diffidence to ever greater confidence in our knowledge claims), we end up (perhaps after a couple of intermediate positions) at the extreme of (4) dogmatism or dogmatic certainty. Where would you situate Socrates, Plato, and Descartes on this continuum?
5. Does human knowledge really need a foundation of absolute certainty? Or is human science, as fallibilists maintain, an inherently shaky structure, and is Descartes searching for something that cannot be found?
6. Descartes proposes to reject as false anything that could *conceivably* turn out to be untrue. Is it indeed conceivable, as he suggests, that the whole of one's life might just be a well-ordered, lucid dream (from which one may still wake up)?
7. Consider: You cannot advance reasons for mistrusting your reason without contradicting yourself; and you cannot give reasons for trusting reason without begging the question. What is the significance of this (if any)?
8. Discuss the meanings of 'thought' and 'consciousness' in standard English. Are they synonyms? How do they differ? Are they synonyms for Descartes? How do they differ for Descartes?
9. It has been suggested that Descartes went too far when he said '*I* think'; that he ought to have been content to assert that 'there is thinking going on' as his first truth; that he asserted something uncertain when he maintained '*I* think.' What is the point of this criticism? Would you agree?
10. Would 'I walk, therefore I am' do as well as 'I think, therefore I am'? Why or why not?
11. Give some examples of truths that you consider to be immediate insights, not involving any inference at all. Now give examples of truths that are not immediate insights or intuitions, but inferences or deductions. Which category does 'I think, therefore I am' fall into? Why?
12. Has Descartes convinced you that your existence is more certain than that of

the table right in front of you that you see and touch? Can anything be more certain than the existence of that table is right now? Does anything *need* to be more certain than this?

13 Repeat Descartes's analysis of the ball of wax, substituting another object (say an eraser) for the wax. What do you arrive at as the essence of body?
14 What is solipsism? Distinguish different varieties of solipsism. Can more than one of these be ascribed to Descartes? Why or why not?
15 What is the correct order of knowing according to instinct and common sense? Has Descartes shaken your confidence in this order?
16 Explain Descartes's 'truth rule.' Is it a reliable criterion of truth?
17 What is meant by 'the Cartesian circle'? Distinguish some different charges of circularity that can be brought against Descartes. How can he respond to them?
18 What are empiricism and rationalism? On the face of it, which of the two seems a more reasonable account of the origins of human knowledge?
19 What do 'a priori' and 'a posteriori' mean when applied to arguments? When applied to propositions?
20 What does 'objectively real' mean in ordinary speech? And in Descartes?
21 Descartes was proud of the proof of God's existence presented in the Third Meditation. And he had reason to be, quite apart from whether the proof establishes what it sets out to demonstrate. Do you agree, or do you find the proof trivial?
22 In your opinion, is the existence of God something that can be proved by unassisted human reason? Does it need to be proved?
23 Is the idea of God innate or do we acquire it in childhood from our parents and teachers? Is it plausible of Descartes to suggest that this idea is innate in all human minds?
24 Explain the difference between causal, representational, and ontological realism. What is meant by 'scientific' and 'naive realism'?
25 Does it make sense to doubt the existence of the external world? Why, in your opinion, does Descartes think he must do so?
26 Does Descartes's proof of the existence of the external world depend on the proof of God's existence and veracity? How?
27 What lies behind the pilot-and-ship model of mind–body union evoked in the Sixth Meditation? Who held such a view? Why did Descartes reject it?
28 Identify the sources of the mind–body problem in Descartes.
29 What affinities do you observe between Descartes and Plato on the subject of the human soul?

PART FOUR

HUME AND THE ROAD BACK TO COMMON LIFE

Philosophy, ... if just, can present us only with mild and moderate sentiments; and if false and extravagant, its opinions are merely the objects of a cold and general speculation, and seldom go so far as to interrupt the course of natural propensities ... Generally speaking, the errors in religion are dangerous, those in philosophy only ridiculous.

Hume, *A Treatise of Human Nature*

28

Philosophical Works and Outlook

28.1 Philosophical works

Hume was a Scotsman and thus the first author to be studied who actually wrote in English. Born in 1711, he was a precocious genius, producing his philosophical masterpiece *A Treatise of Human Nature* (published anonymously in 1739) by the time he was twenty-five. This very long and complex work was a literary flop of grand proportions; in Hume's memorable phrase, it "fell dead-born from the press." In a desperate attempt to resuscitate his brainchild, Hume took the highly unorthodox step of publishing an anonymous, laudatory review of his own work under the title *An Abstract of A Treatise of Human Nature* (1740). This did little to generate the interest he had hoped for. Putting the failure of his book down to its great length, complexity, and style, Hume undertook to present his ideas afresh in a more accessible form.

Accordingly, some of the material of Book I of the *Treatise* was recast as a work entitled *Philosophical Essays concerning Human Understanding* (1748), retitled *An Enquiry concerning Human Understanding* for the 1758 edition, and generally known as 'the First *Enquiry*.' In it Hume omitted certain especially difficult portions of the *Treatise*, but added some new material as well, including a treatment of the classic problem of the freedom of the will and the essays "Of Miracles" and "Of a Particular Providence and a Future State." These sections of the work were probably based on materials Hume had suppressed in the *Treatise* for fear they would be branded irreverent or impious—the age-old charge first brought against philosophy in the person of Socrates. Some of the materials from Books II and III of the *Treatise* were recast as the so-called Second *Enquiry*, whose full title is *An Enquiry concerning the Principles of Morals* (1751). Hume's efforts were rewarded, and the *Philosophical Essays* in particular made his philosophical and literary reputation as well as his personal fortune. He died a wealthy not-so-old man in 1777.

In the principal sections of the First *Enquiry*, Hume defines his philosophical tasks as those of (1) a mental geographer (section I), (2) an empiricist epistemologist (section II), (3) an associationist psychologist (sections III, V, VI, and IX), and (4) a sceptical critic of causal reasonings about matter of fact and existence in the empirical or experimental sciences (section IV and VII). This critique of the conception of causality and law prevalent in the modern natural sciences is generally regarded as the heart of the work, for which the preceding sections are merely preparatory. On it follow three sections in which Hume dons the dangerous mantle of (5) secular critic of religious philosophy. These sections deal with the problem of freedom and necessity and its implications for religion and morality (section VIII), as well as with miracles (section X), and with divine justice and the afterlife (section XI). The whole *Enquiry* culminates in (6) a blistering critique of metaphysics, that is, an assault on the alleged intuitive insights (in Descartes's terms, "common notions" or "axioms") and deductive inferences or proofs regarding matter of fact and existence (especially the existence of God) to be found in virtually all traditional systems of metaphysics (section XII).

In chapters 30 and 31, we shall focus our attention on (5), Hume's critique of religious philosophy in sections X and XI of the First *Enquiry*. This is the main business of the present part. However, to follow Hume's argument in these two essays, some familiarity with his general philosophical outlook and ideas is necessary. This can be garnered from a consideration of some of the other items in the above list, starting with a brief examination of (4) and (6) in the present chapter. Hume's (1) mental geography—the term will be explained in 28.6 below—and (2) empiricist epistemology will be discussed along with his (3) associationist psychology in the next chapter.

28.2 General philosophical outlook

In order to prepare ourselves for the radically different type of philosophizing found in Hume's works, we cast a swift backward glance at the philosophies of Socrates, Plato, and Descartes, noting a few significant parallels and contrasts.

In the philosophy of Socrates, we encountered a wholesale and quite deliberate rejection of speculative philosophical thinking about nature. Abandoned, too, was all religious debate about theoretical rather than practical and specifically moral questions. Socrates, we said, was interested exclusively in moral philosophy or ethics (including moral theology). For him, philosophy was *man-centred* and strictly *practical* or *this-worldly*, concerned with the morally good life and the happy life for man *here and now*.

With Plato the scene changed drastically. Here we found the still-powerful Socratic legacy completely overwhelmed by the combined influence of (a) Pythagorean and Orphic religious mysticism (including mathematical theorizing) and (b) the speculative ideas of two prominent Presocratics, Heraclitus and Parmenides. The 'twin pillars' of Platonism are (1) the theory of Forms, that is, a two-world metaphysics, and (2) the doctrine of the immortality of the human soul. According to the first, this world is less real than the world of transcendent universals or Forms; while not completely unreal, as Parmenides maintained, it is nevertheless entirely unknowable, as Heracleitus or his follower Cratylus held. According to the second, the human person is a soul temporarily confined within the prison of the body; the soul or person is not really 'of' this world at all, belonging rather to the world of Forms, from which it came. If we were to sum up Plato's philosophical outlook in the *Phaedo*, we should have to describe it as *other-worldly* or speculative in the extreme, and as soul-centred or *spiritualistic*.

In our study of Descartes, finally, we encountered a philosophy whose focus is twofold: (a) God, the creator of all things, even of their natures or essences (the eternal truths), and (b) the human mind or soul. Or, to put Descartes's dual focus in a single word: *the supersensible*, divine and human, as opposed to the sensible, material world. The chief aims of the *Meditations* are to show (1) that the soul is a finite immaterial substance capable of existing in its own right, that is, "really distinct" from the body; (2) that God, the infinite immaterial substance, actually exists; (3) that we can know the soul and God more reliably than sensible material things; and (4) that we can know *nothing else* with perfect certainty unless and until we know them.

Summing up Descartes's philosophical outlook, we can say that it is *more* this-worldly or *less* other-wordly than Plato's, since there is at least *some* "true and certain knowledge" of this world, of material or sensible things, as there is not for Plato (see 20.2). Moreover, man is *more* than just a spirit or a soul for Descartes; he is a material body, too, and since his body is entirely *of this world*, man himself is at least partly so (see 27.11). At bottom, though, Descartes's philosophical outlook is still other-worldly, *spiritualistic* and *God*-centred.

Contrasting now Hume's philosophical outlook with those just described, we can say that Hume is (1) *sceptical* about our knowledge of this world, (2) *agnostic* about knowledge of God and the next world, and, therefore, (3) totally *man-centred and this-worldly*. We shall consider these points in turn in the next three sections

28.3 Scepticism

The study of man or human nature convinced Hume that our capacity to achieve rational certainty either through experience (the senses) or by the intellect (reasoning) is in fact much more narrowly circumscribed than had been suspected by anyone since the ancient sceptics (see 9.1.4). Hume actually went beyond Descartes in *scepticism with regard to the senses*. For Descartes reinstated the senses as trustworthy at the end of the *Meditations*, contenting himself with reasonable in lieu of strict rational certainty. Hume, for his part, insisted to the end that the various doubts about ordinary sense experience raised by Descartes and the sceptics were simply unanswerable by philosophical means (see section XII, part I of the First *Enquiry*).

As for Hume's *scepticism with regard to the intellect or reason*, it rests primarily on the demonstration that although certain widely shared and strongly held beliefs about this world, namely the cause-and-effect relations embodied in natural scientific laws, may in fact be true, they cannot be *shown* to be so with strict rational certainty. For neither the senses nor the intellect can furnish the materials for demonstration of the metaphysical principles underlying all causal laws, namely (a) everything that begins to exist has some cause, and (b) the same cause always produces the same effect. Along with (i) scientific and (ii) metaphysical, (iii) mathematical reasoning, too, is subjected to doubt by Hume, chiefly owing to the insoluble paradoxes of space, time, and the infinite in which mathematical reasoning inevitably bogs down (see section XII, part II).

Of course, Descartes too questioned the reliability of mathematical reasoning *remembered*, devising the infamous Deceiving God argument just for this purpose. Yet he regarded *actual* clear and distinct perception of mathematical truths and the causal axioms of metaphysics as absolutely certain. As for the truth of the causal laws of the physical sciences, these he doubted only by questioning the actual existence of their objects. That was the purpose of the dreaming argument, which was ultimately overcome. The chief difference between Descartes and Hume is that the latter mounted his sceptical attack on reason from a completely secular viewpoint, without resorting to anything so extravagant as the suppositions that life is a long, coherent dream or that a deceiving God exists. Hume's typical procedure is to point out either (1) that certain beliefs or conclusions do not follow in logic from the evidence or premises available for them; or (2) that the premises from which they would follow are themselves incapable of being rendered certain. Moreover, where Descartes dispelled his doubts about reason in the end, Hume stood by his right to the finish, just as with his doubts about the senses. Scepticism, in short, is the outcome for Hume; for Descartes, it is only a methodological device and starting point (25.2).

28.3.1 Sceptical critic of metaphysics

As a sceptical critic of *science*, Hume cast doubt on two causal principles of *metaphysics* that are implicitly taken for granted in all scientific investigations. But the critique of metaphysics is also undertaken for its own sake. Apart from the two principles just mentioned, it extends to all the alleged intuitive insights and deductive inferences or proofs regarding matter of fact and existence found in the traditional systems of metaphysics. Such purported insights and inferences include: (1) the existence of an immaterial soul-substance (alleged to be intuitively evident by Descartes, Leibniz, and others); (2) the a priori and a posteriori proofs of the existence of God found in Anselm, Aquinas, Descartes, Spinoza, Leibniz, and others; and (3) the self-evident axioms or common notions employed in such demonstrations, including, but not restricted to, the two causal maxims.

In the First *Enquiry* Hume does not mention (1) or (2) explicitly. Both receive close attention in the *Treatise*, however. As for (3), the *Enquiry* pays particular attention to the two causal maxims, even though traditional metaphysics, both before and after Descartes, abounds in axioms or principles concerning existence, and in demonstrations based on such allegedly self-evident axioms and principles. We distinguished earlier (see 25.5) between three types of principles. First, there are (1) mathematical axioms like 'if equals are added to (or subtracted from) equals the sums (remainders) are equal' and 'the whole is greater than its part $(a + b > a)$,' which do not assert the existence of anything. Neither do (2) metaphysical axioms or principles like (a) 'if anything thinks, then it exists,' (b) 'nothing comes from nothing,' (c) 'nothing has no properties,' or (d) 'an infinite causal series is impossible.' Only (3) the *cogito*-principle asserts existence: 'I am.' Still, all the principles under (2) *have to do with existence*, and that is why they too must be regarded as metaphysical principles, principles of being. After all, (a) is just a consequence of (c), which asserts that properties or states *cannot exist* without substances for them to belong to; if (c) is true, that is, if some property or state of thinking exists, then something that does the thinking *must exist* as well. As for (b), this principle, fully spelled out, asserts that for anything that begins to exist there *must exist* also a cause of its beginning to be. And (d) was frequently understood as stating that an infinite causal series *cannot exist*, that the series of states in which the world has existed must be finite. All such metaphysical principles, then, assert a priori that something must or cannot happen or exist. That is what they have in common with the two causal principles on which Hume focuses attention in the *Enquiry*.

Regarding the most basic causal principle, the "impious [causal] maxim *ex nihilo nihil fit* ['nothing comes from nothing,' or 'something cannot arise from nothing']" (194), this, as we have seen, plays a key role in Descartes's proof of God's existence in the Third Meditation. Kant called it the *crux metaphysicorum*, the crux or cross of the metaphysicians. For if this principle regarding the *necessary existence* of a cause is groundless, there is at least a strong presumption that *all* metaphysical principles, that metaphysics as a whole, may be similarly groundless. After all, the metaphysical principles in (a)–(d) serve as key premises in metaphysical demonstrations. For example, (b) serves as a premise in Descartes's, while (d) is the key premise in Aquinas's, proof for the existence of God. And they are allegedly based on reason or rational intuition *alone*, that is, known to be true independently of all experience. Moreover, in some cases, they, or the demonstrations in which they figure, run counter to sensory evidence and plain common sense. So if Hume's critique of these alleged principles or insights, and of all demonstrations in which they are employed, is justified, it strikes at the very heart of metaphysics. Or so Kant believed.

28.3.2 Sceptical critic of natural science

So much for the thrust of Hume's general assault on metaphysics, item (6) in the enumeration above (see 28.1). It may be worth considering item (4) in that list as well, the sceptical critique of natural science.

According to Hume, all empirical or experimental science presupposes in its explanations certain causal principles that are neither (a) intuitively self-evident nor (b) demonstrable by any a priori reasoning nor (c) justifiable by inner and outer experience together with a posteriori or inductive reasoning. One such principle is that (as Hume puts it in the *Abstract of A Treatise of Human Nature*) "like causes, in like circumstances, will always produce like effects" or that "the course of nature must continue uniformly the same, and ... the future must be conformable to the past" (34). This has been dubbed the 'Principle of the Uniformity of Nature' or the 'Same-Cause-Same-Effect Principle' in order to distinguish it from the 'Every-Event-Some-Cause Principle,' that is, the "impious maxim" of metaphysics cited earlier as *ex nihilo nihil fit*. ("Whatever has a beginning" or "whatever begins to exist, must have a cause of existence," are the ways Hume puts it in the *Treatise*.) On the Same-Cause-Same-Effect Principle rest all those strictly universal statements of law-like regularity employed in the natural sciences both to explain particular observed events and to predict or retrodict such events. Unless this metaphysical principle is perfectly certain, therefore, all the less general (but still exceptionless) laws of nature, and hence all explanations, predictions, and retrodictions, are merely probable, not certain, that is, possibly false. Yet the causal principle itself, Hume argues, is without any justification that could render it more than very highly probable. Accordingly everything that depends upon it is no more than probable, not rationally certain.

28.4 Agnosticism

If there is good reason to be sceptical even about our beliefs concerning *this* world, concerning the "experimental reasonings" of empirical science, how much more reason might there be, then, for scepticism regarding our beliefs concerning God and the afterlife? Here Hume's procedure is the same: examine the arguments used by others and show them to be *unsound*.

It is important to note the differences among the following: (a) showing an argument to be *unsound* owing either to false or doubtful premises, or to logical invalidity, or both; (b) showing its conclusion to be *false*; and (c) showing the denial of its conclusion to be *more reasonable* (given the evidence) than the conclusion itself. Now since Hume carefully confined himself to (a), he should perhaps be called an 'agnostic' rather than an 'atheist' or even a 'crypto-atheist.' (On the term 'agnostic,' see above 11.12.1.) However, if, in the spirit of (c), we ask ourselves what Hume's privately held convictions were, it seems likely that he considered a belief in the bare existence of some intelligent deity, about whom nothing else is known ('deism'), to be at least as reasonable as complete atheism. So with regard to anything that goes beyond simple deism, as traditional religions, including Christianity, invariably do, Hume would have considered it more reasonable to reject such teachings outright (for example, transubstantiation, resurrection or immortality, the Holy Trinity, immaculate conception, the divinity of Christ, etc.) than to accept them, even with reservations. While not an out-and-out philosophical atheist, therefore, Hume would, as far as the teachings of Christianity were concerned, probably not have been content merely to suspend belief either; he clearly *dis*believed all such dogmas. Probably, he rejected even the deists' conclusions about God's existence too—that is more controversial—but if he did so, he did so as a matter of private conviction rather than public philosophical doctrine. For that reason we shall do well to speak of 'agnosticism' rather than 'atheism' or 'crypto-atheism' in Hume's case.

28.5 Man-centred view of philosophy

The upshot of this sketch of Hume's philosophical outlook can be put in some such way as this. If (so one can imagine Hume saying) we cannot even achieve the kind of certainty that philosophers and scientists have for the most part taken to be the hallmark of genuine knowledge *with regard to this world*—for example, in the realm of science—how can we expect to fare better (or even as well!) in matters that lie completely outside the sphere of human experience and observation? Examples, apart from (1) the existence of God and (2) the fate of the human soul after death, are (3) the origin or cause of the universe (*Enquiry*, section VIII) and (4) the reconciliation of human freedom with divine foreknowledge or foreordination (ibid.). Given the limits of our knowledge, should we not rather abandon speculative metaphysics and theology altogether, concentrating our efforts on improving such restricted and uncertain knowledge as we have of 'common life' for the betterment of the lot of mankind? The real business of philosophy is precisely to help us discover the "proper province of human reason" (59), persuading us to abandon the "abstract and profound" (56) questions of metaphysics and philosophical theology for those subjects to which human reason is naturally suited. "Happy if she," says Hume of human reason,

> be ... sensible of her temerity [that is, boldness], when she pries into these sublime mysteries; and leaving a scene so full of obscurities and perplexities, return, with suitable modesty, to her true and proper province, the examination of common life; where she will find difficulties enough to employ her enquiries, without launching into so boundless an ocean of doubt, uncertainty, and contradiction! (138)

Or again, in the concluding section of the First *Enquiry*:

The *imagination* of man is naturally sublime, delighted with whatever is remote and extraordinary, and running, without control, into the most distant parts of space and time in order to avoid the objects, which custom has rendered too familiar to it. A correct *Judgement* observes a contrary method, and avoiding all distant and high enquiries, confines itself to common life, and to such subjects as fall under daily practice and experience; leaving the more sublime topics to the embellishment of poets and orators, or to the arts of priests and politicians ... While we cannot give a satisfactory reason, why we believe, after a thousand experiments, that a stone will fall, or fire burn; can we ever satisfy ourselves concerning any determination, which we may form, with regard to the origin of worlds, and the situation of nature, from, and to eternity? (192)

These passages epitomize Hume's philosophical outlook. It is an outlook that reverses the trend we have just traced from Socrates through Plato to Descartes, returning to the man-centred outlook of Socrates by focusing attention on what Hume calls 'moral science,' the science of human nature. The path of Hume's philosophy can, accordingly, be called the road back to common life.

Unlike Socrates before him, however, Hume sought to lay philosophical foundations for the man-centred and practically oriented outlook he espoused. This made it necessary to go into theoretical and speculative matters at least far enough to show that there is no point in attempting to penetrate any further, that all efforts in this domain are utterly futile, so that there is no justification for venturing beyond the sphere of common life. Thus, while speculative religious questions occupy Hume greatly (and Socrates not at all), his aim is negative, and his real intent to establish no more than that (as his contemporary Alexander Pope famously put it) "the proper study of mankind is man." (Hume, incidentally, sent Pope a copy of his *Treatise*.)

The philosophical foundations referred to a moment ago are the work of Hume the mental geographer and mental scientist in sections II, III and VI of the First *Enquiry*. They are the subject of the next chapter. The remainder of the present chapter can be devoted to Hume's conception of philosophical science and metaphysics as described in section I of the *Enquiry* and in the *Abstract of A Treatise of Human Nature*.

28.6 Metaphysics and the science of human nature

For Hume, philosophy or "philosophical science" includes all knowledge of man, God, and the world, but not the knowledge "of quantity and number" (102) found in the mathematical sciences, arithmetic, geometry, and algebra. The expressions 'moral philosophy' and 'moral science' are interchangeable with 'the science of human nature,' which comprises four branches: (1) theory of knowledge, or what Hume calls "logic" or "logics" (39), the "sole end" of which is "to explain the principles and operations of our reasoning faculty, and the nature of our ideas" (30); (2) political theory, or what Hume calls "politics," which considers "men as united in society and dependent on each other" (ibid.); (3) theory of art, or aesthetics (Hume calls this "criticism"); and, finally, (4) ethics (called "morals" by Hume). The latter two "regard our tastes and sentiments" (ibid.)—a shocking claim to make about ethics, though perfectly conventional regarding aesthetics.

As moral science treats of "the principles of the human mind" (102), 'metaphysics' contains all the *first* principles of moral science, all the most basic laws *of human nature*. In other words, if we trace logic, politics, aesthetics, or morals back to their first principles, we come at last to certain *basic facts* about human nature or the nature of the human mind, ultimate truths about the way the intellect works or the will and passions operate. If we ask why the human mind is like this, no answer can be given. We have to stop somewhere in the sequence of why-questions, and this, according to Hume, is the point at which all enquiry ends, "those original principles, by which, in every science, all human curiosity must be bounded" (54). Hume's psychological first principles make up what he understands by 'metaphysics.'

In this connection it may be interesting to recall what was traditionally understood by the term 'metaphysics': the philosophical study of *being* (as *existence* and as *essence*) in general, and especially of the existence and essence of the *supersensible* or *immaterial* (i.e., God, if he exists, and the human soul, if there is such a thing) and of first principles or axioms (see 20.7). The only element of this working definition of 'metaphysics' to be met with in Hume's conception of it is the last, the notion of *first principles*. So Hume's idea of metaphysics is very remote from the traditional one; in fact, it is pretty clearly intended as *an assault* upon it, as a radical narrowing of the scope of metaphysics, designed to "bring philosophy back down to earth," back to the human domain—much as did Socrates. Formerly, metaphysics had been the universal science that encompassed all being as well as the science of the supersensible; with Hume, it comes to be the study of the first principles of moral science or the science of human nature.

The word 'metaphysics' is explicitly used in this way in section I of the *Enquiry*:

Were the generality of mankind contented to prefer the easy philosophy to the abstract and profound, without throwing any blame on the latter, it might not be improper perhaps, to comply with this general opinion, and allow every man to enjoy, without opposition, his own tastes and sentiment. But as the matter is often carried farther, even to the absolute rejecting of all *profound reasonings, or what is commonly called metaphysics*, we shall now proceed to consider what can reasonably be pleaded in their behalf. (56 e.a.)

Here 'metaphysics' is a synonym for 'philosophy that engages in profound reasonings,' this having been described a little earlier as the "accurate and abstruse philosophy" in contrast with the "easy and obvious" one (54). Where the latter cultivates fine sentiments and good conduct by proceeding from concrete example to general precept, the former reverses the order, starting from general precepts regarding "truth and falsehood, vice and virtue, beauty and deformity" (ibid.) and proceeding to "the source of these distinctions," that is, to the very "foundations of morals, reasoning, and criticism" (ibid.), the "original principles by which, in every science, all human curiosity must be bounded" (ibid.). This "accurate and abstruse philosophy" is "the science of human nature." In view of its first principles, it is occasionally given the name 'metaphysics' by Hume, who at one point even uses the expression "philosophy of the *moral or metaphysical* kind" (76 e.a.). 'Moral philosophy' is equivalent to the 'science of human nature' for Hume, its first principles being 'metaphysics' in Hume's use of that term.

It turns out, however, that Hume has a dual conception of metaphysics, comprising true and false metaphysics. True metaphysics is equivalent to the science of human nature, that is, the "accurate scrutiny into the powers and faculties of the human mind" (59), based on what Hume calls "mental geography" (60). This unusual expression refers to the business of locating the exact 'province' (that is, the faculty) of the mind from which certain ideas or beliefs hail, identifying their point of origin on the 'map' of the mind. By this means it is possible to achieve "certainty and solidity" in exploring "the secret springs and principles, by which the human mind is actuated in its operations" (61). False metaphysics is just so much metaphysical jargon mixed up with popular superstition, that is, with popular religion (59). It is "uncertain and chimerical" (60), a "shelter to superstition, and a cover to absurdity and error" (62), "the most contentious science" (131). True metaphysics, Hume argues, is the only effective remedy for false metaphysics; instead of shunning the abstruse sort of philosophy altogether, then, one must lay bare the true foundations of the philosophical sciences, thereby exposing and dispelling bad metaphysics. What follows is Hume's conception of science and philosophy set out in diagram form:

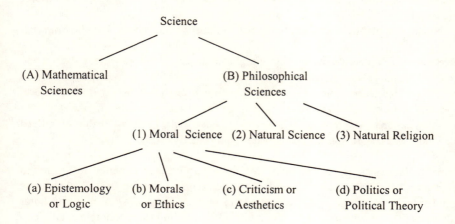

29

An Empiricist Critique of Reason

29.1 Introductory

The preceding chapter provided a very rough general orientation. We are still not ready to focus attention on the detail of Hume's attack on religious philosophy or "bad metaphysics," however. For while his idea of philosophy may be clearer, more needs to be said about religion and about the philosophical tools with which Hume mounts his attack on the alleged rational bases of religion, indeed on the claims of reason itself. That is the task of the present chapter.

Revealed religion, religion based solely on faith, tradition, and revelation, is not at issue, except obliquely, where Hume recommends it (with mock piety) as the only type of religious belief open to a rational human being. *Natural* religion or theology, that is, religion based on "mere natural and unassisted reason" (138), bears the full brunt of Hume's withering critique.

Religion or theology, so understood, is "nothing but a species of philosophy" (179), called "religious philosophy" by Hume. It includes all attempts to argue rationally for the truth of religion, whether by demonstrative or only probable means. The difference between this and religion based upon the teaching authority of the Church or on the divine origin of sacred books was already well established in the thought of two of the greatest of Hume's seventeenth-century predecessors, Leibniz and Descartes. "The theologians," writes Leibniz, "distinguish rational grounds for belief, along with the *natural assent* which can arise only from such grounds and cannot have higher probability than they have, from the *supernatural assent* which is brought about by divine grace" (e.a.). In a similar vein, Descartes distinguished between the "natural light" of human reason and the "supernatural light" of divine illumination or grace.

29.2 The twin prongs of Hume's attack

Hume's assault on natural religion is twin-pronged. To understand it, we have to distinguish between (1) the truth of religion in general, that is, belief in God's existence, which Hume calls "the religious hypothesis" (173); and (2) the truth of the Christian religion in particular. Both belong to natural theology insofar as the knowledge in question is supposed to be obtainable by means of natural human reason alone, without either miraculous revelation through scripture or divine illumination through grace.

Clearly, if (2) the truth of the Christian religion could really be established as rationally warranted by solid evidence, then all the Christian scriptures and authoritative teachings of the Church could be used to supplement our bare (1) knowledge of God's *existence*, furnishing further knowledge of many particulars concerning God's nature, his attributes, his actions, commandments, purposes, and so forth—even though much would still remain beyond our ken, God not having revealed himself completely. Thus, the same Leibniz quoted a moment ago also wrote that "the greatest mysteries [of the Christian faith] are made known to us by God's testimony [or revelation], *through those rational grounds for belief on which our religion rests*" (e.a.). Mysteries, of course, remain mysteries; we can never penetrate them, though we can know what they reveal to be true, Leibniz maintains, since reason rightly persuades us of the truth of Christianity, and thus of the truth of the Christian mysteries. Leibniz remarks with evident pride that the age in which he lives has "many fine works on the truth of the Christian religion." Hume, accordingly, is keenly interested in whether (1) and (2) above can be substantiated by "unassisted reason," as the "religious philosophers" (169) staunchly maintain, Leibniz perhaps foremost among them.

29.2.1 The first prong

The first prong of Hume's attack is directed against (1) the two traditional types of argument for God's existence, namely (a) the wholly a priori argument from his nature or essence, that is, the ontological argument from essence to existence pioneered by St Anselm and renewed by Descartes (see chap. 26); and (b) the a posteriori or causal arguments for God's existence (from effect to cause), including (i) Descartes's Third Meditation argument (ibid.), (ii) the causal arguments employed in St Thomas's famous Five Ways (ibid.), and (iii) the argument used by the deists of the eighteenth century and known as the 'Argument from Design.' This last-named argument has not come before us yet. It is the subject of a major posthumous work by Hume, entitled *Dialogues Concerning Natural Religion*. A contemporary of Descartes, Gassendi, styled it "the principal argument for establishing by the natural light [of reason] the wisdom, providence and power of God, and indeed his existence." This opinion reflects the outlook of the eighteenth century as well. We shall consider the Argument from Design in more detail below (see 31.5.1).

We have already dealt with Hume's criticism of (a) the a priori or ontological argument for God's existence based on a consideration of his nature or essence (see 26.9.3). The argument is decisively rejected in section XII of the First *Enquiry* on the strength of a counter-argument that runs roughly as follows. All knowledge of the actual *existence* of anything is derived from the senses, or from memory, or from a posteriori reasoning, whether from an observed cause to its usual effect, or from an observed effect to its customary cause, or from an observed effect to its customary concomitant effect. All knowledge of *necessity*, by contrast, depends on a priori reasoning, that is, on the intuition or demonstration that the denial of a certain proposition involves contradiction. Accordingly, the conclusion of the ontological argument, 'God exists necessarily,' is simply unintelligible, a muddle; for the existence of anything whatever may be denied without the slightest contradiction. In more contemporary terms, necessity may be predicated *of propositions* when they or their denials are self-contradictory (necessarily false and necessarily true propositions, respectively); it may *not* be predicated *of things* and their existence, not even of God. This way of putting the point would have been quite congenial to Hume, though it is actually that adopted by Bertrand Russell in a famous debate with the Jesuit priest and historian of philosophy Frederick Copleston concerning the existence of God. Or, to put Hume's point in the colloquial terms used earlier: necessity and existence just 'don't mix' (see 26.9.3). We saw in the last part why Descartes would have lost very little sleep over this argument, which he anticipated and even tried to rebut (see 26.10.3).

As for (b), the grounds on which Hume rejected all three a posteriori arguments are likewise set out in section XII of the *Enquiry*. They can be summed up this way. We cannot know a priori, without experience, either that every event has a cause or what sort of cause a given event (or effect) must have; rather, these are things we learn and know through experience, a posteriori. And what experience teaches us is never absolutely certain, however probable it may be. So we cannot simply help ourselves to premises concerning what sort of cause *must* have created a certain idea in the mind, or the whole universe for that matter, as though this were self-evident a priori; it is not evident at all, but probable, at best, and thus not known with certainty.

This is obviously devastating to (ii) Descartes's Third Meditation causal proof, which turns crucially on the assumption that only a certain kind of cause, God himself, could produce the idea of God in the mind. It is similarly destructive of St Thomas's Five Ways. For they too assume that only a certain type of cause, a necessary being or unmoved mover, is adequate to produce the whole sequence of secondary causes. The only a posteriori argument for God's existence for which Hume had a measure of respect was (iii) above, the causal argument known as the Argument from Design. For proponents of the latter at least have experience to back up their claims about what sort of thing is required to produce a certain effect; both Descartes and Aquinas appealed to reason alone.

That is not to say that Hume *accepted* the Argument from Design. But though the inference from the observable signs of a pervasive order in the universe to a rational and benevolent creator God is not strictly probative, it is not unreasonable, in Hume's view, to accept the conclusion (as does the deist) since it at least accords with what experience teaches us about the kind of cause required to produce an intricately contrived effect like the physical universe as we observe it to be. Of course, advances in astronomy and in the study of the natural history of the earth, along with the emergence of a scientific theory of evolution, all give us other explanations today, explanations that Hume could not have known about. However, in Hume's day deism seemed reasonable (even to him!), though he himself almost certainly did not accept the deists' conclusion. Nevertheless, his assessment of the logic of the Argument from Design stands as a model of philosophical analysis to this day.

29.2.2 The second prong

So much for the first prong, the attack on all three major types of proof of God's existence. The second prong is a critique of arguments for the truth of the Christian religion in particular. Here there are just two principal types of arguments to consider: (a) a posteriori arguments from historical (testimonial) evidence for miracles wrought by Jesus to the truth of Christian revelation, and (b) a posteriori arguments from the signs of wisdom and goodness in the universe to the existence of a wise and benevolent creator God who will mete out reward and punishment in the afterlife. This last argument goes beyond just establishing the existence of an intelligent creator of the world as we know it; it involves a further inference to a perfect justice to be realized by him in the hereafter.

The diagram on page 501 summarizes Hume's twin-pronged attack on the rational bases of religion. The sections of the First *Enquiry* entitled "Of Miracles" and "Of a Particular Providence and a Future State" concern (a) and (b) of the second prong, respectively. Nothing more need be said of the alleged proofs of the truth of Christianity at this stage, since they are the subject of the next two chapters. The remainder of the present chapter is devoted to the tools Hume employs to mount his attack upon natural religion, beginning with a sketch of the empiricist and associationist psychologist, and ending with another look at Hume's famous critique of the empirical or experimental sciences (see 28.1).

29.2.3 Technical preliminaries

Consideration of the technical means Hume employs in his assault on natural religion furnishes a welcome pretext for a section-by-section summary of the *Enquiry* up to

Chapter 29: An Empiricist Critique of Reason 501

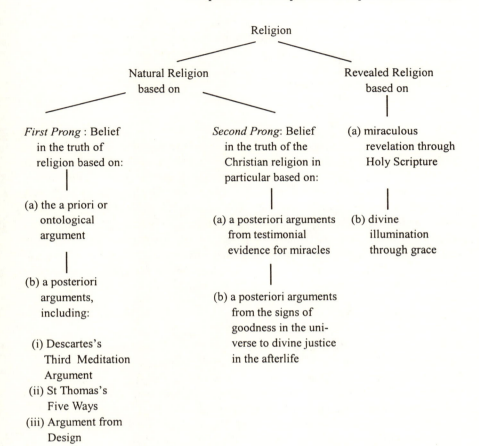

the onset of the second prong in sections X and XI. No treatment of Hume's philosophy can afford to omit discussion of these themes, though some readers may wish to proceed immediately to the following chapters on miracles and divine justice in the afterlife, referring back to the relevant sections of this chapter as the need arises.

We shall consider first two fundamental tenets of Hume's philosophy, to be labelled (1) 'the great divide' and (2) the 'principle of the priority of impressions to ideas,' respectively. On these follows a consideration of four further doctrines: (3) the principle of the liberty of the imagination to transpose and change its ideas; (4) the distinction between two kinds of truths or propositions (also known as 'Hume's Fork'); (5) Hume's classification of the various sources or "branches of human knowledge" (79); and (6) Hume's distinction among three different degrees of evidence or certainty, (a) demonstration, (b) proof, and (c) probability. This last is of vital importance for the understanding of the essay "Of Miracles." The chapter concludes with a look at (7) Hume's characteristic mode of psychological and logical analysis as illustrated by his most famous piece in the genre, the analysis of the idea of causality or 'necessary connection.'

29.3 Hume's empiricism

Both (1) the great divide and (2) the principle of the priority of impressions to ideas are found in section II of the First *Enquiry* and in the *Abstract of A Treatise of Human Nature* (31–2). Together they make clear the precise extent of Hume's commitment to empiricist principles like those championed by Locke. Not that Hume merely took over Locke's doctrines; on the contrary, he had an acute sense of where they were open to attack, and sought to shore them up by means of a more sophisticated theory of his own. This, Hume believed, allowed him to clear up once and for all the point at issue in the swirling debate about innate ideas between Locke and the followers of Descartes (see 29.3.3 below). As we shall see, his solution to this thorny question is anything but persuasive.

29.3.1 The great divide

Hume's use of the key philosophical term 'idea' is different from Descartes's. Where for Descartes (1) 'perception' is just the equivalent of 'idea' as the name for one species of the genus 'thought,' the others being (2) volition, (3) judgment, and (4) emotion, in the *Enquiry* Hume uses 'idea' interchangeably with 'thought' to refer to one species of a new highest genus, 'perception' (see the diagram on page 503). The other species of perception is impressions. This division of all the contents of the mind ('perceptions') into just two species ('impressions' and 'ideas') is what we refer to as 'the great divide.' The word 'reflection' is a further synonym of 'thought,' 'reflecting upon' something being in Hume much the same as 'thinking of' it.

It will again be useful to provide a table summarizing this important bit of "mental geography" (60) or, as we should say, Hume's classification of all mental phenomena, psychic states, conscious experiences, or mental acts. For purposes of orientation, this chart should be compared with that depicting Descartes's classification in 27.3 above. Despite marked changes in vocabulary, Hume subscribes at bottom to the Cartesian conception of the mind, soul, self, or psyche as self-consciousness, including the Cartesian conception of the mind's basic faculties and modalities. His main scruple concerns the Cartesian 'I' that thinks—but this issue is to be left aside here.

The class of mental phenomena belonging to the species designated 'impressions' comprises in the essentials two things: (1) the deliverances of outer sense or sensation

Chapter 29: An Empiricist Critique of Reason   503

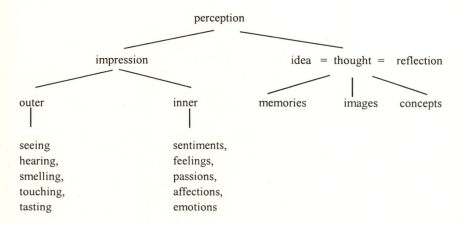

('sense perception' in the customary sense) and (2) the data of inner sense or sensation, of introspection, as we say nowadays. 'Impression' is thus coextensive with 'sensation' or 'sentiment' or 'feeling' in a *wide* sense that includes both "inward" and "outward sentiment" (65), since all this is immediately given and 'felt' by the mind. Hume also speaks of "sensations, either outward or inward" (67) and "the internal and external senses" (90; see 102) when distinguishing between perceptions of the sensible qualities of external things and those of our own states of mind. Locke spoke of inner and outer 'experience.'

On the other side of the great divide are what Hume terms 'ideas' or 'thoughts,' the products of reflection upon an inner or outer object as opposed to actually sensing or feeling its presence. These are our "less forcible and lively" (63) or "fainter and weaker" (31) perceptions, being mere "copies" (102) of our impressions and hence somewhat less vivid than they, as copies tend to be. When we just reflect on the objects of which we have had impressions in the past—for example, when we (a) imagine, or (b) remember (say) the Niagara Falls or (c) just understand what is meant by the words 'the Niagara Falls,' without actually feeling the corresponding sensory impressions, then what is before or in the mind is, technically speaking, an *idea* of that great torrent rather than the *impressions* we have when actually standing before and gazing at it. And since the mind comes to be stocked with a wealth of ideas or thoughts in this sense, all of them derived from antecedent impressions of "outward or inward sentiment," it is clear that their being in the mind is not just a matter of being actually entertained at the moment, but of one's being *capable* of calling them up at will. This is why, in the *Abstract of A Treatise of Human Nature* (36), Hume speaks of all our ideas as being dependent upon the will, unlike our impressions or feelings, which, apart from being more lively and forceful, do not so depend.

29.3.2 The priority of impressions to ideas

From given ideas, as the "materials afforded us by the senses and experience" (64), the mind is able to form many new ideas unlike anything that it has actually experienced through "mixing" (32), that is, through "compounding, transposing, or diminishing" (64) the raw materials originally acquired through sensation. What were earlier impressions remain in the mind as ideas; yet the mind is incapable of ever furnishing itself with a single new idea that is not either (a) copied from some new impression or (b) fashioned (by one or more of the operations just mentioned) out of the ideas it already has. Thus, according to Hume, all our fictitious or factitious ideas ('golden mountain,' 'satyr,' 'mermaid,' 'unicorn,' and so on), but likewise all our abstruse philosophical notions ('substance,' 'causality,' and so on) are formed by certain operations of the mind performed upon the raw materials of inner and outer sensation or experience. Some of this is done consciously and deliberately, as when we indulge in fantasy; some, however, takes place unbeknownst to us through the spontaneous power of the faculty of imagination acting under the influence of habit. We shall return to this point in discussing Hume's associationist psychology (see 29.4).

The foregoing gives the gist of Hume's empiricism as a thesis about the origin of ideas. He rests his case on two key philosophical principles. In the *Treatise*, he calls them the "principle of the priority of impressions to ideas" and the "principle of the liberty of the imagination to transpose and change its ideas." The latter will be discussed in the next section (see 29.4). As for the first, it finds expression in section II of the *Enquiry*, although the clearest and best formulation of it is to be found in section VII:

all our ideas are nothing but copies of our impressions, or, in other words ... it is impossible for us to *think* of anything, which we have not antecedently *felt*, either by our external or internal senses. (102)

29.3.3 Innate ideas

With the help of his new technical use of the familiar terms 'impression' and 'idea,' Hume tries to present the controversy between Locke and the followers of Descartes over innate ideas as a verbal quibble, due largely to the failure of both sides to define their terms adequately. Thus, in the *Abstract* he remarks, apparently sincerely: "I am persuaded [that] whoever would take the question in this light" (that is, take the word 'idea' in Hume's rather than Locke's sense), would be easily able to reconcile all parties. Father Malebranche [a follower of Descartes] would find himself at a loss to point out any thought of the mind which did not represent something antecedently felt by it, either internally or by means of the external senses, and must allow that however we compound, and mix, and augment, and diminish our ideas, they are all derived from these sources [inner and outer impressions]. Mr. Locke, on the other hand, would readily acknowledge that all our passions are a kind of natural instincts, derived from nothing but the original constitution of the human mind. (32)

This is really too facile. Leibniz, too, was apt to suggest, rather lamely, that the disagreement was only apparent, surmising with characteristic optimism that Locke meant by 'reflection' much the same thing as he, namely attending to certain universal notions already innate within ourselves, such as 'being,' unity,' 'substance,' 'duration,' 'change,' 'action,' and "a thousand other objects of our intellectual ideas." This is just preposterous. There is a real difference of opinion between Locke and Leibniz concerning a whole range of metaphysical ideas, including that of God. Like Leibniz, Hume is reluctant to acknowledge the fact. To avoid becoming embroiled in what he considers a verbal dispute (on which he nevertheless clearly takes Locke's side), Hume states his own position (at the end of section II of the *Enquiry*) in the form of a series of hypothetical propositions of the form: if by 'idea' is meant x and by 'innate' y, then there are (or there are not) innate ideas. He considers four alternative antecedents.

1 If by 'innate' is meant 'natural' (as opposed either to 'extraordinary,' 'artificial,' or 'miraculous,' i.e., supernatural), then *all* perceptions of the mind, including both impressions and all ideas or thoughts, are innate.

Obviously, this was never what the 'nativist' or 'innatist' followers of Descartes had in mind, though it may apply to something like Plato's doctrine of recollection of concepts acquired during one's prenatal existence in the realm of the divine, and to some theories of divine or supernatural inspiration. As far as the real issue is concerned, 1 is just beside the point.

2 If by 'innate' is meant 'existing in the mind at the instant of birth,' then the dispute is of no consequence ('frivolous'), it being useless to enquire at what exact point in time those perceptions properly called 'ideas' actually begin to occur in the mind, whether before, at, or immediately after birth, since this cannot be determined by any means at our disposal.

This was never the issue either, though, again, it has a certain relevance to Plato's Recollection Argument. Generally, Cartesians posited no more than *dispositions* in all men to have certain ideas ('God,' 'cause and effect,' 'substance,' etc.) *whenever* the appropriate stimuli for their actualization occurred.

3 If by 'innate' is meant 'instinctive' and by 'idea' any perception (in Hume's broad sense) whatever (including, emotions, desires), then there are many innate ideas,

e.g., feelings of self-love, anger at a hurt, friendship, desire for sexual union, etc.

Again, the real issue concerns what Descartes called "seeds of truth," that is, *knowledge* of truths, or materials for such knowledge, not derived from experience in the manner of adventitious ideas. Everybody acknowledges the existence of innate instincts like those Hume alludes to here. This is another non-issue.

4 If by 'innate' is meant 'being an original perception copied from no antecedent perception' and by 'idea' any 'perception' whatever, then all our impressions are innate and none of our ideas or thoughts are innate.

This too is irrelevant. No nativist would wish to apply the term 'innate' to inner and outer impressions in the manner proposed here.

Hume's own position on the innateness question is in fact clearly and dogmatically staked out in his principle of the priority of impressions to ideas; all the above is just an elaborate attempt to separate this substantive position from a number of unimportant verbal issues. Hume's contention that once the equivocations are exposed the substantive disagreements simply vanish is quite incredible. The philosophical issue between empiricists and rationalists is anything but a verbal quibble (see 26.2).

29.4 Hume's associationism

Section III of the *Enquiry* is entitled "Of the Association of Ideas." It corresponds to a couple of much more detailed sections of the *Treatise*. Hume treats association as a universal force of attraction in the mind analogous to the force of gravitation in the physical universe. It is here that "mental geography" gives way to what might be called 'mental science' or 'mental mechanics.' Here is how Hume himself develops the analogy:

But may we not hope, that philosophy, if cultivated with care, and encouraged by the attention of the public, may carry its researches still farther, and discover, at least in some degree, the secret springs and principles, by which the human mind is actuated in its operations. Astronomers had long contented themselves with proving from the phaenomena, the motions, order, and magnitude of the heavenly bodies: Till a philosopher [Sir Isaac Newton], at last rose, who seems from the happiest reasoning, to have also determined the laws and forces, by which the revolutions of the planets are governed and directed. The like has been performed with regard to other parts of nature. And there is no reason to despair of equal success in our enquiries concerning the mental powers and economy, if prosecuted with equal capacity and caution. (61)

Employing the principle of the association of ideas as his universal force of attraction,

Chapter 29: An Empiricist Critique of Reason 507

Hume proposes to explain all those complex ideas that arise from the simple ones without deliberate "compounding, transposing, or diminishing" (64). The associationist psychology sketched in section III of the *Enquiry* and applied in sections V, VI, and IX is based on the second of the two principles cited earlier (see 29.3.2): the "principle of the liberty of the imagination to transpose and change its ideas," that is, to join together those that, in experience, are separate and distinct, and to separate those that, in experience, are conjoined in one idea.

The imagination, for Hume, is a *productive* faculty of the mind. Yet it is not just productive of new ideas through "mixing, compounding, separating, and dividing" (91) given ideas; it is productive of *new impressions* as well. From such new impressions *genuinely* new ideas derive. Imagination, in other words, is the source of a special sort of "fictions" which are *absolutely new creations of the mind* rather than just the result of reworking given materials in various ways.

Here Hume goes beyond Locke. His brand of associationism acknowledges that the imagination has the ability to fashion, if not new simple ideas of properties or qualities in things, then at least *new ideas of relations among such properties*, that is, new *complex* or *compound* ideas involving new simple impressions. These genuinely new ideas incorporate a felt propensity of the mind to pass from one idea to another that has become associated with it through habit or custom. And this *felt* propensity is itself just a *new impression* due entirely to the power of the imagination. But the productive imagination that spawns new simple impressions of inner sense is a source of error. Judgment or belief is itself just "something felt by the mind, which distinguishes the ideas of the judgement [ideas of really existing things and states of affairs] from the fictions of the imagination" (92). Accordingly, erroneous judgments about the way things are arise from a failure to distinguish what the mind itself produces (the merely 'subjective,' as we say) from what exists in things outside the mind (the 'objective'). This proves to be of great importance in explaining the psychological origin of the idea of the relation of "cause and effect" or "necessary connexion" (section VII), which is of particular importance for Hume as a sceptical critic of natural science.

In the third section of the *Enquiry* Hume provides only a much-scaled-down version of the detailed theory of association developed in the *Treatise*. He begins with the fact that some ideas are found to be conjoined and connected with others, and proceeds to identify as the law governing their connection the law of the association of ideas on the basis of (1) resemblance, (2) contiguity in time or place, and (3) cause and effect. These three are called 'principles' of the association of ideas. 'Resemblance' just means 'sameness' of quality or nature, sameness between two ideas in respect of *what* they represent. Its opposite is 'contrariety' (or 'contrast'). 'Contiguity,' on the other hand, covers all spatial and temporal relations among the objects of ideas; not just 'near' in time and space, as the word suggests, but also 'far' or 'distant,' 'above' or 'below,' 'to the right' or 'to the left of,' and 'before' and 'after' in time. 'Cause and effect' or 'causation' will be discussed later (see 29.8.2).

In the two principles discussed in this and the previous section, "the priority of impressions" and "the liberty of the imagination," Hume has all he needs to construct a theory of knowledge and the mind: (a) irreducible elements as starting points; (b) a power of separating them, where they occur in combination, and of recombining them in new ways; and (c) the psychological 'cement' for certain new combinations, namely habit or custom, which is not just a cohesive force, but also a source of altogether new impressions (and hence ideas) like the ideas 'substance' and 'necessary connection' or 'cause and effect,' many of which were thought to be innate ideas in the earlier tradition. But another, even more important, tool of Hume's critical enterprise remains to be considered.

29.5 Hume's Fork

So far we have sketched (1) Hume's division of all perceptions into impressions and ideas, (2) the principle of the priority of impressions to ideas, and (3) that of the liberty of the imagination to transpose and change its ideas. All are found in sections II and III of the *Enquiry*. In the first two paragraphs of section IV, Hume draws another justly famous distinction that has since come to be known as (4) 'Hume's Fork.'

As he divides all perceptions into two classes, so Hume divides all propositions (or truths) into two kinds. First, are propositions expressing relations (of ideas). These are (a) perfectly certain and necessary as well as (b) discoverable by the "mere operation of thought," that is, through purely logical (conceptual) analysis of our ideas or concepts. Moreover, they (c) do not entail the actual existence of anything. Non-trivial truths of this kind are confined wholly to the mathematical sciences, according to Hume, the sciences of "quantity and number" (102, 193), as he calls them. Examples are simple arithmetical and geometrical truths such as '$2 + 2 = 4$' and 'a triangle has three sides.' These are perfectly certain and cannot be denied without contradiction; they depend only on the understanding or analysis of the meanings of 'two,' 'plus,' 'four,' 'triangle,' 'three,' and so on; and they are perfectly true whether or not any entities corresponding to the concepts 'two,' 'triangle,' and so forth actually exist.

The second class of propositions or truths is composed of all those that correctly describe matters of fact, asserting some thing or some state of affairs to exist. These are (a) at best only very highly probable and contingent rather than certain and necessary; moreover, they are (b) based on (i) "the testimony of the senses," or (ii) the "records of the memory," or (iii) causal reasonings (inductive or probable inferences) from observed and remembered sequences of events to similar sequences of events, observed and unobserved. Finally, (c) they depend for their truth upon the actual existence of the things and properties that the propositions are about. If the things designated by the words in the subject position of these propositions do not exist at all, the propositions about them cannot be true; while if they do exist, the propositions *may* be true, though not perfectly certain. Whether or not they are true in fact can only be determined by observation.

This should be easily recognizable as a form of the distinction between conceptual and factual propositions or truths drawn in 7.4 above. Or, in the language of Leibniz, it is a form of the distinction between truths of reason and truths of fact. However, it differs from Leibniz's manner of drawing the distinction in two respects. First, it confines non-trivial truths of reason to the mathematical sciences. Leibniz, following Descartes, insisted that there are non-trivial metaphysical truths of reason. Moreover, Hume's propositions expressing "relations of ideas" tell us nothing whatever about anything actually existent: even if true, they do not entail the existence of anything. At least some of Leibniz's metaphysical axioms are truths of reason that are informative about the real world (see 20.2). Although we have spoken of truths here, following both Leibniz and Hume, false propositions, too, may either express relations of ideas (e.g., '2 + 2 = 5') or misreport matters of fact (e.g., 'cows are bipeds,' 'unicorns exist').

29.6 The sources of human knowledge

We have seen already that Hume distinguishes reasoning in general from three other main sources or "branches of human knowledge" (79): observation, memory, and imagination. These and all other sources of human knowledge recognized by Hume are described in the following paragraphs and summarized in a table below.

The first source is experience, which is either (a) outer observation, that is, *sense perception* of extra-mental, material objects, including my own body, or (b) inner observation, *internal perception*, introspection of what is going on in my own mind (my perceptions, emotions, volitions, judgments, reasonings). From (a) I get my concepts of extra-mental physical objects: a dog, a house, a river, a mountain; from (b) I derive psychological concepts like 'perception,' 'memory,' 'emotion,' 'belief,' and so on, that is, concepts of mental states, operations, events, faculties, and the like.

Further "branches of human knowledge" are memory and the imagination, that is, (c) the capacity to retain and reawaken ideas of external and internal objects I have perceived before, without their being present and perceived right now (say, the Niagara Falls); and (d) the capacity to imagine such objects as I have never in fact perceived by fashioning new ideas out of the materials derived from the senses and memory, that is, forming new ideas like those of "a golden mountain" (64), "an enchanted castle" (93), a centaur, dragon, ghost, ghoul, hobgoblin, and so on. Imagination, as we have seen, may also be the source of new impressions.

The fourth main source of knowledge is *reasoning* or, equivalently, the exercise of the *understanding*, which is again "of two kinds" (79), a priori and a posteriori (or experiential) reasoning. A priori reasoning is also called "demonstrative" (81) or "abstract" (76) by Hume, who refers to it also as "ratiocination" (82), "reasoning from mere ideas" (48), and "scientific reasoning" (50). This is the kind of reasoning found in the mathematical sciences. It is, of course, also met with in metaphysics and natural theology. There, however, it furnishes no legitimate extension of our knowledge according to Hume.

Such a priori reasoning can further be divided into 'intuitive' and 'demonstrative,' that is, (e) a priori understanding of self-evident truths and (f) a priori deduction of further truths by means of direct or indirect inferences. The former is not usually thought of as 'reasoning,' but it is a function of reason for Hume, as it was for Descartes and many other thinkers, going right back to Plato. Hume, of course, was a sceptic about many principles traditionally regarded as self-evident, but simple truths expressing genuinely self-evident relations of ideas unquestionably fall into this category. As for a posteriori (inductive or experiential) reasoning, it is also called "causal reasoning," "moral reasoning" (79, 194), "probable reasoning" (79, 80), "reasoning concerning matters of fact [and real existence]" (77, 79), "arguments from experience" (80), "experimental conclusions" (80), and reasonings "founded on the relation of cause and effect" (72, 77, 80). Here Hume distinguishes between (g) merely probable arguments, for example, 'raising interest rates will bring down inflation,' and (h) full proofs (where the probability equals one), for example, 'unsupported bodies near the earth's surface fall,' or 'the sun will rise and set within a twenty-four-hour period.'

Putting all this together, we get the following list of sources of human knowledge:

1 sense experience
   (a) outer observation
   (b) inner observation
2 (c) memory
3 (d) imagination
4 reason or the understanding
   a priori reasoning
   (e) intuition
   (f) deduction
   a posteriori reasoning
   (g) probable reasoning
   (h) proof

It is worth noting that Hume assigns 3(d), the imagination, such "great authority over our ideas" (43), that he is very apt to blur the boundaries between sense and imagination, on the one hand, and reasoning and imagination, on the other. As he himself puts it at one place in the *Treatise*: "The memory, senses, and understanding are, therefore, all of them founded on the imagination." In the *Enquiry* he is generally more circumspect than this.

29.7 The degrees of evidence or certainty

Three of the "branches of knowledge" ranged under item 4, reasoning, in the above table—(f), (g), and (h)—point to a threefold distinction among *degrees of evidence*: (i) demonstration, (ii) proof, and (iii) probability. The differences are elaborated in section VI of the First *Enquiry*.

A *demonstration*, according to Hume, is an argument in which the evidence stated in the premise(s) logically entails the conclusion such that to affirm the premise(s) and deny the conclusion would be to contradict oneself: "wherever a demonstration takes place, the contrary is impossible, and implies contradiction" (34). This is tantamount to a definition of a formally valid inference. In Hume's view, demonstration as a means of acquiring new knowledge is strictly confined to the mathematical sciences, in which neither observation nor causal reasoning play any role at all: "It seems to me, that the only objects of the abstract sciences or of demonstration are quantity and number" (193). The mathematical sciences furnish no knowledge of any matter of fact or existence; mathematical demonstration is "founded merely on the comparison of ideas" (34); they have to do solely with "relations of ideas," never with matters of fact and existence. Outside mathematics, in the other sciences, demonstrative reasoning may be useful in spelling out the implications of, or the logical relations between, various truths; but it cannot produce any *new* knowledge. Thus, to illustrate, one can say (taking the example from another of Hume's works) *"that where there is no property, there can be no injustice."* If injustice is defined, say, as 'an unfair distribution of property,' then it is demonstratively true, though trivial and uninformative, that "where there is no property, there can be no injustice," much as if one said, "where there is no property, there can be no theft." For this simply spells out what 'theft' means (say, 'depriving another of his property by illegal means'). Outside mathematics, then, observation and causal or experimental reasoning are the sole sources of whatever non-trivial knowledge is obtainable about matter of fact and existence, that is, about the world.

A *proof*, by contrast, is an argument the conclusion of which *goes beyond* (is not logically entailed by) the experiential evidence stated or summarized in the premises. A proof is therefore not a 'demonstration' in Hume's sense, though the terms are often used interchangeably by others. Where *all* the known evidence supports the conclusion and *no* evidence tells against it, an argument amounts to a full and complete proof. As demonstrations are confined to the mathematical sciences, so proofs are found only in the non-mathematical sciences, for example, in the sciences of nature. The laws of physics or biology, insofar as they are constantly corroborated by all past and by all new experience, and not contradicted by *any* contrary instances, amount to complete and perfect proofs. An example is the law of *physics*: All unsupported bodies near the earth's surface fall (or gravitate) toward the earth. Or in biology: All human beings (or all animal organisms) die.

A merely *probable* argument, finally, is one the conclusion of which again *goes beyond* the experiential evidence stated in the premises. In this respect it is like a proof. But while *all* the evidence supports the conclusion in a complete and perfect proof, in a probable argument there is *at least some* evidence against the conclusion drawn. To the extent that there is more evidence for than against it, the conclusion is probable. For example, it is a law in economics that if interest rates are raised, spending and thus inflation will decrease (since people stop spending and start saving to take advantage of the high interest rates); while if interest rates are lowered, spending and inflation will increase. Of course, there have been plenty of cases in which this has not happened, but, by and large, it is what those who set economic policy continue to expect as a highly likely outcome.

In sum, then, it is *demonstrably certain* that the internal angles of a triangle equal two right angles, but not that high interest rates will slow inflation or that the sun will rise and set within a twenty-four-hour period or that all men die. It is *only probable*, not demonstrably certain, that raising interest rates will curb inflation, or that rhubarb will purge and opium induce sleep (Hume's examples). After all, rhubarb may not have this effect, and so with the other examples. On the other hand, it would be odd to say that it is only probable that the sun will rise in the next twenty-four hours or that I shall die, or even that bread will nourish me. Hence, Hume speaks in such cases, not of probability, but of *proof*, since there is no contrary evidence whatsoever.

29.8 Hume's characteristic mode of argument

So much for six of the seven technical preliminaries to the interpretation of the two essays constituting the second prong of Hume's attack on natural religion (see 29.2.2). Now for the last, the way in which these tools are put to work.

It was remarked earlier that, whatever Hume himself may have thought of the Argument from Design, his analysis of its *logic* stands as a lasting philosophical achievement. The same might be said of other typically Humean analyses. In this final section, we shall briefly set out the typical pattern of logical and psychological analysis employed by Hume, illustrating it with reference to Hume's most famous analysis of all. In the next two chapters we shall have to consider the extent to which the pattern is employed in the two essays "Of Miracles" and "Of a Particular Providence and a Future State."

29.8.1 A typically Humean pattern of argument

The characteristic pattern of Humean analysis can be set out roughly this way:

Step 1: Question. From a given truth, T1, some, most, or practically all people infer another, T2. (Often it is not an inference but a conviction that is analyzed, and sometimes one held only by philosophers.) The questions are: (a) What operation of the mind is responsible for the belief in T2 ("mental geography"), and (b) Is that belief rationally justified (logical analysis)? These questions, the first psycho-genetic, the second logical or epistemological, are seldom sharply distinguished by Hume.

Step 2: Investigation. Consideration, one after the other, of various 'candidate' operations of the mind, namely one or more of the following: (a) inner or (b) outer observation, (c) memory, (d) a priori intuition, (e) a priori or demonstrative reasoning, a posteriori or causal reasoning amounting to (f) probability or (g) proof.

Step 3: Sceptical Answer. Neither observation, nor memory, nor any form of reasoning actually justifies the inference from T1 to T2. Or: only the use of a further suppressed premise, say, T3, would render the inference a valid piece of deductive reasoning, and this premise is something that we are just not entitled to assume. Thus, there just is *no adequate rational justification* for the conclusion.

Step 4: Psychological Explanation. What actually *causes* people to draw this conclusion is, say, a flight of fancy (imagination), or the force of habit, or both, or some other psychological mechanism of the mind having nothing to do with reason. This completes the psycho-genetic or causal explanation typically begun in Step 2.

The most famous instance of this pattern of argument is undoubtedly Hume's analysis of the grounds for the belief in the relation of "cause and effect" or "necessary connexion" in sections IV and VII of the First *Enquiry*.

29.8.2 Causal reasonings in science

Extensively, the laws of nature are just those causal laws set forth in abundance in natural sciences like physics, biology, and so on. They are commonly understood as rules governing the sequence of events in nature, rules as to what must or cannot produce what in the natural order of events. Such laws are often expressed in the form: 'B-like events depend on A-like events as their causally necessary and sufficient conditions.' This means, roughly: '*never, as a matter of physical or natural necessity*, can there be a B that is not preceded by an A, or an A that is not followed by a B.' Or, in other words, 'the existence of A is *necessarily* connected with that of B such that if one exists, the other *must* exist (or must have existed) too.' Yet unlike conceptual truths or propositions expressing relations of ideas, universal laws of nature concerning what must or cannot exist involve physical, not logical, necessity. Logically, the laws of nature are contingent universal truths.

Belief in "necessary connexion" is the basis of a great many particular scientific inferences about what must or cannot occur under specified conditions. Yet it itself is the conclusion of an inference. The question that corresponds to Step 1 is: What does this widely held belief in necessary connections rest on? This is ambiguous between: What faculty or faculties of the mind are operative in its formation ("mental geography")? and Is the belief rationally justified, that is, warranted by the evidence, by the premises from which it is inferred (logical analysis)?

Hume identifies two necessary conditions, both based on sense perception and memory, under which A is said to 'cause' or be 'necessarily connected' with B: (a) event A is observed to be *followed* by event B, in other words, the cause precedes its effect in time (temporal sequence); and (b) *all* events similar to B have been observed to be preceded by events similar to A (constant conjunction). That is as far as Hume's official analysis goes. In one place in the *Enquiry* (115), however, he alludes to a third condition: (c) if event A had not occurred, then event B would not have occurred either (necessity of A for the production of B, or necessity of B given A). This seems indeed to be an essential condition of saying that A is a causally necessary and sufficient condition of B. Yet this is precisely what cannot be justified by sense perception, memory, and/or any mode of reasoning, according to Hume. We are thus left with (a) and (b) as the sole but logically inadequate basis of the belief in necessary connection. Why inadequate?

Hume was quite prepared to allow that statements like the following are justified by experience or observation and memory: 'never *as a matter of fact* has there been an observed B not preceded by an observed A or an observed A not followed by an observed B,' since this judgment merely sums up or epitomizes a great many present and past experiences. But 'never *as a matter of physical or natural necessity* can there be a B not preceded by an A or an A not followed by a B' is a different matter. This goes *beyond* what has been observed; it asserts that something *must always* be the case. And this, Hume saw clearly, just does not follow in logic from the observational evidence (a limited number of observations of what has *thus far* always been the case). Naturally, it *would* follow if we had at our disposal a metaphysical Principle of the Uniformity of Nature to guarantee that the same sort of cause *must always* produce the same sort of effect (see 28.3.2). But no a priori insight or rational demonstration can render this causal principle certain. Its denial does not involve contradiction, so it is not self-evident; and from what higher principle could it be validly deduced? It cannot be justified by appeal to past experience ('nature has always been uniform up to now') either. For it is supposed to justify inferences from past observation to all events of the same kind. The appeal to experience would thus be circular, that is, no justification at all.

So much for the second and third steps in the pattern of argument outlined above: having asked what the belief in the existence of necessary connections rests upon, Hume uncovered the sources of knowledge from which it in fact derives, demonstrating by logical analysis that they cannot justify it. The sceptical conclusion is: while we may be justified *for all practical purposes* in believing in strictly universal, exceptionless laws of nature (and while we can hardly help doing so and had better continue doing so if we wish to survive), there is just no adequate *theoretical justification* for the belief in any physical necessity.

The fourth and last step is to provide a psychological explanation of this unwarranted conviction. True to his associationist principles, Hume reassigns to custom or habit what has hitherto been ascribed to human reason. The association of two ideas owing to their regular sequence and constant conjunction gives rise to a new impression, an inner or felt (psychological) necessity of passing in thought from the idea of A, as given in experience, to that of B, not so given (or vice versa). This impression we mistake for a real physical necessity connecting A itself with B, or A-like events and B-like events in the real world. In short, what is merely a subjective feature of inner experience is mistaken for an objective feature of external things. The belief in question stems, not from any real causal connection between events in the world, either observed or validly inferred, but from an inner impression arising from the association of ideas such that on perceiving one event the mind imagines that which customarily precedes, accompanies, or follows upon it with a vividness amounting to belief that it too exists, has existed, or will exist.

29.9 Conclusion

It should be clear by now that the alleged necessity or impossibility of the existence of anything was Hume's special bugbear. As the first prong of his critique of religious philosophy includes an attack on the idea of *logically* necessary existence (God as the being who cannot *not* exist), so his attack on the standard conception of scientific law focuses on that of *physically* necessary existence. The real target, however, is reason itself, or rather the unwarranted claims made on its behalf by philosophers, theologians, and even scientists. Much that was ascribed to reason is reassigned to habit and the imagination or feeling by Hume.

Faced with Hume's sceptical conclusions, Kant was understandably alarmed (see 28.3.1). For, like Hume, he took metaphysics to consist largely of strictly universal and necessary propositions concerning the real existence of things in the sensible and supersensible realms. Regarding the supersensible—God and an immortal soul—he was entirely of Hume's opinion; here apodictic proof or scientific knowledge is simply out of the question. But if no general method could be devised for proving a priori the necessary truth of metaphysical principles concerning the existence and nature of *sensible* things, Kant believed, then the whole metaphysical enterprise would fall into the same well-deserved disrepute into which rash claims to knowledge of the supersensible had long since brought that part of metaphysics concerned with "God, freedom, and immortality." Were this to happen, empirical science, too, would succumb to the Humean scepticism that had discredited the metaphysical first principles on which it rests. These, for Kant, include, but are not restricted to, the causal principle or *crux metaphysicorum* (ibid.).

Given Descartes's pervasive influence, this hankering after apodictically certain demonstration is hardly surprising. Earlier we described metaphysics as forming part of the rational or intellectual basis of human life and yet as possessing a rationality no less different from the mathematical and other formal sciences than from the empirically proceeding natural sciences (see 7.5.2–3). If this was correct, then Kant set his sights too high in demanding a method for *demonstrating* metaphysical principles governing all sensible things. He was similarly mistaken in thinking that apodictically certain foundations were required for the empirical natural sciences. They too have their own kind of rationality.

Hume, for his part, regarded 'bad metaphysics' as aspiring vainly to the condition of mathematics, 'good metaphysics' as capable of achieving that of empirical science. It was Aristotle who said, speaking of the search for a moral basis of human life: "it is the mark of an educated mind to expect that amount of exactness in each kind of discipline which the nature of the particular subject matter admits of." Though simple and obvious, this lesson has proved hard to learn. Otherwise Hume's empiricist critique could never have sparked a defence of reason like that put forward in Kant's *Critique of Pure Reason*. If the future of metaphysics, as the foundation and outer framework of the moral and intellectual basis of human life, depended either on Kant's defence or on the devising of some alternative method of apodictic demonstration of metaphysical truths, the prospects would be bleak indeed. As far as metaphysics is concerned, there is good reason to heed Hume's call to intellectual modesty, even if Hume's own sceptical conclusions go much too far.

30

The Unmaking of Miracles

30.1 Introductory

We turn now to Hume's attack on the alleged rational basis for believing in the truth of the Christian religion, beginning with the essay "Of Miracles." As we do so, it is worth recalling once again the difference between natural and revealed religion (see 29.1).

Roughly speaking, natural theology is based on unassisted human reason, revealed religion on scriptural authority and divine illumination through grace. In this context, 'reason' is understood to comprise *all* the natural faculties of man, including even sensory experience and merely probable inferences. Aristotle called such arguments 'dialectical' (see 9.2.5), and during the Enlightenment many worthy theologians argued for the reasonableness of Christianity by appeal to miracles attested by the human authors of scripture who were witnesses to them. As noted earlier (see 29.1), if the truth of some particular revelation can be reliably established by reasoning, even probable reasoning, then there is a great deal that can be known about God's attributes, purposes, and so on, apart from the little that is allegedly demonstrable by strictly a priori means.

30.2 The structure of Hume's "Of Miracles"

As usual, we begin by setting out the overall structure of the work. Part I of Hume's "Of Miracles" outlines the conditions under which testimonial evidence (the reports of eyewitnesses) would suffice to *prove* the occurrence of a miracle in accordance with the rules of correct reasoning about alleged matters of fact. Part II then shows that the conditions so described have never obtained in the case of any miracle recorded in history, let alone those in the Bible (religious miracles). That, in very

518   Part Four: Hume and the Road Back to Common Life

brief outline, is the argument of the whole essay. We shall confine ourselves to Part I and the conclusion drawn in Part II. The structure of Part I is as follows:

1 Paragraphs 1–2: Adaptation of Tillotson's argument concerning the doctrine of transubstantiation
2 Paragraphs 3–4: The general rule of reasoning or inference from evidence provided by experience
3 Paragraphs 5–14: Application of this rule to the special case of evidence in the form of testimony by witnesses
   a Paragraphs 8–11: Consideration of cases in which the event in question is "extraordinary or marvellous"
   b Paragraphs 12–14: Consideration of the cases in which the event is "miraculous"
4 Paragraph 15: The conditions to be satisfied by testimonial evidence in order to prove the occurrence of a miracle (Conclusion of Part I)

These steps will be followed in order. Although Part II will not be examined (except for Hume's summary and overall conclusion), a brief résumé may be useful for purposes of orientation.

In Part II, Hume cites four considerations that prevent the testimonial evidence for miracles from amounting to anything like a full proof that the miracles reported actually occurred. The focus is upon the greater likelihood, given what we know of the laws of human nature, that some "knavery" (157, 164) on the part of the witnesses and/or excessive "credulity" (157, 162) on the part of the hearers is involved. Thus, as regards the circumstances affecting the reliability of witnesses, Hume points out (1) that there has never yet been a report of a miracle where the reliability of the witnesses was placed utterly beyond all doubt by (a) their level of education and discernment, (b) their honesty or probity, (c) their rank and reputation (such that they stood to lose a great deal by being found out), as well as by (d) corroborating reports of other witnesses.

So much for possible "knavery." As for "credulity," Hume mentions first (2) the "love of wonder," pointing out that the pleasing emotions of wonder and surprise make men eager to believe and repeat stories of certain kinds; this emotion, of course, becomes all the stronger when those stories tend to reinforce agreeable religious feelings. A further point is (3) that most reports of miracles are transmitted by "ignorant and barbarous" peoples in remote times and places rather than among learned and critical people at the present day. Finally, Hume argues (4) that testimony for miracles in favour of the truth of another religion or religious sect must be regarded as testimony *against* the testimonial evidence for the truth of miracles alleged by a given religion or sect. This point bears on religious miracles exclusively, the others on them especially.

Having set out these four telling grounds for suspicion, Hume concludes Part II with a brief summary and an important statement of the conclusion of the whole essay. It will be quoted and interpreted in the next section. We return now to Part I.

30.3 Hume and Tillotson

The expression "real presence" in Hume's opening sentence refers to the Roman Catholic interpretation of the sacrament of the Eucharist as authoritatively decreed by the Council of Trent (1545–1563). The Council belongs to the period of the so-called Catholic Counter-Reformation that emanated from Italy, Spain, and Portugal after Protestantism had taken hold of the north (see 1.3.2). It was a period of bitter reaction against heretics and schismatics. Nothing at all was to be conceded to the criticisms of the reformers; on the contrary, precisely those tendencies within the Roman Church (for example, the veneration of relics, the cult of the saints, the authority of the Pope and clergy) of which the reformers were most sharply critical were defiantly reaffirmed or pushed to new extremes.

According to the interpretation of the Council, the substance of the sacramental bread and wine of the Holy Communion is really, that is, literally, and hence miraculously, transformed into the body and blood of Christ, which are "really present" in the Eucharist, though in the guise of bread and wine. In the words of the Council, the "whole substance of the bread is changed into the substance of the body of Our Lord Christ while the form [i.e., appearance] of the bread remains unaltered." This is the meaning of the word 'transubstantiation' ('one *substance trans*formed into another'), which is virtually synonymous with 'real presence.'

Despite the Council's decree that anyone denying real presence was to be excommunicated (and so condemned to eternal damnation), there was in the early Church, as among the Church Fathers and Christian scholastics, a very considerable body of theological opinion to the effect that, as Christ used the words "This is my body" figuratively at the Last Supper, so Christ's body and blood are not *really or literally* present in the wine and host of the Eucharist at all, but only *symbolically* so. The doctrine of transubstantiation also had a chequered history in Protestant theology after the Reformation. Luther championed it, while the followers of an important sect founded by the Swiss reformer Ulrich Zwingli (1484–1531) denied all versions of it. The Zwinglians maintained that Christ's body was a human body; since a human body cannot be in two places at the same time, Christ's body, being in Heaven at the right hand of God the Father, cannot be really present in the host of the sacrament. This is typical of the whole debate.

30.3.1 Tillotson's argument

The subsequent history of the controversy need not detain us, until we come to John Tillotson (1630–1694), a prominent (first Presbyterian, then Anglican) cleric who

520   Part Four: Hume and the Road Back to Common Life

later became Archbishop of Canterbury. At the end of his long *Discourse against Transubstantiation* (1684), Tillotson marshalled four arguments to show that the doctrine of real presence not only had no basis in scripture and almost none in Christian theology prior to its adoption by the Council, but was "against all the evidence of reason and sense." Of these the third argument seems to have particularly appealed to Hume. It can be formalized in the following way (quotation marks indicate phrases from Tillotson, not Hume):

P1   The "main external evidence" *for* (a) the truth of the Christian religion itself is (b) "the miracles wrought by our Saviour and his apostles."
P2   The evidence for (b) these miracles, in turn, is (c) the observation of eyewitnesses.
C1   Therefore, the "external evidence" *for* the truth of the Christian religion is "resolved into the certainty of sense."

As Tillotson puts it, "if the senses of those who saw them, were deceived, then there might be no miracles wrought; and consequently it may be justly doubted whether that kind of confirmation which God hath given to the Christian religion would be strong enough to prove it." The argument continues:

P3   On the other hand, the "external evidence" *against* the truth of the doctrine of real presence is the report of the senses that the wine of the sacrament is not blood and the bread not flesh.
C2   Thus, the evidence *against* the doctrine of real presence must, in the nature of the case, be just as great as the evidence *for* the Christian religion itself. (In Tillotson's words: "every man hath as great evidence, that transubstantiation is false, as he hath that the Christian religion is true.").

30.3.2 Hume's altered version

Hume took a page out of Tillotson's book, probably not without the mischievous pleasure that a confirmed agnostic and ironist would take in donning the protective mantle of a venerable Archbishop of Canterbury. The argument is reproduced without change down to P3, but before drawing his own altered conclusion Hume weaves in a further premise, not found in Tillotson:

P4   The first-hand testimony of one's own senses is, in the nature of the case, *stronger* than any second-hand testimony (which is in turn stronger than third-hand testimony, and so forth).

From this and the foregoing premises a different conclusion follows:
C3   Even if the doctrine of real presence were clearly attested in scripture (as it is

not), it is impossible that the (*n*-th hand) testimonial evidence *for* that doctrine should even be equal to the (first-hand) evidence *against* it.

If this is a fair summary of Hume's opening paragraph, then he is not wrong in claiming a precedent for the general type of argument he intends to make. For like Tillotson he argues that a certain kind of conclusion cannot be established by evidence of a certain kind. Yet Hume presents Tillotson as arguing that contrary evidence of one kind must *outweigh* supporting evidence of *another kind*; whereas the real Archbishop argued that the one must be *at least as great as* the other, both being of the *same kind*. So Hume reshapes his precedent to fit the more aggressive use of this general pattern of argument that he himself has in mind. This brings us to the question of the *probandum*.

30.3.3 The probandum

Hume's remodelled paradigm prefigures an argument intended to show neither (a) that no miracles can ever have taken place, miracles being impossible; nor yet (b) that no miracle can ever be *proved* to have taken place, it being impossible that the evidence for a miracle should ever amount to proof; nor, finally, (c) that *testimonial* evidence for a miracle can never amount to such a proof. This much is clear from the end of Part II, where Hume states that "[a] there may possibly be miracles ... of such a kind as to [b] admit of proof [c] from human testimony, though, perhaps, it will be impossible to find any such in all the records of history" (163). If the *probandum* is not (a), (b), or (c), then what is it? The answer appears to be (d) "that no human testimony can have such force as to prove a miracle, *and make it a just foundation for any ... system of religion*" (ibid., e.a.), since in the case of all *religious* miracles the evidence to the contrary must, in the nature of the case, outweigh the evidence for the miracle. We shall discuss the difference between miracles and religious miracles later (see 30.8.1).

On the strength of this his official conclusion, Hume presses a further point that is even more alien to Tillotson. It formed no part of the Archbishop's purpose to show that belief in the Christian religion could not be based on "external evidence," but was a matter of *faith*. On the contrary, he is, he says, "well assured [1] of the grounds of religion in general, and [2] of the Christian religion in particular." By (2) Tillotson means "the miracles that were wrought by our Saviour and his apostles, the assurance whereof did depend on the certainty of sense." After all, every rational believer has the same perfectly adequate grounds for rejecting transubstantiation that he has for accepting Christianity: the reliability of the senses.

Hume's inference from his *probandum* is a very far cry from this. For he concludes that Christianity cannot be based on "external," but only on *inner* evidence, on faith as the gift of divine grace or "the operation of the Holy Spirit" (144) upon our minds.

He makes a great show of having to "criticize reason in order to make room for faith," as Kant was later to put it; or, in Locke's words, of urging that matters "beyond the discovery of our natural faculties" are "the proper matter of faith," the truth of Christianity being such a matter:

> I am the better pleased with the method of reasoning here delivered, as I think it may serve to confound those dangerous friends or disguised enemies of the *Christian Religion*, who have undertaken to defend it by the principles of human reason. Our most holy religion is founded on *Faith*, not on reason; and it is a sure method of exposing it to put it to such a trial as it is, by no means, fitted to endure. (165)

It is hard to mistake the irony of this. Where Locke and Kant were sincere believers, Hume pretends to shield Christianity against those merely "pretended Christians" (165)—among whom the Archbishop would have to be counted—who expose it to attack by defending it on grounds of its reasonableness rather than faith. Since he is not trying to fool the intelligent reader, but only to hold would-be persecutors at bay, we are right to speak of irony rather than hypocrisy. In the very last sentence of the essay, Hume goes so far as to suggest that the belief in miracles attested by eyewitness accounts is so profoundly *un*reasonable that only a continuous miraculous intervention of the Holy Spirit can make it possible:

> So that, upon the whole, we may conclude, that the *Christian Religion* not only was at first attended with miracles, but that even at this day cannot be believed by a reasonable person without one. Mere reason is insufficient to convince us of its veracity: And whoever is moved by *Faith* to assent to it, is conscious of a continued miracle in his own person, which subverts all the principles of his understanding [that is, his reason] and gives him a determination to believe what is most contrary to custom and experience. (166)

One can only imagine Hume's sentiments as he wrote this. So it was that the sort of argument originally deployed by Protestant theologians against Roman Catholicism began, in Hume's day, to be used by free-thinkers, sceptics, and atheists to subvert the rational foundation of Christianity itself.

30.4 Hume's canon

We come now to the second step in the argument, Hume's general rule of reasoning or inference from evidence furnished by experience. Earlier we distinguished two types of causal or experiential reasoning from demonstrative reasoning (see 29.6), noting the corresponding degrees of evidence (see 29.7). On that basis, we can understand Hume's rule of experiential reasoning quite readily. It is formulated in various ways, and to begin with we can simply cite them in sequence.

Chapter 30: The Unmaking of Miracles 523

(i) "A wise man ... proportions his belief to the evidence." (144)
(ii) "All probability ... supposes an opposition of experiments and observations, where the one side is found to overbalance the other and, and to produce a degree of evidence, proportioned to the superiority." (145)
(iii) "In all [such] cases, we must balance [or weigh up] the opposite experiments, where they are opposite, and deduct the smaller number from the greater, in order to know the exact force of the superior evidence." (ibid.)
(iv) Where "there is a mutual destruction of arguments [that is, conflicting evidence for and against] ... the superior only gives us an assurance suitable to that degree of force which remains after deducting the inferior." (149)
(v) "The maxim, by which we commonly conduct ourselves in our [experiential] reasonings, is that the objects of which we have no experience resemble those of which we have; that what we have found to be most usual is always most probable; and that where there is an opposition of arguments, we ought to give the preference to such as are founded on the greatest number of past observations." (150)

We can dub this 'the rule of proportioning one's belief to one's evidence' or 'the proportionality principle.' Version (i) applies to both proof and probability, while (ii) through (v) apply to probability alone. This general principle has several corollaries, that is, special rules that follow from it. We can call the principle and its corollaries together 'Hume's canon' of evidence, a canon (with a single 'n') being a set of rules, especially rules of inference, like those employed in formal logic, or rules for the evaluation of inferences. Hume alludes to the subordinate rules of the canon at various places in the essay; they can be explicitly formulated as follows:

Rule 1: No contingent statement (one that could be denied without contradiction, a proposition concerning "matter of fact and existence") should ever be believed true with the maximal degree of conviction except on the basis of a full proof, that is, in the complete absence of any direct or indirect evidence to the contrary.

Rule 2: Whenever there is *even the slightest* evidence to the contrary, such a statement ought to be regarded as only probable and believed only to the precise extent that the evidence for it is greater than the evidence against it.

Rule 3: A statement for the *denial* of which there is a full proof should only be believed *at all* in the event that there is also a full proof *for it* that is even stronger than the proof against it; and it should only be believed to the degree that the full proof for it is superior to that against it.

This last rule will be applied to the case of testimonial evidence for events that are miraculous (see 30.8.2 below), just as the second is applied to the case where the event is only marvellous (see 30.7.2). Of course, how one full proof can be superior to another (as in Rule 3) is not immediately obvious; this will be explained later (see 30.8.2).

30.5 A new ideal of rationality

Three points are worth making about Hume's canon, which is interesting chiefly for the light it sheds on his conception of rationality.

30.5.1 A logic of probability

First, the proportionality principle is primarily a *normative or prescriptive rather than a merely descriptive* rule (see above 10.2.3); it states what men *ought* to do if they want to be rational, not so much what they *in fact* do. Before Hume, no one concerned himself much with the logic of probability or the rationality of probable reasoning. The exception is Leibniz, who repeatedly pointed to the importance of this neglected domain of logic (see Hume's *Abstract of A Treatise of Human Nature*, 30–1). Hume was the first to heed Leibniz's call. Since Hume's time, the mathematical theory of probability has made great strides forward.

Second, Hume's principle, though predominantly normative, *also* describes what men actually do in most, though not in all, circumstances. This is clear from formulation (v) above: "The maxim, by which we commonly conduct ourselves in our [experiential] reasonings." Here Hume is referring to what we do *in fact* ("commonly," though not always). Hence, when men are found to behave otherwise, some explanation is called for. In Part II of "Of Miracles," Hume cites a number of psychological factors to explain, or partially explain, why people abandon the sound practice of proportioning their belief to their evidence as soon as they are confronted with reports of something marvellous or miraculous. Indeed, they often reverse it: the more improbable the story, the stronger some people's propensity to believe it! (Compare the view, attributed to Hitler's propaganda minister, Goebbels, that it is easier to get people to believe a big lie than a small one.)

Third, Hume's canon has a different sphere of application from the more familiar canon of a priori or purely logical (deductive) reasoning. As employed in mathematics, the rules of logical inference *extend* our perfectly certain knowledge of arithmetic, geometry, and algebra through demonstration of new theorems or truths not immediately evident from the definitions, axioms, and postulates of these sciences. Outside the "mathematical sciences," however, logical reasoning can at best *clarify* the meanings of statements by drawing out their logical implications. The importance of deductive procedure for testing scientific theories (see 6.2.3) apparently escaped Hume, for whom the "philosophical sciences" extend our knowledge of matter of fact and existence by experiential reasoning or inductive generalization. In elaborating a canon of such reasoning, Hume understood himself to be extending the method of Newtonian natural science to the sphere of moral science or "the science of human nature." Accordingly, he rather immodestly subtitled his early work, the *Treatise of Human Nature*: "An Attempt to introduce the Experimental Method of Reasoning [in other words, Newton's method] into Moral Subjects," that is, into the study of man and society. His goal, in short, was to become the Newton of moral science (see 29.4).

30.5.2 Rationality

From all this emerges an ideal of rationality different from any encountered thus far. In the tradition stemming from Parmenides and his followers, to which Plato also belongs, to be rational is primarily (1) to exercise one's faculty of non-sensuous intuition, one's *nous*, and to reason consistently from the insights so acquired to further truths, avoiding contradiction and fallacies. Above all, one must not be the dupe of the senses. With Descartes something new was added to this, probably owing to the influence of ancient and modern sceptics. For Descartes, (2) to suspend judgment is another key component of rationality wherever the matter in question is the least bit uncertain, that is, wherever the evidence itself is less than perfectly "clear and distinct," or where it does not "clearly and distinctly" entail some particular conclusion.

Now avoiding contradiction and fallacies is certainly *part* of what 'being rational' means for Hume too—or anybody else, for that matter; so is caution in assenting to matters that are in the least doubtful. But being rational is for Hume above all a matter of (3) *proportioning one's belief to one's evidence*, that is, assenting to or denying a given proposition with precisely the degree of conviction warranted by the arguments and evidence for and against it—neither more nor less—such evidence being, as far as matter of fact and existence are concerned, *at bottom* evidence of the senses.

On closer inspection this actually conflicts with Descartes's 'all or nothing' prescription, which counsels two things: (a) withholding assent altogether wherever there is even the slightest doubt, just as though the matter were plainly understood to be false; and (b) assenting without reserve where anything is perceived clearly and distinctly. Against this, Hume urges *cautious assent*, even to that which is not completely certain, with the degree of caution precisely proportioned to the degree of uncertainty in the case. On the other hand, Hume agrees with Descartes that full and unreserved assent should be given to matters perceived to be true with perfect certainty; yet this kind of certainty, Hume held, is only to be had in propositions asserting "relations of ideas" and in logical inferences. In other words, certainty in *extending* our knowledge is achievable only in mathematics. In all interesting cases of new knowledge about matter of fact and existence, about the real *world*, proof is the most that can be obtained. For the most part, we have to settle for probability.

At bottom, then, Hume's conception of rationality is closest to that of Socrates, who advocated 'following the best argument,' adopting what appears to be the opinion or the course of action with the strongest reasons in its favour, once all the pros and cons have been carefully weighed in the balance. Still, Hume's proportionality principle is different from that laid down in the *Crito*. For once convinced that a certain course of action has the weight of the best reasons behind it, Socrates was ready to adopt it with *complete* confidence, even staking his life on the outcome. Not so Hume, who was diffident to the last—a sceptic, after all.

30.6 Application of Hume's canon to testimonial evidence

We turn now to the third step, Hume's application of his canon to the case of testimonial evidence. The first thing to be cleared up is (A) that any inference from (a) the testimony of witnesses that a certain event has occurred (such testimony being itself a certain kind of event) to (b) the actual occurrence of the event so reported is an instance of a posteriori or experiential rather than a priori or demonstrative reasoning (see 29.6). According to the previous step in the argument, this means (B) that the principle of proportioning one's belief to one's evidence must be applied to all cases of testimonial evidence for the occurrence of unobserved events. Specifically, should the evidence amount to a full proof, we are to believe in the occurrence of the event reported with the last degree of conviction. However, whenever the evidence makes the conclusion only probable, Rule 2 should be applied: the conclusion ought to be believed to the precise extent that the evidence for it is greater than the evidence against it (or for its denial). Finally, should the contrary evidence amount to a full disproof, Rule 3 must be applied: the conclusion should only be believed at all on the basis of a full proof *for it* that is superior to the full proof against it; and it should only be believed to the precise extent that the former proof is superior to the latter.

30.6.1 Assessing testimonial evidence

The first point, (A) that inferences from testimonial evidence are a species of probable or experiential reasoning, is evident from the briefest summary of the conclusions reached in sections IV and VII of the *Enquiry*. There it was shown that knowledge of the actual occurrence of an event that one has not witnessed oneself—a matter "beyond the present testimony of our senses, or the records of our memory" (72)—can only be acquired by a posteriori reasoning. The main points can be briefly recapitulated as follows.

First, all events are *logically unconnected*, there being no strictly logical relationship between events such that one could *deduce* the occurrence of one from that of the other, that is, predict (or retrodict) its occurrence (or its non-occurrence) completely a priori, without experience. The very idea of the strict *logical* necessity or impossibility of any particular event is no less a philosophical muddle, from Hume's perspective, than the alleged necessary existence of God (see 29.2.1). Unfortunately, it is a muddle into which a few philosophers, notably Spinoza, fell through inattention to the difference between physical and logical laws. So while it may seem obvious, the point that "no objects [here: observed events] have any discoverable connexion together" (145) is still worth making, and Hume makes it with his customary concision and elegance.

Second, though logically unconnected, some events are *causally rather than just casually connected* so that we can and do in fact infer one from the other in our *inductive, causal* or a posteriori reasonings. On seeing fire, I expect to find ashes—that is, I infer the existence of the usual effect from that of the cause; on seeing smoke I expect to find fire—that is, I infer the existence of the usual cause from that of its effect; and seeing firelight, I expect to feel warmth on approaching its source, that is, I infer the existence of one effect from that of a collateral effect. If, on the other hand, on seeing a fire in the hearth I wonder about the condition of the chimney, the connection is casual, not causal, a case of the association of ideas (fire and chimney) based on contiguity, not cause and effect.

Third, whenever two events are said to have a causal rather than a casual connection, the inference of the mind from one to the other is based on nothing but a "constant and regular conjunction" (145) of the perception of the one kind of event with the perception of events of the other kind. Such "constant and regular conjunction" is inadequate to justify belief in *physically* necessary connections between events (see 29.8.2), which, in Hume's opinion, is almost as great a muddle as *logically* necessary connections or a logically necessary being.

Applying the findings of these earlier sections to the special case of testimonial evidence (paragraph 5), Hume points out that inferences from the testimony of witnesses to the events they report rest entirely on experience or observation of (a) a more or less "constant and regular conjunction" between eyewitness reports and the events reported, that is, between these two *kinds* of events. He declines to enter into a verbal dispute about whether the relation is one of "cause and effect" or not, so long as it be granted that it is a species of a posteriori or experiential reasoning.

This "constant and regular conjunction" constitutes *direct* evidence for the reliability of such inferences. To some extent, they are also based on observation and experience of (b) human nature in general, that is, of man's cognitive, emotional and moral qualities—for example, the reliability of human memory up to a certain point (cognitive), man's natural inclination to tell the truth rather than lie for no reason (moral), their fear of the shame of being caught in a lie (emotional), and so forth. This constitutes *indirect* evidence for the reliability of testimony. These are the main sorts of evidence we have for our conclusions about the occurrence of events not observed, but reported by eyewitnesses.

30.6.2 Rules for assessing testimonial evidence

Granted, then, (A) that inferences from testimonial evidence are a posteriori or inductive reasonings based on direct and indirect evidence acquired through experience, *not* on a priori reasonings or straight *logical* deductions, it follows (B) that in assessing eyewitness reports Hume's canon is to be applied (see paragraph 6). Specifically, we ought to apply Rule 2, weighing up the probabilities where we have to do with a *probable* argument, and we ought to apply either Rule 1 or Rule 3 wherever the evidence amounts to a full *proof*.

The question that immediately arises is: How is one to decide whether testimonial evidence amounts to a full proof or only to a probability? To explain this, Hume discusses (paragraph 7) various factors affecting the reliability of human testimony in favour of the occurrence of a particular event. To distinguish them from the direct and indirect evidence described above, we can refer to this as *ad hoc* evidence (see 6.2.3). We can simply list the factors in question without elaborate commentary, supplementing the account given in this paragraph with a few relevant considerations mentioned elsewhere in the essay:

1. the tenacity of the witness(es)' memory;
2. a disposition to truthfulness or untruthfulness (honesty or dishonesty) in the witness(es);
3. their fear of shame or punishment for being caught lying;
4. the availability of other witnesses, and whether they give contrary or corroborating testimony;
5. the witness(es)' level of education and good sense;
6. the extent to which the witness(es) stand to profit in some way, materially or otherwise, from the story's being believed;
7. the witness(es)' manner of giving their testimony (too much or too little confidence).

Only if these and like circumstances are uniformly in favour of the testimony can it amount to a proof. "A wise man," after all, "expects the event with the last degree of assurance" only when all "past experience," direct and indirect, amounts to "a full *proof*"(144).

30.7 Application of Hume's canon to testimonial evidence for marvels

Thus far we have considered only (a) factors tending to corroborate or discredit *testimony* for or against the occurrence of a certain event. Yet it is a commonplace that (b) events are *intrinsically* more or less likely to have occurred according as we have past or present experience of (i) events of the same kind or (ii) events of a similar kind. In other words, an event may be *inherently* more or less probable. That too is relevant to the rational assessment of testimonial evidence concerning it. So in

Chapter 30: The Unmaking of Miracles 529

deciding whether to follow Rule 1, reposing "the last degree of assurance" in some testimony, or whether to apply Rule 2 or Rule 3 instead, we must weigh a second and separate set of factors.

30.7.1 Intrinsic probability

Consider the implications of the following situations for the occurrence or non-occurrence of certain events, quite apart from any relevant testimonial evidence.

In case A, I have no experience of events of the *same* kind and no experience of events of a *similar* kind whatever. In other words, I have no evidence one way or the other on the basis of which to assess the intrinsic likelihood or improbability of the event reported. For example, I read a newspaper report that multiple births are increasing. This may well be true, as far as I can tell, but I have no reason to regard the trend reported as probable or improbable.

In case B, I have no experience of events of the *same* kind, but some experience of events of a *similar* kind. This constitutes weak evidence for or against the report, depending on how much of the experience confirms or disconfirms the report. An example might be a report claiming that a man in his nineties has fathered a child. Cases of men in their seventies or eighties fathering children are on record, but there is no record of anything of the kind for men in their nineties.

In hypothetical case C, we have some limited experience of events of the *same* kind. For example, suppose I read a report that a man in his eighties has fathered a child, and I recall similar cases I have heard of.

Finally, in case D, there is a vast amount of experience of events of the same kind, all of it perfectly uniform. In other words, there is a full proof for or against the alleged event. Suppose, for example, that I read a report of a so-called virgin birth. I naturally disbelieve it, there being no case in recorded history (as opposed to religious tradition) of such a thing's having ever occurred.

30.7.2 Marvellous, unusual, or extraordinary events

The sum of the foregoing can be put this way. A first set of experiential factors makes it seem on the whole probable that a particular eyewitness report is true. This includes direct, indirect, and *ad hoc* considerations. However, the cases considered above show that a second set of experiential factors may make it appear inherently likely or unlikely that an event of that sort actually occurred.

Beginning in paragraph 8, Hume considers one specific type of event like those described above: events that are marvellous rather than miraculous, that is, very unusual, without being physically impossible (according to the known laws of nature). Thus, that a woman should give birth to septuplets is marvellous (extremely unusual, though not unprecedented, and certainly not physically impossible according to the known laws of cell fission in biology); while that a woman should give birth to even one child without (natural or artificial) insemination is miraculous (contrary to the known laws of biology). Hume's point is that in such a case, the inherent unlikelihood of the event itself makes it necessary that there be "pretty strong testimony to render it credible" (147) in the eyes of any reasonable judge.

Hume's own example (paragraphs 10–11) is an Indian prince who is informed by European visitors that rivers in Europe freeze over in winter. (Hume may have found this example in Leibniz, who also mentions it.) The prince was right to be incredulous and to require very strong evidence that the witnesses were reliable before believing them. For he himself (a) had *no experience whatever of the same kind of event* (the effect of a *European* winter on water) and (b) the report *contradicted* the experiences he had had of similar kinds of events. For, we may assume, the same *kind* of cause, cooling in the winter months, had frequently been observed to produce cold but *not* hardness in water; that at a certain point it should begin to produce an effect which it had not produced up to that point is directly contrary to what one would reasonably expect, reasoning from experience like that available to the Indian prince. So taking (a) and (b) into account, the prince was right to be very sceptical at first and only to give credence to what he had been told after having convinced himself of the complete reliability of the witnesses.

30.8 Application of Hume's canon to testimonial evidence for miracles

In paragraph 12 Hume begins consideration of events, not merely marvellous or extraordinary, but *miraculous*. The case of *marvellous* events gave him occasion to apply Rule 2 above: the report ought to be believed to the precise extent that the evidence for it is greater than the evidence against it. Such was the rule wisely followed by the Indian prince. In the case of *miraculous* events, where the contrary evidence amounts to a full disproof, Rule 3 must be followed: the report should only be believed at all on the basis of a full proof *for it* that is superior to the full proof against it; and it should only be believed to the degree that the former proof is superior to the latter. That there is in fact always a full proof against the occurrence of a reported miracle is just a consequence of the way Hume defines 'miracle.'

30.8.1 Hume's definition of a miracle

In colloquial English, the word 'miracle' is used loosely for any event that is both (i) very unusual and (ii) very fortunate. Thus, an unexpected recovery from an illness or a very narrow escape from almost certain injury or death may be referred to as a 'miracle,' whether or not the speaker actually believes it to be (iii) contrary to the known laws of nature (of physics or biology, for example), or (iv) owing to the intervention of some supernatural power. Sometimes, no doubt, (iv) may at the back

Chapter 30: The Unmaking of Miracles

of the speaker's mind, even when not asserted; but in ordinary usage, (i) and (ii) are enough for talk of 'a miracle.' This can be called the 'vulgar' use.

In certain philosophical contexts (i) unusualness figures as a necessary, though not a sufficient, condition of miraculousness. Thus, for the English philosopher-theologian and disciple of Newton, Samuel Clarke, everything miraculous is unusual, but not everything unusual (eclipses, monstrous births, certain forms of madness in men) is miraculous. For Leibniz and Hume, (i) unusualness is not even a necessary condition of miraculousness. As for (ii), this is generally regarded as irrelevant by philosophers and theologians. After all, a sudden *mis*fortune, like the one that befell the Pharaoh and his troops pursuing the Israelites, might be just as miraculous as the escape from one; and so might an event that is neither fortunate nor unfortunate—always assuming that conditions (iii) and/or (iv) are met.

Both points are borne out by Leibniz's correspondence with Clarke. Leibniz objected that Newton's force of universal attraction among bodies was (as he put it) "a perpetual miracle." It would be hard to imagine anything less (i) unusual or more neutral in regard to (ii) the fortunes of men than the phenomenon of universal gravitation. What lies behind Leibniz's charge is condition (iii) alone, or rather (iii) understood as entailing (iv). For while Newton had toyed with the idea, he remained unwilling to endorse any strictly mechanical explanation of the law of universal gravitation. For him, it was enough to have established on the basis of observation that bodies do gravitate or accelerate (that is, change speed, direction, or both) toward one another, and to have described their gravitation mathematically, as a function of their respective masses and the distances separating them. What hidden or unobservable mechanical *causes* produce this effect Newton regarded as a speculative matter unbecoming of the natural philosopher. That was the point of his famous dictum *hypotheses non fingo*, mentioned earlier (see 6.2.2-3). Yet for Leibniz, *natural* causes were by definition mechanical. Since nothing happens without a reason or cause—this being Leibniz's famous Principle of Sufficient Reason, more familiar to us as Descartes's causal adequacy principle in its first formulation (see 26.4.4) and as the "impious maxim" pilloried by Hume (see 28.3.2)—if no cause is assigned, or if the cause assigned is not mechanical, the effect must be supernatural, miraculously produced by the action of some higher power.

Hume, for his own part, gives the word 'miracle' a technical sense remote from the vulgar one and different in a key respect from Leibniz's. Initially, he provides only a very rough definition in terms of (iii) alone: (1) "A miracle is a violation of the laws of nature" (148). Later, however, he refines the definition as follows: (2) "A miracle may be accurately defined, *a transgression of a law of nature by a particular volition of the Deity, or by the interposition of some invisible agent*" (149). The difference is not just one of accuracy; (1) is Hume's definition of 'miracle' in general, while (2) defines a 'religious miracle' in particular, that is, one alleged to attest the truth of some particular revelation. Thus, (iv) is not an automatic consequence of (iii), as in

Leibniz, but the distinguishing feature of that particular type of miracle that Hume has set out to discredit.

Note that 'violation' or 'transgression' of a particular law of nature is a genuine rather than merely apparent exception. Any exception not simply owing to a mistaken description of the event in question or to inexactly formulated laws of nature satisfies Hume's first definition of a miracle, whether or not supernatural agency is involved. Note too that there need be nothing at all out of the ordinary about the effect produced; what makes it miraculous is rather *the manner of its production*, which is a violation of a *known* law of nature. Thus, while there is nothing at all extraordinary about a woman's becoming pregnant, for her to do so without some form of insemination would be miraculous in Hume's first sense, given the known laws of biology.

All this is borne out by Hume's remark that a perfectly ordinary natural or mechanical cause like an air current moving a feather, of which no one takes the slightest notice, can still be miraculous in sense (1), provided it is inadequate to produce its effect. Hume is probably thinking of Tillotson's definition here: "there are two things necessary to a miracle—that there be a supernatural effect wrought, and that this effect be evident to sense." From Hume's perspective, *neither* of these is necessary for a miracle in the first sense:

A miracle may either be discoverable by men or not. This alters not its nature and essence. The raising of a ship into the air is a visible miracle. The [very ordinary] raising of a feather, when the wind wants ever so little of a force requisite for that purpose, is as real a miracle [in itself], though not so sensible with regard to us. (149)

As for religious miracles, however, both conditions apply. They must not only be "discoverable" but actually "discovered" or witnessed if they are to be employed as "external evidence" of the truth of some particular religion. Of course, Tillotson is *only* concerned with religious miracles; and if we take Hume at his word, these are the only miracles that he wishes to deny, employing an argument derived from Tillotson. Hence two separate definitions are called for.

30.8.2 Miraculous events

Now for the main point of Part I. Suppose an event is correctly describable as a violation of a known law of nature. It is then, in the nature of the case, necessary that there be experiential evidence amounting to a *full proof* that the event did not occur; otherwise events of that kind would not be miracles at all. In order for a reasonable man to assent to testimony that such an event had occurred, therefore, such testimony would have to amount to a full proof that is even stronger. In Hume's own words:

There must, therefore, be a uniform experience against every miraculous event, otherwise the event would not merit that appellation [would not correctly be called 'a miracle']. And as a uniform experience amounts to a proof [since that is what 'proof' means], there is here a direct and full *proof*, from the nature of the fact, against the existence of any miracle; nor can such a proof be destroyed, or the miracle rendered credible, but by an opposite proof, which is superior. (148)

Note Hume's insistence that testimonial evidence for a miracle *can* amount to a full proof, even one that is "superior" to the contrary evidence. This was almost certainly intended to spike the guns of pious critics who might charge him with having denied either the possibility of miracles or that they can be proved on the basis of testimonial evidence. These are things he concedes, even with a certain fanfare.

Note too the echoes of Tillotson here, with proof set over against proof much as the testimony of the senses was opposed to the testimony of the senses by the Archbishop. The question of a standoff versus inevitable superiority on one side is rather murky. It is difficult to see what "superiority" might mean here if not that it would violate a greater number of laws of nature, especially *human* nature, for the testimony to be false than for the report of a miraculous event to be true. Granted that such a thing is logically possible (conceivable without contradiction), one is left to consider for oneself the circumstances in which it might be an even *greater miracle* for the testimony to be false than for the report of a miracle to be true. This much, however, is clear: in *any other* circumstances, the "superiority" must be on the other side, that is, *against* the miracle. The closing words of Part I leave little room for doubt on this score:

[N]o testimony is sufficient to establish a miracle, unless the testimony be of such a kind that its falsehood would be more miraculous than the fact which it endeavours to establish; and even in that case there is a mutual destruction of arguments, and the superior only gives us an assurance suitable to that degree of force which remains after deducting the inferior. When anyone tells me, that he saw a dead man restored to life, I immediately consider with myself whether it be more probable, that this person should either deceive or be deceived, or that the fact, which he relates, should really have happened. I weigh the one miracle against the other; and according to the superiority, which I discover, I pronounce my decision, and always reject the greater miracle. If the falsehood of his testimony would be more miraculous, than the event which he relates; then, and not until then, can he pretend to command my belief and opinion. (149)

The irony of the reference to weighing miracle against miracle is typical of Hume. It is easy enough to proclaim one's readiness to admit something when one has already demonstrated the impossibility of ever being called upon to do so.

30.9 Conclusion

Throughout Part I Hume writes as though he considered it more than an empty logical possibility that testimonial evidence might be good enough to establish a miracle. In Part II, however, he reflects that this may have been "a great deal too liberal" (150), going on to show (1) that the evidence for a miraculous event has never, in any known case, amounted to full proof, and (2) that testimonial evidence for *religious* miracles in particular must inevitably be considerably less than that for other miraculous events.

This certainly comes up well short of asserting either (a) that miracles are impossible or even (b) that it could not be reasonable to believe in the occurrence of one. As for (a), Hume would be the last one to assert any matter of fact to be either necessary or impossible (see 29.9). Regarding (b), we may suppose that in the event that one actually witnessed a miracle in circumstances where it would be unreasonable to suspect illusion or deceit, even Hume would allow (though he does not say) that it would be more reasonable to believe in a violation of the known laws of nature than to disbelieve one's senses. Even the possibility of (c) a full proof of a miracle on the basis of testimonial evidence is explicitly allowed, though the concession does not amount to much in the light of (1) and (2), not to mention the fact that the evidence to the contrary (a full proof) must still be deducted from this full proof, leaving nothing at all in the case of a religious miracle, and precious little otherwise. Here is the conclusion of the whole essay as Hume formulates it at the end of Part II:

Upon the whole, then, it appears that no testimony *for any kind of miracle* [even non-religious ones] has ever amounted to a probability, much less to a proof; and that, even supposing it amounted to a proof, it would be opposed by another proof, derived from the very nature of the fact, which it would endeavour to establish. It is experience only, which gives authority to human testimony; and it is the same experience which assures us of the laws of nature. When, therefore, these two kinds of experience are contrary, we have nothing to do but subtract the one from the other, and embrace an opinion, either on one side or the other, with that assurance which arises from the remainder. But according to the principle here explained, this subtraction, with regard to all popular religions [that is, religious miracles], amounts to an entire annihilation; and therefore we may establish it as a maxim, that no human testimony can have such force as to prove a miracle, and make it a just foundation for any such system of religion. (163)

Note the care Hume takes to bring the full weight of the essay to bear on *religious* miracles in particular:

I beg that the limitation here made may be remarked, when I say, that a miracle can never be proved so as to be the foundation of a system of religion. For I own, that otherwise, there may possibly be miracles, or violations of the usual course of nature, of such a kind as to admit of proof from human testimony, though, perhaps it will be impossible to find any such in all the records of history. (ibid.)

One might think Hume's real intentions too transparent to take in any but the simple-minded. In allowing the possibility of miracles proved on the basis of testimony he makes concessions that he knows to be quite empty, hoping to deal religious miracles, at least, a killing blow—which, it seems, he does. Sincere Christian apologists, though probably somewhat puzzled by his irony, were in little doubt about the real thrust of Hume's essay. They were quick to respond with indignant refutations. One wonders about the reasons for so much artifice on Hume's part. The question will come up again in the next chapter.

31

The Undoing of Divine Justice

31.1 Introductory

As noted earlier (see 29.2), Hume's attack on the rational bases of religion is twin-pronged. Directed against (1) natural religion in general, it also targets (2) rational arguments in favour of the truth of the Christian religion. The second prong is again double. Having dealt with (a) a posteriori arguments from historical (testimonial) evidence for miracles in the last chapter, we turn now to (b) a posteriori arguments from the signs of wisdom and goodness in the universe to the existence of an all-wise and all-good creator God (such as Christianity posits) who will mete out justice (rewards or punishment) in the afterlife. The philosophical term for proofs of divine justice is 'theodicy' (from *theos*, 'God,' and *dikē*, 'justice').

The title of the second essay to be studied (section XI of Hume's First *Enquiry*, actually a dialogue rather than essay) is an allusion to (b). In a theological context, the word 'providence' means 'divine foresight'; a 'particular providence,' accordingly, is a special plan for perfect distributive justice instituted by the deity. Perfect distributive justice amounts to an exact allocation of rewards and punishments in accordance with men's deserts. According to an influential argument advanced by the "religious philosophers" (169), since perfect justice is not realized in this life, where the righteous often suffer and the wicked prosper, there must be another life yet to come where it will be realized after all. The talk of 'a future state' alludes to the afterlife; it has nothing at all to do with the state as a political entity.

Although Hume's title has an odd ring to it, similar expressions for related ideas are found in other contemporary authors and even in earlier sources. In the *Essay concerning Human Understanding*, Hume's great empiricist predecessor, Locke, had used the expression "a future state" exactly as Hume uses it here. Acknowledging that there is nothing in the *Essay* about the evidence for immortality, Locke writes that he has "forborne to mention any thing of the certainty, or probability of a future state." And Leibniz, writing around the turn of the eighteenth century, considers the effects of the belief in God and the afterlife on moral conduct in terms very similar to Hume's (translating from the French): "believing themselves to be relieved of the inhibiting fear of an overseeing Providence and of a threatening future, they give their brutish passions free rein," and so on. The parallel is interesting, for not only is Hume's wording similar to Leibniz's, so is the context in which he situates his argument: religious belief as an inducement to morality. On this subject, it is worth looking again at the epigraph to the previous part, from which it is plain that Descartes is entirely of Leibniz's opinion on this subject.

31.2 Four themes

There are four themes in Hume's dialogue, united by this common thread: all have to do with a posteriori reasonings of one sort or another (Hume's signature motif!).

The first concerns (1) the a posteriori argument from (i) the evidence of design in the fabric of the universe to (ii) the existence of a divine artificer—that bare theism (or deism) that Hume dubs "the religious hypothesis" (173). Since it forms part of the first prong, Hume only touches on it here, leaving the fuller elaboration of his doubts for his (posthumously published) *Dialogues concerning Natural Religion*. The conclusion reached there might be put this way. The inference from (i) the signs of order and design in the universe to (ii) the existence of an all-wise and all-powerful creator God is not unreasonable, though it is *uncertain*; the "religious hypothesis" is *at best just as probable* as atheistic 'materialism'—the belief that the world as we know it came about by the blind or chance operation of material, unintelligent causes—but it is no *more* probable than the latter.

The centrepiece of the dialogue, however, is (2) the a posteriori argument from (ii) God's existence to (iii) divine or perfect justice in the afterlife—"a particular providence and a future state." Even if the inference from (i) design to (ii) God's existence were itself rationally justified, Hume argues, the *further inference* from (ii) God's existence to (iii) divine justice is not. While the Argument from Design is treated as *uncertain*, Hume devotes his energies principally to showing that the further inference to divine justice commits a pretty gross *fallacy*. Of course, to show that an argument is fallacious is not to show that its conclusion is *false*. It may be perfectly true. The point is that it *does not follow* from the premises alleged to establish its truth. The main point is the fallacy behind, not the falsity of, (iii), which may, for all Hume professes to know, be true.

In the third place, the dialogue examines (3) the a posteriori argument that belief in (ii) God's existence and (iii) his justice provides (iv) the only effective inducement to leading a moral life—the Leibnizian theme mentioned above. Here Hume examines the logical consequences of religious belief for public and private morality in order to determine whether religion provides any (let alone the only adequate) answer to the question, 'Why be moral?' To understand Hume's argument here, we must bear in mind the distinction between belief in (ii) God's *existence* (theism) and belief in (iii) divine *justice*. Hume is perfectly willing to concede that (iii) provides the faithful with (iv) the strongest practical inducement to lead a moral life. After all, it would be very imprudent to behave immorally if an omnipotent and omniscient God were going to mete out eternal punishment for such actions in the next life; rational self-interest would dictate the choice of a moral way of life. Hume's point, however, is that (iii) *does not follow* from (ii) as supported by (i), the signs of intelligent and benevolent contrivance in the universe; so whatever the practical consequences of (iii) for public or private morality, the mere belief in (ii) cannot *legitimately* be supposed to have those consequences as well, since (ii) does not entail (iii). Conversely, the denial of (ii) by atheists cannot deprive anyone but a bad reasoner of an inducement to morality. In point of fact, those who accept *and* those who reject (ii) have *exactly the same inducements to lead a moral life, so long as they reason correctly*. So a perfectly rational theism and a perfectly rational atheism have exactly the same *practical* consequences: none whatsoever.

Finally, some attention is paid to a fourth theme that is closely related to the third: the argument that the state has a legitimate interest in curbing philosophical speculation that might undermine the belief in God. The issue, then, is (4) toleration and censorship, and the question discussed is whether it is necessary to curb philosophical speculation about "the origin and government of worlds" (169), censoring "philosophical disputes concerning metaphysics and religion" (179) in the interests of political stability and public morality. The answer follows immediately from the treatment of the previous theme. For the conclusion there was: theists *if they are rational*, not *jumping* to unwarranted conclusions about divine justice (theodicy) from the evidence for divine existence (theism), have no more reason to be moral than atheists. Or, to put it the other way round: atheists have no less reason to be moral and to adhere to the rules of public morality than rational theists. On this basis Hume urges that the state can and should let philosophers argue about religious matters as much as they like. In this connection, it is worth translating the Latin motto from the Roman poet Tacitus that Hume selected for his major work, *A Treatise of Human Nature*: "Rare the happiness of times when to think what you like and to say what you think is permitted."

In arguing that belief in God's existence is not only *uncertain* in itself (as an item of speculative or theoretical philosophy), but also *useless* (devoid of *validly derived* consequences for practical philosophy), Hume disregards the very material circumstance that human beings (alas?) are *not* perfectly rational; that even those who base their belief in God on the Argument from Design eagerly believe in providence and a future state despite the fact that their theism does not entitle them to do so; and that *this fallacy of theirs may in fact be beneficial to public and private morality*.

Chapter 31: The Undoing of Divine Justice 539

Only in the third-from-last paragraph does Hume actually confront this (for him) rather awkward fact. Even there, however, he does not try to weaken the force of the objection but, instead, makes an unrelated argument in favour of toleration or freedom of thought, the last theme of the dialogue.

31.3 The structure of the dialogue

Broadly speaking, then, the dialogue concerns itself with the theoretical and practical consequences of a theism based on the Argument from Design. *Theoretically*, the point is that the empirical considerations which render a belief in God's existence reasonable though not certain (theme 1), do not suffice to justify belief in divine justice (theme 2). *Practically*, this means that "the religious hypothesis" has no consequences for public or private morality (theme 3), whence no restrictions can legitimately be placed on the liberty of philosophical thought and expression in the interest of law and order (theme 4).

The structure of the dialogue is as follows:

1 Paragraphs 1–7: Opening Discussion
2 Paragraphs 8–22: Epicurus's Defence of Toleration
3 Paragraphs 23–26: Objection and Reply
4 Paragraph 27: Further Psychological Explanation of the Fallacy Uncovered in 2
5 Paragraphs 28–29: Query of the General Conclusion of 2
6 Paragraph 30: Concluding Criticism of the Argument from Design

We shall confine ourselves to the speech of Epicurus (with a brief allusion to stage 4). This portion of the dialogue constitutes a defence of the philosophic life such as we have already encountered in the *Apology* and the *Phaedo*. It also sheds some fresh and interesting light on the question of the relation between philosophy and religion or theology, a central theme in every part of this work so far.

31.4 The opening discussion

In the opening discussion, Hume accuses his imaginary friend of denying

> that a wise magistrate can justly be jealous of certain tenets of philosophy, such as those of Epicurus, which, denying a divine existence, and consequently a providence and a future state, seem to loosen in great measure, the ties of morality, and may be supposed, for that reason, pernicious to the peace of civil society. (168)

This one sentence introduces all the themes of the dialogue. In order to refute the charge, Hume's friend adopts the *persona* of Epicurus, whom he imagines to be defending himself before the Athenian populace, much as Socrates once defended himself before his fellow citizens on similar charges. Plato's *Apology* is probably not far from Hume's mind here; he even mentions Socrates in the second paragraph. It may not be far-fetched, therefore, to suggest that we are dealing here with a third and very different defence of philosophy from those studied earlier.

Notice too the effect of the setting: Hume obviates the need for irony by cautiously putting all arguments to the effect that "the religious hypothesis" is theoretically weak and practically sterile in the mouth of "a friend who loves sceptical paradoxes" (167). The unnamed friend, in turn, speaks, not in his own person, but wearing the mask of the ancient materialist philosopher Epicurus. Thus, Hume places himself at two removes from the opinions being expressed. That he should have thought it wise to do so suggests that the persecution of philosophy—one of the themes of the dialogue—was still very much a live issue in Hume's day. This may go some way toward explaining Hume's use of artifice in "Of Miracles." To quote Tacitus again: "Rare the happiness of times when ... to say what you think is permitted." Hume was not about to take chances.

The third paragraph articulates (and the ninth takes up again) a threefold distinction between (a) religion as established on tradition and authority (for example, the "traditional belief" or "established superstition" of the state religion of the Greeks); (b) philosophical speculation based on reason alone; and (c) philosophical religion, that is, the attempt by "religious philosophers" to establish the conclusions of traditional religion "upon the principles of reason" (169). Hume's friend argues that (a) and (b) are never at odds; (b) is the choice of "the learned and the wise" (168), (a) of the "vulgar and illiterate" (ibid.). Only when (b) gives rise to (c), philosophical religion, do the religious authorities begin to persecute these philosophers. This we might describe as Hume's 'natural history' of the conflict between philosophy and theology.

31.5 Epicurus's defence of philosophy

With the main themes introduced and his brief natural history in place, Epicurus's defence of philosophy can begin.

31.5.1 The causal argument for divine existence

The starting point is the alleged rational basis of theism. Hume takes it for granted that the only rational argument for God's existence worthy of serious consideration is the Argument from Design. This he rightly identifies as a type of experiential or *causal argument*, an argument *from effect* (the apparent order, beauty, and purposiveness in the universe) *to cause* (the existence of an intelligent, benevolent divine Purposer). Once the rational basis of religion (belief in God's existence) is laid

Chapter 31: The Undoing of Divine Justice 541

bare, Hume can go on to consider whether or not the same argument provides rational grounds for providence and a future state (belief in a perfect divine justice) as well. That, as we have seen, is his main business.

Establishing divine justice was taken by some to be the *main* use of the Argument from Design. One has only to recall Gassendi (see 29.2.1), who described the Argument from Design as "the principal argument for establishing by the natural light [of reason] the *wisdom, providence and power of God*, and indeed his existence" (e.a.). Here existence is almost an afterthought, the main thing being providence—Hume's target. Gassendi, incidentally, was a materialist and a follower of the ancient atomists Leucippus, Democritus, and Epicurus (among the Greeks), and of their Roman disciple, the philosopher-poet Lucretius. In his objections to Descartes's *Meditations*, he sketches the Argument from Design in the following terms:

Leaving aside the entire world, the heavens and its other main parts, how or where will you be able to get any better evidence for the existence *of such a God* than from the function of the various parts in plants, animals, man, and yourself (or your body) ... We know that certain great thinkers have been led by a study of anatomy not just to achieve a knowledge of God but also to sing thankful hymns to him for having organized all the parts and harmonized their functions in such a way as to deserve the highest praise *for his care and providence*. (e.a.)

This sets the main thrust of the argument in a clear light: from the intricately contrived structure of organisms an intelligent and benevolent creator is inferred, the only alternative explanation being the blind operation of unintelligent causal factors like atoms colliding randomly in a void. What might Gassendi have thought of Darwin's principles of random variation and natural selection?

Of course, this version of the Argument from Design deliberately leaves out of account the wondrous beauty and order of "the heavens"—as Gassendi himself notes in the first sentence. This version of the argument, based on planetary astronomy, is not affected by objections based on evolutionary theory. A breathtakingly brief example is found in Newton's *Principia*: "it is not to be conceived that mere mechanical causes could give birth to so many regular motions ... This most beautiful system of the sun, planets, and comets could only proceed from the counsel and dominion of an intelligent and powerful Being" (General Scholium). Or again: "Blind metaphysical necessity, which is certainly the same always and everywhere, could produce no such variety of things. All the diversity of natural things which we find suited to different times and places could arise from nothing but the ideas and will of a Being necessarily existing" (ibid.).

Both versions of the Argument from Design would have been familiar to Hume. And both are apparently intended by the words with which Hume's Epicurus launches into his "harangue":

You, then, who are my accusers, have acknowledged that the chief or sole argument for a divine existence (which I never questioned) is derived from the order of nature; where there appear such marks of intelligence and design that you think it extravagant to assign for its cause, either chance, or the blind and unguided force of matter. You allow, that this is an argument drawn from effects to causes. From the order of the work, you infer, that there must have been a project and forethought in the workman. If you cannot make out this point, you allow, that your conclusion [namely, that God exists] fails. (170)

Hume's task is quite simply is to show that the basis of this particular argument for divine existence, even were it sufficient to establish that there is a God, is still inadequate for the further inference to a perfect divine justice in the afterlife.

31.5.2 Epicurean naturalism

Around 306 BC Epicurus founded a philosophy school at Athens not unlike Plato's Academy, Aristotle's Lyceum, and Zeno's Stoa (see 2.1). To call someone an 'Epicurean' nowadays is to imply that he is a *bon vivant*, a gourmet, a sensualist, one who attaches great importance to sensual enjoyment, particularly food and drink. Epicurus in fact taught the opposite: a life of frugality, simplicity, and respect for others as a means of avoiding pain and achieving the greatest and most enduring of pleasures: friendship and serenity or tranquillity of mind. Still, Epicurus was a hedonist in the technical philosophical sense, pleasure being for him the only intrinsic good (see 12.9.1); so the colloquial use of 'Epicurean' contains at least a grain of historical truth.

Relevant to Hume's essay is not so much Epicurus's ethics as the (1) philosophy of nature and (2) theology that he derived from his overriding practical concern with achieving a truly good or happy life. Together, (1) and (2) exemplify a philosophical outlook that can be described as 'naturalism.' The term implies, on the face of it, rejection of any appeal to the *super*natural, that is, adoption of the rule that everything that can be explained at all must be explained in terms of *natural* (as opposed to supernatural) causes.

The central tenet of Epicurus's (1) philosophy of nature is that everything is composed of material atoms. This includes all living bodies as well as human and animal souls. The human soul is immortal only in the sense that its material atoms, like all atoms, are indestructible. Hence, we speak of *materialistic* atomism of a reductive sort (see 27.9.1). The ordered universe came to be through chance collisions of atoms in a void. The atoms themselves, however, are eternal, that is, ungenerable as well as indestructible. It is at this level that Epicurus, following Leucippus and Democritus, located something possessing certain of those Parmenidean properties of true being that Plato ascribed only to the Forms (see 20.4.2).

As for his (2) theology, Epicurus had no intention of "denying divine existence," as Hume misleadingly states. Socrates took for granted the *moral* superiority of the gods; Epicurus went a step further, regarding divinities as truly blessed beings, utterly indifferent to, and hence in no way involved in, human affairs or the course of events in this world. So blissfully happy are they, lacking and hence desiring nothing, that they can have no interest in distributing reward and punishment to men for their actions. Only natural causes operate within the physical world and in the sphere of human agency; the gods do not intervene either miraculously or in the ordinary course of events. As men come to understand these truths, Epicurus believed, they overcome their fear of the supernatural, death, and punishment after death. This is the key to the attainment of genuine happiness in this life.

If we are justified in calling this outlook 'naturalism' or 'naturalistic' in order to highlight the denial of the operation of *super*natural causes, Hume too must be considered a naturalist, though, as we shall see, of a rather different sort. For one thing, he is no materialist or atomist. For another, he probably would have denied, not just the influence, but the very existence, of the supernatural. But that, as already noted, is controversial.

31.5.3 Hume's Razor

As in the essay "Of Miracles," the crucial step in the speech of Epicurus is the laying down of a rule of correct causal reasoning. In "Of Miracles" it was the rule of proportioning one's belief to one's evidence (Hume's canon); here it is the rule of proportioning the cause to the effect, or proportioning the inferred cause to the effect from which it is inferred. In Hume's words: "The cause must be proportioned to the effect" (171). In view of one of its corollaries, to be discussed in a moment, this further proportionality principle can be called 'Hume's Razor.' It is not to be confused with the famous metaphysical razor of Ockham (roughly: "do not multiply entities beyond necessity") encountered earlier (see 21.3.2).

The proportionality principle has both a positive and a negative corollary. The former can be put this way: "If the cause, assigned for any effect, be not sufficient to produce it, we must either reject that cause, or add to it such qualities as will give it a just proportion to the effect" (170). Despite a superficial resemblance, this must not be confused with the causal adequacy principle of Descartes, discussed earlier. On the likeliest interpretation, that principle meant that the cause of anything must possess, not the same degree and kind of being or reality as its effect, but *any* kind, provided it is of at least the same degree or greater (see 27.10). Hume's point is simpler and not obviously metaphysical. Since conclusions about what is sufficient or insufficient to produce an effect can only be based on experience, if causal factors of a certain kind have not, in our past experience, been found to suffice to produce an effect of a certain kind, we should not, in any new case, posit such a cause as sufficient, but either reject it or augment it in such a way as to make it sufficient.

The second and negative corollary of Hume's proportionality principle runs: "If the cause be known only by the effect, we never ought to ascribe to it any qualities, beyond what are precisely requisite to produce the effect" (171). The two corollaries are complementary. The first states that the cause must be *great enough* to produce the effect, the second that it should be presumed *no greater than just great enough* to produce that effect (unless there are other known effects of the same cause to justify this assumption). The source of both principles is experience. It is the negative corollary that Hume wields as an offensive weapon against divine justice in the afterlife.

31.5.4 Application of Hume's Razor

Having set out the rule and its corollaries, Hume/Epicurus applies it to three cases of causal reasoning concerned with the past, the present, and the future, respectively: (1) the Stoic doctrine, derived from Hesiod's *Works and Days*, of a Golden Age in the distant past; (2) the doctrine of theodicy, or divine justice in the present, another idea with roots in the Stoics and Neoplatonism, though best known in the eighteenth century in the form it took in the philosophy of Leibniz; and (3) the question of providence, or perfect divine justice in a "future state." In all three cases the formal process of reasoning involves two stages. Schematically:

Stage 1:   From a given observed effect the existence of a cause of that effect is inferred.

Of this the Argument from Design for the existence of a wise and good creator God is the contemporary instance of particular interest to Hume.

Stage 2:   From the nature of the inferred cause the existence (past, present, or future) of certain other (unobserved) effects is inferred.

The cause in the Argument from Design is an intelligent and benevolent deity, the effect a future state of perfect justice. The pattern of inference can be represented more simply thus:

Stage 1: Effect 1 → Cause 1
Stage 2: Cause 1 → Effect 2   (where Effect 2 > Effect 1 and unobservable)

Or even more simply still:

Lesser Effect 1 → Cause 1 → Greater Effect 2

How does Hume's Razor invalidate all such inferences?

According to the positive and negative corollaries stated above, one must attribute to the cause of a given effect *just enough and no more power* than is requisite to produce its observed effect. So (to take the instance that interests Hume) the God whose existence is inferred from the order and design in the universe must possess just enough intelligence and goodness to produce the degree of order and design actually found there *and no more*. From the existence of this cause, however, the existence of *another, unobserved effect* is inferred, *which is greater than the observed effect*. But since *more* intelligence and goodness are required to produce this greater effect, there is no rational justification for assuming that the cause is adequate to produce it, let alone that the effect actually will exist. Hence the inference is fallacious.

31.5.5 Psychological analysis of this reasoning

Having analyzed the causal inference and exposed the fallacy at the heart of it, Hume's Epicurus offers a brief psychological explanation of the conclusion. Thus, the typical Humean pattern of argument described above (see 29.8), though not obvious in "Of Miracles," is followed quite closely here. It is not *reasoning* that causes us to draw this inference; rather, the *imagination adds* attributes to the cause beyond those that reason could legitimately infer it to possess judging solely by its effects. This done, reason then infers the probable effects of the *enhanced* cause to which it has added these imagined attributes. In other words, once the theist arrives at the bare idea of God as intelligent benevolent creator, he embellishes that idea with all sorts of flattering attributes derived from our knowledge of human beings; but human beings are so unlike God that all this must be pure fantasy. Finally, from this heavily embroidered notion of the deity, further, more perfect effects are inferred as probable or even necessary. Put this way, the whole business seems a shallow conjuror's trick by which we fool no one but ourselves.

31.6 Golden Age, theodicy, and divine justice

Having completed his logical analysis and psychological explanation of the fallacy, Hume (or Epicurus) goes on to illustrate the pervasiveness of this kind of reasoning by means of three examples. One has to do with a effect in the past, one with an effect in the present, and one with an effect in the distant future.

The doctrine about the *past* (paragraph 15) is the myth of the Golden Age that was so prevalent in Greek culture, from Hesiod and Empedocles down to the Stoics. This example is selected because the fictional Epicurus is speaking; otherwise Hume might have taken the Judeo-Christian myth of the lost paradise, Eden, as his example. Still, the parallel would have been lost on no reader, and criticizing Greek polytheism was obviously much the safer course in Hume's day.

The *present* effect corresponding to a Golden Age in the past is the existence of greater good in the world than there actually appears to be (paragraph 12). This is the contention of the philosophical doctrine of 'theodicy' (see 31.1). It urges—rather disreputably, some would say—that the apparent imperfections of the universe are an illusion, whether (a) because the presumed evils are really not evils at all when seen in the context of the larger scheme of things that only God can grasp; or (b) because the evils, though indeed evils, were unavoidable, so that this world, even though imperfect in *absolute* terms, is *relatively* perfect: the best *possible* world God could create. As Leibniz put the latter approach to the problem of evil in his correspondence with Newton's disciple Clarke, "every perfection, which God could impart to things without derogating from their other perfections, has actually been imparted to them."

Finally, the *future* effect that parallels these is an afterlife in which perfect distributive justice is fully realized (paragraphs 19–21). This last—providence and a future state—is obviously Hume's real preoccupation; the others are just interesting, but no longer very topical, and hence safer, examples of the same type of fallacious reasoning. For divine justice is the conclusion that has important consequences for practical behaviour—*or rather would have if it were validly inferred*. However, Hume has exposed the fallacy: it may (for all we know) be true that there is a divine providence and a future state; but this cannot be rationally inferred from the order and design in the universe by any competent reasoner.

31.7 Consequences for morality of theism and atheism

With the logical analysis complete, the psychological explanation presented, and the three examples considered, it remains only for Hume's Epicurus to draw the conclusion: the consequences for morality are exactly the same whether we accept or reject the proof of God's existence offered in the Argument from Design. Since no inducement to be moral may be *legitimately* drawn from that argument, the only legitimate inducements are those which ordinary observation of the course of human life provides for theist and atheist alike:

I deny a providence, you say, and supreme governor of the world, who guides the course of events, and punishes the vicious with infamy and disappointment, and rewards the virtuous with honour and success, in all their undertakings. But surely I deny not the course itself of events, which lies open to every one's enquiry and examination. I acknowledge that, in the present order of things, virtue is attended with more peace of mind than vice and meets with a more favourable reception from the world ... I never balance [i.e., waver] between the virtuous and the vicious course of life; but am sensible that, to a well-disposed mind, every advantage is on the side of the former. (173–4)

In short, Epicurus, the naturalist, has all the same inducements to lead a moral life that any believer in the supernatural has, provided both are rational; the believer has *no added inducements*, unless, of course, he jumps to conclusions about divine justice that are not warranted by reason, but a figment of the human imagination.

The conclusion of the dialogue is that the Argument from Design is not just *uncertain*, but *useless*, since it does not *entitle* anyone to believe in providence and a future state, thus providing an added inducement to morally acceptable conduct:

> The experienced train of events is the great standard by which we all regulate our conduct. Nothing else can be appealed to in the field, or in the senate. Nothing else ought ever to be heard of in the school, or in the closet [in private]. In vain would our limited understanding break through those boundaries, which are too narrow for our fond imagination. While we argue from the course of nature, and infer a particular intelligent cause, which first bestowed, and still preserves order in the universe, we embrace a principle which is both uncertain and useless. It is uncertain; because the subject lies entirely beyond the reach of human experience. It is useless; because our knowledge of this cause, being derived entirely from the course of nature, we can never, according to the rules of just reasoning, return back from the cause with any new inference, or making additions to the common and experienced course of nature, establish any new principles of conduct and behaviour. (175)

31.8 Concluding critical reflection

The last part closed with a brief critical reflection on the gulf separating Descartes's metaphysical outlook from our pre-philosophical understanding of what it is to be a human being inhabiting a world given in ordinary sense experience. Does Hume's call for a return to "common life" result in a philosophical outlook less sharply at odds with ordinary experience than Descartes's? In Section XII of the *Enquiry*, Hume states that "philosophical decisions are nothing but the reflections of the common life, methodized and corrected" (192). Does this description fit the philosophy just studied? Against such a conclusion stands Hume's concept of experience. It is not a theme that was discussed in the preceding chapters, despite frequent use of the word 'experience'; our attention was fixed instead on Hume's strictures on reason. Therefore, the first two sub-sections, which are somewhat technical, may be omitted by anyone wishing to proceed straight to a critical reflection on the content of the preceding chapters.

31.8.1 Hume's concept of experience

Although he confessed his inability to make good philosophical sense of either, it apparently never occurred to Hume simply to repudiate the twin tenets of modern philosophy: "that [1] nothing can ever be present to the mind but an image or perception, and that [2] the senses are only the inlets through which images are conveyed, without being able to produce an immediate intercourse [i.e., relation] between the mind and objects" (183). He even employs item (1) and *our ignorance of* item (2) in this characterization of our pre-philosophical understanding of experience: The vulgar "[1] always suppose the very images, presented to the senses, to be external objects," and "never entertain any suspicion, that [2] the one are nothing but [immediately perceived] representations of the other" (ibid.). For the vulgar, Hume alleges, material things are that which is perceived immediately, and that which is perceived immediately are mental images or representations. The philosophers, he adds elsewhere, endorse (1), "that nothing can ever be present to the mind but an image" (ibid.), yet distinguish between mental image and mind-independent material object, affirming (2) that we do not perceive the latter immediately, but only mediately, via interposed perceptions or images of them in the mind, the perceptions being (3) "caused by external objects, entirely different from them though resembling them" (184). While item (3) of this account is already familiar to us as that causal and representative realism discussed earlier (see 27.4), item (2), which has not come before us yet, has been aptly labelled the 'veil of perception doctrine.' It is also known by the name 'representationalism.'

Dismissing Descartes's appeal to God's veracity as a very roundabout way to knowledge of the things right under our noses, Hume had little trouble showing that (2) and (3) lead straight to philosophical scepticism about the world behind the veil of perceptions or ideas. Why, then, did he not reject them in favour of some other account of ordinary perceptual experience and its relation to its object? Probably because sceptical conclusions were welcome to Hume, especially when the theory in question was concocted by philosophers and at odds with "the maxims of common life" (182). Only (1) represents the viewpoint of common sense "corrected and methodized" by philosophy. Or does it?

Surely it never occurred to anyone unacquainted with modern philosophy that the immediate object of sense perception is an image in the mind. This is not because the philosophically uninitiated fail to distinguish representations and things (or representations of images from those of things), but because they believe that they perceive things *and not* images. No one who never darkened the door of a university takes a table, say, for a collection of mental images (brown, rectangular, and large to sight; hard, smooth, and heavy to touch, and so on); nor would there be any point in trying to persuade such a person that in calling tables 'bodies' or 'material things' he is just endowing his fleeting and constantly changing perceptions with a mind-independent existence and a constant, uniform nature that they in truth lack. In fact, prior to Malebranche and Berkeley, no *philosopher*, not even the Father of Modern Philosophy himself, ever espoused (1) either in defence or in defiance of common sense. On the contrary, the outlook of common sense and most philosophy right down to the eighteenth century was the opposite of (1). 'Epistemological direct realism' is the name customarily given both the ordinary and the philosophical conviction that we perceive material things, not images of them, immediately.

Hume derived his preposterous idea of "the primary opinion of all men" (183) from Berkeley, who dwelt mercilessly on the contradiction involved in ascribing mind-independent existence to material things understood as mental images immediately perceived. This contradiction Berkeley laid to the blame of the philosophers alone; when ordinary folk speak of a table's existing or having certain properties when no one is around to perceive it, they just mean that certain mental images are, or would be, perceiv*able* under the right conditions. Thus, Berkeley himself retained the view (1) that all we ever perceive are mental images, yet rejected (2) and (3) as inherently absurd and the high road to scepticism about the world behind the veil of perception. He presented his idealism as *both* a defence of common sense and the antidote to scepticism. If Hume saw through any of this, it was at most the idea that common sense was free of the error of philosophy. The sceptic in him could not rest until even "the maxims of common life" were shown to be "a blind and powerful instinct of nature" (183) to believe something quite unwarranted by the evidence, and in fact incapable of being made philosophically coherent. Only then could the psychological task of explaining the beliefs of everyday life along with "the most profound principles of or conclusions of metaphysics and theology" (182) begin.

The plain fact is that neither Berkeley nor Hume was in any position to either defend or criticize the "reflections of common life," since neither got even close to a correct understanding of ordinary perceptual experience and its object—though Hume, admittedly, got somewhat closer than Berkeley.

31.8.2 The analysis of experience

A different sort of philosophical analysis, with stronger claims to reflect and refine our commonsense understanding of perceptual experience and its object than either Hume's or Berkeley's, was sketched earlier in the part on Descartes (see 29.4). In ordinary perceptual experience things actually *present* in the world are *re-presented* in the human mind. When I see a table, for example, the representation of the table is not itself again represented as an intermediate object; rather, the table alone is represented, and represented immediately, in the mind. The table-perception is not a perception of a mental image of the table, but a mental act, an occurrence or process through which a table really and physically present in the external world becomes immediately but only representationally present to the conscious human mind as well. Despite the figurative talk of 'having the table in mind,' things like tables are never literally *in* the mind; only the representations or experiences of them are, that is, the corresponding mental acts or events. The thing or object may nevertheless be said to be 'in' the mind *figuratively*. For that is only to say that the table exists there *representationally* for as long as the act of representing it exists there *really*, as a real part of the stream of consciousness. Indeed, to say that the representation of the table exists in the mind really or literally is just another way of saying that the table itself exists there representationally or figuratively. As for the table's real existence outside the mind, this does not depend on the mind or its acts at all.

All this was perfectly clear to Descartes, as his distinction between the formal and objective reality of ideas and things clearly shows (see 26.4.1–2). He took it over from his scholastic predecessors, who in turn derived it from Aristotle, the first to distinguish *immaterial* existence in the mind (literally, being there 'without matter') from real existence outside the mind or *in matter*—though, for Aristotle, it was not the represented thing that so existed but its form. Similarly, it was well recognized long before Descartes that whenever things present in the world are represented in the mind, there is a concomitant awareness of the act of representing. However, only the perception of things was termed 'experience' (*empeiria*); it was Descartes who first dubbed these concurrent modes of outer and inner awareness 'outer' and 'inner *experience*,' reserving the word *especially* for the latter and insisting on the primacy of such *self*-consciousness within the order of knowing.

That was the first important departure from the pre-philosophical understanding of experience as analyzed in pre-modern philosophy: two objects, corresponding to two different kinds of experience. It inevitably introduced a sceptical note into the interpretation of outer experience or sense perception, which had always been regarded as reliable (though not infallible) in the Aristotelian tradition. Yet this is still nothing like a dual object theory of outer experience: an immediately perceived image in the mind, as in (1), the alleged view of both the vulgar and the philosophers; and a mediately perceived thing outside the mind, as in (2), the alleged view of the philosophers but not the vulgar.

It is one thing to institute a new *order* of knowing in which acts of thinking are the immediate objects of inner experience and prior to the immediate objects of outer experience in the order of knowing. This much Descartes did. It is quite another to posit a new object of *outer* experience, the immediately given *image* or representation in the mind, or *two* objects, the one immediately and certainly known, the other only mediately given and irremediably doubtful. This further departure from the old Aristotelian idea of experience seems to have been instituted by Malebranche. It was this chilling spectre that drove Berkeley to idealism and a completely fanciful distortion and defence of common sense. It led Hume to a scepticism that engulfed common sense itself. Yet the point is worth repeating: neither Berkeley nor Hume criticized or defended anything even remotely resembling common sense and ordinary experience.

Concerning our primary experience of the external world, then, we may perhaps say that of these four ways of presenting "the reflections of common life, corrected and methodized" by philosophy, Hume's is less bizarre than Berkeley's, though still a poor third behind Descartes's and the non-sceptical direct epistemological realism of the Aristotelian tradition. Whether we can get closer to the way we actually understand ourselves and the world in pre-philosophical experience by replacing the perceiving subject/material object schema common to all four theories with a notion of *pre-cognitive* experience as Being-in-the-world is a question we shall consider in the next part on Sartre's existentialism.

31.8.3 Hume's critique of reason

Obviously, the *main* critical thrust of Hume's philosophy is not directed against experience and common sense, but at the unwarranted claims made in metaphysics, theology, and science on behalf of human *reason*. Yet as he misunderstood common sense, so Hume distorted the nature of reason, construing the latter much too narrowly.

Hume's discussion of physical, or what is also called 'hypothetical,' necessity is one of those milestones in the analysis of causal reasoning that all subsequent writers on the subject feel compelled to acknowledge. It had never occurred to anyone to doubt what Hume doubted; and what he demonstrated—the logical gap between fact and necessity, or between restrictedly universal premises and an unrestrictedly universal conclusion—he demonstrated irrefutably. Although Hume has been much criticized for presenting so-called induction as a failed deduction, a kind of broken-backed syllogism, his stature as a pioneer in the analysis of the logic of the empirical sciences is undiminished today, centuries later.

Regarding his strictures on absolute or logical necessity in the domain of matter of fact and existence, Hume's statement of his position is so simple and compelling that others have only rephrased, never surpassed, it. Of course, the position itself turns crucially on a division of all propositions into just two classes and all sciences into two kinds: the deductive, a priori, demonstrative mathematical disciplines concerned with "relations of ideas," and the empirical, inductive, a posteriori or probable sciences concerned with "existence and matter of fact." Of anything that fits into neither category, Hume says, in the uncharacteristically purple passage that concludes the whole *Enquiry*, "commit it ... to the flames" for it is "nothing but sophistry and illusion" (195).

This conclusion gives very short shrift to mankind's efforts to create, in science, religion, philosophy, literature, and the arts, an intellectual and moral basis for life, the foundation and outer framework of which is metaphysics. While metaphysics has much to do with experience, especially with "the reflections of common life, methodized and corrected," it cannot be empirical science; nor is it likely to gain admittance to the ranks of the demonstrative sciences by pleading a new method of apodictic demonstration different from that of mathematics. Kant's efforts to this end were lost labour if metaphysics has a unique texture of rationality all its own.

It takes no very profound knowledge of the history of thought to realize that the "good metaphysics" that Hume recommends (the first principles of the "science of human nature") is metaphysics in name only. It is more than just armchair psychology, however, since it involves a great deal of acute logical analysis of the sort philosophers have always engaged in. Yet regarding the tools of Hume's analysis—the great divide, the principle of the priority of impressions to ideas, and Hume's Fork, in particular—extreme caution is indicated. Apodictic certainty such as Descartes and Kant insisted on may not be for us; but if we commit ourselves uncritically to Hume's principles, we shall almost certainly have to resign ourselves to sitting by and musing upon "the whimsical condition of mankind, who must act and reason and believe; though they are not able, by their most diligent enquiry, to satisfy themselves concerning the foundation of these operations, or to remove the objections which may be raised against them" (191).

Here Hume may be forgetting his own sage counsel: "The wise man proportions his belief to his evidence." In the previous chapter (see 30.5.2), a parallel was drawn between this and Socrates's admonition to 'follow the best argument.' In fact, the parallels do not stop there, and it is worth recalling, in this final assessment, Hume's wit and irony, his intellectual playfulness and prowess, his remarkable eloquence, his exemplary personal life, the fortitude with which he faced a relatively early fatal illness (see the letter from Adam Smith to William Strahan that is included in our edition of the *Enquiry*), his hatred of cant and intellectual pretension, his sincere love of clarity of thought—all reminiscent of Plato's great teacher and qualities that it is hard *not* to admire. The similarities between the two men extend, unfortunately, even to their animus towards speculative metaphysics. It is this that makes it hard to regard Hume's efforts sympathetically.

The animus would be even harder to understand were what Hume writes in the epigraph to this part true: "The errors in religion are dangerous, those in philosophy only ridiculous." That a philosophy that slips its moorings in common life thereby becomes an object of ridicule seems mistaken. Even common sense is not as resistant to the entreaties of transcendent metaphysics as Hume suggests—especially when the entreater is a Plato or a Descartes. Hume's animus toward metaphysics would presumably have been less had he entertained the possibility of a naturalistic or immanent metaphysics worthy of that ancient name. Kant must have understood this. For in order to rebut Hume he set out to demonstrate the possibility of a naturalistic metaphysics.

Recommended readings and references

Cornford, F.M. 1965. *Principium Sapientiae. A Study of the Origins of Greek Philosophical Thought*. New York: Harper Torchbook. (Chapter II contains an excellent, brief discussion of Epicurus's philosophy.)

Flew, Antony. 1961. *Hume's Philosophy of Belief*. London: Routledge & Kegan Paul. (Fairly advanced, but still the only section-by-section commentary devoted exclusively to Hume's *Enquiry concerning Human Understanding*. The approach is analytic and linguistic rather than historical.)

Hick, John, ed. 1964. *The Existence of God*. London: Macmillan. (A reader with extracts drawn from the whole history of thought. Contains the debate between Russell and Copleston mentioned in the text.)

Hume, David. 1992. *Writings on Religion*. Introduction, notes, and editorial arrangement by Antony Flew. Lasalle, IL.: Open Court. (A collection of writings that includes the two essays studied here and the posthumously published *Dialogues concerning Natural Religion*. Flew's introduction to "Two Scandalous Sections" is very helpful, as is his introduction to the edition as a whole.)

McGiffert, A.C. 1961. *Protestant Thought before Kant*. New York: Harper Torchbook. (A very readable survey that touches on the doctrine of real presence in a variety of contexts.)

Smith, Norman Kemp. 1941. *The Philosophy of David Hume. A Critical Study of Its Origins and Central Doctrines*. London: Macmillan. (A classic study by one of the leading historians of ideas of the twentieth century. The approach is historical rather than analytic.)

Tillotson, John. 1820. *The Works of Dr. John Tillotson, late Archbishop of Canterbury*. With the life of the Author by Thomas Birch, M.A. Also a Copious Index, and the Texts of Scripture Carefully Compared. In Ten Volumes. (Vol. II contains "A Discourse Against Transubstantiation.")

Wilson, Fred. 1997. *Hume's Defence of Causal Inference*. Toronto: University of Toronto Press. (Contains an instructive, though rather technical, discussion of miracles and testimony. Informed by the author's interest in contemporary epistemology and philosophy of science. Too advanced for beginners.)

Wright, J.P. 1983. *The Sceptical Realism of David Hume*. Minneapolis: University of Minnesota Press. (Historically well informed, philosophically original and insightful.)

Yolton, J.W. 1984. *Perceptual Acquaintance. From Descartes to Reid*. Minneapolis: University of Minnesota Press. (Contains valuable chapters on ideas and imagination in Hume, focusing mainly on the *Treatise*.)

Questions for reflection, discussion, and review

1. Philosophies are commonly divided into empiricist or rationalist types, based on their estimate of the role of the senses in attaining knowledge. Discuss the three philosophies studied so far from this perspective.
2. Philosophies can also be divided into philosophies of immanence ('this-wordly') and transcendence ('other-worldly'). Again, discuss the thinkers studied so far in this light.
3. How do natural and revealed religion differ? In your opinion, is there any basis for such a distinction, or is religion based exclusively on faith?
4. Hume writes that "all our ideas are nothing but copies of our impressions, or, in other words, that it is impossible for us to *think* of anything, which we have not antecedently *felt*, either by our external or internal senses." What does this mean? Is it persuasive? Can you think of a counter-example?
5. Explain how one might use Hume's 'principle of priority of impressions to ideas' as a formula for clarifying obscure ideas. Can it also be used to show that someone literally doesn't know what he is talking about? How?
6. Explain Hume's concept of 'mental geography' and the corresponding idea of a 'mental mechanics.' Is there, or can there be, a *science* of the human mind analogous to geography or mechanics?
7. What is meant by 'Hume's Fork'? What is Hume's restriction of all truths to these two kinds intended to *deny*? Is it an expression of his empiricist outlook? How?
8. How do we use the terms 'proof' and 'demonstration' in standard English today? How does Hume use them? Is there anything odd about standard usage such that we need to improve upon it?
9. Explain Hume's canon for evaluating experiential or probable arguments.
10. What is the difference between the marvellous and the miraculous according to Hume? Give examples of events that would have to be regarded as (a) marvellous and (b) miraculous by Hume's definitions.
11. How does Hume's use of 'miracle' differ from colloquial usage today? Give examples of contemporary colloquial usage.
12. Have you ever heard a report of a miracle? Have you ever actually experienced something that you thought might be miraculous?
13. What might Gassendi or Hume himself have thought of the Argument from Design had they heard of Darwin's principles of random variation and natural selection? What might Newton have thought about the 'Big Bang' Theory?
14. Contrast Hume's conception of rationality with that met with in the reasoning of Socrates and Descartes.
15. Was Hume's Indian prince right to be sceptical of stories of rivers freezing over in winter in Europe? What factors prompted his scepticism? What factors

induced him to accept the account in the end?
16 What is meant by 'Hume's Razor'? Is there anything analogous to this in Descartes?
17 Does a sort of reasoning underlie the stories of the Garden of Eden, heaven, and hell, , as Hume suggests, or are these just age-old stories, myths?
18 Does the state have any business monitoring the expressions of opinion of its citizens in the name of the common good? How far might this be permissible? When does it become dangerous?
19 To what extent do the two essays "Of Miracles" and "Of a Particular Providence and a Future State," follow the typical pattern of analysis associated with Hume?

PART FIVE

SARTRE AND THE ROAD TO FREEDOM

Man is condemned to be free. Condemned, because he did not create himself, yet is nevertheless at liberty, and from the moment that he is thrown into this world he is responsible for everything he does.

Sartre, *Existentialism and Humanism*

32

Life, Work, and Basic Philosophical Outlook

32.1 Life, writings, and influences

Jean-Paul Sartre (1905–1980), like Descartes, a Frenchman, was not just a philosopher, but a novelist, dramatist, and literary critic as well as a political commentator and left-wing social activist for most of his life. He began his philosophical studies in Paris, completing them in Germany (Berlin and Freiburg) before taking up a variety of teaching posts in various French *lycées* (see 2.1) or secondary schools (at which philosophy is still a subject of instruction today), both in his native Paris and elsewhere. As a young man he published some notable philosophical studies on the emotions, the self, and the imagination. These were mainly influenced by Edmund Husserl, the founder of the philosophical school or movement of the early twentieth century known as 'phenomenology.' He also published a famous philosophical novel (translated into English as *Nausea*) and some remarkable short stories, all before the Second World War. At the outbreak of war in 1939, Sartre enlisted in the French army. He was captured by the Germans, and, following a period of internment in a German prisoner-of-war camp, returned to Paris at war's end, where he once again began to teach and write, taking a very active part in French life, letters, and political debate right up to his death.

Sartre was one of the key figures of the so-called existentialist movement, and perhaps the only so-called existentialist to have welcomed the label. Others often referred to as 'existentialists' are: Søren Kierkegaard (Danish, 1813–1855), Nietzsche, and Heidegger. Still other names frequently associated with the movement are Martin Buber (German/Jewish, 1883–1965), Gabriel Marcel (French, 1889–1973), and Karl Jaspers (German, 1883–1969). The first two are deeply religious thinkers, Marcel being perhaps the foremost Christian existentialist after Kierkegaard, though the latter was a Protestant and Marcel a Catholic. Buber may have been the greatest Jewish thinker after Spinoza, though the latter is hardly a religious thinker in the same sense as Buber. Jaspers, a physician and psychiatrist by training, wrote an important early work on psychopathology (1913) and another influential study of the psychology of world-views (1919). He actually coined the phrase 'philosophy of existence' early in the twentieth century, from which the popular name 'existentialism' was derived. Another author frequently mentioned in discussions of French existentialism in particular is Albert Camus (Algerian, 1913–1960), who was, however, primarily a novelist and essayist—a thinker of some note, but perhaps not a philosopher so much as a Nobel Prize–winning man of letters.

Sartre's post-war work falls into two phases, the early period of existential phenomenology and the later, Marxist phase. The major influences on the first phase were Husserl and especially Heidegger, who was the chief continuator of the phenomenological school founded by Husserl and the thinker generally credited with having laid the foundations of twentieth-century existentialism. The main work of Sartre's early period is *Being and Nothingness* (1943), a huge tome and a classic of twentieth-century philosophy. We shall study a short piece from the same period entitled *Existentialism and Humanism* (1946), which outlines the philosophical position of Sartre's major work and defends it against the criticisms of Christian and communist intellectuals of the post-war era. The later Marxist phase of Sartre's career will not concern us.

32.2 Philosophical outlook

In the previous part we contrasted Hume's philosophical outlook with those of Socrates, Plato, and Descartes, noting that Hume was (1) *sceptical* even about our knowledge of this world, whether through reason or the senses; (2) *agnostic* about knowledge of God and the next world (although almost certainly a complete unbeliever); and therefore (3) totally *man-centred and this-worldly*. If we now contrast Sartre with Hume, we might describe the former as (1) not just sceptical about certain types of knowledge, but a *relativist*; (2) not just agnostic, but an *atheist*; and finally, (3) not just man-centred, but *humanistic*. This way of contrasting the two is intended to convey that, despite important differences, Sartre heightens certain tendencies already present in Hume, pushing them further than the latter would have been prepared to go. The same can be said of the relationship of both thinkers to Descartes. That is why Hume's scepticism and Sartre's relativism are to be treated as varieties of Cartesian subjectivism in the next section. It is not that Hume and Sartre are not both overtly critical of Descartes, or that either understood him correctly; on the contrary, their criticisms are the index of both their debt to him and their failure to grasp his basic metaphysical and epistemological position.

In the next chapter we shall examine (2) and (3) together under the heading 'atheistic humanism.' For present we shall confine our attention to (1) Sartre's subjectivism, which forms the basis of his whole philosophical outlook as presented in this and the next chapter.

32.3 Varieties of subjectivism

The move from Humean scepticism to Sartre's sceptical relativism involved the denial that there exists any objective truth to be known (about some or all things) or any objective moral and non-moral value to be discovered. For the relativist, truth and goodness are the products of human subjects' individual or collective *wills*. They are accordingly subjective, that is, relative to, and alterable by, the decisions of the individual or community. This is very different from admitting that there is or may be objective or absolute truth and value while denying that it can be reliably known; that is as far as scepticism need go (see 3.3.1).

Admittedly Hume's scepticism went further, stressing the role of feeling or sentiment and the imagination in shaping men's fundamental convictions about both theoretical and valuational matters. He thus abandoned the long-dominant *cognitivist standpoint* of most ancient and medieval philosophy. From that standpoint, the true and the good exist objectively, either in particular things (their formal/final causes), or in things *and* apart from them in their own right (Platonic Forms), or in the mind of God. Moreover, they are knowable through rational intuition or some other intellectual process of the human mind. Nevertheless, (1) making *beliefs* concerning the true and the good depend upon *sentiment* comes up well short of (2) making *truth and value themselves* dependent upon the *will* alone; for the former at least leaves open the possibility of objective truth and goodness, however inaccessible it may be to the likes of us. It is only the latter type of non-cognitivism that we shall call 'relativism' here—that is, *voluntarism about truth and value*—the will in question being human will, not, as in Descartes, God's will, which is absolute, immutable, and perfectly arbitrary in its decrees.

It is largely a terminological decision whether to speak of two forms of relativism concerning truth and value (relative to human sentiment and relative to man's will), or of scepticism and relativism as two forms of subjectivism. The latter usage has the advantage of setting in a clear light an important trend toward voluntarism in modern philosophy as it evolved from Descartes via Hume to Sartre (see the Conclusion). Nevertheless, it is open to misunderstanding unless the logical relationships are clear.

32.3.1 Subjectivism, scepticism, and sceptical relativism

As noted earlier (see chap. 22), Descartes was responsible for the *subjective turn* that inaugurated modern philosophy, that is, the reorientation of metaphysics toward the human subject, mind, or self as the first item in the order of knowing. Yet Descartes regarded the natural light of reason as the source of absolutely certain knowledge of the existence and essence of *everything*; his point of departure may have been the human subject, but he eventually extended the sphere of perfect certainty to the existence and natures of all things, starting with God. As subjectivism was to be the antidote to scepticism (see 23.4), so the doctrine of divine creation of truth and goodness was to administer a decisive check to sceptical relativism of every kind (see 11.11 and 25.8).

If by 'subjectivism' we mean no more than situating the *starting point of knowledge in thoughts rather than extra-mental things*, there is no difficulty about calling both Hume and Sartre 'subjectivists.' The logical relationships may then be put this way. While scepticism and relativism are forms of subjectivism, not all subjectivism is either sceptical or relativistic (for example, Descartes's is not). As for the denials (i) that objective truth and goodness can be known (Humean scepticism) and (ii) that there is any objective truth to be known (Sartrean relativism), the logical relationship is more straightforward. While all relativism is sceptical about objective truth and values (hence 'sceptical relativism'), not all scepticism is relativistic (for example, Hume's is not). Obviously, *modern* scepticism and relativism alone are meant; the ancient forms of both, which obviously owe nothing to Descartes, are not in question here.

32.3.2 Absolutism and relativism

In denying that there is any objective truth or value to be known about some things at least, Sartre specifically denies (a) a transcendent realm of Platonic Forms (essences, including valuational essences) independent of human volition; (b) a transcendent divine intellect and will in which such essences and moral commandments exist independently of human volition; and (c) a timeless, unchanging set of descriptive and prescriptive principles rooted in the human mind or reason, that is, innate or a priori axioms and norms that man *discovers* through the exercise of reason rather than *producing* them by acts of will.

Now (a) and (b) obviously correspond roughly to certain tenets of the philosophies of Plato and of the Christian Middle Ages, respectively; (c), by contrast, reflects, on the practical side, Kant's categorical imperative as a basic norm or rule of action (see above 12.8.5). Of course, Kant also posited a set of purely theoretical principles or axioms (including the principle of causality: 'every event has some cause') as indigenous to the human mind; and before him others had posited *innate* principles of both a theoretical and a practical kind. So in denying (a), (b), and (c), Sartre is championing the point of view that all moral and other values, and some theoretical truths concerning the essences or natures of things (namely, those concerning *human* nature), are not *objective*, but *subjective*, and moreover *freely created by man* himself. They are therefore relative to the human will.

Now it is one thing to deny that (1) there is any such thing as objective or absolute truth and value in *these three traditional senses*; it is quite another to deny (even if only for a restricted range of object) that (2) there exist objective truths and objective values *in any sense at all*. Sartre, as we shall see, slides illegitimately from (1) to (2). Hume himself would have been the first to dispute the knowledge of (1) objective truth and objective value in the specifically Platonic, Christian, or nativist senses, though he would not have denied (2) the very possibility of objective truth and objective value in *any* sense whatever. His sceptical point concerns our inability to *get at* the true or the good in any such sense, without denying that they exist; Sartre, by contrast, holds that there can be no objective truth (at least about a fixed and determinate human nature) and no objective values *in any sense*, having considered only the three emblematic positions just mentioned.

This is typical of the intellectually shoddy way in which Sartre proceeds at times, setting up and knocking down convenient straw men. Moreover, instead of despairing at the conclusions so reached, Sartre welcomes them as grounds for hope, as an *opportunity*: in this situation it becomes possible for man to *create freely his own nature* and *to establish values of his own choosing*. Radical subjectivism or relativism is a form of human emancipation for Sartre; it amounts to liberating man from the myths and illusions of Platonism, Christianity, and traditional rationalism, restoring man's radical freedom to create values and to create human nature through acts of will.

One cannot help but think of Hume's satisfaction at reaching sceptical conclusions that most philosophers would be understandably reluctant to embrace. Sartre's evocation of radical freedom and emancipation from the illusions of the past has an appeal that is lacking in Hume's sober insistence on our intellectual limitations. It remains to be seen whether his relativism is better warranted philosophically than Hume's scepticism.

32.4 Sartre's moral relativism and other varieties of moral scepticism

In the theoretical domain, Sartre's radical subjectivism is fairly innocuous, since it is only truth about *human* nature that is relativized; the idea that there exists no human nature is troubling enough, since sciences like psychology seem to presuppose the opposite, but at least the objectivity of scientific beliefs about the nature of matter or the laws of physics is unaffected by relativism. In the all-important ethical domain, however, Sartrean subjectivism issues in a new form of that moral relativism first hinted at in the 'Man is the measure' doctrine of Protagoras (see chap. 3) and espoused by others of the sophists as well. To make this clearer, it may be helpful to distinguish Sartre's moral relativism from a variety of other forms of moral scepticism, both more and less extreme.

Generally speaking, the moral sceptic holds that there are no objectively valid, and hence universally binding, moral norms or principles at which we can arrive by means of unassisted human reason. This is to say that the distinctions customarily drawn between right and wrong, morally good and bad actions, or virtue and vice are incapable of *either rational justification or criticism*. When it comes to *explaining* the existence in most or all societies of moral distinctions and codes of ethical conduct, moral sceptics may cite religious, psychological, anthropological, sociological, or political factors, stressing the effects of priestcraft, superstition, gullibility, fear, social conditioning, or the self-seeking desire of certain individuals and groups to dominate and exploit others; but the underlying philosophical position, beyond which the moral sceptic need not go, is that such codes and distinctions are not susceptible of rational justification or criticism. It is this idea of the impossibility of *rational* criticism of the actions of, say, the sweatshop owner, the slaveholder, the brutal dictator, the genocidal imperialist, and so on that brings home to us why we must be reluctant to accept the conclusions of the moral sceptic unless there are compelling reasons to do so; for we want to be able to say that these things are wrong, and to back up our condemnation with reasons.

32.4.1 Amoralism and immoralism

One very pointed way of stating the moral sceptic's conclusion is to say "everything is permitted." This is how a character in a novel by Dostoevsky puts it, and the remark is quoted by Sartre at one point in our text (33/353). We noted in passing earlier (see 9.2.3) the advantage of having different means of negation at our disposal ('a-' as well as 'un-' or 'im-'), and the best term for the attitude that "everything is permitted," even the most complete selfishness and disregard for others, is perhaps '*a*moralism.' An *a*moral individual need not behave in ways others would consider *im*moral, since he may not think it in his best interests to do so, given that he may be found out; his is basically a theoretical position concerning *what* is moral—although, again, only in that rather odd sense in which *a*theism may be called a theological position concerning God (see 20.10.2). Nevertheless, the likelihood is that the amoralist will be a complete egotist (see 38.2), behaving in ways that most of us would consider immoral whenever he believes he can get away with it.

Amoralism, then, is to be distinguished from immorality, but also from *im*moralism: the practice of deliberately flouting accepted moral norms. This is well illustrated by a character in a famous novel entitled *The Immoralist* by the French writer André Gide (1869–1951), whom Sartre also mentions (48/363). On witnessing a base act, Gide's protagonist discovers to his surprise that he feels no repugnance whatsoever;

thereafter he feels compelled to act contrary to accepted moral norms himself. His is the reverse of the Kantian maxim of acting from the motive of reverence for the law; his motive is something like flouting the law for its own sake. The immoralist, so understood, is obviously very different from your garden variety of immoral individual, who is so called on account of a disposition to behave in certain ways often or for the most part, not whenever possible and on principle.

In the same place, Sartre mentions Gide's theory of the "gratuitous" or "unmotivated action" (*acte gratuit* in French). The reference is to another novel in which Gide's protagonist pushes a man off a speeding train for no reason—or rather just *because* he has no reason to do so. A figurative 'flip of a coin' determines him to act. To his mind, the crime underscores the existence of a perfect human liberty: action that is so far from being determined in advance by a chain of causes, including psychological motives, that it is performed despite the fact that there is no motive for it at all. (Of course, the desire to prove the existence of such liberty may constitute a motive.) Interestingly, this is the sort of liberty ascribed by theological voluntarists to *all* God's actions: complete arbitrariness, acting without a reason (see 11.11 and 28.5); apparently, some critics took Sartre to be reverting to Gide's idea of the *acte gratuit* in his own account of moral choice. Sartre took exception to this, and not without reason; nevertheless his critics may have spotted a real parallel between his and Descartes's voluntarisms of which Sartre was unaware (see chap. 36).

32.4.2 Emotivism and voluntarism

Amoralism and immoralism are obviously extremes of moral scepticism. The moral scepticism of Hume is moderate by comparison—even by comparison with Sartre. In the Second *Enquiry* Hume gives an analysis of what he calls "Personal Merit," that is, moral and non-moral excellence or virtue, arguing that there is an underlying standard or measure governing our moral and non-moral appraisals, namely *utility* in a wide sense that includes all things useful and/or agreeable to oneself and/or others. This preference for utility is by no means arbitrary; it is founded upon a constant and universal law or principle of human nature. Hume's main point is that the underlying principle is not self-love or rational self-interest, as others had maintained, but a disinterested benevolence, a sentiment of humanity or fellow feeling that is universal in mankind and the source of all our moral and non-moral value judgments. While men's selfish sentiments drive them apart, their common benevolence unites them, furnishing a basis for widespread agreement about morals and value judgments generally. The main casualty of Hume's theory is universal human reason, which, typically, is supplanted by a universal sentiment.

Through the importance he attached to utility, Hume was among the precursors of a very influential normative ethical theory to be described in the last chapter as utilitarianism (see 38.2). Yet by explaining psychologically, in terms of feeling or sentiment, what allegedly cannot be justified by reason, Hume set the stage for a type of meta-ethical theory that was to enjoy a great vogue among twentieth-century empiricists under the title 'emotivism.' In its crassest form, emotivism holds that moral value judgments (say, 'Killing is wrong' or 'Saving lives is good') are the expressions of negative or positive feelings, attitudes, or wishes; for the underlying pro and con attitudes (as distinct from the factual beliefs they presuppose) no reasons can be given. Its detractors have accordingly dubbed this 'the Boo-Hooray Theory' of morality. Its consequences are again such that one should only be prepared to accept them if there is no reasonable alternative.

Emotivism is often lumped together with voluntarism as a related non-cognitivist meta-ethical theory. According to voluntarists, particular ethical judgments and/or general moral rules are merely the expressions of more or less blind or arbitrary commitments, volitions, or decisions on the part of the individual or the moral community. From this meta-ethical perspective, which he bases on metaphysical considerations regarding the priority of existence to essence in man (see chap. 35), Sartre develops a normative ethical theory usually called 'decisionism.' It too will be discussed in the final chapter. Its basic rule or maxim can be stated roughly this way: 'Choose freely, without deceiving yourself concerning your freedom, and you thereby make your choice morally right.'

At the meta-ethical level, there is a difference between emotivism and voluntarism that is often overlooked. Both are non-cognitivist theories that stress the impossibility of rational justification; but in appealing to the *will* rather than feeling, Sartre means to set alongside those familiar patterns of *rational* justification found in the various families of sciences another type of justification based on the human *will*. Accordingly, his theory presents incompatible moral judgments and principles, not as alike *un*warranted, but as *equally warranted* or valid *relative to certain individuals*. This sets his voluntarism apart not only from emotivism, but also from Gide's *acte gratuit*, to which it nevertheless bears a certain resemblance.

32.4.3 Meta-ethical, normative, and descriptive moral relativism

Decisionism is a type of (1) normative ethical relativism, while emotivism and voluntarism are forms of (2) meta-ethical scepticism and sceptical relativism, respectively. Normative and meta-ethical relativism must be distinguished from another variety, so-called (3) descriptive relativism.

Descriptive moral relativism is not a normative ethical theory but a descriptive social-scientific hypothesis (see 10.2.3). It involves the empirical claim that moral values vary widely from society to society and from culture to culture, and even within the same society or culture at different times. Now this much seems to be an incontestable matter of anthropological and sociological fact. The contentious point is whether the moral rules that differ are *basic*. After all, observable differences in *derivative* moral duties might spring from underlying moral beliefs that are in fact identical yet generate different derivative rules according as social circumstances differ. For different circumstances may call for very different means of achieving the same moral ends. The key tenet of descriptive moral relativism, therefore, is that the *de facto* differences in moral rules or values, of which anthropologists and sociologists inform us, *cannot* be adequately accounted for in terms of differences in circumstances or factual beliefs or clarity of thought, but really involve different *underlying* moral outlooks. All this is obviously very difficult to prove, and most sociological and anthropological testimony goes almost no way toward establishing anything of the kind.

32.5 Conclusion

So much for the varieties of moral scepticism and relativism. As we shall see in chapter 35, one of the main charges levelled at Sartre's existentialism concerns relativism. It is a charge the force of which Sartre will be not be able to escape entirely. But who is to say that moral scepticism and relativism are not perfectly justified? In assuming the opposite, those who make the charge seem to beg the question.

If 'rational justification' is understood narrowly enough, in terms of observation and inductive generalization or immediate rational intuition and logical deduction, then the moral sceptic's doubts will be hard to allay without establishing an equivalence of moral judgments with non-ethical ones of a factual or conceptual sort. This has been tried, without success. Theories that acknowledge the distinctiveness of moral judgments, positing a faculty of rational insight into good and evil, have not fared much better in trying to quell the riot of moral scepticism. It seems that in the moral domain, as in the metaphysical, we are faced with a special type of enquiry having a pattern of rationality of its own. When we argue from a metaphysical point of view, the standard of rigour and the type of rational justification sought are different from the proof and demonstration that Hume showed to be characteristic of empirical and mathematical sciences. And we may quite reasonably adopt the same attitude when engaging in enquiry and debate from a moral point of view. The onus is on the sceptic or the relativist to show that such confidence in reason is misplaced, even on a broader understanding of reason than his own. If this is correct, then the charge may not be question-begging after all.

33

Atheistic Humanism

33.1 Some senses of 'humanism'

'Humanism' is a vague and notoriously elusive term; not only does it have several different meanings, but the meanings tend to overlap. Still, we can distinguish three important strands of meaning.

1. Humanism is spoken of in the sense of 'humanistic studies,' the pursuit of the 'humanities' or 'human sciences,' of 'general culture' as opposed to practical skills and professional competence, on the one hand, and to knowledge of the natural sciences on the other. In some European languages (German, for example), 'humanistic' is employed even more narrowly for the study of *ancient* languages and culture, that is, for the discipline called 'classics' in English. The nineteenth-century German F.J. Niethammer coined the term 'humanism' in this sense; but the Renaissance already knew the Latin phrase *studia humanitatis*, comprising grammar, rhetoric, poetry, history, and philosophy, all taught on the basis of classical texts (see 1.3.2), so Niethammer was only providing a convenient German equivalent for an expression already in use in learned circles.
2. 'Humanism' is sometimes used in a sense very close to 'humanitarianism,' 'philanthropy' (see 13.4 on Kant's use of this term). In this sense, humanism is opposed to the so-called inhumane; it is the attempt to *free* men from suffering, poverty, ignorance, superstition, intolerance, and subjugation to illegitimate authority—in fact, all forms of inhumane treatment—through practical-political efforts to improve the social condition of the whole or some part of mankind. Humanism in the sense of kindness and compassion, especially towards those less fortunate than ourselves, seems to be another nineteenth-century innovation. One thinks of the movements that led to the abolition of the slave trade and then of slavery itself in early-nineteenth-century Britain, or of the novels of Dickens on child labour and the abhorrent condition of the urban poor. That is not to say that it was unknown

in earlier times. The parable of the Good Samaritan and the Sermon on the Mount have been around for a good long time, and charity, or beneficent love of one's fellow human beings, is a traditional Christian virtue. While Socrates may have turned a blind eye to slavery, others in his time were duly incensed. The point, then, is that humanitarianism only became a powerful social force in the nineteenth century.

3 'Humanism' can be used to designate an extreme form of man-centred philosophical and practical outlook, stressing (a) the this-worldly, the human sphere, the realm of human culture, that is, imaginative, intellectual, and practical activity rather than the realms of (b) physical nature or (c) the supernatural (divine) or other-worldly (be it Descartes's God or Plato's Forms). In this use, 'humanism' is tantamount to extreme anthropocentrism.

Thus, the three senses of 'humanism' are, in capsule form: (1) human studies, the study of man and society; (2) philanthropy or humanitarianism; (3) extreme anthropocentrism, a narrowly man-centred outlook. Are all three senses in play in the title of Sartre's work?

33.2 The sense of 'humanism' in the title of Sartre's work

Sartre's use of 'humanism' in the title *Existentialism and Humanism* would appear to be an amalgam of the latter two senses alone (the first is largely irrelevant). For, on the one hand, we find in the work a flat *denial of the supernatural, together with a complete indifference towards questions regarding the non-human, natural sphere*—in short, a refocusing of philosophy on the 'human milieu' in a manner even more extreme than Hume's return to 'common life' or Socrates's preoccupation with man and moral matters. This much corresponds to 3 above. On the other hand, we have a philosophy of human emancipation, directed toward opening man's eyes to his real liberty and, at the same time, to the illusions and crippling religious superstitions and social conditions that restrict human freedom. This corresponds roughly to sense 2.

Thus, when Sartre proclaims, in the French title of the work, that "Existentialism *is a* humanism," he is recommending it as clearing away the old other-worldly metaphysical and religious lumber by refocusing philosophy on man, on the concrete 'here and now.' This is what existentialism has in common with Marxism. But beyond this, it recommends itself as providing the best basis for social activism directed toward the betterment of the lot of mankind individually and collectively. In this it far surpasses Marxism, according to the early Sartre.

33.3 From theocentrism to atheistic humanism

Sartre's atheistic humanism is at bottom a radicalization of certain anthropocentric tendencies already in evidence in Descartes and Hume. It is possible to distinguish two main stages in the overall post-Greek development of philosophy down to Sartre. The first is the transition *from theocentrism to anthropocentrism*, that is, from the god-centred philosophical outlook of the Christian Middle Ages, particularly the earlier Middle Ages, to the man-centred focus of Hume. In this development Descartes's subjectivism is the real watershed. The second stage is the development *from anthropocentrism to humanism*, or from Hume and the eighteenth-century Enlightenment to Sartre and the twentieth-century subjectivism and relativism.

It is worth taking a closer look at these historical developments. They have to do with the way man orientates himself within the totality of what is—arguably, the distinctive thing about metaphysical as opposed to all other kinds of thinking (see chap. 3 above). Accordingly, the two phases of radical *re*orientation just mentioned can be set in a clear light by contrasting the philosophies of the Middle Ages, of Descartes, Hume, and Sartre in three key respects: (1) the scope of philosophy, its subject matter; (2) the order of knowing; and (3) the order of being.

33.4 From theocentrism to anthropocentrism

To begin with, let us juxtapose the philosophical outlook of the Middle Ages with those of Descartes and Hume in the three respects just mentioned. For our purposes here, we shall equate medieval with scholastic philosophy, although there were many other important periods and currents of medieval thought, some of them sharply at odds with mainstream scholasticism.

33.4.1 Medieval thought

As regards the *scope* of philosophy, medieval thought, like ancient Greek philosophy before and after Socrates, was 'synoptic' or 'holistic' in tendency: it strove, in accordance with the Aristotelian conception of metaphysics outlined earlier (see 20.6.1), after a comprehensive understanding of *all being*, of being as a whole. For this purpose, it divided the All into God (the uncreated being) and the created world, assigning man (and the human soul) a special place within creation, human redemption or salvation being the chief goal or purpose of the whole created order of things. Despite its universality of scope, the *supersensible* enjoyed a certain pre-eminence among the objects of philosophy.

In the *order of knowing*, by contrast, what comes first, in scholasticism as in Aristotle, is precisely the *sensible* world around us. From this starting point, it is possible to know the human mind as well, through attending to our thinking about sensible things while focusing attention on the mind itself rather than the things thought about (see 22.3.1). Similarly derivative or indirect is our knowledge of the divine through reasoning from the created world, as an effect, to the uncreated first cause of all things. The starting point of *all* knowledge is those ordinary physical or material things accessible in simple sense perception.

As regards the *order of being*, we find a striking innovation among the medievals. Greek, especially Aristotelian, science regarded the cosmos as eternal, that is, as independent, as far as its existence is concerned, of any cause. By contrast, the Christian philosophy of the Middle Ages was decisively shaped by the biblical creation story. Accordingly, God, the uncreated Creator, is first in the order of being. On him the material world and the human soul depend for their existence. The whole world was created "out of nothing" by God "in the beginning," and it is sustained in existence from moment to moment by the same creative act through which it was brought into being in the first place. As for mind and body, human thought depends for its existence on the body (brain) and on the sensible things it thinks about. So the whole order of being discernible in medieval thought is: first, God, then the sensible world, and finally human thought or the soul.

33.4.2 Descartes's philosophical outlook

If the preceding sketch is accurate, one can indeed speak of medieval *theocentrism* regarding the order of being, but not with regard to either the order of knowing or the scope of philosophy. We turn now to Descartes and modern philosophy.

For his own part, Descartes still takes a synoptic or holistic view of reality and its three principal domains: God, the world, and the human soul. While Descartes undoubtedly gave new prominence to the problem of knowledge, his philosophy is still concerned *primarily* (see 22.2) with being and the totality of what is. His ontology can be summed up this way: Everything that is is either (1) a thinking substance (whether infinite or finite), (2) a material substance, (3) an attribute of such a thinking or material substance (thought or extension, respectively), or (4) a mode of such an attribute (the varieties of knowing and willing in the case of thought, and of shape and motion in that of extension). To these must be added (5) the eternal truths, which do not exist outside the human mind *in rerum natura* ('in nature' or 'in the nature of things'), though they exist in the mind of God as well as (at least latently) in all human minds in which God has implanted them. To establish this general ontology in opposition to the reigning scholastic orthodoxy was the principal aim of what is known as 'Cartesian dualism,' though, as noted earlier (see 27.8.3), this term is often used for Descartes's view of the human being as a composite of mind and body.

As for the starting point of knowledge in Descartes, it obviously shifted away from the sensible things to the human mind or soul (*cogito, ergo sum*). Here we see the emergence of a new *anthropocentrism* regarding the order of knowing. Still, a non-deceiving God is needed if there is to be any stable and permanent knowledge that does not immediately become subject to doubt when no longer clearly and distinctly perceived; for a deceptive God, having created the eternal truths, could change them, unbeknownst to me. Even my own existence is thus subject to doubt when I do not actually attend to the grounds for my belief in it. So, despite the *cogito, ergo sum*, the anthropocentric shift is not complete; a strong element of theocentrism still pervades the Cartesian order of knowing. The theocentrism of medieval philosophy, as we have just seen, was focused on the order of being; Descartes introduces a kind of theocentrism into the order of knowing, even though the self, the soul, becomes the first item and new starting point of all knowledge, even of the knowledge of God.

As for the *order of being*, the order expressed as 'first God, then the world' remains unaltered in Descartes, since the old creation story of the Judeo-Christian Bible is retained throughout the seventeenth century. But the mind–matter split within the created realm gets a fresh interpretation in Cartesian dualism. The traditional dependence of thought on the existence of sensible things is denied: human thought and material things become two mutually independent domains: each depends on God, but neither depends upon the other. That is, once again, the main contention of the substance dualism described above.

33.4.3 Hume's outlook

All things considered, the theocentrism of the Middle Ages emerges very largely, though not entirely, unscathed from the Cartesian revolution. Nevertheless, the thin edge of the anthropocentric wedge has now been inserted. Hume enhances Descartes's anthropocentric tendencies in two of the respects under consideration, but actually curbs them in a third.

Hume understood the subject matter of philosophy as the "science of human nature" or "moral science," taking metaphysics to comprise all the first principles of that science: of epistemology, ethics, aesthetics, and politics (see 28.6). This already represents a great narrowing of the scope of philosophy. Philosophy is no longer the synoptic attempt to orientate oneself within the totality of what is; it is the science of human nature alone. Here begins the flowering of that anthropocentric tendency the seeds of which were sown by Descartes. Of Hume it would be correct to say, as it would not of Descartes, that epistemological and psychological questions occupy a central, even controlling position in philosophy.

Being the *sole* object of philosophy, the study of the human *mind* is also *the first* object of knowledge for Hume. Everything except one's own passing mental states and their internal object is engulfed in sceptical doubts (see 31.8.1). The *order of knowing* starts with thinking (*cogito*) *and stops there too*, even before it gets to *sum* (a thinking thing or mental substance, which Hume denies). In relation to observation and memory, neither of which is absolutely reliable, scientific knowledge of universal laws is even more precarious. Only the psychological laws of human nature are excepted, since knowledge of our own irremediable ignorance qualifies as scientific knowledge. Hume's all-corroding scepticism is more man-centred, more *mind*-centred in fact, than anything to be found in Descartes; for owing to his representationalism (ibid.), Hume *ends up* in a scepticism not unlike that from which Descartes begins.

As for the *order of being*, the Argument from Design and all other proofs of God's existence used to underpin some version of the biblical creation story are shown by Hume to be either inconclusive or patently fallacious. As a result, the God–World split becomes insignificant. As for the Mind–Matter split, however, Hume believed, though he acknowledged himself unable to justify the belief, in an independent realm of material things on which the thoughts in human minds depended causally for their existence. This is a return from Descartes's position to something more like the position of the Middle Ages (dependence of thought on things).

Summing up, then, with regard to the scope of philosophy and the order of knowing, Hume is more man- or mind-centred than Descartes, while with regard to the order of being (in which mind again depends upon body) his is less so.

33.5 From anthropocentrism to atheistic humanism

We can now compare Sartre with Descartes and Hume in the same three respects.

As for the *scope of philosophy*, an existential philosophy simply coincides with the philosophy of man. Man alone 'exists'; other things 'are.' This is obviously a new technical use of 'existence' that is much narrower than traditional usage. Whereas, traditionally, existence was opposed to essence, here it is applied to the particular mode of being actual that is distinctive of human as opposed to non-human entities. Accordingly, philosophy of existence or existential philosophy is the ontology of man; it is a regional rather than a universal study of being such as Aristotle envisaged. Hence, we have much the same radical restriction on the scope of philosophy as in Hume: the proper subject matter of philosophy is man alone.

In the *order of knowing*, philosophical knowledge starts (as in Descartes and Hume) with the human *and also ends there* (as with Hume, though not Descartes). The big difference is that Sartre balks at the idea of taking *the human* as *the mental*, that is, understanding man (a) as a worldless, bodiless, solipsistic mind characterized by cognitive, volitional, and emotional states, and (b) as only *accidentally* related, via those states, to a world (including his own body) and to other human beings, both of which *just happen* to be there too. Instead, Sartre follows Heidegger in attempting to understand man as he exists *physically and concretely* in the real world of everyday practical and social activity. So understood, human life is not primarily a sequence of lived experiences (knowing, willing, and feeling), but above all a set of actualized and as yet unactualized possibilities of existing practically, that is, as a physical being with desires, emotions, and a will, in a world populated by other persons and by non-human things. To these persons and things man is related *essentially*, not accidentally; they, the 'not-I,' make up an essential dimension of our own 'human reality' as the only 'existers.'

This captures well enough what Heidegger means when he describes man as a 'Being-in-the-world.' Philosophical understanding of other humans, of non-human things, even of God (or of God's non-existence), is absorbed into the knowledge of one's own 'human reality' or existence, into self-knowledge. There is thus no *order* of knowing, such as one finds in Descartes, proceeding from self to God to sensible things, including human others; things and other human beings are indeed present in the world, but the being-for-me of *things* and the being-together-with-me of *others* are taken as integral parts of my own human reality, as dimensions of *my* Being-in-the-world-with-others. Accordingly, they become comprehensible in understanding my own being. As for God, he simply does not exist.

How faithful Sartre remains to this new Heideggerian starting point is a question that will occupy us later. Turning now to the *order of being*, we ask, What are the consequences of the fact that, in the order of knowing, the only *world* philosophy has to investigate is a dimension of 'human reality' itself, the world of those Beings-in-the-world that we ourselves are? Or again, what follows from the fact that the only God that comes within the purview of philosophy is the God who is dead (in Nietzsche's famous phrase), the God by whom man feels himself "abandoned," as Sartre puts it? Proofs of the existence of the external world or the existence of God are, from Sartre's perspective, equally worthless; the former because they are unnecessary, since the world is in any case part of my human reality and its reality therefore just as certain as my own existence; the latter because the conclusion, 'God exists,' is dogmatically assumed to be false. The question of God's existence is in any case irrelevant to the main concern of existential philosophy: for "man ... to find himself" (56/369), not God. So in the order of knowing, as in the order of being, man is the starting point and endpoint; nothing else either is or is knowable apart from our human reality.

Thus, in respect of the scope of philosophy, the order of knowing, and the order of being, we have in Sartre the *most extreme anthropocentrism* ever encountered in philosophy. It is this that we have been referring to as 'humanism' or 'atheistic humanism.'

33.6 The structure of *Existentialism and Humanism*

So much for Sartre's philosophical outlook. What is meant by 'humanism,' specifically 'atheistic humanism,' has now been clarified, at least in preliminary fashion; so too what we have called Sartre's *basic* philosophical outlook, his subjectivism. We conclude this chapter with a quick sketch of the overall structure of Sartre's *Existentialism and Humanism*.

The work is built around four criticisms brought against existentialism by Christian and/or Marxist philosophers. Sartre begins the first stage of rebuttal with a very brief response to each criticism. Then, in the middle section of the work, he elaborates the central doctrines of existentialism. He concludes with an examination of the four criticisms in much more depth, this time based squarely on the detailed exposition of the middle section. Thus, we have the following overall structure (the numbers in parentheses refer to paragraphs):

I. Criticisms of Existentialism

1 Four Criticisms (1–4)

(i) Quietism
(ii) Pessimism
(iii) Cartesianism
(iv) Relativism

2 Brief Reply to these Criticisms (5)

II. The Basic Doctrines Explained and Exemplified by Key Phenomena

3 Basic Doctrines: Subjectivism and Decisionism (Existence precedes Essence) (6–10)
4 Anguish (11–12)
5 Abandonment (13)
6 Example (14–16)
7 Despair (17–18)

III. Reply to the Four Criticisms

8 Reply to the Charge of Quietism (19)
9 Reply to the Charge of Pessimism (20–21)
10 Reply to the Charge of Cartesianism (22–25)
11 Reply to the Charge of Relativism (26–32, first half)
12 Existentialism and Humanism (32, second half–end)

34

Criticisms of Existentialism

34.1 Introductory

Existentialism and Humanism begins with a consideration of four "reproaches" (23/345) made by Christian or Marxist philosophers or both. Here at the outset Sartre replies in a fairly perfunctory manner, dismissing the first three charges as either disingenuous or based on misunderstandings. These criticisms and replies need only be examined briefly at this stage; Sartre's fuller response, as outlined in the third and final segment of the work (see 33.6), will be interpreted in the following chapters. The last of the four charges will only be touched on here, since, in this opening gambit, Sartre does not even attempt to reply to it.

34.2 The reproach of the communists: quietism

The reproach of the communists is summed up in this way: "First, it [existentialism] has been reproached as an invitation to people to dwell in the quietism of despair" (23/345). The point is that existentialism is a philosophy that presents the human condition as something *inescapable*, thus dwelling upon man's *impotence* rather than his power. The whole emphasis is on the utter *futility* of attempts to rise above the limitations of the universal human condition. As a consequence, so these communist critics allege, existentialism is a philosophy that hobbles the will to act, to transform human reality, inviting instead adoption of an attitude of passive (perhaps brooding, even despairing) acceptance, resignation, and contemplation of the inevitable.

This is obviously an objection based on pragmatic considerations that are arguably irrelevant. The real or imagined communist objector does not say (though he may in fact believe) that the existentialist's description of the human condition is mistaken; he says only that, from his point of view, it has undesirable, perhaps disastrous, *practical* consequences. For it leads, and apparently can only lead, to passive acquiescence in the immutability of things as they now are. While this is strictly irrelevant to the question of truth, Sartre, as we shall see, attempts to meet the objection on its own ground.

Historically, quietism was a seventeenth-century movement within Roman Catholicism that stressed passive contemplation and complete surrender of the self to the will of God, "like a feather blown about by all the winds of grace," in the phrase of François Fénelon (1651–1715), its chief exponent in France. In this way the soul of the believer achieves a truly blessed state, abandoning all earthly desires and purposes. An avowed atheist like Sartre could hardly be expected to use the word in this technical theological sense. Instead, he employs 'quietism' loosely to designate a general attitude of resignation and passive submission. This gives a mistaken impression of the original quietists, though the error is understandable enough; even their contemporary, Leibniz, who should have known better, accused the quietists of reprehensible sloth. They were in fact anything but idlers and layabouts, however; when it came to propagation of their own views, they could be so extraordinarily energetic that, according to one waggish historian, the "chief complaint made against the quietists by their adversaries was that they would not keep quiet."

Later, Sartre defines what he means by 'quietism' in this way: "Quietism is the attitude of people who say 'let others do what I cannot do'" (41/358). This, from the communists' perspective, is the very thing that distinguishes so-called bourgeois philosophies from Marxist activism. "Philosophers," writes Marx in the eleventh of his *Theses on Feuerbach*, "have only *interpreted* the world in various ways; the point, however, is to *change* it." Sartre's philosophy, it is alleged, belongs to those that merely interpret the world in new ways, acquiescing in the social and political *status quo*.

All that Sartre has to say in reply to this charge is that "existentialism ... is a doctrine that does render human life possible" (24/346). What he means by this is that it is a philosophy that stresses the possibility of *free* human action by removing the old Platonic, Christian, and rationalist obstacles to man's understanding of his own freedom. As rendering human *freedom* possible, it renders a genuinely human life possible; that appears to be the point of Sartre's enigmatic rejoinder.

34.3 The reproach of the Catholics: pessimism

The reproach of the Catholics is altogether different. "From another quarter," writes Sartre, "we are reproached for having underlined all that is ignominious in the human situation, for depicting what is mean, sordid, base to the neglect of certain things that possess charm and beauty and belong to the brighter side of human nature" (23/346), for example, "how an infant smiles."

The basis for this charge is most apparent from Sartre's fiction and drama, which present what can only be considered a very bleak picture of human life and relationships. For example, in the novel *The Age of Reason* the Sartrean 'hero,' having just learned that his mistress is pregnant, makes the rounds of his friends and acquaintances in Paris trying to borrow the money to pay for an illegal back-street abortion. The story "The Wall" deals with the terror of a group of political prisoners awaiting execution in the morning. Even in his philosophical works Sartre attaches great importance to emotions like shame and anguish, or to discreditable actions springing from so-called bad faith or self-deception. Little attention is paid to corresponding positive emotions and behaviours, and even at that they tend be given a perversely negative twist. We shall consider the reasons for this apparent one-sidedness later (see chap. 37).

To the charge that existentialism displays a penchant for grim or morbid themes, Sartre's initial response is twofold. First, he argues that the people who level this charge at existentialist philosophy are not really put off by its pessimism at all, since they in fact delight in fiction of a similar kind (for example, the works of the French realist novelist Émile Zola) and in popular sayings of a decidedly pessimistic turn. (Some examples of the latter are given in the text. They tend to show that proverbs are untranslatable. Home-grown English examples might be 'Money makes the world go round' and 'Misery loves company.') But beyond this *ad hominem* retort, Sartre suggests that what is really troubling these critics is the inherent *optimism* of existentialism, the disturbing freedom it ascribes to man and the burden of responsibility that results from recognizing that freedom. Later (42/359–60) Sartre clarifies this, indicating that, in the case of the social realism of Zola, the blame for the sordid aspects of life is put on hereditary, social, and economic circumstances, whereas Sartre's own philosophy assigns responsibility to no one but the agents themselves. Hence, what these critics are really objecting to, Sartre suggests, is not the pessimism of existentialism but its extreme optimism, of which they are afraid.

34.4 The reproach of Christians and communists: Cartesianism

The next charge is common to both Christian (Catholic) and communist critics:

Both from this side [that is, Catholics] and the other [communists] we are also reproached for leaving out of account the solidarity of mankind and considering man in isolation. And this ... is because we base our doctrine on pure subjectivity—upon the Cartesian 'I think': which is the moment in which solitary man attains to himself; a position from which it is impossible to regain solidarity with other men who exist outside the self. The *ego* cannot reach them through the *cogito*. (23/346)

The reproach here is that existentialism ignores the *community* with others (be it the solidarity of the working classes or the fellowship of Christ) that is supposed to be co-

Chapter 34: Criticisms of Existentialism 579

constitutive of the individual's own humanity; it ignores completely, in other words, the undeniable fact that man is essentially a social being. Existentialism lapses from man-centredness (already a marked trend in modern philosophy, as we have seen) into *self-centredness*, that is, *into egocentrism* and even *solipsism*. This, according to these critics, is tantamount to a return to the highly artificial and long-since-discredited starting point of Cartesian philosophy.

To this Sartre replies that existentialism is "a doctrine ... which affirms that every truth and every action imply both an environment and a human subjectivity" (24/346). The point of this dark saying is this. Man, according to existentialism, is not a worldless *ego* (considered abstractly, by abstracting from the environment to which he is *essentially* related); nor is he a solipsistic *ego* (conceived by abstracting from the other human beings to whom he is *essentially* related as well). In fact, he is not a bodiless *ego* or thinking thing at all. Rather, he is a Being-in-the-world with others. The fuller meaning of this was hinted at earlier (see 33.5); we shall consider it in more detail later (see 36.4). First, however, we must at least mention the final reproach, to which Sartre offers no response at this stage.

34.5 The reproach of the Christians: moral relativism

The fourth and last reproach stems again from the Christian or Catholic camp:

From the Christian side, we are reproached as people who deny the reality and seriousness of human affairs. For since we ignore the commandments of God and all values prescribed as eternal, nothing remains but what is strictly voluntary [i.e., dependent upon the *human* will]. Everyone can do what he likes, and will be incapable, from such a point of view, of condemning either the point of view or the action of anyone else. (23–4/346)

The charge, in short, is *voluntarism*, the implied consequence of which is relativism: the denial that there are or can be any objective standards or norms of conduct, any moral action guides that are not man-made, the products of a human will. Only if there is an "eternal" and unalterable standard that is ascertainable by us, so the criticism goes, is there a universally valid criterion of right and wrong by which to condemn a code of conduct of the sort deemed vicious, or particular actions of the sort deemed wicked by the vast majority of moral communities. Failing this, all codes and actions are either equally unwarranted or else capable of the same or equivalent justifications.

To this, as we shall see later (chap. 38), Sartre cannot give any fully *adequate* reply, since the charge is at bottom justified. It would certainly have been open to Sartre to reply, even at this early stage, that the implicit demand for "eternal" God-given moral absolutes aims too high; that all that is required to evade the charge of relativism is that there be some scope for rational justification and/or criticism, a pattern of rational argumentation appropriate to the nature of the moral subject matter. Instead, Sartre tries to meet these critics on their own ground—and fails. As we shall see (chap. 38), his voluntarism rules out the possibility of meeting even the lesser requirement: leaving room for *some* form of rational debate about morals.

34.6 Conclusion

So much for the charges *Existentialism and Humanism* sets out to answer. None is really defused by Sartre's initial retorts, and the most serious of all is not even addressed. Since the exposition of the following chapters deals with Sartre's detailed replies to these criticisms, we shall assess the force of the criticisms and the adequacy of the responses as we go along rather than postpone our critical reflections, as in the preceding parts, to a separate chapter or section at the end. The point of view remains that adopted in the last two parts. As we shall see, Sartre, following Heidegger, succeeds to a greater extent than any thinker studied so far in hewing close to that understanding of ourselves and our natural and social environment that is primary. Whether he illuminates or distorts everyday experience with his voluntarism and pessimism is a harder question to answer.

35

Slogan and Basic Doctrines

35.1 Introductory

In an effort to clear up the misunderstandings behind the reproaches outlined in the last chapter, Sartre first divides existentialists into two camps: Christian existentialists like Jaspers and Marcel, and atheistic existentialists like Heidegger and himself. This is typical of the half-truths Sartre is apt to proclaim even about the recent history of philosophy. That Jaspers's "philosophy of existence" (*Existenzphilosophie* in German) is 'Christian' seems mistaken; and Heidegger expressly denied being an atheist in anything like the customary sense of the word. It is true, however, that Marcel was a Catholic thinker, that Jaspers retained a non-denominational attitude of belief in God, and that the Christian faith perspective plays no role at all in Heidegger's thought.

What both camps share, according to Sartre, is the conviction that "existence comes before" (26/348) or "precedes essence" (28/349). Here again extreme caution is indicated. When it was first reported to him by one of his French disciples, Heidegger explicitly rejected the slogan and the existentialist label that goes with it. Like the label, then, the slogan "existence precedes essence" is Sartre's alone. The present chapter examines the broader historical context of the slogan, which sums up *two basic doctrines*, a (1) theory of human reality and a (2) normative ethical theory, to be examined in the chapters to follow.

The first thing to note is that the existentialist slogan claims to reverse the order of precedence between existence and essence in (a) the Christian philosophies of the Middle Ages and (b) the dominant philosophies of the seventeenth century, by which Sartre means those of Descartes and Leibniz, both of whom are mentioned by name (27/348). What (a) and (b) share, apart from the conviction that essence precedes existence, is a belief in God; the reversal of the order of precedence between essence and existence is just the logical consequence of a consistent philosophical atheism.

Here again we must take care not to be misled by Sartre. For reasons that cannot be considered here, "existence precedes essence" would be a fitting slogan for the Christian philosophy of St Thomas Aquinas. For present purposes, however, we can go along with Sartre's view that the essence of created things is prior to their existence in the traditional creation story of medieval Christian theology. Lumping Descartes and Leibniz together with the medievals is, however, another matter. So is the misleading claim that a reversal of the order of existence and essence is just a *logical* consequence of the denial of God's existence. These are things we will not be able to go along with.

35.2 The Aristotelian and medieval syntheses

Despite the biblical theism that unites them, the Christian philosophies of the Middle Ages and the seventeenth-century were sharply divided over Greek science. By the seventeenth century, the medieval synthesis of (i) the Judeo-Christian Bible with (ii) Greek, particularly Aristotelian, science (sometimes referred to as the synthesis of Faith and Reason) was beginning to come undone. While the major philosophies of the period remained committed to a philosophical creation story loosely based on the Bible, they were adamant in their rejection of the Aristotelian science of the Middle Ages as incompatible with the new mechanistic mathematical natural science of Copernicus, Kepler (1571–1630), and Galileo. Of course, Aristotelian science was itself the product of an older synthesis (see 8.2.1), its basic tendency diametrically opposed to that of the new science.

35.2.1 Aristotelian and modern science

The fundamental tendency of the new science of the early modern period was not altogether new; it consisted in a return to the mathematical, mechanistic, and materialist outlook pioneered by the ancient Greek atomists, especially Epicurus. Thus, at the dawn of the modern era, thinkers as disparate as Descartes and Locke again (i) reduced the qualitative richness and variety of things to quantitatively describable powers acting mechanically on the human sense organs to produce sensory responses in the mind. At the same time, a renewed attempt was made to (ii) reduce living or vital forces to the mechanical motions of inert matter, notably by Descartes, who maintained that animals were just highly complex machines (see 24.6.4). Finally, (iii) the whole realm of the mental was reduced to the "dance of material particles" (see 27.13) by such thinkers as Hobbes and Gassendi. This time, however, the entire enterprise was crowned with a success undreamt of in ancient times, owing partly to important advances in microphysics and physiology, partly to innovations in technology like microscopes and telescopes.

Throughout the early modern era Aristotelian science was derided by progressive thinkers as having retarded the emergence of an exact mathematical science of nature by some two millennia—a charge still heard on occasion from historians of science today. It was indeed Aristotle who, at the end of the classical age, pulled Greek science back from the brink of a reductivist mathematical, mechanistic, and materialistic outlook, purging it at the same time of the spiritualist and other-wordly tendencies of Plato by restoring to the idea of nature (*physis*) the associations of growth and life that it has in ordinary experience—and still had in the thought of the first *physiologoi* (see 5.5.2). Aristotle's own synthesis of all he deemed worthy of preservation in earlier Greek thought ensured that the philosophical investigation of formal and final causes continued to enjoy pride of place vis-à-vis the study of the efficient, mechanical causes of change right down through the medieval period. He set the seal of his authority on the irreducible reality of qualities and relations as well as on the primacy of sense perception in the cognitive process. Little wonder, then, that the name 'Aristotle' became synonymous with all that seemed outmoded or retrograde to the philosophers and scientists of the early modern period.

35.2.2 The medieval Christian creation story

If Aristotelian science was starkly at odds with the new mechanistic natural philosophy and with the actual physical science of the seventeenth century, the other component of the medieval synthesis, the biblical creation story, was not so to anything like the same extent. Like the thirteenth, the century of Descartes, Leibniz, and Newton produced philosophical creation stories of its own. Only in the eighteenth century did the idea of divine creation become the object of scathing philosophical criticism. And only in the following century, with advances in biological science (in particular, the evolutionary theory of Darwin), was this second component of the medieval synthesis completely discredited and almost universally discarded by philosophers and scientists—whatever those same individuals may have held privately as believing Christians, which most still were. Of course, the philosophical creation story of the Middle Ages was itself a complex synthesis of biblical and Greek elements, as that of the moderns was an amalgam of biblical and scientific ideas.

The influence of Plato's late dialogue, *Timaeus*, on medieval Christian theology has been mentioned several times already (see especially 25.8). Numerous Christian Platonists of the Middle Ages had surprisingly little difficulty adapting this pagan Greek myth to the biblical account of divine creation *ex nihilo*. Of course, in bringing forth a rational order from chaos, Plato's divine craftsman (the 'Demiurge,' as he is called, from the Greek *demiurgos* 'artisan') looks away to separate Forms as models already existing somewhere outside himself. He is thus (a) the *necessary*, not the sufficient, (b) cause of *order*, not of the existence of anything, be it of the separately existing patterns of rational order or of the disorderly matter arranged. Moreover, he

(c) acts from the necessity of his own nature, because, as Plato says, "he was good," not from the exercise of free will.

By removing the Forms from the Platonic heaven and sticking them in the mind of God, the Christian Middle Ages made the divine being what the Demiurge had never been for Plato, (a) the *sufficient* as well as necessary condition or (b) cause of the *existence* rather than of the order of everything in the universe. Unlike the Demiurge of the *Timaeus*, moreover, the creator God of Christian theology (c) acts freely, by choice, not from the necessity of his nature. God the creator does not create the forms or essences of things, since these exist eternally in the divine mind as part of his creative essence; in order to grasp them, he has only to contemplate his own nature. God thus brings forth the world and every entity in it, including man, *ex nihilo* by causing the form, essence, or nature that exists eternally in his Mind to exist temporally outside it in created matter; to the form that is the essence, God adds a new 'form' in another sense, what Aquinas called the 'act of existence.'

35.3 Sartre on theism, creation, and human nature

Of the two great syntheses just described, only the latter involves a definite order of priority of essence and existence, the distinction, while not unknown, having been of only minor importance in the Greek sources on which the medievals drew (see 26.8.2). For present purposes we can say, without too much distortion, that in the medieval synthesis of biblical and Platonic elements the essence or nature that exists from eternity in the divine intellect, as part of God's creative nature, is prior to the so-called act of existence conferred by God's creative will. It is not hard to see how Aristotle's conception of the first Unmoved Mover as "thought thinking itself" (see 20.5.2) may have contributed to the medieval notion of God's exemplar causality (see 25.8). Less obvious is how the model of human manufacture shaped all three cosmologies, the Ancient Greek, biblical, and medieval Christian alike. That it did so, positively and/or negatively, seems clear enough; but the full story is apt to be complex. It is surprising, therefore, that Sartre treats *the* theistic model of creation (as though there were only one) as based squarely on the model of human manufacture of artefacts and nothing else:

When we think of God as the creator, we are thinking of him, most of the time, as a supernal [that is, a higher kind of] artisan. Whatever doctrine we may be considering [including the medieval?], whether it be a doctrine like that of Descartes, or of Leibnitz himself [the spelling of the text], we always imply that the will follows, more or less, from the understanding or at least accompanies it, so that when God creates he knows precisely what he is creating [i.e., knows in advance the essence of the thing that he will cause to exist]. Thus, the conception of man in the mind of God is comparable to that of the paper-knife in the mind of the artisan: God makes man according to a procedure and a conception, exactly as the artisan manufactures a

Chapter 35: Slogan and Basic Doctrines   585

paper-knife, following a definition and a formula. Thus each individual man is the realization of a certain conception that dwells in the divine understanding. (27/348)

As developed here, the key point of the analogy with human manufacture is that the form, essence, or nature comes *first*; it must be present already, however vaguely, in the intellect of the artisan—for instance, the idea of a knife for cutting the pages of a book (purpose), including a knowledge of the steps involved in its production (a recipe or "formula," as Sartre calls it). Only *then* comes the act of producing the artefact *in accordance with* the paradigm by following the steps in the formula for its production. Sartre's emphasis here is squarely upon the implications of the alleged model for the creation *of man*. A definite, circumscribed concept or definition of man must pre-exist in God's intellect (like that of the paper-knife in the mind of the human artisan) *before* man can be brought into existence by an act of the divine will. But secondarily he is objecting to the traditional notion that will is subsequent to, or only simultaneous with ("accompanies"), the intellect. The priority of volition will be the subject of the next chapter.

According to Sartre, then, the essence of man precedes his existence in *all* those theistic philosophies that develop or retain some form of the biblical creation story that he takes to be based strictly on the model of human manufacture. The point he is leading up to is that once the craft model of theism is abandoned, consistency demands that the idea of a universal human nature and the priority of essence to existence be abandoned as well:

In the philosophic atheism of the eighteenth century, the notion of God is suppressed, but not, for all that, the idea that essence is prior to existence; something of that idea we still have everywhere, in Diderot, Voltaire and even Kant. Man possesses a human nature; that "human nature," which is the conception of human being, is found in every man, which means that every man is a particular example of a universal conception, the conception of Man.

Atheistic existentialism, of which I am a representative, declares with greater consistency that if God does not exist, there is at least one being whose existence comes before its essence, a being which exists before it can be defined by any conception of it. (27/348-9)

Thus, we are told, a straight reversal of the traditional order of existence and essence—at least in the case of man—follows logically once God is erased from the standard picture of creation of which Descartes and Leibniz were the last pre-Enlightenment apostles. That both Descartes and Leibniz followed the medievals in asserting the priority of essence to existence is true enough; but the former flouts, while the latter reasserts, the standard view described above. On closer examination, Sartre's assertion of the priority of existence to essence turns out to be not so much a reversal of Christian teaching as a sort of *Cartesian voluntarism without God*. That is why we can easily ignore the distorting features of his picture of medieval thought, but not the conflation of Descartes and Leibniz.

35.4 Descartes and Leibniz on creation

Even granting Sartre's assumption concerning the priority of essence to existence in the medieval Christian account of creation, how could it be read off from the craft model in anything like the way Sartre maintains for all theistic accounts? A human artisan only (a) works pre-existing materials up into a new form or pattern, (b) without creating *ex nihilo* the materials out of which the artefact is made. Moreover, unlike the creator God who grasps through reflection a pattern existing from eternity in his own mind, the human artisan *may* actually create an idea or form *ex nihilo*, bringing forth something genuinely new through the exercise of natural human ingenuity. This seems to be the case for artistic production in particular. Still, 'looking away' to an already existing model outside him (a table, say) is the norm for most other craft production; and this is more reminiscent of Plato's Demiurge than of the creator God of standard Christian theology. Naturally, (c) the human craftsman acts freely, by choice, not, like the Demiurge, from any necessity of his nature.

On the whole, then, the medieval conception of the creator strikes a reasonable balance (partial sameness, partial difference) between the model of human craft production (anthropomorphism) and a creator God whose activity is so utterly foreign to us as to seem almost totally incomprehensible (agnosticism). On this spectrum, it falls somewhere between the quasi-anthropomorphic conception of the Platonic Demiurge and, at the other end of the scale, the utterly remote and self-absorbed Aristotelian First Mover, 'thought thinking itself.'

Leibniz, for his part, understood and adhered closely to the orthodox model, rejecting the Cartesian heresy of divine creation of the essences of things. Descartes had moved unacceptably close to the anthropomorphic end of the scale by following the craft model on the key point (b): as the human artist freely invents the idea of the object to be produced, so the Cartesian God creates the essences of things. By eliminating God from the story of man altogether, Sartre indeed reverses what he takes to be the order of priority of essence and existence in all theistic philosophies, but in a way that issues in a *human* voluntarism: Sartre bestows on man the sheer omnipotence—at least as regards his own nature and all values—that belonged to the Cartesian creator God and no other. This goes well beyond the anthropocentrism of Hume and the Enlightenment, justifying our earlier ascription to Sartre of the most extreme form of man-centred outlook possible (see 32.2). A closer look at Descartes and Leibniz will make this clearer.

35.4.1 Descartes on the creation of the world

Descartes's philosophical creation story departs from the medieval doctrine in several ways. First and foremost, (1) God is the efficient cause both of the essences of things (including, as we shall see, the universal essence of man) and of the things whose essences they are (for example, each individual existing man). For eternal truths about "true and immutable natures" are no less dependent upon God's will than contingent truths about matters of fact or existence—what there is and what happens in the world. That is the sense of Descartes's notorious doctrine that intellect and will are one and the same in God though distinct in humans (see 25.8): God makes the true true; the act of the intellect by which he *understands* that something is so is the very act by which he *wills* that it be so. For the medievals, by contrast, the divine intellect and will are distinct (ibid.), the former prior to the latter. So while in Descartes, as in medieval thought, there are no essences (possible entities) that are independent of God, this is not because they are part of God's creative essence, but rather because God creates them too, just as he creates all contingent existents.

To the extent that the human artist, too, invents the idea of the object to be brought into being, this Cartesian teaching comes closer to the model Sartre has in mind than does the orthodox Christian view. And as with truth so with value or goodness: as there are no essences that exist independently of God, so (2) there are no values either. God does not make certain possible things actual because they are good (or better than other possible things); rather, he chooses arbitrarily to create certain things and *makes them good simply by choosing them* (ibid.). That is Descartes's second departure from standard Christian orthodoxy.

The third and final point of divergence concerns the doctrine that (3) God continues to maintain what he has created in existence *at every subsequent moment* by an act of conservation that is identical with his original act of creation (creation is continuous creation for Descartes), even though *we* limited human creatures must conceive the acts of creation and conservation as different. For Descartes, this is true even of the eternal truths, including those having to do with good and bad, right and wrong in the moral sense: they are created/conserved at every moment of time by God's free will.

35.4.2 Leibniz on the creation of the world

Leibniz's philosophical creation story involves the deliberate rejection of *all three* Cartesian heresies. First, (1) the essences or natures of things and the eternal truths of logic and mathematics are not dependent on God's will. They become again part of the divine nature. Even the divine intellect has to avoid logical contradiction in conceiving the essences of things (the possible things or natures, of which some are made actual); only what is actual or existent, not, as in Descartes, what is possible, depends upon the divine will. When Leibniz writes: "He [God] is the source of possibilities and existents alike, the one [the essences of things] by his essence [that is, his exemplar causality], the other [the existence of things] by his will" or efficient causality, he is just returning to the orthodox theological view that intellect and will are separate in God and humans alike. Furthermore, (2) God chooses to make this world actual because it is good, or at least better than other possible worlds—in fact the *best* of all possible worlds; it is not good or best simply because he chooses it, as Descartes had maintained. Finally, (3) God chooses the whole sequence of events that will take place in the world "in the beginning." He does not need to intervene in the course of nature at each moment to decide the state of the world at the next; instead, he decides everything at the moment of creation, 'pre-programming' the world, so to speak, to endure and to change in ways of his choosing. Kant accordingly spoke of Leibniz's 'Preformation Theory.' Eternal truths, not being created, are not conserved by God's will either.

35.4.3 Descartes and Leibniz on the creation of man

We can highlight the first two differences between Descartes and Leibniz in terms of the Euthyphro dilemma (see 11.8). Is the true true because God affirms it? Or does God affirm it because it is true? Is the good good because God chooses it? Or does God choose it because it is good? Descartes takes the first horn (theological voluntarism), Leibniz, like Euthyphro, the second.

Turning now to the *creation of man* in particular, we note that, for Descartes, God first creates man's essence and then the individual man in accordance with his "true and immutable" idea; the divine will *first* determines what the divine intellect conceives (will and intellect being one and the same in God) and *then* makes it actual *outside* the divine intellect *in rerum natura* through another act of volition. Here we have a model of man's coming-into-being that indeed mirrors human artistic creation. For Leibniz, by contrast, the essence of man is independent of the divine will; it is one possible human nature among an infinite variety of others surveyed in a single act of intuition by the divine intellect. The divine will then actualizes an entity having the one that is *best*.

Thus, Sartre ascribes to man that power of creating his own nature and all values that only Descartes was bold enough to assign to God. He thus gives to human beings a sphere of absolute freedom and an omnipotence of the sort that Leibniz and most traditional philosophy denied even to God! To that extent the result may be described as a creation story without God. It is not really surprising, therefore, that Sartre develops an extensive comparison with the work of art:

[D]oes anyone reproach an artist, when he paints a picture, for not following the rules established *à priori*? ... As everyone knows, there is no pre-defined picture for him to make ... [T]he picture that ought to be made is precisely that which he will have made. As everyone knows, there are no aesthetic values *à priori*, but there are values which will appear in due course in the coherence of the picture in relation to the will to create ... What has that to do with morality? We are in the same creative situation. We never speak of a work of art as irresponsible; when we are discussing a canvas by Picasso, we understand very well that the composition became what it is at the time when he was painting it ...

It is the same on the plane of morality. There is this in common between art and morality, that in both we have to do with creation and invention ... Man makes himself; he is not found ready-made; he makes himself by the choice of his morality. (49/364)

The nature of morality will be discussed in more detail in chapter 38. At this stage, two comments may be in order. First, there seems to be "this in common between art and morality," that judgments of each kind, aesthetic and moral, admit of a pattern of rational justification of their own; neither can be understood in terms of the other, let alone in terms of those patterns of scientific rationality considered in chapter 6. Sartre may be over-hasty in concluding that what they have in common is that neither requires nor admits of rational justification. The other comment concerns the mistaken assumption that all rational justification must appeal to a priori principles.

35.5 The logical consequences of atheism

So much for the medieval and seventeenth-century background of the existentialist slogan. How much of this Sartre actually understood is hard to say. The seventeenth century having broken with Aristotelian science, the Enlightenment (Sartre mentions Diderot, Voltaire, and Kant, but could also have mentioned Hume) abandoned the remaining component of the great medieval synthesis of Faith and Reason, the biblical creation story. About this latter point Sartre is right. The eighteenth century was an era of philosophic and scientific *atheism* or *agnosticism*, like our own. True, too, is Sartre's statement that the Enlightenment did not at all abandon the idea of a *timeless, unchanging human nature* that is (a) the same for all men, civilized and savage, (b) throughout all ages, recent and remote, and (c) in all inhabited parts of the globe. The divine intellect and will of the creation story are both dispensed with in the atheistic or agnostic philosophies of the period, but not the belief in a *universal human nature* and universal human reason. This is rather a hallmark of Enlightenment thinking. What is not true is that it is inconsistent.

Sartre would have us believe that (1) the denial of a fixed, determinate, universal human nature and (2) the denial of any objective rules of moral conduct are the *logical* consequences of agnosticism or atheism. In the very last paragraph of the essay, he writes: "Existentialism is nothing else but an attempt *to draw the full conclusions from a consistently atheistic position*" (56/369). And elsewhere he notes: "we only mean to say that God does not exist, and that it is necessary to draw the consequences of his absence right to the end" (32–3/352). The "conclusions," or "consequences," are: (1) "If God does not exist ... [m]an is nothing else but that which he makes of himself" (27–8/349)—in other words, there is *no timeless, unchanging human nature*; and (2) "If God did not exist ... then everything would be permitted" (33/353)—that is, there are *no strictly objective rules of conduct or moral values*. Or, as Sartre also puts this latter point: "The existentialist ... finds it extremely embarrassing that God does not exist, for there disappears with Him all possibility of finding values in an intelligible heaven" (ibid.). Somehow, one feels that Sartre is not really very embarrassed by this alleged fact at all.

The reference to an "intelligible heaven" is an unmistakable allusion to the Platonic theory of Forms (see *Phaedrus* 247c), though here it is may be intended to cover the Christian creator God as well, in whose mind ideas of the good and the true exist from eternity. On the face of it, Sartre's inference is a pretty gross non sequitur ('non sequitur' is Latin for 'it does not follow,' so a non sequitur is a fallacious inference): If there are no Platonic Forms and there is no divine mind in which timeless ideas of man and values exist, then there is no human nature and the search for rationally warranted values is futile. What this way of arguing overlooks is the possibility of other models of rational justification. In the passage cited at the end of the last section, Sartre commits the same non sequitur in speaking of the rationalist tradition: if no a priori principles on which to base moral or aesthetic judgments, then no rational justification whatever. We noted earlier (see 32.3.2) that it is an illegitimate slide from: (1) no objective standards of the Platonic, Christian, or rationalist sort, to (2) no objective standards whatsoever. In the light of the foregoing, it will be hard to exonerate Sartre of this fallacy. At work is just the same old hankering after absolute rational certainty of the sort only the mathematical sciences afford. It haunted Kant no less than Plato and Descartes, as we have seen, and even Sartre, despite his disdain for tradition, is not able to work himself sufficiently free of it to recognize other patterns of objective rational justification.

35.6 Conclusion

According to the standard account of creation, the divine intellect first grasps what is possible in reflecting upon itself, whereupon the divine will makes certain of those possible natures or essences actual through an act of efficient causality. On Descartes's *un*orthodox view, God first creates the essences of things (including man); only then does he make certain of those natures, including man's, actual, causing them to exist not only in his mind, but also outside it, in the created world. Thus, for Descartes, intellect and will, conception and volition, though separate in man, are one and the same in God; God's very act of conceiving essences as possible is *at the same time* an act of will by which those essences are brought into being.

Sartre ascribes to man, within a restricted sphere, the sort of sheer omnipotence that Descartes ascribed to God. 'Theological voluntarism' is replaced with what may be called 'non-theological' or 'anthropological voluntarism': both man's own nature and all values depend for their existence upon the *human will and on nothing else*. The

'Divine Command Theory' becomes (so to speak) a 'Human Command Theory.' In terms of the Euthyphro dilemma: What is true of human nature is true because man makes it so; and what is (morally) right is right because man wills it, commits himself to it as a value.

That is what it means to say that "existence precedes essence." In what follows we shall consider the alleged "consequences" of atheism further. *Logical* consequences they are not, whatever Sartre maintains to the contrary. One could perfectly consistently eliminate God, embracing a this-wordly humanistic outlook, without falling into anything so extravagant as anthropological voluntarism. Of that the Enlightenment is proof. The consequences are rather the conclusions to which Sartre *jumps*, embodying them in his slogan "existence precedes essence."

There are *two* chief consequences built into this slogan: (1) a theory of man, of the 'human condition' rather than human nature, which can be conveniently summed up under the heading 'Sartre's theory of human reality'; and (2) a meta-ethical theory already described as 'voluntarism.' The latter forms the basis of a normative ethical theory called 'decisionism.' Sartre's theory of human reality is the subject of chapter 36, while his voluntarism and decisionism are discussed in chapter 38. Two important corollaries linking the first doctrine with the second, (a) the supremacy of the will and (b) the significance of the emotions, will be examined together in chapter 37.

36

Human Reality

36.1 Introductory

It is important to remember that Sartre has no desire to dispute the existence of a universal human nature in *any* sense whatever; he merely denies the existence of a fixed, static, or objectively given nature that is related to human action as a sufficient cause to its effect. Were there in all mankind some such set of unalterable traits and dispositions, then what man *is* would strictly determine what he *does*. Sartre's denial that this is so *at all* is tantamount to the assertion of a perfect or absolute human freedom. For he does not simply deny the proposition that what man is determines what he does; he asserts the converse: what man *does* determines what he *is*—and nothing else does so.

This is built right into the doctrine that existence precedes essence. It entails a universal human condition—a condition of absolute freedom to create oneself *ex nihilo*, so to speak. Moreover, what is thus fashioned out of nothing is not just one's individual character, existence, or human nature, but, as we shall see, a model or image of all mankind, a *universal* form of man. That is why it is not going too far to speak of a quasi-divinity of man on the Cartesian model of creation.

Of course, in speaking of this condition of absolute freedom, we run a constant risk of assimilating Sartre's theory to more traditional, including Enlightenment, views of 'human nature.' 'Human reality,' 'human existence,' 'the human condition' may therefore be preferable expressions. In Sartre's own words, the salient point is that

although it is impossible to find in each and every man a universal essence that can be called human nature, there is nevertheless a human universality of *condition*. (45–6/361–2)

There is human universality, but it is not something given; it is being perpetually made. I make this universality by choosing myself. (47/362)

Here we see how Sartre turns things around, much as with the relation between essence and existence. Instead of the traditional 'What man is (his universal human nature) determines what he does,' we have 'What man does (his free choices, his freely chosen actions) determines what he is.' This reversal implies a metaphysical conception of man that is different from *all* traditional theories of human nature in several important respects.

In view of the charge (see above 34.4) that existentialism presupposes a Cartesian starting point and concept of the subject, 'human reality' is perhaps a better designation even than 'human subjectivity' for Sartre's theory of man, although he himself still speaks of "human subjectivity" (55/368). This is symptomatic. For as we shall see in the present chapter, Sartre's conception of the human condition aims to recede as far as possible from the strict Cartesian concept of the self as "a thinking, unextended [bodiless] thing" (see 27.10)—and yet only falls somewhere between the completely un- and anti-Cartesian outlook of Heidegger and that of Descartes himself.

36.2 Thrownness and projection

The first consequence of atheism, (1) "If God does not exist … [m]an is nothing else but that which he makes of himself" (27–8/349), Sartre elaborates as follows:

if God does not exist, there is at least one being whose existence comes before its essence, a being which exists before it can be defined by any conception of it. That being is man or, as Heidegger has it, the human reality. What do we mean by saying that existence precedes essence? We mean that man [1] first of all exists, encounters himself, surges up in the world—and [2] defines himself afterwards. If man as the existentialist sees him is not definable, it is because [3] to begin with he is nothing. He will not be anything until later, and then [4] he will be what he makes of himself. Thus, there is no human nature because there is no God to have a conception of it. Man simply is. Not that he is simply what he conceives himself to be, but [5] he is what he wills, and as he conceives himself after *already* existing—as he wills to be after that leap toward existence. Man is nothing else but that which he makes of himself. That is the first principle of existentialism. (ibid.)

This key passage contains five puzzling claims (see the interpolated numbers in the cited passage): (1) man "first of all exists, encounters himself, surges up in a world"; (2) man "defines himself afterwards," that is, after "surging up in a world"; (3) "to begin with man is nothing"; (4) later "he will be what he makes of himself"; (5) he will be "what he wills." All these points can be subsumed under *two heads*. We call them, for convenience, by the names Heidegger gave them: 'thrownness' and 'projection.' The former coincides with (1), while the latter covers (2) through (5).

36.2.1 Thrownness

Sartre does not actually use this Heideggerian term in the quoted passage, though he comes close to doing so later, when he states that man is "thrown into this world" (34). Thrownness is that condition in which man *finds himself* at the moment of first becoming aware of himself at all—or, as Sartre and Heidegger prefer to say, the moment he first "encounters himself." He finds himself thrown *into a concrete existential situation*, and that means, above all, into a *world*, a natural and social environment made up of non-human things and other human beings. The reflexive talk of 'encountering *oneself*' signalizes that the notion of thrownness replaces the traditional Cartesian concept of the subject as the object of *self*-consciousness. The warrant for the substitution lies in the plain fact that man, as he *originally* discovers or becomes aware of himself, is nothing like a bodiless, worldless, solipsistic Cartesian mind that does *not yet* know whether anything else exists apart from it. The self in the sense of an abiding and relatively permanent 'I' in a stream of successive states or modes of thinking is a bloodless theoretical abstraction concocted by Descartes for purposes of achieving absolutely certain knowledge of the existence of a substance. The concrete human reality of which each of us is immediately, though perhaps only dimly, aware in day-to-day living is very different.

About this Sartre (or rather Heidegger) is undoubtedly right. If we attend carefully to the way we actually understand ourselves in everyday life (before being exposed to Cartesian philosophy or modern psychology), we can hardly deny that we understand ourselves as (a) having a human body and being in a world together with other human beings with whom that world is shared; furthermore we find ourselves existing already (b) in certain definite ways, that is, in some set of already actualized possibilities, some specific situation, whether freely chosen or somehow imposed. In short, we understand ourselves as *already involved* with things and with other human beings in various ways of coexisting in the world. Moreover, if we are perfectly honest about it, we discover ourselves as (c) ignorant of the 'whence' and 'whither' (as Heidegger puts it) of our being here, that is, not knowing where we came from or why we are here. In a word: thrown. True, religion and science may provide us with elaborately detailed accounts of our 'whence' and our 'whither'; and we may embrace them eagerly as either the gift of faith or the fruits of scientific understanding. But these are solutions, devised later, to a fundamental question that is there already when we first 'surge up' in a world. This primordial perplexity is just a fact.

All three of these points are implicit in Sartre's remark that (1) man "first of all exists, encounters himself, surges up *in a world*." If he speaks of 'thrownness' to designate these features of our Being-in-the-world, then it is mainly because, according to (c), we have not *brought ourselves by choice* into (a) the concrete world and (b) the situation in which we find ourselves. Even if we readily reassure ourselves (as we do) that our parents made us, or (as we may) that God made us, or both (our parents made our bodies and God our souls), this, to repeat, cannot alter the *brute fact* that at any given moment we continue to *find* ourselves as having a *past*, as being *already* in a world and in a situation that is not of our making, together with others in the midst of things, without knowing where we came from or what we are here for. That is the brute fact almost totally disguised by Descartes's misdescription of everyday immediate self-awareness as 'I think that I am thinking (something).'

This brute fact is called man's 'facticity' or 'factical existence' by Heidegger. The 'facticity' of existence and man's 'thrownness' into a world are different expressions for exactly the same thing. Behind both lies the philosophical attempt to break the hold of the Cartesian notion of the bodiless, worldless, solipsistic self of inner awareness. The self that only acquires a world *after the fact*, through a process of inference, is supplanted by a concept of 'selfhood' or 'personhood' that better reflects the concrete reality of our day-to-day self-understanding: Being-in-the-world.

If Descartes's notion of the self is a pure abstraction, a theoretical construct that is starkly, even wildly, at odds with ordinary experience, the notion of thrown Being-in-the-world springs from an effort to remain as faithful as possible to the phenomena themselves, to the way we actually experience and think about ourselves in our day-to-day living. The "door of reason" (see 27.13), on this view of philosophy, does not open on an altogether different image of self and world from those given in immediate lived experience. The task of philosophy is rather to make the phenomena of our pre-philosophical experience conceptually transparent, to articulate philosophically or discursively what immediate, so-called naive experience constantly understands at a pre-philosophical level. This is what the phenomenological method is all about, at least as Heidegger practised it; and Sartre's theory of human reality in *Being and Nothingness* attempts to follow Heidegger's lead, calling itself an "essay in phenomenological ontology" (see 32.1). This much seems indeed to represent philosophical progress. More will be said about the phenomenological method later (see 37.4.1).

36.2.2 Projection

The other general feature of human existence or reality as Being-in-the-world was termed 'projection' by Heidegger. Again, Sartre does not actually use the Heideggerian term in the long passage cited above, although he does say, somewhat later, that "man is, before all else, something which propels itself towards a future and is aware that it is doing so. Man is, indeed *a project* which possesses a subjective life, instead of being a kind of moss, or a fungus, or a cauliflower" (28/349).

'Projecting' (literally: 'throwing before oneself') is, as the nominal word meaning suggests, the opposite of 'thrownness' ('being thrown'); the two notions *complement* one another in the following way. In encountering myself as *already* something definite and as having a definite past, I come *at the same time* to the realization that I am *in a certain sense* "nothing," that is, that the future is open. I realize that I am *not yet* fully actualized in the present, so that I have to actualize myself *in the future* through my own choices among different possible ways of being in a body and different possibilities of being in a world together with others. That is the primary sense of the deliberate overstatement that "to begin with man is nothing": at the heart of human existence is an ineliminable '*not* yet.' No matter how many or how far-reaching the choices we in fact make, no matter how far we give determinateness to our being through willing what we shall be, we remain always, to a very large extent, indeterminate; our concrete being is always something that has *yet* to be achieved, always open.

In the next chapter we shall consider another important aspect of the talk of "nothing"; the frequency with which it occurs in the present work is to some extent explained by the fact that *Existentialism and Humanism* is a defence of the philosophy first presented in *Being and Nothingness*. What concerns us just now is Sartre's remark in the long passage cited earlier that (3) "to begin with man is nothing." The key to this is the concept of projection. That "[m]an is ... a project" alludes to the immediately experienced *fact* that the situation in which I find myself 'already' is *not* something definitive; I understand myself as thrown, to be sure, but also as projecting, as holding before myself a range of *un*actualized possibilities that I am 'not yet.' This is the source of man's so-called responsibility for what he is, the burden of having to create himself *ex nihilo*, 'out of nothing,' having to make himself what he is not yet. Although (3) "to begin with man is nothing," he (2) "defines himself afterwards." But this 'defining' is not just a matter of forming a mental idea of what one is going to be; it is rather a matter of making concrete practical *choices* among the various possible ways of existing, of living, that are open to one. *Projecting* what one is is a matter of *willing* what one will be much more than just conceiving or understanding what one can be. As Sartre puts it: (4) "he will be what he makes himself," or (5) he will be "what he wills." The will is the subject of the next chapter. Nevertheless, it is worth noting that the traditional notion of man as a knowing, willing, feeling being cannot have been entirely left behind if Sartre can still write as he writes here. Nothing of this kind is found in Heidegger.

36.3 Transcendence (self-surpassing)

The concept of the human project projecting is taken up again later and equated with that of transcendence in Sartre's peculiar sense of the word. "Man," writes Sartre, "is all the time outside himself [beyond himself, reaching out beyond what he already is toward what he is not yet]: it is in projecting and losing himself beyond himself that he makes man to exist; and, on the other hand, it is by pursuing transcendent aims that he himself is able to exist" (55/368). Or again:

Since man is thus self-surpassing ... he is himself the heart and center of his transcendence. There is no other universe [no Platonic realm of Forms, no Divine Being] except the human universe, the universe of human subjectivity. (ibid.)

The term 'transcendence' already had several well-established uses in philosophy before Sartre (once again following Heidegger) took it over and gave it a new, man-centred meaning. For example, in Platonism the realm of the Forms is regarded as 'transcendent.' In Christian philosophy, God is 'the transcendent being.' In Christian Platonism (such as that of St Augustine), the transcendent Forms are relocated in the mind of the transcendent Creator God as Divine Ideas. In Sartre, by contrast, man, not God or Form, is the transcendent (self-surpassing) being. For man alone of all beings is always *more* potentially than he is actually, always "ahead of himself," as Heidegger puts it, always projecting *future* possibilities *as determinative of what he is now*. This use of 'transcendence' is the only one still possible in a philosophy that has broken with other-wordliness in all its forms. Before leaving Sartre's theory of human subjectivity we must consider whether he provides an adequate response to the third of the four criticisms of existentialism outlined in chapter 34: Cartesian subjectivism.

36.4 Sartrean and Cartesian subjectivity

Summing up all the foregoing, we can say that, at any given moment of the present, man understands himself both in terms of ways of existing in a world with others that are *already* actualized (thrownness) and also in terms of other *not yet* actualized possibilities of existing (projecting). Both are determinative of what man *is*, the latter no less than the former. Human existence—as distinct from the being of the moss, the fungus, and the cauliflower—is *thrown projecting*.

These complementary features of human existence can be spoken of as belonging to "human subjectivity" as well, since Sartre, unlike Heidegger, uses the terms 'subject,' 'human subject,' and 'consciousness' with reference to man. Heidegger avoids them altogether, designating man instead by the German word, *Dasein*, which Sartre translates as 'human reality.' The retention of the word 'subject' obviously need not mean that Sartre thinks of man in exactly the same terms as Descartes or Hume; on the contrary, Sartre is trying to stick close to what Heidegger understands by *Dasein*: the Sartrean 'subject' is not the *abstract, worldless, bodiless, solitary thinking thing* of Descartes's *cogito*-principle, but the *concrete, embodied, person coexisting with others in a shared world*, a Being-in-the-world, as Heidegger says.

The difference is more vivid if we say that the Cartesian subject understands itself as 'self-aware object awareness,' including among its objects other minds and non-living and living bodies, not least its own (see 24.6.4). By contrast, the Sartrean subject understands itself as coexisting with others in various concrete ways of being together in a shared world and having constantly to choose among further possibilities of existing together with them in a world. When Sartre glosses the slogan "existence precedes essence" as "we must begin from the subjective" (26/348), therefore, he is *not* advocating a Cartesian starting point—contrary to the criticism of both the Christians and the Marxists—although it is hard to see how anyone who had worked himself entirely free of Descartes could put the point this way.

Negatively speaking, 'beginning from the subjective' means *not* starting from some objective idea of the human essence in the divine mind (Christian metaphysics), or some Idea 'laid up' as a model in a Platonic heaven, or from some Kantian (or Enlightenment) conception of 'universal human reason' stocked with a priori theoretical axioms and practical norms. And it purports to mean *not* starting from an isolated, worldless Cartesian subject either. *Positively* speaking, 'beginning from the subjective' is starting from what is really given in the way man "exists, encounters himself, surges up in the world" (28/349). It means starting from the fact that one is "nothing," so that what one will be has yet to be determined by one's choices.

What Sartre's enriched notion of subjectivity retains from Descartes is the purely formal structure of *self*-consciousness, a being that is *related to itself*, that 'understands itself' (as a moss and a fungus do not). But just how far Sartre remains faithful to that *as which* we understand ourselves in the *primary* self-awareness that characterizes everyday existence is a different question. He has undoubtedly got closer to something like the ordinary experience of the self than Descartes, but he seems unable to think outside the Cartesian box; he borrows freely from Heidegger, but owes almost as much to Descartes. We can confirm this assessment by bringing the Sartrean notion of *inter-subjectivity* together with that of transcendence.

36.5 Subjectivity and inter-subjectivity

As already noted, man, as 'thrown,' finds himself already related in manifold concrete ways to *other human beings* as well as to non-human things within his immediate environment. His possibilities, actualized and unactualized, involve both. That is just to say that all his (1) *own* possibilities of being are at one and the same time also (2) possibilities of dealing *with things* in his non-human environment and also (3) possibilities of being together with *other humans*, that is, dealing with these things in concert with others, in addressing *shared*, *common* concerns and pursuing common goals. Under attack here is obviously the notion of a sharp subject–object dichotomy. To put the point somewhat differently: the human subject in Sartre differs from the solipsistic Cartesian *ego* in that human existence is essentially, not just accidentally,

Chapter 36: Human Reality 599

coexisting with others alongside non-human entities. The others 'co-define' my being in the sense that what I am *for them* co-determines what I am *for myself*. This is true also of the non-human things of my environment, my personal milieu, so to speak, though it is the relation to others that is of interest right now.

Now Sartre takes this sound insight so far as to say that each individual subject is *essentially related to all others*, in fact *to all humanity*. Where we have repeatedly referred to human existence as 'coexistence,' Sartre himself speaks (less happily) of human subjectivity as "inter-subjectivity" (45/361). He even makes his point with specific reference to the Cartesian *cogito*, as follows:

Contrary to the philosophy of Descartes, contrary to that of Kant, when we say 'I think' we are attaining to ourselves in the presence of the other, and we are just as certain of the other as we are of ourselves. Thus the man who discovers himself directly in the *cogito* also discovers all the others, and discovers them as the conditions of his own existence. He recognizes that he cannot be anything (in the sense in which one says that one is spiritual, or that one is wicked or jealous) unless others recognize him as such. I cannot obtain any truth whatever about myself, except through the mediation of another. The other is indispensable to my existence, and equally so to any knowledge I can have of myself. Under these conditions, the intimate discovery of myself is at the same time the revelation of the other as a freedom which confronts mine. Thus, at once, we find ourselves in a world which is, let us say, that of 'inter-subjectivity.' (ibid.)

We can surely conclude from this that the third reproach, Cartesianism, starting from an isolated subject instead of a human being existing in solidarity with others, is on the whole misleading. Sartre's own trenchant criticism of the Cartesian notion of the subject as an empty philosophical abstraction having little to do with the way we think of ourselves in our day-to-day living has all the marks of genuine philosophical insight—if indeed it is the business of philosophy not to *replace* our everyday self-understanding of things with a completely different story told in the refined concepts of the philosophers, but to enhance and deepen our grasp of what we already know ourselves to be, however vaguely.

Nevertheless, the troubling fact remains that Sartre's criticism of Descartes takes the form of a reinterpretation of the Cartesian *cogito*. The language is Descartes's language. Cartesianism stood on its head is, willy-nilly, Cartesianism of a sort. This is not the way to break the spell of Descartes. It was open to Sartre to go further. Heidegger had already done so. Vestiges of Cartesian subjectivism remain, though hardly enough to justify the reproach of the communists or the Christians.

36.6 Conclusion

We have not yet spelled out everything that is contained in Sartre's notions of subjectivity and inter-subjectivity. In thrownness the individual discovers himself through the others; in projecting, man projects not just what he will be, but also an "image of man such as he believes he ought to be" (29/350). In Sartre's words: "When we say that man chooses himself, we do mean that every one of us must choose himself; but by that we also mean that in choosing for himself he chooses for all men" (ibid.). Thus, projecting, willing, choosing "concerns mankind as a whole" (ibid.). "In fashioning myself I fashion man" (ibid.).

We spoke earlier (see 36.2.2) of man's "responsibility" for what he is, the burden of having to create himself 'out of nothing,' to make himself what he is 'not yet.' We now see that the individual subject's responsibility is all the more burdensome as it extends, according to Sartre, to *all mankind*. This burden is first revealed, not by philosophical reflection, but pre-philosophically, in certain key human emotions. The same is true of absolute freedom of the will, even if, for the most part, we attempt to disguise the fact from ourselves. Will and emotion are the subjects of the next chapter.

37

Will and Emotion

37.1 Introductory

The present chapter rounds out the sketch of the theory of human reality begun in the last by examining two aspects of Sartre's regional ontology (see 33.5) of man that are deserving of special attention: (1) the great metaphysical weight assigned volition and (2) the methodological importance of the emotions in the elaboration of Sartre's existential ontology.

The expressions 'theory of human reality,' 'regional ontology of man,' and 'existential ontology' are, incidentally, all used synonymously here. The allusion to a *philosophy of freedom* in the title of Part Five ("Sartre and the Road to Freedom") is prompted by (1). This philosophy of freedom was characterized as 'non-theological' or 'anthropological voluntarism' in chapter 35, where we exploited the Cartesian doctrine of God's omnipotence and the Euthyphro dilemma to put it in a broader historical perspective. It remains now to consider its bearing on the first charge levelled at existentialism by its critics, quietism (see chap. 34).

In the second half of the chapter we shall consider (2) the special cognitive significance assigned certain emotions—chiefly negative ones like anguish and despair—in *Existentialism and Humanism* and elsewhere in Sartre's literary and philosophical works. To claim that such emotions are philosophically important for what they reveal about the human condition, and then to point to those very emotions as confirming the philosophical theory based upon them, sounds circular. In assessing Sartre's reply to the second charge of his critics, pessimism, we shall have to consider whether his procedure is indeed viciously circular.

Whatever the outcome, by asserting as he does the sovereignty of the will and the special cognitive significance of the emotions Sartre challenges a long-dominant philosophical tradition in which the supremacy of reason over both will and feeling is more or less taken for granted. (Hume is a predecessor only as far as feeling is concerned.) That is why these two aspects of Sartre's thought deserve special consideration. For all its excesses, the first embodies, as we shall see, a conception of human autonomy and freedom worthy of Socrates, the patron saint of philosophy, while the latter is a salutary protest against the dismissive treatment too often accorded the emotions in the philosophies of the past.

37.2 The sovereignty of the will

The extraordinary emphasis Sartre places on the will reverses the priority of intellect over will in popular psychology and most traditional philosophy. Normally, we think of acts of will, that is, a person's choices, decisions, and actions, as *following* from his or her nature: what is chosen reflects one's individual 'personality' or 'character' no less than our common humanity. Sartre typically turns this around: through free choices each of us determines what he or she is; there is just no prior nature, neither a universal human nature nor any individual character or personality; we create both freely, *ex nihilo*, so to speak. Accordingly, we can only *understand* what we are, our own natures, after *having willed* what we shall be. The will is prior to intellect or reason, at least as far as *self*-understanding is concerned. If this is true, it follows that neither intellect nor reason, neither knowledge of one's own nature nor of universal human nature, can provide us with the slightest guidance in making decisions.

Man, Sartre insists, cannot create, actualize, or realize himself in accordance with any pre-given idea of human nature or ideal of the best human life; there just is no such formula, recipe, or ideal to be ascertained in advance by the human intellect, neither in a Platonic heaven nor in the mind of the creator God, nor anywhere else for that matter. About this the Greek and all later moralists, right down to the Enlightenment, were simply mistaken, even inconsistent. Through his choices man wills *blindly*, without any rational guidance; and he wills into being not just his own but the universal human essence.

One has only to state the upshot of Sartre's creation story without God in this way in order to see how extreme it is. If Sartre is right, then no one can be said to have a nature or character different from that actually exhibited in his or her actions: your actions *are* your character; they show what you are, because *you are in fact nothing else but what you do*. There are therefore *no excuses* (34/353; see 12.9.3 for the Socratic analogue to this). You cannot, without deliberate "self-deception" (31/351; see also 51/365), allege, as we are only too apt to do, that you behaved in a certain way (say, in a cowardly or a selfish manner), but, 'really are not like that.' Sartre states categorically: "there is no [human] reality except in action ... Man is nothing else but what he purposes [to do], he exists only in so far as he realizes himself, he is therefore nothing else but the sum of his actions, nothing else but what his life is" (41/358). Or again: "You are nothing else but what you live" (42/359), and "[l]ife is nothing until it is lived" (54/367). These are just different ways of making the same point about the absolute primacy of action and the will. They reveal the full import of the statement, cited earlier (see 36.2.2), that man is "nothing." The point is at bottom metaphysical or ontological rather than psychological; it has to do with the relation between essence and existence, not with describing, explaining, or evaluating observable behaviour, though Sartre is apt to run the metaphysical, psychological, and ethical points of view together at times. The specifically meta-ethical implications of Sartre's voluntarism will be considered in the next chapter, along with his normative ethical theory. Here we shall examine Sartre's voluntarism in the light of the first two charges brought against existentialism by its critics.

37.3 Voluntarism, quietism, and pessimism

We have already quoted Sartre's rough-and-ready definition: "Quietism is the attitude of people who say 'let others do what I cannot do'" (41/358). From the foregoing it is plain that Sartre is so far from urging the futility of action that he in fact holds that there is nothing else but action, no other human reality at all. His position is, accordingly, the antithesis of quietism as it is understood in this essay. Whether it goes too far in the other direction is a separate question; the first charge, at least, seems unjustified.

As for the second charge, pessimism, the stress laid upon will and deed constitutes, Sartre maintains, the only genuine *optimism*: a clear-sighted, sober realization that 'nothing is written,' that human potential exceeds or transcends any existing reality, and that human history remains to be written by our deeds:

You have seen that it [existentialism] cannot be regarded as a philosophy of quietism since it defines man by his action, nor as a pessimistic description of man, for no doctrine is more optimistic, the destiny of man is placed within himself. Nor is it an attempt to discourage man from action since it tells him that there is no hope except in his action, and that the one thing which permits him to have life is the deed. Upon this level therefore, what we are considering is an ethic of action and self-commitment. (44/360)

The word 'action' here is neither just a psychological event, a 'decision to act' in the ordinary sense, nor the publicly observable event resulting from such a decision. All so-called actions are, for Sartre, concrete modes or actualized possibilities of Being-in-the-world with others, that is, Being-alongside the entities with which we and they are practically involved in a multitude of ways. It requires a special effort or therapy to keep present to mind the nature of that thrown-projecting that Sartre, following Heidegger, sets over against the modes of consciousness of the worldless solipsistic ego of Descartes. This is only made more difficult by the fact that, unlike Heidegger, Sartre constantly lapses into psychological and Cartesian jargon.

Such is the purported optimism of existentialism. It is hard to be certain that this is more than a verbal dispute. Sartre's communist critics might be placated by this sort of optimism; but the fact remains that his works assign great importance to such negative emotions as shame, guilt, anguish, despair, the sense of abandonment, and so on. This is what earned him the reproach of pessimism from his Catholic critics. We turn now to the other theme of this chapter, the emotions.

37.4 The significance of the emotions

A good portion of Sartre's exposition of the central doctrines of existentialism is devoted to certain *moods, feelings, or emotions*, terms used interchangeably here. As noted repeatedly, Sartre, despite his indebtedness to Heidegger, still thinks of man as a knowing, willing, feeling being, much in the manner of Descartes (see 27.3). The difference is that these are no longer conceived *purely* as modes of thought or consciousness, as fleeting psychical states, but rather as different dimensions of thrown-projecting Being-in-the-world along with others. In short, the inter-subjective and, as we might say, 'wordly' dimensions of cognition, volition, and emotion come to the fore in Sartre's account of them. We have just seen, in outline at least, how this is so for volition, and we must now do the same in the case of emotion.

While volition may be the key factor in *determining* what man is, existentialism nevertheless ascribes a very important role to the emotions in *revealing* the human situation, including the sovereignty of the will. In practically the whole prior tradition of philosophy, emotion, feeling, or mood was regarded as something that 'gets in the way of' and 'clouds' cognition, preventing us from grasping our situation clearly. One has only to recall Socrates's admonition to Crito not to allow himself to be frightened by 'bogeys,' but to think clearly about the rights and wrongs of the course of action under consideration (see 12.3.1). This is echoed, in one form or another, right down through the philosophical tradition. For Sartre, by contrast, it is precisely the *dominant emotions of man* that reveal his inescapable condition of radical freedom. So while the emotions may *often* be an obstacle to clear-sighted judgment, when it comes to understanding the human condition, mood or feeling plays a decisive, positive role. In *Existentialism and Humanism* three emotions are singled out for particular comment in this regard: the mood of anguish, the sense of abandonment, and the feeling of despair.

37.4.1 The mood of anguish

What has been said already about subjectivity and inter-subjectivity (see 36.5) is the key to understanding the concept of anguish or anxiety, which plays an important role in other so-called existentialist philosophies as well, notably in Kierkegaard and Heidegger. In the question-and-answer period that followed the oral presentation of

Existentialism and Humanism, Sartre discussed two connotations of his use of 'anguish.' The first should be clear without further comment: (a) total *absence of justification*, that is, of 'objective' standards for thought or action, since the true and the good are true and good because we choose them, not vice-versa. (By 'the true' is meant, it must be remembered, only truth concerning *human* nature.) This is also described as our not being able to "pass beyond human subjectivity" (29/350) to something non-relative or objective. The second connotation is (b) responsibility, not just for myself, but *toward all mankind*: each individual is "legislator deciding for the whole of mankind" (30/351; see also 56/369). This latter point requires a brief explanatory comment.

At first sight, Sartre's insistence that the individual chooses, not for himself alone, but for all mankind, seems puzzling. After all, few of us would be inclined to say that all others are bound to make the same choices in life as we do. Yet Sartre may in fact be invoking something akin to Kant's famous universalizability criterion here (see below 38.6.1–2). If so, he his not employing it quite as Kant did, but in a manner that arguably comes closer to its true significance. For Kant, the willingness to universalize the maxim of one's action is a positive criterion or test of right and wrong, whereas in truth it is at most a reliable test for distinguishing moral from non-moral decisions and choices. Thus, in matters of religious duty, etiquette, taste, or personal preference, few of us would say that all others are bound to choose and act as we do; but it is a defining feature of *moral* decisions that what I identify as right in certain circumstances is right for *every* moral agent in relevantly similar circumstances. So perhaps Sartre is here just distinguishing properly moral decisions from non-moral choices and preferences by saying that when I make a choice that can be correctly described as a moral choice, or (as he might say) an 'existential decision,' I must, in the nature of the case, be willing to universalize my maxim; that is, I must choose for the whole of humanity. It remains only to make clear what all this has to do with anguish.

According to Sartre, it is through the emotion of anguish that each individual human being discovers his or her own personal responsibility for all mankind. And this fundamental truth about the human condition is brought home to us in the mood of anguish more immediately, more intimately, and more powerfully than by any philosophical doctrine like Kant's. Indeed, philosophical theory always comes afterwards, formulating in conceptual terms—whether faithfully or in a distorting manner—knowledge that is primordially or pre-theoretically acquired in the mood of anguish that suffuses all human Being-in-the-world, only breaking through to the surface now and then, at rare moments, to disrupt our customary complacency.

Here we see once again what is distinctive of the phenomenological method as the existentialist understands it: not imposing on the phenomena (literally, 'what shows itself') preconceived conceptual schemes of one's own, or of some cherished tradition, but allowing the choice of philosophical terms and concepts to be guided (or corrected, since we are never without preconceptions) by immediate experience of the phenomena themselves (see 36.2.1). This seems indeed to be the only reliable recipe for bringing our philosophical understanding of ourselves and our natural and social environment into accord with immediate pre-philosophical experience. But while the formula is sound, the question must remain open whether Sartre applies it as he should, or whether he simply imposes a different set of preconceptions of his own on what the mood of anguish reveals.

One thing that should be immediately apparent is that the procedure is circular. In conceptualizing through theoretical reflection what is already known pre-theoretically through emotion, for example, and then appealing to the emotions as corroborating our theoretical account of the human condition, we only make clear to ourselves what we already know, appealing to immediate experience as the source and touchstone of our theory. However, there is nothing vicious about this circle. It is exactly what we should expect from existential phenomenology. It is a circle of the kind referred to earlier (see 7.7.3) as 'hermeneutical.' Heidegger himself spoke, in this regard, of the "hermeneutics of facticity" or of "factical existence" (36.2.1) to describe the method pioneered in his *Being and Time*.

37.4.2 The sense of abandonment

The feeling of abandonment is singled out for analysis, much as was anguish, because of an important Heideggerian precedent. But as in the case of anguish, it is given a somewhat different sense than in Heidegger. The connotations in Sartre are: (1) man is forlorn, abandoned, left alone, without God and without objective standards to guide his thought and action; (2) man is without excuse, since there is "no determinism" (34/353), no fixed human nature on which to pin the blame for what we make of ourselves; and finally, (3) man is "condemned to be free" (ibid.). This last point means that there is no escaping our freedom: the one thing man is *not* free to do is to evade his responsibility for creating man; he can conceal it from himself in self-deception, but he cannot shirk it: "what is not possible is not to choose. I can always choose, but I must know that if I do not choose, that is still a choice" (48/363).

These are, to repeat, existential insights actually gained, not, in the first instance, through reflection and philosophical analysis, but rather through the *feeling* of abandonment; philosophy only spells them out for us in non-emotive, conceptual terms. It is likely that Sartre had the Enlightenment figure Jean-Jacques Rousseau (1712–1788), a contemporary and acquaintance of Hume, in mind when he coined the phrase "condemned to be free" (34/353). For it was Rousseau who remarked: "It may be necessary to compel men to be free." In Rousseau's view, human nature had been so corrupted by bad social institutions that, even if all the checks on freedom were removed at once, men would still not embrace their freedom but would have to be forced to do so. From Sartre's perspective, by contrast, men cannot escape their freedom, though by nature they wish to do so. So the faint allusion to Rousseau signals not a debt but yet another typical reversal of a classical perspective.

As for (1) and (2), both points, embodying the denials of theism and determinism, respectively, should be clear enough without further elaboration. There is little need at this stage to reiterate the point that "man is nothing" represents the complete antithesis of that rigorous scientific determinism which regards all human choices and decisions as necessitated in advance, the product of inner (psychological and biological) and outer (societal and physical) forces over which the individual has little or no control. As for Sartre's not recognizing the existence of a God who creates man in his own image, the sense of abandonment, of inhabiting a human universe from which the gods have fled, or rather in which "God is dead" (Nietzsche), is just the primary way in which this feature of the human condition reveals itself *emotively*, long before the philosopher and theologian come along to either deny it by providing proofs of the contrary or, in Sartre's case, to enshrine it as a core philosophical doctrine. Here again the procedure is manifestly circular, but not viciously so.

37.4.3 *The feeling of despair*

The significance of the emotion of despair is summed up in Sartre's notion of acting "without hope" (39/357) or, as he also puts it, somewhat more fully:

It [despair] simply means that we limit ourselves to a reliance upon that which is within our wills, or within the sum of the probabilities which render our action feasible. (ibid.)

This means that we cannot rely (1) on some allegedly higher instance, on divine providence, for example, to ensure the victory of good over evil or to guarantee justice in this life or the next. (On this point, recall Hume.) Nor can we place our trust (2) in the goodness of human nature. If we do, we are deceiving ourselves. Nor, finally, can we count on (3) the goodwill of those others who share our fundamental convictions and purposes. The sense of despair that pervades our lives, even when we are unaware of it, reveals that we can "count upon nothing" (41/358) *but ourselves*, on nothing more than what we ourselves do and on the knowledge of probabilities—not certainties!—without reliance on which human action, indeed human survival, would be impossible. Sartre's point is that whatever assurances religion or anthropology or personal experience may give us to the contrary, the ever-present sense of despair lurking just below the surface of our lives testifies, with an insistence not to be outbidden, that such hopes are groundless.

To illustrate this point it may be interesting (since Sartre is so chary of details) to consider a passage from the essay "A Free Man's Worship" by the British philosopher Bertrand Russell. In basic philosophical outlook, Russell is as close to Hume and as remote from Sartre as can be imagined; nevertheless, Sartre would endorse the attitude Russell adopts in drawing the consequences of what he takes to be the scientific view of the human condition, even if the scientific outlook itself is much more alien to Sartre than to Russell:

That Man is the product of causes which had no prevision of the end they were achieving; that his origin, his growth, his hopes and fears, his loves and his beliefs, are but the outcome of accidental collocations of atoms; that no fire, no heroism, no intensity of thought and feeling, can preserve an individual life beyond the grave; that all the labours of the ages, all the devotion, all the inspiration, all the noonday brightness of human genius, are destined to extinction in the vast death of the solar system, and that the whole temple of Man's achievement must inevitably be buried beneath the debris of a universe in ruins—all these things, if not quite beyond dispute, are yet so nearly certain, that no philosophy which rejects them can hope to stand. Only within the scaffolding of these truths, only on the firm foundation of unyielding despair, can the soul's habitation henceforth be safely built.

The prevalence of the mood of despair in the emotional experience of modern man—witness the literature of the twentieth century—may point to a subliminal understanding of the human condition not unlike that described by Russell here. We may hide it from ourselves by denying some or all of those alleged "truths" that Russell proclaims, be it in the name of faith in God or in the human spirit, or on other grounds; still, what is thus denied in words may break through, at times violently, as despair. Phenomenological philosophy merely seizes on the fact of its ever-lurking presence, making explicit, clarifying, and conceptualizing what is primordially revealed about human existence by this emotion. What phenomenological philosophy thus captures is already 'known' pre-philosophically, in everyday life, at least at some level, however much we may try to conceal the fact from ourselves and others.

Or so Sartre would have us believe. It is very hard to say whether he is right about this since anything alleged to the contrary would almost certainly be dismissed as wishful thinking and self-deception. Accordingly, the Catholic critics' point about "how an infant smiles" (see 34.3) is sure to fall on deaf ears. Yet might it not be said, with equal justice, that a mood of confidence, optimism, even joy, pervades pre-philosophical human experience at some level? Perhaps it only comes luminously to the fore in circumstances like those the Catholic critic accuses Sartre of ignoring. If so, then it seems only fair to ask what facets of human existence may be disclosed in positive emotions of this kind.

It seems, in short, that the charge of one-sided pessimism may have some basis after all. Is the alleged pervasiveness of the moods of anguish, abandonment, and despair an incontestable fact of human experience? Or is it a reflection of the unprecedented horrors of twentieth-century history, coupled with the pall thrown over human life by the cold, scientific picture that Russell paints so vividly? These are questions one would do well to ask in pondering Sartre's account of the emotions. One way to gain what we nowadays call 'perspective' is to adopt a very different point of view, be it that of Sartre's Catholic critic, or better still the Greek view of life sketched in Part One. That cannot be attempted here. In conclusion, we must consider the other alleged consequence of atheism embodied in the existentialist slogan: the claim that there are no absolute or objective rules of conduct; that the individual creates moral values, whose validity is therefore relative to his own will.

38

Decisionism

38.1 Introductory

We have now completed our examination of the first three criticisms of existentialism. Despite the influence of Heidegger, Sartre apparently still understands human reality in *modified* Cartesian terms; and his intent seems to be primarily to *understand* rather than transform the human condition. Nevertheless, he is on reasonably strong ground in rejecting the charges of quietism and Cartesian subjectivism. As for the third charge, Sartre's choice of themes does seem one-sided; unless it is justified by the special importance of the negative phenomena singled out for attention, there may be something to the reproach of undue pessimism after all. Moral relativism remains to be considered. It is the target of the fourth charge levelled at Sartre's philosophy and the subject of the present chapter.

What we have referred to as Sartre's 'decisionism' (see 32.4.2) is a type of normative ethical theory (see 10.2.1) that is labelled 'deontic' or 'deontological' in the customary classification almost universally employed by moral philosophers today. The other main type of normative ethical theory is generally called 'consequentialist' or 'teleological.' Since 'teleology' and 'teleological' were used earlier to characterize a certain type of causal explanation (see 5.5.3), we shall use the term 'consequentialist' (along with 'consequentialism') here. The two main subspecies of consequentialist theories are act and rule consequentialism. So too with deontological theories: some focus primarily on *general rules or action guides*, others on the *particular actions* to be taken in concrete situations. Decisionism is a type of *act* deontological theory that lays particular stress on the human will (volition) as opposed to both reason (cognition) and feeling (emotion). Before we consider the charge of relativism, it will be useful to situate decisionism on a wider spectrum of competing normative ethical theories.

38.2. Egoism, altruism, utilitarianism

For all moral theories of the consequentialist type, the rightness, wrongness, or permissibility of a particular action (act consequentialism) or of a general rule of behaviour (rule consequentialism) is a function of its non-morally good or bad *consequences* (benefit and harm). Such theories differ, however, according as the consequences to be considered are those (1) for the agent alone or (2) for others, but not the agent, or (3) for all concerned, that is, for the agent *and* all others, for *everyone* affected by the action or rule in any way, no matter how remotely or indirectly.

Version (1) is commonly known as 'moral egoism,' (2) as 'moral altruism,' and (3) as 'utilitarianism.' The morality of Jesus, requiring as it does beneficent love towards all mankind, comes closest to (2) altruism. Historically, (3) the utilitarian theory arose among the nineteenth-century English social reformers in the circle of Jeremy Bentham (1748–1832) and James Mill (1773–1836) and John Stuart Mill. If Jesus's morality of selflessness—indeed, self-sacrifice for others' sakes—sets the standard of moral conduct too high (see 12.8.3), utilitarianism, many would argue, brings it down to something more like the right level (see 12.8.6). For it requires, not self-denial, but disinterestedness and impartiality; not altruism, but consideration of the effects of rules or actions in a detached and neutral manner, such that each individual, including oneself, counts only for one, and the happiness of others matters every bit as much as, yet no more than, one's own.

As compared with (2) and (3), the trouble with (1) egoism is not so much that it sets the moral bar too low as that it cannot really be called a *moral* theory at all. For at least some measure of disinterested concern for the well-being of others seems to be essential to what has aptly been called (by the moral philosopher Kurt Baier and others) 'the moral point of view.' This is absent in moral egoism. Indeed, the egoist's view that one ought always to act so as to secure the greatest overbalance of good over bad consequences *for oneself* seems tantamount to what was earlier called 'amoralism' (see 32.4.1). If one were to acknowledge it, for argument's sake, as a moral theory, the resulting standard would be so low as to subvert practically the whole of traditional morality, sanctioning a great deal of what we should consider highly immoral conduct.

All things considered, though, it is probably better to contest the moral egoist's claim to be advancing a *moral* theory at all. It will be recalled (see above 12.8.5) that Kant said much the same thing of *all* consequentialist theories, including the various forms of eudaemonism (see 12.9.1) espoused by the Greek moralists. Now it is certainly true that eudaemonist theories stress enlightened or rational *self*-interest above all else, that is, consequences *for the agent*; yet the appeal to self-interest figures in the answer to the question, Why be moral? With regard to the central question of normative ethical theory, What is moral? most eudaemonist theories are very far from suggesting that one need only consult one's own interests. Thus, the chief focus of Socrates's normative ethical theory is on not harming *others*, whether friends or foes. So with regard to what counts as right, wrong, or permissible, the eudaemonists were by no means moral egoists, even if their answer to the question, Why be moral? is at bottom: because being moral is an indispensable condition of, or a key part of, or identical with, happiness, the achievement of the best life of which one is capable.

Of course, the eudaemonist theory of Socrates answers the other question, What is moral? in terms of harm and consequences for others, and this, for Kant, would be enough to disqualify it as a moral theory. Kant was convinced that any theory that includes the non-morally good consequences of actions, whether for ourselves or others or everyone, among their good-making features is no *moral* theory at all. He calls this 'heteronomy,' literally, subordinating the moral law (Greek: *nomos*) to something else (Greek: *heteron*). However appealing Kant's ideal of the autonomy of morals, he is surely mistaken here. From a moral point of view, consequences matter, provided they are not just consequences for the agent, as in egoism. Kant went decidedly too far in insisting that all morally good actions must be intrinsically so, that is, good just in virtue of the motive for which they were performed (reverence for the law), irrespective of consequences (see 12.8.5).

From the foregoing it appears that *all* eudaemonist theories can be styled forms of egoism with respect to the question, Why be moral? But regarding the question, What is moral? some are consequentialist, though not egoistic, since they stress—even, as in the case of Socrates, *over*-stress—consequences for people other than the agent himself. Only egoism regarding the question, What is moral? should be discounted on the grounds that it does not take a moral viewpoint at all. As for altruism and utilitarianism, they certainly qualify as *moral* theories by almost any standard except Kant's, even if the former pretty clearly sets the standard of moral conduct much too high. The latter adjusts it to something more like the right level. One problem with utilitarianism is that it involves a principle of distributive justice (roughly, 'everyone counts for one' or 'counts equally') that apparently cannot be grounded on considerations of utility alone (see 13.2). For who is to say an unfair distribution of benefits may not at times result in a greater overall amount of utility produced? It seems, then, that this sort of consequentialism is not the whole story about morals. Some deontic principles have to be recognized as well. Even the principle that maximizing utility is good may be best regarded as such a deontic principle.

38.3 Deontic or deontological theories

According to deontic or deontological moral theories like Kant's, the moral rightness or wrongness of particular actions or general rules does not depend on consequences at all. Certain things are just *inherently* right and wrong, regardless of consequences, like justice, for example. Of course, there are also mixed theories involving both consequences and deontic principles. They seem to be on the right track.

'Deontic' and 'deontological' come from the Greek *to deon* 'what must be,' a term for obligation first introduced by Democritus of Abdera (see 5.7). Deontic moral principles are absolute, that is, binding always, everywhere, and on everyone, regardless of circumstances or consequences. One deontic theory with which we are already familiar is the Divine Command Theory or theological voluntarism. It might be objected that this is not a deontic theory at all, since nothing is *inherently* right or wrong unless and until God commands or proscribes it. However, adherents of the theory are apt to say that what anything is 'inherently' or 'by nature' is just what God's creative will has made it; so certain kinds or rules of behaviour are inherently right or wrong regardless of circumstances and consequences. But the most famous deontological theory, and the only one much discussed nowadays, is Kant's.

38.3.1 Rigourism

All the moral principles derivable from Kant's categorical imperative are supposed to be absolute duties incumbent upon every rational agent and admitting of no exceptions, even when the direst of consequences ensue. Thus, lying, stealing, or taking a life are inherently bad. To say that the duty to refrain from these actions is 'absolute' is to say that lying, for example, is wrong irrespective of the fact that, in particular circumstances, a lie may have no bad, indeed may even have beneficial, consequences, such as shielding someone from embarrassment, humiliation, or harm. And so too with theft and killing. Stealing, even from the rich to feed the starving poor, and killing, even in order to save many lives, are inherently wrong. This outlook is sometimes referred to as 'rigourism.' A famous example is that of lying to a murderer who enquires the whereabouts of his intended victim. Kant maintained that even in such circumstances, where the chief consequence is saving an innocent life, to lie is just inherently wrong.

Now, in a sense different from Kant's, the view that lying is always wrong, regardless of circumstances, is in fact perfectly defensible. Following the British philosopher and Aristotle scholar Sir David Ross, it is customary for defenders of deontic moral principles to draw a distinction between prima facie and actual duties. 'Prima facie' is just Latin for 'at first sight,' while by 'actual duties' are meant those actions that turn out to be duties 'at the end of the day,' after a full consideration of all the morally relevant facts and circumstances. Thus, to say that truth-telling (or respect for life or for property) is an absolute prima facie duty just means that the fact that a certain course of action involves telling a lie (or breaking a promise, or taking a life, or theft) is *always* a wrong-making feature of the actions in question. Of course, the same action may, under another description, be an act of protecting a victim from harm or preserving someone from starvation. This is obviously a right- or good-making feature. Considering the action under every possible description or from every perspective, the agent must weigh up all the right- and wrong-making features in order to determine what his or her actual duty is. On doing so, lying may be found to be the right course of action, one's actual duty, even though prima facie wrong—as in the case of the murderer enquiring after his intended victim. On this account of moral deliberation, there are no absolute or exceptionless *actual* duties, as in Kant's rigourism, though there are exceptionless or absolute *prima facie* duties.

38.3.2 Act and rule deontologism

If we now distinguish *rule* from *act* deontologism, as in the case of consequentialist theories, then the Divine Command Theory, as it is usually understood, is a *rule* deontological theory. God, after all, does not stand at one's elbow telling one what to do in particular situations. Cases like Sartre's example of God commanding Abraham to kill Isaac (see below) are, supposing they occur at all, well outside the moral experience of most of us. On most versions of the Divine Command Theory, therefore, God only gives human beings general rules or commandments, moral precepts to apply in particular cases using one's own judgment.

Apart from the Divine Command and other rule deontological theories like Kant's, there are so-called *act* deontological theories, of which Sartre's is a well-known example. Such theories take it that there are no universal rules for moral agents to apply in concrete situations; that every moral situation is somehow unique. Particular judgments about what is right and wrong in the circumstances always *precede* rather than follow upon general moral rules. The latter are at best only 'rules of thumb' derived from past experience of moral decisions actually made in concrete situations, the rightness or wrongness of those decisions having been immediately apparent to the agent at the time.

According to act deontologists generally, then, we must choose our course of action in each particular situation without the guidance of any rules at all, relying either (a) on a special sort of rational intuition (of the peculiarly moral features of the situation) or (b) on some special sentiment or feeling for what is right in the circumstances. These—(a) intuitionism and varieties of the so-called (b) moral sense theory—are the most widely known act deontological theories. Alternatively, the deontologist may stress neither cognition nor feeling, but, as in Sartre, (c) volition, a more or less blind commitment to act in a certain way. This sort of act deontological theory is usually referred to as 'decisionism.' It is the type of ethical theory advocated in *Existentialism and Humanism*, where it is defended against the charge of relativism.

The salient features of Sartre's decisionism can now be placed under four heads, to be examined individually in the remainder of this chapter: (1) blindness, (2) arbitrariness, (3) universalizability, and (4) authenticity. These points of view should give us a fair idea of the nature of Sartre's moral theory and of whether Sartre is in a position to furnish a satisfactory rebuttal of the charge of relativism.

38.4 Blindness

Moral choice, for Sartre, is always and inescapably *blind*. This means that there can be no internal or external guidance or justification for moral choices: not in the form of (a) valid general rules grounded either in Platonic Forms, or in God's will, or in universal human reason; nor in the form of (b) particular commands or concrete advice specific to the situation, be it from God or some human authority; nor, finally, in the form of (c) promptings of powerful passions or sentiments.

The question Sartre does not ask in this work (and we shall confine ourselves in the following to it alone) is whether there might not be a form of rational justification different from these three. If so, then to infer the blindness of moral choice from the inadmissibility of these particular types of justification is just the same old non sequitur all over again (see 32.3.2 and 35.5). This is obviously not the place to try to work out the pattern of rational justification appropriate to moral value judgments or decisions—assuming there is one. We must confine ourselves to Sartre's reasons for rejecting the above options. For even if there is a non sequitur here, at least Sartre attempts to state his objections to several traditional types of moral theory rather than just dismissing them as no longer worthy of serious consideration.

The basic objection to (a), (b), and (c) is the same and can be put this way. Even if there were such norms, such authorities, and such feelings to prompt us as to how to act in a given situation, we still *choose* freely to follow the norm, the command, the advice, or the feeling, and *this* higher-order choice is irremediably blind. In other words, there are no *other* (still higher-order) norms, commands, or feelings to guide us in deciding *which* rules to apply, *whom* (what human or Divine authority) to follow, or *how* to give fitting expression to a dominant passion; and even if there were, this would only push the decision back a stage. We would still have to decide to follow that higher-order rule, without the guidance of any still-higher-order rule to justify our choice. Whatever norms we follow, *ultimately* we choose blindly, without justification, to follow a certain course of action.

Let us now look at (a), (b), and (c) individually, and at one or two interesting examples by which Sartre illustrates his central point.

38.4.1 No general ethical principles

First, then, (a) there are *no general ethical rules* of the sort posited by rule deontological theories to follow in making moral decisions. There are no external Divine Commands, since God does not exist; nor is there a categorical imperative, the dictate of human reason itself. Each concrete situation in which action is called for is describable in so many different ways, as falling under so many different rules, that even if there were some general rules or principles (as there are not!), the decision regarding a particular course of action would already have been made the moment it was decided to treat it as an instance of this rather than that rule, as subject to this rather than that principle. In short, each situation is unique, and the decision is, in the final analysis, *always* taken in view of its unique character and circumstances. Rules, if any, come *afterwards*; they are no more than approximative generalizations based on what has been learned from particular situations. The agent must, accordingly, decide in the first instance without the benefit of such rules to guide him.

A case in point is the young man torn between staying home to care for his grieving mother and going off to war to avenge the death of his fallen brother. Sartre describes the situation as follows:

Christian doctrine says: Act with charity, love your neighbour, deny yourself for others, choose the way which is hardest, and so forth. But which is the harder road? ... To whom does one owe more? ... Which is the more useful aim? ... Who can give an answer to that a priori? No one. Nor is it given in any ethical scripture. The Kantian ethic says, Never regard another as a means, but always as an end. Very well; if I remain with my mother, I shall be regarding her as the end and not as a means: but by the same token, I am in danger of treating as means those who are fighting on my behalf; and the converse is also true, that if I go to the aid of the combatants I shall be treating them as the end at the risk of treating my mother as a means. (36/355)

Sartre's point here is that the decision as to which rules to apply and how to interpret and apply them in the concrete circumstances must be taken blindly. For one and the same action can be considered under different descriptions as falling under different rules. At bottom, 'abandoning one's aging mother,' 'avenging one's brother,' and 'fighting to liberate one's fellow citizens' are all possible descriptions of the young man's decision to leave home and join the French Free Forces. Obviously, the decision to consider the action predominantly in one light rather than another, as falling under this rather than that rule, is his alone. Nothing and no one tells him which is the correct description. He chooses without guidance.

Sartre's description of this moral quandary is instructive. However, whether, had he considered the action from all vantage points in this way, the young man's decision would still have to be regarded as blind rather than informed and rational is not easy to decide. Given Sartre's narrow conception of rationality, his conclusion seems warranted; but, as we have seen, it is possible to have grave doubts about the models of rationality assumed by Sartre to be the only ones.

38.4.2 No external authority

The second point was that (b) there are no specific moral imperatives that can be

Chapter 38: Decisionism 617

taken over from any external authority. Even if it seemed to me that (i) God himself were commanding me to do something in a specific situation, I would still have to decide for myself, first, whether the command really comes *from God* and, second, whether it is really a directive *to me*. In other words, I still have to make a decision that is blind. Similarly, if (ii) I seek advice from a priest or from a teacher, I have in fact already made the decision facing me by deciding whose advice to ask (which teacher, what sort of priest), since I know beforehand what kind of advice to expect.

To illustrate (i), Sartre reverts to the biblical example of Abraham, already discussed by Kierkegaard:

An angel commanded Abraham to sacrifice his son: and obedience was obligatory, if it really was an angel who had appeared and said, "Thou, Abraham, shalt sacrifice thy son." But anyone in such a case would wonder, first, whether it was indeed an angel and secondly, whether I am really Abraham. (31/351)

This is carelessly worded, even for Sartre. Since Abraham would not normally be in any doubt about whether he is Abraham, Sartre must mean by the latter question: whether I am the one to whom God's command is addressed. This is something Abraham must decide for himself, just as he must decide whether the command comes from God, or from the devil, or from his own overactive imagination. But what of the case in which some miraculous sign attests the divine origin of the command? "Neither," Sartre replies, "will an existentialist think that a man can find help through some sign being vouchsafed upon earth for his orientation: for he thinks that the man himself interprets the sign as he chooses. He thinks that every man, without any support or help whatever, is condemned at every instant to invent man" (34/353–4).

As for the other case, (ii) human authority, the example of the young man illustrates Sartre's point particularly well:

You may say that the youth did, at least, go to a professor to ask for advice. But if you seek counsel—from a priest, for example—you have selected that priest; and at bottom you already knew, more or less, what he would advise. In other words, to choose an adviser is nevertheless to commit oneself by that choice. If you are a Christian, you will say, Consult a priest; but there are collaborationists, priests who are resisters and priests who wait for the tide to turn: which will you choose? Had this young man chosen a priest of the resistance, or one of the collaboration, he would have decided beforehand the kind of advice he was to receive. Similarly, in coming to me, he knew what advice I should give him. (37–8/356)

Again, it is hard to fault Sartre's description and analysis, which are indeed very damaging to certain rather simplistic accounts of moral deliberation based on reflection, consultation, fact-gathering, and the like. The question is, once again, whether such a decision should not be said to have been made to some extent rationally rather than, as Sartre would have it, quite blindly, at least to the extent that different kinds of advice are considered and the consequences of acting on each weighed carefully in the balance.

38.4.3 No guiding passions

So much for (a) general rules derived from God or universal human reason and (b) specific commands or advice provided by some divine or human authority in a concrete situation. The final point was that (c) no *passion*, however great, can relieve us of the onerous responsibility of choosing blindly, since we are not only responsible for choosing *which* passions to give free rein to, but also *how* we do so.

The pertinent examples are Maggie Tulliver in George Eliot's *The Mill on the Floss* and Stendhal's duchess of Sanseverina in *The Charter House of Parma* (53–4/367). Here we have two women whose romantic, passionate natures are thwarted by circumstances; yet they choose almost diametrically opposed courses of action. The one (Maggie Tulliver) is prepared to smother her love for the sake of loyalty; the other (La Sanseverina) is prepared to resort to any means (including incitement to murder) to save the man she loves. Contrasting the two cases (about which he should have said more), Sartre concludes: "The existentialist does not believe in the power of passion. He will never regard a grand passion as a destructive torrent on which a man is swept into certain actions as by fate, and which, therefore, is an excuse for them. He thinks that man is responsible for his passions" (34/353). In short, we choose to allow a certain emotion to become a dominant passion in our lives, sweeping everything before it, and we choose this by deciding how to act on the passion in question, either in some particular case or as a general rule.

Relevant to this point is Sartre's comment on Gide's distinction between false and true sentiment (37/355–6). Gide's point was that what we really feel and what we just pretend to feel are so close at times as to be almost indistinguishable, even by us. Sartre disagrees. There is an absolute standard of what we really feel, and that standard is our actions: "Feeling is formed by the deeds that one does; therefore I cannot [without circularity] consult it as a guide to action" (ibid.).

38.5 Arbitrariness

The underlying principle of Sartre's act deontological normative ethical theory was put this way earlier (see 32.4.2): 'Choose freely, for all mankind, without deceiving yourself concerning your freedom, and you thereby make your choice morally right.' Accordingly, whatever one chooses is right, provided only that the choice is made in the right way. The proviso of "authenticity" (52/366), as Sartre calls it, borrowing another term from Heidegger, will be discussed in detail later (see 38.7); here it may be instructive to examine the main contention as if it were not qualified in any way.

That it renders moral choice not just blind but arbitrary can be seen in the light of the Euthyphro dilemma. For the main contention can be put this way: What is right is right because it is chosen; it is not chosen because it is right. The textual support for ascribing this view to Sartre is unambiguous:

To choose between this and that is at the same time to affirm the value of that which is chosen; for we are unable ever to choose the worse. What we choose is always the better; and nothing can be better for us [in a moral sense] unless it is better for all. (29/350)

Sartre is not just making the long-familiar point of the eudaemonists that a rational agent always chooses what *seems* good to him and cannot, insofar as he is rational, do otherwise. Rather, he is saying that simply choosing something in a certain way *makes it the better*. It is thus not only reasonable to choose the good; with a certain proviso, it is *logically* impossible to do otherwise on Sartre's theory. This is perhaps clearest in another brief passage:

the action presupposes that there is a plurality of possibilities, and in choosing one of these they realize that it has value only because it is chosen. (32/352)

On the face of it, this would appear to involve the very things with which Sartre's critics reproach him: (1) voluntarism and (2) relativism (see 34.5). Regarding (1), all moral choice is indeed *arbitrary*, since nothing is good or even better than anything else before, but rather because and only because, it is chosen. Accordingly, one cannot have any good reason for choosing one thing over another. That is precisely the arbitrariness ascribed to God's choices by theological voluntarists like Descartes (see 25.8). Since Sartre places human choice on exactly the same footing while dispensing with God, the talk of non-theological voluntarism seems perfectly apt. Arbitrariness of this sort goes beyond the mere blindness of moral choice described in the previous section. For there the point was only that we are without any secure guidance in making the right decision; here the claim is that we cannot make the wrong decision—always subject to the proviso that we choose authentically.

Regarding (2), the cited passages apparently make moral values entirely dependent upon, and hence *relative* to, the individual will. Now relativism is one consequence that *theological* voluntarism did not have. God's choices or commands, though perfectly arbitrary, provide an absolute standard by which to measure human choices or actions. We shall postpone consideration of (2) until section 38.7.

38.6 Universalizability

Before we can assess the exact bearing of the authenticity proviso on the charge of relativism, we must first examine Sartre's notion of universalizability. For the puzzling assertion (see 37.4.1) that "[w]hen a man commits himself to anything . . . he is not only choosing what he will be, but is thereby at the same time a legislator deciding for the whole of mankind" (30/351) apparently articulates a necessary and sufficient condition of authentic choice. Of course, the normative injunction of existentialism, "one ought always to ask oneself what would happen if everyone did as one is doing" (30–1/351), cannot be identical with the famed Kantian procedure of universalizing the maxim of one's action in order to determine whether the action is right, wrong, or permissible. For Sartre rejects Kantian ethics in no uncertain terms. It may be a useful preliminary, therefore, to compare and contrast his notion of "deciding for the whole of mankind" with Kant's universalizability criterion.

38.6.1 Kant's universalizability criterion

The basic principle of Kant's normative ethical theory, alluded to several times already, receives explicit mention where Sartre describes the situation of the young man: act so as to treat others as ends and not just as means to your own ends (see 38.4.1). But Kant's categorical imperative is usually formulated in two other ways: "act only on that maxim through which you can at the same time will that it should become a universal law" and "act as if the maxim of your action were to become through your will a *universal law of nature*." These rather than the first formulation express what is known as 'Kant's universalizability criterion.' Although he neither quotes them nor uses the word 'universalizability,' Sartre cannot have been unaware of the Kantian overtones of the existentialist injunction cited above.

For Kant, the agent's *ability* to universalize the maxim (rule) of his action, making it a universal law for all mankind, is a test or criterion of moral rightness, wrongness, or permissibility. Simply put, it is *permissible* to act on a certain maxim if and only if one can will that it be a universal law (that is, if it is possible to will that everyone act that way in relevantly similar circumstances); it is *wrong* to act on a maxim or rule if and only if one cannot will that it be a universal law; and it is *obligatory* to act on a maxim if and only if it is impossible to will that its contradictory *opposite* be a universal law.

What 'cannot' and 'impossible' mean is unfortunately left unclear. That is the first and chief problem with Kant's universalizability criterion. Apart from a few straightforward applications, like lying, for instance, the criterion is so ambiguous as to be unworkable. Clearly, I cannot, for logical reason, will that everyone lie or go back on his word whenever convenient, since, if everyone did so, all promise-making would cease. Here there may indeed to be a hidden contradiction of sorts in what is willed. But there are plenty of other cases of morally reprehensible conduct where it is difficult to see how a similar difficulty arises. And yet unless it covers all cases, the alleged rule is not a necessary and sufficient condition of morally good, bad, and permissible actions at all. This brings us to the other main problem with Kant's universalizability criterion: there seems to be a muddle as to what it is a criterion *of*.

Had Kant employed universalizability as a criterion *not* of (1) morally good, bad, and permissible actions but of (2) moral as opposed to non-moral actions, his point would have been the perfectly correct one that if the maxim of an action is *not* one that holds universally for *all* rational agents (who ought therefore to behave in the same way in relevantly similar circumstances), the maxim or rule in question is not a moral but a *non*-moral one: it is, at best, a "counsel of prudence," as Kant puts it, a way to promote good (one's own or other's) or to avoid harm, not a moral law or rule. Or it may be a religious duty, incumbent only on the faithful (on moral and religious duties, see above 10.2.6, 11.3, and 13.4). Or it may simply be a matter of taste, preference, courtesy, etiquette, or the like.

Universalizability of one's maxim is, moreover, only a necessary, not a sufficient, condition of a rule's being a moral rather than a non-moral action guide. For if an action is *morally* right (permissible or obligatory) for person A in such-and-such circumstances, then the same must be true for person B (or any other moral agent) under relevantly similar circumstances. Yet what is at least a necessary condition of an action's or a rule's being a moral *rather than non-moral* action or rule is interpreted by Kant as a *sufficient* condition of its being a moral (in the sense of 'permissible' or 'obligatory') *rather than immoral* (wrong) act or rule. And this seems mistaken, a muddle in fact, quite apart from the problem of what 'being able to universalize one's maxim' actually means.

38.6.2 Sartre's universalizability criterion

As regards the first difficulty, it is clearly not the *ability or inability* to universalize one's maxim or rule of action that counts for Sartre, but the agent's *willingness or unwillingness* to choose for everyone, to have others, indeed all mankind, act as he or she is acting. So the puzzles about possibility and impossibility disappear. Sartre recognizes the unworkability of Kant's criterion when he points out, apropos of the young man, that one and the same action can be considered under widely different descriptions and subsumed under various rules (see 38.4.1). It is a little harder to determine whether he avoids the second difficulty. Minimally, the *willingness* to universalize serves to distinguish moral from non-moral choices, decisions, and actions. This is the use to which Kant *should* have put the notion, and Sartre seems to have precisely this in mind when he emphasizes the burden of anguish-laden responsibility that comes of being a *moral* agent and choosing, not just for oneself alone, but for humanity as a whole:

If I am a worker, for instance, I may choose to join a Christian rather than a Communist trade union. And if, by that membership, I choose to signify that resignation is, after all, the attitude that best becomes a man, that man's kingdom is not upon this earth, I do not commit myself alone to that view. Resignation is my will for everyone, and my action is, in consequence, a commitment on behalf of mankind. Or if, to take a more personal case, I decide to marry and to have children ... I am thereby committing not only myself but humanity as a whole, to the practice of monogamy. (29–30/350)

Sartre *may* just be saying here that what makes these *moral* decisions (rather than morally *right* choices) is the fact that I am committing the *whole* human race through my individual choice. Instead of moral decisions, it would be more in keeping with the general tenor of Sartre's philosophy to speak of 'existential decisions.' Not every decision, however trivial, is such that in making it I choose for all mankind; that would be absurd. If this minimal reading is correct, however, Sartre's examples are rather poorly chosen. The decision to join this or that trade union, or to marry and have children, seems a doubtful example of the sort of thing that one must be willing to universalize. Sartre would have been well advised to steer clear of examples that are better regarded as political or life-style choices. Still, on this minimal interpretation, there is no confusion of a necessary condition of an action's being an existential decision with a sufficient condition of its being morally right.

However, if Sartre wishes to assert that willingness to choose for all mankind is sufficient for authentic choice, which in turn suffices to *make* the decision morally *right* (see 38.5), then willingness to universalize is a criterion for moral rightness after all. In that case, the problem is moral relativism. For if deciding authentically *makes* what is decided right, it is impossible for one individual to be justified—not rationally justified, of course, but justified in virtue of his authentic moral commitments—in criticizing or condemning the *authentic* choices of another. Of course, the charge of relativism was interpreted to mean that condemnation could *never* be warranted *in any circumstances*, so Sartre may have at least a partial defence, even if he cannot evade the charge altogether. This, as we shall see, is indeed the outcome.

38.7 Authenticity

The detailed reply to the charge of relativism has two parts. First, Sartre (1) affirms—without supporting argument of any kind—the existence of a basic moral value that is non-relative or absolute. On this basis, he then (2) shows that derivative moral values, too, are non-relative. This succeeds reasonably well for (a) moral choices that are inauthentic; but in the case of (b) actions authentically willed for mankind as a whole, we are left with an ineliminable residue of relativism.

38.7.1 Freedom as absolutely good

In the first place, then, Sartre (1) asserts dogmatically that there is one absolute moral value—meaning by 'value' either (i) some way of acting that is absolutely good, or

(ii) that which makes that particular way of acting absolutely good (the criterion of goodness), or (iii) both. If there exists such an absolute moral value, then we have something by which to appraise men's actions and moral characters in a manner that is not merely relative—even after traditional moral theories involving Forms, God, eternal verities, and the like have been relegated to the scrapheap where they belong. That *basic* uncreated value, "the foundation" (51/366) of all derivative values created by man, is *freedom itself*. It is described in the terms traditionally applied to the supreme good or *summum bonum* of classical moral theory, things like (a) pleasure, (b) knowledge, and (c) virtue, among the ancients, or (d) utility and (e) duty among the moderns:

I can pronounce a moral judgment [that is absolute]. For I declare that freedom ... can have no other end and aim but itself [in other words, freedom is an end or good in itself] ... [W]hen a man has seen that [all other] values depend upon himself, in that state of forsakenness he can will only one thing, and that is freedom as the foundation of all [such] values. (ibid.)

Into the select company of things identified by prominent moral theorists of the past as good or as ends *in themselves*, things desired, willed, or chosen *for their own sakes*, all others being desired merely as means to one of these ends, Sartre thus introduces—by his choice of language, if not in so many words—a new candidate: (f) freedom. That in itself may entitle him to a place in the history of moral theory; whether it is a place of honour remains to be seen.

In Sartre's case, it would be better to say that freedom is the only thing desir*able* or choice*worthy* for its own sake, stressing the normative over the descriptive dimension, as in the case of ancient eudaemonism (see 10.3). For in certain of the moral theories that Sartre is alluding to here, what men *in fact* choose (whether always, or for the most part, or only under certain circumstances) is a key consideration in determining what they *ought* to choose. As for freedom, this is, by Sartre's own admission, precisely what people do *not* choose, what they *avoid* choosing for the most part. That is at least a minor, if not an insuperable, difficulty for his theory. For although few people ever will freedom, to say that they *ought* to do so means that they *would* do so if enlightened, clear-sighted, and courageous—as most are not. Hence, furnishing a credible account of why people in fact flee freedom is, for Sartre, an integral part of the task of making his absolute standard plausible.

If the intent of the above passage is indeed to propose freedom as the highest good, then the alleged arbitrariness of choice is subject to a very important qualification or proviso. It seemed earlier that the goodness of morally good things must be relative to the individuals *by whom* they are chosen and *made* good or right simply *by* being chosen; for, as we put it in terms of the Euthyphro dilemma: they are not chosen because they are good, but good because and only because they are chosen. Yet if freedom, and it alone, is good in itself, those ways of acting designated morally 'good' or 'bad' have an objective, non-relative measure of their moral worth in *how* they are chosen. The question is *not* whether they are chosen freely, since that is invariably the case, man being "condemned to be free" (34/353); the question is rather whether or not they are chosen *for the sake of* freedom, as means to the end of freedom, or, as Sartre will put it later: whether or not in willing them, the agent wills freedom for its own sake.

38.7.2 Willing freedom for its own sake

In the immediate sequel to the above passage, Sartre explains what it means to "will freedom" for its own sake:

We will freedom for freedom's sake ... Thus, in the name of that will to freedom which is implied in freedom itself, I can form judgments upon those who seek to hide from themselves the wholly voluntary nature of their existence and its complete freedom. Those who hide from this total freedom, in a guise of solemnity or with deterministic excuses, I shall call cowards. Others, who try to show that their existence is necessary, when it is merely an accident of the appearance of the human race on earth—I shall call scum. But neither cowards nor scum can be identified except upon the plane of strict authenticity. (51–2/366)

At a first approximation, 'willing freedom for its own sake' means 'choosing not to deceive oneself about one's total freedom.' This is not just a matter of *knowing* the truth about the contingency of human existence, about our state of abandonment, our inability to "pass beyond human subjectivity" (29/350), and our responsibility for humanity as a whole; for every human being knows these things implicitly, even if most try to avoid facing up to that which mood has always already revealed. The existentialist philosopher, for his part, knows these things explicitly; and yet choosing freedom for its own sake can hardly be the prerogative of the philosopher. No, choosing freedom for its own sake is rather a matter of *acting* from the *motive* of exercising one's freedom "to invent man" (34/354) and to create values for all mankind. In the above passage this is equated with choosing authentically rather than inauthentically. This every moral agent is capable of, even if few exercise their freedom in this way and most deliberately avoid doing so.

If this interpretation is correct, then choosing *freedom* for its own sake, acting from the motive of freedom, is almost the antithesis of acting for the sake of *duty*, or from the motive of *obedience* to the moral law, as described by Kant (see 12.8.5). It amounts to acting in the anguished realization that there simply is no moral law to guide us in the concrete situations we must face; that there are no moral rules or values antecedent to those actually brought into existence and made universal by the individual who 'legislates' for all mankind. Freedom itself cannot provide such guidance; as an absolute value, it governs *how*, not *what*, we ought to choose.

38.7.3 The metaphysical basis of morals

That is the main point made in the passage cited above, the first part of which nevertheless sheds some interesting light on the missing justification for the absolute value of choosing freedom for its own sake. For what can be meant by the "will to freedom *which is implied in freedom itself*" (e.a.)? This must mean that the value of freedom is somehow entailed by the very *nature* of man. For man, according Sartre, *is* "nothing," that is, nothing but the freedom to create man himself and universal values *ex nihilo*. Of course, some such normative injunction as 'Become (choose to be) what you are' must be operative here as well; for, as Sartre realizes, no normative conclusion can be validly derived from descriptive metaphysical premises alone. Nevertheless, the missing justification is primarily metaphysical.

Freedom, then, has absolute value in virtue of what man *is* rather than what he *wills*, while all else is dependent for its worth on being willed. Freedom is not created by man, as are *all* derivative moral values; it is *given* rather than *created*. In trying to meet the charge of relativism in this way, Sartre is at least qualifying, if not abandoning, his anthropological voluntarism. For it turns out that not *all* values, but all *except one*, are freely created by man. Still, freedom is at least brought into being by man's existence as a knowing-willing-feeling Being-in-the-world; and this is probably enough to make the exception palatable to Sartre. For it fits in with his general anthropocentric and voluntaristic tendency, even though it is not strictly consistent with the theory of unqualified anthropological voluntarism that he asserts at times. Sartre is simply not the rigorous thinker that, say, Kant is.

38.7.4 Inauthentic choice

So much for the (1) assertion of the absolute value of freedom. The remaining task is (2) to show that derivative, created values may be assessed, and moral praise and blame assigned, in a way that is non-relative. We have seen that, apart from (i) *what* is decided upon in a concrete existential situation, there are two basic (ii) *ways* in which existential decisions may be taken: authentically, by willing freedom for its own sake, or inauthentically, by disguising the fact that one has chosen blindly and arbitrarily for all mankind. At most, Sartre has furnished grounds for condemning inauthentic action or, assuming most human action falls between the extremes of authenticity and inauthenticity, for condemning actions to the precise extent that they are inauthentic. Yet, as far as we know up to this point, *anything* may be willed authentically. Only if it turns out that some choices cannot be made authentically, and if these coincide roughly with those actions that we must be able to condemn on any satisfactory moral theory, has Sartre successfully met the charge of relativism.

To determine whether these conditions are met, let us consider the two ways in which Sartre describes inauthentic action, namely (a) as disavowing responsibility for one's own actions by invoking some "deterministic doctrine" (51/365), and (b) as disavowing responsibility for the whole of mankind by *not* asking the question, "What would happen if everyone did so [as I am doing now]?" (31/351).

Under (a) Sartre probably means to include, not only (i) appeals to philosophical or psychological doctrines that deny or restrict total freedom, but all (ii) "deterministic excuses" (51/366) such as 'my upbringing is at fault,' 'my hormones were out of whack,' 'I was overcome by passion,' 'man is a fallen creature owing to original sin,' 'human nature is corrupted by social conditions,' and so forth. The range of such excuses seems almost limitless. Sartre would presumably also want to include here (iii) any action taken in the mistaken belief that one's concrete choices are dictated in advance by some such standard as Kant's categorical imperative, or by the rule of Christian love, or by knowledge of the supreme good. So too (iv) any theory that invokes a pre-ordained purpose for which man has been put on earth—assuming, for the moment, that this is what Sartre has in mind when he speaks of those who try to "show that their existence is necessary, when it is merely an accident of the appearance of the human race on earth" (52/366). All the above are tantamount to "bad faith," hiding from oneself the "wholly voluntary nature of existence and its complete freedom" (ibid.)—though it may be question-begging to assume that such theories and excuses involve "error," as in this passage:

[I]n certain cases choice is founded upon an error, and in others upon the truth. One can judge a man by saying that he deceives himself. Since we have defined the situation of man as one of free choice, without excuse and without help, any man who takes refuge behind the excuse of his passions, or by inventing some deterministic doctrine, is a self-deceiver. One may object: 'But why should he not choose to deceive himself?' I reply that it is not for me to judge him morally, but I define his self-deception as an error. Here one cannot avoid pronouncing a judgment of truth. The self-deception is evidently a falsehood, because it is a dissimulation of man's complete liberty of commitment. (50–1/365)

From this it is apparent just how fluid is the boundary between true and false ("error," "falsehood"), on the one hand, and right and wrong, on the other—in short, between metaphysics and morality in Sartre. However, if the "judgment of truth" is to provide grounds for *moral* condemnation of certain actions, not just of certain motives (which we may or may not be able to ascertain), it has to be shown that certain recognizable sorts of actions cannot be chosen authentically. The first description of inauthenticity goes almost no way toward showing anything of the kind.

To this end the other description of inauthentic action is more serviceable: (b) disavowing responsibility for the whole of mankind by *not* asking the question, What if everybody behaved as I am now behaving? For no one *would* (rather than could) will that those of his own actions that are harmful to others be a law for all mankind, since in so willing he would choose that all others harm him under relevantly similar circumstances. Here Sartre appeals tacitly to the psychological fact, noticed already by eudaemonist theorists, that no one willingly harms himself. That is apparently why actions harmful to others cannot be chosen authentically:

> nor can one escape from that disturbing thought ['what if everyone did as I am doing?'] except by a kind of self-deception. The man who lies in self-excuse, by saying 'Everyone will not do it' must be ill at ease in his conscience, for the act of lying implies the universal value [for all mankind] which it denies [does *not* universalize]. (31/351)

Unfortunately, Sartre invites misunderstanding by suggesting that what is at issue is *truth* or *logical consistency*, since the agent both "implies" and "denies" the same thing. The point is rather that in refusing to will that *what* he chooses become a normative law for all mankind (as he must, given the psychological make-up of human beings), the agent is rejecting his absolute freedom to create values for all mankind, his own quasi-omnipotence. He is rejecting, in other words, the absolute sovereignty of the will that makes each human being a Cartesian God of sorts, the creator of man and of universal human values *ex nihilo*. If he assumes his responsibility for all mankind, on the other hand, he will never treat others as he would be unwilling to be treated himself. What makes harmful actions wrong is neither the harmful consequences themselves, nor the supposed inconsistency of affirming and denying the same thing, but the bad faith or inauthenticity involved in *not* choosing freedom for its own sake.

If this is correct, then Sartre has managed to avoid moral relativism of the 'anything goes' variety. It is no good objecting: even the worst moral reprobate can choose authentically, so who is to say that his anguished choice of evil as a positive good for all mankind is wrong? Anyone who treats others as he would not be willing to be treated himself is acting inauthentically and can be condemned by the absolute standard of freedom. So the worry that, on Sartre's theory, one is in no position to condemn the tyrant, the torturer, the murderer, the exploiter, the extortionist, the embezzler, and so on is successfully dispatched.

38.7.5 Authentic choice

Yet Sartre himself is prepared to concede that those who bring the charge of relativism have a point: "people say to us, 'You are unable to judge others.' This is true in one sense and false in another" (50/365). The sense in which it is false has now been explained. As for that in which it is true, all Sartre says at this stage is: "we do not believe in progress." This short and enigmatic response presumably means that the *authentic* choices of all epochs are on the same footing; whatever system of values is chosen authentically is made right—for a particular epoch—by the *way* it is chosen. No later epoch can legitimately condemn it, adopting an attitude of superiority based on the belief in moral progress. Elsewhere Sartre speaks explicitly of "the relativity of each epoch" (47/362). The concession is important, since, if this much is granted, the same conclusion follows for the authentic choices of individuals within the same epoch and even the same milieu.

If so, an important residue of relativism clings to authentic choices at least. For what happens when I cannot fault another's existential decisions on the grounds that he or she is acting in bad faith—as I clearly cannot in some cases of earnest moral disagreement among decent people? Given what *makes* moral choice right on Sartre's theory, it seems that all I can legitimately say is: 'What you choose freely and in good faith for all mankind is right, and so is what I choose in the same manner.' Even incompatible moral choices are thus right relative to the chooser.

This, surely, sells human reason rather short. We are left in some, and by no means the least important, cases with an irresolvable clash of wills. In the case of moral disagreement over core values authentically chosen, one cannot even argue or attempt to come to an understanding; one can only affirm over and over again one's own moral commitments, acknowledging the other's right to differ. Should there be a limit to one's tolerance for the dissenting authentic choices of others, there is nothing left but to fall to name-calling of the sort Sartre himself indulges in toward inauthentic choosers ('cowards,' 'scum'). The next step may be violence. From benign tolerance the way to insults and blows may not be very far at all.

38.8 Conclusion

While certain choices can be recognized and condemned as inauthentic, it being impossible for human beings, given their psychological make-up, to make such choices authentically, we are still left with a wide range of options or values that are simply immune to criticism or rejection since they are made right by being chosen in a certain way. Ultimately, the unpalatable consequences of voluntarism are only mitigated, not avoided, by the distinction between authenticity and inauthenticity. As Sartre was able to respond with some plausibility to the charges of quietism and Cartesianism, so he has at least a partial response—no more—to the most serious charge of his critics, a thoroughgoing moral relativism.

The road to freedom thus ends in a largely featureless landscape in which we must choose our direction without benefit of signposts. We have obviously come a very long way from the confines of that prison cell in which two old friends, meeting for the last time, settled an earnest moral disagreement to their mutual satisfaction by carefully examining the options open to them in the light of certain ground rules and guiding principles. What has become of the Socratic idea of 'following the best argument'? By way of conclusion, it may be worth considering this along with certain other developments noticed on the long road from ancient to contemporary philosophy.

Recommended readings and references

Desan, Wilfrid. 1960. *The Tragic Finale. An Essay on the Philosophy of Jean-Paul Sartre*. New York: Harper Torchbook.

Fell, Joseph P. 1981. *Heidegger and Sartre: An Essay on Being and Place*. New York: Columbia University Press.

Foster, M.B. 1934. "The Christian Doctrine of Creation and the Rise of Modern Natural Science." *Mind*. (An interesting scholarly account of the importance of the craftsman model in ancient philosophy.)

Frankena, William. 1963. *Ethics*. The Foundations of Philosophy Series. Englewood Cliffs, New Jersey: Prentice-Hall. (Superb critical survey of ethics. Develops a mixed deontological-consequentialist theory.)

Gilson, Étienne. 1952. *Being and Some Philosophers*. Toronto: Pontifical Institute of Medieval Studies.

Greene, Norman N. 1963. *Jean-Paul Sartre: The Existentialist Ethic*. Ann Arbor: The University of Michigan Press (Ann Arbor Paperbacks). (Offers a simplified but useful overview of existentialism in its initial chapter.)

Heidegger, Martin. 1977. *Basic Writings*. New York and San Francisco: Harper & Row, Publishers. (Contains "A Letter on Humanism," which formulates an oblique reply to Sartre's *Existentialism and Humanism*.)

Murdoch, Iris. 1989. *Sartre: Romantic Rationalist*. Hammondsworth: Penguin. (Examines the literary works in relation to the philosophical.)

Owens, Joseph, CssR. 1985. *An Elementary Christian Metaphysics*. Houston: Center for Thomistic Studies. (A subtle treatment of the priority of existence to essence in Aquinas. Difficult, but rewarding.)

Sartre, Jean-Paul. 1957. *The Transcendence of the Ego. An Existentialist Theory of Consciousness*. Translated and Annotated with an Introduction by Forrest Williams and Robert Kirkpatrick. New York: Farrar Strauss and Company (The Noonday Press).

Sartre, Jean-Paul. 2001. *Being and Nothingness*. Translated by Hazel E. Barnes. New York: Citadel Press.

Snell, Bruno. 1982. "The Discovery of *Humanitas*, and Our Attitude toward the Greeks." Chapter 11 of *The Discovery of the Mind*. New York: Dover Publications. (On the history of the concept of humanism.)

Warnock, Mary. 1971. *The Philosophy of Sartre*. London: Hutchinson University Library. (Sympathetic, yet sensible where scepticism is called for. The essay *Existentialism and Humanism* is unfortunately dismissed in less than a page. Could be more informative about the German philosophical influences.)

Questions for reflection, discussion, and review

1. What is the difference between moral scepticism and relativism? If the latter is just a species of the former, what is the relevant specific difference?
2. Is descriptive relativism an incontestable fact, or do different codes of conduct in different cultures have some underlying shared principles?
3. Granted that people will always disagree about moral matters, is that because there just is no basis for agreement or because it is as yet undiscovered?
4. What do you understand by 'the humanities'? What, if anything, do the humanities have to do with the word 'humanism' in Sartre's title?
5. Must humanism be atheistic? What might a theistic humanism be like?
6. Which of the four criticisms of existentialism outlined by Sartre at the beginning of his work seems most serious to you? Why?
7. Try to put the slogan "existence comes before essence" in a historical context by contrasting Descartes's theological with Sartre's anthropological voluntarism.
8. In what sense are 'thrownness' and 'projection' complementary concepts?
9. When Sartre writes that man is "nothing" is he overstating a valid point? If so, why? If not, why not? Can you think of any other examples?
10. Is there a kernel of truth to Sartre's claim each individual chooses for the whole of humanity? What might he be driving at?
11. Of the various types of consequentialist theories, which seems to you the most plausible?
12. Is there any plausibility to Kant's claim that lying to a murderer enquiring as to the whereabouts of his intended victim is wrong? Is rigourism more justifiable when it comes to taking a life?
13. Is some degree of disinterestedness essential to 'the moral point of view'? Or are even egoistic and hedonistic theories moral theories too?
14. Consider the moral situation of Abraham? Is Sartre correct in saying that even in this situation the decision to take his son's life is taken blindly?
15. Consider the situation of the young man who came to Sartre for advice. Had he already decided what he would do when he turned to his teacher? Or was this just part of a process of deliberation that was rational rather than blind?
16. What sense can you make of André Gide's distinction between false and true sentiment? Is Sartre right to reject it?

Conclusion

The most fitting conclusion may be a brief reflection on the career of philosophy in the light of the major trends and perennial postures noticed in the five main parts of this book. The trend toward voluntarism and relativism that culminated in the atheistic humanism of Sartre is just a stream in that larger current of thought called 'anthropocentrism' and 'subjectivism' throughout this work. Of course, such 'isms' are just terms of art (see 2.7) coined by intellectual historians to register the peculiar stress laid by certain thinkers or schools on one side or the other of a philosophical dichotomy. It may be the priority of man over the rest of the universe ('humanism'); of the human subject over the objects of knowledge ('subjectivism'); of the human over the non-human and superhuman realms ('anthropocentrism'); of the will over the intellect ('voluntarism'); of the relative and mind-dependent over the absolute or independent ('relativism'), and so on. In these cases, as perhaps in that of realism and idealism as well, there seems to be good reason to speak of a historical *trend*; whereas when it comes to empiricism and rationalism, or philosophies of immanence and transcendence, it seems preferable to speak of perennial philosophical *postures* of the sort that vie with each other in every age. There is admittedly something facile about labels, but without them we cannot even begin to *interpret* what we have seen in the foregoing. That is what is to be attempted here by way of conclusion.

Of the major trends noticed, the one of which the others seem to be separate but interwoven strands is the momentous shift in focus from (1) metaphysical questions concerning the existence and nature of all *things* to (2) psychological and epistemological questions concerning human *thought* or knowledge—to the study of man, whether as a mind, a psycho-physical being, or a Being-in-the-world. Subjectivism and anthropocentrism still had not run their course as far as Husserl and Sartre when, early in the twentieth century, (3) *language* (and with it, logic) began to supplant both things and thought as the starting point and principal focus of philosophical reflection. This final stage was only hinted at in the references to Quine and contemporary Anglo-American nominalism or linguisticism (see 21.3.2); not mentioned at all was the fact that it had an important parallel on the European continent, in what is called 'hermeneutics' or 'hermeneuticism' and in so-called post-modernism. What unites these three movements within twentieth-century philosophy is a shared focus on the linguistic dimension of human thought and experience.

In post-modernism, moreover, linguisticism takes on its most radical cast, fostering a sceptical relativism not confined to values and human nature, as in Sartre, but affecting every domain of truth expressible in language. This should be enough to cause at least mild alarm. There is no good reason to struggle against the conclusion that there is no such thing as truth that is not somehow 'constructed' by us as language users, if this is indeed the only or the most reasonable conclusion open to us; but before dismissing as outdated a starting point in things whose natures are discoverable through rational reflection on human experience, we ought to have pretty compelling reasons for doing so.

The same goes for the scepticism, especially regarding metaphysics itself, that was the outcome of the transition from (1) things to (2) thought. There may be something to Hume's influential idea that we ought to abandon efforts to encompass in thought the unrestricted totality of things. In turning instead to psychology, sociology, epistemology, or the study of the history of philosophical and scientific ideas, we at least have to do with ourselves and our thought rather than with things in the world around us. Some such starting point and focus may seem wise given the spectacular errors and excesses of the great synoptic metaphysical systems of the past. Still, it is just not clear either that the holistic impulse need be fallacious, or that it has actually abated under the strictures of the last few centuries, or that it is ever capable of doing so. Kant, who was one of the principal architects of a new metaphysics with its starting point and principal object in human thought, once described man as the *animal metaphysicum*. By this he meant that the urge to grasp the totality of things was ineradicably rooted in human nature. The dogged persistence of metaphysics from the birth of philosophy to the present day certainly bears him out. The critic Northrop Frye once remarked of painting that it had been around at least since the last ice age, and that he, for one, hoped it would be around until the next. In the case of metaphysics, we can say with perfect confidence that there has almost always been and—barring another natural or man-made catastrophe—will always be some metaphysics. No compelling argument has yet been produced for stifling rather than channelling the metaphysical impulse; and until one is, it seems premature to abandon efforts to orientate ourselves within the totality of what is, especially if this can help provide an intellectual and moral basis for human life and flourishing.

Another aspect of the same trend toward subjectivism and relativism is the growing estrangement from the notion, apparently so obvious to the Greeks, that philosophy can shed light on the vital question of the good life for man. This assumption has gradually given way to the idea of the pursuit of individual happiness. Hume's emotivism and Sartre's decisionism are, in different ways, steps in this direction (see 37.2); yet nothing could be further from the outlook of the Greeks. Before dismissing it as quaint or naive, we ought to give the ancient point of view careful consideration.

For on the face of it, it seems as plausible today as it was in Greek times that while every human being must seek to be happy after his or her own fashion, there are nevertheless certain universal truths, discoverable through rational reflection, to guide us in the conquest of a happiness truly worth having. If the question of 'the meaning of life' is one that can still be made intellectually respectable today, this may be the content to give it. In any case, the study of Socrates and the Greek moralists provides a valuable check on the impulse to accept uncritically the conclusions widely proclaimed by the apostles of contemporary subjectivism and relativism.

Another side-stream in the same broad current of thought is the tendency toward voluntarism. For the human subject that was at first understood primarily as a knowing (Descartes) and then as a feeling being (Hume) was at last conceived primarily under the aspect of will or volition (Sartre). Yet looking back to our point of departure, it is hard to imagine a more thoroughgoing subordination of will to intellect than that embodied in the Socratic paradoxes (see 12.9.2). From Socrates's perspective, there is just no such thing as a good or bad will, only insight and lack of it. The fully rational human being pursues the moral good first and above all; for it is not just an indispensable means to, but the sufficient condition of, genuine human thriving or happiness. There is accordingly no wickedness, only blindness and foolishness, and no inducement to moral goodness except *knowing* what is really in one's best interests. This Socratic intellectualism is just the first stage in an ever-increasing valorization of theoretical knowledge among the Greek thinkers of the classical period. We noted its influence on Plato (see 19.3.2), for whom the highest vocation of man is the theoretical contemplation of the eternal Forms. For Aristotle, too, the life of intellectual contemplation is the consummate form of *eudaimonia*. For the purest manifestation of this contemplative ideal, we must look to the life not of man but of the divine Intelligences (see 20.5.2).

Of this Aristotelian conception of divinity the Cartesian God is virtually the antithesis. For God's infinite intellect is totally absorbed into his will. Divine goodness has nothing to do with grasping what is best by means of the intellect, and everything with making the good good through willing it arbitrarily. And as with the good, so with the true. God creates the eternal verities by assenting to them; he does not assent to them because they are true. Something of this trickles down to the human level via the *imago Dei* doctrine (that man was created in God's image). In mankind, it is the will, not the intellect, that is perfect, the image of the creator. For the human intellect is confined within the narrow limits of the clearly and distinctly perceived; beyond these limits it is constantly dogged by error. The divine intellect, by contrast, understands everything clearly and distinctly. However, the human will knows no such limits as human understanding is subject to; its power to affirm, to doubt, or to deny extends to absolutely everything. That is the doctrine of the Fourth Meditation, which we did not stop to consider in Part Three: although an infinitely great distance separates us both from God's intellect and from his power, in respect of willing we are in no way inferior to the creator. Even if we cannot know clearly and distinctly everything we wish to, by withholding our assent from anything not clearly and distinctly perceived we can at least avoid ever being deceived, even by an omnipotent deceiver. There is no need to rehearse yet again the manner in which Sartre ups the ante on the Cartesian supremacy of the will by transposing a simulacrum of divine omnipotence to the human level; the point just now is that Descartes unwittingly set the stage for such voluntarism.

In Hume, though to some extent in Sartre as well, we met another tendency of thought that is part and parcel of the anthropocentrism of modern philosophy. It might be described, in picturesque terms, as a return from the flights of philosophical fancy to the here and now of ordinary human experience. 'Immanentism' may be a better designation than 'naturalism' for those thinkers, represented here by Hume and Sartre, who oppose the philosophies of transcendence typified by Plato and Descartes. Philosophies of immanence understand themselves as deepening that pre-philosophical understanding of ourselves and the world that arises out of everyday experience. Aristotle is another who—despite occasional flights of transcendence in his discussions of minds or intelligences, including the human soul (see 16.2 and 20.5.1)—is essentially a philosopher of immanence. In this basic tendency of thought he is followed by the whole Peripatetic tradition. The funny thing about Hume's call for a return to "common life" is that he thoroughly misunderstood the ordinary experience he so prized (see 31.8.1).

The fundamental trait of all philosophies of immanence, not excepting Hume's, is the conviction that philosophy is essentially continuous with ordinary experience and common sense. Typical of philosophies of transcendence, on the other hand, is the tendency to subvert our ordinary understanding of ourselves and the world, replacing it with conclusions drawn from principles furnished by reason alone. Thus, for the Plato of the *Phaedo*, a flesh-and-blood human being like Socrates, who is born, lives seventy years, and perishes, is in truth a divine or semi-divine (but in any case imperishable) soul, temporarily imprisoned in a body and confined to a world of changing material things of which he forms no part. For Descartes, such a man is not even *one* being, but two, a composite of two separate substances, mind and body, each capable of existing in its own right. Cartesian man, moreover, is the furthest thing from what we normally take to be a person: a worldless, solipsistic, disembodied centre of conscious activity that is accidentally lodged in a foreign substance or material body.

Such teachings plainly stand common sense on its head, as does the philosophical doctrine that the material world is unreal, or less than completely real (Plato); or that material things in space are not really distinct from the space they occupy—that they are, rightly understood, pure extension, devoid of all those sensory qualities ordinarily ascribed to them (Descartes). And so too when it comes to the philosopher's idea of the divine: like Aristotle's 'thought thinking itself,' the 'necessary being' of later philosophical theology is about as remote as can be imagined from the personal God of faith and scripture. In every region of being, then, the pre-philosophical understanding of things is overturned in philosophies of transcendence. Like the born-again Christians of recent times, the philosopher of Plato or Descartes is a twice-born mortal, reborn through initiation into philosophy. Aristotle was only the first to rebel against this whole tendency of thought. He stressed that common humanity that unites the philosopher with the rest of mankind, treating ordinary existence in a world of sensible things as *the* fully human way of being and attempting, through philosophical reflection, to understand it, not to explain it away. In this he was followed by a long line of thinkers right down to Heidegger. That is why, in the case of philosophies of immanence and transcendence, it is better to speak, not of a historical trend, but of two perennial philosophical postures that coexist in every era. The same is true, as noted above, for philosophies that stress experience at the expense of reason, or vice versa.

What guarantees the perenniality of philosophies of immanence is a different sort of holistic tendency from that identified by Kant. As beginning philosophers it is only natural for us to wish to understand all things as we experience them. In turning to philosophy, we expect some enrichment of that understanding of ourselves, of the world, perhaps also of the divine, already acquired through pre- and extra-philosophical experience. From this point of view, any philosophy that seeks to supplant our natural understanding with another that is altogether unlike it must seem suspect. As mankind's attempt to orientate itself within the totality of what is, philosophy naturally takes its footing in lived experience and in the innate desire of men to find an intellectual and moral basis for life by pondering the big questions. This is once again what Aristotle meant when he began his *Metaphysics* with the simple sentence: "All men desire by nature to know" (see 10.2.9).

Enquiry in other domains has its foundation and outer framework in philosophy (see 1.2.3), and no philosophical questions are more universal or fundamental than those concerning (1) the order of knowing, (2) the order of being, (3) the concept of experience, and (4) the idea of being itself (see chaps. 3 and 4). Following the example set by the established usage of 'ethical' and 'meta-ethical' (see 10.2.2), we may call these two pairs of questions 'metaphysical' (or 'ontological') and 'meta-metaphysical' (or 'meta-ontological'), respectively (see 20.10.2). Unlike the order of knowing and of being, the meta-metaphysical ideas of being and experience are only implicit in the major systems of philosophical thought; to make them explicit may be to achieve the deepest level of understanding of our intellectual heritage of which we are capable. Of meta-metaphysical enquiry one can say with even greater justification what Aristotle said of metaphysics itself: "although all the other sciences are more necessary than this, none is more excellent."

Little enough has been accomplished in the course of the long history of thought toward settling any of the perennial issues in a manner that even suggests growing consensus among members of the philosophical community. That may be the best indication of the difficulty of the task. Rather than become despondent at this state of affairs, we shall do well to ponder the advice that Plato has Simmias offer the dispirited company assembled in the prison cell of Socrates, for it may still be the most fitting response yet devised to the many who allege that the asking of such abstruse philosophical questions is at bottom no more excellent than it is necessary:

[P]recise knowledge on that subject is impossible or extremely difficult ... [B]ut ... it surely shows a very poor spirit not to examine thoroughly what is said about it, and to desist before one is exhausted by an all-round investigation. One should achieve one of these things: learn the truth about these things [from one who knows it] or find it out for oneself, or, if that is impossible, adopt the best and most irrefutable of men's theories, and, borne upon this, sail through the dangers of life as upon a raft, unless someone should make that journey safer and less risky upon a firmer vessel of some divine doctrine.

Glossary of Philosophical Terms

accident. See *substance* and *proprium*.

ad hominem. Meaning, literally, 'to' or 'against the man,' the term is generally applied to arguments that are informally invalid owing to the fallacy of irrelevance: they attack the person who advances an argument instead of criticizing (as they should) the argument itself. One type of *ad hominem* argument is valid, however. It consists in showing not that the implications of the argument under examination are mistaken but that those implications must be unacceptable to the person or persons putting the argument forward. See 7.7.1, 9.2.4, 20.2, 34.3.

agnosticism. See *atheism*.

amoralism. An extreme form of moral scepticism according to which "everything is permitted," there being no valid moral norms or principles of any kind. One who believes that "everything is permitted" will never be concerned about right and wrong in the conventional or any other moral sense. However, an *a*moral individual may not behave in ways that others regard as *im*moral, since he may not deem it to be in his best interests to do so, especially considering the penalties (including shame) if found out. However, it is likely that such a person would breach moral norms whenever convinced that it is advantageous to do so. Nevertheless, amoralism as a theoretical conviction differs from immorality as a practice or way of behaving and from immoralism as the practice of behaving that way as a matter of principle. See 32.4.1, 38.2.

anachronism. Etymologically derived from Greek words meaning 'against [the flow, for example]' and 'time,' this is the error of reading back into an earlier age or phase of history or of a particular individual's thought, problems, concepts, and distinctions that belong to a later stage in the development of the discipline or of that individual thinker. See 20.3, 20.11.

analytic, analyticity. Various fairly involved philosophical disputes are associated with this term, but, roughly speaking, a proposition is analytic only if it can be known to be true (or false) in virtue of the meanings of the non-logical terms involved—e.g., 'All mothers are female' or 'No mothers are male.' Since 'mother' is defined as a female parent, the former proposition only asserts that all female parents are female—that is, it is reducible to a tautology (see *tautology*) by the simple substitution of definitions. 'Analytic truths' are sometimes defined as those knowable by means of the principle of contradiction alone. They are said to tell us nothing about the world as it is (so-called non-linguistic reality), but only about the meanings of words. They are therefore regarded as vacuous or uninformative, since they elucidate knowledge we already have rather than extending it. Analytic truths are also called 'truths of reason' or 'necessary truths,' though identifying analytic, necessary, rational truths assumes not just that all analytic truths are truths of reason and necessary (which is uncontroversial) but that all truths of reason and all necessary truths are analytic. This is highly debatable. Take, for example, 'everything that happens has a cause' or 'material objects are spatial.' It seems clear that these are necessary truths in some sense. Moreover, they do not seem to be vacuous. Are they analytic? It is difficult to see how they could be, though some would maintain that they are, perhaps in an extended sense of 'analytic.' See 7.4, 7.5.2.

animism. See *panpsychism*.

anthropogony. From the Greek *anthropos* 'man' and *genesthai* 'to generate,' 'beget,' or 'cause to be.' A story or theory of the origin—whether 'creationist' or 'evolutionary'—of the human race on earth. See 5.3.1.

anthropomorphism. From the Greek *anthropos* 'man,' and *morphē*, 'form.' Anthropomorphism is the tendency to represent the divine (or anything non-human) in human form, in human terms. This applies particularly to the *personified* deities of the Greek myths, who have all the good and bad characteristics of human beings, but alleged anthropomorphizing tendencies have been the subject of criticism in Christian theology as well. See 5.3.2, 5.5.1–3, 5.7, 11.12.1, 20.5.1, 25.8, 35.4.

apodictic, apodicticity. The term can be applied either to truths (propositions) or to arguments. It designates the highest degree of certainty, or what might be called 'rational' (as opposed to merely 'reasonable') certainty. Thus, apodicticity is opposed to all degrees of probability (or merely reasonable certainty). See 6.2.1–2, 6.4.1, 7.4, 7.5.1–3, 9.2.5, 27.13, 28.9, 31.8.3.

aporia. From the Greek word *poros* 'path' or 'way,' and the syllable *a*, the Greek negation corresponding to our 'un-.' Thus, *aporia* means literally: 'the state of *not* knowing any *way* out,' in other words, a state of puzzlement or befuddlement, being dumbfounded, stunned, or dazed. This (according to Meno) is the usual result of undergoing one of Socrates's cross-examinations. See 9.2.3, 9.4.2, 15.4.1, 20.12.1.

a priori / a posteriori. These terms are adopted from Latin. Literally, they mean 'from the earlier' (or 'beforehand') and 'from the later' (or 'after the fact'), respectively. They are already so much a part of the philosopher's vocabulary that they are not usually italicized as foreign words any longer. One has to be cognizant both of their original use and of the sense they acquired in the eighteenth century.

Beginning in medieval times, and continuing right down to the seventeenth century, both terms were applied to *reasoning* from cause ('the earlier) to effect ('the later') or from an effect to its cause ('from the later to the earlier'). In other words, they were applied primarily to *arguments*. Since the eighteenth century they have been applied not so much to arguments as to *propositions* or *truths*. In this use they designate the manner in which such propositions are known to be true (or false). Those known to be *true or false* in a manner that does not depend upon experience are called a priori knowledge. 'Earlier' or 'in advance of experience' thus means neither (1) *'from the (earlier) cause to the (later) effect,'* nor even (2) *'temporally prior to,'* but rather (3) *simultaneous with, though independent of,* experience. Knowledge acquired through experience or observation, on the other hand, is called a posteriori knowledge.

On the basis of this modern sense of a priori and a posteriori, we can also classify arguments as a priori or a posteriori in the modern sense. An argument that employs a priori propositions *exclusively* as premises is an a priori argument, while one in which at least one premise is based on experience or observation is an a posteriori argument. See 4.8, 21.1, 21.3.3, 26.1–10, 27.7.6, 28.3.1–2, 29.2.1–2, 29.6, 29.8.1–2, 30.1, 30.5.1, 30.6.1–2, 31.8.3, 32.3.2, 35.4.3, 35.5, 36.4, 38.4.1.

Archimedean point. A phrase coined by Descartes. Archimedes, the ancient Greek scientist who discovered the principle of the lever, is supposed to have said: "Give me a place to stand [that is, a fixed, immovable point], and a lever long enough, and I will lift the world." By analogy, Descartes is searching for an absolutely certain starting point from which to rebuild the system of the sciences. That fixed point is the *first principle* of *metaphysics, cogito, ergo sum*. The requirements that any principle that is to serve as an Archimedean point must satisfy are three. First, as a *metaphysical* first principle it must assert the existence of something. Second, it must be an assertion of the existence of a substance or thing rather than a mere property or quality or accident of a thing. And, finally, what it asserts it must assert with perfect certainty. See 24.2, 24.4.

asceticism. From the Greek word *askēsis*, meaning 'practice,' 'training,' 'mode of life,' particularly the mode of life prescribed by certain religious sects and consisting in abstention from the satisfaction of all bodily wants in order to achieve otherwise unattainable heights of 'spirituality,' communion with the non-bodily, the non-sensible, the supersensible or spiritual (soul and God). See 14.2, 15.4.2.

atheism. Roughly, the unbeliever's denial of the existence of God. Atheists may be declared or just crypto-atheists (like Hume). Like theism (belief in God's existence), atheism is a doctrinal or dogmatic position (even a theological one in an odd sense). It must be distinguished from agnosticism (from the Greek *agnoein* 'not to know,' 'to be ignorant'), the suspension of judgment on the issue of God's existence as beyond our capacities to decide. See 5.5.3, 9.1.1–2, 10.3, 11.1, 11.12.1, 28.4, 31.2, 31.7, 32.4.1, 35.1–6, 36.2, 37.4.3.

begging the question. See *circularity*.

behaviourism. The view that all talk of mental states or events and processes is meaningful only to the extent that it is explicable in terms of overt, observable linguistic and other human behaviour. This is philosophical or logical behaviourism, such as that espoused by Gilbert Ryle. Psychological behaviourism, whose principal exponent is B.F. Skinner, is essentially a methodological injunction that scientific psychology concern itself with the description and explanation of overt behaviour, not with supposed causal relations between unobservable mental and observable physical events. See 27.12.

Being-in-the-world. The term is a neologism of the German philosopher Martin Heidegger. It was coined to embody his concept of man and to distinguish it from the dominant traditional concept stemming from Descartes. The hyphens are intended to convey the idea that being related through all sorts of *practical* activities to both (1) the non-human things or objects of use and (2) the human others that together make up one's own environment or 'world' is not just an accidental feature of each individual human being's own being, but part and parcel of (3) the self. Being-in-the-world does not result from the fact that things and others happen to exist too; rather *human* being is essentially being-in, i.e., being-practically-related-to things, whose being is unlike our own, and to others like ourselves, such that both (the *world* and the others *sharing* it) are essential to one's *own* being. This is the furthest remove from the Cartesian notion of a world*less*, solipsistic thinking (rather than practical) thing. See 31.8.2, 33.5, 34.4, 36.2.1–2, 36.4, 37.3, 37.4.1, 37.4.1, 38.7.3.

categorial, categorical. An adjective applied to those properties of an entity that are necessary and strictly universal for all members of the class to which that entity belongs, and that *make* them the sort of entity that they are. 'Categorial' in this sense is a synonym for 'essential' properties. Examples are: 'unchanging' as a property of

Forms in Plato or 'extended' as a property of bodies in Descartes. 'Categor*ial*' as an epithet applied to properties should not be confused with 'categor*ical*' as applied to propositions of the basic form '*S* is *P*.' These are distinct from hypothetical and disjunctive propositions ('If *S* is *P*, then *Q* is *R*,' 'Either *S* is *P*, or *S* is *R*' etc.), as in Kant's use of the expression 'categorical imperative' for one that commands us to do something absolutely, 'no ifs, ands, or buts.' See 12.8.5, 20.4.1, 24.5.1, 32.3.2, 38.3.1, 38.4.1, 38.6.1, 38.7.4.

circularity. In philosophy, this term is used to designate an informal fallacy that consists in taking for granted the very thing to be demonstrated or proved. It is also called 'begging the question' or (in Latin) *petitio principii*. The fallacy in all its forms consists, at bottom, in 'using x in order to prove x,' whereby 'x' may be either a faculty of knowledge whose reliability is to be demonstrated, a proposition whose truth is to be demonstrated, or a form of argument whose validity is to be established. Obviously, one cannot use the very faculty whose reliability is to be established in order to establish its reliability without taking for granted the very thing in dispute. Similarly, one cannot use as a premise in an argument a proposition whose truth depends upon the truth of the conclusion to be established by that argument. Nor can one establish the validity of a certain form of argument by means of an argument that has that form. In the same way, one cannot define a word using the very word to be defined without taking for granted that its meaning is already clear. Such a definition is circular and therefore accomplishes nothing at all. Like definitions, explanations can be called circular when they lead to an infinite regress, that is, just confront us with same problem over and over again at various removes from the starting point. See 7.7.2–3, 7.8.1, 9.2.2, 11.6, 11.6.2–3, 11.7, 18.10.1–2, 20.2, 23.11, 24.3.2, 25.1–10, 26.8.4, 26.9.1, 26.10.2, 29.8.2, 37.1, 37.4.1–2, 38.4.3.

conceptualism. According to conceptualists, universals exist only in the mind, as general concepts (concepts of genera like 'animal' and species like 'man'); they do not exist in things as well, let alone apart from them. Individual things have similarities on the basis of which *we* group them into certain classes or collections; but only ideas or class concepts in the mind are universal; everything mind-independent is particular. Of course, not all the contents of the mind are universal; universal concepts (from the Latin *concipio* 'seize or take together') must be distinguished from those contents of the mind, like sense perceptions, that have concrete individuals as their objects. Locke and Kant are conceptualists, as were the ancient Stoics. See 4.8.

consequentialism. A general type of normative ethical theory according to which the rightness and wrongness either of particular actions (act consequentialism) or of general rules of moral behaviour (rule consequentialism) are a function of its non-morally good or bad *consequences* (benefit and harm). Such theories differ depending on whether the consequences considered are those (1) for the agent alone (egoism) or (2) for others, but not the agent (altruism), or (3) for *everyone* affected by the action or rule in any way, no matter how distantly (utilitarianism). Since they make morality dependent upon non-moral considerations (benefit and harm), Kant famously labelled all such theories 'heteronomous' (involving dependence of moral on non-moral considerations) and rejected them as not really moral theories at all. The opposing type of normative ethical theory considers moral principles (and hence morality itself) as strictly autonomous—because valid and binding regardless of consequences. It is called 'deontic' or 'deontological,' from the Greek *to deon* 'what must be.' See 10.2.1, 38.1–2.

contingent. Meaning, literally, 'touching together,' the term is applied both to propositions or statements (*de dicto* contingency) and to things (*de re* contingency). As applied to propositions, it means that they just happen to be true, to 'hit on' (*contingere*) an existing state of affairs that might be otherwise. Opposed to such truths of fact (as Leibniz called them) are truths of reason or eternal truths—these being different designations for the same class of *necessary* truths. As just noted, in addition to the propositions that correctly describe them, the existing states of affairs and things described are also called 'contingent' ('contingent beings' or 'contingent states of affairs') if it is logically possible (or conceivable) for them to be otherwise. In traditional Christian metaphysics, God is the only being to possess necessary existence: whereas in the case of all other things, actual existence and nature or essence just 'touch together' (making them contingent 'might-not-have-beens'), in the case of God they are identical. God therefore cannot *not* be. For convenience, only contingent truth and contingent existence have been mentioned here. Parallel considerations apply to falsity and non-existence. See 7.4–5, 26.3.2, 26.8.3, 26.9.3, 26.10.1–2, 29.5, 29.8.2, 30.4, 35.4.1.

contradiction. Not to be confused with contradictories (see *contraries*), contradictions arise between or among statements or propositions rather than terms or predicates. In the simplest terms, a contradiction is formed by any two statements whose meaning is such that exactly one must be true and one false. But it is also correct to speak of three or more propositions forming a contradiction when any two of them entail the denial of a third (that is, when any two together, if true, imply that another statement is false). Less technically, a contradiction is the assertion and denial of the same thing, or what amounts to the same thing, though perhaps in other words. Non-technically (in everyday speech) any sort of tension or opposition between opposed forces or motives is called a 'contradiction.' This loose sense is largely irrelevant to philosophy (and totally so to logic). (See *principle of (non-)contradiction* below. On so-called contradictions in terms, see 26.9.3, and 27.10 for examples of contradictions involving three statements.) See 6.3.1, 7.4, 7.10, 17.5.2, 20.6.1, 25.5, 25.6.1.

contradictories. See *contraries*.

contraries. Contraries or contrary predicates (terms like 'red' and 'blue') cannot both be true of one and the same thing (in exactly the same respect), although they may both be false (a thing can be neither red nor blue, say, yellow). As for contradictories or contradictory predicates (terms like 'red' and 'not-red'), they too cannot both be true of one and the same thing in exactly the same respect, but they cannot both be false either. So exactly one is true and one is false. See 7.10, 17.5.1–2.

cosmogony. A theory of the source(s) or origin(s) of the universe as a whole. Originally, this was not distinguished from cosmology, the source being understood both as the origin and the governing principle of all things. The first cosmogonies arose among the earliest civilizations and were mythico-religious in nature. Philosophical cosmogonies began to emerge among the Greeks in the sixth century BC. Scientific cosmogonies began to be developed in the seventeenth and eighteenth centuries and are still with us in the form of theories like that of the 'Big Bang.' See 5.3.1, 5.4, 5.5.1, 5.5.4, 5.6, 5.7, 9.1.2.1, 16.2.

cosmology. A branch of philosophy concerned with the understanding of the physical universe (*cosmos*) as an ordered, law-governed totality. Issues usually include the (finite or infinite) extent of the universe in space and time, the nature of contingency and necessity in the real world, the most universal principles or laws governing everything, principles more encompassing than even the laws of physics. See 1.2.1, 2.4, 5.3–10, 9.1.2.1, 16.2, 20.5.1–2, 20.6.2.

critical rationalism. The critical rationalist holds (i) that there is objective truth and (ii) that we can get at it. He *may*, in addition, grant (iii) that we have in fact got it, that is, that we do have at least some knowledge. He denies, however, (iv) that, having got it, we could ever *know that we have got it*. So what the critical rationalist denies is not that objective truth exists, like the relativist, nor that we can get it, like the sceptic, but that we can ever be certain that we have got it *even when we have*. See 3.3.1, 6.3.3, 9.1.5.

crypto-atheism. See *atheism*.

deism, deist. A type of religious belief according to which the bare existence of a divine being can be known by unassisted human reason, but not those alleged truths about the divine nature and will that make up the doctrines of all institutionalized

deontic, deontological. See *consequentialism*.

descriptive. A term applied to a type of statement or enquiry concerned with what is (or is not) the case, that is, with matters of fact, as opposed to what ought to be the case, right and wrong (in the moral sense) or good and bad (in the non-moral sense). The latter are called normative enquiries and statements. Thus a descriptive enquiry is concerned with how people *in fact* behave (perhaps also with why), while a normative investigation has to do with how they *ought to* behave either for moral or for prudential reasons. See 10.2.3–4, 10.3, 20.3, 30.5.1, 32.3.2, 32.4.3, 38.7.1, 38.7.3.

dialectics, dialectical. From the Greek *dialegesthai* 'to discuss or converse,' 'to exchange words (or even arguments).' An elusive term for an (or *the*) argumentative method of philosophy, with different meanings when applied to (or by) Socrates, Plato, Aristotle, Kant, Hegel, and Marx. The meaning of the term in a Kantian, Hegelian, or Marxian context cannot be considered here. In a Socratic or Platonic setting the term may be taken to designate the question-and-answer method of philosophical enquiry as such, whether carried on by more than one individual or by a single individual who successively adopts different standpoints. In Aristotle, dialectical arguments are opposed to peirastic and apodictic proofs (such as are found in mathematics). They are (1) negative or 'refutative' and refute (2) by showing the view under discussion to be, or to have consequences that are, inconsistent with certain widely held views that are presumed true. As a consequence, dialectical arguments are (3) not strictly probative; i.e., their conclusions are uncertain. See 1.5, 5.6, 9.2.5, 12.3.1, 30.1.

dilemma. Not strictly a philosophical term, a 'dilemma' is any choice situation involving a pair of alternatives (hence *di*lemma from the Greek *dia* 'two') that are equally fraught with problems or unpleasantness. In philosophy, what is usually meant is a form of argument that places an adversary before two equally undesirable alternatives (the so-called horns of the dilemma). The main philosophical dilemma examined here is the Euthyphro dilemma. See 11.8, 12.4, 35.4.3, 35.6, 37.1, 38.5, 38.7.1.

distinction. Scholastic philosophy developed a variety of distinctions among distinctions, mainly in the context of the discussion of the way in which God's existence differs from his essence. Descartes added to the list. In Descartes, however, the distinctions among distinctions come into play not in a theological but in an

Glossary of Philosophical Terms 645

anthropological context: the question of the distinction between matter (the body) and the mind, with particular reference to human nature. The two most important kinds of distinction are (1) conceptual and (2) real distinctions. A and B are conceptually distinct (or: there obtains between them a distinction of reason) when they can be separated in thought only, but not in fact, that is, when they can be conceived independently of one another but cannot exist separately. On the other hand, things are said to be 'really distinct' when they can actually exist apart from one another. There are some important differences in the way Aquinas and Descartes handled this particular distinction between distinctions. See 22.2, 26.8.2, 27.8.1.

element. This term can be used (1) loosely for any *more or less* basic form of matter or (2) strictly for a form of matter that is *absolutely* basic, that is, not reducible to any other more basic form. While the periodic table of modern chemistry contains 103 elements, the early Greek thinkers recognized only four: earth, water, air, and fire, associated with the earth, the seas and rivers, the lower atmosphere, and the outer heaven, respectively. For them, water was an element, while blood was not; for us neither is an element, water being analyzable into two hydrogen and one oxygen molecule. In the strict sense, certain early Greek thinkers may only have recognized a single element, water (Thales) or air (Anaximenes), for example. See 5.5.1–3, 5.7–8, 20.5.1.

elenchus. A transliteration of the Greek word *elenchos*, the term is applied to the Socratic manner of cross-examination and refutation of an adversary by peirastic argument. (See *peirastic*.) Essentially, it is a technique of compelling one's adversary to abandon some particular proposition by drawing out of it implications that he cannot accept, either because they are self-contradictory or because they entail the denial of some other proposition that he accepts and cannot readily give up, thus forcing him to abandon the proposition under examination. See 9.2.4–5, 9.4.2, 9.5.4.

empiricism, empiricist. Derived from the Greek word *empeiria* (meaning 'experience,' whence the adjectival form 'empirical'), the name 'empiricist' is given to those epistemologists (see next entry) who maintain that experience is the *only source* of the *simple* ideas and concepts in the mind and hence of whatever knowledge we can acquire by means of such concepts and others formed out of them by the mind itself. Negatively speaking, this is to deny that reason or the intellect is a *separate* source of knowledge about the world (say, knowledge of certain universal principles of thought like the principle of non-contradiction or of the things thought about, like the causal principle 'nothing happens without a cause'). In Locke (the first of the three so-called British Empiricists, the others being Berkeley and Hume), this is tantamount to the denial of innate ideas and principles in the mind. The role of reason (or the intellect or understanding) is thus confined to concept formation based on pre-given (sensory) materials. There are varying degrees of empiricism, right up to those who (like John Stuart Mill) have maintained that even logic and mathematics are derived from empirical sources. See 1.3.1, 3.3.2, 3.4, 4.8, 7.5.1–2, 21.3.1–2, 26.2, 27.7.3, 29.1–9.

epistemology, epistemologist. Literally, 'theory of knowledge.' A sub-discipline of philosophy concerned with the problem of knowledge. This includes (1) the necessary and sufficient conditions of knowledge (as distinct from opinion or true belief); (2) the various degrees of evidence or certainty attainable in different types of enquiry; (3) questions regarding the order of knowing such as are debated between epistemological realists and idealists. See 1.2.4, 2.4, 3.1–2, 3.4–5, 4.1–2, 4.5, 18.3, 22.2, 25.2, 27.4, 28.6, 29.8.1, 31.8.1, 33.4.3.

equivocation. A fallacy consisting in using the same word in different senses in successive premises of an argument. For example, 'some cars are expensive, my car is some car, therefore my car is expensive.' In the first premise, the word 'some' is the logical quantifier; in the second it is a slang expression for 'exceptional.' Of course, this argument would be invalid even without the equivocation. See 7.7.4, 17.5.2, 18.6, 18.8–9, 29.3.3.

essence. See *proprium*.

essentialism. A metaphysical position on the question of universals according to which the universal essences of things do not merely exist in the mind (see *conceptualism*), nor just as universal terms in our language (see *nominalism*), but are really existent in particular things themselves outside the mind whose real essences they constitute. Also known as 'immanent realism' as distinct from Platonic or transcendent realism. (See *realism*.) See 4.7.1, 4.7.3, 4.8, 8.2.1, 11.5, 20.4.2, 20.7, 20.13.2, 21.3.1–2, 24.7.3.

eternal truths. The traditional designation, in Descartes and the scholastics, for a class of propositions now usually described as necessary truths. Such propositions do not just *happen* to be true, given the way the world is; it is impossible even to conceive of their being false. Thus, they are true in all possible, not just this actual world. Leibniz called them 'truths of reason' as opposed to contingent 'truths of fact.' Uncontroversial examples are the simple truths of mathematics (e.g., $2 + 3 = 5$; a square has four sides), though, traditionally, the principles of logic (e.g., the principle of non-contradiction) and even metaphysical principles (e.g., 'something cannot come from nothing') belong to this class as well. All propositions that assert something necessarily true about the essences of things (e.g., 'all mothers are female') can be regarded as eternal truths or truths of reason, though usually this class is restricted to truths that (unlike the example) are non-trivial. Descartes notoriously regarded such truths as dependent on God's will. See 25.8 and 35.4.1 (on Descartes's doctrine). See 7.4, 7.5.1–2, 25.4–8, 26.2, 26.4.4, 26.8, 27.9.1, 28.2, 33.4.2, 35.4.1–2.

eternal, eternity. One of the two meanings of 'forever,' eternity, or non-temporal existence, existence outside time, as opposed to everlastingness, or existence throughout all time. (See *sempiternal*.) Anything is called 'eternal' all the parts or phases of whose existence are coexistent or simultaneous rather than successive; of it we can correctly say 'it is' but not 'it was' or 'it will be.' Whatever exists in this way (if anything does) remains immutably the same in an 'eternal present' or 'permanent now' (*nunc stans*), as it is sometimes called. See 16.5.1, 18.8–9.

eudaemonism. A type of moral theory whose basic premise is that all men, insofar as they are rational, desire and pursue what is or seems to be good, what they believe will make them happy. This looks like a *factual belief* about human behaviour and motivation, about the end at which all rational human action *in fact* aims. But Greek moral theorists probably did not distinguish it from a basic normative rule or action guide: You *ought* (see *norm, normative*) never to do what you know is harmful to yourself, what impairs or destroys your own (chances of) happiness, or even what produces more harm than good for you (since that would be irrational). Particular eudaemonistic theories differ with regard to what *is* moral, but all give the same answer to the question, Why be moral? That answer can be put this way: rationality dictates that we do what is in our own best interests, what will best secure our own happiness, and it is in one's best interests to lead a moral life. Thus all eudaemonist moral theories hold that *leading* a good life (moral virtue) is (a) identical with or (b) a significant part of or (c) an *indispensable* part of *having* a good life, a happy life. Minimally, it is (d) the most important means to having such a life. See 9.2.2, 9.2.4, 10.2.1, 10.3, 10.4.3–4, 11.12.2, 12.1, 12.8.5, 12.9.1–3, 13.3, 14.2, 19.3.2, 20.3, 38.2, 38.5, 38.7.4.

fallacy. A fallacy is a logical error in reasoning from one proposition (a premise or premises) to another (a conclusion). The fallacy may be either informal (like circularity, equivocation, *ad hominem* argument, and the like) or it may be a formal fallacy, that is, a violation of the rules of correct reasoning as laid out in some system of logic. The latter is often called 'a non-sequitur,' which is Latin for 'it does not follow' ('it' being the conclusion drawn). Fallacy should not be confused with falsity. Even an argument whose conclusion is true may be fallacious. See 7.6.2, 7.7.1–6, 7.9, 30.5.2.

formal mode of speech. See *material mode of speech*.

hedonism. From the Greek word *hēdonē*, meaning 'pleasure,' this term is used to designate the view that pleasure (or the absence of pain) is the good, or the only intrinsic good, or the only thing good in itself. See 10.2.5, 10.2.9, 12.9.1, 38.7.1.

heteronomy. See *consequentialism*.

hylozoism. The view that the matter of the universe (*hylē*) is alive, living stuff, and the universe itself therefore a living thing (*zōon*) or animal. See 5.5.3–4.

idealism. There are two main types of idealism, epistemological and ontological. According to the epistemological idealist, (1) all that we experience directly are ideas of things in the mind, not the extra-mental material things themselves. Our judgments about the latter are sometimes causal, sometimes logical, inferences from other, more secure judgments about occurrences in our own mind. Since direct apprehension of extra-mental things is impossible, (2) the criteria for distinguishing true from false judgments have to do with the order of perceptions within the totality of experience rather than their agreement with mind-independent things. The name 'epistemological idealism' may be applied either to (1) alone or to (1) and (2) together.

While epistemological idealism has to do with the order in which things are known by us, ontological idealism is a thesis about the order in which they stand to one another. In other words, it has to do with the order of dependence, independence, interdependence, or inter-independence among different sorts of things: among material and immaterial things, for example, or among finite things (whether material or immaterial) and the infinite being, God—if God exists. According to the ontological idealist, material things depend for their existence on perceiving minds. For Bishop Berkeley, this is because material things are at bottom nothing but collections of ideas, and ideas can be said to exist only insofar as they are perceived or perceivable: *esse est percipi*. Such ontological idealism *reduces* material things to ideas in the mind. See 1.3.1, 3.4–5, 4.3–8, 20.4.3, 20.7, 20.3.1, 22.3.2, 24.6.4, 25.2, 25.9–10, 27.8.3, 27.12, 31.8.1–2.

immoral. See *moral*.

innate, innateness*:* Ideas (concepts) or principles (truths) are said to be 'innate' or 'in-born' when not acquired through sensory experience but indigenous to the mind itself. There are various theories of innateness. The oldest (Platonic-Stoic-Ciceronian) theory regards the mind as 'furnished' with some ideas from birth. We bring them into the world with us. According to Descartes's theory, an idea is innate if it is not acquired through *external* sensation (via the five bodily senses) but simply through reflection on the mind's own operations and what is implicit in them. It is in this way that we acquire the innate ideas of the mind, of thinking, doubting, etc., and even of

God and of matter. Such ideas are implicit in our thinking as soon as we begin to think (i.e., even in the womb), though only on reaching maturity do we actually attend to, or reflect upon, them. See 4.8, 21.1, 21.3.3, 26.2, 26.7.1–2, 26.10.1, 26.10.3, 27.3, 27.9.1, 29.3.3, 29.4, 32.3.2.

introspection. A synonym for 'inner experience,' that is, the immediate reflective (sometimes also called 'pre-reflective') awareness one has, insofar as one is conscious at all, of the goings-on (cognitive, volitional, and emotional states or acts) in one's own mind. See 3.3.2, 25.10, 29.3.1, and 29.6.

justice. For the Greeks, justice (*dikē*) was not distinct at all from rightness or goodness in the moral sense. However, it is possible to distinguish them in the following way. Rightness or moral goodness is a matter of having good moral precepts, while (distributive) justice is a matter of applying them fairly and equitably to all people, that is, not discriminating in any way. As for divine justice, this is a matter of making the reward or punishment fit the virtue or vice. See 11.3, 13.2, 29.7, 31.1, 31.5.2, 31.6, 38.2–3.

law of (non-)contradiction. See *principle of (non-)contradiction*.

material mode of speech. Distinguished from the formal mode of speech (FMS) preferred by contemporary logicians and philosophers of language, the material mode of speech (MMS) was favoured by classical metaphysicians. This is alleged to have been the source of many errors. By reducing statements made in the MMS to equivalent statements in the FMS it can allegedly be shown that what were taken for ontological statements or implications are in fact no more than logical points about what cannot be asserted or denied without contradiction. See 21.3.1.

mechanism (mechanicism). Roughly speaking, a mechanical explanation is one restricted to such causal factors as the size, shape, position, speed, and direction of the moving or quiescent parts of matter and their action by contact, that is, collisions and rebounds. These can be described more picturesquely as 'push-and-pull' or 'pulley-and-lever' efficient causal transactions. Such explanations are opposed to those in terms of internal powers of change analogous to vital powers of growth, development, and self-motion in living bodies (formal and final causes). (See *teleology*.) But they are opposed, too, to mysterious physical forces by which one body might be thought to act upon another at a distance, by a power not reducible to any combination of mechanical forces. (Both magnetism and gravitation have been thought of in this way). 'Mechanicism' is the refusal to acknowledge any but mechanical forces as primitive, that is, the project of eliminating all other causes by reducing them to those of the mechanical sort. See 5.5.3, 30.8.1, 35.2.1.

meta-ethics. A sub-discipline of ethics (along with normative ethics and applied ethics) concerned with the nature or *status* of moral knowledge or moral value judgments (their subjectivity or objectivity) and the *meanings* of moral terms like 'good,' 'right,' 'just,' 'duty,' 'freedom,' 'responsibility,' and so on. See 10.2, 11.10–11, 32.4.2–3, 35.6.

metaphysics. According to the working definition developed in chapter 20, metaphysics is the philosophical study of *being* (as *existence* and as *essence*) in general, that is, of *all* beings, but especially the existence and essence of the *supersensible* or *immaterial* (for example, God and the human soul), and of *first principles*. Elsewhere (see chaps. 3 and 4) metaphysics was defined as mankind's attempt to orientate itself within, or to encompass in thought, the totality of what is by determining the correct order of knowing and of being. From the metaphysical questions concerning the order of knowing and being, we may distinguish the meta-metaphysical questions regarding the idea of experience and of being itself. See 1.2, 1.2.3–4, 3.1–5, 4.1–9, 5.5.2–3, 7.5.1–3, 20.1–13, 22.2–3, 28.6, and Conclusion.

metempsychosis. The doctrine of the soul's survival of the death of the body and its reincarnation in other bodies in a cycle of births and rebirths. The first occurrence of the doctrine in western philosophy is early Pythagoreanism. 'Metempsychosis,' 'transmigration (of souls),' and 'reincarnation' are all used synonymously. See 5.6–8, 14.6, 16.3–4, 17.2, 19.1–3, 24.6.6.

moral. The moral must be distinguished from the immoral, the non-moral, and the amoral. When 'the moral' refers to moral goodness, that is, morally good or (as we say) 'ethical' behaviour, 'immoral' just designates its opposite: moral evil, morally wicked or unethical behaviour. Persons who behave in these ways are designated 'moral' and 'immoral,' the actions themselves 'right' and 'wrong,' respectively.

Moral good and evil are not to be confused with *non*-morally good and bad things. The latter are pursued or shunned, not as virtuous or vicious, but as beneficial or harmful. The corresponding actions or rules of action are designated 'prudent' and 'imprudent' (or 'foolish') rather than 'moral' and 'immoral.' They may be called 'right' and 'wrong,' respectively, just as with moral and immoral action, but here in a non-moral sense. Non-morally good and bad things may be divided into classes—for example, the private or personal and the public or social, with the former divided again into the good and bad things of the body and those having to do with the mind or soul, and so forth. Separating morally from non-morally good and bad things is a necessary precondition for determining whether the former are independent of or dependent upon (see *consequentialism*) the latter.

To call someone 'amoral' rather than 'immoral' is to say that he regards all moral considerations and teachings as equally mistaken, rejecting the moral point of view

Glossary of Philosophical Terms   651

altogether (see *amoralism*). Thus, an amoral code of conduct excludes moral considerations, leaving only considerations of non-moral goodness to govern one's actions. From the moral point of view, a person who behaves in this way may or may not perform actions considered immoral by others, depending on how he assesses the consequences of doing so; but from his own point of view he will be neither moral nor immoral but at most prudent or imprudent. See 1.2, 1.2.2–4, 10.1–3, 38.1–3.

moral paradox. See *paradox*.

nativism. See *innateness, innate*.

naturalism, naturalistic. This word has a variety of uses. In the case of the early Greek philosophers whom Aristotle referred to collectively as the 'physiologists,' it refers to the denial of a *transcendent* divine (God or gods) beyond this world. The thinkers in question (Thales, Anaximander, Anaximenes, for example) regarded nature itself as divine. (See *pantheism*.) In its most general sense, the term implies the rejection of any appeal to the supernatural (supernatural causes or forces) for purposes of explanation, that is, adoption of the prescriptive rule that everything that can be explained must be explained in terms of natural (rather than supernatural or preternatural) causes. Such 'naturalism' is typical of science in the modern era, but it has a long history going right back to the birth of philosophy. In the Conclusion, 'naturalistic' philosophies are equated with 'philosophies of immanence' and opposed to 'philosophies of transcendence.' See 5.5.2–4, 9.1.2.1, 31.5.2, 31.7.

neologism. The expression used for a new word coinage (invention of a word) but also for an innovation in religious matters. Thus Socrates, who was formally charged with "not believing in the Gods that the City believes in" is sometimes said to have been accused of 'neologism.' See 9.2.4 on the charges brought against Socrates.

nominalism. Nominalists dispute the existence even of abstract general ideas, maintaining that the contents of the mind are invariably particular. Universals are a feature of our language, words (Latin, *nomen*, whence 'nominalism') being either proper names for particulars or else universal names for classes or groups of things. For the nominalist there are no natural, let alone inborn, concepts or dispositions of thought, much less universal natures really existing in things or apart from them. (See *realism*.) See 4.7.1, 4.8, 11.5, 20.7, 20.12.2, 21.3.1–3.

non-sequitur. See *fallacy*.

norm, normative. Philosophers distinguish two types of propositions or statements, as well as two types of enquiry: (1) descriptive or factual statements simply assert (accurately or mistakenly) that something is true, that is, describe (correctly or incorrectly) what *is* the case, perhaps also explaining it, without however saying that it is good or bad; (2) prescriptive or normative statements assert something to be *good or bad,* prescribe or prohibit it, justify or condemn it, express approval or disapproval of some kind and degree. The latter are more familiar under the everyday name 'value judgments.' Questions the answers to which are descriptive or prescriptive are descriptive (factual) and normative questions or enquiries. (See *normative* and the references given there.)

normative ethics. The attempt to establish the basic norms or rules of moral conduct (from which all others are derivable). A normative ethical theory will be either (a) *a theory of obligation (or duty)* or (b) *a theory of virtue (or the virtues)*. A theory of obligation sets out the basic rules or duties, the observance of which is required by morality and from which all our other duties may be derived. A theory of virtue, on the other hand, sets out the basic character traits or personal qualities which belong to a morally excellent human being and from which the virtuousness of other traits may be derived. See 10.2, 10.4, 34.2.2–3, 38.1–3.

Ockham's Razor. The principle of ontological parsimony, ascribed to William of Ockham, that in developing philosophical theories to account for known facts one ought not to multiply entities beyond necessity. See 21.3.2 and 31.5.3.

ontological difference. A technical term coined by Heidegger for the distinction between beings (entities) and the universal structures, necessary features, and various modes of their being. The latter must be understood as non-entitative principles rather than as beings. Historically, the distinction emerged only gradually. All of Plato's principles of being (the Forms) are themselves beings—save one, the highest, which is explicitly said to be 'beyond being.' In Aristotle the idea is implicit in the distinction between principles (like form and matter) and entities (the composites made up of form and matter). In Christian theology, the being of entities *qua* existence is itself an entity: God is existence for St Thomas Aquinas, for example. Heidegger charges the whole tradition with having blurred the ontological difference between being (a 'cause' or explanatory principle that is not itself *a* being) and beings (the things whose being is explained by means of that principle). See 5.5.2.

ontology. Coined in the seventeenth century by the German Cartesian Johannes Clauberg, the term is taken from the Greek words *on* 'a being' or 'entity,' and *logos* 'the study or science of.' 'Ontology' is thus the designation for what Aristotle called 'the science or study of being as being,' the most universal science which studies all beings simply with respect to the principles or causes of their being. A distinction is drawn in the Conclusion between ontology and meta-ontology. The former deals with the questions, What is there? and In what does the being (reality) of what is consist? The latter deals with the guiding ideas of being underlying various ontologies. See 4.1, 4.3–6, 20.4.3, 20.6–7, 20.10.2, 21.3.1–2, 22.2, 33.5, 37.1.

panpsychism. From the Greek words *pan* ('everything,' 'all') and *psychē* ('soul' or 'mind'). This can mean that the whole material universe is animate or alive, *soul* being understood as the life principle. In that case, it is very close in meaning to both 'animism' and 'hylozoism.' If, however, 'soul' is understood as the principle of sentience or consciousness (roughly, feeling, thought, and volition, where sense perception is included under feeling), then panpsychism maintains that not just men and animals but absolutely everything in the material universe is sentient or conscious. The former sense of 'panpsychism' fits the hylozoism of several Ionian thinkers, while the latter is the stronger sense of the panpsychism found in Empedocles, for example. See 5.5.3, 5.7.

pantheism. From the Greek words *pan* 'everything,' and *theos* 'god,' this term is applied to the view that the world itself is a god, or that the whole of nature is divine. See 5.5.3–4, 5.7, 16.2.

paradox. Literally, anything which runs counter to (Greek: *para*) popular belief or opinion (Greek: *doxa*). Thus, Socrates's view that, for example, a good man can never be harmed by a bad one is paradoxical, since most people naturally think otherwise. Apart from (1) this non-technical sense, the term also has two technical uses. According to the first, (2) a statement is a paradox if its truth entails its falsehood. Thus (to cite a famous ancient paradox), when the Cretan Epimenides says 'All Cretans are liars,' if what he says is true, then it is false. But if what he says is false, i.e., if some Cretans are not liars, nothing follows. In the second technical sense, (3) a statement is a paradox only if its truth entails its falsehood *and* its falsehood entails its truth. Thus, if I say: 'Everything I say today is false' and I say nothing further the rest of the day, then if what I have said is true, it is false (as in the case of Epimenides), but if what I have said is false, then it is true. The most famous of the Socratic paradoxes are the moral and the prudential paradoxes. According to the former, no one really desires morally wicked things; all who pursue such things are simply blinded by ignorance and pursue them therefore involuntarily. According to the prudential paradox, no one desires non-morally bad things (things bad *for oneself*) either; if they seem to pursue them willingly (as when one drinks to excess, for example, thereby destroying one's health), they in fact do so without knowing that they are bad for them. And pursuing them out of ignorance, they do so involuntarily. See 12.9.2.

peirastic. A term coined by Aristotle (from the Greek verb *peirao* 'to make trial of,' 'to put to the test') to describe the Socratic manner of cross-examination and refutation. Like the dialectical, peirastic arguments are negative or refutative, using as their premises only probable opinions; but unlike dialectical arguments the opinions are those of the discussant himself. These are shown either to be, or to have consequences that are, inconsistent with the opinion under examination. See 9.2.5

petitio principii. See *circularity*.

physiology. A transliteration of *physiologoi*, a term used by Aristotle (along with *physikoi*) for the early Greek thinkers who developed theories (*logoi*) about nature (*physis*). He contrasts them with the earlier *theologoi* or mythologists. Something akin to the Aristotelian contrast is preserved in Kant, who still uses 'physiology' to designate the study of nature as opposed to supernatural or (as he says) 'hyperphysical' investigation of the supersensible, especially the divine. When he means physiology in the contemporary sense, Kant employs the expression "medical physiology." See 5.5.2, 9.1.2.1, 11.12.1, 35.2.1.

principle of (non-)contradiction. A basic law of logic, sometimes referred to as 'Aristotle's axiom,' since Aristotle was the first to formulate it: 'The same attribute cannot at the same time belong and not belong to the same subject and in the same respect,' or, more concisely, 'It is impossible for the same thing to both be and not to be.' Modern logicians formulate it as: 'It is not the case that p and *not-p* (where p stands for any proposition).' (For references, see *contradiction*.)

probandum. A technical philosophical term meaning 'that which is to be proved.' In other words, the thing to be established, the conclusion to be demonstrated by an argument. See 15.2.

projection. A term borrowed by Sartre from Heidegger, 'projecting' (literally: 'throwing out before oneself') is opposed to 'thrownness' ('being thrown'). The two notions *complement* each other. Becoming aware of or encountering myself as *already* something definite in the present and as having a past is *at the same time* a realization that I am *in a certain sense* "nothing," that the future is open. It is the realization that I am '*not yet*' fully actualized, so that I have to actualize myself *in the future* through my own choices among different possible ways of being in a body and different possibilities of being in a world together with others. This is the other feature of human existence captured by the term 'projection.' See 36.2.

proprium. According to a doctrine of the third century AD, the (1) essence of a thing must be distinguished from its (2) accidents and from its (3) *propria* or properties. Naturally, (3) is called a 'property' in a special sense, since (1) can also be understood as comprising the essential properties of a thing and (2) as referring to its accidental properties. As opposed to both essential and accidental properties, a (3) *proprium* is a property which belongs to *all and only* the members of a certain class or type of thing, but which is nevertheless not the very thing that makes them what they are, nor just a feature they happen to have. That which makes them what they are is (1) the essence, while properties possessed by some, but not necessarily all, members of the class of things in question are (2) accidents. As an example of a *proprium*, take being a featherless biped (or being capable of learning grammar). This is true of every human being; and, conversely, every featherless biped is a human being. So being a featherless biped is a *proprium* of human beings. But unless being two-footed and lacking feathers is what *makes* a man a man, this is only a *proprium* rather than the essence of man. The essence could be (and is, according to a very old definition) being rational, rationality, while being white or being elderly is clearly an accident. See 7.14, 8.2.1, 11.8–9, 18.2, 20.9, 24.7.3.

prudential paradox. See *paradox*.

rationalist. From the Latin word *ratio* 'reason.' Philosophers and philosophies classified as 'rationalist' (usually opposed to 'empiricist') have two chief features. First, they subscribe to a pretty robust version of the innateness of certain ideas (concepts) and/or principles (truths). (See *innateness*.) That is, they stress the role of reason (*ratio*) itself as a source of some of the basic building blocks of human knowledge, denying that *all* knowledge is derived from experience. (Extreme rationalists like Plato deny that *any* knowledge worthy of the name is derived from experience.) Secondly, they generally conceive all genuine sciences or scientific knowledge on the model of formal sciences like arithmetic, geometry, and algebra, that is, as having a formal axiomatic structure, beginning with definitions and axioms, from which theorems are logically derived by deduction. (See also *critical rationalism*. On Cartesian rationalism in particular, see 27.13. On rationalism in general, see 1.3.1, 3.3.2, 3.4, 26.2, 32.3.2, 34.2, 35.5.

realism. As with idealism, there are two main types of realism, epistemological and ontological. According to *epistemological* realism, (1) we perceive or experience things directly (not via the intermediary of directly experienced ideas in the mind) and, for the most part, reliably. Moreover, we judge truly about such things when we judge them to be as they really are in themselves. The rules for distinguishing true from false judgments may be fairly elaborate, but (2) truth, for the epistemological realist, consists in the agreement of thought with mind-independent objects.

As for *ontological* realism, it has to do with the relations of dependence, independence, interdependence, and inter-independence between the mind (mental particulars) and the body (material or physical particulars or things). Common sense suggests that the mind and the living human body are interdependent. Descartes held that they are separate and independent entities (hence: inter-independent), *each* capable of existing in its own right, without the other. Both views, however, agree in taking material things to exist in their own right, independently of their being thought about by, and of the very existence of, any minds. This much is common to all forms of ontological realism, including materialists who deny the existence of anything but physical entities.

Causal realism is the view that at least some of the ideas in the mind are caused by mind-independent, extra-mental material things that act on the mind by means of the bodily sense organs and central nervous system (ultimately, the brain). *Representative* realism posits a relation of similarity or resemblance between those ideas and their extra-mental objects (or causes). If the relation of similarity is restricted to *some* ideas only, one can speak of *qualified* representative realism; otherwise, that is, if it extends to *all* ideas, the representative realism is *unqualified* or unrestricted. The latter, when combined with causal realism, may be called *naive* realism. The former, unqualified representative realism, may be called *scientific* realism. *Epistemological direct realism* is the name customarily given both the ordinary and the philosophical conviction that we perceive material things, not images of them, immediately. The opposing view (that all we ever perceive directly are ideas in the mind) is sometimes referred to as the 'veil of perception doctrine,' but more commonly as 'representationalism.'

Finally, there is *Platonic realism*. This last type of realism has to do, not with the relations between particulars, namely between minds and bodies, as in the case of all the varieties of realism considered so far, but with the relationship of universals to particulars of both kinds, psychic and physical. Plato avers that such universal features as belong to the definitions of certain species of entities are themselves things, *res* in Latin, that is, entities capable of existing in their own right, apart from the many particular things whose essence they constitute. This stands in sharp contrast to the immanent realism of both Socrates and Aristotle (see *essentialism*), but also the view that universals and particulars are only two kinds of terms (*nomen* in Latin) that occur in our language. This is called 'nominalism' (see *nominalism*). It contrasts also with the view (see *conceptualism*) that universals and particulars may be distinguished not only with respect to words but also with respect to ideas or concepts in the mind. See 3.4–5, 4.3, 4.5–9, 8.2.1, 11.5, 16.2, 20.4.3, 20.7, 21.3, 24.7.3, 27.4–8, 31.8.1–2.

real presence. A theological term that refers to the Roman Catholic interpretation of the sacrament of the Eucharist as laid down in the decrees of the Council of Trent (1545–1563). According to Catholic teaching, the substance of the sacramental bread and wine is changed into the body and blood of Christ, which are "really present" in the Eucharist, though under the guise of bread and wine. Hence 'real presence' is virtually synonymous with 'transubstantiation.' See 30.3.

relativism. As distinct from the sceptic (see *scepticism*), who believes that there is such a thing as truth, a way things are just in themselves, but denies that we humans can know it reliably, the relativist denies that there exists any objective truth to be known at all. The first such relativist was Protagoras, who reportedly said "Man is the measure of all things, of what is that it is, of what is not, that it is not." *Moral* relativism is more prevalent than relativism about truth, although Protagoras's dictum presumably concerned both. While denying objective truth and/or values, the relativist commonly holds that both may exist 'in the eye of the beholder,' that is, relative to the human subject, or 'subjectively,' as we say. However, philosophers like Hume who make truth and/or value a function of human feeling are better called sceptics, while those, like Sartre, who make (some or all) truth and/or value dependent on the individual or collective human will are relativists in the stricter sense given the term here. There are three basic types of moral relativism: meta-ethical, normative, and descriptive. See 3.3.1, 3.5, 4.5, 4.8, 6.1, 6.3.1, 11.1, 32.2–4, 34.5, 38.1, 38.4–7.

representationalism. See *realism*.

scepticism. Classical scepticism dates back to the Hellenistic period, when certain observations and criticisms of earlier Greek thinkers were shaped into a battery of standard arguments designed to show either (1) that no knowledge is possible (apart from the knowledge of our ignorance) or (2) that it is impossible to determine *whether* any knowledge is possible. (1) is known as 'Academic' scepticism, while (2) is called 'Pyrrhonian' scepticism (after the legendary figure Pyrrho of Elis). Pyrrho was the complete doubter who was content to follow the appearances of things but refused to commit himself to the *truth* or certainty of any judgment whatsoever. His followers criticized both the Academic sceptics for saying that nothing can be known and the dogmatists for holding that some things can be known. As an alternative, they proposed complete suspension of judgment on all questions—including the question whether anything can be known. From Academic and Pyrrhonist as two forms of doctrinal scepticism we can further distinguish the methodological scepticism ('method of doubt') of Descartes, the aim of which is to permit us to attain certainty about first principles. In Hume we encounter a new form of doctrinal scepticism having affinities with classical Academic scepticism. See 3.3.1, 3.5, 4.5, 5.5.4, 5.10, 6.1, 6.3.1, 23.4, 28.3, 29.1–9, 32.3.1–2, 32.4.

scholasticism. The word used to refer to the period in the high Middle Ages (particularly the twelfth and thirteenth centuries) when a new form of Christian Aristotelianism was codified in the works of the great philosopher-theologians of the period (the 'scholastics' as they are called), the chief among them being St Thomas Aquinas. The movement was centred in the great medieval universities or 'schools' of Oxford, Paris, and Cologne, whence the scholastics are also referred to as the 'schoolmen.' Scholasticism continued in one form or another for many centuries. There was a resurgence in the fifteenth and sixteenth centuries, particularly during the Catholic Counter-Reformation in Spain and Portugal. A related form of Protestant scholasticism grew up in Germany in the seventeenth and eighteenth centuries, flourishing there until its fate was sealed by the withering critique of Kant. In Roman Catholic circles, a new scholasticism has thrived ever since the Middle Ages, and continues to do so today. See 1.3.1, 1.5, 2.1, 33.4, 35.2.2.

scientism. The term applied to the view that the boundaries of human knowledge are coextensive with the frontiers of scientific discovery. All knowledge is scientific knowledge; what cannot be known scientifically cannot genuinely be said to be known at all. See 5.3.2, 6.4.3.

semantic, semantics. Having to do with the 'meaning' or 'reference' of words or terms and the way in which it may affect the truth-values of the statements in which they occur. See 7.2, 7.4, 7.14.

sempiternal, sempiternity. From the Latin *semper*, meaning 'always,' these terms mean literally 'everlastingness' and 'everlasting,' respectively. They thus represent an alternate interpretation of 'forever' to that represented by 'eternal' (see). While 'eternal' means 'outside of time altogether' and therefore 'neither coming to be, enduring, nor passing away,' 'sempiternal' means 'perpetual existence' or 'existence throughout all time,' that is, existence *in* time, not outside it, but without ever ceasing to exist. The sempiternal may (but need not) have a *beginning*; yet if it begins it begins *with* rather than *in* time. And it has no end, except with time itself. The successive phases of its duration, past, present, and future, coincide exactly with those of time itself. See 16.5.1, 18.8, 19.1, 20.5.1–2, 20.6.1, 20.6.4, 26.3.

solipsism. The term is derived from the Latin *solus ipse*, meaning 'himself (or oneself) alone.' Solipsism can be (1) a metaphysical or (2) an epistemological position, or (as in Descartes's case) (3) a methodological device. As a metaphysical or *doctrinal* position, solipsism entails that I am alone in the world, that apart from me there is nothing else, that I am all there is 'in' the universe or, in other words, that I *am* the universe (the 'all'). As an epistemological posture, solipsism means that the only thing the existence of which I can *know* is with certainty is myself, my own mind. This is not to deny that there may *be* other thing in the universe, but only that other things (besides my mind) can be *known* to exist with apodictic certainty. Finally, as a methodological device for sorting out the order of knowing, solipsism is the view that the *first* (but not the only) thing of which I can *know* the existence or nature is myself alone, and that this knowledge is the basis of the knowledge of other things, which is possible as well. See 25.2, 34.4, 36.5.

subjectivism. A general designation for (1) the historical trend toward idealism (see *idealism*) on either the epistemological or the ontological front, or on both fronts simultaneously; and for (2) the further trend from idealism to scepticism and relativism (see above). As far as the order of knowing is concerned, the subjectivist trend means that knowledge of the subject is the starting point. If it is also the end point, as in Hume and Sartre, then we have scepticism (there is other truth, but we cannot know it) or relativism (all truth, even about the subject, is relative, what we choose to make it). As against this, Descartes's subjectivism implies that knowledge of the subject or self provides a secure starting point for other, exact, objective, certain, reliable knowledge. See 3.5, 4.2, 4.5,4.8, 6.1, 22.3.1, 25.10, 33.2–3, 33.3, 36.4–5.

substance. The philosopher's technical term for what we ordinarily call a 'thing,' be it an inanimate object of a natural (a stone) or of an artificial (a table) kind, a living plant (a rose, for instance), or a living animal (a horse, a man). A substance is anything that is capable of existing independently or in its own right, apart from something else. In an absolute sense, this may be true only of the totality of what is or of the first being on whom all others depend for their existence (God in the Judeo-Christian tradition), and not at all of those things listed above. But in a relative or looser sense, those things just mentioned may be called 'substances' in order to distinguish them from essential and accidental properties and relations. The latter are incapable of existing 'in themselves'; they exist rather 'in another' (or, in the case of a relation, between two others). A major issue in metaphysics is whether the human mind or soul is a substance in this relative sense, or whether it depends for its existence upon a body. See 3.3–4, 4.2–3,15.4.3.

supererogatory. A philosopher's technical term for 'above and beyond' the call of (moral) duty.' The supererogatory is that which is undoubtedly good and commendable (even saintly), but which goes beyond what morality *minimally* requires of us. See 12.8.6.

syntactic, syntax. The system of rules governing the construction of grammatically correct sentences in a natural language is called the 'syntax' of that language. Apart from grammatical rules, there are certain rules of what is called 'logical syntax' that prevent us from combining certain kinds of predicates with certain kinds of subjects, even when the combination is grammatically correct. Thus, we cannot meaningfully say 'Caesar is a prime number' or that an argument is false (rather than fallacious) or that a proposition is fallacious (rather than false) or that a command is true or false, or that someone scored a goal in baseball, and so on. See 7.2–4, 7.5.1.

tautology. From the Greek *t'auton*, meaning 'the same,' and *logos*, meaning (in this case not 'theory of' or 'science of' but) 'proposition' or 'statement.' A tautology is a proposition that merely 'says over again' (in the predicate position) the very thing said already in the subject position, for example, 'A rose is a rose' (Gertrude Stein) or 'A man is a man' (Bertholt Brecht), and so forth. Thus, tautologies are regarded as uninteresting because completely vacuous. Like analytic truths, they tell us nothing about the real world, but, unlike them, they tell us nothing about the meanings of the non-logical terms involved either. 'Tautology' can be defined somewhat more technically as a proposition that is true in virtue of the meanings of the logical terms (connectives or operators) involved. This makes possible a distinction between analytic truths and tautologies. See 11.11.

teleology. This term, and the cognate adjective 'teleological,' are used both in ethics for a certain kind of normative ethical theory and in theoretical philosophy and the philosophy of science for a certain pattern of explanation in terms of function and purpose. (Only the latter use concerns us here. On the former, see *consequentialism*.) Teleological, including vitalistic, explanations are distinguished from mechanical explanations. (See *mechanism*.) The difference is plain from two senses of 'acting for a reason,' namely (a) acting from a cause, as when a billiard ball begins to move on being struck by another, and (b) acting for a purpose. Purposive action can again be sub-divided into (i) functional and (ii) intentional modalities. Thus, when a plant absorbs water or an animal nourishes itself, the purpose is to sustain and optimize life, growth, flourishing; while when a human being consciously decides to grow food for consumption, the process is conscious or intentional. Advocates of teleology hold that no mechanical explanation of (b) can be adequate. See 5.5.3, 5.7, 10.2.1, 20.5.2, 20.6.4, 38.1.

theodicy. From *theos* ('God') and *dikē* ('justice'), theodicy is the branch of moral theology concerned with the difficult task of providing a rational explanation and justification for all the imperfection and downright evil in the world, given that it is the creation of an all-powerful, omniscient, and omnibenevolent creator God. See 31.1–2, 31.5.4, 31.6.

theogony. A story or mythical account of the origin (*gon*, from the Greek word *genesthai* 'to beget' or 'to create') of the Gods (*theoi*). See 5.3.1.

theological voluntarism. So called as having to do with the *will* (Latin *voluntas*) of God (Greek *theos*), this moral theory is also known as 'The Divine Command

Theory.' It holds, in essence, that our *basic* moral duty is to obey God's will or commands; all our *derivative* moral duties are just the specific commands of God—for example, the Ten Commandments. More precisely: All and only those things are morally good and right which God commands, while all and only those things are wrong which God prohibits. Furthermore, the *only* thing that makes those actions right or wrong is the fact that God commands or forbids them. Or, in simpler terms still: all morally good things are morally good *if and only if* and *because* and *only* because a god, the gods, or God command(s) them. So God does not command us to do or not do certain things because they are good or bad; they are good or bad because *and only because* he commands us to do them; his commands *make* certain things good or bad, and they are *the only thing* that makes those things good or bad. The consequence of this theory is that unless and until commanded by God, acts like (refraining from) murder, theft, and so on are neither good nor bad. Hence God's commands are the *only* and *ultimate* standard of right and wrong. As a meta-ethical theory about the meaning of the ethical terms 'right' and 'wrong,' 'good' and 'bad,' the Divine Command Theory implies that 'good' may be defined as 'commanded by God,' while 'bad' may be defined as 'forbidden by God.' See 11.10–12, 25.7.2, 25.8, 32.4.1, 35.4.3, 35.6, 38.3, 38.5.

theology. As the name implies, 'theology' is the study (or science) of the divine. In this general sense, it antedates by far the rise of monotheistic religions (and Christianity in particular—a relative latecomer). Thus, we can speak of the 'Olympian theology' of the Homeric and Hesiodic poems or of the 'theology' of the early Greek thinkers or that of Plato and Aristotle. Around the time that Aristotle's writings on the divine or supersensible Intelligences became known in Europe, a distinction began to be drawn between natural theology, that is, religion based on argument or natural human reason alone, and revealed theology, the 'science of Sacred Scripture.' The former, natural or rational theology, is a branch of philosophy or metaphysics. Moral theology is concerned with the moral goodness or badness of God or the gods, e.g., divine justice or theodicy. See 5.1–10, 9.1.2.1, 11.12.1, 13.4, 20.6, 29.1, 30.1.

thrownness. A locution borrowed by Sartre from Heidegger, 'thrownness' refers to the condition in which man *finds himself* the moment he first becomes 'aware' of himself at all. The main point is that man is not a bodiless, worldless, solipsistic Cartesian mind that does not yet know whether anything else exists apart from itself and its stream of successive states or modes of consciousness. Rather, as soon as we are aware of ourselves at all, we are aware of ourselves as already existing in a world with others, that is, as related to (involved with) them in manifold ways, not just accidentally, but essentially. That is to say, being so involved with things and others is part of our own being as a Being-in-the-world, and the evidence for this is the fact that this is what we discover ourselves as being first and how we understand ourselves for the most part, provided we do not let Cartesian and other philosophical interpretations distort 'the phenomenal facts of the case.' 'Thrownness' and 'projection' are complementary concepts. See 36.2, 36.4–5.

Index of Names

This index is confined to philosophers and writers discussed or referred to in the text and omits (a) the fictional and historical figures, both gods and men, mentioned in Plato's dialogues or in Homer's epics as well as (b) all names that occur in the sections entitled "Recommended readings and references" and "Questions for reflection, discussion, and review." Omitted also are (c) historical names used in examples (for example, 'Caesar') and (d) the names of the five main authors studied in this book. Occurrences of a name in the Glossary are recorded. The dates (year of birth and death) for each historical figure are given in parentheses after the first occurrence of the name in the text.

Aeschylus, 90
Alexander of Aphrodisias, 319
Alexander of Hales, 447
Allen, R.E., ix, xxii, 259, 355
Allen, Woody, 283, 285
Anaxagoras, 20, 81, 85–9, 159, 161, 222
Anaximander, 19, 73–5, 78–80, 160, 224, 649
Anaximenes, 19, 73, 79, 81–2, 161, 644, 649
Antisthenes, 242–3
Antoninus, Marcus Aurelius, 243, 372
Aquinas, St Thomas, xiv, xvi–xvii, xxii, 15, 16, 21, 64, 152, 282, 286, 326, 365, 370, 426–30, 439, 446–54, 468–9, 472–3, 491, 498–501, 582, 584, 644, 650, 655
Arcesilaus, 91, 166
Aristippus, 242–3
Aristophanes, 90, 150, 160, 162
Aristotle, x, xi, xiv, xvi, xvii–xix, xxii, 7, 12, 20–2, 24–6, 37, 51–2, 56, 59–61, 63–5, 67, 73, 76–7, 80, 84–5, 90, 110, 121, 122, 137, 141,149–54, 156, 160, 175–8, 195, 205, 209–10, 233, 242–3, 250, 262, 260, 262, 282, 286, 296, 314–15, 318–19, 322– 37, 340–8, 351, 353, 364–6, 389, 391–3, 423, 426, 428, 445, 459, 473–4, 476, 516–17, 542, 550, 570, 573, 583–4, 613, 633–5, 643, 649–52, 654, 658
Armstrong, A.H., xxii, 46, 56
Augustine, xvii, 16, 22, 45, 260, 351, 372, 430, 597

Averroës, 280, 282

Baier, Kurt, 611
Bentham, Jeremy, 611
Berkeley, George (Bishop of Cloyne), 22, 51–2, 54–56, 59, 61–2 , 65, 89, 91, 334, 364, 367, 423, 470, 548–50, 644, 647
Bonaventure, St, xvii, 447
Brecht, Bertholt, 657
Buber, Martin, 559-60
Buddha, The, 235
Burnet, John, 161
Butler, Joseph (Bishop of Bristol, later Durham), 240

Camus, Albert, 560
Carneades, 166
Cicero, 14, 160, 166, 183, 222, 243, 264, 647
Clifford, C.K., 222
Comte, Auguste, 70
Copernicus, Nicholas, 324, 582
Copleston, Frederick, 499
Cornford, F.M., xviii, xxii, 259, 480
Cratylus, 336–8, 489

Democritus of Abdera, 20, 87, 160, 472, 541–2, 613
Diogenes, Laertius, 264, 338
Diogenes of Sinope, 91, 243
Dodds, E.R., 149, 278

Empedocles, 20, 84–8, 282, 545, 651
Engels, Friedrich, 124, 370
Epicurus, xx, 22, 25, 87, 90–1, 242–3, 280, 472, 539–46, 582
Epimenides, 71, 244, 651
Erasmus, 15

Euripides, 90, 232
Fénelon, François, 577
Flew, Antony, ix, xxi
Frege, Gottlob, 136
Freud, Sigmund, 189, 440
Frye, Northrop, 36, 632

Galilei, Galileo,14–15, 460, 582
Gallop, David, ix, xi
Garber, Daniel, 364
Gassendi, Pierre, 55, 62, 370, 372, 440, 472, 498, 541, 582
Gewirth, Alan, 380
Gide, André, 564–6, 618
Gorgias of Leontini, 40, 162, 170

Hegel, Gottfried Wilhelm Friedrich, xvii, 16, 54–5, 59, 67, 152, 643
Heidegger, Martin, ix–xi, xviii–xix, 16, 22, 27, 65, 67, 75, 89, 152, 305, 328, 458, 479, 559–60, 573–4, 580–1, 593–9, 610, 618, 635, 640, 650, 652, 658
Heracleitus of Ephesus, 19–20, 22, 80–4, 160, 222, 264, 282–3, 335–7, 339, 391, 489
Herodotus, 90
Hesiod, 68–70, 72–4, 76, 79–80, 161–2, 203, 222, 233, 282, 544–5, 658
Hobbes, Thomas, xv, xxii, 55, 62, 225, 235–40, 44o, 472, 582
Homer, 68–70, 72–3, 76, 70–81, 161–2, 203, 222–3, 233, 253, 276, 278–9, 281, 310, 396, 658
Husain, Martha, x, xv
Husserl, Edmund, 16, 559–60, 631
Hutcheson, Francis, 240

Jaeger, Werner, 72, 314
Jaspers, Karl, 559–60, 581

Index of Names

Jesus (of Nazareth), 225, 234–5, 237–9, 500, 611
Johnson, Dr Samuel, 183

Kant, Immanuel, xiv–xvii, 5, 10, 13, 18–19, 21, 39, 49, 54–5, 59, 61–2, 65, 89, 110, 115–16, 118–20, 129, 182, 188, 192, 225, 236–40, 249, 252, 285, 288, 304, 319–20, 329–30, 333–4, 350, 352, 357, 364, 367, 376, 396, 403, 408, 422–4, 443–4, 447, 449–50, 452, 454–5, 491, 515–16, 522, 551–2, 562, 564, 568, 585, 588–590, 598–9, 605, 611–14, 616, 620–1, 624–6, 632, 635, 640–1, 643, 652, 655
Kenny, Anthony, xxii, 364
Kepler, Johannes, 582
Kierkegaard, Søren, 559, 604, 617
Kneale, William, 141, 143

Lao-Tse, 235
Leibniz, Gottfried Wilhelm, 22, 54–5, 59, 62, 64, 89, 98, 103, 115–16, 280, 334, 395–6, 413, 424, 447, 475, 490–1, 497–8, 505, 509, 524, 530–2, 537, 544, 546, 577, 581–3, 585–8, 641, 645
Leonardo, 13
Leucippus, 20, 87, 338, 541–2
Locke, John, 51, 61, 95, 124, 296, 425–6, 460, 502–5, 507, 522, 536, 582, 641, 644
Loyola, Ignatius, 372
Lucretius, 22, 87, 541
Luther, Martin, 15, 372, 519

Malebranche, Nicholas, 22, 504, 548, 550
Mao-Tse-Tung, 370
Marcel, Gabriel, 559, 581
Marion, J.-L., 364
Marx, Karl, 124, 370, 440, 577, 643
Melissus of Samos, 20, 63, 83–4, 339
Michelangelo, 12
Mill, James, 611
Mill, John Stuart, 426, 611, 644
Moore, G.E. 19
Murray, Gilbert, 278
Musaeus, 71

Newton, Sir Isaac, 15, 64, 95–6, 105, 506, 525, 531, 541, 546, 583
Newton-Smith, W.H., 93
Niethammer, Friedrich, 568
Nietzsche, Friedrich, 16, 22, 238, 351, 559, 574, 607

Ockham, William of, 62, 355–6, 420, 543, 650
Orpheus, 71
Owens, Joseph, x

Parmenides, xi, 20, 40, 64, 76, 80, 82–3, 85, 87–9, 264, 276, 320–2 330, 333, 335–41, 391, 489, 525
Pascal, Blaise, 22
Pericles, 82, 90, 161, 178
Plotinus, 77, 91
Pope, Alexander, 494
Popper, Sir Karl, 41, 97, 167
Porphyry, 91
Proclus, 55, 91
Protagoras, 40, 45, 161–2, 222, 563, 654
Pyrrho of Elis, 91, 166, 655

666 Index of Names

Pythagoras of Samos, 19, 82, 265, 277, 282
Quine, Willard van Orman, xxii, 105, 348–9, 353–5, 357, 361
Quintillian, 183
Reid, Thomas, 240
Robinson, Thomas, ix
Ross, Sir David, 613
Rousseau, Jean-Jacques, 606–7
Russell, Bertrand, 19, 71, 107, 136–7, 354, 499, 607–8
Ryle, Gilbert, xix, 479, 640

Schopenhauer, Arthur, 22
Scotus, John Duns, 420, 447
Sellars, Wilfrid, xvii, 1
Sextus (Empiricus), 166
Skinner, B.F., 479, 640
Snell, Bruno, 167
Sophocles, 90
Spinoza, Baruch, 22, 77, 103, 110, 447, 491, 527, 560
Stein, Gertrude, 657
Stephanus, xxi
Suarez, Francisco, 21
Swift, Jonathan, 393

Tacitus, 538, 540
Thucydides, 90, 233
Tillotson, John, 518–521, 532–3
Timon of Phleius, 166

Vlastos, Gregory, ix
Voltaire, 440, 585, 589

Williams, Bernard, 18
Wittgenstein, Ludwig, 354

Xenophanes of Colophon, 40–1, 80–1, 83, 160–1, 167, 222, 280, 283, 338

Xenophon, 20, 149–52, 233

Zeno of Citium, 25, 90, 243, 542
Zeno of Elea, 20, 40, 63, 83–4, 87
Zola, Émile, 578
Zwingli, Ulrich, 519